FUNDAMENTALS OF LOGIC DESIGN

THIRD EDITION

FUNDAMENTALS OF LOGIC DESIGN

THIRD EDITION

Charles H. Roth, Jr.
University of Texas at Austin

WEST PUBLISHING COMPANY
St. Paul • New York • Los Angeles • San Francisco

Cover: *Takht-i-Sulayman I*, 1967 by Frank Stella reproduced courtesy of the Menil Foundation, Houston, Texas. Design by The Quarasan Group, Inc.

COPYRIGHT © 1985
By WEST PUBLISHING CO.
   50 West Kellogg Boulevard
   P. O. Box 64526
   St. Paul, Minnesota 55164-0526

Library of Congress Cataloging in Publication Data

Roth, Charles H.
   Fundamentals of logic design.
   (West series in electrical engineering)
   Bibliography: p.
   Includes index.
   1. Logic circuits. 2. Logic design. I. Title

TK7868.L6R67   1985   621.3819'58'35   84-27102
ISBN 0-314-85292-1

PREFACE

After studying this text, you should be able to apply switching theory to the solution of logic design problems. This means that you will learn both the basic theory of switching networks and how to apply it. After a brief introduction, you will study Boolean algebra, which provides the basic mathematical tool needed to analyze and synthesize an important class of switching networks. Starting from a problem statement, you will learn to design networks of logic gates which have a specified relationship between signals at the input and output terminals. Then you will study the logical properties of flip-flops, which serve as memory devices in sequential switching networks. By combining flip-flops with networks of logic gates, you will learn to design counters, adders, sequence detectors and similar networks.

This text is designed so that it can be used in either a standard lecture course or in a self-paced course. In addition to the standard reading material and problems, study guides and other aids for self-study are included in the text. The content of the text is divided into 28 study units. These units form a logical sequence so that mastery of the material in one unit is generally a prerequisite to the study of succeeding units. Each unit consists of four parts. First, a list of objectives states precisely what you are expected to learn by studying the unit. Next, the study guide contains reading assignments and study questions. As you work through the unit, you should write out the answers to these study questions. The text material and problem set which follow are similar to a conventional textbook. When you complete a unit, you should review the objectives and make sure that you have met them.

The 28 study units are divided into three main groups. The first 11 units treat Boolean algebra and the design of combinational logic networks. Units 12 through 22 and 28 are mainly concerned with the analysis and design of clocked sequential logic networks, including networks for arithmetic operations. Units 23 through 27 cover the special problems encountered in the analysis and design of asynchronous sequential networks. The first 22 units can typically be covered in a one semester course taught at the Sophomore or Junior level. The remaining units can then be used as enrichment material for the better students, or they can be covered in the first part of a second course in digital systems design.

Several of the units include laboratory exercises. These exercises provide an opportunity to design a logic network and then test its operation in lab. The equipment required includes a logic patchboard with flip-flops and several types of logic gates. If such equipment is not available, the lab exercises can be assigned as design problems. This is especially important for Units 10, 17 and 27 since the comprehensive design problems in these units help to review and tie together the material in several of the preceding units.

This text is written for a first course in the logic design of digital systems. It is written on the premise that the student should understand and learn thoroughly certain fundamental concepts in a first course. Examples of such fundamental concepts are the use of Boolean algebra to describe the signals and interconnections in a logic network, use of systematic techniques for simplification of a logic network, interconnection of simple components to perform a more complex logic function, analysis of a sequential logic network in terms of timing charts or a state graph, and use of a control network to control the sequence of events in a digital system.

The text attempts to achieve a balance between theory and application. For this reason, the text does not overemphasize the mathematics of switching theory; however, it does present the theory which is necessary for understanding the fundamental concepts of logic design. After completing this text, the student should be prepared for a more advanced digital systems design course which stresses more intuitive concepts like the development of algorithms for digital processes, partitioning of digital systems into subsystems, and implementation of digital systems using currently available hardware. Alternatively, the student should be prepared to go on to a more advanced course in switching theory which further develops the theoretical concepts which have been introduced here.

This new edition offers a number of improvements over the second edition. The SM chart method for designing state machines, or sequential control networks, is presented as an alternative to standard state graph techniques. The material on programmable logic arrays has been expanded to include use of PALs, a new type of programmable array logic that is rapidly gaining favor with logic designers. Three-state logic is introduced and applied to transferring data between registers using a bus. The new IEEE standard notation for logic symbols is explained in Appendix B. The material on simplification of switching expressions has been reorganized to permit more flexibility in coverage. New exercises and problems have been added to most units, and several sections have been rewritten to clarify the presentation.

The text is suitable for both computer science and engineering students. All material relating to circuit aspects of logic gates is contained in Appendix A so that this material can conveniently be omitted by computer science students or other students with no background in electronic circuits. The text is organized so that Unit 4 on Algebraic Simplification and Unit 7 on the Quine-McCluskey procedure may be omitted without loss of continuity. Instructors who wish to place less emphasis on logic simplification can omit one or both of these units to allow more time for study of digital design techniques presented in the later units. The following diagram illustrates the unit prerequisite structure for the third edition:

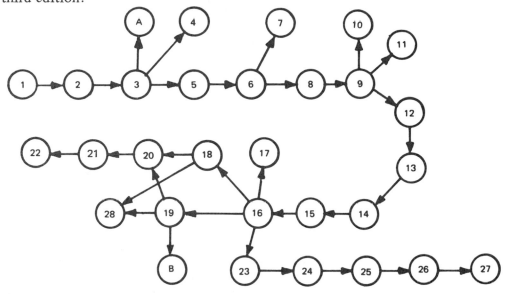

  Although many texts are available in the areas of switching theory and logic design, this text was developed specifically to meet the needs of a self-paced course in which students are expected to study the material on their own. Each of the units has undergone extensive class testing in a self-paced environment and has been revised based on student feedback. Study guides and text material have been expanded as required so that students can learn from the text without the aid of lectures and so that almost all of the students can achieve mastery of all of the objectives. Supplementary materials were developed as the text was being written. An instructor's manual is available which includes suggestions for using the text in a standard or self-paced course, quizzes on each of the units, and suggestions for laboratory equipment and procedures. The instructor's manual also contains solutions to problems, to unit quizzes and to lab exercises.

HOW TO USE THIS BOOK FOR SELF - STUDY

If you wish to learn all of the material in this text to mastery level, the following study procedures are recommended for each unit:

1. Read the **Objectives** of the unit. These objectives provide a concise summary of what you should be able to do when you complete study of the unit.

2. Work through the **Study Guide**. After reading each section of the text, *write* out the answers to the corresponding study guide questions. In many cases, blank spaces are left in the study guide so that you can write your answers directly in this book. By doing this, you will have the answers conveniently available for later review. The study guide questions will generally help emphasize some of the important points in each section or will guide you to a better understanding of some of the more difficult points. If you cannot answer some of the study guide questions, this indicates that you need to study the corresponding section in the text more before proceeding. The answers to selected study guide questions are given in the back of this book; answers to the remaining questions can generally be found within the text.

3. Several of the units (Units 3, 4, 6, 7, 12, 14, 15, 21, 24 and 25) contain one or more programmed exercises. Each programmed exercise will guide you step-by-step through the solution of one of the more difficult types of problems encountered in this text. When working through a programmed exercise, be sure to write down your answer for each part in the space provided before looking at the answer and continuing with the next part of the exercise.

4. Work the **Problems** at the end of the unit. Check your answers against those at the end of the book and rework any problems which you missed.

5. Reread the **Objectives** of the unit to make sure that you can meet all of them. If in doubt, review the appropriate sections of the text.

6. If you are using this text in a self-paced course, you will need to pass a readiness test on each unit before proceeding with the next unit. The purpose of the readiness test is to make sure that you have mastered the objectives of one unit before moving on to the next unit. The questions on the test will relate directly to the objectives of the unit, so that if you have worked through the study guide and written out answers to all of the study guide questions and to all of the problems, you should have no difficulty passing the test.

7. If you are using this text for self-study or in a self-paced course, you may wish to use *Introduction to Boolean Algebra and Logic Design** by Hoernes and Heilweil as a supplement to the first 7 units in this text. The Hoernes and Heilweil book is written in a programmed instruction format and provides an opportunity for additional drill and practice in some of the fundamental concepts of Boolean algebra and logic design. Since Hoernes and Heilweil is written on a very elementary level, it should not be needed unless you find the material in this text difficult to study on your own. Correspondence between units in this text and chapters in the Hoernes and Heilweil book is as follows:

Roth Unit 1 – H & H Chapter 1
Roth Unit 2 – H & H Chapters 2, 3, 4
Roth Unit 3 – H & H Chapter 5
Roth Unit 5 – H & H Chapters 6 and 7
Roth Unit 6 – H & H Chapters 10, 11, 12
Roth Unit 7 – H & H Chapters 8 and 9

---

*Hoernes, Gerhard E. and Heilweil, Melvin F., *Introduction to Boolean Algebra and Logic Design*, McGraw-Hill, 1964 (paperback edition).

ACKNOWLEDGMENT

To be effective, a book designed for self-study cannot simply be written. It must be tested and revised many times to achieve its goals. The author wishes to express his appreciation to the many professors, proctors and students who participated in this process. A special thanks goes to Dr. Erwin A. Reinhard for a thorough review of an earlier version of the text and for class-testing at the University of Alabama. The author is especially grateful to Bill Shellorne, one of the graduate student proctors, who made major contributions to the development of the book. In addition to working out solutions to most of the problems and tests, he has offered many suggestions for improving the clarity and consistency of the presentation. And finally, the author wishes to thank Dr. Billy Koen, whose enthusiasm for the PSI method of self-paced instruction first induced the author to try out PSI, and hence indirectly helped to create the need for this book.

CONTENTS

1

INTRODUCTION
NUMBER SYSTEMS AND CONVERSION

OBJECTIVES

1. Introduction

   The first part of this unit introduces the material to be studied later. In addition to getting an overview of the material in the first part of the course, you should be able to explain:

   a. The difference between analog and digital systems and why digital systems are capable of greater accuracy.

   b. The difference between combinational and sequential networks.

   c. Why two-valued signals and binary numbers are commonly used in digital systems.

2. Number systems and conversion

   When you complete this unit, you should be able to solve the following types of problems:

   a. Given a positive integer, fraction, or mixed number in any base (2 through 16), convert to any other base. Justify the procedure used by using a power series expansion for the number.

   b. Add, subtract, and multiply positive binary numbers. Explain the addition and subtraction process in terms of carries and borrows.

   c. Represent a decimal number in BCD, 6-3-1-1 code, excess-3 code, etc. Given a set of weights, construct a weighted code.

STUDY GUIDE

1. Study Section 1.1, *Digital Systems and Switching Networks,* and answer the following study questions:

   a. What is the basic difference between analog and digital systems?

   b. Why are digital systems capable of greater accuracy than analog systems?

   c. Explain the difference between combinational and sequential switching networks.

   d. What common characteristic do most switching devices used in digital systems have?

   e. Why are binary numbers used in digital systems?

2. Study Section 1.2, *Number Systems and Conversion.* Answer the following study questions as you go along:

   a. Is the first remainder obtained in the division method for base conversion the most or least significant digit?

   b. Work through all of the examples in the text as you encounter them and make sure that you understand all of the steps.

   c. An easy method for conversion between binary and octal is illustrated in Equation (1-1). Why should you start forming the groups of 3 bits at the binary point instead of the left end of the number?

   d. Why is it impossible to convert a decimal number to binary on a digit by digit basis as can be done for octal or hexadecimal?

   e. Complete the following conversion table.

Binary (base 2)	Octal (base 8)	Decimal (base 10)	Hexadecimal (base 16)
0	0	0	0
1			
10			
11			
100			
101			
110			
111			
1000			
1001			
1010			
1011			
1100			
1101			
1110			
1111			
10000	20	16	10

    f.   Work Problems 1.1, 1.2, 1.4 and 1.5.

3. Study Section 1.3, *Binary Arithmetic.*

    a. Make sure that you can follow all of the examples, especially the propagation of borrows in the subtraction process.

    b. To make sure that you understand the borrowing process, work out a detailed analysis in terms of powers of 2 for the following example:

$$\begin{array}{r} 1100 \\ -101 \\ \hline 111 \end{array}$$

4. Work Problems 1.3 and 1.9.

5. Study Section 1.4, *Binary Codes*.

   a. Represent 187 in BCD code, excess-3 code, 6-3-1-1 code, and 2-out-of-5 code.

   b. Verify that the 6-3-1-1 code is a weighted code. Note that for some decimal digits, two different code combinations could have been used. For example, either 0101 or 0110 could represent 4. In each case the combination with the smaller binary value has been used.

   c. How is the excess-3 code obtained?

   d. How are the ASCII codes for the decimal digits obtained? What is the relation between the ASCII codes for the capital letters and lower-case letters?

   e. Work Problem 1.6.

6. If you are taking this course on a self-paced basis, you will need to pass a readiness test on this unit before going on to the next unit. The purpose of the readiness test is to determine if you have mastered the material in this unit and are ready to go on to the next unit. Before you take the readiness test

   a. Check your answers to the problems against those provided at the end of this book. If you missed any of the problems, make sure that you understand why your answer is wrong and correct your solution.

   b. Make sure that you can meet all of the objectives listed at the beginning of this unit.

1. INTRODUCTION
NUMBER SYSTEMS AND CONVERSION

1.1 Digital Systems and Switching Networks

Digital systems are used extensively in computation and data processing, control systems, communications, and measurement. Because digital systems are capable of greater accuracy and reliability than analog systems, many tasks formerly done by analog systems are now being performed digitally.

In a digital system, the physical quantities or signals can only assume discrete values, while in analog systems the physical quantities or signals may vary continuously over a specified range. For example, the output voltage of a digital system might be constrained to take on only two values such as 0 volts and 5 volts, while the output voltage from an analog system might be allowed to assume any value in the range −10 volts to +10 volts.

Because digital systems work with discrete quantities, in many cases they can be designed so that for a given input, the output is exactly correct. For example, if we multiply two 5-digit numbers using a digital multiplier, the 10-digit product will be correct in all 10 digits. On the other hand, the output of an analog multiplier might have an error ranging from a fraction of one per cent to a few per cent depending on the accuracy of the components used in construction of the multiplier. Furthermore, if we need a product which is correct to 20 digits rather than 10, we can redesign the digital multiplier to process more digits and add more digits to its input. A similar improvement in the accuracy of an analog multiplier would not be possible because of limitations on the accuracy of the components.

The design of digital systems may be divided roughly into three parts — system design, logic design, and circuit design. System design involves breaking the overall system into subsystems and specifying the characteristics of each subsystem. For example, system design of a digital computer could involve specifying the number and type of memory units, arithmetic units, and input-output devices as well as the interconnection and control of these subsystems. Logic design involves determining how to interconnect basic logic building blocks to perform a specific function. An example of logic design is determining the interconnection of logic gates and flip-flops required to perform binary addition. Circuit design involves specifying the interconnection of specific components such as resistors, diodes and transistors to form a gate, flip-flop, or other logic building block. This book is largely devoted to a study of logic design and the theory necessary for understanding the logic design process. Some aspects of system design are treated in Units 20 and 21. Circuit design of logic gates is discussed briefly in Appendix A.

Many of the subsystems of a digital system take the form of a switching network (Fig. 1-1). A switching network has one or more inputs and one or more outputs which take on discrete values. In this text, we will study two types of switching networks — combinational and sequential. In a combinational network, the output values depend only on the present value of the inputs and not on past values. In a sequential network, the outputs depend on both the present and past input values. In other words, in order to determine the output of a sequential network, a sequence of input values must be specified. The sequential network is said to have memory because it must "remember" something about the past sequence of inputs, while a combinational network has no memory. In general, a

Fig. 1-1. Switching network

sequential network is composed of a combinational network with added memory elements. Combinational networks are easier to design than sequential networks and will be studied first.

The basic building blocks used to construct combinational networks are logic gates. The logic designer must determine how to interconnect these gates in order to convert the network input signals into the desired output signals. The relationship between these input and output signals can be described mathematically using Boolean algebra. Units 2 and 3 of this text introduce the basic laws and theorems of Boolean algebra and show how they can be used to describe the behavior of networks of logic gates.

Starting from a given problem statement, the first step in designing a combinational logic network is to derive a table or algebraic logic equations which describe the network outputs as a function of the network inputs (Unit 5). In order to design an economical network to realize these output functions, the logic equations which describe the network outputs generally must be simplified. Algebraic methods for this simplification are described in Unit 4, and other simplification methods (Karnaugh map and Quine-McCluskey procedure) are introduced in Units 6 and 7. Implementation of the simplified logic equations using several types of gates is described in Unit 8, and alternative design procedures using integrated circuits are developed in Unit 9.

The basic memory elements used in the design of sequential networks are called flip-flops (Unit 12). These flip-flops can be interconnected with gates to form counters and registers (Unit 13). Analysis of more general sequential networks using timing diagrams, state tables, and graphs is presented in Unit 14. The first step in designing a sequential switching network is to construct a state table or graph which describes the relationship between the input and output sequences (Unit 15). Methods for going from a state table or graph to a network of gates and flip-flops are developed in Units 16 and 17, and alternative methods of implementing sequential networks are discussed in Unit 19. In Units 20 and 21, combinational and sequential design techniques are applied to the realization of networks for performing binary addition, subtraction, multiplication and division. The last part of the book (Units 23–27) deals with the design of asynchronous sequential networks. Such networks present special timing problems and are more difficult to design than the synchronous sequential networks described in earlier units.

The switching devices used in digital systems are generally two-state devices; that is, the output can assume only two different discrete values. Examples of switching devices are relays, diodes, transistors and magnetic cores. A relay can assume two states — closed or open — depending on whether power is applied to the coil or not. A diode can be in a conducting state or a non-conducting state. A transistor can be in a cut-off or saturated state, with a corresponding high or low output voltage. Of course, transistors can also be operated as linear amplifiers with a continuous range of output voltages, but in digital applications greater reliability is obtained by operating them as two-state devices. A magnetic core can be magnetized in one direction or in the opposite direction. Because the outputs of most switching devices assume only two different values, it is natural to use binary numbers internally in digital systems. For this reason binary numbers will be discussed first before proceeding with the design of switching networks.

1.2 Number Systems and Conversion

When we write decimal (base 10) numbers, we use a positional notation; each digit is multiplied by an appropriate power of 10 depending on its position in the number. For example,

$$953.78_{10} = 9 \times 10^2 + 5 \times 10^1 + 3 \times 10^0 + 7 \times 10^{-1} + 8 \times 10^{-2}$$

Similarly, for binary (base 2) numbers, each binary digit is multiplied by the appropriate power of two:

$$1011.11_2 = 1 \times 2^3 + 0 \times 2^2 + 1 \times 2^1 + 1 \times 2^0 + 1 \times 2^{-1} + 1 \times 2^{-2}$$

$$= 8 + 0 + 2 + 1 + \frac{1}{2} + \frac{1}{4} = 11\frac{3}{4} = 11.75_{10}$$

Note that the binary point separates the positive and negative powers of two just as the decimal point separates the positive and negative powers of ten for decimal numbers.

Any positive integer R ($R > 1$) can be chosen as the *radix* or *base* of a number system. If the base is R then R digits $(0, 1, \ldots, R-1)$ are used. For example, if $R = 8$, then the required digits are 0, 1, 2, 3, 4, 5, 6 and 7. A number written in positional notation can be expanded in a power series in R. For example,

$$N = (a_4 a_3 a_2 a_1 a_0 . a_{-1} a_{-2} a_{-3})_R = a_4 \times R^4 + a_3 \times R^3 + a_2 \times R^2 + a_1 \times R^1$$

$$+ a_0 \times R^0 + a_{-1} \times R^{-1} + a_{-2} \times R^{-2} + a_{-3} \times R^{-3}$$

where a_i is the coefficient of R^i and $0 \leqslant a_i \leqslant R-1$. If the arithmetic indicated in the power series expansion is done in base 10, then the result is the decimal equivalent of N. For example,

$$147.3_8 = 1 \times 8^2 + 4 \times 8^1 + 7 \times 8^0 + 3 \times 8^{-1} = 64 + 32 + 7 + \frac{3}{8}$$

$$= 103.375_{10}$$

For bases greater than 10, more than 10 symbols are needed to represent the digits. In this case, letters are usually used to represent digits greater than 9. For example, in hexadecimal (base 16), A represents 10_{10}, B represents 11_{10}, C represents 12_{10}, D represents 13_{10}, E represents 14_{10}, and F represents 15_{10}. Thus,

$$A2F_{16} = 10 \times 16^2 + 2 \times 16^1 + 15 \times 16^0 = 2560 + 32 + 15 = 2607_{10}$$

Next, we will discuss conversion of a decimal *integer* to base R using the division method. The base R equivalent of a decimal integer N can be represented as

$$N = (a_n a_{n-1} \ldots a_2 a_1 a_0)_R = a_n R^n + a_{n-1} R^{n-1} + \ldots + a_2 R^2 + a_1 R^1 + a_0$$

If we divide N by R, the remainder is a_0:

$$\frac{N}{R} = a_n R^{n-1} + a_{n-1} R^{n-2} + \ldots + a_2 R^1 + a_1 = Q_1, \text{ remainder } a_0$$

Then we divide the quotient Q_1 by R:

$$\frac{Q_1}{R} = a_n R^{n-2} + a_{n-1} R^{n-3} + \ldots + a_3 R^1 + a_2 = Q_2, \text{ remainder } a_1$$

Next we divide Q_2 by R:

$$\frac{Q_2}{R} = a_n R^{n-3} + a_{n-1} R^{n-4} + \ldots + a_3 = Q_3, \text{ remainder } a_2$$

This process is continued until we finally obtain a_n. Note that the remainder obtained at each division step is one of the desired digits and the *least* significant digit is obtained first.

Example: convert 53_{10} to binary

$$
\begin{array}{ll}
2\underline{|\,53} & \\
2\underline{|\,26} & \text{rem.} = 1 = a_0 \\
2\underline{|\,13} & \text{rem.} = 0 = a_1 \\
2\underline{|\,\ 6} & \text{rem.} = 1 = a_2 \qquad 53_{10} = 110101_2 \\
2\underline{|\,\ 3} & \text{rem.} = 0 = a_3 \\
2\underline{|\,\ 1} & \text{rem.} = 1 = a_4 \\
\ \ \ 0 & \text{rem.} = 1 = a_5
\end{array}
$$

Conversion of a decimal *fraction* to base R can be done using successive *multiplications* by R. A decimal fraction F can be represented as

$$F = (.a_{-1} a_{-2} a_{-3} \ldots a_{-m})_R = a_{-1} R^{-1} + a_{-2} R^{-2} + a_{-3} R^{-3} + \ldots + a_{-m} R^{-m}$$

Multiplying by R yields

$$FR = a_{-1} + a_{-2} R^{-1} + a_{-3} R^{-2} + \ldots + a_{-m} R^{-m+1} = a_{-1} + F_1$$

where F_1 represents the fractional part of the result and a_{-1} is the integer part. Multiplying F_1 by R yields

$$F_1 R = a_{-2} + a_{-3} R^{-1} + \ldots + a_{-m} R^{-m+2} = a_{-2} + F_2$$

Next, we multiply F_2 by R:

$$F_2 R = a_{-3} + \ldots + a_{-m} R^{-m+3} = a_{-3} + F_3$$

This process is continued until we have obtained a sufficient number of digits. Note that the integer part obtained at each step is one of the desired digits and the *most* significant digit is obtained first.

Example: convert $.625_{10}$ to binary

$$F = .625 \qquad F_1 = .250 \qquad F_2 = .500$$
$$\underline{\times\ 2} \qquad\quad \underline{\times\ 2} \qquad\quad \underline{\times\ 2}$$
$$1.250 \qquad\quad 0.500 \qquad\quad 1.000 \qquad\qquad .625_{10} = .101_2$$
$$(a_{-1} = 1) \qquad (a_{-2} = 0) \qquad (a_{-3} = 1)$$

This process does not always terminate, but if it does not terminate the result is a repeating fraction.

Example: convert 0.7_{10} to binary

$$.7$$
$$\underline{2}$$
$$(1)\ .4$$
$$\underline{2}$$
$$(0)\ .8$$
$$\underline{2}$$
$$(1)\ .6$$
$$\underline{2}$$
$$(1)\ .2$$
$$\underline{2}$$
$$(0)\ .4 \longleftarrow \text{process starts repeating here since .4 was previously}$$
$$\underline{2} \qquad\qquad\quad \text{obtained above}$$
$$(0)\ .8 \qquad 0.7_{10} = 0.1\ \underline{0110}\ \underline{0110}\ \underline{0110}\ \ldots_2$$

Conversion between two bases other than decimal can be done directly by using the procedures given; however, the arithmetic operations would have to be carried out using a base other than ten. It is generally easier to convert to decimal first and then convert the decimal number to the new base.

Example: convert 231.3_4 to base 7

$$231.3_4 = 2 \times 16 + 3 \times 4 + 1 + \frac{3}{4} = 45.75_{10}$$

$$7\underline{|\ 45} \qquad\qquad\qquad .75$$
$$7\underline{|\quad 6} \qquad \text{rem. 3} \qquad \underline{7}$$
$$\qquad 0 \qquad \text{rem. 6} \qquad (5).25 \qquad\qquad 45.75_{10} = 63.5151 \ldots_7$$
$$\qquad\qquad\qquad\qquad\qquad \underline{7}$$
$$\qquad\qquad\qquad\qquad (1).75$$
$$\qquad\qquad\qquad\qquad\quad \underline{7}$$
$$\qquad\qquad\qquad\qquad (5).25$$
$$\qquad\qquad\qquad\qquad\quad \underline{7}$$
$$\qquad\qquad\qquad\qquad (1).75$$

Conversion from binary to octal (and conversely) can be done by inspection since each octal digit corresponds to exactly 3 binary digits (bits). Starting at the binary point, the bits are divided into groups of 3 and each group is replaced by an octal digit:

$$11010111110.0011_2 = \underbrace{011}_{3}\underbrace{010}_{2}\underbrace{111}_{7}\underbrace{110}_{6}.\underbrace{001}_{1}\underbrace{100}_{4} = 3276.14_8 \qquad (1\text{-}1)$$

Similarly, binary to hexadecimal conversion is accomplished by dividing the binary number into groups of 4 bits and replacing each group by a hexadecimal digit:

$$1001101.0101 11_2 = \underbrace{0100}_{4}\ \underbrace{1101}_{D}.\ \underbrace{0101}_{5}\ \underbrace{1100}_{C} = 4D.5C_{16} \qquad . \quad (1\text{-}2)$$

1.3 Binary Arithmetic

Arithmetic operations in digital systems are usually done in binary because design of logic networks to perform binary arithmetic is much easier than for decimal. Binary arithmetic is carried out in much the same manner as decimal, except the addition and multiplication tables are much simpler.

The addition table for binary numbers is

$$0 + 0 = 0$$
$$0 + 1 = 1$$
$$1 + 0 = 1$$
$$1 + 1 = 0 \quad \text{and carry 1 to the next column}$$

Example: add 13_{10} and 11_{10} in binary

$$
\begin{array}{r}
1111 \longleftarrow \text{carries} \\
13_{10} = \quad 1101 \\
11_{10} = \quad \underline{1011} \\
11000 = 24_{10}
\end{array}
$$

The subtraction table for binary numbers is

$$0 - 0 = 0$$
$$0 - 1 = 1 \qquad \text{and borrow 1 from the next column}$$
$$1 - 0 = 1$$
$$1 - 1 = 0$$

Borrowing 1 from a column is equivalent to subtracting 1 from that column.

Examples of binary subtraction:[*]

(a)		(b)	(c)
$1 \longleftarrow$ (indicates		$1111\longleftarrow$ borrows	$111 \longleftarrow$ borrows
11101	a borrow	10000	111001
-10011	from the	-11	-1011
1010	3rd column)	1101	101110

Note how the borrow propagates from column to column in the second example. In order to borrow 1 from the second column, we must in turn borrow 1 from the third column, etc.

Binary subtraction sometimes causes confusion, perhaps because we are so used to doing decimal subtraction that we forget the significance of the borrowing process. Before doing a detailed analysis of binary subtraction, we will review the borrowing process for decimal subtraction.

If we number the columns (digits) of a decimal integer from right to left (starting with 0), then if we borrow 1 from column n, what we mean is that we subtract 1 from column n and add 10 to column $n-1$. Since $1 \times 10^n = 10 \times 10^{n-1}$,

---

[*]An alternative to binary subtraction is the use of 2's complement arithmetic, as discussed in Section 20.1.

the value of the decimal number is unchanged, but we can proceed with the subtraction. Consider, for example, the following decimal subtraction problem:

$$
\begin{array}{r}
\text{column 2} \qquad \text{column 1} \\
2\ 0\ 5 \\
-\ 1\ 8 \\
\hline
1\ 8\ 7
\end{array}
$$

A detailed analysis of the borrowing process for this example, indicating first a borrow of 1 from column 1 and then a borrow of 1 from column 2, is as follows:

205 − 18

$= [2 \times 10^2 + 0 \times 10^1 + 5 \times 10^0]$

$- [\qquad\qquad 1 \times 10^1 + 8 \times 10^0]$

note borrow from column 1

$= [2 \times 10^2 + (0 - 1) \times 10^1 + (10 + 5) \times 10^0]$

$- [\qquad\qquad 1\ \times 10^1 + \qquad 8\ \times 10^0]$

note borrow from column 2

$= [(2 - 1) \times 10^2 + (10 + 0 - 1) \times 10^1 + 15 \times 10^0]$

$- [\qquad\qquad\qquad\qquad 1\ \times 10^1 + \ 8 \times 10^0]$

$= [1 \times 10^2 \qquad + \ 8 \times 10^1 \qquad + \ 7 \times 10^0] = 187$

The analysis of borrowing for binary subtraction is exactly the same, except that we work with powers of 2 instead of powers of 10. Thus for a binary number, borrowing 1 from column n is equivalent to subtracting 1 from column n and adding 2 (10_2) to column $n-1$. The value of the binary number is unchanged because $1 \times 2^n = 2 \times 2^{n-1}$.

A detailed analysis of binary subtraction example (c) follows. Starting with the rightmost column, $1 - 1 = 0$. In order to subtract in the second column, we must borrow from the third column. Rather than borrow immediately, we place a 1 over the third column to indicate that a borrow is necessary, and we will actually do the borrowing when we get to the third column. (This is similar to the way borrow signals might propagate in a computer.) Now since we have borrowed 1, the second column becomes 10, and $10 - 1 = 1$. In order to borrow 1 from the third column, we must borrow 1 from the fourth column (indicated by placing a 1 over column 4). Column 3 then becomes 10, subtracting off the borrow yields 1, and $1 - 0 = 1$. Now in column 4, we subtract off the borrow leaving 0. In order to complete the subtraction, we must borrow from column 5, which gives 10 in column 4, and $10 - 1 = 1$.

The multiplication table for binary numbers is

$$
\begin{array}{l}
0 \times 0 = 0 \\
0 \times 1 = 0 \\
1 \times 0 = 0 \\
1 \times 1 = 1
\end{array}
$$

The following example illustrates multiplication of 13_{10} by 11_{10} in binary:

$$
\begin{array}{r}
1101 \\
1011 \\
\hline
1101 \\
1101 \\
0000 \\
1101 \\
\hline
10001111 = 143_{10}
\end{array}
$$

Note that each partial product is either the multiplicand (1101) shifted over the appropriate number of places or is zero.

The following example illustrates division of 145_{10} by 11_{10} in binary:

$$
\begin{array}{r}
1101 \\
1011\,\overline{\smash{)}\,10010001} \\
1011 \\
\hline
1110 \\
1011 \\
\hline
1101 \\
1011 \\
\hline
10
\end{array}
$$

The quotient is 1101 with a remainder of 10.

1.4 Binary Codes

Although most large computers work internally with binary numbers, the input-output equipment generally uses decimal numbers. Since most logic circuits only accept two-valued signals, the decimal numbers must be coded in terms of binary signals. In the simplest form of binary code, each decimal digit is replaced by its binary equivalent. For example, 937.25 is represented by

$$
\begin{array}{ccccc}
9 & 3 & 7 & . & 2 & 5 \\
1001 & 0011 & 0111 & . & 0010 & 0101
\end{array}
$$

This representation is referred to as binary-coded-decimal (BCD) or more explicitly as 8-4-2-1 BCD. Note that the result is quite different than that obtained by converting the number as a whole into binary.

Table 1-1 shows several possible sets of binary codes for the ten decimal digits. Many other possibilities exist since the only requirement for a valid code is that each decimal digit be represented by a distinct combination of binary digits. To translate a decimal number to coded form, each decimal digit is replaced by its corresponding code. Thus 937 expressed in excess-3 code is 1100 0110 1010. The 8-4-2-1 (BCD) code and the 6-3-1-1 code are examples of weighted codes. A 4-bit weighted code has the property that if the weights are w_3, w_2, w_1 and w_0, the code $a_3 a_2 a_1 a_0$ represents a decimal number N, where

$$
N = w_3 a_3 + w_2 a_2 + w_1 a_1 + w_0 a_0
$$

Table 1-1. Binary Codes for Decimal Digits

decimal digit	8-4-2-1 code (BCD)	6-3-1-1 code	excess-3 code	2-out-of-5 code	Gray code
0	0 0 0 0	0 0 0 0	0 0 1 1	0 0 0 1 1	0 0 0 0
1	0 0 0 1	0 0 0 1	0 1 0 0	0 0 1 0 1	0 0 0 1
2	0 0 1 0	0 0 1 1	0 1 0 1	0 0 1 1 0	0 0 1 1
3	0 0 1 1	0 1 0 0	0 1 1 0	0 1 0 0 1	0 0 1 0
4	0 1 0 0	0 1 0 1	0 1 1 1	0 1 0 1 0	0 1 1 0
5	0 1 0 1	0 1 1 1	1 0 0 0	0 1 1 0 0	1 1 1 0
6	0 1 1 0	1 0 0 0	1 0 0 1	1 0 0 0 1	1 0 1 0
7	0 1 1 1	1 0 0 1	1 0 1 0	1 0 0 1 0	1 0 1 1
8	1 0 0 0	1 0 1 1	1 0 1 1	1 0 1 0 0	1 0 0 1
9	1 0 0 1	1 1 0 0	1 1 0 0	1 1 0 0 0	1 0 0 0

For example, the weights for the 6-3-1-1 code are $w_3 = 6$, $w_2 = 3$, $w_1 = 1$ and $w_0 = 1$. The binary code 1011 thus represents the decimal digit

$$N = 6 \cdot 1 + 3 \cdot 0 + 1 \cdot 1 + 1 \cdot 1 = 8$$

The excess-3 code is obtained from the 8-4-2-1 code by adding 3 (0011) to each of the codes. The 2-out-of-5 code has the property that exactly 2 out of the 5 bits are 1 for every valid code combination. This code has useful error-checking properties since if any one of the bits in a code combination is changed due to a malfunction of the logic circuitry, the number of 1 bits is no longer exactly two. The table shows one example of a Gray code. A Gray code has the property that the codes for successive decimal digits differ in exactly one bit. For example, the codes for 6 and 7 differ only in the fourth bit, and the codes for 9 and 0 differ only in the first bit. A Gray code is often used when translating an analog quantity such as a shaft position into digital form. In this case, a small change in the analog quantity will change only one bit in the code, which gives more reliable operation than if two or more bits changed at a time. The Gray and 2-out-of-5 codes are *not* weighted codes. In general, the decimal value of a coded digit *cannot* be computed by a simple formula when a non-weighted code is used.

Many applications of computers require processing of data which contains numbers, letters and other symbols such as punctuation marks. In order to transmit such alphanumeric data to or from a computer, or store it internally in a computer, each symbol must be represented by a binary code. One common alphanumeric code is the ASCII code (American Standard Code for Information Interchange). This is a 7-bit code, so 2^7 (128) different code combinations are available to represent letters, numbers and other symbols. Table 1-2 shows a portion of the ASCII code; the code combinations not listed are used for special control functions like "form feed" or "end of transmission". The word "Start" is represented in ASCII code as follows:

1010011	1110100	1100001	1110010	1110100
S	t	a	r	t

Table 1.2   ASCII Code

char-acter	ASCII code $A_6 A_5 A_4 A_3 A_2 A_1 A_0$	char-acter	ASCII code $A_6 A_5 A_4 A_3 A_2 A_1 A_0$	char-acter	ASCII code $A_6 A_5 A_4 A_3 A_2 A_1 A_0$
space	0 1 0 0 0 0 0	@	1 0 0 0 0 0 0	`	1 1 0 0 0 0 0
!	0 1 0 0 0 0 1	A	1 0 0 0 0 0 1	a	1 1 0 0 0 0 1
"	0 1 0 0 0 1 0	B	1 0 0 0 0 1 0	b	1 1 0 0 0 1 0
#	0 1 0 0 0 1 1	C	1 0 0 0 0 1 1	c	1 1 0 0 0 1 1
$	0 1 0 0 1 0 0	D	1 0 0 0 1 0 0	d	1 1 0 0 1 0 0
%	0 1 0 0 1 0 1	E	1 0 0 0 1 0 1	e	1 1 0 0 1 0 1
&	0 1 0 0 1 1 0	F	1 0 0 0 1 1 0	f	1 1 0 0 1 1 0
'	0 1 0 0 1 1 1	G	1 0 0 0 1 1 1	g	1 1 0 0 1 1 1
(	0 1 0 1 0 0 0	H	1 0 0 1 0 0 0	h	1 1 0 1 0 0 0
)	0 1 0 1 0 0 1	I	1 0 0 1 0 0 1	i	1 1 0 1 0 0 1
*	0 1 0 1 0 1 0	J	1 0 0 1 0 1 0	j	1 1 0 1 0 1 0
+	0 1 0 1 0 1 1	K	1 0 0 1 0 1 1	k	1 1 0 1 0 1 1
,	0 1 0 1 1 0 0	L	1 0 0 1 1 0 0	l	1 1 0 1 1 0 0
-	0 1 0 1 1 0 1	M	1 0 0 1 1 0 1	m	1 1 0 1 1 0 1
.	0 1 0 1 1 1 0	N	1 0 0 1 1 1 0	n	1 1 0 1 1 1 0
/	0 1 0 1 1 1 1	O	1 0 0 1 1 1 1	o	1 1 0 1 1 1 1
0	0 1 1 0 0 0 0	P	1 0 1 0 0 0 0	p	1 1 1 0 0 0 0
1	0 1 1 0 0 0 1	Q	1 0 1 0 0 0 1	q	1 1 1 0 0 0 1
2	0 1 1 0 0 1 0	R	1 0 1 0 0 1 0	r	1 1 1 0 0 1 0
3	0 1 1 0 0 1 1	S	1 0 1 0 0 1 1	s	1 1 1 0 0 1 1
4	0 1 1 0 1 0 0	T	1 0 1 0 1 0 0	t	1 1 1 0 1 0 0
5	0 1 1 0 1 0 1	U	1 0 1 0 1 0 1	u	1 1 1 0 1 0 1
6	0 1 1 0 1 1 0	V	1 0 1 0 1 1 0	v	1 1 1 0 1 1 0
7	0 1 1 0 1 1 1	W	1 0 1 0 1 1 1	w	1 1 1 0 1 1 1
8	0 1 1 1 0 0 0	X	1 0 1 1 0 0 0	x	1 1 1 1 0 0 0
9	0 1 1 1 0 0 1	Y	1 0 1 1 0 0 1	y	1 1 1 1 0 0 1
:	0 1 1 1 0 1 0	Z	1 0 1 1 0 1 0	z	1 1 1 1 0 1 0
;	0 1 1 1 0 1 1	[	1 0 1 1 0 1 1	{	1 1 1 1 0 1 1
<	0 1 1 1 1 0 0	\	1 0 1 1 1 0 0	ı	1 1 1 1 1 0 0
=	0 1 1 1 1 0 1	]	1 0 1 1 1 0 1	}	1 1 1 1 1 0 1
>	0 1 1 1 1 1 0	^	1 0 1 1 1 1 0	~	1 1 1 1 1 1 0
?	0 1 1 1 1 1 1	_	1 0 1 1 1 1 1	delete	1 1 1 1 1 1 1

PROBLEMS

1.1   Convert to octal and then to binary:

   a. 757.25_{10} b. 123.17_{10} c. 356.89_{10} d. 1063.5_{10}

1.2 Convert to octal and then to decimal:
    a. 10111011.1_2
    b. 1101101.011_2
    c. 10000011.11_2
    d. 11101111.101_2

1.3 Add, subtract and multiply in binary:
    a. 1111 and 1011
    b. 1001001 and 111010
    c. 110100 and 11011

1.4 Convert to base 5: 165.2_7
    (do all of the arithmetic in decimal)

1.5   a. Convert to hexadecimal: 701.12_{10}

    b. Devise a scheme for converting hexadecimal directly to base 4 and convert your answer to base 4.

    c. Convert to decimal: $ABC.D_{16}$

1.6 Construct a table for a 5-3-2-1 weighted code and write 9371 using this code.

1.7 Convert to base 3: 375.54_8
    (do all of the arithmetic in decimal).

1.8 Convert to hexadecimal and then to binary:
    a. $2983\frac{63}{64}$
    b. 93.70

1.9 Subtract in binary. Place a 1 over each column from which it was necessary to borrow.
    a. 11011011 - 1101101
    b. 10001100 - 1100101
    c. 11101010 - 110111101

1.10 Divide in binary:
    a. $1011110 \div 1001$
    b. $110000001 \div 1110$
    c. $1110010 \div 1001$
    Check your answers by multiplying out in binary and adding the remainder.

1.11 Is it possible to construct a 5-4-1-1 weighted code? A 5-3-2-1 weighted code? Justify your answers.

1.12 Construct a 6-2-2-1 weighted code for decimal digits. What number does 1001 0110 represent in this code?

1.13 Devise a scheme for converting base 3 numbers directly to base 9. Use your method to convert the following number to base 9: 210120221001.121_3

1.14 Convert to hexadecimal, and then give the ASCII code for the resulting hexadecimal number (including the code for the hex point): 234.71_{10}

2

BOOLEAN ALGEBRA

OBJECTIVES

A list of 17 laws and theorems of Boolean algebra is given on page 37 of this unit. When you complete this unit, you should be familiar with and be able to use any of the first 11 of these. Specifically, you should be able to:

1. Understand the basic operations and laws of Boolean algebra.

2. Relate these operations and laws to networks composed of AND gates, OR gates, and INVERTERS. Also relate these operations and laws to networks composed of switches.

3. Prove any of these laws using a truth table.

4. Apply these laws to the manipulation of algebraic expressions including:

   a. multiplying out an expression to obtain a sum of products

   b. factoring an expression to obtain a product of sums

   c. simplifying an expression by applying one of the laws.

STUDY GUIDE

1. In this unit you will study Boolean algebra, the basic mathematics needed for logic design of digital systems. Just as when you first learned ordinary algebra, you will need a fair amount of practice before you can use Boolean algebra effectively. However, by the end of the course, you should be just as "at home" with Boolean algebra as with ordinary algebra. Fortunately, many of the rules of Boolean algebra are the same as for ordinary algebra, but watch out for some surprises!

2. Study Sections 2.1 and 2.2 of this unit, *Introduction* and *Basic Operations*.

   a. How does the meaning of the symbols 0 and 1 as used in this unit differ from the meaning as used in Unit 1?

   b. Two commonly-used notations for the inverse or complement of A are $\overline{A}$ and A'. The latter has the advantage that it is much easier for typists, printers and computers. (Have you ever tried to get a computer to print out a bar over a letter?) We will use A' for the complement of A. You may use either notation in your work, but please don't mix notations in the same equation. Most engineers use $+$ for OR and $\cdot$ (or no symbol) for AND, and we will follow this practice. An alternative notation, often used by mathematicians, is $\vee$ for OR and $\wedge$ for AND.

   c. Many different symbols are used for AND, OR, and INVERTER logic blocks.* We will use:

   The shapes of these symbols conform to those commonly used in industrial and military practice. We have added the $+$ and $\cdot$ for clarity. The above symbols point in the direction of signal flow. This makes it easier to read the network diagrams in comparison with the square or round symbols used in some books.

   d. Determine the output of each of the following gates:

   e. Determine the unspecified inputs to each of the following gates if the outputs are as shown:

3. Study Section 2.3, *Boolean Expressions and Truth Tables*.

   a. How many *variables* does the following expression contain? _____
   How many *literals*? _____

   $$A'BC'D + AB + B'CD + D'$$

   _____

   *See Appendix B.1 for a discussion of alternative gate symbols.

b. For the following network, if $A = B = 0$ and $C = D = E = 1$, indicate the output of each gate (0 or 1) on the network diagram.

c. Derive a Boolean expression for the network output. Then substitute $A = B = 0$ and $C = D = E = 1$ into your expression and verify that the value of F obtained in this way is the same as that obtained on the network diagram in b.

d. Write an expression for the output of the following network and complete the truth table:

$F = $ _____

$A\ B$	A'	$A'B$	$(A'B)'$

e. When filling in the combinations of values for the variables on the left side of a truth table, always list the combinations of 0's and 1's in binary order. For example, for a 3-variable truth table, the first row should be 000, the next row 001, then 010, 011, 100, 101, 110, and 111. Write an expression for the output of the following network and complete the truth table:

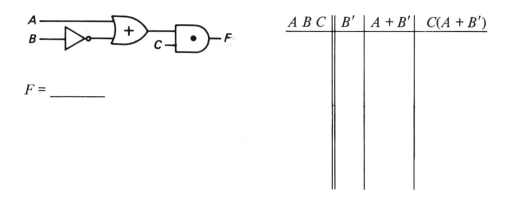

$F = $ _____

$A\ B\ C$	B'	$A + B'$	$C(A + B')$

f. Draw a gate network which has an output
$$Z = [BC' + F(E + AD')]'$$
(*Hint:* Start with the innermost parentheses and draw the network for AD' first.)

4. Study Section 2.4, *Basic Theorems.*

a. Prove each of the theorems (2-4) through (2-8D) by showing that it is valid for both $X = 0$ and $X = 1$.

b. Determine the output of each of the following gates:

c. State which of the basic theorems was used in simplifying each of the following expressions:

$(AB' + C) \cdot 0 = 0$ $A(B + C') + 1 = 1$

$(BC' + A)(BC' + A) = BC' + A$ $X(Y' + Z) + [X(Y' + Z)]' = 1$

$(X' + YZ)(X' + YZ)' = 0$ $D'(E' + F) + D'(E' + F) = D'(E' + F)$

5. Study Section 2.5, *Commutative, Associative and Distributive Laws.*

a. State the associative law for OR.

b. State the commutative law for AND.

c. Simplify the following network by using the associative laws. Your answer should require only two gates.

d. For each gate determine the value of the unspecified input(s):

e. Using a truth table, verify the distributive law, Equation (2-11).

f. Illustrate the distributive laws, Equation, (2-11) and (2-11D), using AND and OR gates.

g. Verify Equation (2-3) using the second distributive law.

h. Show how the second distributive law can be used to factor $RS + T'$.

6. Study Section 2.6, *Simplification Theorems*.

   a. By completing the truth table, prove that $XY' + Y = X + Y$.

X Y	XY'	XY' + Y	X + Y
0 0			
0 1			
1 0			
1 1			

   b. Which of the theorems (2-12) through (2-14D) was applied to simplify each of the following expressions? Identify X and Y in each case.

   $$(A + B)(DE)' + DE = A + B + DE$$

   $$AB' + AB'C'D = AB'$$

   $$(A' + B)(CD + E') + (A' + B)(CD + E')' = A' + B$$

   $$(A + BC' + D'E)(A + D'E) = A + D'E$$

   c. Simplify the following network to a single gate:

   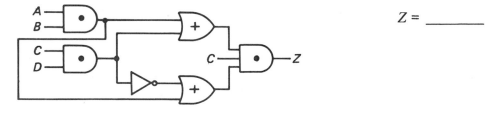

   $Z = \underline{\hspace{2cm}}$

   d. Work Problems 2.1, 2.2, 2.3, and 2.7a and b.

7. Study Section 2.7, *Multiplying Out and Factoring*.

   a. Indicate which of the following expressions are in product-of-sums form, sum-of-products form, or neither.

   $$AB' + D'EF' + G$$
   $$(A + B'C')(A' + BC)$$

$$AB'(C' + D + E')(F' + G)$$
$$X'Y + WX(X' + Z) + A'B'C'$$

Your answer to this question should include one product-of-sums, one sum-of-products, and two "neither", not necessarily in that order.

b. When multiplying out an expression, why should the second distributive law be applied before the ordinary distributive law when possible?

c. Factor as much as possible using the ordinary distributive law:

$$AD + B'CD + B'DE$$

Now factor your result using the second distributive law to obtain a product of sums.

d. Work Problems 2.4a and b, 2.5, and 2.6.

8. Probably the most difficult part of the unit is using the second distributive law for factoring or multiplying out an expression. If you have difficulty with problems 2.4 or 2.5, or you cannot work them *quickly*, study the examples in Section 2.7 again, and then work the following problems.

Multiply out:

a. $(B' + D + E)(B' + D + A)(AE + C')$

b. $(A + C')(B' + D)(C' + D')(C + D)E$

As usual, when we say multiply out, we don't mean multiply out by brute force, but rather use the second distributive law whenever you can to cut down on the amount of work required.

Answer to 8a above should be of the following form: $XX + XX + XX$ and 8b of the form: $XXX + XXXXX$, where each X represents a single variable or its complement.

Now factor your answer to 8a to see that you can get back the original expression.

9. Review the first 11 laws and theorems on p. 37. Make sure that you can recognize when to apply them even if an expression has been substituted for a variable.

10. Reread the objectives of this unit. If you are satisfied that you can meet these objectives, take the readiness test.

   (*Note:* You will be provided with a copy of the theorem sheet (p. 37) when you take the readiness test this time. However, by the end of Unit 3, you should know all the theorems by memory.)

2. BOOLEAN ALGEBRA

2.1 Introduction

   The basic mathematics needed for the study of logic design of digital systems is Boolean algebra.* Boolean algebra has many other applications including set theory and mathematical logic, but we will restrict ourselves to its application to switching networks in this text. Since all of the switching devices which we will use are essentially two-state devices (such as a transistor with high or low output voltage), we will study the special case of Boolean algebra in which all of the variables assume only one of two values. This two-valued Boolean algebra is often referred to as switching algebra.

   We will use a Boolean variable, such as X or Y, to represent the input or output of a switching network. We will assume that each of these variables can take on only two different values. The symbols "0" and "1" are used to represent these two different values. Thus, if X is a Boolean (switching) variable, then either $X = 0$ or $X = 1$.

   Although the symbols 0 and 1 used in this chapter *look* like binary numbers, they are not. They have no numeric value, but rather are just two symbols which represent the two values of a switching variable. The symbol 0, for example, might correspond to a low voltage and 1 might correspond to a high voltage. F and T could be used just as well as 0 and 1.

2.2 Basic Operations

   The basic operations of Boolean algebra are AND, OR, and complement (or inverse). The complement of 0 is 1, and the complement of 1 is 0. Symbolically, we write

$$0' = 1 \text{ and } 1' = 0$$

where the prime (') denotes complementation. If X is a switching variable,

$$X' = 1 \text{ if } X = 0, \text{ and } X' = 0 \text{ if } X = 1.$$

An alternate name for complementation is inversion, and the electronic circuit which forms the inverse of X is referred to as an inverter. Symbolically, we represent an inverter by

---

*George Boole developed Boolean algebra in 1847 and used it to solve problems in mathematical logic. Claude Shannon first applied Boolean algebra to the design of switching networks in 1939.

$$X —\!\!\!\triangleright\!\!\circ\!— X'$$

where the circle at the output indicates inversion. If a logic 0 corresponds to a low voltage and a logic 1 corresponds to a high voltage, a low voltage at the inverter input produces a high voltage at the output and vice versa. Complementation is sometimes referred to as the NOT operation since $X = 1$ if X is *not* equal to 0.

The AND operation can be defined as follows:

$$0 \cdot 0 = 0, \quad 0 \cdot 1 = 0, \quad 1 \cdot 0 = 0, \quad 1 \cdot 1 = 1$$

where "$\cdot$" denotes AND. (Although this looks like binary multiplication, it is not since 0 and 1 here are Boolean constants rather than binary numbers.) If we write the Boolean expression $C = A \cdot B$, then given the values of A and B, we can determine C from the following table:

A B	$C = A \cdot B$
0 0	0
0 1	0
1 0	0
1 1	1

Note that $C = 1$ iff (if and only if) A *and* B are both 1, hence the name AND operation. A logic gate which performs the AND operation is represented by

$$A,\ B \longrightarrow \boxed{\cdot} \longrightarrow C = A \bullet B$$

The "$\cdot$" symbol is frequently omitted in a Boolean expression, and we will usually write AB instead of $A \cdot B$. The AND operation is also referred to as logical (or Boolean) multiplication.

The OR operation can be defined as follows:

$$0 + 0 = 0 \quad 0 + 1 = 1 \quad 1 + 0 = 1 \quad 1 + 1 = 1$$

where "+" denotes OR. If we write $C = A + B$, then given the values of A and B we can determine C from the following table:

A B	$C = A + B$
0 0	0
0 1	1
1 0	1
1 1	1

Note that $C = 1$ iff A *or* B (or both) is 1, hence the name OR operation. This type of OR operation is sometimes referred to as "inclusive OR". A logic gate which performs the OR operation is represented by

$$A,\ B \longrightarrow \boxed{+} \longrightarrow C = A + B$$

The OR operation is also referred to as logical (or Boolean) addition. Electronic circuits which realize inverters and AND and OR gates are described in Appendix A.

We will next apply switching algebra to describe networks containing switches. We will label each switch with a variable. If switch X is open, then we will define the value of X to be 0; if switch X is closed, then we will define the value of X to be 1.

$X = 0 \rightarrow$ switch open

$X = 1 \rightarrow$ switch closed

Now consider a network composed of two switches in series. We will define the transmission between the terminals as $T = 0$ if there is an open circuit between the terminals and $T = 1$ if there is a closed circuit between the terminals.

$T = 0 \rightarrow$ open circuit between terminals 1 and 2

$T = 1 \rightarrow$ closed circuit between terminals 1 and 2

Now we have a closed circuit between terminals 1 and 2 ($T = 1$) iff (if and only if) switch A is closed *and* switch B is closed. Stating this algebraically,

$$T = A \cdot B$$

Next consider a network composed of two switches in parallel.

In this case, we have a closed circuit between terminals 1 and 2 iff switch A is closed *or* switch B is closed. Using the same convention for defining variables as above, an equation which describes the behavior of this network is

$$T = A + B$$

Thus, switches in series perform the AND operation and switches in parallel perform the OR operation.

2.3 Boolean Expressions and Truth Tables

Boolean expressions are formed by application of the basic operations to one or more variables or constants. The simplest expressions consist of a single constant or variable, such as 0, X, Y', etc. More complicated expressions are formed by combining two or more other expressions using AND or OR, or by complementing another expression. Examples of expressions are

$$AB' + C \tag{2-1}$$

$$[A(C + D)]' + BE \tag{2-2}$$

Parentheses are added as needed to specify the order in which the operations are performed. When parentheses are omitted, complementation is performed first followed by AND and then OR. Thus in (2-1), B' is formed first, then AB' and finally $AB' + C$.

Each expression corresponds directly to a network of logic gates. Fig. 2-1 gives the networks for expressions (2-1) and (2-2) above.

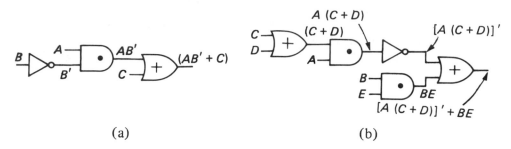

(a)   (b)

Fig. 2-1.   Networks for expressions (2-1) and (2-2)

An expression is evaluated by substituting a value of 0 or 1 for each variable. If $A = B = C = 1$ and $D = E = 0$, the value of expression (2-2) is

$$[A(C + D)]' + BE = [1(1 + 0)]' + 1 \cdot 0 = [1(1)]' + 0 = 0 + 0 = 0$$

Each appearance of a variable or its complement in an expression will be referred to as a *literal*. Thus the following expression, which has 3 variables, has 10 literals:

$$ab'c + a'b + a'bc' + b'c'$$

When an expression is realized using logic gates, each literal in the expression corresponds to a gate input.

A *truth table* (also called a table of combinations) specifies the values of a Boolean expression for every possible combination of values of the variables in the expression. The name truth table comes from a similar table which is used in symbolic logic to list the "truth" or "falsity" of a statement under all possible conditions. We can use a truth table to specify the output values for a network of logic gates in terms of the values of the input variables. The output of the network in Fig. 2-2(a) is $F = A' + B$. Figure 2-2(b) shows a truth table which specifies the output of the network for all possible combinations of values of the inputs A and B. The first two columns list the four combinations of values of A and B, and the next column gives the corresponding values of A'. The last column, which gives the values of $A' + B$, is formed by ORing together corresponding values of A' and B in each row.

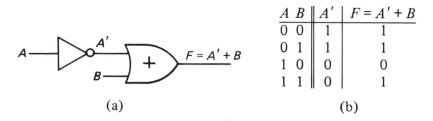

A B	A'	F = A' + B
0 0	1	1
0 1	1	1
1 0	0	0
1 1	0	1

(a)   (b)

Fig. 2-2.   2-input network and truth table

Next, we will use a truth table to specify the value of expression (2-1) for all possible combinations of values of the variables A, B and C. On the left side of Table 2-1, we list the values of the variables A, B and C. Since each of the three variables can assume the value 0 or 1, there are $2 \times 2 \times 2 = 8$ combinations of values of the variables. These combinations are easily obtained by listing the binary numbers $000, 001, \ldots, 111$. In the next three columns of the truth table, we compute B', AB' and $AB' + C$ respectively.

Table 2-1

A B C	B'	AB'	$AB' + C$	$A + C$	$B' + C$	$(A + C)(B' + C)$
0 0 0	1	0	0	0	1	0
0 0 1	1	0	1	1	1	1
0 1 0	0	0	0	0	0	0
0 1 1	0	0	1	1	1	1
1 0 0	1	1	1	1	1	1
1 0 1	1	1	1	1	1	1
1 1 0	0	0	0	1	0	0
1 1 1	0	0	1	1	1	1

Two expressions are equal if they have the same value for every possible combination of the variables. The expression $(A+C)(B' + C)$ is evaluated using the last three columns of Table 2-1. Since it has the same value as $AB' + C$ for all eight combinations of values of the variables A, B and C, we conclude

$$AB' + C = (A + C)(B' + C) \qquad (2\text{-}3)$$

If an expression has n variables, and each variable can have the value 0 or 1, the number of different combinations of values of the variables is

$$\underbrace{2 \times 2 \times 2 \times \ldots}_{n \text{ times}} = 2^n$$

Therefore, a truth table for an n-variable expression will have 2^n rows.

2.4 Basic Theorems

The following basic theorems of Boolean algebra involve only a single variable:

Operations with 0 and 1:

$X + 0 = X$	(2-4)	$X \cdot 1 = X$	(2-4D)
$X + 1 = 1$	(2-5)	$X \cdot 0 = 0$	(2-5D)

Idempotent laws

$X + X = X$	(2-6)	$X \cdot X = X$	(2-6D)

Involution law

$(X')' = X$ \qquad (2-7)

Laws of complementarity:

$$X + X' = 1 \qquad (2\text{-}8) \qquad\qquad X \cdot X' = 0 \qquad (2\text{-}8D)$$

Each of these theorems is easily proved by showing that it is valid for both of the possible values of X. For example, to prove $X + X' = 1$, we observe that if

$$X = 0,\ 0 + 0' = 0 + 1 = 1,\ \text{and if } X = 1,\ 1 + 1' = 1 + 0 = 1.$$

Any expression can be substituted for the variable X in these theorems. Thus, by theorem (2-5),

$$(AB' + D)E + 1 = 1$$

and by theorem (2-8D),

$$(AB' + D)(AB' + D)' = 0$$

We will illustrate some of the basic theorems by networks of switches. As before, 0 will represent an open circuit or open switch and 1 will represent a closed circuit or closed switch. If two switches are both labeled with the variable A, this means that both switches are open when $A = 0$ and both are closed when $A = 1$. Thus the network

can be replaced with a single switch

This illustrates the theorem $A \cdot A = A$. Similarly,

which illustrates the theorem $A + A = A$. A switch in parallel with an open circuit is equivalent to the switch alone

$$(A + 0 = A)$$

while a switch in parallel with a short circuit is equivalent to a short circuit

$$(A + 1 = 1)$$

If a switch is labeled A', then it is open when A is closed and conversely.

Hence A in parallel with A' can be replaced with a closed circuit since one or other of the two switches are always closed:

$$(A + A' = 1)$$

Similarly, switch A in series with A' can be replaced with an open circuit: (Why?)

$$(A \cdot A' = 0)$$

2.5 Commutative, Associative and Distributive Laws

Many of the laws of ordinary algebra, such as the commutative and associative laws, also apply to Boolean algebra. The commutative laws for AND and OR, which follow directly from the definitions of the AND and OR operations, are

$$XY = YX \qquad (2\text{-}9) \qquad\qquad X + Y = Y + X \qquad (2\text{-}9D)$$

This means that the order in which the variables are written will not affect the result of applying the AND and OR operations.

The associative laws also apply to AND and OR:

$$(XY)Z = X(YZ) = XYZ \qquad (2\text{-}10)$$

$$(X + Y) + Z = X + (Y + Z) = X + Y + Z \qquad (2\text{-}10D)$$

When forming the AND (or OR) of three variables, the result is independent of which pair of variables we associate together first, so parentheses can be omitted as indicated in Equations (2-10) and (2-10D).

We will prove the associative law for AND by using a truth table (Table 2-2). On the left side of the table, we list all combinations of values of the variables X, Y and Z. In the next two columns of the truth table, we compute XY and YZ for each combination of values of X, Y and Z. Finally, we compute $(XY)Z$ and $X(YZ)$. Since $(XY)Z$ and $X(YZ)$ are equal for all possible combinations of values of the variables, we conclude that Equation (2-10) is valid.

Table 2-2. Proof of Associative Law for AND

X	Y	Z	XY	YZ	(XY)Z	X(YZ)
0	0	0	0	0	0	0
0	0	1	0	0	0	0
0	1	0	0	0	0	0
0	1	1	0	1	0	0
1	0	0	0	0	0	0
1	0	1	0	0	0	0
1	1	0	1	0	0	0
1	1	1	1	1	1	1

Figure 2-3 illustrates the associative laws using AND and OR gates. In Fig. 2-3(a) two 2-input AND gates are replaced with a single 3-input AND gate. Similarly, in Fig. 2-3(b) two 2-input OR gates are replaced with a single 3-input OR gate.

(a)

(b)

Fig. 2-3. Associative laws for AND and OR

When two or more variables are ANDed together, the value of the result will be 1 iff all of the variables have the value 1. If any of the variables have the value 0, the result of the AND operation will be 0. For example,

$$XYZ = 1 \text{ iff } X = Y = Z = 1$$

When two or more variables are ORed together, the value of the result will be 1 if any of the variables have the value 1. The result of the OR operation will be 0 iff all of the variables have the value 0. For example,

$$X + Y + Z = 0 \text{ iff } X = Y = Z = 0$$

Using a truth table, it is easy to show that the distributive law is valid:

$$X(Y + Z) = XY + XZ \tag{2-11}$$

In addition to the ordinary distributive law, there is a second distributive law which is valid for Boolean algebra but not for ordinary algebra:

$$X + YZ = (X + Y)(X + Z) \tag{2-11D}$$

Proof of the second distributive law follows:

$$(X + Y)(X + Z) = X(X + Z) + Y(X + Z) = XX + XZ + YX + YZ$$

$$\text{(by 2-11)}$$

$$= X + XZ + XY + YZ = X \cdot 1 + XZ + XY + YZ$$

$$\text{(by 2-6D and 2-4D)}$$

$$= X(1 + Z + Y) + YZ = X \cdot 1 + YZ = X + YZ$$

$$\text{(by 2-11 and 2-5)}$$

The ordinary distributive law states that the AND operation distributes over OR, while the second distributive law states that OR distributes over AND. This second law is very useful in manipulating Boolean expressions. In particular, an expression like $A + BC$ which cannot be factored in ordinary algebra is easily factored using the second distributive law:

$$A + BC = (A + B)(A + C)$$

2.6 Simplification Theorems

The following theorems are useful in simplifying Boolean expressions:

$XY + XY' = X$	(2-12)	$(X + Y)(X + Y') = X$	(2-12D)
$X + XY = X$	(2-13)	$X(X + Y) = X$	(2-13D)
$(X + Y')Y = XY$	(2-14)	$XY' + Y = X + Y$	(2-14D)

In each case, one expression can be replaced by a simpler one. Since each expression corresponds to a network of logic gates, simplifying an expression leads to simplifying the corresponding logic network.

Each of the above theorems can be proved by using a truth table, or they can be proved algebraically starting with the basic theorems.

Proof of (2-13): $X + XY = X \cdot 1 + XY = X(1 + Y) = X \cdot 1 = X$

Proof of (2-13D): $X(X + Y) = XX + XY = X + XY = X$

(by 2-6D and 2-13)

Proof of (2-14D): $Y + XY' = (Y + X)(Y + Y') = (Y + X)1 = Y + X$

(by 2-11D and 2-8)

Proof of the remaining theorems is left as an exercise.

We will illustrate theorem (2-14D) using switches. Consider the following network:

Its transmission is $T = Y + XY'$ since there is a closed circuit between the terminals if switch Y is closed *or* switch X is closed and switch Y' is closed. The following network is equivalent because if Y is closed ($Y = 1$) both networks have a transmission of 1; if Y is open ($Y' = 1$) both networks have a transmission of X.

The following example illustrates simplification of a logic gate network using one of the theorems. In Fig. 2-4, the output of network (a) is

$$F = A(A' + B)$$

By theorem (2-14), the expression for F simplifies to AB. Therefore, network (a) can be replaced with the equivalent network (b).

(a) (b)

Fig. 2-4. Equivalent gate networks

Any expressions can be substituted for X and Y in the theorems.

Example 1:   Simplify $Z = A'BC + A'$

This expression has the same form as (2-13) if we let $X = A'$ and $Y = BC$. Therefore, the expression simplifies to $Z = X + XY = X = A'$.

Example 2:   Simplify $Z = [A + B'C + D + EF]\ [A + B'C + (D + EF)']$

Substituting: $Z = [\quad X \quad + \quad Y \quad]\ [\quad X \quad + \quad Y' \quad]$

Then, by (2-12D), the expression reduces to

$$Z = X = A + B'C$$

Example 3:   Simplify $Z = (AB + C)(B'D + C'E') + (AB + C)'$

Substituting: $Z = \qquad Y' \qquad X \qquad + \qquad Y$

By (2-14D): $Z = X + Y = B'D + C'E' + (AB + C)'$

Note that in this example we let $Y = (AB + C)'$ rather than $(AB + C)$ in order to match the form of (2-14D).

2.7   Multiplying Out and Factoring

The two distributive laws are used to multiply out an expression to obtain a sum-of-products form. An expression is said to be in *sum-of-products* form when all products are the products of single variables only. This form is the end result when an expression is fully multiplied out. It is usually easy to recognize a sum-of-products expression since it consists of a sum of product terms:

$$AB' + CD'E + AC'E' \qquad (2\text{-}15)$$

However, in degenerate cases, one or more of the product terms may consist of a single variable. For example,

$$ABC' + DEFG + H \qquad (2\text{-}16)$$

and

$$A + B' + C + D'E \qquad (2\text{-}17)$$

are still considered to be in sum-of-products form. The expression $(A + B)CD + EF$ is not in sum-of-products form because the $A + B$ term enters into a product but is not a single variable.

When multiplying out an expression, the second distributive law should be applied first when possible. For example, to multiply out $(A + BC)(A + D + E)$ let

$$X = A,\ Y = BC,\ Z = D + E$$

Then $(X + Y)(X + Z) = X + YZ = A + BC(D + E) = A + BCD + BCE.$

Of course, the same result could be obtained the hard way by multiplying out the original expression completely and then eliminating redundant terms:

$$(A + BC)(A + D + E) = A + AD + AE + ABC + BCD + BCE$$

$$= A(1 + D + E + BC) + BCD + BCE$$

$$= A + BCD + BCE$$

You will save yourself much time if you learn to apply the second distributive law as above instead of doing the problem the hard way.

Both distributive laws can be used to factor an expression to obtain a product-of-sums form. An expression is in *product-of-sums* form when all sums are the sums of single variables. It is usually easy to recognize a product-of-sums expression since it consists of a product of sum terms:

$$(A + B')(C + D' + E)(A + C' + E') \qquad (2\text{-}18)$$

However, in degenerate cases, one or more of the sum terms may consist of a single variable. For example,

$$(A + B)(C + D + E)F \qquad (2\text{-}19)$$

and

$$AB'C(D' + E) \qquad (2\text{-}20)$$

are still considered to be in product-of-sums form, but $(A + B)(C + D) + EF$ is not in product-of-sums form. An expression is fully factored if and only if it is in product-of-sums form. Any expression not in this form can be factored further.

The following examples illustrate how to factor using the second distributive law:

(a) Factor $A + B'CD$. This is of the form $X + YZ$ where $X = A$, $Y = B'$ and $Z = CD$
so $\qquad A + B'CD = (X + Y)(X + Z) = (A + B')(A + CD)$

$A + CD$ can be factored again using the second distributive law, so

$$A + B'CD = (A + B')(A + C)(A + D)$$

(b) Factor $AB' + C'D$

$\qquad AB' + C'D = (AB' + C')(AB' + D)$ $\qquad \leftarrow$ note how $X + YZ = (X + Y)(X + Z)$ was applied here

$\qquad = (A + C')(B' + C')(A + D)(B' + D)$ $\qquad \leftarrow$ the second distributive law was applied again to each term

(c) Factor $C'D + C'E' + G'H$

$\qquad C'D + C'E' + G'H = C'(D + E') + G'H$ $\qquad \leftarrow$ first apply the ordinary distributive law, $XY + XZ = X(Y + Z)$

$\qquad = (C' + G'H)(D + E' + G'H)$ $\qquad \leftarrow$ then apply the 2nd distributive law

$\qquad = (C' + G')(C' + H)(D + E' + G')(D + E' + H)$ $\leftarrow$ now identify X, Y and Z in each expression and complete the factoring

As in example (c) above, the ordinary distributive law should be applied before the second law when factoring an expression.

A sum-of-products expression can always be realized directly by one or more AND gates feeding a single OR gate at the network output. Figure 2-5 shows the networks for Equations (2-15) and (2-17). Inverters required to generate the complemented variables have been omitted.

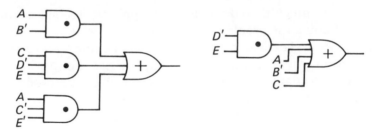

Fig. 2-5. Networks for Equations (2-15) and (2-17)

A product-of-sums expression can always be realized directly by one or more OR gates feeding a single AND gate at the network output. Figure 2-6 shows the networks for Equations (2-18) and (2-20). Inverters required to generate the complements have been omitted.

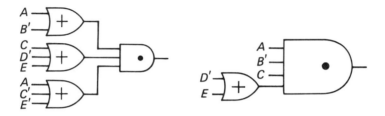

Fig. 2-6. Networks for Equations (2-18) and (2-20)

The networks shown in Figs. 2-5 and 2-6 are often referred to as two-level networks since they have a maximum of two gates in series between an input and the network output.

PROBLEMS

2.1 Prove the following theorems algebraically:

   a. $XY + XY' = X$ c. $X(X' + Y) = XY$

   b. $(X + Y)(X + Y') = X$ d. $(A + B)(A + C) = A + BC$

2.2 Illustrate the following theorems using networks of switches:

   a. $X + XY = X$ b. $X + YZ = (X + Y)(X + Z)$

   In each case, explain why the networks are equivalent.

2.3 Simplify each of the following expressions by applying one of the theorems. State the theorem used (see p. 37).

   a. $ABC' + (ABC')'$ d. $AB'(C + D) + (C + D)'$

   b. $(AB + CD')(AB + D'E)$ e. $[(EF)' + AB + C'D'](EF)$

   c. $A + B'C + D'(A + B'C)$ f. $(AB + C) + (D + EF)(AB + C)'$

2.4 Multiply out to obtain a sum of products:
 a. $(A + B)(A + C')(A + D)(BC'D + E)$
 b. $(A + B' + C)(B' + C + D)(A' + C)$
 c. $(A + B'C + D')(B'C + D' + E)(A + E')(AD + E')$
 d. $(A'+BE')(BE' + C + D)(E + C')$

2.5 Factor each of the following expressions to obtain a product of sums:
 a. $DE + F'G'$ e. $AC'D + C'D' + A'D'$
 b. $WX' + WY'Z' + WYZ$ f. $(H + IJ') + K'L$
 c. $A'CD + E'F + BCD$ (answer should be a product
 d. $ABE + D'E + AC'E$ of 4 terms, each a sum of
                         3 variables)

2.6 Draw a network to realize each of the following functions using only one AND gate and one OR gate.
 a. $(A + B + C + D)(A + B + C + E)(A + B + C + F)$
 b. $WXYZ + VXYZ + UXYZ$

2.7 For each of the following networks, find the output and design a simpler network having the same output. (Find the network output by first finding the output of each gate, going from left to right, and simplifying as you go.)

(a)

(b)

(c)

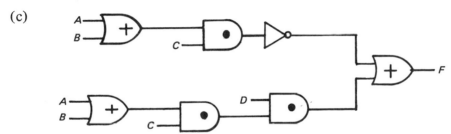

2.8 Simplify each of the following expressions by applying one of the theorems. State the theorem used.

    a. $(A'B + C)(A'B + C)'$

    b. $(AB' + C' + DE')(AB' + C')$

    c. $CD'(A + B') + CD'(A + B')'$

    d. $(CD + A' + B')(CD + A' + B)$

    e. $(A'C + B + D + E)(A'C + D)'$

    f. $(A + B'C + DF)(C + E' + F) + (A + B'C + DF)$

2.9 Multiply out to obtain a sum of products:

    a. $(X' + Y)(X' + Z)(W + Y)(W + Z)$

    b. $(X + Y' + Z)(W + X + Z)(Y' + Z)$

2.10 Factor each of the following expressions to obtain a product of sums:

    a. $AB'C + D$ c. $BC'D + A'BE + BEF$

    b. $W + X'Y + VZ$ d. $D'EF' + A'D' + B'D'E$

2.11 Draw a network to realize the following function using two OR gates and two AND gates:

    $F = (E + A + C)(E + B + C)(E + D)$

2.12 Prove the following equation using a truth table:

    $(A + CD)(A' + B) = A'CD + AB$

LAWS AND THEOREMS OF BOOLEAN ALGEBRA

Operations with 0 and 1:

1. $X + 0 = X$ 1D. $X \cdot 1 = X$

2. $X + 1 = 1$ 2D. $X \cdot 0 = 0$

Idempotent laws:

3. $X + X = X$ 3D. $X \cdot X = X$

Involution law:

4. $(X')' = X$

Laws of complementarity:

5. $X + X' = 1$ 5D. $X \cdot X' = 0$

Commutative laws:

6. $X + Y = Y + X$ 6D. $XY = YX$

Associative laws:

7. $(X + Y) + Z = X + (Y + Z)$
$$= X + Y + Z$$
7D. $(XY)Z = X(YZ) = XYZ$

Distributive laws:

8. $X(Y + Z) = XY + XZ$ 8D. $X + YZ = (X + Y)(X + Z)$

Simplification theorems:

9. $XY + XY' = X$ 9D. $(X + Y)(X + Y') = X$

10. $X + XY = X$ 10D. $X(X + Y) = X$

11. $(X + Y')Y = XY$ 11D. $XY' + Y = X + Y$

DeMorgan's laws:

12. $(X + Y + Z + \ldots)' = X'Y'Z' \ldots$ 12D. $(XYZ \ldots)' = X' + Y' + Z' + \ldots$

13. $[f(X_1, X_2, \ldots, X_n, 0, 1, +, \cdot)]' = f(X_1', X_2', \ldots, X_n', 1, 0, \cdot, +)$

Duality:

14. $(X + Y + Z + \ldots)^D = XYZ \ldots$ 14D. $(XYZ \ldots)^D = X + Y + Z + \ldots$

15. $[f(X_1, X_2, \ldots, X_n, 0, 1, +, \cdot)]^D = f(X_1, X_2, \ldots, X_n, 1, 0, \cdot, +)$

Theorem for multiplying out and factoring:

16. $(X + Y)(X' + Z) = XZ + X'Y$ 16D. $XY + X'Z = (X + Z)(X' + Y)$

Consensus theorem:

17. $XY + YZ + X'Z = XY + X'Z$ 17D. $(X + Y)(Y + Z)(X' + Z)$
$$= (X + Y)(X' + Z)$$

3

BOOLEAN ALGEBRA (Continued)

OBJECTIVES

When you complete this unit, you should know from memory and be able to use any of the first 16 laws and theorems of Boolean algebra listed at the end of Unit 2. Specifically, you should be able to:

1. Apply these laws and theorems to manipulation of algebraic expressions including:

   a. Simplifying an expression.

   b. Finding the complement or the dual of an expression.

   c. Multiplying out and factoring an expression.

2. Prove any of the theorems using a truth table or give an algebraic proof if appropriate.

3. Define the exclusive-OR and equivalence operations. State, prove and use the basic theorems which concern these operations.

4. Define positive and negative logic; apply the negative logic theorem.

STUDY GUIDE

1. Study Section 3.1, *Inversion.*

2. Find the complement of each of the following expressions as indicated. In your answer, the complement operation should only be applied to single variables.

   a. $(ab'c')' =$

   b. $(a' + b + c + d')' =$

   c. $(a' + bc)' =$

   d. $(a'b' + cd)' =$

   e. $[a(b' + c'd)]' =$

3. Since $(X')' = X$, if you complement each of your answers to part 2 you should get back the original expression. Verify that this is true.

   a.

   b.

   c.

   d.

   e.

4. a. State a single rule which can be used to form the complement of a Boolean expression in one step.

   b. In the following equation, each AND and OR operation has been given a number for reference:

   $$F = A \cdot B + C \cdot [D + E \cdot F + G \cdot (H + I \cdot J)]$$
   $$ 1 2 3 4 5 6 7 8 9$$

   When the expression is evaluated, which of the following pairs of operations is performed first?

   8 or 9 _____   6 or 7 _____   4 or 5 _____   2 or 3 _____
   1 or 2 _____

   By the one-step rule,

   $$F' = A' + B' \cdot C' + D' \cdot E' + F' + G' + H' \cdot I' + J'$$
   $$ 1 2 3 4 5 6 7 8 9$$

   Fill in the required parentheses in F' so that each pair of operations is performed in the same order as above. For example, since 9 is performed before 8 in F, add parentheses so 9 is performed before 8 in F'. Then add four more pairs of parentheses.

   c. When this rule was applied in Equation (3-8), which parentheses (or brackets) were added in order to preserve the proper hierarchy of operations?

   Verify that Equation (3-8) is correct by using Equations (3-1) and (3-2).

5. Given that $F = a'b + b'c$, $F' =$ _____ .
   Complete the following truth table and verify that your answer is correct:

$$F =$$

a b c	a'b	b'c	a'b + b'c	(a + b')	(b + c')	F'
0 0 0						
0 0 1						
0 1 0						
0 1 1						
1 0 0						
1 0 1						
1 1 0						
1 1 1						

6. Work Problem 3.3 using the "one-step" method. Work Problem 3.9.

7. Read Section 3.2, *Duality.* You will find an interesting application of duality when we study positive and negative logic.

   a. How does the dual of an expression differ from the complement?

   b. How are the constants 0 and 1 treated when forming the dual?

   When forming the complement?

   c. Observe that the theorems listed at the end of Unit 2 are listed in dual pairs. (Mentally verify that each pair is a dual.) This means that you really have only half as many theorems to learn, since if you know one, you can form its dual by inspection.

   d. Work Problem 3.4.

8. Study Section 3.3, *Multiplying Out and Factoring Expressions.*

   a. List three laws or theorems which are useful when multiplying out or factoring expressions.

   b. Use Equation (3-12) to factor each of the following:
      $ab'c + bd =$
      $abc + (ab)'d =$

   c. In the following example, first group the terms so that (3-11) can be applied two times.
      $$F_1 = (x + y' + z)(w' + x' + y)(w + x + y')(w' + y + z')$$

After applying (3-11), apply (3-12) and then finish multiplying out using (3-10).

If we did not use (3-11) and (3-12) and used only (3-10) on the above expression we would generate many more terms:

$$F_1 = (w'x + w'y' + w'z + xx' + x'y' + x'z + xy + yy' + yz)$$
$$(ww' + w'x + w'y' + wy + xy + yy' + wz' + xz' + y'z')$$
$$= (w'x + w'xy' + w'xz + \ldots + yzy'z')$$

$$\underbrace{}$$

49 terms in all

This is obviously a *very inefficient* way to proceed! The moral to this story is first group the terms and apply (3-11) and (3-12) where possible.

d. Work Programmed Exercise 3.1. Then work Problem 3.6 being careful not to introduce any unnecessary terms in the process.

e. In Unit 2, you learned how to factor a Boolean expression using the two distributive laws. In addition, this unit has introduced use of the theorem

$$XY + X'Z = (X + Z)(X' + Y)$$

in the factoring process. Careful choice of the order in which these laws and theorems are applied may cut down the amount of work required to factor an expression. When factoring, it is best to apply Equation (3-10) first, using as X the variable or variables which appear most frequently. Then Equations (3-11) and (3-12) can be applied in either order depending on circumstances.

f. Work Programmed Exercise 3.2. Then work Problem 3.7(a) and (b).

Checking your answers:

A good way to partially check your answers for correctness is to substitute in 0's or 1's for some of the variables. For example, if we substitute $A = 1$ in the first and last expression in Equation (3-14), we get:

$$1 \cdot C + 0 \cdot BD' + 0 \cdot BE + 0 \cdot C'DE$$
$$= (1 + B + C')(1 + B + D)(1 + D' + E)(0 + C)$$
$$C = 1 \cdot 1 \cdot 1 \cdot C \quad \checkmark$$

Similarly substituting $A = 0$, $B = 0$ we get:

$$0 + 0 + 0 + C'DE = (0 + C')(0 + D)(D' + E)(1 + C)$$
$$= C'DE \quad \checkmark$$

Verify that the result is also correct when $A = 0$ and $B = 1$.

10. The *method* which you use to get your answer is very important in this unit. If it takes you two pages of algebra and one hour of time to work a problem which can be solved in ten minutes with three lines of work, you have not learned the material in this unit! Even if you get the answer correct, your work is not satisfactory if you worked the problem by an excessively long and time-consuming method. It is important that you learn to solve simple problems in a simple manner — otherwise, when you are asked to solve a complex problem you will get bogged down and never get the answer.

When you are given a problem to solve, don't just plunge in, but rather first ask yourself, "What is the easiest way to work this problem?" For example, when you are asked to multiply out an expression, don't just multiply it out term by term by brute force. Instead, ask yourself, "How can I group the terms and which theorems should I apply first so as to reduce the amount of work?" (See Study Guide question 8.) After you have worked out Problems 3.6 and 3.7, compare your solutions with those in the solution book.
If your solution required substantially more work than the one in the solution book, rework the problem and try to get the answer in a more straight-forward manner.

11. Study Section 3.4, *Exclusive-OR and Equivalence Operations.*

   a. Prove theorems (3-17) through (3-21). You should be able to prove these both algebraically and by using a truth table.

   b. Show that $(xy' + x'y)' = xy + x'y'$. Memorize this result.

   c. Prove theorem (3-23).

   d. Show that $(x \equiv 0) = x'$, $(x \equiv x) = 1$, and $(x \equiv y)' = (x \equiv y')$.

   e. Express $(x \equiv y)'$ in terms of exclusive OR.

   f. Work Problems 3.12 and 3.13.

12. Study Section 3.5, *Positive and Negative Logic.*

   a. Note the definitions of positive and negative logic.
      If logic $1 = -3$ volts and logic $0 = -6$ volts, is this $+$ or $-$ logic?

      If logic $1 = +3$ volts and logic $0 = +6$ volts, is this $+$ or $-$ logic?

Does the sign of the voltages have anything to do with whether the logic is + or −?

b. If a logic gate circuit realizes

$$Z = [(A + B')C'D + A'BD'](E' + F)$$

for negative logic, what function does it realize for positive logic?

c. Why does an inverter for positive logic also act as an inverter for negative logic?

d. Work Problems 3.16 and 3.17.

13. When you take the readiness test, you will be expected to know from memory the first 16 laws and theorems listed at the end of Unit 2. Where appropriate, you should know them "forward and backward"; i.e., given either side of the equation you should be able to supply the other. Test yourself to see if you can do this.

14. Reread the objectives stated at the beginning of the lesson. If you are satisfied that you can meet these objectives, take the readiness test.

3. BOOLEAN ALGEBRA (Continued)

In this unit, we continue our study of Boolean algebra to learn additional methods for manipulating Boolean expressions. After methods for finding the inverse and dual of a Boolean expression have been examined, the consensus theorem is introduced. This is one of the key theorems used for algebraic simplification of switching expressions. Finally, conversion between product-of-sums form and sum-of-products form is accomplished by multiplying out or factoring. Such algebraic manipulations permit us to realize a switching function by a variety of switching network forms.

3.1 Inversion

The inverse or complement of any Boolean expression can easily be found by successively applying the following theorems, which are frequently referred to as DeMorgan's laws:

$$(X + Y)' = X'Y' \qquad (3\text{-}1)$$
$$(XY)' = X' + Y' \qquad (3\text{-}2)$$

We will verify these laws using a truth table:

$X\ Y$	$X'\ Y'$	$X + Y$	$(X + Y)'$	$X'Y'$	XY	$(XY)'$	$X' + Y'$
0 0	1 1	0	1	1	0	1	1
0 1	1 0	1	0	0	0	1	1
1 0	0 1	1	0	0	0	1	1
1 1	0 0	1	0	0	1	0	0

DeMorgan's laws are easily generalized to n variables:

$$(X_1 + X_2 + X_3 + \ldots + X_n)' = X_1'X_2'X_3' \ldots X_n' \qquad (3\text{-}3)$$

$$(X_1\,X_2\,X_3 \ldots X_n)' = X_1' + X_2' + X_3' \ldots + X_n' \qquad (3\text{-}4)$$

For example, for $n = 3$,

$$(X_1 + X_2 + X_3)' = (X_1 + X_2)'X_3' = X_1'X_2'X_3'$$

Referring to the OR operation as the logical sum and the AND operation as the logical product, DeMorgan's laws can be stated as

> The complement of the product is the sum of the complements.
>
> The complement of the sum is the product of the complements.

To form the complement of an expression containing both OR and AND operations, DeMorgan's laws are applied alternately.

Example 1: To find the complement of $(A' + B)C'$, first apply (3-2) and then (3-1).

$$[(A' + B)C']' = (A' + B)' + (C')' = AB' + C$$

Example 2:
$$
\begin{aligned}
[(AB' + C)D' + E]' &= [(AB' + C)D']'E' && \text{(by 3-1)}\\
&= [(AB' + C)' + D]E' && \text{(by 3-2)}\\
&= [(AB')'C' + D]E' && \text{(by 3-1)}\\
&= [(A' + B)C' + D]E' && \text{(by 3-2)} \qquad (3\text{-}5)
\end{aligned}
$$

Note that in the final expressions, the complement operation is only applied to single variables.

The inverse of $F = A'B + AB'$ is

$$F' = (A'B + AB')' = (A'B)'(AB')' = (A + B')(A' + B)$$

$$= AA' + AB + B'A' + BB' = A'B' + AB$$

We will verify that this result is correct by constructing a truth table for F and F':

$A\ B$	$A'B$	AB'	$F = A'B + AB'$	$A'B'$	AB	$F' = A'B' + AB$
0 0	0	0	0	1	0	1
0 1	1	0	1	0	0	0
1 0	0	1	1	0	0	0
1 1	0	0	0	0	1	1

In the above table, note that for every combination of values of A and B for which $F = 0$, $F' = 1$; and whenever $F = 1$, $F' = 0$.

We can combine the two forms of DeMorgan's law into a single rule which will enable us to complement an entire expression in one step:

> To form the complement of a Boolean expression, replace each variable with its complement, replace 0 with 1, 1 with 0, + with $\cdot$, and $\cdot$ with + .

In applying this rule, we must be careful to preserve the proper hierarchy of operations by adding (or deleting) parentheses as required. In a Boolean expression, the normal hierarchy of operations is that AND is performed before OR, unless parentheses indicate otherwise. For the example of Equation (3-5), applying the one-step rule for forming the complement gives

$$[(AB' + C)D' + E]' = [(A' + B)C' + D]E' \qquad (3\text{-}6)$$

AND is done before OR

add parentheses here so OR is done before AND

On the left side of Equation (3-6), C is ORed with AB'. Thus, parentheses were added on the right side to assure that C' is ANDed with the complement of AB'.

The "one-step" rule for applying DeMorgan's laws can be written symbolically as

$$[f(X_1, X_2, \ldots, X_n, 0, 1, +, \cdot)]' = f(X_1', X_2', \ldots, X_n', 1, 0, \cdot, +) \qquad (3\text{-}7)$$

This notation simply means that to form the complement of an expression containing variables $X_1, X_2, \ldots, X_n$, constants 0 and 1, and operations + and $\cdot$, replace X_1 with X_1', X_2 with X_2', \ldots, X_n with X_n', 0 with 1, 1 with 0, + with $\cdot$, and $\cdot$ with + .

In the following example, again note how parentheses are added and deleted so that the proper hierarchy of operations is preserved after applying the "one-step" rule.

$$[(a'b + c')(d' + ef') + gh + w]' = [(a + b')c + d(e' + f)](g' + h')w' \qquad (3\text{-}8)$$

Verify that the above answer is correct by carrying out the complementation one step at a time.

3.2 Duality

Given a Boolean expression, the dual is formed by replacing AND with OR, OR with AND, 0 with 1, and 1 with 0. Variables and complements are left unchanged. This rule for forming the dual can be summarized as follows:

$$[f(X_1, X_2, \ldots, X_n, 0, 1, +, \cdot)]^D = f(X_1, X_2, \ldots, X_n, 1, 0, \cdot, +) \qquad (3\text{-}9)$$

Example: if $F = ab' + c + 0 \cdot d'(1 + e)$

then the dual expression is $F^D = (a + b')c(1 + d' + 0 \cdot e)$

Note that the method of forming the dual is similar to the method for forming the complement except that the variables are *not* complemented when forming the dual. An alternate method for forming the dual of an expression is to first form the complement of the expression and then replace each variable by its complement. In the above example,

$$F' = (a' + b)c'(1 + d + 0 \cdot e')$$

from which $F^D = (a + b')c(1 + d' + 0 \cdot e)$

Given that two Boolean expressions which contain the same variables are equal, the duals are also equal. To show that this is true for expressions F and G, first observe that if $F = G$, then $F' = G'$. If we replace each variable in F' and G' by its complement, this will not destroy the equality since this is equivalent to substituting one variable for another on both sides of the equation. Therefore, we can conclude that if $F = G$, then $F^D = G^D$. This means that if a theorem is true, so is its dual. For example, given that $(X + Y')Y = XY$ (Theorem 11), it follows immediately by duality that $XY' + Y = X + Y$ (Theorem 11D).

3.3 Multiplying Out and Factoring Expressions

Given an expression in product-of-sums form, the corresponding sum-of-products expression can be obtained by "multiplying out" using the two distributive laws:

$$X(Y + Z) = XY + XZ \qquad (3\text{-}10)$$

$$(X + Y)(X + Z) = X + YZ \qquad (3\text{-}11)$$

In addition, the following theorem is very useful for factoring and multiplying out:

$$(X + Y)(X' + Z) = XZ + X'Y \qquad (3\text{-}12)$$

Note that the variable that is paired with X on one side of the equation is paired with X' on the other side, and vice versa.

Proof:

If $X = 0$, (3-12) reduces to $Y(1 + Z) = 0 + 1 \cdot Y$ or $Y = Y$.

If $X = 1$, (3-12) reduces to $(1 + Y)Z = Z + 0 \cdot Y$ or $Z = Z$.

Since the equation is valid for both $X = 0$ and $X = 1$, it is always valid.

The following example illustrates the use of theorem (3-12) for factoring:

$$AB + A'C = (A + C)(A' + B)$$

Note that the theorem can be applied when we have two terms, one which contains a variable and another which contains its complement.

Theorem (3-12) is very useful for multiplying out expressions. In the following example, we can apply (3-12) because one factor contains the variable Q, and the other factor contains Q':

$$(Q + AB')(C'D + Q') = QC'D + Q'AB'$$

If we simply multiplied out by using the distributive law, we would get four terms instead of two:

$$(Q + AB')(C'D + Q') = QC'D + QQ' + AB'C'D + AB'Q'$$

Since the term $AB'C'D$ is difficult to eliminate, it is much better to use (3-12) instead of the distributive law.

In general, when we multiply out an expression, we should use (3-12) along with (3-10) and (3-11). To avoid generating unnecessary terms when multiplying out, (3-11) and (3-12) should generally be applied before (3-10), and terms should be grouped to expedite their application.

Example:

$$(A + B + C')(A + B + D)(A + B + E)(A + D' + E)(A' + C)$$

$$= (A + B + C'D)(A + B + E) \,[AC + A'(D' + E)]$$

$$= (A + B + C'DE)(AC + A'D' + A'E)$$

$$= AC + ABC + A'BD' + A'BE + A'C'DE \tag{3-13}$$

(What theorem was used to eliminate ABC? *Hint*: let $X = AC$)

In this example, if the ordinary distributive law (3-10) had been used to multiply out the expression by "brute force", 162 terms would have been generated and 158 of these terms would then have to be eliminated.

The same theorems that are useful for multiplying out expressions are useful for factoring. By repeatedly applying (3-10), (3-11) and (3-12) any expression can be converted to a product-of-sums form.

Example of factoring:

$$AC + A'BD' + A'BE + A'C'DE = AC + A' \,(BD' + BE + C'DE)$$

$$\underset{XZ \quad X'}{\qquad} \underset{Y}{\qquad}$$

$$= (A + BD' + BE + C'DE)(A' + C) = [A + C'DE + B(D' + E)](A' + C)$$

$$\underset{X}{\qquad} \underset{Y \quad Z}{\qquad}$$

$$= (A + B + C'DE)(A + C'DE + D' + E)(A' + C)$$

$$= (A + B + C')(A + B + D)(A + B + E)(A + D' + E)(A' + C) \tag{3-14}$$

This is the same expression we started with in (3-13).

3.4   Exclusive-OR and Equivalence Operations

The *exclusive-OR* operation ($\oplus$) is defined as follows:

$$0 \oplus 0 = 0 \qquad\qquad 0 \oplus 1 = 1$$
$$1 \oplus 0 = 1 \qquad\qquad 1 \oplus 1 = 0$$

The truth table for $X \oplus Y$ is

X Y	$X \oplus Y$
0 0	0
0 1	1
1 0	1
1 1	0

From this table, we can see that $X \oplus Y = 1$ iff $X = 1$ or $Y = 1$, but *not* both. The ordinary OR operation, which we have previously defined, is sometimes called inclusive OR since $X + Y = 1$ iff $X = 1$ or $Y = 1$, or both.

Exclusive OR can be expressed in terms of AND and OR. Since $X \oplus Y = 1$ iff X is 0 and Y is 1 *or* X is 1 and Y is 0, we can write

$$X \oplus Y = X'Y + XY' \qquad\qquad (3\text{-}15)$$

The first term in (3-15) is 1 if $X = 0$ and $Y = 1$; the second term is 1 if $X = 1$ and $Y = 0$. Alternatively, we can derive Equation (3-15) by observing that $X \oplus Y = 1$ iff $X = 1$ or $Y = 1$ *and* X and Y are not both 1. Thus,

$$X \oplus Y = (X + Y)(XY)' = (X + Y)(X' + Y') = X'Y + XY' \qquad (3\text{-}16)$$

In (3-16), note that $(XY)' = 1$ if X and Y are not both 1.

We will use the following symbol for an exclusive-OR gate:

The following theorems apply to exclusive-OR:

$$X \oplus 0 = X \qquad\qquad\qquad\qquad\qquad\qquad (3\text{-}17)$$
$$X \oplus 1 = X' \qquad\qquad\qquad\qquad\qquad\qquad (3\text{-}18)$$
$$X \oplus X = 0 \qquad\qquad\qquad\qquad\qquad\qquad (3\text{-}19)$$
$$X \oplus X' = 1 \qquad\qquad\qquad\qquad\qquad\qquad (3\text{-}20)$$
$$X \oplus Y = Y \oplus X \quad \text{(commutative law)}$$
$$(X \oplus Y) \oplus Z = X \oplus (Y \oplus Z) = X \oplus Y \oplus Z \quad \text{(associative law)} \qquad (3\text{-}21)$$
$$X(Y \oplus Z) = XY \oplus XZ \quad \text{(distributive law)} \qquad\qquad (3\text{-}22)$$
$$(X \oplus Y)' = X \oplus Y' = X' \oplus Y = XY + X'Y' \qquad\qquad (3\text{-}23)$$

Any of these theorems can be proved by using a truth table or by replacing $X \oplus Y$ by one of the equivalent expressions from Equation (3-16). Proof of the distributive law follows:

$$XY \oplus XZ = XY(XZ)' + (XY)'XZ = XY(X' + Z') + (X' + Y')XZ$$
$$= XYZ' + XY'Z$$
$$= X(YZ' + Y'Z) = X(Y \oplus Z)$$

The *equivalence* operation ($\equiv$) is defined by

$$(0 \equiv 0) = 1 \qquad\qquad (0 \equiv 1) = 0 \qquad\qquad\qquad (3\text{-}24)$$
$$(1 \equiv 0) = 0 \qquad\qquad (1 \equiv 1) = 1$$

The truth table for $X \equiv Y$ is

X Y	$X \equiv Y$
0 0	1
0 1	0
1 0	0
1 1	1

From the definition of equivalence, we see that $(X \equiv Y) = 1$ iff $X = Y$. Since $(X \equiv Y) = 1$ iff $X = Y = 1$ or $X = Y = 0$, we can write

$$(X \equiv Y) = XY + X'Y' \qquad\qquad\qquad (3\text{-}25)$$

Equivalence is the complement of exclusive-OR:

$$(X \oplus Y)' = (X'Y + XY')' = (X + Y')(X' + Y)$$
$$= XY + X'Y' = (X \equiv Y) \qquad\qquad\qquad (3\text{-}26)$$

Just as for exclusive-OR, the equivalence operation is commutative and associative.

We will use the following symbol for an equivalence gate:

Since equivalence is the complement of exclusive-OR, an alternate symbol for the equivalence gate is an exclusive-OR gate with a complemented output:

The equivalence gate is also called an exclusive-NOR gate.

In order to simplify an expression which contains AND and OR as well as exclusive OR and equivalence, it is usually desirable to first apply (3-15) and (3-25) to eliminate the $\oplus$ and $\equiv$ operations. As an example, we will simplify

$$F = (A'B \equiv C) + (B \oplus AC')$$

By (3-15) and (3-25),

$$F = [(A'B)C + (A'B)'C'] + [B'(AC') + B(AC')']$$
$$= A'BC + (A + B')C' + AB'C' + B(A' + C)$$
$$= B(A'C + A' + C) + C'(A + B' + AB') = B(A' + C) + C'(A + B')$$

When manipulating an expression that contains several exclusive-OR or equivalence operations, it is useful to note that

$$(XY' + X'Y)' = XY + X'Y' \qquad\qquad\qquad (3\text{-}27)$$

For example, $A' \oplus B \oplus C = [A'B' + (A')'B] \oplus C$
$$= (A'B' + AB)C' + (A'B' + AB)'C$$
$$= (A'B' + AB)C' + (A'B + AB')C \qquad \text{(by 3-15)}$$
$$= A'B'C' + ABC' + A'BC + AB'C \qquad \text{(by 3-27)}$$

3.5 Positive and Negative Logic

Logic gates can be constructed using diodes, transistors or other switching elements. Several types of logic gate circuits are analyzed in Appendix A. In this section we will discuss the relationship between the voltage levels at the gate inputs and outputs and the logic function performed by the gate.

Under normal operating conditions, the voltage applied to any input terminal of a logic gate is restricted to have one of two nominal values. When the proper input voltages are applied to a logic gate, the voltage at the output terminal will assume one of the two possible nominal values.

Table 3-1* shows the input and output voltages for the logic gate of Fig. 3-1. We have assumed that each input and output voltage can have one of two nominal values, 0 volts or $+V$ volts. Since there are three input terminals, 8 different combinations of values of input voltages can be applied to the gate. For example, if the input voltages are $e_1 = 0$, $e_2 = +V$ and $e_3 = +V$, the output voltage is $e_o = 0$.

Fig. 3-1

Table 3-1

e_1	e_2	e_3	e_o
0	0	0	0
0	0	$+V$	0
0	$+V$	0	0
0	$+V$	$+V$	0
$+V$	0	0	0
$+V$	0	$+V$	0
$+V$	$+V$	0	0
$+V$	$+V$	$+V$	$+V$

In order to determine the logic function realized by the gate, we must interpret the voltage levels as logic values. Two ways of doing this are:

a. let $+V$ represent a logic 1 and 0 volts represent a logic 0 *or*
b. let $+V$ représent a logic 0 and 0 volts represent a logic 1.

These two ways are called positive and negative logic, respectively. In general if we have two voltage levels, positive and negative logic are defined as follows:

positive logic — the higher of the two voltage levels represents a logic 1 and the lower of the two voltage levels represents a logic 0

negative logic — the lower of the two voltage levels represents a logic 1 and the higher of the two voltage levels represents a logic 0

Both systems are used in practice, so we should be familiar with both.

*See Appendix A.1 for an example of a diode circuit which realizes this table.

If we translate Table 3-1 according to positive logic (0 volts is a logic 0 and $+V$ volts is a logic 1), we obtain:

e_1	e_2	e_3	e_o
0	0	0	0
0	0	1	0
0	1	0	0
0	1	1	0
1	0	0	0
1	0	1	0
1	1	0	0
1	1	1	1

Since e_o is 1 iff e_1, e_2 *and* e_3 are all 1, $e_o = e_1 e_2 e_3$ and the gate performs the AND function for positive logic.

If we translate Table 3-1 according to negative logic (0 volts is a logic 1 and $+V$ volts is a logic 0), we obtain:

e_1	e_2	e_3	e_o
1	1	1	1
1	1	0	1
1	0	1	1
1	0	0	1
0	1	1	1
0	1	0	1
0	0	1	1
0	0	0	0

Since e_o is 1 iff e_1, e_2 *or* e_3 is 1, $e_o = e_1 + e_2 + e_3$, and the gate performs the OR function for negative logic. Note that the function realized for negative logic is the dual of the function for positive logic. Later we will prove that this is true in general for any logic network.

Next, we will consider another type of logic gate which has input and output voltages related as shown in Table 3-2(a).*

Table 3-2

(a) Voltages				(b) Positive logic				(c) Negative logic			
e_1	e_2	e_3	e_o	e_1	e_2	e_3	e_o	e_1	e_2	e_3	e_o
0	0	0	0	0	0	0	0	1	1	1	1
0	0	$+V$	$+V$	0	0	1	1	1	1	0	0
0	$+V$	0	$+V$	0	1	0	1	1	0	1	0
0	$+V$	$+V$	$+V$	0	1	1	1	1	0	0	0
$+V$	0	0	$+V$	1	0	0	1	0	1	1	0
$+V$	0	$+V$	$+V$	1	0	1	1	0	1	0	0
$+V$	$+V$	0	$+V$	1	1	0	1	0	0	1	0
$+V$	$+V$	$+V$	$+V$	1	1	1	1	0	0	0	0

*See Appendix A.1 for an example of a diode circuit which realizes this table.

Tables 3-2(b) and 3-2(c) show the results when Table 3-2(a) is translated according to positive and negative logic, respectively. For positive logic, e_o is 1 iff e_1, e_2 or e_3 is 1 so $e_o = e_1 + e_2 + e_3$, and Table 3-2(a) represents an OR gate. For negative logic, $e_o = e_1 e_2 e_3$, and Table 3-2(a) represents an AND gate.

If we know the function realized by a switching network for positive logic, we can easily determine the function realized by the same network for negative logic by applying the *negative logic theorem*:

> If a given combinational network realizes a function F when input and output variables are defined according to positive logic, the same network will realize the dual function (F^D) when the input and output variables are defined according to negative logic.

Example:

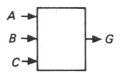

Input and output voltage levels are 0 and +5 volts. If for positive logic (logic 0 = 0 volts, logic 1 = 5 volts) the network output is

$$G = ABC' + A'B'C$$

then for negative logic (logic 1 = 0 volts, logic 0 = 5 volts) the network output is

$$G = (A + B + C')(A' + B' + C)$$

For a given set of input *voltages*, the output *voltage* is the same in both cases. It is just the logical interpretation of these voltages that differs in the two cases.

Proof:

Consider the following network where positive logic is used for all variables:

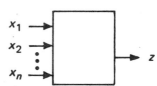

Now re-label the inputs and output using negative logic variables:

For a given input voltage applied to terminal i, if $x_i = 1$, $w_i = 0$ and if $x_i = 0$, $w_i = 1$. Therefore, $w_i = x_i'$ and similarly, $y = z'$. For the positive logic variables, let $z = f(x_1, x_2, \ldots, x_n)$. Then for the negative logic variables,

$$y' = f(w_1', w_2', \ldots, w_n')$$

Therefore,

$$y = [f(w_1', w_2', \ldots, w_n')]' = f^D(w_1, w_2, \ldots, w_n)$$

*See Appendix A.1 for an example of a diode circuit which realizes this table.

since the dual of a function can be formed by complementing a function and then replacing all variables by their complements. If, as was done in the example, we use the same variable names for both positive and negative logic, then for negative logic,

$$z = [f(x_1', x_2', \ldots, x_n')]' = f^D(x_1, x_2, \ldots, x_n)$$

By applying the negative logic theorem, we can see that a logic circuit which realizes an AND gate for positive logic realizes an OR gate for negative logic and vice versa. Since the dual of exclusive OR is

$$(x \oplus y)^D = (x'y + xy')^D = (x' + y)(x + y') = x'y' + xy = (x \equiv y) \quad (3\text{-}28)$$

a gate which realizes exclusive OR for positive logic realizes equivalence for negative logic.

Programmed Exercise 3.1

Cover the bottom part of this page with a sheet of paper and slide it down as you check your answers.

    The following expression is to be multiplied out to form a sum of products:

$$(A + B + C')(A' + B' + D)(A' + C + D')(A + C' + D)$$

First, find a pair of sum terms which have two literals in common and apply the second distributive law. Also apply the same law to the other pair of terms.

Answer: $(A + C' + BD)[A' + (B' + D)(C + D')]$

(*Note:* This answer was obtained by using $(X + Y)(X + Z) = X + YZ$.)

Next, find a pair of sum terms which have a variable in one and its complement in the other. Use the appropriate theorem to multiply these sum terms together without introducing any redundant terms. Apply the same theorem a second time.

Answer: $(A + C' + BD)(A' + B'D' + CD) = A(B'D' + CD) + A'(C' + BD)$

    or $A(B' + D)(C + D') + A'(C' + BD) = A(B'D' + CD) + A'(C' + BD)$

(*Note:* This answer was obtained using $(X + Y)(X' + Z) = XZ + X'Y$.)

Complete the problem by multiplying out using the ordinary distributive law.

Final answer: $AB'D' + ACD + A'C' + A'BD$

Programmed Exercise 3.2

Cover the bottom part of this page with a sheet of paper and slide it down as you check your answers.

The following expression is to be factored to form a product of sums:

$$WXY' + W'X'Z + WY'Z + W'YZ'$$

First, factor as far as you can using the ordinary distributive law.

Answer: $$WY'(X + Z) + W'(X'Z + YZ')$$

Next, factor further by using a theorem which involves a variable and its complement. Apply this theorem twice.

Answer: $(W + X'Z + YZ')[W' + Y'(X + Z)]$
$\qquad = [W + (X' + Z')(Y + Z)][W' + Y'(X + Z)]$

or $\quad WY'(X + Z) + W'(X' + Z')(Y + Z)$
$\qquad = [W + (X' + Z')(Y + Z)][W' + Y'(X + Z)]$

(*Note:* This answer was obtained by using $AB + A'C = (A + C)(A' + B)$.)

Now, complete the factoring by using the second distributive law.

Final answer: $\quad (W + X' + Z')(W + Y + Z)(W' + Y')(W' + X + Z)$

PROBLEMS

3.3 Find the complement of each of the following expressions (do not simplify the result):

a. $wx(y'z + yz') + w'x'(y' + z)(y + z')$

b. $(ab + c')(d'e + 1) + g(h' + 0) + w$

c. $[ab' + d(e'f' + g'h)][a' + bcd(e' + f'g)]$

3.4 Find the dual of each of the expressions in Problem 3.3 (do not simplify the result).

3.5 Find the dual and the complement of the following expressions. (Do not simplify.)

a. $F = [(AB + C'D + E' + 0)(A' + BC) + 1(D'E + B)](C + E')$

b. $F = (A' + B \cdot 0 + 1)[1 \cdot (AB' + C)D + E \cdot 0] + A'B \cdot 1$

c. $F = [AB'(C + DE') \cdot 0] + AC(1 + CD + B'E)$

3.6 a. Multiply out to obtain a sum of four terms:

$$(A' + B + D)(A + C)(A + B' + D)(A' + C' + D')(A' + B)$$

(*Hint:* Apply $X(X + Y) = X$ to eliminate a term before you start multiplying.)

b. Multiply out to obtain a sum of four terms:

$$(B' + C' + D')(A' + B' + C')(A + B + C)(B + C + D)$$

c. Multiply out to obtain a sum of three terms:

$$(A' + C' + D)(A' + C)(B + C' + D')(A' + B + C)(C + D)$$

3.7 a. Factor to obtain a product of four terms: $A'B'C' + A'D' + ABC' + AD$

b. Factor to obtain a product of four terms: $ACD + A'B'D + A'BC + AC'D'$

c. Factor to obtain a product of four terms:
$A'C'D' + AB'D' + A'CD' + BD$

3.8 Simplify each of the following expressions:

a. $AB' + A'B'D + A'CD'$

b. $(A' + C' + D)(A + B' + C')(B + C')$

c. $AB' + AB'CD + ABC'D'$

d. $CE(A' + B + C' + E')(B + C' + D + E')(A + B + C' + E')$

3.9 Find F and G and simplify:

(a)

(b)

3.10 Convert the following expression to product-of-sums form:

$$AB' + A'CD + BC'D$$

3.11 Convert the following expression to sum-of-products form:

$$(V + Y + Z)(V' + W + X')(V' + X + Y')(V + X')$$

3.12 Write an expression for F and simplify.

3.13 Answer the following:

    a. Is the following distributive law valid? $X \oplus YZ = (X \oplus Y)(X \oplus Z)$
       Prove your answer.

    b. State and prove the associative law for the equivalence operation.

3.14 Simplify to obtain a sum of 2 terms:
    a. $(A \oplus C)(B \oplus C) + (A \oplus B)(B \oplus C)$
    b. $[(B + C) \equiv A'B][C \oplus (A + B')]$

3.15 Find an expression for F which uses only the exclusive-OR and complement operations.

$$F = xyz' + x'y'z' + xy'z + x'yz$$

3.16 The following table shows the input and output voltages for a two-input logic gate circuit.

    a. Translate this table to a truth table using positive logic. What logic function is realized for positive logic?

    b. Translate this table to a truth table using negative logic. What logic function is realized for negative logic?

e_1	e_2	e_o
−5	−5	+5
−5	+5	−5
+5	−5	−5
+5	+5	+5

3.17 The following table shows the input and output voltages for a 3-input logic gate circuit.

    a. If 0 volts is a logic 1, and −5 volts is a logic 0, what logic operation does the gate realize?

    b. If −5 volts is a logic 1, and 0 volts is a logic 0, what logic operation does the gate realize?

e_1	e_2	e_3	e_o
0	0	0	0
0	0	−5	−5
0	−5	0	−5
0	−5	−5	−5
−5	0	0	−5
−5	0	−5	−5
−5	−5	0	−5
−5	−5	−5	−5

4

ALGEBRAIC SIMPLIFICATION

OBJECTIVES

1. Use the consensus theorem to delete terms from and add terms to a switching expression.

2. Simplify a switching expression using the laws and theorems of Boolean algebra.

3. Given an equation, prove algebraically that it is valid or show that it is not valid.

STUDY GUIDE

1. Study Section 4.1, *The Consensus Theorem*. The consensus theorem is an important method for simplifying switching functions.

   a. In each of the following expressions, find the consensus term and eliminate it:

   $$abc'd + a'be + bc'de$$

   $$(a' + b + c)(a + d)(b + c + d)$$

   $$ab'c + a'bd + bcd' + a'bc$$

   b. Eliminate two terms from the following expression by applying the consensus theorem:

   $$A'B'C + BC'D' + A'CD + AB'D' + BCD + AC'D'$$

   (*Hint*: First compare the first term with each of the remaining terms to see if a consensus exists, then compare the second term with each of the remaining terms, etc.)

   c. Study the example given in Equations (4-3) and (4-4) carefully.
   Now let us start with the 4-term form of the expression (Equation 4-3):

   $$A'C'D + A'BD + ABC + ACD'$$

   Can this be reduced directly to three terms by application of the consensus theorem?

Before we can reduce the above expression, we must add another term. Which term can be added by applying the consensus theorem?

Add this term, and then reduce the expression to three terms. After this reduction can the term which was added be removed? Why not?

d. Eliminate two terms from the following expression by applying the dual consensus theorem:

$$(a' + c' + d)(a' + b + c)(a + b + d)(a' + b + d)(b + c' + d)$$

Use brackets to indicate how you formed the consensus terms. (*Hint*: First find the consensus of the first two terms and eliminate it.)

e. Derive theorem (3-12) by using the consensus theorem.

f. Work Programmed Exercise 4.1. Then work Problem 4.4.

2. Study Section 4.2, *Algebraic Simplification of Switching Expressions.*

   a. What theorems are used for:

      combining terms?

      eliminating terms?

      eliminating literals?

      adding redundant terms?

      factoring or multiplying out?

   b. Note that in the example of Equation (4-8), the redundant term WZ' was added and then was eliminated later after it had been used to eliminate another term. Why was it possible to eliminate WZ' in this example?

      If a term has been added by the consensus theorem, it may not always be possible to eliminate the term later by the consensus theorem. Why?

   c. You will need considerable practice to develop skill in simplifying switching expressions. Work through Programmed Exercises 4.2 and 4.3.

   d. Work Problems 4.6 and 4.8.

e. When simplifying an expression using Boolean algebra, two frequently asked questions are:

(1) Where do I begin?

(2) How do I know when I am finished?

In answer to (1), it is generally best to try simple techniques such as combining terms or eliminating terms and literals before trying more complicated things like using the consensus theorem or adding redundant terms. Question (2) is generally difficult to answer since it may be impossible to simplify some expressions without first adding redundant terms. We will usually tell you how many terms to expect in the minimum solution so that you won't have to waste time trying to simplify an expression which is already minimized. In Units 6 and 7, you will learn systematic techniques which will guarantee finding the minimum solution.

3. Study Section 4.3, *Proving Validity of an Equation.*

   a. When attempting to prove that an equation is valid, is it permissible to add the same expression to both sides? Explain.

   b. Work Problem 4.13.

   c. Show that (4-14) and (4-15) are true by considering both $x = 0$ and $x = 1$.

   d. Given that $a'(b + d') = a'(b + e')$, the following "proof" shows that $d = e$:

   $$a'(b + d') = a'(b + e')$$
   $$a + b'd = a + b'e$$
   $$b'd = b'e$$
   $$d = e$$

   State two things that are wrong with the "proof." Give a set of values for a, b, d, and e that demonstrates that the result is incorrect.

4. Reread the objectives of this unit. When you are satisfied that you can meet the objectives, take the readiness test.

4. ALGEBRAIC SIMPLIFICATION

4.1 The Consensus Theorem

The consensus theorem is very useful in simplifying Boolean expressions. Given an expression of the form $XY + X'Z + YZ$ the term YZ is redundant and can be eliminated to form the equivalent expression $XY + X'Z$.

The term which was eliminated is referred to as the "consensus term." Given a pair of terms for which a variable appears in one term and the complement of that variable in another, the consensus term is formed by multiplying the two original terms together, leaving out the selected variable and its complement. For example, the consensus of ab and $a'c$ is bc; the consensus of abd and $b'de'$ is $(ad)(de') = ade'$. The consensus of terms $ab'd$ and $a'bd'$ is 0.

The consensus theorem can be stated as follows:

$$XY + X'Z + YZ = XY + X'Z \tag{4-1}$$

Proof:

$$XY + X'Z + YZ = XY + X'Z + (X + X')YZ = (XY + XYZ) + (X'Z + X'YZ)$$
$$= XY(1 + Z) + X'Z(1 + Y) = XY + X'Z$$

The consensus theorem can be used to eliminate redundant terms from Boolean expressions. For example, in the following expression, $b'c$ is the consensus of $a'b'$ and ac, and ab is the consensus of ac and bc', so both consensus terms can be eliminated:

$$a'b' + ac + bc' + b'c + ab = a'b' + ac + bc'$$

The dual form of the consensus theorem is

$$(X + Y)(X' + Z)(Y + Z) = (X + Y)(X' + Z) \qquad (4\text{-}2)$$

The brackets indicate how the consensus terms are formed.

Note again that the key to recognizing the consensus term is to first find a pair of terms, one of which contains a variable and the other its complement. In this case, the consensus is formed by adding this pair of terms together leaving out the selected variable and its complement. In the following expression, $(a + b + d')$ is a consensus term and can be eliminated by using the dual consensus theorem:

$$(a + b + c')(a + b + d')(b + c + d') = (a + b + c')(b + c + d')$$

The final result obtained by application of the consensus theorem may depend on the order in which terms are eliminated.

Example: $A'C'D + A'BD + BCD + ABC + ACD' \qquad (4\text{-}3)$

First we eliminate BCD as shown. (Why can it be eliminated?)

Now that BCD has been eliminated, it is no longer there, and it *cannot* be used to eliminate another term. Checking all pairs of terms shows that no additional terms can be eliminated by the consensus theorem.

Now we start over again:

$$A'C'D + A'BD + BCD + ABC + ACD' \qquad (4\text{-}4)$$

This time, we do not eliminate BCD; instead we eliminate *two* other terms by the consensus theorem. After doing this, observe that BCD can no longer be eliminated. Note that the expression reduces to four terms if BCD is eliminated first, but that it can be reduced to three terms if BCD is not eliminated.

Sometimes it is impossible to directly reduce an expression to a minimum number of terms by simply eliminating terms. It may be necessary to first add a term using the consensus theorem and *then* use the added term to eliminate other terms. For example, consider the expression

$$F = ABCD + B'CDE + A'B' + BCE'$$

If we compare every pair of terms to see if a consensus term can be formed, we find that the only consensus terms are $ACDE$ (from $ABCD$ and $B'CDE$) and $A'CE'$ (from $A'B'$ and BCE'). Since neither of these consensus terms appears in the original expression, we cannot directly eliminate any terms using the consensus theorem. However, if we first add the consensus term $ACDE$ to F we get

$$F = \overbrace{\underbrace{ABCD}_{} + \overbrace{B'CDE}^{} + \overbrace{A'B'}^{} + BCE'}^{} + \underbrace{ACDE}_{}$$

Then we can eliminate $ABCD$ and $B'CDE$ using the consensus theorem and F reduces to

$$F = A'B' + BCE' + ACDE$$

The term $ACDE$ is no longer redundant and cannot be eliminated from the final expression.

4.2 Algebraic Simplification of Switching Expressions

In this section we will apply the theorems of Boolean algebra to simplifying switching expressions. This is important because simplifying an expression reduces the cost of realizing the expression using gates. Later we will learn graphical methods for simplifying switching functions, but we will learn algebraic methods first. In addition to multiplying out and factoring, three basic ways of simplifying switching functions are combining terms, eliminating terms and eliminating literals.

a. *Combining terms.* Use the theorem $XY + XY' = X$ to combine two terms.

   Example: $abc'd' + abcd' = abd'$ $[X = abd', Y = c]$ (4-5)

   When combining terms by this theorem as above, the two terms to be combined should contain exactly the same variables, and exactly one of the variables should appear complemented in one term and not in the other. Since $X + X = X$, a given term may be duplicated and combined with two or more other terms.

   Example: $ab'c + abc + a'bc = ab'c + abc + abc + a'bc = ac + bc$

   The theorem still can be used, of course, when X and Y are replaced with more complicated expressions.

   Example: $(a + bc)(d + e') + a'(b' + c')(d + e') = d + e'$
   $$[X = d + e', Y = a + bc, Y' = a'(b' + c')]$$

b. *Eliminating terms.* Use the theorem $X + XY = X$ to eliminate redundant terms if possible; then try to apply the consensus theorem ($XY + X'Z + YZ = XY + X'Z$) to eliminate any consensus terms.

   Examples: $a'b + a'bc = a'b$ $[X = a'b]$

   $a'bc' + bcd + a'bd = a'bc' + bcd\,[X = c,\ Y = bd,\ Z = a'b]$ (4-6)

c. *Eliminating literals.* Use the theorem $X + X'Y = X + Y$ to eliminate redundant literals. Simple factoring may be necessary before the theorem is applied.

Example: $A'B + A'B'C'D' + ABCD'$

$$= A'(B + B'C'D') + ABCD' = A'(B + C'D') + ABCD'$$

$$= B(A' + ACD') + A'C'D' = B(A' + CD') + A'C'D'$$

$$= A'B + BCD' + A'C'D' \qquad (4\text{-}7)$$

The expression obtained after applying a, b and c above will not necessarily have a minimum number of terms or a minimum number of literals. If it does not, and no further simplification can be made using a, b and c, deliberate introduction of redundant terms may be necessary before further simplification can be made.

d. *Adding redundant terms.* Redundant terms can be introduced in several ways such as adding xx', multiplying by $(x + x')$, adding yz to $xy + x'z$, or adding xy to x. When possible, the terms added should be chosen so that they will combine with or eliminate other terms.

Example: $WX + XY + X'Z' + WY'Z'$ (add WZ' by consensus theorem)

$$= WX + XY + X'Z' + WY'Z' + WZ' \text{ (eliminate } WY'Z')$$

$$= WX + XY + X'Z' + WZ' \text{ (eliminate } WZ')$$

$$= WX + XY + X'Z' \qquad (4\text{-}8)$$

The following comprehensive example illustrates the use of all four methods.

$$A'B'C'D' + A'BC'D' + A'BD + \cancel{A'BC'D} + ABCD + ACD' + B'CD'$$

$$\underbrace{\hphantom{A'B'C'D' + A'BC'D'}}_{① \ A'C'D'} \qquad ②$$

$$= A'C'D' + BD(A' + \cancel{A}C) + ACD' + B'CD'$$

$$③$$

$$= A'C'D' + A'BD + \underbrace{BCD + ACD' + B'CD'}_{}$$

$$+ ABC \ ④ \qquad \text{consensus } ACD'$$

$$= A'C'D' + A'BD + \underbrace{\cancel{BCD} + \cancel{ACD'} + B'CD' + ABC}_{\text{consensus } \ BCD}$$

$$= A'C'D' + A'BD + B'CD' + ABC \qquad (4\text{-}9)$$

What theorems were used in steps 1, 2, 3 and 4?

If the simplified expression is to be left in a product-of-sums form instead of a sum-of-products form, the duals of the theorems used above should be applied.

Example: $\underbrace{(A' + B' + C')(A' + B' + C)}_{① \ (A' + B')}(B' + C)(A + C)\underbrace{(\cancel{A + B + C})}_{②}$

$$= (A' + B')(\cancel{B' + C})(A + C) = (A' + B')(A + C) \qquad (4\text{-}10)$$

$$③$$

What theorems were used in steps 1, 2, and 3?

In general, there is no easy way of determining when a Boolean expression has a minimum number of terms or a minimum number of literals. Systematic methods for finding minimum sum-of-products and minimum product-of-sums expressions will be discussed in Units 6 and 7.

4.3   Proving Validity of an Equation

Often we will need to determine if an equation is valid for all combinations of values of the variables. Several methods can be used to determine if an equation is valid:

a.   Construct a truth table and evaluate both sides of the equation for all combinations of values of the variables. (This method is rather tedious if the number of variables is large, and it certainly is not very elegant.)

b.   Manipulate one side of the equation by applying various theorems until it is identical with the other side.

c.   Reduce both sides of the equation independently to the same expression.

d.   It is permissible to perform the same operation on both sides of the equation provided that the operation is reversible. For example, it is all right to complement both sides of the equation, but it is *not* permissible to multiply both sides of the equation by the same expression. (Multiplication is not reversible since division is not defined for Boolean algebra.) Similarly, it is not permissible to add the same term to both sides of the equation since subtraction is not defined for Boolean algebra.

To prove that an equation is *not* valid, it is sufficient to show one combination of values of the variables for which the two sides of the equation have different values. When using methods b or c above to prove that an equation is valid, a useful strategy is to:

a.   First reduce both sides to a sum of products (or a product of sums)

b.   Compare the two sides of the equation to see how they differ

c.   Then try to add terms to one side of the equation that are present on the other side

d.   Finally, try to eliminate terms from one side that are not present on the other.

Whatever method is used, frequently compare both sides of the equation and let the difference between them serve as a guide as to what steps to take next.

Example 1:   Show that $A'BD' + BCD + ABC' + AB'D = BC'D' + AD + A'BC$

Starting with the left side, we first add consensus terms, then combine terms and finally eliminate terms by the consensus theorem.

$$A'BD' + BCD + ABC' + AB'D$$
$$= A'BD' + BCD + ABC' + AB'D + BC'D' + A'BC + ABD$$

(add consensus of $A'BD'$ and ABC')⟍
   (add consensus of $A'BD'$ and BCD)⟍
      (add consensus of BCD and ABC')⟍

$$= AD + A'BD' + BCD + ABC' + BC'D' + A'BC = BC'D' + AD + A'BC \quad (4\text{-}11)$$

(eliminate consensus of $BC'D'$ and AD)
   (eliminate consensus of AD and $A'BC$)
      (eliminate consensus of $BC'D'$ and $A'BC$)

Example 2:   Show that the following equation is valid:

$$A'BC'D + (A' + BC)(A + C'D') + BC'D + A'BC'$$
$$= ABCD + A'C'D' + ABD + ABCD' + BC'D$$

First, we will reduce the left side:

$$A'BC'D + (A' + BC)(A + C'D') + BC'D + A'BC' =$$

(eliminate $A'BC'D$ using (2-13))

$$(A' + BC)(A + C'D') + BC'D + A'BC' =$$

(multiply out using (3-12)

$$ABC + A'C'D' + BC'D + A'BC' =$$

(eliminate $A'BC'$ by consensus)

$$ABC + A'C'D' + BC'D =$$

Now we will reduce the right side:

$$ABCD + A'C'D' + ABD + ABCD' + BC'D$$

(combine $ABCD$ and $ABCD'$)

$$= ABC + A'C'D' + ABD + BC'D$$

(eliminate ABD by consensus)

$$= ABC + A'C'D' + BC'D$$

Since both sides of the original equation were independently reduced to the same expression, the original equation is valid.

As we have previously observed, some of the theorems of Boolean algebra are not true for ordinary algebra. Similarly, some of the theorems of ordinary algebra are not true for Boolean algebra. Consider, for example, the cancellation law for ordinary algebra:

$$\text{If } x + y = x + z, \text{ then } y = z. \qquad (4\text{-}12)$$

The cancellation law is *not* true for Boolean algebra. We will demonstrate this by constructing a counterexample in which $x + y = x + z$ but $y \neq z$. Let $x = 1, y = 0, z = 1$. Then

$$1 + 0 = 1 + 1 \qquad \text{but } 0 \neq 1$$

In ordinary algebra, the cancellation law for multiplication is

$$\text{If } xy = xz, \text{ then } y = z \qquad (4\text{-}13)$$

This law is valid provided x $\neq$ 0.

In Boolean algebra, the cancellation law for multiplication is also not valid when $x = 0$. (Let $x = 0$, $y = 0$, $z = 1$; then $0 \cdot 0 = 0 \cdot 1$, but $0 \neq 1$). Since $x = 0$ about half of the time in switching algebra, the cancellation law for multiplication cannot be used.

Even though statements (4-12) and (4-13) are generally false for Boolean algebra, the converses

$$\text{If } y = z, \text{ then } x + y = x + z \qquad (4\text{-}14)$$
$$\text{If } y = z, \text{ then } xy = xz \qquad (4\text{-}15)$$

are true. Thus, we see that although adding the same term to both sides of a Boolean equation leads to a valid equation, the reverse operation of cancelling or subtracting a term from both sides generally does not lead to a valid equation. Similarly, multiplying both sides of a Boolean equation by the same term leads to a valid equation, but not conversely. When we are attempting to prove that an equation is valid, it is *not* permissible to add the same expression to both sides of the equation or to multiply both sides by the same expression, because these operations are not reversible.

Programmed Exercise 4.1

Cover the lower part of this page with a sheet of paper and slide it down as you check your answers. *Write* your answer in the space provided before looking at the correct answer.

The following expression is to be simplified using the consensus theorem:

$$AC' + AB'D + A'B'C + A'CD' + B'C'D'$$

First, find all of the consensus terms by checking all pairs of terms.

Answer: The consensus terms are indicated below.

$$AC' + AB'D + A'B'C + A'CD' + B'C'D'$$

Can the original expression be simplified by direct application of the consensus theorem?

Answer: No, since none of the consensus terms appear in the original expression.

Now add the consensus term $B'CD$ to the original expression. Compare the added term with each of the original terms to see if any consensus exists. Eliminate as many of the original terms as you can.

Answer:

$$AC' + AB'D + A'B'C + A'CD' + B'C'D' + B'CD$$

with $(AB'D)$ over $AB'D$ and $(A'B'C)$ under the terms

Now that we have eliminated two terms, can $B'CD$ also be eliminated? What is the final reduced expression?

Answer: No, since the terms used to form $B'CD$ are gone. Final answer is

$$AC' + A'CD' + B'C'D' + B'CD$$

Programmed Exercise 4.2 (top half of this and the next 4 pages)

Problem: The following expression is to be simplified·

$$ab'cd'e + acd + acf'gh' + abcd'e + acde' + e'h'$$

State a theorem which can be used to combine a pair of terms and apply it to combine two of the terms in the above expression.

Turn to the next page and check your answer.

Programmed Exercise 4.3 (bottom half of this and the next 4 pages)

$$Z = (A + C' + F' + G)(A + C' + F + G)(A + B + C' + D' + G)$$
$$(A + C + E + G)(A' + B + G)(B + C' + F + G)$$

The above is to be simplified to the form

$$(X + X + X)(X + X + X)(X + X + X)$$

where each X represents a literal.

State a theorem which can be used to combine the first two sum terms of Z and apply it. (*Hint:* The two sum terms differ in only one variable.)

Turn to the next page and check your answer.

Answer to 4.2:

Apply $XY + XY' = X$ to the terms $ab'cd'e$ and $abcd'e$ which reduces the expression to

$$acd'e + acd + acf'gh' + acde' + e'h'$$

Now state a theorem (other than the consensus theorem) which can be used to eliminate terms and apply it to eliminate a term in the above expression.

Turn to the next page and check your answer.

Answer to 4.3:

$$(X + Y)(X + Y') = X$$
$$Z = (A + C' + G)(A + B + C' + D' + G)(A + C + E + G)(A' + B + G)$$
$$(B + C' + F + G)$$

Now state a theorem (other than the consensus theorem) which can be used to eliminate a sum term and apply it to the above expression.

Turn to the next page and check your answer.

Answer to 4.2:

Apply $X + XY = X$ to eliminate $acde'$. (What term corresponds to X?) The result is

$$acd'e + acd + acf'gh' + e'h'$$

Now state a theorem that can be used to eliminate literals, and apply it to eliminate a literal from one of the terms in the above expression. (*Hint:* It may be necessary to factor out some common variables from a pair of terms before the theorem can be applied.)

Turn to the next page and check your answer.

Answer to 4.3:

$$X(X + Y) = X$$
$$Z = (A + C' + G)(A + C + E + G)(A' + B + G)(B + C' + F + G)$$

Next, eliminate one literal from the second term, leaving the expression otherwise unchanged. (*Hint:* This cannot be done by direct application of one theorem; it will be necessary to partially multiply out the first two sum terms before eliminating the literal.)

Now turn to the next page and check your answer.

Answer to 4.2:

Use $X + X'Y = X + Y$ to eliminate a literal from $acd'e$. To do this, first factor ac out of the first two terms: $acd'e + acd = ac(d + d'e)$. After eliminating d', the resulting expression is

$$ace + acd + acf'gh' + e'h'$$

---

a. Can any term be eliminated from this expression by direct application of the consensus theorem?

b. If not, add a redundant term using the consensus theorem, and use this redundant term to eliminate one of the other terms.

c. Finally, reduce your expression to three terms.

Turn to the next page and check your answer.

Answer to 4.3:

$$(A + C' + G)(A + C + E + G) = A + G + C'(C + E) = A + G + C'E$$
Therefore, $Z = (A + C' + G)(A + E + G)(A' + B + G)(B + C' + F + G)$

---

a. Can any term be eliminated from this expression by direct application of the consensus theorem?

b. If not, add a redundant sum term using the consensus theorem, and use this redundant term to eliminate one of the other terms.

c. Finally, reduce your expression to a product of three sum terms.

Now turn to the next page and check your answer.

Answer to 4.2:

    a. No

    b. Add the consensus of ace and $e'h'$:

$$ace + acd + acf'gh' + e'h' + ach'$$

       Now eliminate $acf'gh'$ (by $X + XY = X$)

$$ace + acd + e'h' + ach'$$

    c. Now eliminate ach' by the consensus theorem. The final answer is

$$ace + acd + e'h'$$

Answer to 4.3:

    a. No

    b. Add $B + C' + G$ (consensus of $A + C' + G$ and $A' + B + G$)
       Use $X(X + Y) = X$, where $X = B + C' + G$, to eliminate $B + C' + F + G$

    c. Now eliminate $B + C' + G$ by consensus. The final answer is

$$Z = (A + C' + G)(A + E + G)(A' + B + G)$$

PROBLEMS

4.4 Simplify each of the following expressions using only the consensus theorem (or its dual):

    a. $BC'D' + ABC' + AC'D + AB'D + A'BD'$ (reduce to three terms)

    b. $W'Y' + WYZ + XY'Z + WX'Y$ (reduce to three terms)

    c. $(B + C + D)(A + B + C)(A' + C + D)(B' + C' + D')$

4.5 Simplify the following expressions using only the consensus theorem or its dual:

    a. $W'Y'Z + W'X'Y + W'XY' + X'YZ'$

    b. $(W + X)(W + Y + Z)(W' + X' + Y)(W' + X' + Z')$

    c. $ABC + AB'CE + ACDE + A'B'D + B'CDE$

    d. $(A + B)(A + C)(A' + D)(B + C')(B + D)(C + D)$

4.6 Simplify each of the following expressions:

    a. $xy + x'yz' + yz$

    b. $(xy' + z)(x + y')z$

    c. $xy' + z + (x' + y)z'$

    d. $a'd(b' + c) + a'd'(b + c') + (b' + c)(b + c')$

    e. $w'x' + x'y' + yz + w'z'$ (reduce to a sum of 3 terms)

    f. $A'BCD + A'BC'D + B'EF + CDE'G + A'DEF + A'B'EF$ (reduce to a sum of 3 terms)

    g. $[(a' + d' + b'c)(b + d + ac')]' + b'c'd' + a'c'd$ (reduce to 3 terms)

4.7 Factor to obtain a product of four terms and then reduce to three terms by applying the consensus theorem: $ABC + A'B'C'$

4.8 Factor $Z = ABC + DE + ACF + AD' + AB'E'$ and simplify it to the form $(X + X)(X + X)(X + X + X + X)$ (where each X represents a literal). Now express Z as a minimum sum of products in the form:

$$XX + XX + XX + XX$$

4.9 Simplify to a sum of three terms:

$$A'C'D' + AC' + BCD + A'CD' + A'BC + AB'C'$$

4.10 Reduce to a minimum sum of products:

$$F = (A \oplus BC) + (A'B' \equiv D) + A'BD$$

4.11 Simplify: $F = a'b \oplus bc \oplus ab \oplus b'c'$

4.12 Prove algebraically that the following equation is valid:

$$(A' + B' + D')(A' + B + D')(B + C + D)(A + C')(A + C' + D)$$
$$= A'C'D + ACD' + BC'D'$$

4.13 Determine which of the following equations are always valid (give an algebraic proof):

 a. $a'b + b'c + c'a = ab' + bc' + ca'$

 b. $(a + b)(b + c)(c + a) = (a' + b')(b' + c')(c' + a')$

 c. $abc + ab'c' + b'cd + bc'd + ad = abc + ab'c' + b'cd + bc'd$

4.14 Prove algebraically:

 a. $(A \oplus B)(B + C) + (A \equiv B)(B' + C') = A' + (B \oplus C)$

 b. $ABC + A'B'C' + ABD + B'C'D = (B + C')(A + B')(A' + C + D)$

 c. $XZ + Y'Z' + WYZ + WX'Y = (X + W + Y')(X + Y + Z')(X' + Z + Y')$

4.15 Which of the following statements are always true? Justify your answers.

 a. If $x = y$, then $a(b + x') = a(b + y')$.

 b. If $a(b + x') = a(b + y')$, then $x = y$.

4.16 Which of the following statements are always true?

 a. If $A + B + D = C + D$, then $A + B = C$.

 b. If $A + B = C$, then $A + B + D = C + D$.

 c. If $B + C = E$, then $A'B + A'C = A'E$.

 d. If $A'B + A'C = A'E$, then $B + C = E$.

 Justify your answers.

4.17 Simplify each of the following expressions:

 a. $F = A'B' + BC + AC + AB$

 b. $F = A'B'D + ABC' + AB'CD + BC + A'CD + BCD$

 c. $F = (A' + B + C' + D')(A + C + D)(A' + C' + D')(A + B' + C + D)$
 (reduce to a sum of 3 terms)

 d. $F = B'C'D' + B'D + ABC + BC'D' + ABD' + A'B'D$
 (reduce to 3 terms)

5

WORD PROBLEMS
MINTERM AND MAXTERM EXPANSIONS

OBJECTIVES

1. Given a word description of the desired behavior of a logic network, write the output of the network as a function of the input variables. Specify this function as an algebraic expression or by means of a truth table as is appropriate.

2. Given a truth table, write the function (or its complement) as both a minterm expansion (standard sum of products) and a maxterm expansion (standard product of sums). Be able to use both alphabetic and decimal notation.

3. Given an algebraic expression for a function, expand it algebraically to obtain the minterm or maxterm form.

4. Given one of the following: minterm expansion for F, minterm expansion for F', maxterm expansion for F, maxterm expansion for F', find any of the other three forms.

5. Write the general form of the minterm and maxterm expansion of a function of n variables.

6. Explain why some functions contain "don't care" terms.

STUDY GUIDE

1. Study Section 5.1, *Conversion of English Sentences to Boolean Equations*.

   a. Use braces to identify the phrases in each of the following sentences:

(1) The tape reader should stop if the manual stop button is pressed,

if an error occurs, or if an end-of-tape signal is present.

(2) He eats eggs for breakfast if it is not Sunday and

he has eggs in the refrigerator.

(3) Addition should occur iff an add instruction is given and

the signs are the same, or if a subtract instruction is given and

the signs are not the same.

    b. Write a Boolean expression which represents each of the sentences in part a. Assign a variable to each phrase, and use a complemented variable to represent a phrase which contains "not".

    (Your answers should be in the *form* $F = S'E$, $F = AB + SB'$, and $F = A + B + C$, not necessarily in that order.)

    c. If X represents the phrase "N is greater than 3", how can you represent the phrase "N is less than or equal to 3"?

    d. Work Problems 5.1 and 5.2.

2. Study Section 5.2, *Combinational Network Design Using a Truth Table.* Previously, you have learned how to go from an algebraic expression for a function to a truth table; in this section you will learn how to go from a truth table to an algebraic expression.

    a. Write a product term which is 1 iff $a = 0$, $b = 0$, and $c = 1$.

    b. Write a sum term which is 0 iff $a = 0$, $b = 0$, and $c = 1$.

c. Verify that your answers to a and b are complements.

d. Write a product term which is 1 iff $a = 1$, $b = 0$, $c = 0$, and $d = 1$.

e. Write a sum term which is 0 iff $a = 0$, $b = 0$, $c = 1$, and $d = 1$.

f. For the given truth table, write F as a sum of four product terms which correspond to the four 1's of F.

g. From the truth table, write F as a product of four sum terms which correspond to the four 0's of F.

a	b	c	F
0	0	0	1
0	0	1	1
0	1	0	0
0	1	1	1
1	0	0	1
1	0	1	0
1	1	0	0
1	1	1	0

h. Verify that your answers to both f and g reduce to
$F = b'c' + a'c$.

3. Study Section 5.3, *Minterm and Maxterm Expansions.*

   a. Define the following terms:
   minterm (for n variables)

   maxterm (for n variables)

   b. Study Table 5-2 and observe the relation between the values of A, B, and C and the corresponding minterms and maxterms.
   If $A = 0$, then does A or A' appear in the minterm?   In the maxterm?
   If $A = 1$, then does A or A' appear in the minterm?   In the maxterm?
   What is the relation between minterm m_i and the corresponding maxterm M_i?

   c. For the table given in Study Guide question 2f, write the minterm expansion for F in m-notation and in decimal notation.

For the same table, write the maxterm expansion for F in M-notation and in decimal notation.

Check your answers by converting your answer to 2f to m-notation and your answer to 2g to M-notation.

d. Given a sum-of-products expression, how do you expand it to a standard sum of products (minterm expansion)?

e. Given a product of sums, how do you expand it to a standard product of sums (maxterm expansion)?

f. In Equation (5-11), what theorems were used to factor f to obtain the maxterm expansion?

g. Why is the following expression *not* a maxterm expansion:
$$f(A, B, C, D) = (A + B' + C + D)(A' + B + C')(A' + B + C + D')$$

h. Assuming that there are 3 variables (A, B, C), identify each of the following as a minterm expansion, maxterm expansion, or neither:

(1) $AB + B'C'$ (4) $(A' + B)(B' + C)(A' + C)$

(2) $(A' + B + C')(A + B' + C)$ (5) $A'BC' + AB'C + ABC$

(3) $A + B + C$ (6) $AB'C'$

Note that it is possible for a minterm or maxterm expansion to have only one term.

4. a. Given a minterm in terms of its variables, the procedure for conversion to decimal notation is

(1) Replace each complemented variable with a _____ and replace each uncomplemented variable with a_____.

(2) Convert the resulting binary number to decimal.

b. Convert the minterm $AB'C'DE$ to decimal notation.

c. Given that m_{13} is a minterm of the variables A, B, C, D and E write the minterm in terms of these variables.

d. Given a maxterm in terms of its variables, the procedure for conversion to decimal notation is
   (1) Replace each complemented variable with_____ and replace each uncomplemented variable with a_____ .
   (2) Group these 0's and 1's to form a binary number and convert to decimal.

e. Convert the maxterm $A' + B + C + D' + E'$ to decimal notation.

f. Given that M_{13} is a maxterm of the variables A, B, C, D and E write the maxterm in terms of these variables.

g. Check your answers to b, c, e and f by using the relation $M_i = m_i'$.

h. Given $f(a, b, c, d, e) = \Pi M(0, 10, 28)$, express f in terms of a, b, c, d and e. (Your answer should contain only 5 complemented variables.)

5. Study Section 5.4, *General Minterm and Maxterm Expansions.* Make sure that you understand the notation here and can follow the algebra in all of the equations. If you have difficulty with this section, ask for help *before* you take the readiness test.

a. How many different functions of 4 variables are possible?

b. Explain why there are 2^{2^n} functions of n variables.

c. Write the function of Table 5-1 in the form of Equation (5-13) and show that it reduces to Equation (5-3).

d. For Equation (5-19), write out the indicated summations in full for the case $n = 2$.

e. Study Tables 5-4 and 5-5 carefully and make sure you understand why each table entry is valid. Use the truth table for f and f' (Table 5-1) to verify the entries in Table 5-5. If you understand the relation between Table 5-4 and the truth table for F and F', you should be able to perform the conversions without having to memorize the table.

f. Given that $f = \Sigma m(0, 1, 3, 4, 7)$

   The maxterm expansion for f is _____

   The minterm expansion for f' is _____

   The maxterm expansion for f' is _____

6. Study Section 5.5, *Incompletely Specified Functions.*

   a. State two reasons why some functions have "don't care" terms.

   b. Given the following table, write the minterm expansion for Z in decimal form.

   c. Write the maxterm expansion in decimal form.

A	B	C	Z
0	0	0	1
0	0	1	X
0	1	0	0
0	1	1	X
1	0	0	X
1	0	1	1
1	1	0	0
1	1	1	0

   d. Work Problem 5.12.

7. Study Section 5.6, *Examples of Truth Table Construction.* Finding the truth table from the problem statement is probably the most difficult part of the process of designing a switching network. Make sure that you understand how to do this.

8. Work Problems 5.3 through 5.9.

9. Read the following and then work Problem 5.10 or 5.11 as assigned:

When looking at an expression to determine the required number of gates, keep in mind that the number of required gates is generally *not* equal to the number of AND and OR operations which appear in the expression. For example,

$$AB + CD + EF(G + H)$$

contains four AND operations and three OR operations, but it only requires three AND gates and two OR gates:

10. *Laboratory Exercise.* (Must be completed before you take the readiness test.) The purpose of this lab exercise is to acquaint you with the laboratory and some of the available lab equipment which you will be using later in a more complex lab design problem.

 a. Obtain a "Laboratory Information" study unit and follow the instructions in Part I of the study guide attached to the unit.

 b. Build the network which you designed in Problem 5.10 or 5.11 in the lab. Test the network for all 16 combinations of values for the input variables. Enter the results of your lab testing in a truth table.

11. Reread the objectives of this unit. Make sure that you understand the difference in the procedures for converting maxterms and minterms from decimal to algebraic notation. When you are satisfied that you can meet the objectives, take the readiness test. When you come to take the readiness test, turn in a copy of your solution to Problem 5.10 or 5.11 and the results of lab testing.

5. WORD PROBLEMS
MINTERM AND MAXTERM EXPANSIONS

In this unit, you will learn how to design a combinational switching network starting with a word description of the desired network behavior. The first step is usually to translate the word description into a truth table or into an algebraic expression. Given the truth table for a Boolean function, two standard algebraic forms of the function can be derived — the standard sum of products (minterm expansion) and the standard product of sums (maxterm expansion). Simplification of either of these standard forms leads directly to a realization of the network using AND and OR gates.

5.1   Conversion of English Sentences to Boolean Equations

Logic design problems are often stated in terms of one or more English sentences. The first step in designing a logic network is to translate these sentences into Boolean equations. In order to do this, we must break down each sentence into phrases and associate a Boolean variable with each phrase. If a phrase can have a value of "true" or "false", then we can represent that phrase by a Boolean variable. Phrases like "she goes to the store" or "today is Monday" can be either true or false, but a command like "go to the store" has no truth value. If a sentence has several phrases, we will mark each phrase with a brace. The following sentence has three phrases:

Mary watches TV if it is Monday night and she has finished her homework.

The "if" and "and" are not included in any phrase; they show the relationships among the phrases.

We will define a two-valued variable to indicate the truth or falsity of each phrase:

$F = 1$ if "Mary watches TV" is true; otherwise, $F = 0$
$A = 1$ if "it is Monday night" is true; otherwise, $A = 0$
$B = 1$ if "she has finished her homework" is true; otherwise $B = 0$

Since F is "true" if A and B are both "true", we can represent the sentence by

$$F = A \cdot B$$

The three main steps in designing a single-output combinational switching network are:

a. Find a switching function which specifies the desired behavior of the network.

b. Find a simplified algebraic expression for the function.

c. Realize the simplified function using available logic elements.

For simple problems, it may be possible to go directly from a word description of the desired behavior of the network to an algebraic expression for the output function. In other cases, it is better to first specify the function by means of a truth table and then derive an algebraic expression from the truth table.

The following example illustrates how to go from a word statement of a problem directly to an algebraic expression which represents the desired network behavior. An alarm circuit is to be designed which operates as follows:

The alarm will ring iff the alarm switch is turned on and the door is not closed, or it is after 6 p.m. and the window is not closed.

The first step in writing an algebraic expression which corresponds to the above sentence is to associate a Boolean variable with each phrase in the sentence. This variable will have a value of 1 when the phrase is true and 0 when it is false. We will use the following assignment of variables:

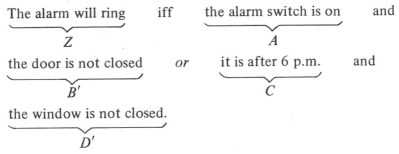

This assignment implies that if $Z = 1$, the alarm will ring. If the alarm switch is turned on, $A = 1$, and if it is after 6 p.m., $C = 1$. If we use the variable B to represent the phrase "the door is closed", then B' represents "the door is *not* closed". Thus $B = 1$ if the door is closed, and $B' = 1$ ($B = 0$) if the door is not closed. Similarly, $D = 1$ if the window is closed and $D' = 1$ if the window is *not* closed. Using this assignment of variables, the above sentence can be translated into the following Boolean equation:

$$Z = AB' + CD'$$

This equation corresponds to the following network:

In the above network, A is a signal which is 1 when the alarm switch is on, C is a signal from a time clock which is 1 when it is after 6 p.m., B is a signal from a switch on the door which is 1 when the door is closed, and similarly D is 1 when the window is closed. The output Z is connected to the alarm so that it will ring when $Z = 1$.

5.2 Combinational Network Design Using a Truth Table

The next example illustrates network design using a truth table. A switching network has three inputs and one output as shown. The inputs A, B, and C represent the first, second, and third bits, respectively, of a binary number N. The output of the network is to be $f = 1$ if $N \geqslant 011_2$ and $f = 0$ if $N < 011_2$. The truth table for f is as follows:

Table 5-1

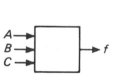

A	B	C	f	f'
0	0	0	0	1
0	0	1	0	1
0	1	0	0	1
0	1	1	1	0
1	0	0	1	0
1	0	1	1	0
1	1	0	1	0
1	1	1	1	0

Next we will derive an algebraic expression for f from the truth table by using the combinations of values of A, B, and C for which $f = 1$. The term $A'BC$ is 1 only if $A = 0$, $B = 1$, and $C = 1$. Similarly, the term $AB'C'$ is 1 only for the combination 100, $AB'C$ is 1 only for 101, ABC' is 1 only for 110, and ABC is 1 only for 111. ORing these terms together yields

$$f = A'BC + AB'C' + AB'C + ABC' + ABC \qquad (5\text{-}1)$$

The above expression equals 1 if A, B, and C take on any of the five combinations of values 011, 100, 101, 110, or 111. If any other combination of values occurs, f is 0 because all five terms are 0.

Equation (5-1) can be simplified by first combining terms and then eliminating A':

$$f = A'BC + AB' + AB = A'BC + A = A + BC \qquad (5\text{-}2)$$

Equation (5-2) leads directly to the following network:

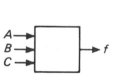

Instead of writing f in terms of the 1's of the function, we may also write f in terms of the 0's of the function. The function defined by Table 5-1 is 0 for three combinations of input values. Observe that the term $A + B + C$ is 0 only if $A = B = C = 0$. Similarly, $A + B + C'$ is 0 only for the input combination 001, and $A + B' + C$ is 0 only for the combination 010. ANDing these terms together yields

$$f = (A + B + C)(A + B + C')(A + B' + C) \qquad (5\text{-}3)$$

The above expression equals 0 if A, B, and C take on any of the combinations of values 000, 001, or 010. For any other combination of values, f is 1 because all three terms are 1. Since Equation (5-3) represents the same function as Equation (5-1) they must both reduce to the same expression. Combining terms and using the second distributive law, Equation (5-3) simplifies to

$$f = (A + B)(A + B' + C) = A + B(B' + C) = A + BC \qquad (5\text{-}4)$$

which is the same as Equation (5-2).

Another way to derive Equation (5-3) is to first write f' as a sum of products, and then complement the result. From Table 5-1, f' is 1 for input combinations $ABC = 000, 001$ and 010, so

$$f' = A'B'C' + A'B'C + A'BC'$$

Taking the complement of f' gives Equation (5-3).

5.3   Minterm and Maxterm Expansions

Each of the terms in Equation (5-1) is referred to as a minterm. In general, a *minterm* of n variables is a product of n literals in which each variable appears exactly once in either true or complemented form, but not both. (A *literal* is a variable or its complement.) Table 5-2 lists all of the minterms of the three variables A, B and C. Each minterm has a value of 1 for exactly one combination of values of the variables A, B and C. Thus if $A = B = C = 0$, $A'B'C' = 1$; if $A = B = 0$ and $C = 1$, $A'B'C = 1$; etc. Minterms are often written in abbreviated form — $A'B'C'$ is designated m_0, $A'B'C$ is designated m_1, etc. In general, the minterm which corresponds to row i of the truth table is designated m_i (i is usually written in decimal).

Table 5-2.   Minterms and Maxterms for Three Variables

Row no.	ABC	Minterms	Maxterms
0	0 0 0	$A'B'C' = m_0$	$A + B + C = M_0$
1	0 0 1	$A'B'C = m_1$	$A + B + C' = M_1$
2	0 1 0	$A'BC' = m_2$	$A + B' + C = M_2$
3	0 1 1	$A'BC = m_3$	$A + B' + C' = M_3$
4	1 0 0	$AB'C' = m_4$	$A' + B + C = M_4$
5	1 0 1	$AB'C = m_5$	$A' + B + C' = M_5$
6	1 1 0	$ABC' = m_6$	$A' + B' + C = M_6$
7	1 1 1	$ABC = m_7$	$A' + B' + C' = M_7$

When a function f is written as a sum of minterms as in Equation (5-1), this is referred to as a *minterm expansion* or a *standard sum of products.* *
If $f = 1$ for row i of the truth table, then m_i must be present in the minterm expansion because $m_i = 1$ only for the combination of values of the variables corresponding to row i of the table. Because the minterms present in f are in one-to-one correspondence with the 1's of f in the truth table, the minterm expansion for a function f is unique. Equation (5-1) can be rewritten in terms of m-notation as

$$f(A, B, C) = m_3 + m_4 + m_5 + m_6 + m_7 \qquad (5\text{-}5)$$

---

*Other names used in the literature for standard sum of products are *canonical sum of products* and *disjunctive normal form*. Similarly, a standard product of sums may be called a *canonical product of sums* or a *conjunctive normal form*.

This can be further abbreviated by listing only the decimal subscripts in the form

$$f(A, B, C) = \Sigma m(3, 4, 5, 6, 7) \tag{5-5a}$$

Each of the sum terms (or factors) in Equation (5-3) is referred to as a *maxterm*. In general, a *maxterm* of n variables is a sum of n literals in which each variable appears exactly once in either true or complemented form, but not both. Table 5-2 lists all of the maxterms of the three variables A, B and C. Each maxterm has a value of 0 for exactly one combination of values for A, B and C. Thus if $A = B = C = 0$, $A + B + C = 0$; if $A = B = 0$ and $C = 1$, $A + B + C' = 0$; etc. Maxterms are often written in abbreviated form using M-notation. The maxterm which corresponds to row i of the truth table is designated M_i. Note that each maxterm is the complement of the corresponding minterm; i.e., $M_i = m_i'$.

When a function f is written as a product of maxterms as in Equation (5-3), this is referred to as a *maxterm expansion* or *standard product of sums*. If $f = 0$ for row i of the truth table, then M_i must be present in the maxterm expansion because $M_i = 0$ only for the combination of values of the variables corresponding to row i of the table. Note that the maxterms are multiplied together so that if any one of them is 0, f will be 0. Because the maxterms are in one-to-one correspondence with the 0's of f in the truth table, the maxterm expansion for a function f is unique. Equation (5-3) can be rewritten in M-notation as

$$f(A, B, C) = M_0 M_1 M_2 \tag{5-6}$$

This can be further abbreviated by listing only the decimal subscripts in the form

$$f(A, B, C) = \Pi M(0, 1, 2) \tag{5-6a}$$

Since if $f \neq 1$, $f = 0$, it follows that if m_i is *not* present in the minterm expansion of f, then M_i *is* present in the maxterm expansion. Thus, given a minterm expansion of an n-variable function f in decimal notation, the maxterm expansion is obtained by listing those decimal integers ($0 \leqslant i \leqslant 2^n - 1$) not in the minterm list. Using this method, Equation (5-6a) can be obtained directly from Equation (5-5a).

Given the minterm or maxterm expansions for f, the minterm or maxterm expansions for the complement of f are easy to obtain. Since f' is 1 when f is 0, the minterm expansion for f' contains those minterms not present in f. Thus, from Equation (5-5),

$$f' = m_0 + m_1 + m_2 = \Sigma m(0, 1, 2) \tag{5-7}$$

Similarly, the maxterm expansion for f' contains those maxterms not present in f. From Equation (5-6),

$$f' = \Pi M(3, 4, 5, 6, 7) = M_3 M_4 M_5 M_6 M_7 \tag{5-8}$$

Since the complement of a minterm is the corresponding maxterm, Equation (5-8) can be obtained by complementing Equation (5-5):

$$f' = (m_3 + m_4 + m_5 + m_6 + m_7)' = m_3' m_4' m_5' m_6' m_7' = M_3 M_4 M_5 M_6 M_7$$

Similarly, Equation (5-7) can be obtained by complementing Equation (5-6):

$$f' = (M_0 M_1 M_2)' = M_0' + M_1' + M_2' = m_0 + m_1 + m_2$$

A general switching expression can be converted to a minterm or maxterm expansion either using a truth table or algebraically. If a truth table is constructed by evaluating the expression for all different combinations of values of the variables, the minterm and maxterm expansions can be obtained from the truth table by the methods just discussed. Another way to obtain the minterm expansion is to first write the expression as a sum of products and then introduce the missing variables in each term by applying the theorem $X + X' = 1$.

Example: Find the minterm expansion of $f(a, b, c, d) = a'(b' + d) + acd'$

$$f = a'b' + a'd + acd'$$
$$= a'b'(c + c')(d + d') + a'd(b + b')(c + c') + acd'(b + b')$$
$$= a'b'c'd' + a'b'c'd + a'b'cd' + a'b'cd + \overline{a'b'c'd} + \overline{a'b'cd} + a'bc'd$$
$$+ a'bcd + abcd' + ab'cd' \tag{5-9}$$

Duplicate terms have been crossed out, since $X + X = X$. The above expression can then be converted to decimal notation:

$$f = a'b'c'd' + a'b'c'd + a'b'cd' + a'b'cd + a'bc'd + a'bcd + abcd' + ab'cd'$$
$$\quad\ 0\,0\,0\,0 \qquad 0\,0\,0\,1 \qquad 0\,0\,1\,0 \qquad 0\,0\,1\,1 \quad 0\,1\,0\,1 \quad 0\,1\,1\,1 \quad 1\,1\,1\,0 \qquad 1\,0\,1\,0$$
$$f = \Sigma m(0, 1, 2, 3, 5, 7, 10, 14) \tag{5-10}$$

The maxterm expansion for f can then be obtained by listing the decimal integers (in the range 0 to 15) which do not correspond to minterms of f:

$$f = \Pi M(4, 6, 8, 9, 11, 12, 13, 15)$$

An alternate way of finding the maxterm expansion is to factor f to obtain a product of sums, introduce the missing variables in each sum term by using $XX' = 0$, and then factor again to obtain the maxterms. For the above example,

$$f = (a' + cd')(a + b' + d) = (a' + c)(a' + d')(a + b' + d)$$
$$= (a' + bb' + c + dd')(a' + bb' + cc' + d')(a + b' + cc' + d)$$
$$= (a' + bb' + c + d)(a' + bb' + c + d')(\overline{a' + bb' + c + d'})(a' + bb' + c' + d')$$
$$\quad (a + b' + cc' + d)$$
$$= (a' + b + c + d)(a' + b' + c + d)(a' + b + c + d')(a' + b' + c + d')$$
$$\qquad\ 1000 \qquad\qquad 1100 \qquad\qquad 1001 \qquad\qquad 1101$$
$$\quad (a' + b + c' + d')(a' + b' + c' + d')(a + b' + c + d)(a + b' + c' + d)$$
$$\qquad 1011 \qquad\qquad 1111 \qquad\qquad 0100 \qquad\qquad 0110$$
$$= \Pi M(4, 6, 8, 9, 11, 12, 13, 15) \tag{5-11}$$

Note that when translating the maxterms to decimal notation, a primed variable is first replaced with a 1 and an unprimed variable with a 0.

Since the terms in the minterm expansion of a function F correspond one-to-one with the rows of the truth table for which $F = 1$, the minterm expansion of F is unique. Thus, we can prove that an equation is valid by finding the minterm expansion of each side and showing that these expansions are the same.

Example: Show that $a'c + b'c' + ab = a'b' + bc + ac'$

We will find the minterm expansion of each side by supplying the missing variables. For the left side,

$$a'c(b + b') + b'c'(a + a') + ab(c + c') =$$
$$a'bc + a'b'c + ab'c' + a'b'c' + abc + abc' =$$
$$m_3 + m_1 + m_4 + m_0 + m_7 + m_6$$

For the right side,

$$a'b'(c + c') + bc(a + a') + ac'(b + b') =$$
$$a'b'c + a'b'c' + abc + a'bc + abc' + ab'c' =$$
$$m_1 + m_0 + m_7 + m_3 + m_6 + m_4$$

Since the two minterm expansions are the same, the equation is valid.

5.4 General Minterm and Maxterm Expansions

Table 5-3 represents a truth table for a general function of three variables. Each a_i is a constant with a value of 0 or 1. To completely specify a function, we must assign values to all of the a_i's. Since each a_i can be specified in two ways, there are 2^8 ways of filling the F column of the truth table; therefore, there are 256 different functions of three variables (this includes the degenerate cases, F identically equal to 0 and F identically equal to 1). For a function of n variables there are 2^n rows in the truth table, and since the value of F can be 0 or 1 for each row, there are $2^{(2^n)}$ possible functions of n variables.

Table 5-3. General Truth Table for Three Variables

ABC	F
0 0 0	a_0
0 0 1	a_1
0 1 0	a_2
0 1 1	a_3
1 0 0	a_4
1 0 1	a_5
1 1 0	a_6
1 1 1	a_7

From Table 5-3, we can write the minterm expansion for a general function of three variables as follows:

$$F = a_0 m_0 + a_1 m_1 + a_2 m_2 + \ldots + a_7 m_7 = \sum_{i=0}^{7} a_i m_i \qquad (5\text{-}12)$$

Note that if $a_i = 1$, minterm m_i is present in the expansion; if $a_i = 0$, the corresponding minterm is not present. The maxterm expansion for a general function of three variables is

$$F = (a_0 + M_0)(a_1 + M_1)(a_2 + M_2) \ldots (a_7 + M_7) = \prod_{i=0}^{7} (a_i + M_i) \quad (5\text{-}13)$$

Note that if $a_i = 1$, $a_i + M_i = 1$, and M_i drops out of the expansion; however, M_i is present if $a_i = 0$.

From Equation (5-13), the minterm expansion of F' is

$$F' = \left[\prod_{i=0}^{7} (a_i + M_i) \right]' = \sum_{i=0}^{7} a_i' M_i' = \sum_{i=0}^{7} a_i' m_i \quad (5\text{-}14)$$

Note that all the minterms which are not present in F are present in F'. From Equation (5-12), the maxterm expansion of F' is

$$F' = \left[\sum_{i=0}^{7} a_i m_i \right]' = \prod_{i=0}^{7} (a_i' + m_i') = \prod_{i=0}^{7} (a_i' + M_i) \quad (5\text{-}15)$$

Note that all the maxterms which are not present in F are present in F'. Generalizing Equations (5-12), (5-13), (5-14), and (5-15) to n variables, we have

$$F = \sum_{i=0}^{2^n - 1} a_i m_i = \prod_{i=0}^{2^n - 1} (a_i + M_i) \quad (5\text{-}16)$$

$$F' = \sum_{i=0}^{2^n - 1} a_i' m_i = \prod_{i=0}^{2^n - 1} (a_i' + M_i) \quad (5\text{-}17)$$

Given two different minterms of n variables, m_i and m_j, at least one variable appears complemented in one of the minterms and uncomplemented in the other. Therefore, if $i \neq j$, $m_i m_j = 0$. For example, for $n = 3$, $m_1 m_3 = (A'B'C)(A'BC) = 0$.

Given minterm expansions for two functions

$$f_1 = \sum_{i=0}^{2^n - 1} a_i m_i \qquad f_2 = \sum_{j=0}^{2^n - 1} b_j m_j \quad (5\text{-}18)$$

the product is

$$f_1 f_2 = \left(\sum_{i=0}^{2^n-1} a_i m_i \right) \left(\sum_{j=0}^{2^n-1} b_j m_j \right) = \sum_{i=0}^{2^n-1} \sum_{j=0}^{2^n-1} a_i b_j m_i m_j$$

$$= \sum_{i=0}^{2^n-1} a_i b_i m_i \quad \text{(since } m_i m_j = 0 \text{ unless } i = j) \tag{5-19}$$

Note that all of the cross-product terms ($i \neq j$) drop out so that $f_1 f_2$ contains only those minterms which are present in both f_1 and f_2. For example, if

$$f_1 = \sum m(0, 2, 3, 5, 9, 11) \text{ and } f_2 = \sum m(0, 3, 9, 11, 13, 14)$$
$$f_1 f_2 = \sum m(0, 3, 9, 11)$$

Table 5-4 summarizes the procedures for conversion between minterm and maxterm expansions of F and F', assuming that all expansions are written as lists of decimal numbers. When using this table, keep in mind that the truth table for an n-variable function has 2^n rows so that the minterm (or maxterm) numbers range from 0 to 2^n-1. Table 5-5 illustrates the application of Table 5-4 to the three-variable function given in Table 5-1.

Table 5-4. Conversion of Forms

DESIRED FORM

	minterm expansion of F	maxterm expansion of F	minterm expansion of F'	maxterm expansion of F'
minterm expansion of F	———	maxterm nos. are those nos. not on the minterm list for F	list minterms not present in F	maxterm nos. are the same as minterm nos. of F
maxterm expansion of F	minterm nos. are those nos. not on the maxterm list for F	———	minterm nos. are the same as maxterm nos. of F	list maxterms not present in F

GIVEN FORM

Table 5-5. Application of Table 5-4

DESIRED FORM

	minterm expansion of f	maxterm expansion of f	minterm expansion of f'	maxterm expansion of f'
$f = \Sigma m(3,4,5,6,7)$	————	$\Pi M(0,1,2)$	$\Sigma m(0,1,2)$	$\Pi M(3,4,5,6,7)$
$f = \Pi M(0,1,2)$	$\Sigma m(3,4,5,6,7)$	————	$\Sigma m(0,1,2)$	$\Pi M(3,4,5,6,7)$

GIVEN FORM

5.5 Incompletely Specified Functions

A large digital system is usually divided into many subnetworks. Consider the following example in which the output of network N_1 drives the input of network N_2.

Let us assume that the output of N_1 does not generate all possible combinations of values for A, B, and C. In particular, we will assume that there are no combinations of values for w, x, y, and z which cause A, B, and C to assume values of 001 or 110. Hence, when we design N_2 it is not necessary to specify values of F for $ABC = 001$ or 110, since these combinations of values can never occur as inputs to N_2. For example, F might be specified by Table 5-6.

Table 5-6

ABC	F
0 0 0	1
0 0 1	x
0 1 0	0
0 1 1	1
1 0 0	0
1 0 1	0
1 1 0	x
1 1 1	1

The x's in the table indicate that we don't care whether the value of 0 or 1 is assigned to F for the combinations $ABC = 001$ or 110. In this example, we don't care what the value of F is because these input combinations never occur anyway. The function F is then *incompletely specified*. The minterms $A'B'C$ and ABC' are referred to as "don't care" terms, since we don't care whether they are present in the function or not.

When we realize the function, we must specify values for the don't cares. It is desirable to choose values which will help simplify the function. If we assign the value 0 to both X's, then

$$F = A'B'C' + A'BC + ABC = A'B'C' + BC$$

If we assign 1 to the first X and 0 to the second, then

$$F = A'B'C' + A'B'C + A'BC + ABC = A'B' + BC$$

If we assign 1 to both X's then

$$F = A'B'C' + A'B'C + A'BC + ABC' + ABC = A'B' + BC + AB$$

The second choice of values leads to the simplest solution.

We have seen one way in which incompletely specified functions can arise, and there are many other ways. In the above example, don't cares were present because certain combinations of network inputs did not occur. In other cases, all input combinations may occur, but the network output is used in such a way that we don't care whether it is 0 or 1 for certain input combinations.

When writing the minterm expansion for an incompletely specified function, we will use "m" to denote the required minterms and "d" to denote the don't care minterms. Using this notation, the minterm expansion for Table 5-6 is

$$F = \Sigma m(0, 3, 7) + \Sigma d(1, 6)$$

For each don't care minterm there is a corresponding don't care maxterm. For example, if $F = x$ (don't care) for input combination 001, m_1 is a don't care minterm and M_1 is a don't care maxterm. We will use "D" to represent a don't care maxterm and write the maxterm expansion of the function in Table 5-6 as

$$F = \Pi M(2,4,5) \cdot \Pi D(1,6)$$

which implies that maxterms M_2, M_4 and M_5 are present in F and don't care maxterms M_1 and M_6 are optional.

5.6   Examples of Truth Table Construction

Example 1: We will design a simple binary adder that adds two 1-bit binary numbers, a and b, to give a two-bit sum. The numeric values for the adder inputs and output are as follows:

a	b	sum	
0	0	00	$(0 + 0 = 0)$
0	1	01	$(0 + 1 = 1)$
1	0	01	$(1 + 0 = 1)$
1	1	10	$(1 + 1 = 2)$

We will represent inputs to the adder by the logic variables A and B, represent the 2-bit sum by the logic variables X and Y, and construct a truth table:

A	B	XY
0	0	00
0	1	01
1	0	01
1	1	10

Since a numeric value of 0 is represented by a logic 0 and a numeric value of 1 by a logic 1, the 0's and 1's in the truth table are exactly the same as in the previous table. From the truth table,

$$X = AB \text{ and } Y = A'B + AB' = A \oplus B$$

Example 2: An adder is to be designed which adds two 2-bit binary numbers to give a 3-bit binary sum. Find the truth table for the network. The network has four inputs and three outputs as shown:

Truth table:

N_1		N_2		N_3		
A	B	C	D	X	Y	Z
0	0	0	0	0	0	0
0	0	0	1	0	0	1
0	0	1	0	0	1	0
0	0	1	1	0	1	1
0	1	0	0	0	0	1
0	1	0	1	0	1	0
0	1	1	0	0	1	1
0	1	1	1	1	0	0
1	0	0	0	0	1	0
1	0	0	1	0	1	1
1	0	1	0	1	0	0
1	0	1	1	1	0	1
1	1	0	0	0	1	1
1	1	0	1	1	0	0
1	1	1	0	1	0	1
1	1	1	1	1	1	0

Inputs A and B taken together represent a binary number N_1.
Inputs C and D taken together represent a binary number N_2.
Outputs X, Y and Z taken together represent a binary number N_3, where $N_3 = N_1 + N_2$ (+ of course represents ordinary addition here).

In this example we have used A, B, C and D to represent both numeric values and logic values, but this should not cause any confusion because the numeric and logic values are the same.

In forming the above table, the variables were treated like binary numbers having *numeric* values. Now we wish to derive the switching functions for the output variables. In doing so, we will treat A, B, C, D, X, Y and Z as switching variables having non-numeric values 0 and 1. (Remember that in this case the 0 and 1 may represent low and high voltages, open and closed switches, etc.)

From inspection of the table, the output functions are:

$$X(A, B, C, D) = \Sigma m(7, 10, 11, 13, 14, 15)$$

$$Y(A, B, C, D) = \Sigma m(2, 3, 5, 6, 8, 9, 12, 15)$$

$$Z(A, B, C, D) = \Sigma m(1, 3, 4, 6, 9, 11, 12, 14)$$

Example 3: Design an error detector for 6-3-1-1 binary-coded-decimal digits. The output (F) is to be 1 iff the four inputs (A, B, C, D) represent an invalid code combination.

The valid 6-3-1-1 code combinations are listed in Table 1-1. If any other combination occurs this is not a valid 6-3-1-1 binary-coded-decimal digit and the network output should be $F = 1$ to indicate that an error has occurred. This leads to the following truth table.

$A\,B\,C\,D$	F
0 0 0 0	0
0 0 0 1	0
0 0 1 0	1
0 0 1 1	0
0 1 0 0	0
0 1 0 1	0
0 1 1 0	1
0 1 1 1	0
1 0 0 0	0
1 0 0 1	0
1 0 1 0	1
1 0 1 1	0
1 1 0 0	0
1 1 0 1	1
1 1 1 0	1
1 1 1 1	1

The corresponding output function is

$$F = \Sigma m(2, 6, 10, 13, 14, 15)$$

$$= A'B'CD' + A'BCD' + AB'CD' + ABCD' + ABC'D + ABCD$$

$$= A'CD' + ACD' + ABD = CD' + ABD$$

The network realization using AND and OR gates is

Example 4: The four inputs to a network (A, B, C, D) represent an 8-4-2-1 binary-coded decimal digit. Design the network so that the output (Z) is 1 iff the decimal number represented by the inputs is exactly divisible by 3. Assume that only valid BCD digits occur as inputs.

The digits 0, 3, 6 and 9 are exactly divisible by 3, so $Z = 1$ for the input combinations $ABCD = 0000, 0011, 0110$, and 1001. The input combinations 1010, 1011, 1100, 1101, 1110, and 1111 do not represent valid BCD digits and will never occur, so Z is a don't care for these combinations. This leads to the following truth table:

$ABCD$	Z
0 0 0 0	1
0 0 0 1	0
0 0 1 0	0
0 0 1 1	1
0 1 0 0	0
0 1 0 1	0
0 1 1 0	1
0 1 1 1	0
1 0 0 0	0
1 0 0 1	1
1 0 1 0	x
1 0 1 1	x
1 1 0 0	x
1 1 0 1	x
1 1 1 0	x
1 1 1 1	x

The corresponding output function is
$$Z = \Sigma m(0,3,6,9) + \Sigma d(10,11,12,13,14,15)$$
In order to find the simplest network which will realize Z, we must choose some of the don't cares (x's) to be 0 and some to be 1. The easiest way to do this is to use a Karnaugh map as described in Unit 6.

PROBLEMS

5.1   Represent each of the following sentences by a Boolean equation:

a. The air conditioner should be turned on iff the temperature is greater than 75°, the time is between 8 a.m. and 5 p.m., and it is not a holiday.

b. The product of A and B is negative iff A is negative and B is positive *or* A is positive and B is negative. (Use only two independent variables.)

c. The tape drive motor should be running iff

    (1) the tape is properly threaded,

    (2) an end-of-tape signal is not present, and

    (3) the tape drive is in the manual mode and the manual start button has been pressed, *or* it is in the automatic mode and a "tape-on" signal from the computer is present.

d. The sound system will squeal if the microphone is turned on, *and* the microphone is too close to the speaker or the volume control is set too high.

5.2 A paper tape reader used as an input device to a computer has 5 rows of holes as shown below. A hole punched in the tape indicates a logic 1 and no hole indicates a logic 0. As each hole pattern passes under the photocells, the pattern is translated into logic signals on lines A, B, C, D, and E. All patterns of holes indicate a valid character with two exceptions. A pattern consisting of none of the possible holes punched is not used because it is impossible to distinguish between this pattern and the unpunched space between patterns. An incorrect pattern punched on the tape is "erased" by punching all 5 holes in that position. Therefore, a valid character punched on the tape will have at least 1 hole punched, but will not have all five holes punched.

a. Write an equation for a variable Z which is 1 iff a valid character is being read.

b. Write an equation for a variable Y which is 1 iff the hole pattern being read has holes punched only in rows C and E.

5.3 A switching network has 3 inputs and 2 outputs. The output variables, a and b, represent the first and second bits, respectively, of a binary number, N. N equals the number of inputs which are "1". For example, if $w = 1, x = 0, y = 1$, then $a = 1, b = 0$.

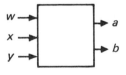

a. Find the minterm expansion for a and for b.

b. Find the maxterm expansion for a and for b.

Express each answer in abbreviated notation and also write it out in terms of w, x, and y.

5.4 A switching network has 4 inputs as shown below. A and B represent the first and second bits of a binary number N_1. C and D represent the first and second bits of a binary number N_2. The output of the network is to be 1 only if the product $N_1 \times N_2$ is greater than two.

a. Find the minterm expansion for F.

b. Find the maxterm expansion for F.

5.5 Given $f(a, b, c) = a' + bc'$

a. Express f as a minterm expansion (use m notation).

b. Express f as a maxterm expansion (use M notation).

c. Express f' as a minterm expansion (use m notation).

d. Express f' as a maxterm expansion (use M notation).

5.6 Repeat Problem 5.5 for $f(a, b, c, d) = (a + c + d)(b' + d')(a' + c' + d)(a' + b + c + d)$

5.7 Four chairs are placed in a row: $\boxed{A}\ \boxed{B}\ \boxed{C}\ \boxed{D}$

Each chair may be occupied ("1") or empty ("0"). Write a logic function $F(A, B, C, D)$ which is "1" iff there are two (or more) adjacent chairs that are empty. Express F

a. as a minterm expansion (standard sum of products) and

b. as a maxterm expansion (standard product of sums)

5.8 Given $F_1 = \Pi M(0, 1, 3, 5)$ and $F_2 = \Pi M(0, 2, 5, 7)$
find the maxterm expansion for $F_1 F_2$.

State a general rule for finding the maxterm expansion of $F_1 F_2$ given the maxterm expansions of F_1 and F_2.

Prove your answer by using the general form of the maxterm expansion.

5.9 a. How many switching functions of two variables (x and y) are there?

b. Give each function in truth table form and in reduced algebraic form. (Include degenerate cases like $F(x, y) = 0$, $F(x, y) = x$, $F(x, y) = y'$, etc.)

5.10 A combinational switching network has four inputs (A, B, C and D) and one output Z. The output is 1 iff 3 or more of the inputs are 1. Design the network using two AND gates and three OR gates. Assume that each gate has a maximum of 3 inputs so that it will be necessary to partially factor your logic equation before you realize it.

5.11 A combinational switching network has four inputs (A, B, C, and D) and one output Z. The output is to be 0 if the input combination is a valid excess-3 coded decimal digit. If any other combination of inputs occurs, the output is to be 1. Design the network using two AND gates and three OR gates. Assume that each gate has a maximum of 3 inputs so that it will be necessary to partially factor your logic equation before you realize it.

5.12 A combinational network is divided into two subnetworks, N_1 and N_2, as shown below. Network N_1 has the given truth table. Note that when $D = 0$, the values of E and F have no effect on the output Z. Also, assume that the input combinations $ABC = 001$ and $ABC = 101$ will never occur. Change as many of the values of D, E and F to don't cares as you can without changing the output Z.

ABC	DEF
000	001
001	110
010	111
011	000
100	110
101	111
110	010
111	101

5.13 Given that $F'(A, B, C, D) = \Sigma m(0, 1, 2, 6, 7, 13, 15)$
   a. Find the minterm expansion for F (both decimal and algebraic form).
   b. Find the maxterm expansion for F (both decimal and algebraic form).

5.14 In each case, determine if $X = Y$:
   a. $X = C(A + B) + AB$, $Y = ABC' + AB'C + BC$
   b. $X = B'C'D' + AB'C + BCD + A'BC'$
      $Y = A'C'D' + AB'D' + ACD + A'BD$

5.15 Each of the following sentences has two possible interpretations depending on whether the AND or OR is done first. Write an equation for each interpretation.
   a. The buzzer will sound if the key is in the ignition switch and the car door is open or the seat belts are not fastened.
   b. You will gain weight if you eat too much or you do not exercise enough and your metabolism rate is too low.

5.16 Work Problem 5.5 using $f(a, b, c) = b'(c + a')$.

5.17 Work Problem 5.5 using
$$f(a, b, c, d) = abd + a'c' + ab'd' + ab'cd$$

5.18 For the given truth table, find the simplest expression for F, and specify the values for the don't cares that lead to this expression.

ABC	F
000	0
001	1
010	x
011	1
100	0
101	x
110	1
111	0

5.19 A combinational network has four inputs (A, B, C, D) and three outputs (X, Y, Z). XYZ represents a binary number whose value equals the number of 1's at the input. For example, if $ABCD = 1011$, $XYZ = 011$.
   a. Find the minterm expansions for X, Y and Z.
   b. Find the maxterm expansions for Y and Z.

5.20 A combinational network has 4 inputs (A, B, C, D), which represent a binary-coded decimal digit. The network has 2 groups of 4 outputs — S, T, U, V and W, X, Y, Z. Each group represents a BCD digit. The output digits represent a decimal number which is 5 times the input number. For example if $ABCD = 0111$, the outputs are 0011 0101. Construct the truth table. Write down minimum expressions for the outputs by inspection of the truth table. *Hint*: Try to match output columns in the table with input columns.

6

KARNAUGH MAPS

OBJECTIVES

1. Given a function (completely or incompletely specified) of 3 to 6 variables, plot it on a Karnaugh map. The function may be given in minterm, maxterm, or algebraic form.

2. Determine the essential (necessary) prime implicants of a function from a map.

3. Obtain the minimum sum-of-products or minimum product-of-sums form of a function from the map.

4. Determine *all* of the prime implicants of a function from a map.

5. Understand the relation between operations performed using the map and the corresponding algebraic operations.

STUDY GUIDE

In this unit we will study the Karnaugh* map. Just about any type of algebraic manipulation we have done so far can be facilitated by using the map, provided the number of variables is small.

1. Study Section 6.1, *Minimum Forms of Switching Functions.*
    a. Define a minimum sum of products.

-----
*Pronounced "*car*-no".

b. Define a minimum product of sums.

c. Work Problem 6.3.

2. Study Section 6.2, *Two- and Three-Variable Karnaugh Maps.*

a. Plot the given truth table on the map. Then loop 2 pairs of 1's on the map and write the simplified form of F.

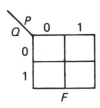

P Q	F
0 0	1
0 1	1
1 0	0
1 1	1

$F =$ _____

Now simplify F algebraically and verify that your answer is correct.

b. $F(a, b, c)$ is plotted below. Find the truth table for F.

a b c	F
0 0 0	
0 0 1	
0 1 0	
0 1 1	
1 0 0	
1 0 1	
1 1 0	
1 1 1	

c. Plot the following functions on the Karnaugh maps given below:

$F_1(R, S, T) = \Sigma m(0, 1, 5, 6)$ $F_2(R, S, T) = \Pi M(2, 3, 4, 7)$

Why are the two maps the same?

d. Plot the following function on the given map:

$$f(x, y, z) = z' + x'z + yz$$

Do *not* make a minterm expansion or a truth table before plotting.

yz \ x	0	1
00		
01		
11		
10		

e. For a 3-variable map, which squares are "adjacent" to square 2?

_____

f. What theorem is used when two terms in adjacent squares are combined?

g. What law of Boolean algebra justifies using a given 1 on a map in two or more loops?

h. Each of the following solutions is *not* minimum.

$$f = ab' + abc$$

$$g = a' + ab$$

In each case, change the looping on the map so that the minimum solution is obtained.

i. Work Problem 6.4.

j. Find two different minimum sum-of-products expressions for the function G which is plotted below.

bc \ a	0	1
00	1	1
01		1
11	1	1
10	1	

G

bc \ a	0	1
00	1	1
01		1
11	1	1
10	1	

G

$$G = \text{_____}$$

$$G = \text{_____}$$

3. Study Section 6.3, *Four-Variable Karnaugh Maps.*

    a. Note the locations of the minterms on 3- and 4-variable maps (Figs. 6-3(b) and 6-10). Memorize this ordering. This will save you much time when you are plotting Karnaugh maps.

    The above ordering is valid only for the order of the variables given. If we label the maps as shown below, fill in the locations of the minterms:

    b. Given the following map, write the minterm and maxterm expansions for *F* in decimal form:

cd\ab	00	01	11	10
00			1	1
01	1	1		1
11		1	1	
10			1	

$F = $ _____

$F = $ _____

    c. Plot the following functions on the given maps:

    (1) $f(w, x, y, z) = \Sigma m(0, 1, 2, 5, 7, 8, 9, 10, 13, 14)$

    (2) $f(w, x, y, z) = x'z' + y'z + w'xz + wyz'$

yz\wx	00	01	11	10
00				
01				
11				
10				

yz\wx	00	01	11	10
00				
01				
11				
10				

Your answers to (1) and (2) should be the same.

    d. For a 4-variable map, which squares are adjacent to square 14? _____ To square 8? _____

e. When we combine two adjacent 1's on a map, this corresponds to applying the theorem $xy' + xy = x$ to eliminate the variable in which the two terms differ. Thus, looping the two 1's indicated on the map below is equivalent to combining the corresponding minterms algebraically:

$a'b'c'd + ab'c'd = b'c'd$

(The term $b'c'd$ can be read directly from the map since it spans the first and last columns (b') and since it is in the second row ($c'd$).)

Loop two other pairs of adjacent 1's on the map above and state the algebraic equivalent of looping these terms. Now read the loops directly off the map and check your algebra.

f. When we combine four adjacent 1's on a map (either four in a line or four in a square) this is equivalent to applying $xy + xy' = x$ three times:

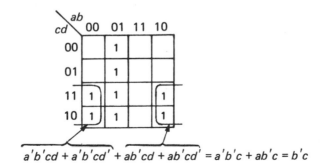

$$a'b'cd + a'b'cd' + ab'cd + ab'cd' = a'b'c + ab'c = b'c$$

Loop the other four 1's on the map and state the algebraic equivalent.

g. For each of the following maps, loop a minimum number of terms which will cover all of the 1's.

ab\cd	00	01	11	10
00		1	1	
01		1	1	1
11	1	1		
10		1		

f_1

ab\cd	00	01	11	10
00				1
01		1		
11	1	1	1	1
10	1			1

f_2

(For each part you should have looped two groups of four 1's and two groups of two 1's).

Write down the minimum sum-of-products expression for f_1 and f_2 from the above maps.

f_1 = _____

f_2 = _____

h. Why is it not possible to combine 3 or 6 minterms together rather than just 2, 4, 8, etc.?

i. Note the procedure for deriving the minimum *product of sums* from the map. You will probably make fewer mistakes if you write down f' as a sum of products first and then complement it as illustrated by the example in Fig. 6-14. Work Problems 6.5 and 6.7.

4. Study Section 6.4, *Determination of Minimum Expressions Using Essential Prime Implicants.*

   a. For the map of Fig. 6-15, list 3 implicants of F other than those which are labeled.

   For the same map, is $ac'd'$ a prime implicant of F?
   Why or why not?

   b. For the given map, are any of the circled terms prime implicants?

   Why or why not?

5. Study Fig. 6-18 carefully and then answer the following questions for the map given below:

   a. How many 1's are adjacent to m_0?

   b. Are all these 1's covered by a single prime implicant?

   c. From your answer to b, can you determine if $B'C'$ is essential?

   d. How many 1's are adjacent to m_9?

   e. Are all of these 1's covered by a single prime implicant?

f. From your answer to e, is $B'C'$ essential?

g. How many 1's are adjacent to m_7?

h. Why is $A'C$ essential?

i. Find two other essential prime implicants and tell which minterm makes them essential.

6. a. How do you determine if a prime implicant is essential using a Karnaugh map?

b. For the following map, why is $A'B'$ *not* essential?

Why is BD' essential?

Is $A'D'$ essential? Why?

Is BC' essential? Why?

CD \ AB	00	01	11	10
00	1	1	1	
01	1	1	1	
11	1			1
10	1	1	1	

Is $B'CD$ essential? Why?

Find the minimum sum of products.

c. Work Programmed Exercise 6.1.

d. List all 1's and x's that are adjacent to 1_0.

CD \ AB	00	01	11	10
00	1_0	1_4	1_{12}	8
01	x_1	1_5	x_{13}	9
11	3	x_7	1_{15}	1_{11}
10	2	6	x_{14}	10

Why is $A'C'$ an essential prime implicant?

List all 1's and x's adjacent to 1_{15}?

Based on this list, why can't you find an essential implicant that covers 1_{15}?

Does this mean that there is no essential prime implicant that covers 1_{15}?

What essential prime implicant covers 1_{11}?

Can you find an *essential* prime implicant that covers 1_{12}? Explain.

Find two prime implicants that cover 1_{12}.

Give two minimum expressions for F.

e. Work Problem 6.6.

7. a. In example 3, p. 90, we derived the following function:
$$Z = \Sigma m(0, 3, 6, 9) + \Sigma d(10, 11, 12, 13, 14, 15)$$
Plot Z on the given map using x's to represent don't cares.

b. Show that the minimum sum of products is
$$Z = A'B'C'D' + B'CD + AD + BCD'$$

Which *four* don't care minterms were assigned the value 1 when forming your solution?

c. Show that the minimum product of sums for Z is
$$Z = (B' + C)(B' + D')(A' + D)(A + C + D')(B + C' + D)$$

Which *one* don't care term of Z was assigned the value 1 when forming your solution?

d. Work Problems 6.8 and 6.9.

8. Study Section 6.5, *Five- and Six-Variable Karnaugh Maps.*

   a. On a five-variable map (Fig. 6-21), what are the five minterms adjacent to minterm 24?

   b. Work through all of the examples in this section carefully and make sure that you understand all of the steps.

   c. Two minimum solutions are given for Fig. 6-24. There is a third minimum sum-of-products solution. What is it?

   d. Read the material on six-variable maps to get the basic idea; however, proficiency in deriving minimum solutions from six-variable maps will not be required in order to pass the readiness test. (*Note:* Proficiency in working with *five*-variable maps will be required.)

   e. Work Programmed Exercise 6.2.

   f.

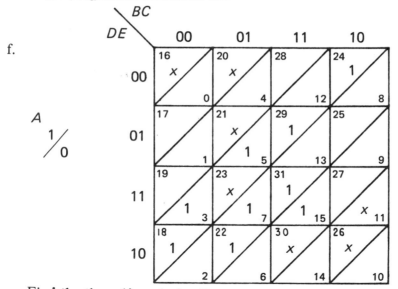

   Find the three 1's and *x*'s adjacent to 1_{18}. Can these all be looped with a single loop?

   Find the 1's and *x*'s adjacent to 1_{24}. Loop the essential prime implicant that covers 1_{24}.

   Find the 1's and *x*'s adjacent to 1_3. Loop the essential prime implicant that covers 1_3.

   Can you find an essential prime implicant that covers 1_{22}? Explain.

   Find and loop two more essential prime implicants.

   Find three ways to cover the remaining 1 on the map and give the corresponding minimum solutions.

9. Study Section 6.6, *Other Uses of Karnaugh Maps*. Refer back to Fig. 6-8 and note that a consensus term exists if there are two adjacent, but non-overlapping, prime implicants. Observe how this principle is applied in Fig. 6-27.

10. Work Problems 6.10 through 6.14. When deriving the minimum solution from the map, always write down the *essential* prime implicants first. If you don't, it is quite likely that you won't get the minimum solution. In addition, make sure you can find *all* of the prime implicants from the map (see Problem 6.10b).

11. Review the objectives and take the readiness test.

6. KARNAUGH MAPS

Switching functions can generally be simplified by using the algebraic techniques described in Units 3 and 4. However, two problems arise when algebraic procedures are used:

a. The procedures are difficult to apply in a systematic way.

b. It is difficult to tell when you have arrived at a minimum solution.

The Karnaugh map method studied in this unit and the Quine-McCluskey procedure studied in Unit 7 overcome these difficulties by providing systematic methods for simplifying switching functions. The Karnaugh map is an especially useful tool for simplifying and manipulating switching functions of 3 or 4 variables, but it can be extended to functions of 5, 6 or more variables. Generally, you will find the Karnaugh map method is faster and easier to apply than other simplification methods.

6.1 Minimum Forms of Switching Functions

When a function is realized using AND and OR gates, the cost of realizing the function is directly related to the number of gates and gate inputs used. The Karnaugh map techniques developed in this unit lead directly to minimum cost two-level networks composed of AND and OR gates. An expression consisting of sum-of-product terms corresponds directly to a two-level network composed of a group of AND gates feeding a single OR gate (see Fig. 2-5, for example). Similarly, a product-of-sums expression corresponds to a two-level network composed of OR gates feeding a single AND gate (see Fig. 2-6, for example). Therefore, in order to find minimum cost two-level AND-OR gate networks, we must find minimum expressions in sum-of-products or product-of-sums form.

A *minimum sum-of-products* expression for a function is defined as a sum of product terms which: (a) has a minimum number of terms, and (b) of all those expressions which have the same minimum number of terms has a minimum number of literals. The minimum sum of products corresponds directly to a minimum two-level gate network which has (a) a minimum number of gates and (b) a minimum number of gate inputs. Unlike the minterm expansion for a function, the minimum sum of products is not necessarily unique; i.e., a given function may have two different minimum sum-of-products forms, each with the same number of terms and the same number of literals. Given a minterm expansion, the minimum sum-of-products form can often be obtained by the following procedure:

  a. Combine terms by using $XY' + XY = X$. Do this repeatedly to eliminate as many literals as possible. A given term may be used more than once since $X + X = X$.

  b. Eliminate redundant terms by using the consensus theorem or other theorems.

Unfortunately, the result of the above procedure may depend on the order in which terms are combined or eliminated so that the final expression obtained is not necessarily minimum.

Example: Find a minimum sum-of-products expression for

$$F(a, b, c) = \Sigma m(0, 1, 2, 5, 6, 7)$$

$$F = a'b'c' + a'b'c + a'bc' + ab'c + abc' + abc$$

$$= a'b' + b'c + bc' + ab \qquad (6\text{-}1)$$

None of the terms in the above expression can be eliminated by consensus. However, combining terms in a different way leads directly to a minimum sum of products:

$$F = a'b'c' + a'b'c + a'bc' + ab'c + abc' + abc$$

$$= a'b' + bc' + ac \qquad (6\text{-}2)$$

A *minimum product-of-sums* expression for a function is defined as a product of sum terms which (a) has a minimum number of factors, and (b) of all those expressions which have the same number of factors has a minimum number of literals. Unlike the maxterm expansion, the minimum product-of-sums form of a function is not necessarily unique. Given a maxterm expansion, the minimum product of sums can often be obtained by a procedure similar to that used in the minimum sum-of-products case, except that the theorem $(X + Y)(X + Y') = X$ is used to combine terms.

Example:

$$(A + B' + C + D')(A + B' + C' + D')(A + B' + C' + D)(A' + B' + C' + D)(A + B + C' + D)(A' + B + C' + D)$$

$$= (A + B' + D') \qquad (A + B' + C') \qquad (B' + C' + D) \qquad (B + C' + D)$$

$$= (A + B' + D') \qquad (A + B' + C') \qquad (C' + D)$$

eliminate by consensus.

$$= (A + B' + D')(C' + D) \tag{6-3}$$

6.2   Two- and Three-Variable Karnaugh Maps

Just like a truth table, the Karnaugh map of a function specifies the value of the function for every combination of values of the independent variables. A two-variable Karnaugh map is shown below. The values of one variable are listed across the top of the map, and the values of the other variable are listed on the left side. Each square of the map corresponds to a pair of values for A and B as indicated.

$A = 0, B = 0$
$A = 1, B = 0$
$A = 0, B = 1$
$A = 1, B = 1$

Figure 6-1 shows the truth table for a function F and the corresponding Karnaugh map. Note that the value of F for $A = B = 0$ is plotted in the upper left square and the other map entries are plotted in a similar way in Fig. 6-1(b).

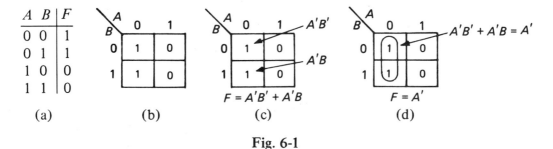

A	B	F
0	0	1
0	1	1
1	0	0
1	1	0

(a)   (b)   (c)   (d)

$F = A'B' + A'B$

$F = A'$

Fig. 6-1

Each 1 on the map corresponds to a minterm of F. We can read the minterms from the map just like we can read them from the truth table. A 1 in square 00 of Fig. 6-1(c) indicates that $A'B'$ is a minterm of F. Similarly, a 1 in square 01 indicates that $A'B$ is a minterm. Minterms in adjacent squares of the map can be combined since they differ in only one variable. Thus, $A'B'$ and $A'B$ combine to form A', and this is indicated by looping the corresponding 1's on the map in Fig. 6-1(d).

Figure 6-2 shows a 3-variable truth table and the corresponding Karnaugh map.* The value of one variable (A) is listed across the top of the map, and the values of the other two variables (B,C) are listed along the side of the map. The rows are labeled in the sequence 00, 01, 11, 10 so that values in adjacent rows differ in only one variable. For each combination of values of the variables, the value of F is read from the truth table and plotted in the appropriate map square. For example, for the input combination $ABC = 001$, the value $F = 0$ is plotted in the square for which $A = 0$ and $BC = 01$. For the combination $ABC = 110$, $F = 1$ is plotted in the $A = 1$, $BC = 10$ square.

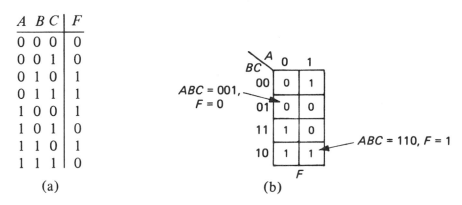

Fig. 6-2.   Truth table and Karnaugh map for 3-variable function

Figure 6-3 shows the location of the minterms on a 3-variable map. Minterms in adjacent squares of the map differ in only one variable and therefore can be combined using the theorem $XY' + XY = X$. For example, minterm 011 ($a'bc$) is adjacent to the three minterms with which it can be combined — 001 ($a'b'c$), 010 ($a'bc'$), and 111 (abc). In addition to squares which are physically adjacent, the top and bottom rows of the map are defined to be adjacent since corresponding minterms in these rows differ in only one variable. Thus 000 and 010 are adjacent, and so are 100 and 110.

---

*See Fig. 6-28 for an alternative way of labeling maps.

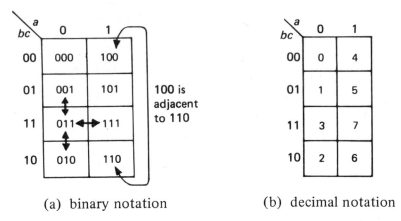

(a) binary notation   (b) decimal notation

Fig. 6-3. Location of minterms on a 3-variable Karnaugh map

Given the minterm expansion of a function, it can be plotted on a map by placing 1's in the squares which correspond to minterms of the function and 0's in the remaining squares (the 0's may be omitted if desired). Figure 6-4 shows the plot of $F(a, b, c) = m_1 + m_3 + m_5$. If F is given as a maxterm expansion, the map is plotted by placing 0's in the squares which correspond to the maxterms and then filling in the remaining squares with 1's. Thus $F(a, b, c) = M_0 M_2 M_4 M_6 M_7$ gives the same map as Fig. 6-4.

Fig. 6-4. Karnaugh map of $F(a, b, c) = \Sigma m(1, 3, 5) = \Pi M(0, 2, 4, 6, 7)$

Figure 6-5 illustrates how product terms can be plotted on Karnaugh maps. To plot the term b, 1's are entered in the four squares of the map where $b = 1$. The term bc' is 1 when $b = 1$ and $c = 0$, so 1's are entered in the two squares in the $bc = 10$ row. The term ac' is 1 when $a = 1$ and $c = 0$, so 1's are entered in the $a = 1$ column in the rows where $c = 0$.

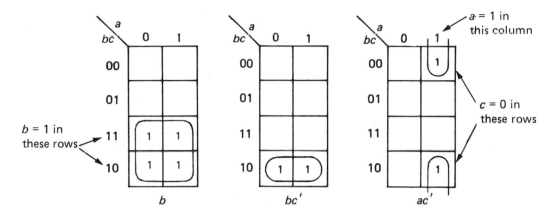

Fig. 6-5. Karnaugh maps for product terms

If a function is given in algebraic form, it is unnecessary to expand it to minterm form before plotting it on a map. If the algebraic expression is converted to sum-of-products form, then each product term can be plotted directly as a group of 1's on the map. For example, given that

$$f(a, b, c) = abc' + b'c + a'$$

we would plot the map as follows:

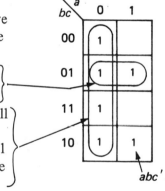

a. The term abc' is 1 when $a = 1$ and $bc = 10$, so we place a 1 in the square which corresponds to the $a = 1$ column and the $bc = 10$ row of the map.

b. The term $b'c$ is 1 when $bc = 01$, so we place 1's in both squares of the $bc = 01$ row of the map.

c. The term a' is 1 when $a = 0$, so we place 1's in all the squares of the $a = 0$ column of the map. (*Note:* since there already is a 1 in the $abc = 001$ square, we do not have to place a second 1 there because $x + x = x$.)

Figure 6-6 illustrates how a simplified expression for a function can be derived using a Karnaugh map. The function to be simplified is first plotted on a Karnaugh map in Fig. 6-6(a). Terms in adjacent squares on the map differ in only one variable and can be combined using the theorem $XY' + XY = X$. Thus $a'b'c$ and $a'bc$ combine to form $a'c$, and $a'b'c$ and $ab'c$ combine to form $b'c$ as shown in Fig. 6-6(b). A loop around a group of minterms indicates that these terms have been combined. The looped terms can be read directly off the map. Thus for Fig. 6-6(b), term T_1 is in the $a = 0$ (a') column and it spans the rows where $c = 1$, so $T_1 = a'c$. Note that b has been eliminated since the two minterms in T_1 differ in the variable b. Similarly term T_2 is in the $bc = 01$ row so $T_2 = b'c$, and a has been eliminated since T_2 spans the $a = 0$ and $a = 1$ columns. Thus the minimum sum-of-products form for F is $a'c + b'c$.

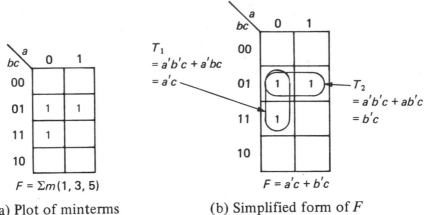

(a) Plot of minterms

(b) Simplified form of F

Fig. 6-6. Simplification of a 3-variable function

The map for the complement of F (Fig. 6-7) is formed by replacing 0's with 1's and 1's with 0's on the map of F. To simplify F', note that the terms in the top row combine to form $b'c'$ and the terms in the bottom row combine to form bc'. Since $b'c'$ and bc' differ in only one variable, the top and bottom rows can then be combined to form a group of four 1's, thus eliminating two variables and leaving $T_1 = c'$. The remaining 1 combines as shown to form $T_2 = ab$, so the minimum sum-of-products form for F' is $c' + ab$.

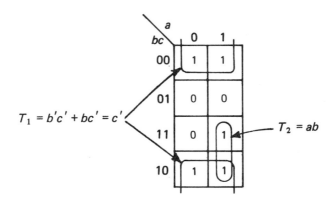

Fig. 6-7. Complement of map in Fig. 6-6(a)

The Karnaugh map can also illustrate the basic theorems of Boolean algebra. Figure 6-8 illustrates the consensus theorem, $XY + X'Z + YZ = XY + X'Z$. Note that the consensus term (YZ) is redundant because its 1's are covered by the other two terms.

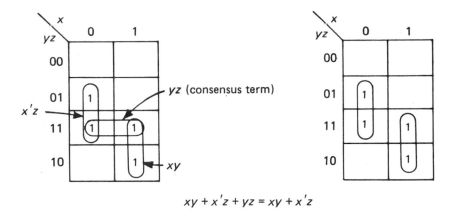

$$xy + x'z + yz = xy + x'z$$

Fig. 6-8. Karnaugh maps which illustrate the consensus theorem

If a function has two or more minimum sum-of-products forms, all of these forms can be determined from a map. Figure 6-9 shows the two minimum solutions for $F = \Sigma m(0, 1, 2, 5, 6, 7)$.

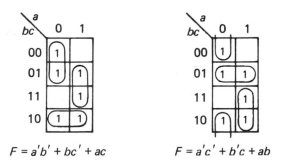

$$F = a'b' + bc' + ac \qquad F = a'c' + b'c + ab$$

Fig. 6-9. Function with two minimum forms

6.3 Four-Variable Karnaugh Maps

Figure 6-10 shows the location of minterms on a 4-variable map. Each minterm is located adjacent to the 4 terms with which it can combine. For example, m_5 (0101) could combine with m_1 (0001), m_4 (0100), m_7 (0111) or m_{13} (1101) because it differs in only one variable from each of the other minterms. The definition of adjacent squares must be extended so that not only are top and bottom rows adjacent as in the 3-variable map, but also the first and last columns are adjacent. This requires numbering the columns in the sequence 00, 01, 11, 10 so that minterms 0 and 8, 1 and 9, etc., are in adjacent squares.

AB CD	00	01	11	10
00	0	4	12	8
01	1	5	13	9
11	3	7	15	11
10	2	6	14	10

Fig. 6-10. Location of minterms on 4-variable Karnaugh map

We will now plot the following four-variable expression on a Karnaugh map (Fig. 6-11):

$$f(a, b, c, d) = acd + a'b + d'$$

The first term is 1 when $a = c = d = 1$, so we place 1's in the two squares which are in the $a = 1$ column and $cd = 11$ row. The term $a'b$ is 1 when $ab = 01$, so we place four 1's in the $ab = 01$ column. Finally, d' is 1 when $d = 0$, so we place eight 1's in the two rows for which $d = 0$. (Duplicate 1's are not plotted since $1 + 1 = 1$.)

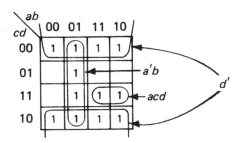

Fig. 6-11. Plot of $acd + a'b + d'$

Next we will simplify the functions f_1 and f_2 given in Fig. 6-12. Since the functions are specified in minterm form, we can determine the locations of the 1's on the map by referring to Fig. 6-10. After plotting the maps, we can then combine adjacent groups of 1's. Minterms can be combined in groups of 2, 4 or 8 to eliminate 1, 2 or 3 variables, respectively. In Fig. 6-12(a), the pair of 1's in the $ab = 00$ column and also in the $d = 1$ rows represents $a'b'd$. The group of four 1's in the $b = 1$ columns and $c = 0$ rows represents bc'.

In Fig. 6-12(b), note that the four corner 1's span the $b = 0$ columns and $d = 0$ rows, and therefore can be combined to form the term $b'd'$. The group of eight 1's covers both rows where $c = 1$, and therefore represents the term c. The pair of 1's which is looped on the map represents the term $a'bd$ since it is in the $ab = 01$ column and spans the $d = 1$ rows.

(a) $f_1 = \Sigma m(1, 3, 4, 5, 10, 12, 13)$

$= bc' + a'b'd + ab'cd'$

(b) $f_2 = \Sigma m(0, 2, 3, 5, 6, 7, 8, 10, 11, 14, 15)$

$= c + b'd' + a'bd$

Fig. 6-12. Simplification of 4-variable functions

The Karnaugh map method is easily extended to functions with don't cares. The required minterms are indicated by 1's on the map, and the don't care minterms are indicated by x's. When choosing terms to form the minimum sum of products, all the 1's must be covered, but the x's are only used if they will simplify the resulting expression. In Fig. 6-13, the only don't-care term used in forming the simplified expression is 13.

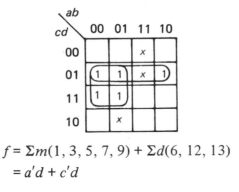

$f = \Sigma m(1, 3, 5, 7, 9) + \Sigma d(6, 12, 13)$

$= a'd + c'd$

Fig. 6-13. Simplification of an incompletely-specified function

Use of Karnaugh maps to find a minimum sum-of-products form for a function has been illustrated in Figs. 6-1, 6-6, and 6-12. A minimum product of sums can also be obtained from the map. Since the 0's of f are 1's of f', the minimum sum of products for f' can be determined by looping the 0's on a map of f. The complement of the minimum sum of products for f' is then the minimum product of sums for f. The following example illustrates this procedure for

$$f = x'z' + wyz + w'y'z' + x'y$$

First, the 1's of f are plotted in Fig. 6-14. Then, from the 0's,

$$f' = y'z + wxz' + w'xy$$

and the minimum product of sums for f is

$$f = (y + z')(w' + x' + z)(w + x' + y')$$

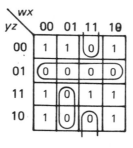

Fig. 6-14

6.4 Determination of Minimum Expressions Using Essential Prime Implicants

Any single 1 or any group of 1's which can be combined together on a map of the function F represents a product term which is called an *implicant* of F.* Several implicants of F are indicated in Fig. 6-15.

Fig. 6-15

A product term implicant is called a *prime implicant* if it cannot be combined with another term to eliminate a variable. In Fig. 6-15, $a'b'c, a'cd'$ and ac' are prime implicants because they cannot be combined with other terms to eliminate a variable. On the other hand, $a'b'c'd'$ is not a prime implicant because it can be combined with $a'b'cd'$. Neither abc' nor $ab'c'$ is a prime implicant since these terms combine together to form ac'.

All of the prime implicants of a function can be obtained from a Karnaugh map. A single 1 on a map represents a prime implicant if it is not adjacent to any

---

*See Section 7.1 for a formal definition of implicant and prime implicant.

other 1's. Two adjacent 1's on a map form a prime implicant if they are not contained in a group of four 1's, four adjacent 1's form a prime implicant if they are not contained in a group of eight 1's, etc.

The minimum sum-of-products expression for a function consists of some (but not necessarily all) of the prime implicants of a function. In other words, a sum-of-products expression containing a term which is not a prime implicant cannot be minimum. This is true because if a non-prime term were present, the expression could be simplified by combining the non-prime term with additional minterms. In order to find the minimum sum of products from a map, we must find a minimum number of prime implicants which cover all of the 1's on the map. The function plotted in Fig. 6-16 has six prime implicants. Three of these prime implicants cover all of the 1's on the map, and the minimum solution is the sum of these three prime implicants.

Minimum solution: $F = a'b'd + bc' + ac$

All prime implicants: $a'b'd, bc', ac, a'c'd,$
$ab, b'cd$

Fig. 6-16. **Determination of all prime implicants**

When writing down a list of *all* of the prime implicants from the map, note that there are often prime implicants which are not included in the minimum sum of products. Even though all of the 1's in a term have already been covered by prime implicants, that term may still be a prime implicant provided that it is not included in a larger group of 1's. For example, in Fig. 6-16, $a'c'd$ is a prime implicant because it cannot be combined with other 1's to eliminate another variable. However, abd is not a prime implicant because it can be combined with two other 1's to form ab. The term $b'cd$ is also a prime implicant even though both of its 1's are already covered by other prime implicants. In the process of finding prime implicants, don't cares are treated just like 1's. However, a prime implicant composed entirely of don't cares can never be part of the minimum solution.

Since all of the prime implicants of a function are generally not needed in forming the minimum sum of products, a systematic procedure for selecting prime implicants is needed. If prime implicants are selected from the map in the wrong order, a non-minimum solution may result. For example, in Fig. 6-17, if CD is chosen first, then BD, $B'C$ and AC are needed to cover the remaining 1's, and the solution contains four terms. However, if the prime implicants indicated in Fig. 6-17(b) are chosen first, all 1's are covered and CD is not needed.

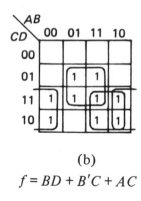

(a)

$f = CD + BD + B'C + AC$

(b)

$f = BD + B'C + AC$

Fig. 6-17

Note that some of the minterms on the map of Fig. 6-17(a) can be covered by only a single prime implicant, but other minterms can be covered by two different prime implicants. For example, m_2 is covered only by $B'C$, but m_3 is covered by both $B'C$ and CD. If a minterm is covered by only one prime implicant, that prime implicant is said to be *essential* and it must be included in the minimum sum of products. Thus, $B'C$ is an essential prime implicant because m_2 is not covered by any other prime implicant. However, CD is *not* essential because each of the 1's in CD can be covered by another prime implicant. The only prime implicant which covers m_5 is BD, so BD is essential. Similarly, AC is essential because no other prime implicant covers m_{14}. In this example, if we choose all of the essential prime implicants, all of the 1's on the map are covered and the non-essential prime implicant CD is not needed.

In general, in order to find a minimum sum of products from a map, we should first loop all of the essential prime implicants. One way of finding essential prime implicants on a map is simply to look at each 1 on the map that has not already been covered, and check to see how many prime implicants cover that 1. If there is only one prime implicant which covers the 1, that prime implicant is essential. If there are two or more prime implicants which cover the 1, we cannot say whether these prime implicants are essential or not without further checking. For simple problems, we can locate the essential prime implicants in this way "by inspection" of each 1 on the map. For example, in Fig. 6-16, m_4 is covered only by the prime implicant bc', and m_{10} is covered only by the prime implicant ac. All other 1's on the map are covered by two prime implicants; therefore, the only essential prime implicants are bc' and ac.

For more complicated maps, and especially for maps with 5 or more variables, we need a more systematic approach for finding the essential prime implicants. When checking a minterm to see if it is covered by only one prime implicant, we must look at all squares adjacent to that minterm. If the given minterm and all of the 1's adjacent to it are covered by a single term, then that term is an *essential* prime implicant.* If all of the 1's adjacent to a given minterm are

---

*This statement is proved in Appendix C.1.

not covered by a single term, then there are two or more prime implicants which cover that minterm and we cannot say whether these prime implicants are essential or not without further checking. Figure 6-18 illustrates this principle.

Fig. 6-18

The adjacent 1's for minterm m_0 (1_0) are 1_1, 1_2, and 1_4. Since no single term covers these four 1's, no essential prime implicant is yet apparent. The adjacent 1's for 1_1 are 1_0 and 1_5 so the term which covers these three 1's ($A'C'$) is an essential prime implicant. Since the only 1 adjacent to 1_2 is 1_0, $A'B'D'$ is also essential. Since the 1's adjacent to 1_7 (1_5 and 1_{15}) are not covered by a single term, neither $A'BD$ nor BCD is essential at this point. However, since the only 1 adjacent to 1_{11} is 1_{15}, ACD is essential. To complete the minimum solution, one of the non-essential prime implicants is needed. Either $A'BD$ or BCD may be selected. The final solution is

$$A'C' + A'B'D' + ACD + \begin{Bmatrix} A'BD \\ \text{or} \\ BCD \end{Bmatrix}$$

If a don't care minterm is present on the map, we do not have to check it to see if it is covered by one or more prime implicants. However, when checking a 1 for adjacent 1's, we treat the adjacent don't cares as if they were 1's since don't cares may be combined with 1's in the process of forming prime implicants. The following procedure can then be used to obtain a minimum sum of products from a Karnaugh map:

    a.   Choose a minterm (a 1) which has not yet been covered.

    b.   Find all 1's and x's adjacent to that minterm. (Check the n adjacent squares on an n-variable map.)

    c.   If a single term covers the minterm and all of the adjacent 1's and x's, then that term is an essential prime implicant, so select that term. (Note that don't cares are treated like 1's in steps b and c but not in step a.)

    d.   Repeat steps a, b and c until all essential prime implicants have been chosen.

e. Find a minimum set of prime implicants which cover the remaining 1's on the map. (If there is more than one such set, choose a set with a minimum number of literals.)

Figure 6-19 gives a flow chart for this procedure.

Fig. 6-19. **Flow chart for determining the minimum sum-of-products using a Karnaugh map**

The following example (Fig. 6-20) illustrates the above procedure.

Fig. 6-20

Starting with 1_4, we see that the adjacent 1's and x's (x_0, 1_5 and 1_6) are *not* covered by a single term, so no essential prime implicant is apparent. However, 1_6 and its adjacent 1's and x's (1_4 and x_7) are covered by $A'B$, so $A'B$ is an essential prime implicant. Next, looking at 1_{13}, we see that its adjacent 1's and x's (1_5, 1_9 and x_{15}) are *not* covered by a single term, so no essential prime implicant is apparent. Similarly, examination of the terms adjacent to 1_8 and 1_9 reveals no essential prime implicants. However, 1_{10} has only 1_8 adjacent to it, so $AB'D'$ is an essential prime implicant since it covers both 1_{10} and 1_8. Having first selected the essential prime implicants, we now choose $AC'D$ since it covers both of the remaining 1's on the map.

Judicious selection of the order in which the minterms are selected (step a) reduces the amount of work required in applying the above procedure. As will be seen in the next section, this procedure is especially helpful in obtaining minimum solutions for 5- and 6-variable problems.

6.5   Five- and Six-Variable Karnaugh Maps

A five-variable map can be constructed in three dimensions by placing one 4-variable map on top of a second one. Terms in the bottom layer are numbered 0 through 15 and corresponding terms in the top layer are numbered 16 through 31, so that terms in the bottom layer contain A' and those in the top layer contain A. To represent the map in two dimensions, we will divide each square in a 4-variable map by a diagonal line and place terms in the bottom layer below the line and terms in the top layer above the line (Fig. 6-21).* Terms in the top or bottom layer combine just like terms on a 4-variable map. In addition, two terms in the same

---

*An alternate representation is to draw the two layers side by side as in Fig. 6-29, but most individuals find adjacencies more difficult to see when this form is used.

square which are separated by a diagonal line differ in only one variable and can be combined. However, some terms which appear to be physically adjacent are not. For example terms 0 and 20 are not adjacent because they appear in a different column and a different layer. Each term can be adjacent to exactly five other terms, four in the same layer and one in the other layer (Fig. 6-22). When checking for adjacencies each term should be checked against the five possible adjacent squares.

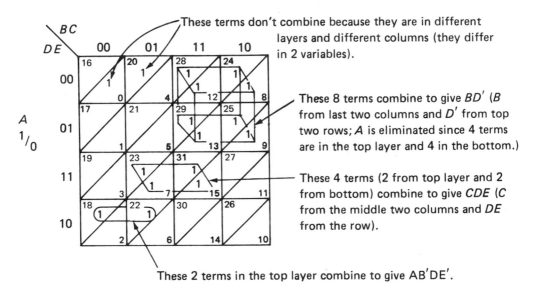

Fig. 6-21.   Five-variable Karnaugh map

Fig. 6-22

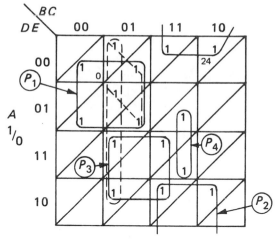

Fig. 6-23

Two examples of five-variable minimization using maps follow. Figure 6-23 is a map of

$$F(A, B, C, D, E) = \Sigma m(0, 1, 4, 5, 13, 15, 20, 21, 22, 23, 24, 26, 28, 30, 31)$$

Prime implicant P_1 is chosen first since all of the 1's adjacent to minterm 0 are covered by P_1. Prime implicant P_2 is chosen next since all of the 1's adjacent to minterm 24 are covered by P_2. All of the remaining 1's on the map can be covered by at least two different prime implicants, so we proceed by trial and error. After a few tries, it becomes apparent that the remaining 1's can be covered by 3 prime implicants. If we choose prime implicants P_3 and P_4 next, the remaining two 1's can be covered by two different groups of 4. The resulting minimum solution is

$$F = A'B'D' + ABE' + ACD + A'BCE + \begin{Bmatrix} AB'C \\ \text{or} \\ B'CD' \end{Bmatrix}$$
$$\quad\;\; P_1 \qquad P_2 \qquad P_3 \qquad P_4$$

Figure 6-24 is a map of

$$F(A, B, C, D, E) = \Sigma m(0, 1, 3, 8, 9, 14, 15, 16, 17, 19, 25, 27, 31)$$

All 1's adjacent to m_{16} are covered by P_1, so choose P_1 first. All 1's adjacent to m_3 are covered by P_2, so P_2 is chosen next. All 1's adjacent to m_8 are covered by P_3, so P_3 is chosen. Since m_{14} is only adjacent to m_{15}, P_4 is also essential. There are no more essential prime implicants, and the remaining 1's can be covered by two terms, P_5 and (1-9-17-25) or (17-19-25-27). The final solution is

$$F = B'C'D' + B'C'E + A'C'D' + A'BCD + ABDE + \begin{Bmatrix} C'D'E \\ \text{or} \\ AC'E \end{Bmatrix}$$
$$\quad\;\; P_1 \qquad\quad P_2 \qquad\quad P_3 \qquad\quad P_4 \qquad\quad P_5$$

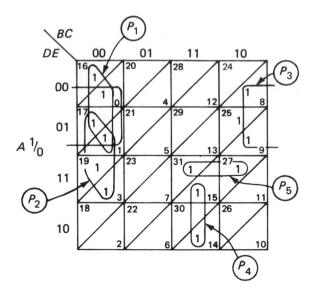

Fig. 6-24

A six-variable map can be constructed in three dimensions by stacking up four 4-variable maps. Plot values of *AB* on the layers and values of *CD* and *EF* on the rows and columns in each layer. Assign *AB* = 00 to the bottom layer, *AB* = 01 to the second layer, *AB* = 11 to the third layer, and *AB* = 10 to the top layer. Then terms in adjacent layers differ in only one of these variables. (In this sense the top and bottom layers are adjacent.) A 6-variable map can be drawn in two dimensions by dividing each square of a 4-variable map into four parts as shown below. Min-terms 0-15 are plotted in the bottom (00 layer), minterms 16-31 in the next (01) layer, 32-47 in the top (10) layer, and 48-63 in the third (11) layer.

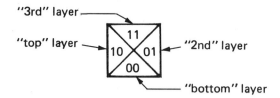

Figure 6-25 shows a six-variable example. Note that terms in adjacent columns (or rows) are adjacent only if they are in the same layer. Term 1 in the 2nd layer is $A'BC'D'E'$. Term 2 spans the 2nd and 3rd layers and is $BCE'F'$. Term 3 in the third layer is $ABEF$. Term 4 spans all four layers, eliminating both A and B. Term 4 is $D'EF'$. The remaining two 1's on the map do *not* combine with another term. They are not adjacent to the nearest terms because these terms are in different layers.

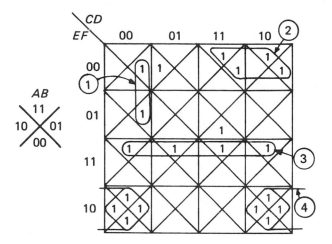

Fig. 6-25. Six-variable map

6.6 Other Uses of Karnaugh Maps

Many operations that can be performed using a truth table or algebraically can be done using a Karnaugh map. If we plot an expression for F on a map, we can read off the minterm and maxterm expansions for F and for F'. From the map of Fig. 6-14, the minterm expansion of f is

$$f = \Sigma m(0, 2, 3, 4, 8, 10, 11, 15)$$

and since each 0 corresponds to a maxterm, the maxterm expansion of f is

$$f = \Pi M(1, 5, 6, 7, 9, 12, 13, 14)$$

We can prove that two functions are equal by plotting them on maps and showing that they have the same Karnaugh map. We can perform the AND operation (or the OR operation) on two functions by ANDing (or ORing) the 1's and 0's which appear in corresponding positions on their maps. This procedure is valid because it is equivalent to doing the same operations on the truth tables for the functions.

A Karnaugh map can facilitate factoring an expression. Inspection of the map reveals terms which have one or more variables in common. For the following map, the two terms in the first column have $A'B'$ in common; the two terms in the lower right corner have AC in common.

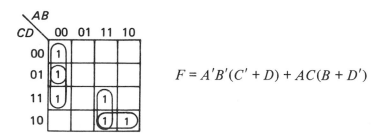

$$F = A'B'(C' + D) + AC(B + D')$$

Fig. 6-26

When simplifying a function algebraically, the Karnaugh map can be used as a guide in determining what steps to take. For example, consider the function

$$F = ABCD + B'CDE + A'B' + BCE'$$

Fig. 6-27

From the map (Fig. 6-27), we see that in order to get the minimum solution, we must add the term $ACDE$. We can do this using the consensus theorem:

$$F = ABCD + B'CDE + A'B' + BCE' + ACDE$$

As can be seen from the map, the above expression now contains two redundant terms, $ABCD$ and $B'CDE$. These can be eliminated using the consensus theorem which gives the minimum solution

$$F = A'B' + BCE' + ACDE$$

6.7   Other Forms of Karnaugh Maps

Instead of labeling the sides of a Karnaugh map with 0's and 1's, some people prefer to use the labeling shown in Fig. 6-28. For the half of the map labeled A, $A = 1$; and for the other half, $A = 0$. The other variables have a similar interpretation. A map labeled this way is sometimes referred to as a Veitch diagram. It is particularly useful for plotting functions given in algebraic form rather than in minterm or maxterm form. However, when using Karnaugh maps to solve sequential network problems (Units 13 through 18), the use of 0's and 1's to label the maps is more convenient.

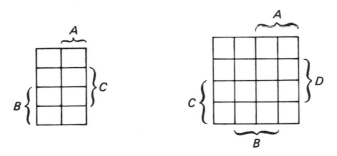

Fig. 6-28. Veitch diagrams

Two alternative forms for 5-variable maps are used. One form simply consists of two four-variable maps side by side as in Fig. 6-29(a). A modification of this uses a "mirror image" map as in Fig. 6-29(b). In this map, the 1st and 8th columns are "adjacent", as are the 2nd and 7th, 3rd and 6th, and 4th and 5th. The same function is plotted on both these maps. Similarly, a six-variable map may be represented as four 4-variable maps arranged in a square.

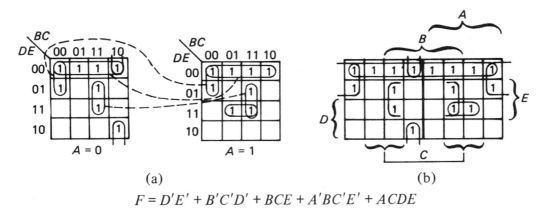

$$F = D'E' + B'C'D' + BCE + A'BC'E' + ACDE$$

Fig. 6-29. Other forms of 5-variable Karnaugh maps

Some people who have trouble visualizing adjacencies on the two-dimensional 5- and 6-variable maps, find 3-dimensional maps helpful. Such maps are constructed using two or four layers of clear plastic, respectively. Colored markers are then used to indicate 1's and don't cares, and to indicate which 1's have already been covered in the process of writing down a minimum solution.

Programmed Exercise 6.1 (top half of this page and next 4 pages)

Problem: Determine the minimum sum of products and minimum product of sums for

$$f = b'c'd' + bcd + acd' + a'b'c + a'bc'd$$

First, plot the map for f.

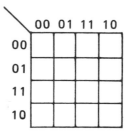

Turn to the next page and check your answer.

Programmed Exercise 6.2 (bottom half of this page and the next 4 pages)

Problem: Determine a minimum sum-of-products expression for

$$f(a, b, c, d, e) = (a' + c + d)(a' + b + e)(a + c' + e')(c + d + e')$$
$$(b + c + d' + e)(a' + b' + c + e')$$

The first step in the solution is to plot a map for f. Since f is given in product-of-sums form, it is easier to first plot the map for f' and then complement the map. Write f' as a sum of products:

$$f' = \underline{\hspace{7cm}}$$

Now plot the map for f'. (Note that there are three terms in the "upper layer", one term in the "lower layer", and two terms which span the two layers.)

Next convert your map for f' to a map for f.

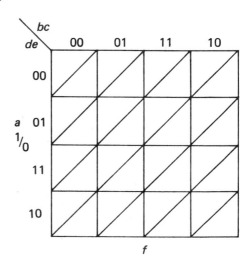

Turn to the next page and check your answer.

Answer to 6.1:

	ab			
cd	00	01	11	10
00	1			1
01		1		
11	1	1	1	
10	1		1	1

a. The minterms adjacent to m_0 on the above map are _____ and _____ .

b. Find an essential prime implicant containing m_0 and loop it.

c. The minterms adjacent to m_3 are _____ and _____ .

d. Is there an essential prime implicant which contains m_3?

e. Find the remaining essential prime implicant(s) and loop it (them).

Turn to the next page and check your answer.

Answer to 6.2:

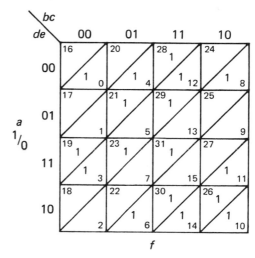

The next step is to determine the essential prime implicants of f.

a. Why is $a'd'e'$ an essential prime implicant?

b. Which minterms are adjacent to m_3? _____ to m_{19}? _____

c. Is there an essential prime implicant which covers m_3 and m_{19}? _____

d. Is there an essential prime implicant which covers m_{21}? _____

e. Loop the essential prime implicants which you have found. Then find two more essential prime implicants and loop them.

Turn to the next page and check your answer.

Answers to 6.1:

a. m_2 and m_8

c. m_2 and m_7

d. no

b.

e.

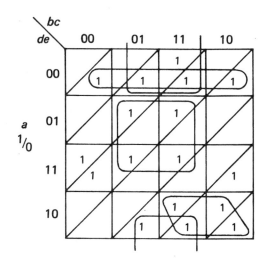

Loop the remaining 1's using a minimum number of loops.

The two possible minimum sum-of-products forms for f are

$f =$ _____ and

$f =$ _____

Turn to the next page and check your answers.

Answers to 6.2:

a. It covers m_0 and both adjacent minterms.

b. m_{19} and m_{11}; m_3 and m_{23}

c. no

d. yes

e.

---

a. Why is there no essential prime implicant which covers m_{11}?

b. Why is there no essential p.i. which covers m_{28}?

Since there are no more essential prime implicants, loop a minimum number of terms which cover the remaining 1's.

Turn to the next page and check your answer.

Answer to 6.1:

$$f = b'd' + a'bd + abc + \begin{Bmatrix} a'cd \\ \text{or} \\ a'b'c \end{Bmatrix}$$

Next, we will find the minimum product of sums for f. Start by plotting the map for f'.

Loop all essential prime implicants of f' and indicate which minterm makes each one essential.

Turn to the next page and check your answers.

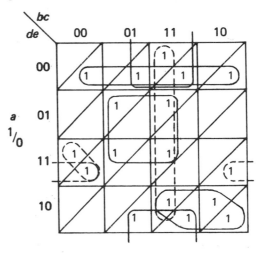

Answers to 6.2:

a. All adjacent 1's of m_{11} (m_3, m_{10}) cannot be covered by one grouping.

b. All adjacent 1's of m_{28} (m_{12}, m_{30}, m_{29}) cannot be covered by one grouping.

Write down two different minimum sum-of-products expressions for f.

$f = $ _____

$f = $ _____

Turn to the next page and check your answer.

Answer to 6.1:

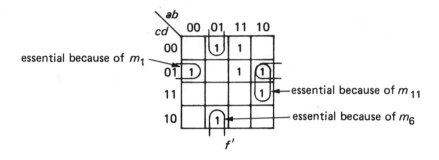

essential because of m_1

essential because of m_{11}

essential because of m_6

f'

Loop the remaining 1's and write the minimum sum of products for f'.

$f' = $ _____

The minimum product of sums for f is therefore

$f = $ _____

(Check your answer against the final answer at the bottom of this page.)

Answer to 6.2:

$$f = a'd'e' + ace + a'ce' + bde' + \begin{Bmatrix} abc \\ \text{or} \\ bce' \end{Bmatrix} + \begin{Bmatrix} b'c'de + a'c'de \\ b'c'de + a'bc'd \\ ab'de + a'c'de \end{Bmatrix}$$

Final answer to 6.1:

$f' = b'c'd + a'bd' + ab'd + abc'$

$f = (b + c + d')(a + b' + d)(a' + b + d')(a' + b' + c)$

PROBLEMS

6.3 A small corporation has 100 shares of stock, and each share entitles its owner to one vote at a stockholders' meeting. Mr. Akins owns 10 shares, Mr. Barnes owns 20 shares, Mr. Clay owns 30 shares, and Mr. Drake owns 40 shares. A two-thirds majority is required in order to pass a measure at a stockholders' meeting. Each of the four men has a switch which he closes to vote "yes" for all his shares and opens to vote "no" for all his shares. A switching circuit is to be designed to turn on a light if the measure passes.

    a. Derive a truth table for the output function (Z).

    b. Write the minterm expansion for Z and simplify algebraically to a minimum sum-of-products form.

    c. Write the maxterm expansion for Z and simplify algebraically to a minimum product-of-sums form.

    d. Check to see that your answer to c is equivalent to the answer to b.

    e. Design a minimum network of switches and a minimum AND-OR gate network to realize Z.

6.4 Find the minimum sum-of-products for each function using a Karnaugh map.

    a. $f_1(a, b, c) = m_1 + m_3 + m_4 + m_6$ c. $f_3(r, s, t) = r't' + rs' + rs$

    b. $f_2(d, e, f) = \Sigma m(1, 4, 5, 7)$ d. $f_4(x, y, z) = M_1 \cdot M_7$

6.5 a. Plot the following function on a Karnaugh map. (Do *not* expand to minterm form before plotting.)

$$F(A, B, C, D) = B'C' + A'BD + ABCD' + B'C$$

    b. Find the minimum sum of products.

    c. Find the minimum product of sums.

6.6 Find the minimum sum-of-products expression for each function.

    a. $f(a, b, c, d) = \Sigma m(0, 1, 2, 4, 6, 7, 8, 9, 13, 15)$

    b. $f(a, b, c, d) = \Pi M(1, 2, 4, 9, 11)$

    c. $f(a, b, c, d) = \Sigma m(0, 1, 5, 8, 12, 14, 15) + \Sigma d(2, 7, 11)$

    d. $f(a, b, c, d) = \Pi M(0, 1, 4, 5, 10, 11, 12) \cdot \Pi D(3, 8, 14)$

6.7 A switching network has two control inputs (C_1, C_2), two data inputs (X_1, X_2), and one output (Z). If $C_1 = C_2 = 0$, the output is $Z = 0$. If $C_1 = C_2 = 1$, the output is $Z = 1$. If $C_1 = 1$ and $C_2 = 0$, $Z = X_1$. If $C_1 = 0$ and $C_2 = 1$, $Z = X_2$.

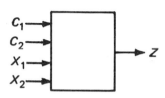

    a. Derive a truth table for Z.

    b. Use a Karnaugh map to find a minimum AND-OR gate network to realize Z.

6.8 For the maps given below:

    a. Find the minimum sum of products for f_1.

    b. Find the minimum *product of sums* for f_2.

cd \ ab	00	01	11	10
00		1		1
01	1	X		1
11	X	1	X	1
10		X		

f_1

cd \ ab	00	01	11	10
00	0	0	X	1
01	X	0	1	1
11	1	0	0	1
10	1	1	X	0

f_2

6.9 Find the minimum sum of products for F. Underline the essential prime implicants in your answer.

cd \ ab	00	01	11	10
00		1	1	
01	X		1	1
11	1	1	X	1
10	1		1	X

F

6.10 $F(a, b, c, d, e) = \Sigma m(0, 3, 4, 5, 6, 7, 8, 12, 13, 14, 16, 21, 23, 24, 29, 31)$

    a. Find the essential prime implicants using a Karnaugh map, and indicate why each one of the chosen prime implicants is essential (there are 4 essential prime implicants).

    b. Find *all* of the prime implicants by using the Karnaugh map (there are 9 in all).

6.11 $F(A, B, C, D, E) = \Sigma m(0, 2, 6, 7, 8, 10, 11, 12, 13, 14, 16, 18, 19, 29, 30)$
$$+ \Sigma d(4, 9, 21)$$

Find the minimum sum-of-products expression for F. Underline the essential prime implicants in this expression.

6.12 $F(A, B, C, D, E) = \Pi M(3,6,7,8,9,10,18,20,21,22,23,25,26,28,29,30)$

Find the minimum sum-of-products expression for F. Underline the essential prime implicants in this expression.

6.13 Given that $F = A'B' + A'C' + C'D' + B'CD$

    a. Use the Karnaugh map to find the maxterm expansion of F (express your answer in both decimal and alphabetic notation).

    b. Use the Karnaugh map to find the minimum sum-of-products form for F'.

    c. Find the minimum product of sums for F.

    d. Given the map for F, we can find a map for the dual of F by complementing all of the 0's and 1's on the map and also complementing all the 0's and 1's in the column and row headings. Use this method to find the minimum sum-of-products form of F^D. (Be careful when reading the F^D map since the column and row headings will not be in the usual order.) Verify algebraically that your expression for F^D is correct.

6.14 $F(A, B, C, D) = A'C' + B'C + ACD' + BC'D$

Find the minimum sum-of-products for F; then make minterm 5 a "don't-care" and verify that the minimum sum-of-products is unchanged. Now start again with the original F and find each single minterm which could be made a "don't-care" without changing the minimum sum-of-products.

6.15 $G = C'E'F + DEF + AD'F' + BCD'E'F$

Find the minimum *product-of-sums* form of G using a 6-variable Karnaugh map.

6.16 Find the minimum sum of products for:

    a. $\Sigma m(0, 1, 2, 3, 7, 8, 9, 10, 11, 12, 13)$

    b. $\Sigma m(2, 4, 6, 10) + \Sigma d(1, 3, 5, 7, 8, 9, 12, 13)$

    c. $\Sigma m(1, 4, 5, 6, 13, 14, 15) + \Sigma d(8, 9)$

6.17 Find the minimum product of sums for:

    a. $\Sigma m(8, 10, 12, 17, 19, 21, 23, 26)$

    b. $\Sigma m(1, 5, 12, 13, 14, 16, 17, 20, 22, 23, 24, 25, 31)$
       $+ \Sigma d(0, 2, 4, 6, 8, 9, 10, 11)$

6.18 A logic network realizes the function
$$F(a, b, c, d) = a'b'cd + a'bd + bc'd' + ab'c'd'$$
Assuming that the network input $a = c = 1$ can never occur, find a simplified expression for F.

6.19 Find all of the prime implicants for each of the functions plotted on p. 133.

6.20 Find all possible minimum sum-of-products expressions for each function:
   a. $f(a, b, c) = \Pi M(2, 3, 4)$
   b. $f(d, e, f) = \Sigma m(1, 6) + \Sigma d(0, 3, 5)$
   c. $f(p, q, r) = (p + q' + r)(p' + q + r')$
   d. $f(s, t, u) = \Sigma m(1, 2, 3) + \Sigma d(0, 5, 7)$

6.21 Find a minimum sum-of-products and a minimum product-of-sums expression for each function:
   a. $f(A, B, C, D) = BC'D + B'CD' + CD + ABC$
   b. $f(A, B, C, D) = \Sigma m(4, 8, 13, 15) + \Sigma d(1, 7, 9, 12, 14)$

6.22 Assuming that the inputs $ABCD = 0001$ and $ABCD = 0010$ never occur, find a simplified expression for:
$$F = ABD + A'B'D + A'CD + A'BC + BCD + AD$$

6.23 For each of the following functions, find the essential prime implicants and then find all of the minimum sum-of-products expressions.
   a. $f(a, b, c, d) = \Sigma m(2, 3, 5, 7, 8, 10, 12, 15)$
   b. $f(w, x, y, z) = \Sigma m(2, 4, 5, 8, 10, 11, 13, 15) + \Sigma d(0, 3, 6)$

6.24 Find a minimum sum-of-products expression for each of the following functions. Underline the essential prime implicants in your answers.
   a. $f(a, b, c, d, e) = \Sigma m(0, 1, 4, 5, 6, 8, 9, 12, 14, 15, 21, 23, 29)$
$$+ \Sigma d(2, 10, 13)$$
   b. $f(a, b, c, d, e) = \Sigma m(3, 4, 5, 11, 12, 13, 14, 15, 17, 21, 25, 27, 29,$
$$31) + \Sigma d(0, 1, 2, 6, 7, 8, 10, 19, 23)$$

6.25 Given $F(a, b, c, d) = \Sigma m(0, 2, 4, 5, 6, 7, 8, 9, 11, 13, 14, 15)$
   a. Find all of the prime implicants.
   b. Find all of the essential prime implicants and tell why each one is essential.
   c. Find two minimum sum-of-products expressions for F.

6.26 Find a minimum *product-of-sums* expression for each of the following functions.
   a. $F(v, w, x, y, z) = \Sigma m(4, 9, 12, 13, 14, 15, 17, 19, 20, 21, 22, 23,$
$$26, 29)$$
   b. $F(a, b, c, d, e) = \Pi M(2, 3, 5, 6, 13, 18, 19, 24, 25, 26, 27, 29) \cdot$
$$\Pi D(4, 9, 12, 14, 17, 21, 28, 31)$$

7

QUINE-McCLUSKEY METHOD

OBJECTIVES

1. Find the prime implicants of a function by using the Quine-McCluskey method. Explain the reasons for the procedures used.

2. Define "prime implicant" and "*essential* prime implicant".

3. Given the prime implicants, find the essential (necessary) prime implicants and a minimum sum-of-products expression for a function using a prime implicant chart.

4. Minimize an incompletely specified function using the Quine-McCluskey method.

5. Find a minimum sum-of-products expression for a function using the method of map-entered variables.

STUDY GUIDE

1. Review Section 6.1, *Minimum Forms of Switching Functions.*

2. Read the introduction to this unit and then study Section 7.1, *Determination of Prime Implicants.*

   a. Using variables A, B, C, D and E, give the algebraic equivalent of

   $$10110 + 10010 = 10{-}10$$

   $$10{-}10 + 10{-}11 = 10{-}1{-}$$

   b. Why won't the following pairs of terms combine?
   $$01101 + 00111$$
   $$10{-}10 + 001{-}0$$

c. When using the Quine-McCluskey procedure for finding prime implicants, why is it only necessary to compare terms from adjacent groups?

d. How can you determine if two minterms from adjacent groups will combine by looking at their decimal representations?

e. When combining terms, why is it permissible to use a term which has already been checked off?

f. In forming Column II of Table 7-1, note that terms 10 and 14 were combined to form 10, 14 even though both 10 and 14 had already been checked off. If this had not been done, which term in Column II could not be eliminated (checked off)?

g. In forming Column III of Table 7-1, note that minterms 0, 1, 8 and 9 were combined in two different ways to form −00−. This is equivalent to looping the minterms in two different ways on the Karnaugh map, as shown below.

h. Using a map, find *all* the prime implicants of Equation (7-2) and compare your answer with Equation (7-3).

i. The prime implicants of $f(a, b, c, d) = \Sigma m(4, 5, 6, 7, 12, 13, 14, 15)$ are to be found using the Quine-McCluskey procedure. Column III is given below; find column IV and check off the appropriate terms in column III.

Column III *Column IV*

(4, 5, 6, 7)	$0\ 1 - -$	
(4, 5, 12, 13)	$- 1\ 0 -$	
(4, 6, 12, 14)	$- 1 - 0$	
(5, 7, 13, 15)	$- 1 - 1$	
(6, 7, 14, 15)	$- 1\ 1 -$	
(12, 13, 14, 15)	$1\ 1 - -$	

	00	01	11	10
00				
01				
11				
10				

Check your answer using a Karnaugh map.

3. a. List all 7 product term implicants of
$$F(a, b, c) = \Sigma m(0, 1, 5, 7)$$
Which of these implicants are prime?

Why is $a'c$ not an implicant?

b. Define a prime implicant.

c. Why must every term in a minimum sum-of-products expression be a prime implicant?

d. Given that $F(A, B, C, D) = \Sigma m(0, 1, 4, 5, 7, 10, 15)$, which of the following terms are *not* prime implicants and why?

$A'B'C'$ $A'C'$ BCD ABC $AB'CD'$

4. Study Section 7.2, *The Prime Implicant Chart*.

    a. Define an *essential* prime implicant.

    b. Find all of the essential prime implicants from the following chart.

	$a\ b\ c\ d$	0	4	5	10	11	12	13	15
(0, 4)	$0-0\ 0$	X	X						
(4, 5, 12, 13)	$-1\ 0\ -$		X	X			X	X	
(13, 15)	$1\ 1-1$							X	X
(11, 15)	$1-1\ 1$					X			X
(10, 11)	$1\ 0\ 1-$				X	X			

    Check your answer using a Karnaugh map.

    c. Why must all essential prime implicants of a function be included in the minimum sum of products?

    d. Complete the solution of Fig. 7-4.

    e. Work Programmed Exercise 7.1.

    f. Work Problems 7.2 and 7.3.

5. Study Section 7.3, *Simplification of Incompletely Specified Functions*.

    a. Why are don't care terms treated like required minterms when finding the prime implicants?

    b. Why aren't the don't care terms listed at the top of the prime implicant chart when finding the minimum solution?

    c. Work Problem 7.4a.

6. Study Section 7.4, *Simplification Using Map-Entered Variables*.

    a. For the following map, find MS_0, MS_1, and F. Verify that your solution for F is minimum by using a 4-variable map.

BC \ A	0	1
00	D	1
01		
11	1	D
10	1	X

b. Use the method of map-entered variables to find an expression for F from the following map. Treat C and C' as if they were independent variables. Is the result a correct representation of F? Is it minimum?

c. Work Problem 7.9.

7. In this unit, you have learned a "turn-the-crank" type procedure for finding minimum sum-of-products forms for switching functions. In addition to learning how to "turn the crank" and grind out minimum solutions, there are several very important concepts you should have learned in this unit. In particular, make sure you know:

a. What a *prime implicant* is.

b. What an *essential* prime implicant is.

c. Why the minimum sum-of-products form is a sum of prime implicants.

d. How don't cares are handled when using the Quine-McCluskey procedure and the prime implicant chart.

8. Reread the objectives of the unit. If you are satisfied you can meet the objectives, take the readiness test.

7. QUINE-McCLUSKEY METHOD

The Karnaugh map method described in Unit 6 is an effective way to simplify switching functions which have a small number of variables. When the number of variables is large or if several functions must be simplified, use of a digital computer is desirable. The Quine-McCluskey method presented in this unit provides a systematic simplification procedure which can be readily programmed for a digital computer.

The Quine-McCluskey procedure reduces the minterm expansion (standard sum-of-products form) of a function to obtain a minimum sum of products. The procedure consists of two main steps:

a. Eliminate as many literals as possible from each term by systematically applying the theorem $XY + XY' = X$. The resulting terms are called prime implicants.

b. Use a prime implicant chart to select a minimum set of prime implicants which, when ORed together, are equal to the function being simplified and which contain a minimum number of literals.

In order to find all of the prime implicants, all possible pairs of minterms should be compared and combined whenever possible. To reduce the required number of comparisons, the binary minterms are sorted into groups according to the number of 1's in each term. Thus,

$$f(a, b, c, d) = \Sigma m(0, 1, 2, 5, 6, 7, 8, 9, 10, 14) \qquad (7\text{-}2)$$

is represented by the following list of minterms:

group 0	0	0000
group 1	1	0001
	2	0010
	8	1000
group 2	5	0101
	6	0110
	9	1001
	10	1010
group 3	7	0111
	14	1110

In the above list, the term in group 0 has zero 1's, the terms in group 1 have one 1, those in group 2 have two 1's, and those in group 3 have three 1's.

Two terms can be combined if they differ in exactly one variable. Comparison of terms in non-adjacent groups is unnecessary since such terms will always differ in at least two variables and cannot be combined using $XY + XY' = X$. Similarly, comparison of terms within a group is unnecessary since two terms with the same number of 1's must differ in at least two variables. Thus, only terms in adjacent groups must be compared.

7.1 Determination of Prime Implicants

In order to apply the Quine-McCluskey procedure to determine a minimum sum-of-products expression for a function, the function must be given as a sum of minterms. (If the function is not in minterm form, the minterm expansion can be found by using one of the techniques given in Section 5.3.) In the first part of the Quine-McCluskey procedure, all of the prime implicants of a function are systematically formed by combining minterms. The minterms are represented in binary notation and combined using

$$XY + XY' = X \qquad (7\text{-}1)$$

where X represents a product of literals and Y is a single variable. Two minterms will combine if they differ in exactly one variable. The examples given below show both the binary notation and its algebraic equivalent.

$AB'CD' + AB'CD = AB'C$

$\underline{1\ 0\ 1\ 0} + \underline{1\ 0\ 1\ 1} = 1\ 0\ 1\ -$ (the dash indicates a missing variable)

$X\ \ Y\ X\ \ Y'\ X$

$A'BC'D + A'BCD'$ (won't combine)

$0\ 1\ 0\ 1 + 0\ 1\ 1\ 0$ (won't combine)

First we will compare the term in group 0 with all of the terms in group 1. Terms 0000 and 0001 can be combined to eliminate the fourth variable, which yields 000–. Similarly, 0 and 2 combine to form 00–0 $(a'b'd')$ and 0, 8 combine to form –000 $(b'c'd')$. The resulting terms are listed in column II of Table 7-1.

Whenever two terms combine, the corresponding decimal numbers differ by a power of 2 (1, 2, 4, 8, etc.). This is true because when the binary representations differ in exactly one column, if we subtract these binary representations, we get a 1 only in the column in which the difference exists, and a binary number with a 1 in exactly one column is a power of 2.

Since comparison of group 0 with groups 2 and 3 is unnecessary, we proceed to compare terms in groups 1 and 2. Comparing term 1 with all terms in group 2, we find that it combines with 5 and 9 but not with 6 or 10. Similarly, term 2 combines only with 6 and 10, and term 8 only with 9 and 10. The resulting terms are listed in column II. Each time a term is combined with another term, it is checked off. A term may be used more than once since $X + X = X$. Even though two terms have already been combined with other terms, they still must be compared and combined if possible. This is necessary since the resultant term may be needed to form the minimum sum solution. At this stage, we may generate redundant terms, but these redundant terms will be eliminated later.

We finish with column I by comparing terms in groups 2 and 3. New terms are formed by combining terms 5 and 7, 6 and 7, 6 and 14, and 10 and 14.

Table 7-1. Determination of Prime Implicants

	Column I		Column II		Column III	
group 0	0	0000 ✓	0, 1	0 0 0 – ✓	0, 1, 8, 9	– 0 0 –
group 1	1	0001 ✓	0, 2	0 0 – 0 ✓	0, 2, 8, 10	– 0 – 0
	2	0010 ✓	0, 8	– 0 0 0 ✓	~~0, 8, 1, 9~~	~~– 0 0 –~~
	8	1000 ✓	1, 5	0 – 0 1	~~0, 8, 2, 10~~	~~– 0 – 0~~
group 2	5	0101 ✓	1, 9	– 0 0 1 ✓	2, 6, 10, 14	– – 1 0
	6	0110 ✓	2, 6	0 – 1 0 ✓	~~2, 10, 6, 14~~	~~– – 1 0~~
	9	1001 ✓	2, 10	– 0 1 0 ✓		
	10	1010 ✓	8, 9	1 0 0 – ✓		
group 3	7	0111 ✓	8, 10	1 0 – 0 ✓		
	14	1110 ✓	5, 7	0 1 – 1		
			6, 7	0 1 1 –		
			6, 14	– 1 1 0 ✓		
			10, 14	1 – 1 0 ✓		

Note that the terms in column II have been divided into groups according to the number of 1's in each term. Again, we apply $XY + XY' = X$ to combine pairs of terms in column II. In order to combine two terms, the terms must have the same variables, and the terms must differ in exactly one of these variables. Thus, it is only necessary to compare terms which have dashes (missing variables) in corresponding places and which differ by exactly one in the number of 1's.

Terms in the first group in column II need only be compared with terms in the second group which have dashes in the same places. Term 000– (0, 1) combines only with term 100–(8,9) to yield –00–. This is algebraically equivalent to $a'b'c' + ab'c' = b'c'$. The resulting term is listed in column III along with the designation 0, 1, 8, 9 to indicate that it was formed by combining minterms 0, 1, 8 and 9. Term (0, 2) combines only with (8, 10), and term (0, 8) combines with both (1, 9) and (2, 10). Again, the terms which have been combined are checked off. Comparing terms from the second and third groups in column II, we find that (2, 6) combines with (10, 14) and (2, 10) combines with (6, 14).

Note that there are three pairs of duplicate terms in column III. These duplicate terms were formed in each case by combining the same set of four minterms in a different order. After deleting the duplicate terms, we compare terms from the two groups in column III. Since no further combination is possible, the process terminates. In general, we would keep comparing terms and forming new groups of terms and new columns until no further terms could be combined.

The terms which have not been checked off because they cannot be combined with other terms are called prime implicants. Since every minterm has been included in at least one of the prime implicants, the function is equal to the sum of its prime implicants. In this example we have

$$f = a'c'd + a'bd + a'bc + \quad b'c' \quad + \quad b'd' \quad + \quad cd' \qquad (7\text{-}3)$$
$$(1, 5) \quad (5, 7) \quad (6, 7) \quad (0, 1, 8, 9) \quad (0, 2, 8, 10) \quad (2, 6, 10, 14)$$

In the above expression, each term has a minimum number of literals, but the number of terms is not minimum. Using the consensus theorem to eliminate redundant terms yields

$$f = a'bd + b'c' + cd' \qquad (7\text{-}4)$$

which is the minimum sum-of-products expression for f. Section 7.2 discusses a better method of eliminating redundant prime implicants using a prime implicant chart.

Next, we will define implicant and prime implicant and relate these terms to the Quine-McCluskey procedure described above.

Definition: Given a function F of n variables, a product term P is an *implicant* of F iff for every combination of values of the n variables for which $P = 1$, F is also equal to 1.

In other words, if for some combination of values of the variables, $P = 1$ and $F = 0$, then P is *not* an implicant of F. For example, consider the function

$$F(a, b, c) = a'b'c' + ab'c' + ab'c + abc = b'c' + ac \qquad (7\text{-}5)$$

If $a'b'c' = 1$, then $F = 1$; if $ac = 1$, then $F = 1$; etc. Hence the terms $a'b'c'$, ac, etc., are implicants of F. In this example, bc is *not* an implicant of F because $bc = 1$ and $F = 0$ when $a = 0$ and $b = c = 1$. In general, if F is written in sum-of-products form, every product term is an implicant. Every minterm of F is also an implicant of F, and so is any term formed by combining two or more minterms. For example, in Table 7-1, all of the terms listed in any of the columns are implicants of the function given in Equation (7-2).

Definition: A *prime implicant* of a function F is a product term implicant which is no longer an implicant if any literal is deleted from it.

In Equation (7-5), the implicant $a'b'c'$ is *not* a *prime* implicant because a' can be eliminated, and the resulting term ($b'c'$) is still an implicant of F. The implicants $b'c'$ and ac are *prime* implicants because if we delete a literal from either term, the term will no longer be an implicant of F. Each prime implicant of a function has a minimum number of literals in the sense that no more literals can be eliminated from it by combining it with other terms.

The Quine-McCluskey procedure illustrated above finds all of the product term implicants of a function. The implicants which are non-prime are checked off in the process of combining terms, so that the remaining terms are prime implicants.

A minimum sum-of-products expression for a function consists of a sum of some (but not necessarily all) of the prime implicants of that function. In other words, a sum-of-products expression which contains a term which is not a prime implicant cannot be minimum. This is true because the non-prime term does not contain a minimum number of literals — it can be combined with additional min-terms to form a prime implicant which has fewer literals than the non-prime term. Any non-prime term in a sum-of-products expression can thus be replaced with a prime implicant, which reduces the number of literals and simplifies the expression.

7.2 The Prime Implicant Chart

The second part of the Quine-McCluskey procedure employs a prime implicant chart to select a minimum set of prime implicants. The minterms of the function are listed across the top of the chart and the prime implicants are listed down the side. A prime implicant is equal to a sum of minterms, and the prime implicant is said to *cover* these minterms. If a prime implicant covers a given minterm, an X is placed at the intersection of the corresponding row and column. Figure 7-1 shows the prime implicant chart derived from Table 7-1. All of the prime implicants (terms which have not been checked off in Table 7-1) are listed on the left. In the first row, X's are placed in columns 0, 1, 8 and 9, since prime implicant $b'c'$ was formed from the sum of minterms 0, 1, 8 and 9. Similarly, X's are placed in columns 0, 2, 8, 10 opposite the prime implicant $b'd'$, and so forth.

		0	1	2	5	6	7	8	9	10	14
(0, 1, 8, 9)	$b'c'$	X	X					X	⊗		
(0, 2, 8, 10)	$b'd'$	X		X				X		X	
(2, 6, 10, 14)	cd'			X		X				X	⊗
(1, 5)	$a'c'd$		X		X						
(5, 7)	$a'bd$				X		X				
(6, 7)	$a'bc$					X	X				

Fig. 7-1. Prime implicant chart

If a minterm is covered by only one prime implicant, then that prime implicant is called an *essential* prime implicant and must be included in the minimum sum of products. Essential prime implicants are easy to find using the prime implicant chart. If a given column contains only one X, then the corresponding row is an essential prime implicant. In Fig. 7-1, columns 9 and 14 each contain one X, so prime implicants $b'c'$ and cd' are essential.

Each time a prime implicant is selected for inclusion in the minimum sum, the corresponding row should be crossed out. After doing this, the columns which correspond to all minterms covered by that prime implicant should also be crossed out. Figure 7-2 shows the resulting chart when the essential prime implicants and the corresponding rows and columns of Fig. 7-1 are crossed out. A minimum set of prime implicants must now be chosen to cover the remaining columns. In this example, $a'bd$ covers the remaining two columns, so it is chosen. The resulting minimum sum of products is

$$f = b'c' + cd' + a'bd$$

which is the same as Equation (7-4). Note that even though the term $a'bd$ is included in the minimum sum of products, $a'bd$ is *not* an *essential* prime implicant. It is the sum of minterms m_5 and m_7; m_5 is also covered by $a'c'd$ and m_7 is also covered by $a'bc$.

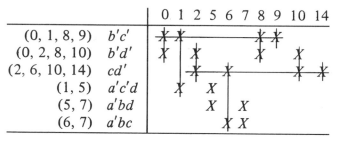

		0 1 2 5 6 7 8 9 10 14
(0, 1, 8, 9)	$b'c'$	
(0, 2, 8, 10)	$b'd'$	
(2, 6, 10, 14)	cd'	
(1, 5)	$a'c'd$	
(5, 7)	$a'bd$	
(6, 7)	$a'bc$	

Fig. 7-2

When the prime implicant chart is constructed, some minterms may be covered by only a single prime implicant, while other minterms may be covered by two or more prime implicants. A prime implicant is *essential* (or necessary) to a function f iff the prime implicant contains a minterm which is not covered by any other prime implicant of f. The essential prime implicants are chosen first since all essential prime implicants must be included in every minimum sum. After the essential prime implicants have been chosen, the minterms which they cover can be eliminated from the prime implicant chart by crossing out the corresponding columns. If the essential prime implicants do not cover all of the minterms, then additional non-essential prime implicants are needed. In simple cases, the non-essential prime implicants needed to form the minimum solution may be selected by trial and error. For larger prime implicant charts, additional procedures for chart reduction can be employed.* Some functions have two or more minimum sum-of-products expressions, each having the same number of terms and literals. The next example shows such a function.

---

*For a discussion of such procedures, see E. J. McCluskey, *Introduction to the Theory of Switching Circuits.* McGraw-Hill, 1965.

Example with a cyclic prime implicant chart: A prime implicant chart which has two or more X's in every column is referred to as "cyclic". The following function has such a chart:

$$F = \Sigma m(0, 1, 2, 5, 6, 7) \tag{7-6}$$

Derivation of prime implicants:

0	000√	0, 1	0 0 −
1	001√	0, 2	0 − 0
2	010√	1, 5	− 0 1
5	101√	2, 6	− 1 0
6	110√	5, 7	1 − 1
7	111√	6, 7	1 1 −

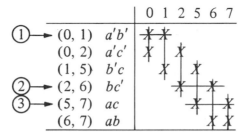

Fig. 7-3

Figure 7-3 shows the resulting prime implicant chart. All columns have 2 X's, so we will proceed by trial and error. Both (0, 1) and (0, 2) cover column 0, so we will try (0, 1). After crossing out row (0, 1) and columns 0 and 1, we examine column 2 which is covered by (0, 2) and (2, 6). The best choice is (2, 6) because it covers two of the remaining columns while (0, 2) covers only one of the remaining columns. After crossing out row (2, 6) and columns 2 and 6, we see that (5, 7) covers the remaining columns and completes the solution. Therefore, one solution is $F = a'b' + bc' + ac$. However, we are not guaranteed that this solution is minimum. We must go back and solve the problem over again starting with the other prime implicant that covers column 0. The resulting table is:

		0	1	2	5	6	7
(0, 1)	$a'b'$	X	X				
(0, 2)	$a'c'$	X		X			
(1, 5)	$b'c$		X		X		
(2, 6)	bc'			X		X	
(5, 7)	ac				X		X
(6, 7)	ab					X	X

Fig. 7-4

Finish the solution and show that $F = a'c' + b'c + ab$. Since this has the same number of terms and same number of literals as the expression for F derived in Fig. 7-3, there are two minimum sum-of-products solutions to this problem. Compare these two minimum solutions for Equation (7-6) with the solutions obtained in Fig. 6-9 using Karnaugh maps. Note that each minterm on the map can be covered by two different loops. Similarly, each column of the prime implicant chart (Fig. 7-3) has two X's, indicating that each minterm can be covered by two different prime implicants.

7.3 Simplification of Incompletely Specified Functions

Given an incompletely specified function, proper assignment of values to the don't care terms is necessary in order to obtain a minimum form for the function. In this section, we will show how to modify the Quine-McCluskey procedure in order to obtain a minimum solution when don't care terms are present. In the process of finding the prime implicants, we will treat the don't care terms as if they were required minterms. In this way, they can be combined with other minterms to eliminate as many literals as possible. If extra prime implicants are generated because of the don't cares, this is all right since the extra prime implicants will be eliminated in the next step anyway. When forming the prime implicant chart, the don't cares are *not* listed at the top. In this way, when the prime implicant chart is solved, all of the required minterms will be covered by one of the selected prime implicants. However, the don't care terms are not included in the final solution unless they have been used in the process of forming one of the selected prime implicants. The following example should clarify the procedure.

Example of simplification of an incompletely specified function:

$$F(A, B, C, D) = \Sigma m(2, 3, 7, 9, 11, 13) + \Sigma d(1, 10, 15)$$

(the terms following d are don't cares)

The don't cares are treated like required minterms when finding the prime implicants:

1	0001 ✓	(1, 3)	0 0 − 1 ✓	(1, 3, 9, 11)	− 0 − 1
2	0010 ✓	(1, 9)	− 0 0 1 ✓	(2, 3, 10, 11)	− 0 1 −
3	0011 ✓	(2, 3)	0 0 1 − ✓	(3, 7, 11, 15)	− − 1 1
9	1001 ✓	(2, 10)	− 0 1 0 ✓	(9, 11, 13, 15)	1 − − 1
10	1010 ✓	(3, 7)	0 − 1 1 ✓		
7	0111 ✓	(3, 11)	− 0 1 1 ✓		
11	1011 ✓	(9, 11)	1 0 − 1 ✓		
13	1101 ✓	(9, 13)	1 − 0 1 ✓		
15	1111 ✓	(10, 11)	1 0 1 − ✓		
		(7, 15)	− 1 1 1 ✓		
		(11, 15)	1 − 1 1 ✓		
		(13, 15)	1 1 − 1 ✓		

The don't cares are omitted when forming the prime implicant chart:

	2	3	7	9	11	13
(1, 3, 9, 11)		X		X	X	
*(2, 3, 10, 11)	X	X			X	
*(3, 7, 11, 15)		X	X		X	
*(9, 11, 13, 15)				X	X	X

$$F = B'C + CD + AD$$

*indicates an essential prime implicant

Note that although the original function was incompletely specified, the final simplified expression for F is defined for all combinations of values for A, B, C and D and is therefore completely specified. In the process of simplification we have automatically assigned values to the don't cares in the original truth table for F. If we replace each term in the final expression for F by its corresponding sum of minterms, the result is

$$F = (m_2 + m_3 + m_{10} + m_{11}) + (\cancel{m_3} + m_7 + \cancel{m_{11}} + m_{15}) + (m_9 + \cancel{m_{11}} + m_{13} + \cancel{m_{15}})$$

Since m_{10} and m_{15} appear in this expression and m_1 does not, this implies that the don't cares in the original truth table for F have been assigned as follows:

for $ABCD = 0001$, $F = 0$; for 1010, $F = 1$; for 1111, $F = 1$

7.4 Simplification Using Map-Entered Variables

Although the Quine-McCluskey method can be used with functions with a fairly large number of variables, it is not very efficient for functions that have many variables and relatively few terms. Some of these functions can be simplified by using a modification of the Karnaugh map method. By using map-entered variables, Karnaugh map techniques can be extended to simplify functions with more than 4 or 5 variables. Figure 7-5(a) shows a 4-variable map with two additional variables entered in the squares in the map. When E appears in a square, this means that if $E = 1$, the corresponding minterm is present in the function G, and if $E = 0$, the minterm is absent. Thus, the map represents the 6-variable function

$$G(A, B, C, D, E, F) = m_0 + m_2 + m_3 + Em_5 + Em_7 + Fm_9$$
$$+ m_{11} + m_{15} \ (+ \text{don't care terms})$$

where the minterms are minterms of the variables $A, B, C,$ and D. Note that m_9 is present in G only when $F = 1$.

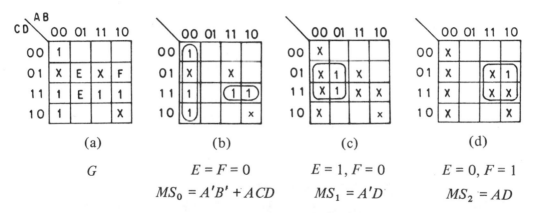

Fig. 7-5. Use of map-entered variables

We will now use a 3-variable map to simplify the function

$$F(A, B, C, D) = A'B'C + A'BC + A'BC'D + ABCD + (AB'C)$$

where the $AB'C$ is a don't care. Since D appears in only two terms, we will choose it as a map-entered variable, which leads to Fig. 7-6(a). We will simplify F by first considering $D = 0$ and then $D = 1$. First set $D = 0$ on the map, and F reduces to $A'C$. Setting $D = 1$ leads to the map of Fig. 7-6(b). The two 1's on the original map have already been covered by the term $A'C$, so they are changed to X's since we don't care whether they are covered again or not. From Fig. 7-6(b), $F = C + A'B$ when $D = 1$. Thus the expression

$$F = A'C + D(C + A'B) = A'C + CD + A'BD$$

gives the correct value of F both when $D = 0$ and when $D = 1$. This is a minimum expression for F, as can be verified by plotting the original function on a 4-variable map; see Fig. 7-6(c).

(a)   (b)   (c)

Fig. 7-6. Simplification using a map-entered variable

Next we will discuss a general method of simplifying functions using map-entered variables. In general, if a variable P_i is placed in square m_j of a map of function F, this means that $F = 1$ when $P_i = 1$ and the variables are chosen so that $m_j = 1$. Given a map with variables $P_1, P_2, \ldots$ entered into some of the squares, the minimum product of sums form of F can be found as follows:

Find a sum-of-products expression for F of the form

$$F = MS_0 + P_1 MS_1 + P_2 MS_2 + \cdots$$
where

MS_0 is the minimum sum obtained by setting $P_1 = P_2 = \cdots = 0$.

MS_1 is the minimum sum obtained by setting $P_1 = 1, P_j = 0 \ (j \neq 1)$,
and replacing all 1's on the map with don't cares.

MS_2 is the minimum sum obtained by setting $P_2 = 1, P_j = 0 \ (j \neq 2)$
and replacing all 1's on the map with don't cares.

(Corresponding minimum sums can be found in a similar way for any remaining map-entered variables.)

The resulting expression for F will always be a correct representation of F. This expression will be minimum provided that the values of the map-entered variables can be assigned independently. On the other hand, the expression will not generally be minimum if the variables are not independent (for example, if $P_1 = P_2'$).

For the example of Fig. 7-5(a), maps for finding MS_0, MS_1 and MS_2 are shown in Figs. 7-5(b), (c), and (d), where E corresponds to P_1 and F corresponds to P_2. The resulting expression is a minimum sum of products for G:

$$G = A'B' + ACD + EA'D + FAD$$

After some practice, it should be possible to write the minimum expression directly from the original map without first plotting individual maps for each of the minimum sums.

7.5 Conclusion

We have discussed three methods for reducing a switching expression to a minimum sum-of-products or a minimum product-of-sums form: algebraic simplification, Karnaugh maps and Quine-McCluskey. Many other methods of simplification are discussed in the literature, but most of these methods are based on variations or extensions of the Karnaugh map or Quine-McCluskey techniques. Karnaugh maps are most useful for functions with 3 to 6 variables. The Quine-McCluskey technique can be used with a high-speed digital computer to simplify functions with up to 15 or more variables. Such computer programs are of most value when used as part of a computer-aided design package that assists with deriving the equations as well as implementing them. Algebraic simplification is still valuable in many cases, especially when different forms of the expressions are required. For problems with a large number of variables and a small number of terms, it may be impossible to use the Karnaugh map, and the Quine-McCluskey method may be very cumbersome. In such cases, algebraic simplification may be the easiest method to use.

The minimum sum-of-products and minimum product-of-sums expressions we have derived lead directly to two-level networks that use a minimum number of AND and OR gates and have a minimum number of gate inputs. As discussed in Unit 8, these networks are easily transformed into networks that contain NAND or NOR gates. Such minimum expressions may also be useful when designing with some types of array logic as discussed in Unit 9. However, many situations exist where minimum expressions do not lead to the best design. For practical designs, many other factors must be considered, such as: What is the maximum number of inputs a gate can have? What is the maximum number of outputs a gate can drive? Is the speed with which signals propagate through the network fast enough? How can the number of interconnections in the network be reduced? Does the design lead to a satisfactory circuit layout on a printed circuit board or on a silicon chip? Up to now we have considered realizing only one switching function at a time. Unit 9 describes design techniques and components that can be used when several functions must be realized by a single network.

Programmed Exercise 7.1

Cover the bottom of the page with a sheet of paper and slide it down as you check your answers.

Find a minimum sum-of-products expression for the following function:

$$f(A, B, C, D, E) = \Sigma(0, 2, 3, 5, 7, 9, 11, 13, 14, 16, 18, 24, 26, 28, 30)$$

Translate each decimal minterm into binary and sort the binary terms into groups according to the number of 1's in each term.

Answer to 7.1:

0	00000✓	0, 2	000–0	Compare pairs of terms in adjacent
2	00010✓			groups and combine terms where
16	10000			possible. (Check off terms which
3	00011			have been combined.)
5	00101			
9	01001			
18	10010			
24	11000			
7	00111			
11	01011			
13	01101			
14	01110			
26	11010			
28	11100			
30	11110			

Turn to the next page and check your answer.

Answer:

0	00000 ✓	0, 2	0 0 0 – 0 ✓	0, 2, 16, 18	– 0 0 – 0
2	00010 ✓	0, 16	– 0 0 0 0		
16	10000 ✓	2, 3	0 0 0 1 –		
3	00011 ✓	2, 18	– 0 0 1 0		
5	00101 ✓	16, 18	1 0 0 – 0 ✓		
9	01001 ✓	16, 24	1 – 0 0 0		
18	10010 ✓	3, 7	0 0 – 1 1		
24	11000 ✓	3, 11	0 – 0 1 1		
7	00111 ✓	5, 7	0 0 1 – 1		
11	01011 ✓	5, 13	0 – 1 0 1		
13	01101 ✓	9, 11	0 1 0 – 1		
14	01110 ✓	9, 13	0 1 – 0 1		
26	11010 ✓	18, 26	1 – 0 1 0		
28	11100 ✓	24, 26	1 1 0 – 0		
30	11110 ✓	24, 28	1 1 – 0 0		
		14, 30	– 1 1 1 0		
		26, 30	1 1 – 1 0		
		28, 30	1 1 1 – 0		

Now compare pairs of terms in adjacent groups in the second column and combine terms where possible. (Check off terms which have been combined.) Check your work by noting that each new term can be formed in two ways. (Cross out duplicate terms.)

Answer: (3rd column)

0, 2, 16, 18	– 0 0 – 0	[check off (0, 2), (16, 18), (0, 16) and (2, 18)]
16, 18, 24, 26	1 – 0 – 0	[check off (16, 18), (24, 26), (16, 24) and (18, 26)]
24, 26, 28, 30	1 1 – – 0	[check off (24, 26), (28, 30), (24, 28) and (26, 30)]

Can any pair of terms in the 3rd column be combined? Complete the given prime implicant chart.

	0 2
(0, 2, 16, 18)	

Turn to the next page and check your answer.

Answer: No terms in the third column combine.

	0	2	3	5	7	9	11	13	14	16	18	24	26	28	30
(0, 2, 16, 18)	X	X								X	X				
(16, 18, 24, 26)										X	X	X	X		
(24, 26, 28, 30)												X	X	X	X
(2, 3)		X	X												
(3, 7)			X		X										
(3, 11)			X				X								
(5, 7)				X	X										
(5, 13)				X				X							
(9, 11)						X	X								
(9, 13)						X		X							
(14, 30)									X						X

Determine the essential prime implicants, and cross out the corresponding rows and columns.

Answer:

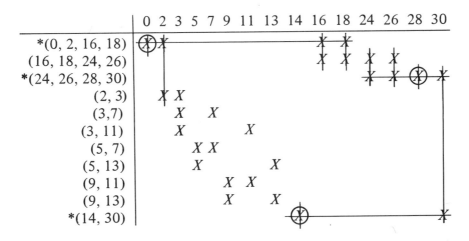

Note that all remaining columns contain two or more X's. Choose the first column which has two X's and then select the prime implicant which covers the first X in that column. Then choose a minimum number of prime implicants which cover the remaining columns in the chart.

Turn to the next page and check your answer.

Answer:

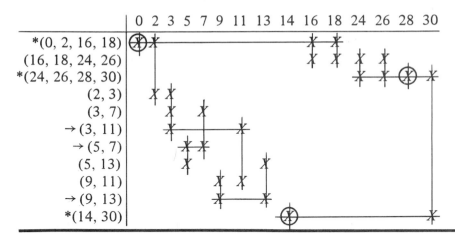

From the above chart, write down the chosen prime implicants in 0, 1,–notation.

Then write the minimum sum of products in algebraic form.

Answer:

$$-1110, -00-0, 11--0, 0-011, 001-1 \text{ and } 01-01$$
$$f = BCDE' + B'C'E' + ABE' + A'C'DE + A'B'CE + A'BD'E$$

The prime implicant chart with the essential prime implicants crossed out is repeated below. Find a second minimum sum-of-products solution.

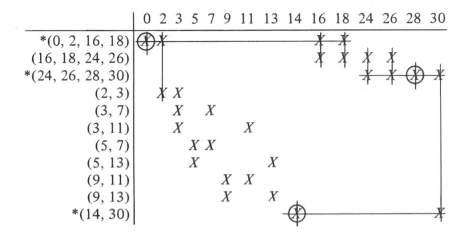

Turn to the next page and check your answer.

Answer:

Start by choosing prime implicant (5, 13).
$$f = BCDE' + B'C'E' + ABE' + A'B'DE + A'CD'E + A'BC'E$$

PROBLEMS

7.2 For each of the following functions, find all of the prime implicants using the Quine-McCluskey procedure.

    a. $f(a, b, c, d) = \Sigma m(1, 5, 7, 9, 11, 12, 14, 15)$

    b. $f(a, b, c, d) = \Sigma m(0, 1, 3, 5, 6, 7, 8, 10, 14, 15)$

7.3 Using a prime implicant chart, find *all* minimum sum-of-products solutions for each of the functions given in Problem 7.2.

7.4 For each function, find a minimum sum-of-products solution using the Quine-McCluskey procedure.

    a. $f(a, b, c, d) = \Sigma m(1, 3, 4, 5, 6, 7, 10, 12, 13) + \Sigma d(2, 9, 15)$

    b. $f(a, b, c, d) = \Sigma m(2, 3, 4, 7, 9, 11, 12, 13, 14) + \Sigma d (1, 10, 15)$

7.5 Using the Quine-McCluskey procedure, find all minimum sum-of-products expressions for

    $f(A, B, C, D, E)$

        $= \Sigma m(0, 1, 2, 3, 6, 8, 9, 10, 11, 17, 20, 21, 23, 25, 28, 30, 31)$

7.6 $F(A, B, C, D, E, F) = \Sigma m(1, 2, 3, 16, 17, 18, 19, 26, 32, 39, 48, 63)$
                           $+ \Sigma d(15, 28, 29, 30)$

    a. Find all minimum sum-of-products expressions for F.

    b. Circle the *essential* prime implicants in your answer.

    c. If there were no don't cares present in the original function, how would your answer to a be changed? (Do this by inspection of the prime implicant chart, do *not* rework the problem.)

7.7 Work Problem 6.16 using the Quine-McCluskey method.

7.8 Work Problem 6.11 using the Quine-McCluskey method.

7.9 Using the method of map-entered variables, use 4-variable maps to find a minimum sum of products expression for

    a. $F(A, B, C, D, E) = \Sigma m(0, 4, 5, 7, 9) + \Sigma d(6, 11) + E(m_1 + m_{15})$, where the m's represent minterms of the variables A, B, C, D.

    b. $Z(A, B, C, D, E, F, G) = \Sigma m(0, 3, 13, 15) + \Sigma d(1, 2, 7, 9, 14) + E(m_6 + m_8) + Fm_{12} + Gm_5$

7.10 a. Rework Problem 7.9a using a 5-variable map.
     b. Rework Problem 7.9a using the Quine-McCluskey procedure.
    Note that you must first express F in terms of minterms of all five variables; the original 4-variable minterms cannot be used.

7.11 Work Problem 6.23 by the Quine-McCluskey method.

7.12 Work Problem 6.24 by the Quine-McCluskey method.

7.13 Work Problem 6.15 using a 4-variable map with map-entered variables.

8

MULTI-LEVEL GATE NETWORKS
NAND AND NOR GATES

OBJECTIVES

1. Design a minimal two-level or multi-level network of AND and OR gates to realize a given function. (Consider *both* networks with an OR gate at the output and networks with an AND gate at the output.)

2. Define a functionally complete set of logic gates and determine if a given set of gates is functionally complete.

3. Design or analyze a two-level gate network using any one of the 8 basic forms (AND-OR, NAND-NAND, OR-NAND, NOR-OR, OR-AND, NOR-NOR, AND-NOR, and NAND-AND).

4. Design or analyze a multi-level NAND-gate or NOR-gate network.

STUDY GUIDE

1. Study Section 8.1, *Multi-Level Gate Networks.*

   a. What are two ways of changing the number of levels in a gate network?

b. By constructing a tree diagram, determine the number of gates, gate inputs and levels of gates required to realize Z_1 and Z_2:

$$Z_1 = [(A + B)C + DE(F + G)]H \qquad\qquad Z_2 = A + B[C + DE(F + G)]$$

Check your answers by drawing the corresponding gate networks.

c. In order to find a minimum two-level solution, why is it necessary to consider both a sum-of-products form and a product-of-sums form for the function?

d. One realization of $H = ABC(D + E) + FG$ is

Redraw the network so that it uses one less gate and so that the output of an AND gate never goes directly to the input of another AND gate.

e. Work Problems 8.1 and 8.2. Unless otherwise specified, you may always assume that both the variables and their complements are available as network inputs.

2. Study Section 8.2, *Other Types of Logic Gates.*

    a. For each gate, specify the missing inputs:

    b. Review the definitions of positive and negative logic, and also review the negative logic theorem (Section 4.4). Make sure that you know the difference between the dual and the inverse. Work Problem 8.3.

    c. Write a logic equation for F.

3. Study Section 8.3, *Functionally Complete Sets of Logic Gates.*

    a. What is meant by a functionally complete set of logic gates?

    b. How can you show that a set of logic gates is functionally complete?

    c. Show that the network given below is functionally complete.

    First, we must find a way to realize the complement of a variable. This means that we must assign constant values to two of the variables in such a way that the complement of the third variable will appear at the output. Find values of Y and Z such that X' will appear at the output.

$$Y = \underline{\hspace{1.5cm}} \qquad Z = \underline{\hspace{1.5cm}}$$

    Next we must find a value for one of the variables such that the AND or OR of the remaining variables (or their complements) will appear at the output. Can you assign a value to X such that $f = YZ$ or $Y'Z$ or YZ' or $Y'Z'$? \underline{\hspace{1.5cm}}

    Assign a value to X such that f reduces to an expression that contains two literals ORed together.

$$X = \underline{\hspace{1.5cm}} \text{ and } f \text{ reduces to } \underline{\hspace{1.5cm}}$$

Now draw a diagram showing how two N networks can be connected to realize $Y \mid Z$ (with appropriate values assigned to the X inputs).

Show how to realize YZ using three N networks.

Explain why N is functionally complete.

d. Work Problems 8.4 and 8.5.

4. Study Section 8.4, *Design of Two-Level NAND- and NOR-Gate Networks.*

a. Draw the network corresponding to Equation (8-18).

b. Derive Equation (8-19).

c. Make sure that you understand the relation between Equations (8-14) through (8-22) and the diagrams of Fig. 8-14.

d. Why is the NOR-NAND form degenerate?

e. What assumption is made about the types of inputs available when the procedures for designing two-level NAND-NAND and NOR-NOR networks are used?

f. For these procedures the literal inputs to the output gate are complemented but not the literal inputs to the other gates. Explain why. Use an equation to illustrate.

g. A general OR-AND network is shown below. Transform this to a NOR-NOR network and prove that your transformation is valid.

h. Work Problem 8.6.

5. Study Section 8.5, *Design of Multi-Level NAND- and NOR-Gate Networks.*

a. Verify that the NAND network of Fig. 8-16 is correct by dividing the corresponding network of AND and OR gates into two-level subnetworks and transforming each subnetwork.

b. If you wish to design a two-level network using only NOR gates, should you start with a minimum sum of products or a minimum product of sums?

c. Note that direct conversion of a network of AND and OR gates to a NAND-gate network requires starting with an OR gate at the output, but direct conversion to a NOR-gate network requires starting with an AND gate at the output. This is easy to remember since a NAND is equivalent to an OR with the inputs inverted:

and a NOR is equivalent to an AND with the inputs inverted:

d. Convert the network of Fig. 8-1(b) to all NAND gates.

e. Work Problems 8.7, 8.8, 8.9 and 8.10.

6. Section 8.6, *Design Using Exclusive-OR Gates,* is optional.

a. Before studying this section, review Section 4.3, *Exclusive-OR and Equivalence Operations.*

b. Rework the design example of Fig. 8-17 using three 2-input equivalence gates.

c. Note that the procedure given on p. 169 applies only to an exclusive-OR sum of terms. If the expression to be simplified contains both OR and exclusive-OR, the procedure should be applied only to the part of the expression containing the exclusive-OR.

d. Work Problem 8.11. Make sure that you understand the relation between the two methods.

7. When you are satisfied that you can meet the objectives of this unit, take the readiness test. The techniques learned in this unit will be applied to a lab design problem in Unit 10.

8. MULTI-LEVEL GATE NETWORKS NAND AND NOR GATES

In the first part of this unit, you will learn how to design networks which have more than two levels of AND and OR gates. In the second part, you will learn techniques for designing with NAND and NOR gates. These techniques generally consist of first designing a network of AND and OR gates and then converting it to the desired type of gates. These techniques are easy to apply *provided* that you start with the proper form of network.

8.1 Multi-Level Gate Networks

The maximum number of gates cascaded in series between a network input and the output is referred to as the number of *levels* of gates (not to be confused with voltage levels). Thus, a function written in sum-of-products form or in product-of-sums form corresponds directly to a two-level gate network. As is usually the case in digital networks where the gates are driven from flip-flop* outputs, we will assume that all variables and their complements are available as network inputs. For this reason, we will not normally count inverters which are connected directly to input variables when determining the number of levels in a network. In this unit we will use the following terminology:

a. *AND-OR network* means a two-level network composed of a level of AND gates followed by an OR gate at the output.

b. *OR-AND network* means a two-level network composed of a level of OR gates followed by an AND gate at the output.

c. *OR-AND-OR network* means a three-level network composed of a level of OR gates followed by a level of AND gates followed by an OR gate at the output.

d. *Network of AND and OR gates* implies no particular ordering of the gates; the output gate may be either AND or OR.

---

* Flip-flops are discussed in Unit 12.

The number of levels in an AND-OR network can usually be increased by factoring the sum-of-products expression from which it was derived. Similarly, the number of levels in an OR-AND network can usually be increased by multiplying out some of the terms in the product-of-sums expression from which it was derived. Logic designers are concerned with the number of levels in a network for several reasons. Sometimes factoring (or multiplying out) to increase the number of levels of gates will reduce the required number of gates and gate inputs and thus reduce the cost of building the network, but in other cases increasing the number of levels will increase the cost. In some applications, the number of gates which can be cascaded is limited by gate delays. When the input of a gate is switched, there is a finite time before the output changes. When several gates are cascaded, the time between an input change and the corresponding change in the network output may become excessive and slow down the operation of the digital system.

The number of gates, gate inputs and levels in a network can be determined by inspection of the corresponding expression. In the example of Fig. 8-1(a), the tree diagram drawn below the expression for Z indicates that the corresponding network will have 4 levels, 6 gates and 13 gate inputs, as verified in Fig. 8-1(b). Each node on the tree diagram represents a gate, and the number of gate inputs is written beside each node. We can change the expression for Z to 3 levels by partially multiplying it out:

$$Z = (AB + C)[(D + E) + FG] + H = AB(D + E) + C(D + E) + ABFG + CFG + H$$

As shown in Fig. 8-2, the resulting network requires 3 levels, 6 gates and 19 gate inputs.

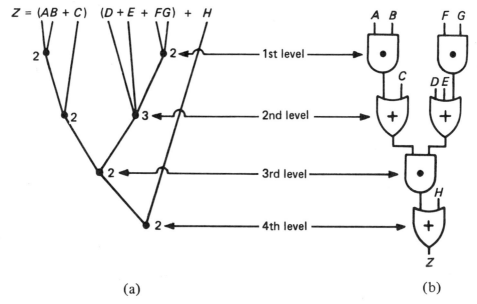

(a)   (b)

Fig. 8-1. Four-level realization of Z

$$Z = AB(D + E) + C(D + E) + A B F G + C F G + H$$

*The same gate can be used for both appearances of $(D + E)$

(a)

(b)

Fig. 8-2. Three-level realization of Z

Example of Multi-Level Design Using AND and OR gates

Problem: Find a network of AND and OR gates to realize

$$f(a, b, c, d) = \Sigma m(1, 5, 6, 10, 13, 14)$$

Consider solutions with two levels of gates and three levels of gates. Try to minimize the number of gates and the total number of gate inputs. Assume that all variables and their complements are available as inputs.

Solution: First simplify f by using a Karnaugh map:

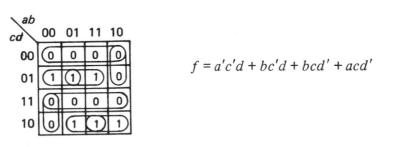

$$f = a'c'd + bc'd + bcd' + acd' \qquad (8\text{-}1)$$

Fig. 8-3

This leads directly to a two-level AND-OR gate network:

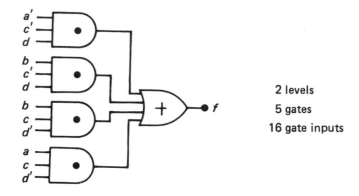

2 levels

5 gates

16 gate inputs

Fig. 8-4

Factoring Equation (8-1) yields

$$f = c'd(a' + b) + cd'(a + b) \qquad (8-2)$$

which leads to the following three-level OR-AND-OR gate network:

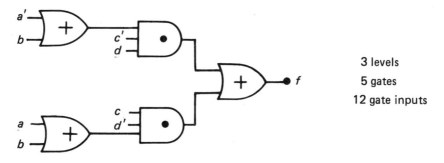

3 levels

5 gates

12 gate inputs

Fig. 8-5

Both of these solutions have an OR gate at the output. A solution with an AND gate at the output might have fewer gates or gate inputs. A two-level OR-AND network corresponds to a product-of-sums expression for the function. This can be obtained from the 0's on the Karnaugh map as follows:

$$f' = c'd' + ab'c' + cd + a'b'c \qquad (8-3)$$

$$f = (c + d)(a' + b + c)(c' + d')(a + b + c') \qquad (8-4)$$

Equation (8-4) leads directly to a two-level OR-AND network:

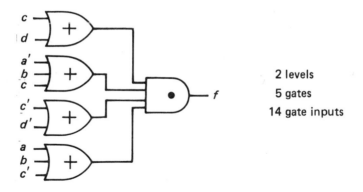

2 levels

5 gates

14 gate inputs

Fig. 8-6

To get a 3-level network with an AND gate output, we partially multiply out Equation (8-4) using $(X + Y)(X + Z) = X + YZ$:

$$f = [c + d(a' + b)][c' + d'(a + b)] \qquad (8\text{-}5)$$

Equation (8-5) would require four levels of gates to realize; however, if we multiply out $d'(a + b)$ and $d(a' + b)$ we get

$$f = (c + a'd + bd)(c' + ad' + bd') \qquad (8\text{-}6)$$

which leads directly to a 3-level AND-OR-AND network:

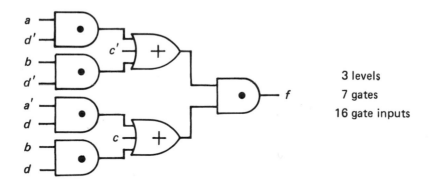

3 levels

7 gates

16 gate inputs

Fig. 8-7

For this particular example, the best two-level solution had an AND gate at the output (Fig. 8-6), and the best three-level solution had an OR gate at the output (Fig. 8-5). In general, to be sure of obtaining a minimum solution, one must find *both* the network with the AND-gate output and the one with the OR-gate output.

If an expression for f' has n levels, the complement of that expression is an n-level expression for f. Therefore, to realize f as an n-level network with an AND-gate output, one procedure is to first find an n-level expression for f' with an OR operation at the output level, and then complement the expression for f'. In the above example, factoring Equation (8-3) gives a 3-level expression for f':

$$f' = c'(d' + ab') + c(d + a'b')$$
$$= c'(d' + a)(d' + b') + c(d + a')(d + b') \qquad (8\text{-}7)$$

Complementing Equation (8-7) gives Equation (8-6), which corresponds to the 3-level AND-OR-AND network of Fig. 8-7.

8.2 Other Types of Logic Gates

Up to this point, we have designed logic networks using AND gates, OR gates and inverters. Exclusive-OR and equivalence gates have also been introduced in Unit 4. In this section, we will define NAND, NOR, majority and minority gates. Logic designers frequently use NAND and NOR gates. These gates can be constructed using transistor logic (Appendix A.2), and they are commonly available in integrated-circuit form (Appendix A.3).

Figure 8-8(a) shows a 3-input NAND* gate. The small circle at the gate output indicates inversion, so the NAND gate is equivalent to an AND gate followed by an inverter as shown in Fig. 8-8(b). The gate output is

$$F = (ABC)' = A' + B' + C'$$

The output of the n-input NAND gate in Fig. 8-8(c) is

$$F = (X_1 X_2 \ldots X_n)' = X_1' + X_2' + \ldots + X_n' \qquad (8\text{-}8)$$

The output of this gate is 1 iff one or more of its inputs are 0.

| (a) 3-input | (b) NAND gate | (c) n-input NAND |
| NAND gate | equivalent | gate |

Fig. 8-8. NAND gates

Figure 8-9(a) shows a 3-input NOR gate.** The small circle at the gate output indicates inversion, so the NOR gate is equivalent to an OR gate followed by an inverter. The gate output is

$$F = (A + B + C)' = A'B'C'$$

---

*A more appropriate name would be an AND-NOT gate, but we will follow common usage and call it a NAND gate.

**A more appropriate name would be an OR-NOT gate, but we will follow common usage and call it a NOR gate.

The output of an n-input NOR gate, shown in Fig. 8-9(c), is

$$F = (X_1 + X_2 + \ldots + X_n)' = X_1'X_2' \ldots X_n' \qquad (8\text{-}9)$$

The output of this gate is 1 iff all inputs are 0.

(a) 3-input NOR gate

(b) NOR gate equivalent

(c) n-input NOR gate

Fig. 8.9. NOR gates

From Equations (8-8) and (8-9), note that the NAND and NOR functions are duals. Thus, by applying the negative logic theorem (Section 4.4), if a given circuit realizes the NAND function for positive logic, it realizes the NOR function for negative logic.

A *majority* gate has an odd number of inputs, and its output is 1 iff a majority of its inputs are 1. Thus, a 3-input majority gate (Fig. 8-10(a)) has an output of 1 if 2 or 3 of its inputs are 1. A *minority* gate has an odd number of inputs, and its output is 1 iff a minority of its inputs are 1. Thus, a 3-input minority gate has an output of 1 if none or one of its inputs is 1.

abc	F_M (majority)	F_m (minority)
000	0	1
001	0	1
010	0	1
011	1	0
100	0	1
101	1	0
110	1	0
111	1	0

(a) Majority gate

(b) Minority gate

(c) Truth table

Fig. 8-10. Majority and minority gates

From the truth table, the function realized by a 3-input majority gate is

$$F_M = a'bc + ab'c + abc' + abc = bc + ac + ab \qquad (8\text{-}10)$$

By inspection of the table, $F_m = F_M'$, so the 3-input minority gate realizes

$$F_m = (bc + ac + ab)' = (b' + c')(a' + c')(a' + b') \qquad (8\text{-}11)$$

8.3 Functionally Complete Sets of Logic Gates

A set of logic operations is said to be *functionally complete* if any Boolean function can be expressed in terms of this set of operations. The set AND, OR and NOT is obviously functionally complete since any function can be expressed in sum-of-products form, and a sum-of-products expression uses only the AND, OR and NOT operations. Similarly, a set of logic gates is functionally complete if all switching functions can be realized using this set of gates. Since the set of operations AND, OR and NOT is functionally complete, any set of logic gates which can realize AND, OR and NOT is also functionally complete. AND and NOT are a functionally complete set of gates since OR can also be realized using AND and NOT:

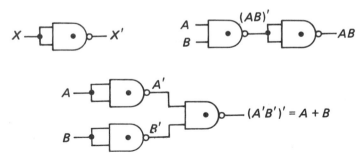

If a single gate forms a functionally complete set by itself, then any switching function can be realized using only gates of that type. The NAND gate is an example of such a gate. Since the NAND gate performs the AND operation followed by an inversion, NOT, AND and OR can be realized using only NAND gates as shown in Fig. 8-11.

Fig. 8-11. NAND gate realization of NOT, AND and OR

Thus, any switching function can be realized using only NAND gates. An easy method for converting an AND-OR network to a NAND network is discussed in the next section.

The following procedure can be used to determine if a given set of gates is functionally complete. First, write out a minimum sum-of-products expression for the function realized by each gate. If no complement appears in any of these expressions, then NOT cannot be realized and the set is not functionally complete. If a complement appears in one of the expressions, then NOT can generally be realized by an appropriate choice of inputs to the corresponding gate. (We will always assume that 0 and 1 are available as gate inputs.) Next, attempt to realize AND or OR, keeping in mind that NOT is now available. Once AND or OR has been realized, the other one can always be realized using DeMorgan's laws if no more direct procedure is apparent. For example, if OR and NOT are

available, AND can be realized by

$$XY = (X' + Y')'$$

Example: Show that all switching functions can be realized using only 3-input minority gates.

Solution: First we will derive the function realized by a 3-input minority gate using a Karnaugh map as shown in Fig. 8-12. The output is 1 if no inputs are 1 or if exactly one of the inputs is 1.

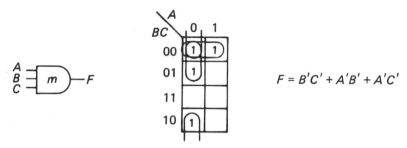

Fig 8-12. Derivation of minority gate output function

We can easily realize the complement of X by letting $A = B = C = X$.

$$F = X'X' + X'X' + X'X' = X'$$

Looking at the expression for F, we see that if $A = 1$, then F reduces to $B'C'$. Therefore the AND operation can be realized in the form shown in Fig. 8-13.

(a) $F = (X')'(Y')' + 0 + 0 = XY$

(b) alternate form for AND
$$F = (X' + Y' + X'Y')' = (X' + Y')' = XY$$

Fig. 8-13. Realization of AND using minority gates

OR can then be realized by using $(X + Y) = (X'Y')'$.

$$(X'Y')' = X + Y$$

Since AND, OR and NOT can all be realized using only minority gates, any switching function can be realized using only minority gates.

8.4 Design of Two-Level NAND- and NOR-Gate Networks

A two-level network composed of AND and OR gates is easily converted to a network composed of NAND gates or of NOR gates. This conversion is carried out by using $F = (F')'$ and then applying DeMorgan's laws:

$$(X_1 + X_2 + \ldots + X_n)' = X_1'X_2' \ldots X_n' \qquad (8\text{-}12)$$

$$(X_1 X_2 \ldots X_n)' = X_1' + X_2' + \ldots + X_n' \qquad (8\text{-}13)$$

The following example illustrates conversion of a minimum sum-of-products form to several other two-level forms:

$$\begin{aligned}
F &= A + BC' + B'CD = [(A + BC' + B'CD)']' & & (8\text{-}14)\\
&= [A' \cdot (BC')' \cdot (B'CD)']' & \text{(by 8-12)} & (8\text{-}15)\\
&= [A' \cdot (B' + C) \cdot (B + C' + D')]' & \text{(by 8-13)} & (8\text{-}16)\\
&= A + (B' + C)' + (B + C' + D')' & \text{(by 8-13)} & (8\text{-}17)
\end{aligned}$$

Equations (8-14), (8-15), (8-16) and (8-17) represent the AND-OR, NAND-NAND, OR-NAND, and NOR-OR forms, respectively, as shown in Fig. 8-14.

Rewriting Equation (8-17) in the form

$$F = \{[A + (B' + C)' + (B + C' + D')']'\}' \qquad (8\text{-}18)$$

leads to a three-level NOR-NOR-INVERT network. However, if we want a two-level network containing only NOR gates, we should start with the minimum product-of-sums form for F instead of the minimum sum of products. After obtaining the minimum product of sums from a Karnaugh map, F can be written in the following two-level forms:

$$\begin{aligned}
F &= (A + B + C)(A + B' + C')(A + C' + D) & & (8\text{-}19)\\
&= \{[(A + B + C)(A + B' + C')(A + C' + D)]'\}' & & \\
&= [(A + B + C)' + (A + B' + C')' + (A + C' + D)']' & \text{(by 8-13)} & (8\text{-}20)\\
&= (A'B'C' + A'BC + A'CD')' & \text{(by 8-12)} & (8\text{-}21)\\
&= (A'B'C')' \cdot (A'BC)' \cdot (A'CD')' & \text{(by 8-12)} & (8\text{-}22)
\end{aligned}$$

Equations (8-19), (8-20), (8-21) and (8-22) represent the OR-AND, NOR-NOR, AND-NOR,* and NAND-AND forms, respectively, as shown in Fig 8-14.

---

*Two-level AND-NOR (AND-OR-INVERT) networks are available in integrated-circuit form. Some types of NAND gates can also realize AND-NOR networks when the so-called "wired OR" connection is used.

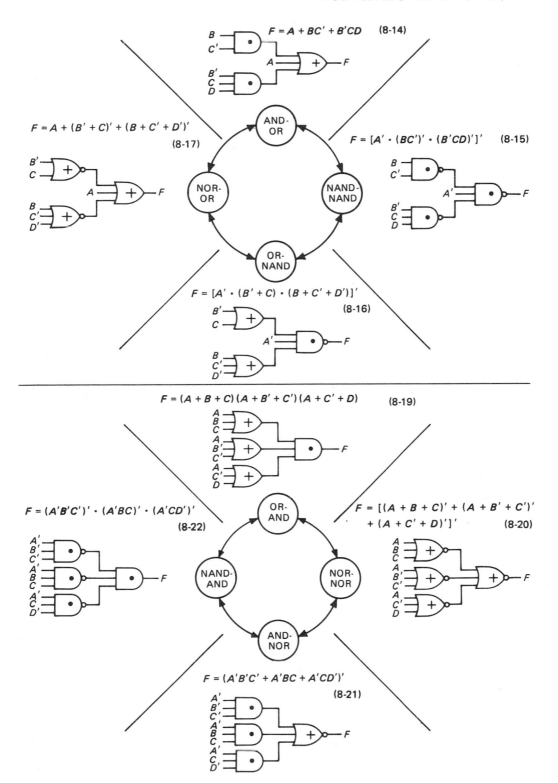

Fig. 8-14. Eight basic forms for two-level networks

The other 8 possible two-level forms (AND-AND, OR-OR, OR-NOR, AND-NAND, NAND-NOR, NOR-NAND, etc.) are degenerate in the sense that they cannot realize all switching functions. Consider, for example, the following NAND-NOR network:

$$F = [(ab)' + (cd)' + e]' = abcde'$$

From the above example, it is clear that the NAND-NOR form can only realize a product of literals and not a sum of products.

Since NAND and NOR gates are readily available in integrated-circuit form, two of the most commonly used network forms are the NAND-NAND and the NOR-NOR. Assuming that all variables and their complements are available as inputs, the following method can be used to realize F with NAND gates:

Procedure for designing a minimum 2-level NAND-NAND network

    a. Find a minimum *sum-of-products* expression for F.

    b. Draw the corresponding two-level AND-OR network.

    c. Replace all gates with NAND gates leaving the gate interconnections unchanged. If the output gate has any single literals as inputs, complement these literals.

Figure 8-15 illustrates the transformation of step c. Verification that this transformation leaves the network output unchanged follows. In general, F is a sum of literals ($\ell_1, \ell_2, \ldots$) and product terms ($p_1, p_2, \ldots$):

$$F = \ell_1 + \ell_2 + \ldots + p_1 + p_2 + \ldots$$

After applying DeMorgan's law,

$$F = (\ell_1' \ell_2' \ldots p_1' p_2' \ldots)'$$

So the output OR gate is replaced with a NAND gate with inputs $\ell_1', \ell_2', \ldots, p_1', p_2', \ldots$. Since product terms $p_1, p_2, \ldots$ are each realized with an AND gate, $p_1', p_2', \ldots$ are each realized with a NAND gate in the transformed network.

    (a) before transformation   (b) after transformation

Fig. 8-15. AND-OR to NAND-NAND transformation

Assuming that all variables and their complements are available as inputs, the following method can be used to realize F with NOR gates:

Procedure for designing a minimum 2-level NOR-NOR network

    a. Find a minimum *product-of-sums* expression for F.

    b. Draw the corresponding two-level OR-AND network.

    c. Replace all gates with NOR gates leaving the gate interconnections unchanged. If the output gate has any single literals as inputs, complement these literals.

The above procedure is similar to that used for designing NAND-NAND networks. Note, however, that for the NOR-NOR network, the starting point is a minimum *product of sums* rather than a sum of products.

8.5 Design of Multi-Level NAND- and NOR-Gate Networks

The following procedure may be used to design multi-level NAND-gate networks:

    a. Simplify the switching function to be realized.

    b. Design a multi-level network of AND and OR gates. The output gate must be OR. AND-gate outputs cannot be used as AND-gate inputs; OR-gate outputs cannot be used as OR-gate inputs.

    c. Number the levels starting with the output gate as level 1. Replace all gates with NAND gates, leaving all interconnections between gates unchanged. Leave the inputs to the 2nd, 4th, 6th, . . . levels unchanged. Invert any literals which appear as inputs to the 1st, 3rd, 5th, . . . levels.

The validity of the above procedure is easily proved by dividing the multi-level network into two-level subnetworks and applying the previous results for two-level networks to each of the two-level subnetworks. The example of Fig. 8-16 illustrates the above procedure. Note that if step b is performed correctly, each level of the network will contain only AND gates or only OR gates.

    The procedure for design of multi-level NOR-gate networks is exactly the same as for NAND-gate networks except the output gate of the network of AND and OR gates must be an AND gate, and all gates are replaced with NOR gates.

Example: $F_1 = a'[b' + c(d + e') + f'g'] + hi'j + k$

(a) Network of AND and OR gates

(b) NAND Network

Fig. 8-16. Multi-level network conversion to NAND gates

8.6 Design Using Exclusive-OR Gates*

Some switching functions can be realized more economically when exclusive-OR gates are used. An example which illustrates this follows:

A switching network has four inputs (a, b, c, d) and one output (F). Design a network such that $F = 1$ if the number of 1 inputs is odd.

cd \ ab	00	01	11	10
00		1		1
01	1		1	
11		1		1
10	1		1	

F

Fig. 8-17

From the resulting Karnaugh map (Fig. 8-17), we see that no terms can be combined, and F can only be simplified by factoring. The map pattern shows that $a'b'$ is common between two terms, $a'b$ is common between another pair of terms, etc. Using this information, we can write F in the form

$$F = a'b'(c'd + cd') + a'b(c'd' + cd) + ab(c'd + cd') + ab'(cd + c'd')$$

---

*This section is optional.

By further factoring, we can write F in terms of exclusive-OR:

$$F = (a'b + ab')(cd + c'd') + (ab + a'b')(c'd + cd')$$
$$= (a'b + ab')(c'd + cd')' + (a'b + ab')'(c'd + cd')$$
$$= (a'b + ab') \oplus (c'd + cd') = a \oplus b \oplus c \oplus d$$

Thus, F can be realized using three 2-input exclusive-OR gates or one 4-input exclusive-OR gate:

A useful theorem for manipulating expressions containing exclusive-OR is

$$\text{If } XY = 0, \text{ then } X \oplus Y = X + Y.$$

Proof: From Equation (4-10), $X \oplus Y = (X + Y)(XY)'$. If $XY = 0$, $(XY)' = 1$ and

$$X \oplus Y = X + Y$$

Example: $abc' \oplus cd'e = abc' + cd'e$ since $(abc')(cd'e) = 0$.

Since $m_i m_j = 0$ $(i \neq j)$, a sum of minterms can be replaced with an exclusive-OR sum:

$$m_1 + m_3 + m_4 = m_1 \oplus m_3 \oplus m_4$$

The following procedure can be used to simplify an exclusive-OR sum of terms:

a. Replace each term by an equivalent sum of minterms.

b. Replace each OR with exclusive-OR.

c. Eliminate duplicate pairs of terms by $X \oplus X = 0$.

d. Replace each exclusive-OR with OR.

e. Simplify the resulting expression.

Example: Simplify $F = AB' \oplus AC \oplus BC$

a. $F = (AB'C + AB'C') \oplus (AB'C + ABC) \oplus (A'BC + ABC)$

b. $= AB'C \oplus AB'C' \oplus AB'C \oplus ABC \oplus A'BC \oplus ABC$

c. $= AB'C' \oplus A'BC$

d. $= AB'C' + A'BC$

All of the above operations can be done using a Karnaugh map. Each term is plotted separately. If two (or an even number of) 1's appear in a square, 0 is entered in that square, since $1 \oplus 1 = 0$. If an odd number of 1's appear in a square, then a single 1 is entered in the square. The result is a Karnaugh map of the function which can then be simplified in the usual manner. For the above example:

Fig. 8-18. Karnaugh map for simplification of exclusive-OR sum of terms

PROBLEMS

8.1 Using AND and OR gates, find a minimum network to realize
$$f(a, b, c, d) = M_1 M_2 M_5 M_9 M_{10} M_{14}$$

  a. using two-level logic

  b. using three-level logic   (12 gate inputs minimum)

8.2 Realize the following functions using AND and OR gates. Assume that there are no restrictions on the number of gates which can be cascaded and minimize the number of gate inputs.

  a. $ACD' + AE + B'CD' + B'E + AC'D$

  b. $ABDF + ABEF + ABG + CDF + CEF + CG$

8.3 The input and output voltages for a given 3-input gate are tabulated below. If the voltages are interpreted according to the positive logic convention, what type of gate is it? What type of gate is it for negative logic?

A	B	C	F
0	0	0	+V
0	0	+V	0
0	+V	0	0
0	+V	+V	0
+V	0	0	0
+V	0	+V	0
+V	+V	0	0
+V	+V	+V	0

8.4 Which of the following sets of operations are functionally complete? (You may assume that 0 and 1 are available as gate inputs.) Justify your answers.

  a. OR and NOT   b. AND and OR

  c. exclusive-OR and OR   d. equivalence and OR

8.5 An IMPLICATION gate has two inputs (X and Y); the output is 1 except when $X = 1$ and $Y = 0$.

a. Show that the implication gate by itself is functionally complete.

b. Realize $F = A'B + AC'$ using only implication gates. (Only A, B, C, 0 and 1 may be used as gate inputs.) Four gates are sufficient.

8.6 Find 8 different minimum two-level gate networks to realize:
$$F = xy'z + x'yz + w$$

8.7 Find a minimum two-level NOR-gate network to realize:
$$f(a, b, c, d, e) = \Sigma m(0, 2, 5, 8, 10, 11, 13, 15, 18, 21, 26, 27, 28, 29, 30, 31)$$
Repeat for a minimum three-level NOR-gate network.

8.8 Design a minimum 3-level NOR-gate network to realize:
$$f = a'b + ad' + ab'c'$$

8.9 Realize the following function using only two-input NAND gates. Minimize the number of gates required.
$$F = A'[B' + C'D' + DE]$$

8.10 Find a minimum network to realize $F = A'B'D' + B'C'D'$ using only two-input NOR gates. Only A, B, C, and D are available and not their complements. (4 gates are sufficient.) (*Hint:* Find a network of 2-input OR and AND gates and convert to NORs.)

8.11 Using the method given in Section 8.6, simplify the following functions both algebraically and by using a Karnaugh map.
a. $F_1 = xy \oplus xyz \oplus wxyz$
b. $F_2 = (AC \oplus B'C \oplus AD') + ACD'$

8.12 Find a minimum 4-level NAND-gate network to realize
$$Z = abe'f + c'e'f + d'e'f + gh$$

8.13 Using AND and OR gates, find a minimum 2-level network to realize
$$F = a'c + bc'd + ac'd$$

8.14 Find 8 different minimum 2-level networks to realize
$$F(a, b, c, d) = \Sigma m(0, 2, 6, 8, 12)$$

8.15 Design a logic network that has a 4-bit binary number as an input and one output. The output should be 1 whenever the input is prime number or zero.

    a. Use a two-level NAND-gate network.

    b. Use a two-level NOR-gate network.

    c. Use only two-input NAND gates.

8.16 Realize each of the functions given in Problem 6.23 using a minimum two-level NAND-gate network and also using a minimum two-level NOR-gate network.

8.17 Realize each of the functions given in Problem 6.21 using a minimum two-level AND-NOR network and also using a minimum two-level OR-NAND network.

8.18 Realize the following function using only 2-input NAND gates. Repeat using only 2-input NOR gates.

$$F = A'BC' + BD + AC + B'CD'$$

8.19 Using AND and OR gates, find a minimum 2-level network to realize

$$F = a'cd' + a'bc + ad$$

9

MULTIPLE-OUTPUT NETWORKS

MULTIPLEXERS, DECODERS, READ-ONLY MEMORIES, AND PROGRAMMABLE LOGIC ARRAYS

OBJECTIVES

1. Design a minimal two-level multiple-output AND-OR, OR-AND, NAND-NAND or NOR-NOR network using Karnaugh maps.

2. Explain the function of a multiplexer. Use a multiplexer to implement a logic function.

3. Explain the operation of a decoder. Use a decoder with added gates to implement a set of logic functions.

4. Explain the operation of a read-only memory (ROM). Use a ROM to implement a set of logic functions.

5. Explain the operation of a programmable logic array (PLA). Use a PLA to implement a set of logic functions. Given a PLA table or an internal connection diagram for a PLA, determine the logic functions realized.

STUDY GUIDE

1. Read Section 9.1, *Introduction.*

2. Study Section 9.2, *Design of Two-Level Multiple-Output Networks.*

   a. In which of the following cases would you replace a term xy' with $xy'z + xy'z'$?

(1) Neither $xy'z$ or $xy'z'$ is used in another function.

(2) Both $xy'z$ and $xy'z'$ are used in other functions.

(3) Term $xy'z$ is used in another function, but $xy'z'$ is not.

b. In the second example (Fig. 9-4), in f_2, c could have been replaced by $bc + b'c$ since bc and $b'c$ were available "free" from f_1 and f_3. Why wasn't this replacement made?

c. In the following example, compute the cost of realizing f_1 and f_2 separately; then compute the cost using the term $a'b'c$ in common between the two functions. Use a two-level AND-OR network in both cases.

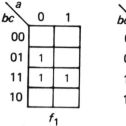

d. Find expressions which correspond to a 2-level, minimum multiple-output, AND-OR realization of F_1, F_2, and F_3. Why should the term cd <u>not</u> be included in F_1?

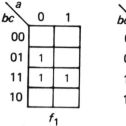

$F_1 =$

$F_2 =$

$F_3 =$

e. Work Problems 9.1, 9.2, 9.3 and 9.4.

f. Work Problem 9.5. (*Hint:* Work with the 0's on the maps and first find a minimum solution for f_1', f_2', and f_3'.)

3. Study Section 9.3, *Multi-Output NAND and NOR Networks.*

   a. Derive expressions for the F_1 and F_2 outputs of the NOR network of Fig. 9.9(b) by finding the equation for each gate output, and show that these expressions reduce to the original expressions for F_1 and F_2.

   b. Work Problem 9.6.

4. Study Section 9.4, *Multiplexers.*

   a. Write the logic equation and draw the internal logic diagrams for a 2-to-1 MUX.

   b. Write the equation for a 4-to-1 MUX with control inputs A and C.

$$Z = \underline{\hspace{6cm}}$$

Realize Equation 9-5 using this MUX. (*Hint:* Expand Equation 9-5 so that each term contains both A and C.)

   c. Write the equation for an 8-to-1 MUX with control inputs B, C and D.

$$Z = \underline{\hspace{7cm}}$$

Use this MUX to realize the function of Fig. 9-14(a). (*Hint:* Draw patches on the map below corresponding to $BCD = 000, 001$, etc.)

d. Realize the same function using a 4-to-1 MUX with control inputs A and C and two added gates. (*Hint:* The map should be divided into 4 square patches.)

e. The 5-variable function shown below is to be realized using a 16-to-1 MUX with control inputs B, C, D and E. Indicate the patches on the map which correspond to I_0, I_1, I_2 and I_8 and determine the values of these I's from the map.

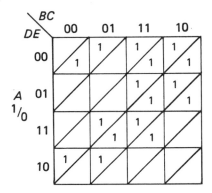

f. Work Problems 9.7 and 9.8.

5. Study Section 9.5, *Decoders.*

a. The 7442 4-to-10 line decoder (Fig. 9-17) can be used as a 3-to-8 line decoder. To do this, which 3 lines should be used as inputs? _____ The remaining input line should be set equal to _____ .

b. Work Problem 9.9.

6. Study Section 9.6, *Read-Only Memories.*

a. The diagram below shows the pattern of 0's and 1's stored in a ROM with 8 words and 4 bits per word. What will be the values of

$$F_1, F_2, F_3 \text{ and } F_4 \text{ if } A = 0, B = C = 1?$$

Give the minterm expansions for F_1 and F_2:

$F_1 =$
$F_2 =$

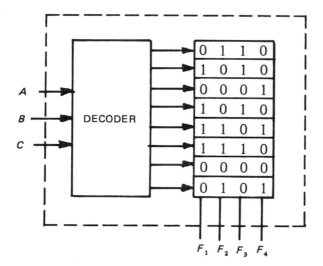

b. When asked to specify the size of a ROM, give the number of words and the number of bits per word.

What size ROM is required to realize 4 functions of 5 variables?

What size ROM is required to realize 8 functions of 10 variables?

c. When specifying the size of a ROM, assume that you are specifying a standard size ROM with 2^n words.

What size ROM is required to convert 8-4-2-1 BCD code to 2-out-of-5 code? (See Table 1-1, p. 13.)

What size ROM would be required to realize the decoder given in Fig. 9-17?

d. Draw an internal connection diagram for a ROM which would perform the same function as the network of Fig. 9-3. (Indicate the presence of switching elements by dots at the intersection of the word lines and output lines.)

e. Explain the difference between a mask-programmable ROM, and PROM and an EPROM. Which would you use for a new design which had not yet been debugged?

7. Study Section 9.7, *Programmable Logic Arrays.* (*Note:* PLAs are also called programmable logic arrays)

   a. When you are asked to specify the size of a PLA, give the number of inputs, the number of product terms, and the number of outputs.

   What size PLA would be required to realize Equations (9-1) if no simplification of the minterm expansions was performed?

   b. If the realization of Equations (9-1) shown in Fig. 9-3 was converted to a PLA realization, what size PLA would be required?

   c. Specify the contents of the PLA of part (b) in tabular form. (Your table should have 4 rows.)

   d. Draw an internal connection diagram for the PLA of part (b). (Use dots to indicate the presence of switching elements in the AND and OR arrays.)

   e. Given the following PLA table, plot maps for Z_1, Z_2 and Z_3.

A B C	Z_1 Z_2 Z_3
– 0 0	1 1 0
0 1 –	1 1 0
1 0 –	1 0 0
1 1 1	0 1 1
0 – 1	1 0 1
0 0 0	0 0 1

   (The Z_1 map should have 6 1's, Z_2 should have 5, and Z_3 should have 4.)

   f. Work Problems 9.10 and 9.11.

8. Study Section 9.8, *Programmable Array Logic* (PAL).

    a. Which fusible links in Fig. 9-29(a) must be blown in order to realize the function shown in Fig. 9-29(b)?

    b. Referring to Table 9-2, which type of PAL could be used to realize the 8-to-1 MUX of Fig. 9-11? The quad MUX of Fig. 9-12?

    c. Verify that the A_2 output function is correctly realized in Fig. 9-31 by tracing all of the signals from the PAL inputs to the A_2 output.

    d. Work Problem 9.15.

9. When you are satisfied that you can meet all of the objectives, take the readiness test.

9. MULTIPLE-OUTPUT NETWORKS MULTIPLEXERS, DECODERS, READ-ONLY MEMORIES AND PROGRAMMABLE LOGIC ARRAYS

9.1 Introduction

In large digital systems, it is frequently necessary to realize several switching functions of the same input variables. Although each function could be realized separately, it is generally more economical to realize the functions using a single network with multiple outputs. Several techniques for doing this are discussed in this unit. First, methods for designing multiple-output gate networks are described. Later in the unit, design techniques using decoders, read-only memories, and programmed logic arrays are developed.

Up to this point we have mainly been concerned with basic principles of logic design. We have illustrated these principles using gates as our basic building blocks. In this unit we introduce the use of more complex integrated circuits in logic design. Integrated circuits may be classified as small-scale integration (SSI), medium-scale integration (MSI), large-scale integration (LSI) or very-large-scale integration (VLSI) depending on the number of gates per integrated circuit package and the type of function performed. SSI functions include NAND, NOR, AND, and OR gates, inverters, and flip-flops*. SSI integrated circuit packages typically contain 1 to 4 gates, 6 inverters, or 1 or 2 flip-flops. MSI integrated circuits, such as adders, multiplexers, decoders, registers and counters*, perform more complex functions. Such integrated circuits typically contain the equivalent of 12 to 100 gates in one package. More complex functions such as memories and microprocessors are classified as LSI or VLSI integrated circuits. An LSI integrated circuit generally contains 100 to a few thousand gates in a single package, and a VLSI integrated circuit contains several thousand gates.

---

*Flip-flops, registers and counters are introduced in Units 12 and 13.

It is generally uneconomical to design digital systems using only SSI integrated circuits. By using MSI and LSI functions, the required number of integrated circuit packages is greatly reduced. The cost of mounting and wiring the integrated circuits as well as the cost of designing and maintaining the digital system may be significantly lower when MSI and LSI functions are used.

After a discussion of multiple output gate networks, this unit introduces the use of MSI multiplexers and decoders in logic design. Then read-only memories (ROMs) and programmable logic arrays (PLAs) are described and used to implement multiple-output combinational logic networks.

9.2 Design of Two-Level Multiple-Output Networks

Solution of digital design problems often requires realization of several functions of the same variables. Although each function could be realized separately, use of some gates in common between two or more functions sometimes leads to a more economical realization. The following example illustrates this:

Design a network with four inputs and three outputs which realizes the functions

$$F_1(A, B, C, D) = \Sigma m(11, 12, 13, 14, 15)$$
$$F_2(A, B, C, D) = \Sigma m(3, 7, 11, 12, 13, 15)$$
$$F_3(A, B, C, D) = \Sigma m(3, 7, 12, 13, 14, 15) \tag{9-1}$$

First, each function will be realized individually. The Karnaugh maps, functions and resulting network are given in Figs. 9-1 and 9-2. The cost of this network is 9 gates and 21 gate inputs.

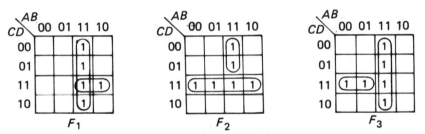

Fig. 9-1. Karnaugh maps for Equations (9-1)

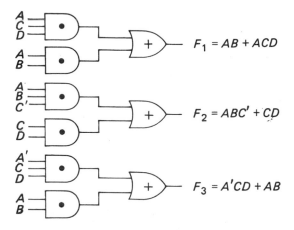

Fig. 9-2. Realization of Equations (9-1)

An obvious simplification is to use the same gate for AB in both F_1 and F_3. This reduces the cost to 8 gates and 19 gate inputs. A further, but less obvious, simplification is possible. Observing that the term ACD is necessary for the realization of F_1 and $A'CD$ is necessary for F_3, if we replace CD in F_2 by $A'CD + ACD$, realization of CD is unnecessary and one gate is saved. Figure 9-3 shows the reduced network, which requires 7 gates and 18 gate inputs.

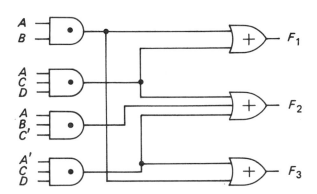

Fig. 9-3. Multiple-output realization of Equations (9-1)

Note that F_2 is realized by the expression $ABC' + A'CD + ACD$ which is *not* a minimum sum of products, and two of the terms are *not* prime implicants of F_2. Thus in realizing multiple-output networks, use of a minimum sum of prime implicants for each function does not necessarily lead to a minimum cost solution for the network as a whole.

When designing multiple-output networks, you should try to minimize the total number of gates required. If several solutions require the same number of gates, the one with the minimum number of gate inputs should be chosen. The next example further illustrates the use of common terms to save gates. A 4-input, 3-output network is to be designed to realize

$$f_1 = \Sigma m(2, 3, 5, 7, 8, 9, 10, 11, 13, 15)$$

$$f_2 = \Sigma m(2, 3, 5, 6, 7, 10, 11, 14, 15)$$

$$f_3 = \Sigma m(6, 7, 8, 9, 13, 14, 15) \tag{9-2}$$

First, we plot maps for f_1, f_2, and f_3 (Fig. 9-4).

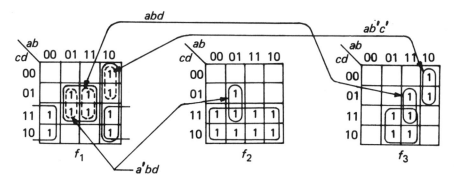

Fig. 9-4

If each function is minimized separately, the result is

$$f_1 = bd + b'c + ab'$$

$$f_2 = c + a'bd \tag{9-2a}$$

$$f_3 = bc + ab'c' + \left\{ \begin{array}{l} abd \\ \text{or} \\ ac'd \end{array} \right\} \qquad \begin{array}{l} \text{10 gates,} \\ \text{25 gate inputs} \end{array}$$

By inspection of the maps, we can see that terms $a'bd$ (from f_2), abd (from f_3) and $ab'c'$ (from f_3) can be used in f_1. If bd is replaced with $a'bd + abd$, then the gate needed to realize bd can be eliminated. Since m_{10} and m_{11} in f_1 are already covered by $b'c$, $ab'c'$ (from f_3) can be used to cover m_8 and m_9, and the gate needed to realize ab' can be eliminated. The minimal solution is therefore:

$$f_1 = \underline{a'bd} + \underline{abd} + \underline{ab'c'} + b'c$$

$$f_2 = c + \underline{a'bd} \qquad\qquad \begin{array}{l} \text{8 gates,} \\ \text{22 gate inputs} \end{array} \tag{9-2b}$$

$$f_3 = bc + \underline{ab'c'} + \underline{abd}$$

(Terms which are used in common between two functions are underlined.)

When designing multiple-output networks, it is sometimes best not to combine a 1 with its adjacent 1's, as illustrated in the example of Fig. 9-5.

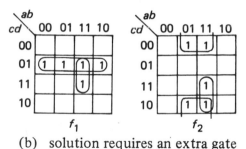

(a) best solution

(b) solution requires an extra gate

Fig. 9-5

The solution with the maximum number of common terms is not necessarily best, as illustrated by the following example:

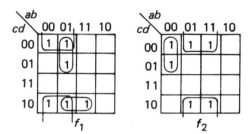

(a) solution with maximum number of common terms requires 8 gates, 26 inputs

(b) best solution requires 7 gates, 18 inputs and has no common terms

Fig. 9-6

Determination of Essential Prime Implicants for Multiple-Output Realization

As a first step in determining a minimum two-level multiple-output realization, it is often desirable to determine essential prime implicants. However, we must be careful because some of the prime implicants essential to an individual function may not be essential to the multiple-output realization. For example, in Fig. 9-4, bd is an essential prime implicant of f_1 (only prime implicant which covers m_5) but it is not essential to the multiple-output realization. The reason that bd is not essential is that m_5 also appears on the f_2 map and hence might be covered by a term which is shared by f_1 and f_2.

We can find prime implicants which are essential to one of the functions *and* to the multiple-output realization by a modification of the procedure used for the single-output case. In particular, when we check each 1 on the map to see if it is covered by only one prime implicant, we will only check for adjacencies those 1's which do not appear on the other function maps. Thus in Fig. 9-5 we find that $c'd$ is essential to f_1 for the multiple-output realization (because of m_1), but abd is not essential because m_{15} also appears on the f_2 map. In Fig. 9-6, the only minterms of f_1 which do not appear on the f_2 map are m_2 and m_5. The only *prime* implicant which covers m_2 is $a'd'$; hence $a'd'$ is essential to f_1 in the multiple-output realization. Similarly, the only prime implicant which covers m_5 is $a'bc'$, and $a'bc'$ is essential. On the f_2 map, bd' is essential (why?). Once the essential prime implicants for f_1 and f_2 have been looped, selection of the remaining terms to form the minimum solution is obvious in this example.

The techniques for finding essential prime implicants outlined above cannot be applied in a problem like Fig. 9-4 where every minterm of f_1 also appears on the f_2 or f_3 map. More sophisticated techniques are available for finding essential multiple-output terms for such problems, but such techniques are beyond the scope of this text.

Design of A Code Conversion Network

Conversion of decimal digits from one code to another is frequently necessary. The following example illustrates design of a network to convert from 8-4-2-1 BCD code to excess-3 code. The network has four inputs and four outputs. The inputs $abcd$ represent one of the ten decimal digits in BCD code, and the outputs $wxyz$ represent one of the ten decimal digits in excess-3 code. The table in Fig. 9-7 specifies the four functions to be realized by the network.

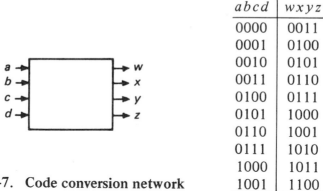

$abcd$	$wxyz$
0000	0011
0001	0100
0010	0101
0011	0110
0100	0111
0101	1000
0110	1001
0111	1010
1000	1011
1001	1100

Fig. 9-7. Code conversion network

It will be assumed that the input combinations which do not correspond to decimal digits will never occur as inputs; therefore w, x, y and z are don't cares for these input combinations. The Karnaugh maps are plotted in Fig. 9-8.

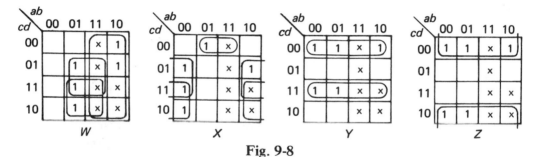

Fig. 9-8

The minimum solution for z is obviously d'. Checking for common terms between the w, x and y maps reveals that use of common terms will not help simplify the network. Therefore, the minimum two-level AND-OR solution (10 gates) is

$$w = a + bc + bd$$
$$x = bc'd' + b'd + b'c$$
$$y = c'd' + cd$$
$$z = d'$$

A 3-level solution with 9 gates is possible if w and x are factored to get the common term $c + d$ as follows:

$$w = a + b(\underline{c + d})$$
$$x = bc'd' + b'(\underline{c + d})$$

9.3   Multi-Output NAND and NOR Networks

The procedure given in Section 8.5 for design of single-output multi-level NAND- and NOR-gate networks also applies to multiple output networks. If all of the output gates are OR gates, direct conversion to a NAND-gate network is possible. If all of the output gates are AND, direct conversion to a NOR-gate network is possible. Figure 9-9 gives an example of converting a 2-output network to NOR gates. Note that the inputs to the first and third levels of NOR gates are inverted.

$$F_1 = [(a + b')c + d](e' + f) \qquad F_2 = [(a + b')c + g'](e' + f)h$$

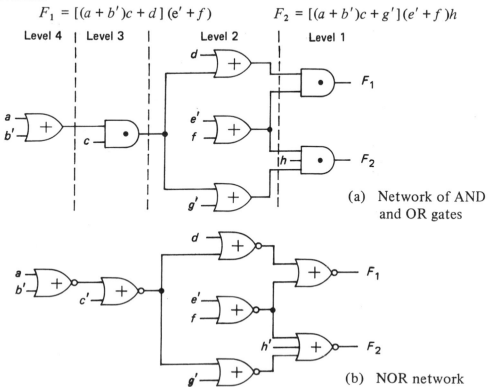

Fig. 9-9.   **Multi-level network conversion to NOR gates**

9.4 Multiplexers

A multiplexer (or data selector) has a group of data inputs and a group of control inputs. The control inputs are used to select one of the data inputs and connect it to the output terminal. Figure 9-10 shows diagrams for a 4-to-1 multiplexer, 8-to-1 multiplexer, and a 2^n-to-1 multiplexer.*

Fig. 9-10. Multiplexers

The 4-to-1 multiplexer (abbreviated as MUX) is described by the equation

$$Z = A'B'I_0 + A'BI_1 + AB'I_2 + ABI_3 \qquad (9\text{-}3)$$

If the control inputs are $AB = 00$, the output is I_0; similarly, the control inputs 01, 10 and 11 give outputs of I_1, I_2 and I_3, respectively. The 8-to-1 MUX is described by the equation

$$Z = A'B'C'I_0 + A'B'CI_1 + A'BC'I_2 + A'BCI_3$$
$$+ AB'C'I_4 + AB'CI_5 + ABC'I_6 + ABCI_7 \qquad (9\text{-}4)$$

When the control inputs are $ABC = 011$, the output is I_3, and other outputs are selected in a similar manner. Figure 9-11 shows an internal logic diagram for the 8-to-1 MUX. In general, a multiplexer with n control inputs can be used to select any one of 2^n data inputs. The general equation for the output of a MUX with n control inputs and 2^n data inputs is

$$Z = \sum_{k=0}^{2^n-1} m_k I_k$$

where m_k is a minterm of the n control variables and I_k is a data input.

---

*IEEE standard symbols for multiplexers, decoders, and other MSI devices are discussed in Appendix B.2.

Fig. 9-11.   Logic diagram for 8-to-1 MUX

Multiplexers are frequently used in digital system design to select the data which is to be processed or stored. Figure 9-12 shows how a quadruple 2-to-1 MUX is used to select one of two 4-bit data words. If the control is $A = 0$, the values of x_0, x_1, x_2 and x_3 will appear at the Z_0, Z_1, Z_2 and Z_3 outputs; if $A = 1$, the values of y_0, y_1, y_2 and y_3 will appear at the outputs.

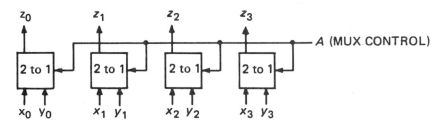

Fig. 9-12.   Quad multiplexer used to select data

Multiplexers can also be used to realize combinational logic functions. A 4-to-1 MUX can realize any 3-variable function with no added logic gates. As an example, we will realize

$$F(A, B, C) = A'B' + AC \qquad (9\text{-}5)$$

Expanding F so that all terms include both control inputs, A and B, yields

$$F = A'B' + AC(B + B') = A'B' \cdot 1 + AB' \cdot C + AB \cdot C \qquad (9\text{-}6)$$

Comparing Equations (9-3) and (9-6), we see that the two equations will be identical if $I_0 = 1$, $I_1 = 0$, $I_2 = C$ and $I_3 = C$. Therefore, Equation 9-5 can be realized as shown in Fig. 9-13.

Fig. 9-13. Realization of Equation 9-5

An 8-to-1 MUX can be used to realize any 4 variable function with no added gates. Three of the variables are used as control inputs to the MUX and the remaining variable is used as required on the data inputs. As an example, consider the 4-variable function (Z) plotted on the Karnaugh map of Fig. 9-14(a). We will select A, B and C as control inputs and then determine the I_k's in Equation (9-4). Setting $ABC = 000$ in Equation (9-4) gives $Z = I_0$, setting $ABC = 001$ gives $Z = I_1$, etc. Performing the corresponding operation on the Karnaugh map identifies "patches" on the map which correspond to I_0, I_1, etc. Thus when the values of ABC are fixed at 000, the 4-variable map reduces down to the 1-variable map labeled I_0 in Fig. 9-14. Similarly, setting $ABC = 001$ means that we have selected the $AB = 00$ column of the map and the $C = 1$ rows, which gives us the 1-variable map labeled I_1. Since we have fixed the values of A, B and C in each case, each 1-variable map gives the value of I_k in terms of D. For the I_0 map, $I_0 = 1$ for both $D = 0$ and $D = 1$, so $I_0 = 1$; for the I_1 map, $I_1 = 1$ only when $D = 1$, so $I_1 = D$. The other values of I_k are read off the map in a similar manner as shown below:

$ABC = 000$	$Z = I_0 = 1$		$ABC = 100$	$Z = I_4 = D'$
$ABC = 001$	$Z = I_1 = D$		$ABC = 101$	$Z = I_5 = D$
$ABC = 010$	$Z = I_2 = 0$		$ABC = 110$	$Z = I_6 = D'$
$ABC = 011$	$Z = I_3 = 1$		$ABC = 111$	$Z = I_7 = D'$

Figure 9-14(c) shows the final realization of Z using an 8-to-1 MUX.

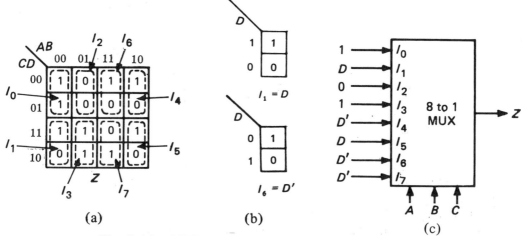

Fig. 9-14. MUX realization of a 4-variable function

If different control inputs are chosen for the multiplexer, the position of the patches on the map will change accordingly. Figure 9-14(d) shows the patches and multiplexer inputs for control inputs A, B and D. For $ABD = 000$, we see that $I_0 = 1$ when $C = 0$, so $I_0 = C'$.

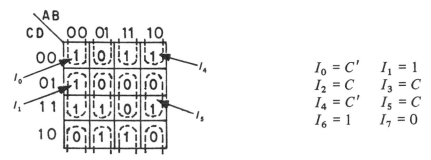

$$
\begin{aligned}
I_0 &= C' & I_1 &= 1 \\
I_2 &= C & I_3 &= C \\
I_4 &= C' & I_5 &= C \\
I_6 &= 1 & I_7 &= 0
\end{aligned}
$$

Fig. 9-14(d) MUX realization with control inputs A, B and D

The function plotted in Fig. 9-14(a) can also be realized using a 4-to-1 MUX with added gates as shown in Fig. 9-15. If we select AB as the control inputs, then Equation (9-3) applies. Setting $AB = 00$, 01, 10, and 11 yields $Z = I_0$, I_1, I_2 and I_3, respectively. The corresponding operation on the map of Fig. 9-15 yields the patches labeled I_0, I_1, I_2 and I_3. Each patch represents a 2-variable map expressing I_k in terms of C and D. Thus, $I_0 = C' + D$, $I_1 = C$, $I_2 = C'D' + CD = C' \oplus D$ and $I_3 = D'$ which gives the realization of Fig. 9-15(b).

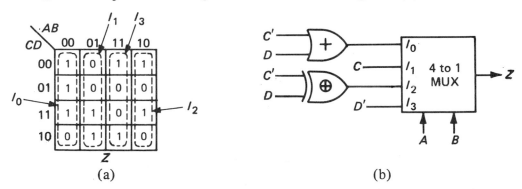

(a) (b)

Fig. 9-15. Realization using a MUX with added gates

In addition to the primary application of data selection in digital systems, we have seen how multiplexers can be used to realize combinational switching functions. Multiplexers are commonly available in integrated circuit packages in the following configurations: quadruple 2-to-1, dual 4-to-1, 8-to-1 and 16-to-1. As we have seen, the 4-to-1 and 8-to-1 multiplexers can be used to realize 3- and 4-variable functions, respectively. Similarly, a 16-to-1 MUX, which has 4 control inputs, can be used to realize any 5-variable function without added gates.

9.5 Decoders

The decoder is another commonly used type of integrated circuit. Figure 9-16 shows the diagram and truth table for a 3-to-8 line decoder. This decoder generates all of the minterms of the 3 input variables. Exactly one of the output lines will be 1 for each combination of values of the input variables.

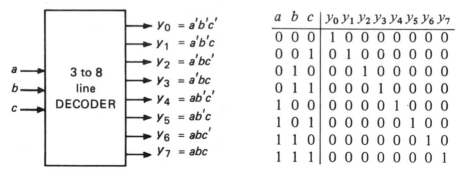

a b c	y_0 y_1 y_2 y_3 y_4 y_5 y_6 y_7
0 0 0	1 0 0 0 0 0 0 0
0 0 1	0 1 0 0 0 0 0 0
0 1 0	0 0 1 0 0 0 0 0
0 1 1	0 0 0 1 0 0 0 0
1 0 0	0 0 0 0 1 0 0 0
1 0 1	0 0 0 0 0 1 0 0
1 1 0	0 0 0 0 0 0 1 0
1 1 1	0 0 0 0 0 0 0 1

$y_0 = a'b'c'$
$y_1 = a'b'c$
$y_2 = a'bc'$
$y_3 = a'bc$
$y_4 = ab'c'$
$y_5 = ab'c$
$y_6 = abc'$
$y_7 = abc$

Fig. 9-16. 3-to-8 line decoder

Figure 9-17 illustrates a 4-to-10 line decoder. This decoder has inverted outputs* (indicated by the small circles). For each combination of values of the inputs, exactly one of the output lines will be 0. When a binary-coded-decimal digit is used as an input to this decoder, one of the output lines will go low to indicate which of the 10 decimal digits is present.

In general, an n-to-2^n line decoder generates all 2^n minterms (or max-terms) of the n input variables. The outputs are defined by the equations

$$y_i = m_i, i = 0 \text{ to } 2^n-1 \qquad \text{(non-inverted outputs)} \tag{9-7}$$

$$\text{or} \quad y_i = m_i' = M_i, i = 0 \text{ to } 2^n-1 \quad \text{(inverted outputs)} \tag{9-8}$$

where m_i is a minterm of the n input variables and M_i is a maxterm.

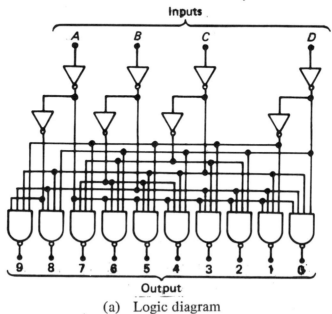

(a) Logic diagram

Fig. 9-17. 4-to-10 line decoder

---
*Most standard integrated circuit decoders, including the type 7442 illustrated in Fig. 9-17, have inverted outputs.

(b) Block diagram

BCD input	decimal output
A B C D	0 1 2 3 4 5 6 7 8 9
0 0 0 0	0 1 1 1 1 1 1 1 1 1
0 0 0 1	1 0 1 1 1 1 1 1 1 1
0 0 1 0	1 1 0 1 1 1 1 1 1 1
0 0 1 1	1 1 1 0 1 1 1 1 1 1
0 1 0 0	1 1 1 1 0 1 1 1 1 1
0 1 0 1	1 1 1 1 1 0 1 1 1 1
0 1 1 0	1 1 1 1 1 1 0 1 1 1
0 1 1 1	1 1 1 1 1 1 1 0 1 1
1 0 0 0	1 1 1 1 1 1 1 1 0 1
1 0 0 1	1 1 1 1 1 1 1 1 1 0
1 0 1 0	1 1 1 1 1 1 1 1 1 1
1 0 1 1	1 1 1 1 1 1 1 1 1 1
1 1 0 0	1 1 1 1 1 1 1 1 1 1
1 1 0 1	1 1 1 1 1 1 1 1 1 1
1 1 1 0	1 1 1 1 1 1 1 1 1 1
1 1 1 1	1 1 1 1 1 1 1 1 1 1

(c) Truth table

Fig. 9-17. **4-to-10 line decoder (cont.)**

Since an n-input decoder generates all of the minterms of n variables, n-variable functions can be realized by ORing together selected minterm outputs from a decoder. If the decoder outputs are inverted, then NAND gates can be used to generate the functions as illustrated in the following example. Realize

$$f_1(a, b, c, d) = m_1 + m_2 + m_4 \text{ and } f_2(a, b, c, d) = m_4 + m_7 + m_9$$

using the decoder of Fig. 9-17. Rewriting f_1 and f_2, we have

$$f_1 = (m_1' m_2' m_4')' \qquad f_2 = (m_4' m_7' m_9')'$$

Then f_1 and f_2 can be generated using NAND gates as shown in Fig. 9-18.

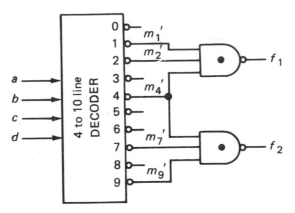

Fig. 9-18.   Realization of a multiple-output network using a decoder

9.6   Read-Only Memories

A read-only memory (ROM) is an LSI circuit which consists of an array of semiconductor devices (diodes, bipolar transistors or field-effect transistors) which are interconnected to store an array of binary data. Once binary data is stored in the ROM, it can be read out whenever desired, but the data which is stored cannot be changed under normal operating conditions. Figure 9-19(a) shows a ROM which has 3 input lines and 4 output lines. Figure 9-19(b) shows a typical truth table which relates the ROM inputs and outputs.

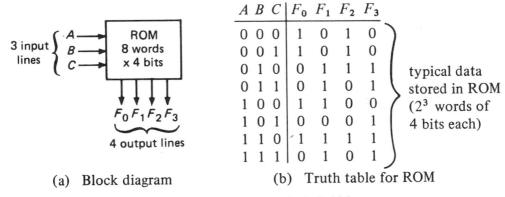

A	B	C	F_0	F_1	F_2	F_3
0	0	0	1	0	1	0
0	0	1	1	0	1	0
0	1	0	0	1	1	1
0	1	1	0	1	0	1
1	0	0	1	1	0	0
1	0	1	0	0	0	1
1	1	0	1	1	1	1
1	1	1	0	1	0	1

typical data
stored in ROM
(2^3 words of
4 bits each)

(a) Block diagram   (b) Truth table for ROM

Fig. 9-19.   8 word X 4 bit ROM

For each combination of input values on the 3 input lines, the corresponding pattern of 0's and 1's appears on the ROM output lines. For example, if the combination $ABC = 010$ is applied to the input lines, the pattern $F_0F_1F_2F_3 = 0111$ appears on the output lines. Each of the output patterns which is stored in the ROM is called a *word*. Since the ROM has 3 input lines, we have $2^3 = 8$ different combinations of input values. Each input combination serves as an *address* which can select one of the 8 words stored in the memory. Since there are 4 output lines, each word is 4 bits long, and the size of this ROM is 8 words X 4 bits.

A ROM which has n input lines and m output lines (Fig. 9-20) contains an array of 2^n words, and each word is m bits long. The input lines serve as an address to select one of the 2^n words. When an input combination is applied to the ROM, the pattern of 0's and 1's which is stored in the corresponding word in the memory appears at the output lines. For the example in Fig. 9-20, if 00 . . . 11 is applied to the input (address lines) of the ROM, the word 110 . . 010 will be selected and transferred to the output lines. A $2^n \times m$ ROM can realize m functions of n variables since it can store a truth table with 2^n rows and m columns. Typical sizes for commercially available ROMs range from 32 words $\times$ 4 bits to 2048 $\times$ 8 bits.

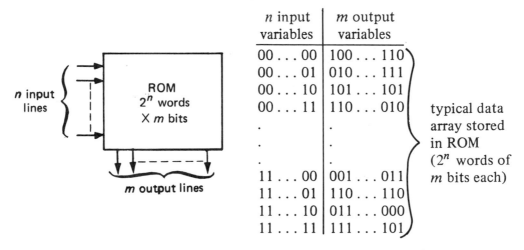

n input variables	m output variables
00 . . . 00	100 . . . 110
00 . . . 01	010 . . . 111
00 . . . 10	101 . . . 101
00 . . . 11	110 . . . 010
.	.
.	.
.	.
11 . . . 00	001 . . . 011
11 . . . 01	110 . . . 110
11 . . . 10	011 . . . 000
11 . . . 11	111 . . . 101

typical data array stored in ROM (2^n words of m bits each)

Fig. 9-20. **Read-only memory with n inputs and m outputs**

A ROM basically consists of a decoder and a memory array as shown in Fig. 9-21. When a pattern of n 0's and 1's is applied to the decoder inputs, exactly one of the 2^n decoder outputs is 1. This decoder output line selects one of the words in the memory array, and the bit pattern stored in this word is transferred to the memory output lines.

Fig. 9-21. **Basic ROM structure**

Figure 9-22 illustrates the internal structure of the 8 word × 4 bit ROM shown in Fig. 9-19. The decoder generates the 8 minterms of the 3 input variables. The memory array forms the 4 output functions by ORing together selected minterms. A switching element* is placed at the intersection of a "word line" and an "output line" if the corresponding minterm is to be included in the output function; otherwise, the switching element is omitted. The switching elements which are connected in this way in the memory array effectively form an OR gate for each of the output functions. For example, m_0, m_1, m_4 and m_6 are ORed together to form F_0. Figure 9-23 shows the equivalent OR gate. In general, those minterms which are connected to output line F_i by switching elements are ORed together to form the output F_i. Thus, the ROM in Fig. 9-22 generates the following functions:

$$F_0 = \Sigma m(0, 1, 4, 6) = A'B' + AC'$$

$$F_1 = \Sigma m(2, 3, 4, 6, 7) = B + AC'$$

$$F_2 = \Sigma m(0, 1, 2, 6) = A'B' + BC' \qquad (9\text{-}9)$$

$$F_3 = \Sigma m(2, 3, 5, 6, 7) = AC + B$$

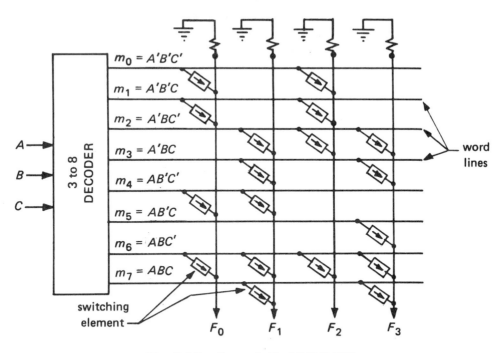

Fig. 9-22. 8-word × 4-bit ROM

---

*Diodes, bipolar transistors or field-effect transistors may be used as switching elements. See Appendix A.

Fig. 9-23.   Equivalent OR gate for F_0

The contents of a ROM is usually specified by a truth table. The truth table of Fig. 9-19(b) specifies the ROM in Fig. 9-22. Note that a 1 or 0 in the output part of the truth table corresponds to the presence or absence of a switching element in the memory array of the ROM.

Multiple-output combinational networks can easily be realized using ROMs. For example, the BCD to excess-3 code conversion network of Fig. 9-7 can be realized using a 4-input, 4-output ROM. The truth table of Fig. 9-7 gives the data to be stored in the first 10 words of the ROM. Since a 4-input ROM has 16 words, the remaining 6 words are don't cares and can be filled with 0's (or 1's). Fig. 9-24 shows an internal diagram of the ROM. The switching elements at the intersections of the rows and columns of the memory array are indicated using dots. A dot indicates that the switching element is present and no dot indicates that the corresponding element is absent.

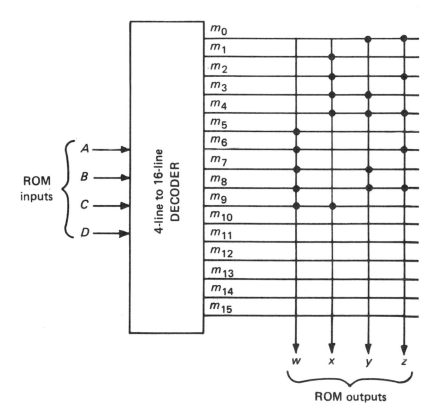

Fig. 9-24.   ROM realization of code converter

Three basic types of ROMs are mask-programmable ROMs, field-programmable ROMs (usually called PROMs) and erasable programmable ROMs (usually called EPROMs). At time of manufacture, the data array is permanently stored in a mask-programmable ROM. This is accomplished by selectively including or omitting the switching elements at the row-column intersections of the memory array. This requires preparation of a special "mask" which is used during fabrication of the integrated circuit. Preparation of this mask is expensive, so use of mask-programmable ROMs is economically feasible only if a large quantity (typically 1000 or more) are required with the same data array.

If only a small quantity of ROMs are required with a given data array, PROMs can be used. PROMs are typically manufactured with all switching elements present in the memory array, but the connection at each row-column intersection is made by means of a fusible link. In order to store data in the PROM, these fusible links are selectively "blown" using appropriate voltage pulses supplied by special equipment called a PROM programmer. Once the links are blown, the data is permanently stored in the memory array.

During developmental phases of a digital system, it is often necessary to modify the data stored in a ROM. To avoid the expense of using a new PROM each time the data must be changed, EPROMs may be used. Instead of fusible links, EPROMs use a special charge-storage mechanism to enable or disable the switching elements in the memory array. In this case, the PROM programmer provides appropriate voltage pulses to store electronic charges in the memory array locations. The data stored in this manner is generally permanent until it is erased using an ultraviolet light. After erasure, a new set of data can be stored in the EPROM.

9.7 Programmable Logic Arrays

A programmable logic array (PLA) performs the same basic function as a ROM. A PLA with n inputs and m outputs (Fig. 9-25) can realize m functions of n variables. The internal organization of the PLA is different from that of the

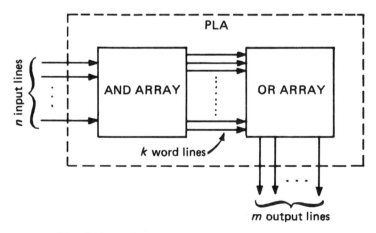

Fig. 9-25. **Programmable logic array structure**

ROM. The decoder is replaced with an AND array which realizes selected product terms of the input variables. The OR-array ORs together the product terms needed to form the output functions.

Figure 9-26 shows a PLA which realizes the same functions as the ROM of Fig. 9-22. Product terms are formed in the AND array by connecting switching elements* at appropriate points in the array. For example, to form $A'B'$, switching elements are used to connect the first word line with the A' and B' lines. Switching elements are connected in the OR array to select the product terms needed for the output functions. For example, since $F_0 = A'B' + AC'$, switching elements are used to connect the $A'B'$ and AC' lines to the F_0 line. The connections in the AND and OR arrays of this PLA make it equivalent to the AND-OR array of Fig. 9-27.

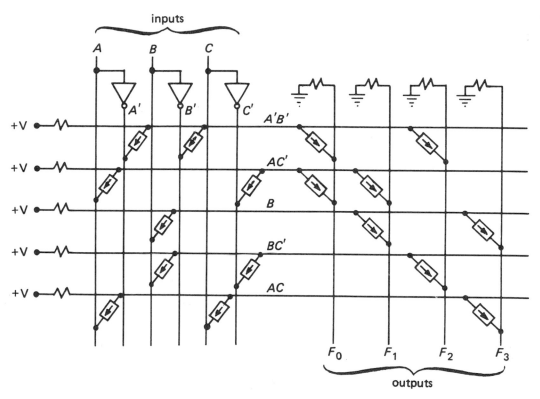

Fig. 9-26. PLA with 3 inputs, 5 product terms, 4 outputs

---

*Either the AND function or OR function may be realized by the switching elements depending on the manner in which they are connected. For example, see the discussion of diode gates in Appendix A.1.

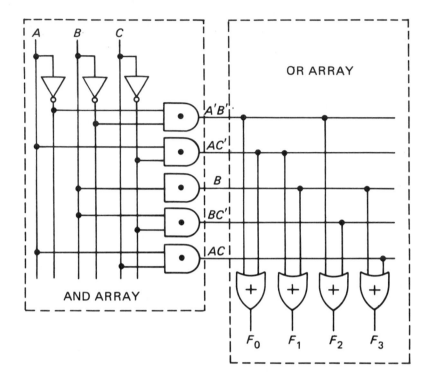

Fig. 9-27. AND-OR array equivalent to Fig. 9-26

The contents of a PLA can be specified by a modified truth table. Table 9-1 specifies the PLA in Fig. 9-26. The input side of the table specifies the product terms. The symbols 0, 1, and − indicate whether a variable is complemented, not complemented, or not present in the corresponding product term. The output side of the table specifies which product terms appear in each output function. A 1 or 0 indicates whether a given product term is present or not present in the corresponding output function. Thus, the first row of Table 9-1 indicates that the term $A'B'$ is present in output functions F_0 and F_2, and the second row indicates that AC' is present in F_0 and F_1.

Table 9-1. PLA Table for Fig. 9-26

product term	inputs A B C	outputs F_0 F_1 F_2 F_3
$A'B'$	0 0 −	1 0 1 0
AC'	1 − 0	1 1 0 0
B	− 1 −	0 1 0 1
BC'	− 1 0	0 0 1 0
AC	1 − 1	0 0 0 1

$$F_0 = A'B' + AC'$$
$$F_1 = AC' + B$$
$$F_2 = A'B' + BC'$$
$$F_3 = B + AC$$

Next we will realize Equations (9-2) using a PLA. Using the minimum multiple output solution given in Equations (9-2b), we can construct a PLA table, Fig. 9-28(a), with one row for each distinct product term. Figure 9-28(b) shows the corresponding PLA structure, which has 4 inputs, 6 product terms and 3 outputs. A dot at the intersection of a word line and an input or output line indicates the presence of a switching element in the array.

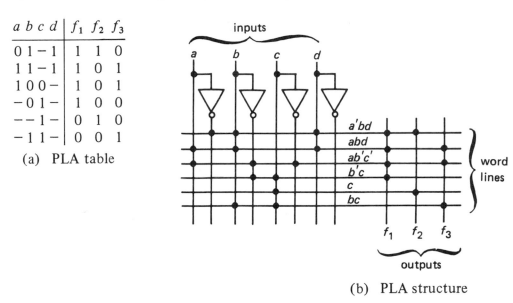

$a\ b\ c\ d$	f_1	f_2	f_3
$0\ 1\ -\ 1$	1	1	0
$1\ 1\ -\ 1$	1	0	1
$1\ 0\ 0\ -$	1	0	1
$-\ 0\ 1\ -$	1	0	0
$-\ -\ 1\ -$	0	1	0
$-\ 1\ 1\ -$	0	0	1

(a) PLA table

(b) PLA structure

Fig. 9-28.. PLA realization of Equations (9-2b)

A PLA table is significantly different than a truth table for a ROM. In a truth table each row represents a minterm; therefore, exactly one row will be selected by each combination of input values. The 0's and 1's of the output portion of the selected row determine the corresponding output values. On the other hand, each row in a PLA table represents a general product term. Therefore, zero, one, or more rows may be selected by each combination of input values. To determine the value of f_i for a given input combination, the values of f_i in the selected rows of the PLA table must be ORed together. The following examples refer to the PLA table of Fig. 9-28(a). If $abcd = 0001$, no rows are selected, and all f_i's are 0. If $abcd = 1001$, only the third row is selected, and $f_1 f_2 f_3 = 101$. If $abcd = 0111$, the first, fifth, and sixth rows are selected. Therefore, $f_1 = 1 + 0 + 0 = 1$, $f_2 = 1 + 1 + 0 = 1$ and $f_3 = 0 + 0 + 1 = 1$.

Both mask-programmable and field-programmable PLAs are available. The mask-programmable type is programmed at the time of manufacture in a manner similar to mask-programmable ROMs. The field-programmable logic array (FPLA) has fusible links which can be blown to store a pattern in the AND and OR arrays. A typical FPLA has 16 inputs, 48 product terms and 8 outputs.

When the number of input variables is small, a ROM is generally more economical to use than a PLA. However, when the number of input variables is large, PLAs often provide a more economical solution than ROMs. For example, to realize 8 functions of 16 variables would require a ROM with 65,536 8-bit words. Since ROMs of this size are not readily available, the functions would have to be decomposed so that they could be realized using a number of smaller ROMs. The same 8 functions of 16 variables could easily be realized using a single PLA provided that the total number of product terms is small. If more terms are required, the outputs of several PLAs can be ORed together.

9.8 Programmable Array Logic (PAL)

The PAL (programmable array logic) is a special case of the programmable logic array in which the AND array is programmable and the OR array is fixed. The basic structure of the PAL is the same as the PLA shown in Fig. 9-25. Because only the AND array is programmable, the PAL is less expensive than the more general PLA, and the PAL is easier to program. For this reason, logic designers frequently use PALs to replace individual logic gates when several logic functions must be realized.

Figure 9-29(a) represents a segment of an unprogrammed PAL. The symbol

represents an input buffer which is logically equivalent to

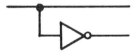

A buffer is used since each PAL input must drive many AND gate inputs. When the PAL is programmed, the fusible links $(F_1, F_2, \cdots F_6)$ are selectively blown to leave the desired connections to the AND gate inputs. Connections to the AND gate inputs in a PAL are represented by X's as shown below:

As example, we will use the PAL segment of Fig. 29(a) to realize the function $I_1 I_2' + I_1' I_2$. The X's indicate that the I_1 and I_2' lines are connected to the first AND gate, and the I_1' and I_2 lines are connected to the other gate (see Fig. 9-29(b)).

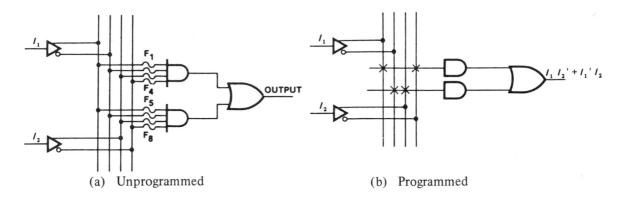

(a) Unprogrammed   (b) Programmed

Fig. 9-29. PAL segment

Table 9-2 gives the characteristics of some of the available types of combinational PALs. Figure 9-30 shows the internal logic diagram for a PAL 14L4, which has 14 inputs and 4 outputs. Each of the 4 output NOR gates is driven from 4 AND gates. The 14H4 is identical to the 14L4, except the NOR gates are replaced with OR gates. The 12H6 (Fig. 9-31) has 12 inputs and 6 outputs. Two of the output OR gates are each driven from 4 AND gates, and four of the OR gates are each driven from 2 AND gates. The X's indicate connections to the AND gates which will be explained in the next example.

Table 9-2. Characteristics of Combinational PALs

type no.	no. of inputs	no. of outputs	gate configuration	no. of inputs per OR gate
10H8	10	8	AND-OR	2
12H6	12	6	AND-OR	4, 2, 2, 2, 2, 4
14H4	14	4	AND-OR	4
16H2	16	2	AND-OR	8
16C1	16	1	AND-OR/NOR	16
20C1	20	1	AND-OR/NOR	16
10L8	10	8	AND-NOR	2
12L6	12	6	AND-NOR	4, 2, 2, 2, 2, 4
14L4	14	4	AND-NOR	4
16L2	16	2	AND-NOR	8
12L10	12	10	AND-NOR	2
14L8	14	8	AND-NOR	4, 2, 2, 2, 2, 2, 2, 4
16L6	16	6	AND-NOR	4, 4, 2, 2, 4, 4
18L4	18	4	AND-NOR	4
20L2	20	2	AND-NOR	8
16L8	16	8	AND-NOR	8
20L8	20	8	AND-NOR	8
20L10	20	10	AND-NOR	4

When designing with PALs, we must simplify our logic equations and try to fit them into one (or more) of the available PALs. Unlike the more general PLA, the AND terms cannot be shared among two or more OR gates; therefore, each function to be realized can be simplified by itself without regard to common terms. For a given type of PAL, the number of AND terms that feed each output OR gate is fixed and limited. If the number of AND terms in a simplified function is too large, we may be forced to choose a PAL with more gate inputs and fewer outputs.

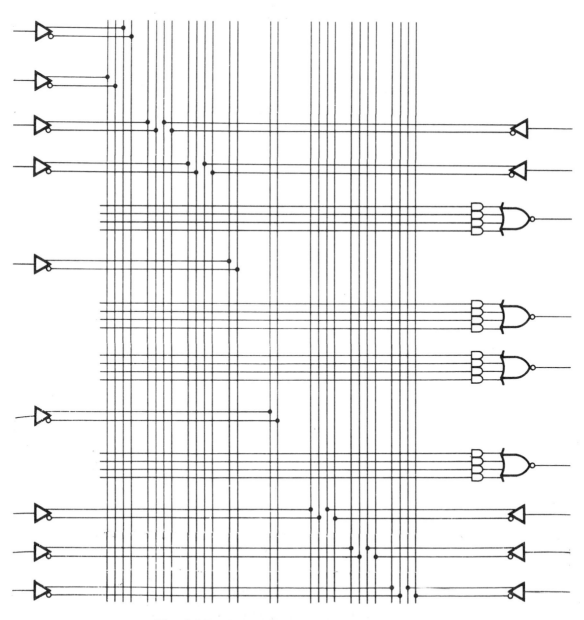

Fig. 9-30. Logic diagram for PAL14L4 (courtesy of Monolithic Memories)

Fig. 9-31. Logic diagram for PAL12H6
(courtesy of Monolithic Memories)

As an example of using a PAL, we will design a network that converts a 4-bit binary number to a hexadecimal digit and outputs the 7-bit ASCII code for the hexadecimal digit. Figure 9-32(a) shows the truth table for the network. Since $A_5 = A_4$ and $A_6 = A_4'$, the PAL only needs to generate 5 functions of 4 variables as shown in Fig. 9-32(b). From Table 9-2, we will tentatively choose a 12H6 or 12L6 PAL, which has 6 outputs and 12 inputs. The next step is to find simplified expressions for the 5 functions using Karnaugh maps, as shown in Fig. 9-33. It appears that the network will not fit in a 12H6 since two of the functions have 3 AND terms and one function has 4 AND terms. One possible solution is to use a 12L6. Since it has inverted outputs, we must start with the functions A_4', A_3', A_2', A_1' and A_0'. Two of these functions require 4 ANDs, and one requires 3 ANDs, so it appears that we cannot use a 12L6 either. Going back to the 12H6, observe that there is one unused output. We can rewrite the equation for A_2 as

$$A_2 = W'X + (XZ + XY) = W'X + B, \text{ where } B = XZ + XY$$

We can then use the extra PAL output to generate B and connect B to one of the PAL inputs as shown in Fig. 9-32(b). In this way, we can generate all 5 functions with a single PAL and no external logic. The X's on the diagram (Fig. 9-31) indicate the variables which are connected to the AND-gate inputs in the PAL. An X inside an AND gate indicates that the gate is not used.

input WXYZ	hex digit	A_6	A_5	A_4	A_3	A_2	A_1	A_0
0000	0	0	1	1	0	0	0	0
0001	1	0	1	1	0	0	0	1
0010	2	0	1	1	0	0	1	0
0011	3	0	1	1	0	0	1	1
0100	4	0	1	1	0	1	0	0
0101	5	0	1	1	0	1	0	1
0110	6	0	1	1	0	1	1	0
0111	7	0	1	1	0	1	1	1
1000	8	0	1	1	1	0	0	0
1001	9	0	1	1	1	0	0	1
1010	A	1	0	0	0	0	0	1
1011	B	1	0	0	0	0	1	0
1100	C	1	0	0	0	0	1	1
1101	D	1	0	0	0	1	0	0
1110	E	1	0	0	0	1	0	1
1111	F	1	0	0	0	1	1	0

The header "ASCII code for hex digit" spans columns A_6 through A_0.

(a) Truth Table

(b) Network

Fig. 9-32. Binary to ASCII converter

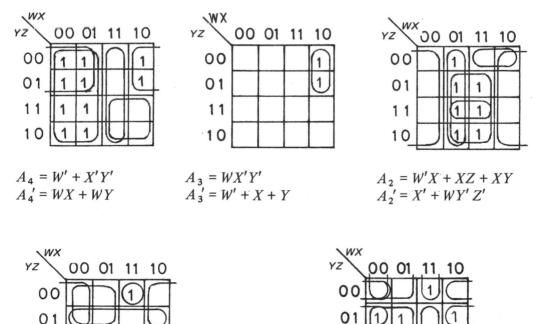

$A_4 = W' + X'Y'$
$A_4' = WX + WY$

$A_3 = WX'Y'$
$A_3' = W' + X + Y$

$A_2 = W'X + XZ + XY$
$A_2' = X' + WY'Z'$

$A_1 = WXY'Z' + YZ + W'Y$
$A_1' = W'Y' + Y'Z + X'Y' + WYZ'$

$A_0 = W'Z + X'Y'Z + WXZ' + WYZ'$
$A_0' = W'Z' + WYZ + WXZ + X'Y'Z'$

Fig. 9-33. Karnaugh maps for binary to ASCII converter

PROBLEMS

9.1   Find a two-level AND-OR gate network to realize

$$f_1 = a'c + a'd' + b'c$$

and $f_2 = c'd' + ab' + ac'$

Minimize the required number of gates. (6 gates)

9.2   Find a minimum two-level multiple-output AND-OR gate network to realize these functions. (11 gates minimum)

$$f_1(A, B, C, D) = \Sigma m(4, 5, 10, 11, 12)$$

$$f_2(A, B, C, D) = \Sigma m(0, 1, 3, 4, 8, 11)$$

$$f_3(A, B, C, D) = \Sigma m(0, 4, 10, 12, 14)$$

9.3 Find a minimum two-level multiple-output AND-OR gate network to realize these functions. (8 gates minimum)

$$f_1(a, b, c, d) = \Sigma m(0, 2, 9, 10) + d(1, 8, 13)$$

$$f_2(a, b, c, d) = \Sigma m(1, 3, 5, 13) + d(0, 7, 9)$$

$$f_3(a, b, c, d) = \Sigma m(2, 8, 10, 11, 13) + d(3, 9, 15)$$

9.4 Design a network of AND and OR gates to convert from excess-3 code to 8-4-2-1 BCD code.

9.5 Find a minimum two-level OR-AND network to realize the functions given in Equations (9-2) on p. 194. (9 gates minimum)

9.6 a. Find a minimum 2-level NAND-NAND network to realize the functions given in Equations (9-2) on p. 194.

b. Find a minimum 2-level NOR-NOR network to realize the functions given in Equations (9-2).

9.7 a. Show how two 2-to-1 multiplexers (with no added gates) could be connected to form a 3-to-1 MUX. Input selection should be as follows:

if $AB = 00$, select I_0

if $AB = 01$, select I_1

if $AB = 1-$ (B is don't care), select I_2

b. Show how two 16-to-1 and one 2-to-1 multiplexers could be connected to form a 32-to-1 MUX with 5 control inputs.

9.8 a. Realize the function of Fig. 6-18 using an 8-to-1 MUX with control inputs A, C and D.

b. Repeat part a using a 4-to-1 MUX. Select the control inputs to minimize the number of added gates.

9.9 Realize a BCD to excess-3 code converter (Fig. 9-7) using a 4-to-10 line decoder (Fig. 9-17) and 4 NAND gates.

9.10 The internal connection diagram for a PLA is given below.

a. Write the equations realized by the PLA.

b. Specify the truth table for a ROM which would realize the same functions as the PLA.

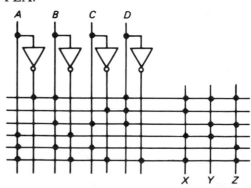

9.11 a An adder for 8 4 2 1 binary-coded decimal digits is to be designed
using a ROM. The adder should add two BCD digits to give the BCD
sum and a carry. For example, $0111 + 0110 = 0011$ with a carry of
1 ($7 + 6 = 13$). Draw a block diagram showing the required ROM inputs
and outputs. What size ROM is required? Indicate how the truth table
for the ROM would be specified by giving some typical rows.

b. If the same adder were implemented using a PLA, what size PLA would
be required? (Assume that only the 10 legal BCD digits can occur as
inputs.)

9.12 Implement your solution to Problem 9.2 using a PLA. Specify the PLA
table and draw the internal connection diagram for the PLA using dots to
indicate the presence of switching elements.

9.13 Realize the function of Problem 6.11
a. using a 16-to-1 MUX
b. using an 8-to-1 MUX with added gates.

9.14 a. Find a minimum 2-level NAND-NAND network to realize
$f_1(a, b, c, d) = \Sigma m(3, 6, 7, 11, 13, 14, 15)$ and $f_2(a, b, c, d) = \Sigma m(3, 4,$
$6, 11, 12, 13, 14)$.
b. Repeat for a minimum 2-level NOR-NOR network.

9.15 Using a PAL14L4, design a code converter that accepts as input the last five
bits of the ASCII code for a hexadecimal number and outputs the
corresponding 4-bit binary code. For example, if the input is 00101, the
output is 1110 (E in hex). Assume that the ASCII codes that do not
represent hex digits will never occur as inputs. Note that the PAL14L4
uses AND-NOR logic. Mark X's on a copy of the PAL logic diagram to
indicate the required fuse pattern.

9.16 A network has four inputs $RSTU$ and four outputs $VWYZ$. $RSTU$
represents a binary-coded decimal digit. VW represents the quotient and
YZ the remainder when $RSTU$ is divided by 3. Realize the network using

a. A minimum two-level NAND-gate network.

b. A PLA (specify the PLA table).

9.17 Show how a quadruple 3-to-1 multiplexer could be implemented using a
PAL14L4. Each MUX has three separate inputs and two control inputs,
which are common to the four multiplexers. Each MUX works as follows:
When the control inputs are $AB = 01$, input 1 is selected; when $AB = 10$,
input 2 is selected; when $AB = 11$, input 3 is selected. The complement
of the selected input appears at the MUX output. Show the PAL fuse
pattern on a copy of the PAL logic diagram.

9.18 a. Find a minimum two-level OR-AND network to realize

$$f_1 = b'd + a'b' + c'd$$
$$\text{and} \quad f_2 = a'd' + bc' + bd'$$

b. Realize the same functions with a minimum two-level NAND-NAND
network.

10

COMBINATIONAL NETWORK DESIGN

OBJECTIVES

Design, construct and test a multi-output NAND or NOR network.

STUDY GUIDE

1. Obtain your design problem assignment from your instructor or proctor.

2. Study Section 10.1, *Design of Networks with Limited Gate Fan-in.*

   a. If a realization of a switching expression requires too many inputs on one or more gates, what should be done?

   b. Assuming that all variables and their complements are available as inputs and that both AND and OR gates are available, does realizing the complement of an expression take the same number of gates and gate inputs as realizing the original expression?

   c. When designing multiple-output networks with limited gate fan-in, why is the procedure of Section 9.2 of little help?

3. Study Section 10.2, *Review of Combinational Network Design.*

4. Generally, it is possible to redesign a network which has two AND gates cascaded or two OR gates cascaded so that AND and OR gates alternate. If this is not practical, the conversion to a NAND or NOR network by the

techniques of Section 8.5 is still possible by introducing a dummy 1-input OR (AND) gate between the two AND (OR) gates. When the conversion is carried out, the dummy gate becomes an inverter. Try this technique and convert the following network to all NAND gates.

5. Study Section 10.3, *Laboratory Testing.* The following network was designed to realize the function

$$F = [A' + B + C'D][A + B' + (C' + D')(C + D)]$$

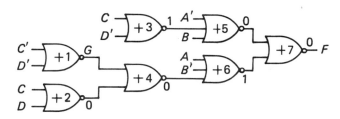

When a student builds the network in lab, he finds that when $A = C = 0$ and $B = D = 1$ the output F has the wrong value and that the gate outputs are as shown above. Determine some possible causes of the incorrect output if $G = 0$ and if $G = 1$.

6. Study your assigned desig.. problem and prepare a design which meets specifications. Note that only 3-input NAND gates (or NOR gates as specified) and inverters are available for this project; therefore, factoring some of the equations will be necessary. Try to make an economical design by using common terms; however, do not waste time trying to get an absolute minimum solution. When counting gates, count both NAND (or NOR) gates and inverters. (Inverters are not needed for the input variables.)

7. Check your design carefully before going to lab. Test it "on paper" by applying some input combinations of 0's and 1's and tracing the signals through to make sure that the outputs are correct. If you wish, ask one of the proctors to look over your design.

8. In designing multi-level, multiple-output circuits of the type used in the design problems in this unit, it is very difficult and time-consuming to find a minimum solution. You are *not* expected to find the best possible solution to these problems. The best known solutions to the design problems in this unit are:

10A.	17 gates and inverters	10D.	13 gates and inverters
10B.	14 gates and inverters	10E.	17 gates and inverters
10C.	13 gates and inverters	10F.	18 gates and inverters

All of these solutions involve some "tricks", and it is unlikely that you could find them without trying a large number of different ways of factoring your equations. Therefore, if you already have an acceptable solution, do *not* waste time trying to find the minimum solution. Since integrated circuit gates are quite inexpensive, it is not good engineering practice to spend a large amount of time finding the absolute minimum solution unless a very large number of units of the same type are to be manufactured.

9. Review the *Laboratory Information unit*, and follow the instructions in Study Guide Part II.

10. COMBINATIONAL NETWORK DESIGN

10.1 Design of Networks with Limited Gate Fan-in

In practical logic design problems, the maximum number of inputs on each gate (or the fan-in) is limited. Depending on the type of gates used, this limit may be 2, 3, 4, 8 or some other number. If a two-level realization of a network requires more gate inputs than allowed, factoring the logic expression to obtain a multi-level realization is necessary.

Example: Realize $f(a, b, c, d) = \Sigma m(0, 3, 4, 5, 8, 9, 10, 14, 15)$ using 3-input NOR gates.

map of f:

$$f' = a'b'c'd + ab'cd + abc' + a'bc + a'cd'$$

As can be seen from the above expression, a two-level realization requires two 4-input gates and one 5-input gate. The expression for f' is factored to reduce the maximum number of gate inputs to 3 and then it is complemented:

$$f' = b'd(a'c' + ac) + a'c(b + d') + abc'$$
$$f = [b + d' + (a + c)(a' + c')] [a + c' + b'd] [a' + b' + c]$$

The resulting NOR-gate network is shown in Fig. 10-1.

Fig. 10-1

The techniques for designing two-level multiple-output networks given in Section 9.2 are not very effective for designing multiple-output networks with more than two levels. Even if the two-level expressions had common terms, most of these common terms would be lost when the expressions were factored. Therefore, when designing multiple-output networks with more than two levels, it is usually best to minimize each function separately. The resulting two-level expressions must then be factored to increase the number of levels. This factoring should be done in such a way as to introduce common terms wherever possible.

Example: Realize f_1, f_2 and f_3 using only 2-input NAND gates and inverters.

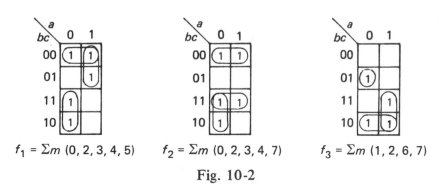

$$f_1 = \Sigma m\ (0, 2, 3, 4, 5) \qquad f_2 = \Sigma m\ (0, 2, 3, 4, 7) \qquad f_3 = \Sigma m\ (1, 2, 6, 7)$$

Fig. 10-2

If we minimize each function separately, the result is

$$f_1 = b'c' + ab' + a'b$$
$$f_2 = b'c' + bc + a'b$$
$$f_3 = a'b'c + ab + bc'$$

Each function requires a 3-input OR-gate, so we will factor to reduce the number of gate inputs:

$$f_1 = b'(a + c') + \underline{a'b}$$
$$f_2 = b(a' + c) + b'c' \quad \text{or} \quad f_2 = (b' + c)(b + c') + \underline{a'b}$$
$$f_3 = a'b'c + b(\underline{a + c'})$$

The second expression for f_2 has a term common to f_1, so we will choose the second expression. We can eliminate the remaining 3-input gate from f_3 by noting that

$$a'b'c = a'(b'c) = a'(b + c')'$$

Figure 10-3(a) shows the resulting network using common terms $a'b$ and $a + c'$. Since each output gate is an OR, conversion to NAND gates, shown in Fig. 10-3(b), is straightforward.

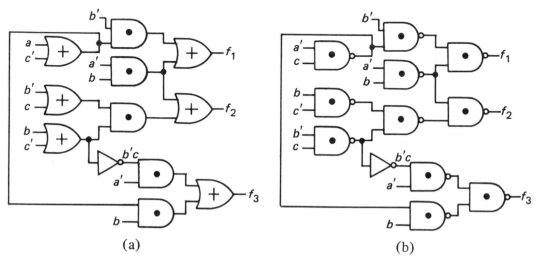

(a)   (b)

Fig. 10-3. Realization of Fig. 10-2

10.2 Review of Combinational Network Design

The first step in the design of a combinational switching network is usually to set up a truth table which specifies the output(s) as a function of the input variables. For n input variables this table will have 2^n rows. If a given combination of values for the input variables can never occur at the network inputs, the corresponding output values are don't cares. The next step is to derive simplified algebraic expressions for the output functions using Karnaugh maps, the Quine-McCluskey procedure, or a similar method. In some cases, particularly if the number of variables is large and the number of terms is small, it may be desirable to go directly from the problem statement to algebraic equations, without writing down a truth table. The resulting equations can then be simplified algebraically. The simplified algebraic expressions are then manipulated into the proper form depending on the type of gates to be used in realizing the network.

The number of levels in a gate network is equal to the maximum number of gates through which a signal must pass going between the input and output terminals. The minimum sum of products (or product of sums) leads directly to a minimum two-level gate network. However, in some applications it is desirable to increase the number of levels by factoring (or multiplying out) because this may lead to a reduction in the number of gates or gate inputs or to a reduction in gate fan-in.

When a network has two or more outputs, common terms in the output functions can often be used to reduce the total number of gates or gate inputs. If each function is minimized separately, this does not always lead to a minimum multiple-output network. For a two-level network, Karnaugh maps of the output functions can be used to find common terms. All of the terms in the minimum multiple-output network will not necessarily be prime implicants of the individual functions. When designing networks with three or more levels, looking for common terms on the Karnaugh maps may be of little value. In this case, the designer will often minimize the functions separately and then use his ingenuity to factor the expressions in such a way to create common terms.

A set of gates which is capable of realizing all switching functions is said to be functionally complete. A set of gates is functionally complete if it can realize AND, OR and NOT. Examples of functionally complete sets are AND and NOT, EXCLUSIVE-OR and AND, NAND, and NOR.

Minimum two-level AND-OR, NAND-NAND, OR-NAND and NOR-OR networks can be realized using the minimum sum of products as a starting point. Minimum two-level OR-AND, NOR-NOR, AND-NOR and NAND-AND networks can be realized using the minimum product of sums as a starting point.

Design of multi-level, multi-output NAND-gate networks is most easily accomplished by first designing a network of AND and OR gates. Usually, the best starting point is the minimum sum-of-products expressions for the output functions. These expressions are then factored in various ways until an economical network of the desired form can be found. If this network has an OR gate at each output and is arranged so that an AND (OR) gate output is never connected directly to an AND (OR) gate input,* direct conversion to a NAND-gate network is possible. Conversion is accomplished by replacing all of the AND and OR gates with NAND gates and then inverting any literals which appear as inputs to the 1st, 3rd, 5th, . . . levels (output gates are the 1st level).

Similarly, design of multi-level, multi-output NOR-gate networks is most easily accomplished by first designing a network of AND and OR gates. In this case the best starting point is usually the minimum sum-of-products expressions for the *complements* of the output functions. *After* factoring these expressions to the desired form, they are then complemented to get expressions for the output functions, and the corresponding network of AND and OR gates is drawn. If this network has an AND gate at each output, and AND (OR) gate outputs are not connected to AND (OR) gate inputs,* direct conversion to a NOR-gate network is possible.

---

*If these conditions are violated, conversion is still possible but extra inverters will have to be added in the conversion process. (See Study Guide question 4.)

10.3 Laboratory Testing

An important part of the design process is verifying that the final design is correct and "debugging" the design if necessary. A combinational logic network with a small number of inputs can easily be tested in lab by checking the output for all possible combinations of values of the input variables. If the network output is wrong for some set of input values, this may be due to several possible causes:

    a.   incorrect design

    b.   gates connected wrong

    c.   defective connecting wire

    d.   wrong input signals to the network

    e.   defective gates

Fortunately, if the output of a combinational logic network is wrong, it is very easy to systematically locate the problem by starting at the output and working back through the network until the trouble is located. For example, if the output gate has the wrong output and its inputs are correct, this indicates that the gate is defective. On the other hand, if one of the inputs is wrong, then either the gate is connected wrong, the gate driving this input has the wrong output, or the input lead is defective.

Example: The function $F = AB(C'D + CD') + A'B'(C + D)$ is realized by the following network:

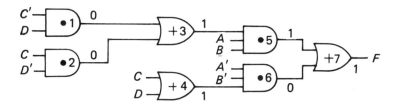

Fig. 10-4. Logic network with incorrect output

When a student builds the network in lab, he finds that when $A = B = C = D = 1$, the output F has the wrong value, and that the gate outputs are as shown in Fig. 10-4. The reason for the incorrect value of F can be determined as follows:

    a.   The output of gate 7 (F) is wrong, but this wrong output is consistent with the inputs to gate 7, i.e., $1 + 0 = 1$. Therefore, one of the inputs to gate 7 must be wrong.

    b.   In order for gate 7 to have the correct output ($F = 0$) both inputs must be 0. Therefore, the output of gate 5 is wrong. However, the output of gate 5 is consistent with its inputs since $1 \cdot 1 \cdot 1 = 1$. Therefore, one of the inputs to gate 5 must be wrong.

c. Either the output of gate 3 is wrong, or the A or B input to gate 5 is wrong. Since $C'D + CD' = 0$, the output of gate 3 is wrong.

d. The output of gate 3 is *not* consistent with the outputs of gates 1 and 2 since $0 + 0 \neq 1$. Therefore, either one of the inputs to gate 3 is connected wrong, gate 3 is defective, or one of the input leads to gate 3 is defective.

The above example illustrates how to find the trouble in a logic network by starting at the output gate and working back until the wrong connection or defective gate is located.

LAB DESIGN PROBLEMS

Seven-Segment Indicator

Several of the lab problems involve the design of a network to drive a 7-segment indicator (See Fig. 10-5). The 7-segment indicator can be used to display any one of the decimal digits 0 through 9. For example, "1" is displayed by lighting segments 2 and 3, "2" by lighting segments 1, 2, 7, 5, and 4, and "8" by lighting all seven segments. A segment is lighted when a logic 1 is applied to the corresponding input on the display module.

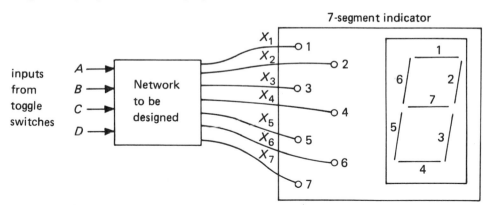

Fig. 10-5. Network driving seven-segment display module

10A. Design an 8-4-2-1 BCD code converter to drive a seven-segment indicator.

The four inputs to the converter network (A, B, C, D in Fig. 10-5) represent an 8-4-2-1 binary-coded decimal digit. Assume that only input combinations representing the digits 0 through 9 can occur as inputs, so that the combinations 1010 through 1111 are don't cares. Design your network using only 2- and 3-input NAND gates and inverters. Try to minimize the number of gates required. The variables A, B, C, and D, will be available from toggle switches.

Use ⟨9⟩ (not ⟨9⟩) for 9. Use ⟨6⟩ (not ⟨6⟩) for 6.

Any solution that uses 21 or fewer gates and inverters (not counting the 4 inverters for the inputs) is acceptable.

10B.   Design an excess-3 code converter to drive a seven-segment indicator.

   The four inputs to the converter network (A, B, C, D in Fig. 10-5) represent an excess-3 coded decimal digit. Assume that only input combinations representing the digits 0 through 9 can occur as inputs, so that the six unused combinations are don't cares. Design your network using only 2- and 3-input NAND gates and inverters. Try to minimize the number of gates and inverters required. The variables A, B, C, and D will be available from toggle switches.

   Use ⌐| (not |⌐|) for 6.   Use ⌐|⌐| (not ⌐|⌐|) for 9.

Any solution with 20 or fewer gates and inverters (not counting the 4 inverters for the inputs) is acceptable.

10C.   Design a circuit which will yield the product of two binary numbers n_2 and m_2, where $00_2 \leqslant n_2 \leqslant 11_2$ and $000_2 \leqslant m_2 \leqslant 101_2$. For example, if $n_2 = 10_2$ and $m_2 = 001_2$, then the product is $n_2 \times m_2 = 10_2 \times 001_2 = 0010_2$.

   Let the variables A and B represent the first and second digits of n_2, respectively (i.e. in the above example $A = 1$ and $B = 0$). Let the variables C, D, and E represent the first, second and third digits of m_2, respectively (in the above example $C = 0$, $D = 0$, and $E = 1$). Also let the variables W, X, Y and Z represent the first, second, third and fourth digits of the product. (In the above example $W = 0$, $X = 0$, $Y = 1$, and $Z = 0$.) Assume that $m_2 > 101_2$ never occurs as a network input.

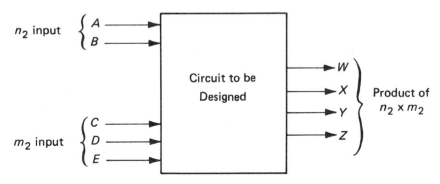

   Design the network using only 2- and 3-input NOR gates and inverters. Try to minimize the total number of gates and inverters required. The variables A, B, C, D, and E will be available from toggle switches. Any solution that uses 16 or fewer gates and inverters (not counting the 5 inverters for the inputs) is acceptable.

10D.   Work Design Problem **10C** using 2- and 3-input NAND gates and inverters instead of NOR gates and inverters. Any solution that uses 16 gates and inverters or less (not counting the 5 inverters for the inputs) is acceptable.

10E. Design a network which multiplies two 2-bit binary numbers and displays the answer in decimal on a 7-segment indicator. In Fig. 10-5, A and B are two bits of a binary number N_1, and C and D are two bits of a binary number N_2. The product $(N_1 \times N_2)$ is to be displayed in decimal by lighting appropriate segments of the 7-segment indicator. For example, if $A = 1$, $B = 0$, $C = 1$, and $D = 0$, the number "4" is displayed by lighting segments 2, 3, 6 and 7.

Use ⑨ (not ⑨) for 9. Use ⑥ (not ⑥) for 6.

Design your network using only 2- and 3-input NAND gates and inverters. Try to minimize the number of gates required. The variables A, B, C, and D will be available from toggle switches. Any solution that uses 23 or fewer gates and inverters (not counting the 4 inverters for the inputs) is acceptable.

10F. Design a Gray code converter to drive a seven-segment indicator.

The four inputs to the converter network (A, B, C, D in Fig. 10-5) represent a decimal digit coded using the Gray code of Table 1.1. Assume that only input combinations representing the digits 0 through 9 can occur as inputs, so that the six unused combinations are don't cares. Design your network using only 2- and 3-input NAND gates and inverters. Try to minimize the numbers of gates and inverters required. The variables A, B, C, and D will be available from toggle switches.

Use ⑥ (not ⑥) for 6. Use ⑨ (not ⑨) for 9.

Any solution with 23 or fewer gates and inverters (not counting the 4 inverters for the inputs) is acceptable.

10G. Design a network that will add either 1 or 2 to a 4-bit binary number N. Let the inputs N_3, N_2, N_1, N_0 represent N. The input K is a control signal. The network should have outputs M_3, M_2, M_1, M_0, which represent the 4-bit binary number M. When $K = 0$, $M = N + 1$. When $K = 1$, $M = N + 2$. Assume that the inputs for which $M > 1111_2$ will never occur.

Design the network using only 2- and 3-input NAND gates and inverters. Try to minimize the total number of gates and inverters required. The input variables K, N_3, N_2, N_1 and N_0 will be available from toggle switches. Any solution that uses 15 or fewer gates and inverters (not counting the 5 inverters for the inputs) is acceptable.

11

REVIEW OF COMBINATIONAL NETWORKS

Before we start the study of sequential switching networks, we will review all of the material on combinational switching networks which we have studied so far. Review of this material is important for two reasons:

a. Review is very important to the learning process. Without adequate review, material once learned is quickly forgotten.

b. Review provides an opportunity for examining the relationship between the various topics which have been studied on an individual basis.

STUDY GUIDE

1. Study the review material (Sections 11.1 through 11.6)*. Refer back to the appropriate study unit if there is anything you do not understand. Also review Section 10.2.

2. Make sure that you understand the meaning of the basic terminology, such as:

minterm	minterm expansion (standard sum of products)
maxterm	maxterm expansion (standard product of sums)
product of sums	minimum product of sums
sum of products	minimum sum of products
prime implicant	essential prime implicant
don't care term	

3. You should be able to go from a word statement of a problem to a truth table, Karnaugh map, minterm and maxterm expansions, minimum product of sums and minimum sum of products, and various types of gate networks.

---

*Omit Section 11.5 and Problem 11.5(d) if you did not study Unit 7.

4. Review the objectives, study questions and problems for each unit. Make sure that you can meet the objectives of each unit.

5. Work the review problems. Try to work rapidly and keep track of the time it takes you to work each problem. Typical times are Problem 11.1—10 min., 11.2—10 min., 11.3—20 min., 11.4—25 min., 11.5—35 min., 11.6—10 min., and 11.7—15 min. If it takes you substantially longer than this to get the correct answers, you are probably not adequately prepared for the review quiz and should spend more time reviewing.

6. Take the *Review Quiz*. The *Review Quiz* will consist of 3 or 4 problems selected from material in different units. (Different forms of the review test will include material from different units.)

11. REVIEW OF COMBINATIONAL NETWORKS

11.1 Number Systems

A number written in base R is easily converted to base 10 by adding up powers of R, doing the arithmetic in decimal:

$$(a_n \ldots a_2 a_1 a_0 \cdot a_{-1} \ldots a_{-m})_R = a_n R^n + \ldots + a_2 R^2 + a_1 R^1 + a_0$$
$$+ a_{-1} R^{-1} + a_{-2} R^{-2} + \ldots + a_{-m} R^{-m}$$

Conversion from decimal to base R is done separately on the integer and fractional parts of the number. To convert the integer, divide it by R and save the remainder as the least significant digit in the answer. Then divide the quotient by R, and the remainder is the next digit in the answer, etc. To convert the fractional part, multiply it by R to obtain an integer and a fraction; the integer is the most significant digit of the fractional part of the base R number. Multiply the new fraction by R and save the integer part of the result as the next digit in the answer, etc. Conversion between binary and octal is easy because each octal digit corresponds to exactly three binary digits. Similarly, conversion between binary and hexadecimal requires division of the binary number into groups of four bits.

11.2 Boolean Algebra and Algebraic Simplification

The basic mathematics used in the analysis of switching networks is Boolean algebra. Two-valued variables are used since most logic networks use switching elements which can assume only two states. The commutative, associative and distributive laws of ordinary algebra also apply to Boolean algebra (with OR taking the place of addition and AND taking the place of multiplication). In Boolean algebra, there is a second distributive law

$$X + YZ = (X + Y)(X + Z)$$

which is used in conjunction with the ordinary distributive law for factoring and multiplying out Boolean expressions. The theorem

$$XY + X'Z = (X + Z)(X' + Y)$$

is also used for factoring and multiplying out. The complement of a Boolean expression is formed by replacing AND with OR, OR with AND, 0 with 1, 1 with 0, and each variable with its complement. The dual is formed in the same way except that the variables are not replaced with their complements.

Algebraic simplification of a Boolean expression can be accomplished by applying the following theorems in addition to multiplying out and factoring:

a. Use $XY + XY' = X$ to combine terms.

b. Use $X + XY = X$ or $XY + X'Z + YZ = XY + X'Z$ (consensus theorem) to eliminate terms.

c. Use $X + X'Y = X + Y$ to eliminate literals.

In some cases, redundant terms must be added before simplification can be accomplished. If the expression is in product-of-sums form, the duals of the above theorems can be used.

Exclusive-OR and equivalence operations can be eliminated from an expression by using

$$X \oplus Y = XY' + X'Y \text{ and } (X \equiv Y) = XY + X'Y'$$

When manipulating such expressions it is useful to note that

$$(XY + X'Y')' = (X' + Y')(X + Y) = XY' + X'Y$$

11.3 Minterm and Maxterm Expansions

Every Boolean function has a unique representation as a sum of minterms and as a product of maxterms. A minterm of n variables is a product of all n variables with each variable either in true or complemented form. Similarly, a maxterm is a sum of all n variables with each variable in either true or complemented form. Each minterm has a value of 1 for exactly one combination of values of the variables; thus the minterm expansion of F contains one minterm for each row of the truth table for which F is 1. Similarly, each maxterm has a value of 0 for exactly one combination of values of the variables, so the maxterm expansion of F contains one maxterm for each row of the truth table for which F is 0.

Minterm and maxterm expansions are often written in abbreviated form using decimal notation. For example, consider m_{11} to be a 5-variable minterm. Then $m_{11} = 1$ iff $abcde = 01011$, so $m_{11} = a'bc'de$. Similarly, if M_{11} is a 5-variable maxterm, $M_{11} = 0$ iff $abcde = 01011$, so $M_{11} = a + b' + c + d' + e'$. Note that $M_{11} = m_{11}'$. Given the minterm expansion of F in decimal notation, the maxterm expansion of F is found by listing the appropriate decimal numbers not in the minterm list.

11.4 Karnaugh Maps

Karnaugh maps are most useful for simplifying functions of 3 to 6 variables. Terms in adjacent squares on the map differ in only one variable and thus can be combined using $XY + XY' = X$. A group of 1, 2, 4, 8, etc. adjacent minterms represents a prime implicant if it cannot be combined with an adjacent group of the same size to eliminate another variable. To find the minimum sum of products of F using a map,

  a. Plot the 1's and don't cares of F on the map.
  b. Determine the essential prime implicants (see Fig. 6-19). Each essential prime implicant contains a 1 which is not included in any other prime implicant.
  c. Choose a minimum set of prime implicants to cover the remaining 1's on the map.

The minimum sum-of-products form for F' can be obtained by the same procedure except that the 0's of F are used instead of the 1's. Then the minimum product of sums for F is easily formed by complementing the minimum sum-of-products form for F'.

11.5   Quine-McCluskey Procedure

The Quine-McCluskey procedure determines a minimum sum-of-products representation of a function starting with its minterm expansion (or truth table). The terms are represented in 0, 1, – notation. The minterms are systematically combined to form a set of prime implicants by repeated application of the theorem $XY + XY' = X$. To reduce the number of pairs of terms which must be compared, the minterms are initially sorted into groups according to the number of 1's in the binary representation. Pairs of terms from adjacent groups are compared and if a pair of terms differs in exactly one column (one term has a 0 and the other has a 1) the corresponding variable is eliminated (replaced with a dash). When no further terms can be combined, the remaining terms are prime implicants. Each prime implicant is formed by combining minterms, and no more literals can be eliminated from it by combining it with other minterms.

A prime implicant chart is then used to find the minimum sum of products by selecting a minimum set of prime implicants which cover all of the minterms. The chart is set up with minterms listed across the top and prime implicants down the side. An "X" placed at the intersection of a row and column indicates that the corresponding prime implicant covers the corresponding minterm. If a column contains only one "X", the corresponding minterm is covered by only one prime implicant. That prime implicant is *essential* and must be included in the minimum sum. After all of the essential prime implicants have been chosen (and the corresponding rows and columns eliminated from the chart), a minimum set of prime implicants which cover the remaining minterms is selected.

The minimum sum of products obtained in this manner thus contains a minimum number of terms (prime implicants) and no term can be replaced with a term which contains fewer literals. The minimum sum of products thus corresponds to a minimum two-level gate network with a minimum number of gates and a minimum number of inputs for each gate.

If the function is incompletely specified because some combinations of the variables can never occur as network inputs, don't care terms will be present in the minterm expansion. The don't cares are treated just like the other minterms when finding the prime implicants. However, the don't cares are not included in the prime implicant chart because selection of prime implicants to cover the don't cares is unnecessary.

11.6 Multiplexers, Decoders, ROMs and PLAs

A 2^n-to-1 multiplexer has n control inputs and 2^n data inputs. Each combination of values applied to the control inputs selects one of the data inputs, and the corresponding input value is transmitted to the multiplexer output. A 2^n-to-1 multiplexer can realize any function of $n + 1$ variables. Each combination of values of the n control variables determines a "patch" on the $n + 1$ variable Karnaugh map of the function. The value of the corresponding data input can be read from this "patch".

An n-input decoder generates some (or all) of the minterms (or maxterms) of the n input variables. For example, a 3-to-8 line decoder has exactly one of its 8 outputs equal to 1 for each combination of values applied to its 3 inputs.

A read-only memory (ROM) with n inputs and m outputs can generate any m functions of n variables. The size of this ROM is 2^n words by m bits. Each of the 2^n combinations of values of the n input variables forms an address which selects one of the 2^n words in the memory array, and the pattern of 0's and 1's stored in this word is transmitted to the ROM outputs.

A programmable logic array (PLA) with n inputs, k word lines and m outputs can realize any m functions of n variables, provided that the total number of product terms required does not exceed k. The PLA consists of an AND array interconnected with an OR array. Switching elements in the AND array are used to realize a set of product terms of the n input variables. Switching elements in the OR array then OR together selected product terms to form the m output functions. A PLA table can be used to specify the contents of a PLA. The following table represents a PLA with 3 inputs, 4 product terms and 2 outputs:

A	B	C	X	Y
0	–	1	1	0
1	0	–	1	1
1	–	0	0	1
0	1	0	1	0

The AND array generates the product terms $A'C$, AB', AC' and $A'BC'$. The output functions are $X = A'C + AB' + A'BC'$ and $Y = AB' + AC'$.

The PAL (programmable array logic) is a special type of PLA with a programmable AND array that provides inputs to a fixed array of OR gates. PALs that have up to 20 input variables and 10 output variables are currently available.

REVIEW PROBLEMS

11.1 Convert to hexadecimal and then to binary: $(544.1)_9$

11.2 Simplify to a sum of two terms; then factor the result to obtain a product of sums.

$$abd'f' + b'cegh' + abd'f + acd'e + b'ce$$

11.3 A combinational switching network has 4 inputs and one output as shown. $F = 0$ iff 3 or 4 of the inputs are 0.

    a. Write the maxterm expansion for F.

    b. Using AND and OR gates, find a minimum 3-level network to realize F. (5 gates, 12 inputs)

11.4 a. Find a minimum two-level NOR gate network to realize F_1 and F_2. Use as many common gates as possible.

$$F_1(a, b, c, d) = \Sigma m(1, 2, 4, 5, 6, 8, 10, 12, 14)$$
$$F_2(a, b, c, d) = \Sigma m(2, 4, 6, 8, 10, 11, 12, 14, 15)$$

    b. Realize F_1 and F_2 using a PLA. Give the PLA table and internal connection diagram for the PLA.

11.5 Given that $f(a, b, c, d, e) = \Sigma m(6, 7, 9, 11, 12, 13, 16, 17, 18, 20, 21, 23, 25, 28)$, using a Karnaugh map,

    a. Find the essential prime implicants. (3)

    b. Find the minimum sum of products. (7 terms)

    c. Find *all* of the prime implicants. (12)

    d. Check your answers using the Quine-McCluskey procedure.

    e. Realize f using a 16-to-1 MUX with no added gates.

11.6 a. Show that $x \oplus y = (x \equiv y)'$.

    b. Realize $a'b'c' + a'bc + ab'c + abc'$ using only 2-input equivalence gates.

11.7 Simplify the following expression first by using a map and then by using Boolean algebra. Use the map as a guide to determine which theorems to apply to which terms for the algebraic simplification.

$$F = a'b'c' + a'c'd + bcd + abc + ab'$$

11.8 Multiply out and simplify to obtain a sum-of-products expression with 3 terms:

$$(a + c)(b' + d)(a + c' + d')(b' + c' + d')$$

11.9 Factor and simplify to obtain a product-of-sums expression with 4 terms:

$$abc' + d'e + ace + b'c'd'$$

11.10 Braille is a system which allows a blind person to "read" alphanumerics by feeling a pattern of raised dots. Design a network that converts BCD to Braille. The table shows the correspondence between BCD and Braille.

a. Use a multiple-output NAND-gate network.

b. Use a PLA. Give the PLA table.

c. Use a PAL. Specify the PAL type and fuse pattern.

A	B	C	D	W	X
D	C	B	A	Z	Y
0	0	0	0		
0	0	0	1		
0	0	1	0		
0	0	1	1		
0	1	0	0		
0	1	0	1		
0	1	1	0		
0	1	1	1		
1	0	0	0		
1	0	0	1		

11.11 The following table gives the input and output voltages for a 3-input logic circuit.

E_1	E_2	E_3	E_4
0	0	0	0
0	0	-5	-5
0	-5	0	0
0	-5	-5	-5
-5	0	0	-5
-5	0	-5	-5
-5	-5	0	0
-5	-5	-5	0

a. What logic function is realized for positive logic?

b. For negative logic?

11.12 $F(V, W, X, Y, Z) = \Pi M(0, 3, 6, 9, 11, 19, 20, 24, 25, 26, 27, 28, 29, 30) \cdot \Pi D(1, 2, 12, 13)$

a. Find two minimum sum-of-products expressions for F.

b. Underline the essential prime implicants in your answer and tell why each one is essential.

12

FLIP-FLOPS

OBJECTIVES

In this unit you will study one of the basic building blocks used in sequential networks—the flip-flop. Some of the basic analysis techniques used for sequential networks are introduced here. In particular, you will learn how to construct timing diagrams which show how each signal in the network varies as a function of time. Specific objectives are:

1. Explain the operation of *S-R, T, J-K*, clocked *J-K*, and clocked *D* flip-flops.

2. Make a table and derive the characteristic (next state) equation for such flip-flops. State any necessary restrictions on the input signals.

3. Draw a timing diagram relating the input and output of such flip-flops.

4. Show how simple flip-flops can be constructed using gates.

5. Explain the advantages of a clocked flip-flop over an unclocked flip-flop.

STUDY GUIDE

1a. Study Section 12.1, *Gate Delays and Timing Diagrams.* Complete the timing diagram for the network given below. Assume that the AND gate has a 30 *ns* propagation delay and the inverter has a 20 *ns* delay.

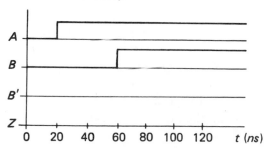

b. In the network shown below, suppose that at some instance of time the inputs to both inverters are zero. Is this a stable condition of the network?

Assuming that the output of the left inverter changes before the output of the right inverter, what stable state will the network reach? (Indicate 0's and 1's on the inverter inputs and outputs.)

c. Work Problem 12.1.

2. Study Section 12.2, *The Set-Reset Flip-Flop.*

   a. Describe in words the behavior of the S-R flip-flop.

   b. For Fig. 12-6(d), what values would P and Q assume if $S = R = 1$?

   c. What restriction is necessary on S and R so that the two outputs of the S-R flip-flop are complements?

   d. State in words the meaning of the equation $Q^+ = S + R'Q$.

   e. Work Problems 12.2 and 12.3.

3. Study Section 12.3, *The Trigger Flip-Flop.*

   a. Describe in words the behavior of the T flip-flop.

   b. Truth tables, such as Figs. 12-7(e), 12-8(a) and 12-10(a) are used in this unit to describe flip-flop behavior. When interpreting these tables, keep in mind that Q^+ and Q both represent the output (state) of the flip-flop; however, Q^+ is measured at a later time than Q. Thus, these tables imply that there is a delay between the time the flip-flop input changes and the time the output changes.

    c.   Trace out the operation of the T flip-flop of Fig. 12-7(b) using the timing diagram of Fig. 12-7(c).

    d.   Work Problem 12.4.

4. Study Section 12.4, *The* J-K *Flip-Flop.*

    a.   Describe in words the behavior of the J-K flip-flop.

    b.   Derive the next state equation for the J-K flip-flop.

    c.   Trace out signals in the network of Fig. 12-8(c) and verify the table of 12-8(a). What timing restriction should be made when J and K are pulsed simultaneously assuming that the S-R flip-flop is the type shown in Fig. 12-7(d)?

5. Study Section 12.5, *The Clocked* J-K *Flip-Flop.*

    a.   Trace signals through the network of Fig. 12-9(c) and verify the timing diagram of Fig. 12-9(d).

    b.   The unclocked *J-K* flip-flop and the clocked *J-K* flip-flop have the same next state equation. Explain the difference in interpretation of the equation for the two flip-flops.

    c.   Is there any restriction on the maximum clock pulse width for a master-slave *J-K* flip-flop? Explain. Compare with the answer to 4c.

    d.   Work Problem 12.5.

6. Study Section 12.6, *The* D *Flip-Flop.*

    a. Describe in words the behavior of the clocked *D* flip-flop.

    b. Given a clocked *D* flip-flop with the following inputs, sketch the waveform for Q.

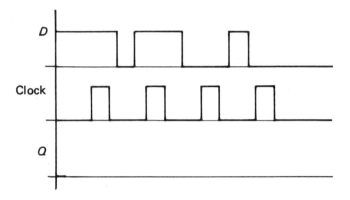

    c. Work Programmed Exercise 12.12.

7. Study Section 12.7, *Clocked Flip-Flops with Clear and Preset Inputs.*

    a. To set the flip-flop of Fig. 12-11 to $Q = 1$ without using the clock, the clear input should be set to_____ and the preset input to_____. To reset the flip-flop of Fig. 12-12(a) to $Q = 0$ without using the clock, the _____ input should be set to_____ .

    b. Work Problem 12.9.

8. Study Section 12.8, *Characteristic Equations.*

    a. To set the flip-flop of Fig. 12-11 to $Q = 1$ without using the clock, the clear be able to derive the characteristic equation which gives the next state of the flip-flop in terms of the present state and inputs. You should understand the meaning of each of the characteristic equations given in Section 12.8.

    b. An *S-R* flip-flop can be converted to a *T* flip-flop by adding gates at the *S* and *R* inputs. The *S* and *R* inputs must be chosen so that the flip-flop will change state whenever *T* is pulsed. In order to determine the *S* and *R* inputs, ask yourself the question, "Under what conditions must the flip-flop be set to 1, and under what conditions must it be reset?" The

flip-flop must be set to 1 if $Q = 0$ and $T = 1$. Therefore, $S =$ _____.
In a similar manner, determine the equation for R and draw the network
which converts an S-R flip-flop to a T flip-flop. Compare your answer
with Fig. 12-7(b).

c. Work Problems 12.8 and 12.11.

9. Optional lab exercise:

   a. Construct an S-R flip-flop using two NOR gates and verify its operation.
   b. Construct the master-slave J-K flip-flop shown in Fig. 12-9(c), using two
      NOR gates for each S-R flip-flop. Verify the timing diagram of Fig.
      12-9(d) by putting in the given sequence of T, J and K signals and ob-
      serving the P and Q outputs. (Use a toggle switch for T as well as
      J and K.)

10. When you are satisfied that you can meet the objectives of this unit, take the
    readiness test.

12. FLIP-FLOPS

Sequential switching networks have the property that the output depends
not only on the present input but also on the past sequence of inputs. In effect,
these networks must be able to "remember" something about the past history of
the inputs in order to produce the present output. Flip-flops are the most commonly used memory devices in sequential networks. Basically, a flip-flop is a
memory device which can assume one of two stable output states, which has a
pair of complementary outputs, and which has one or more inputs that can cause
the output state to change. Several common types of flip-flops are described in
this unit.

12.1 Gate Delays and Timing Diagrams

When the input to a logic gate is changed, the output will not change
instantaneously. The transistors or other switching elements within the gate take
a finite time to react to a change in input, so that the change in the gate output is
delayed with respect to the input change. Figure 12-1 shows possible input and
output waveforms for an inverter. If the change in output is delayed by time ϵ with
respect to the input, we say that this gate has a propagation delay of ϵ. In practice,
the propagation delay for a 0 to 1 output change may be different than the delay
for a 1 to 0 change. Propagation delays for integrated circuit gates may be as
short as a few nanoseconds (1 nanosecond = 10^{-9} seconds), and in many cases
these delays can be neglected. However, in the analysis of some types of sequential networks, even short delays may be important.

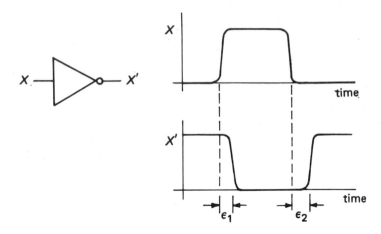

Fig. 12-1. Propagation delay in an inverter

Timing diagrams are frequently used in the analysis of sequential networks. These diagrams show various signals in the network as a function of time. Several variables are usually plotted with the same time scale so that the times at which these variables change with respect to each other can easily be observed.

Figure 12-2 shows the timing diagram for a network with 2 gates. We will assume that each gate has a propagation delay of 20 ns (nanoseconds). This timing diagram indicates what happens when gate inputs B and C are held at constant values 1 and 0, respectively, and input A is changed to 1 at $t = 40$ ns and then changed back to 0 at $t = 100$ ns. The output of gate G_1 changes 20 ns after A changes, and the output of gate G_2 changes 20 ns after G_1 changes.

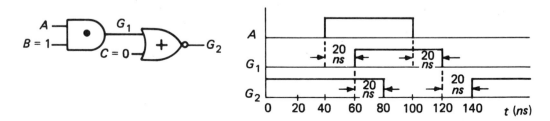

Fig. 12-2. Timing diagram for AND-NOR network

Fig. 12-3 shows a timing diagram for a network with an added delay element. The input X consists of two pulses, the first of which is two microseconds (2×10^{-6} seconds) wide and the second is three microseconds wide. The delay element has an output Y which is the same as the input except that it is delayed by one microsecond. That is, Y changes to a 1 value one microsecond after the rising edge of the X pulse and returns to 0 one microsecond after the falling edge of the X pulse. The output of the AND gate (Z) should be 1 during the time interval in which both X and Y are 1. If we assume a small propagation delay in the AND gate (ϵ), then Z will be as shown in the diagram.

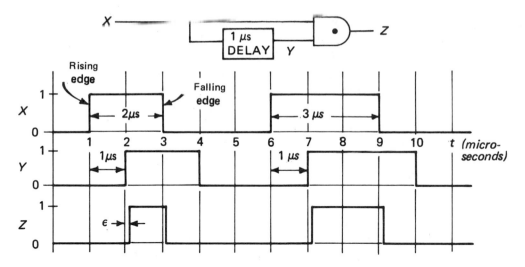

Fig. 12-3. Timing diagram for network with delay

The switching networks we have studied so far have not had feedback connections. In order to construct a switching network that has memory, such as a flip-flop, we must introduce feedback into the network. By feedback we mean that the output of one of the gates is connected back into the input of another gate in the network so as to form a closed loop. For example, in the NOR-gate network of Fig. 12-6(a), the output of the second NOR gate is fed back into the input of the first NOR gate. In simple cases, we can analyze networks with feedback by tracing signals through the network. For example, consider the network in Fig. 12-4(a).

Fig. 12-4(a). Inverter   Fig. 12-4(b). Oscillation at inverter output
with feedback

If, at some instance of time, the inverter input is 0, this 0 will propagate through the inverter and cause the output to become 1. This 1 is fed back into the input, so after the propagation delay, the inverter output will become 0. When this 0 feeds back into the input, the output will again switch to 1, and so forth. The inverter output will continue to oscillate back and forth between 0 and 1 as shown in Fig. 12-4(b), and it will never reach a stable condition. The rate at which the network oscillates is determined by the propagation delay in the inverter.

Next, consider a feedback loop which has two inverters in it, shown in Fig. 12-5(a). In this case, the network has two stable conditions, often referred to as stable states. If the input to the first inverter is 0, its output will be 1. Then the input to the second inverter will be 1, and its output will be 0. This 0 will feed back into the first inverter, but since this input is already 0, no changes will occur. The network is then in a stable state. As shown in Fig. 12-5(b), a second stable state of the network occurs when the input to the first inverter is 1 and the input to the second inverter is 0.

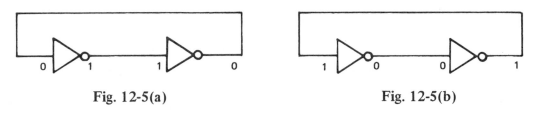

Fig. 12-5(a)   Fig. 12-5(b)

12.2 The Set-Reset Flip-Flop

We can construct a simple flip-flop by introducing feedback into a NOR-gate network, as seen in Fig. 12-6(a). As indicated, if the inputs are $S = R = 0$, the network can assume a stable state with $Q = 0$ and $P = 1$. Note that this is a stable condition of the network because $P = 1$ fed into the second gate forces the output to be $Q = 0$, and $Q = 0$ fed into the first gate allows its output to be 1. Now if we change S to 1, P will become 0. This is an unstable condition or state of the network since both the inputs and output of the second gate are 0; therefore Q will change to 1, leading to the stable state shown in Fig. 12-6(b).

Fig. 12-6(a)   Fig. 12-6(b)

If S is changed back to 0, the network will remain in the above state since $Q = 1$ fed back into the first gate will cause P to remain 0, shown in Fig. 12-6(c).

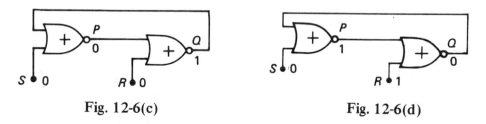

| Fig. 12-6(c) | Fig. 12-6(d) |

Note that the inputs are again $S = R = 0$, but outputs are different than we started with. Thus the network has two different stable states for a given set of inputs. If we now change R to 1, Q will become 0 and P will then change back to 1, as seen in Fig. 12-6(d). If we then change R back to 0, the network remains in this state and we are back where we started.

This network is said to have "memory" because its output depends not only on the present inputs but also on the past sequence of inputs. If we restrict the inputs so that $R = S = 1$ is not allowed, the stable states of the outputs P and Q are always complements, i.e., $P = Q'$. To emphasize the symmetry between the operation of the two gates, the network is often drawn in "cross-coupled" form (see Fig. 12-6(e)). As shown in Figs. 12-6(b) and (d), an input $S = 1$ "sets" the output to $Q = 1$, and an input $R = 1$ "resets" the output to $Q = 0$. When used with the restriction that R and S cannot be one simultaneously, the network is commonly referred to as a set-reset (S-R) flip-flop and given the symbol shown in Fig. 12-6(f).*

Fig. 12-6(e)

Fig. 12-6(f). S-R flip-flop

---

*This type of flip-flop is also called a set-clear (S-C) flip-flop.

If $S = R = 1$, the flip-flop will not operate properly as shown in Fig. 12-6(g). The notation $1 \to 0$ means that the input is originally 1 and then changes to 0. Note that when S and R are both 1, P and Q are both 0. Therefore, P is not equal to Q', and this violates the basic rule of flip-flop operation, which requires the flip-flop outputs to be complements. Furthermore, if S and R are simultaneously changed back to 0, P and Q may both change to 1. If $S = R = 0$ and $P = Q = 1$, then after the 1's propagate through the gates, P and Q will become 0 again, and the flip-flop may continue to oscillate if the gate delays are exactly equal.

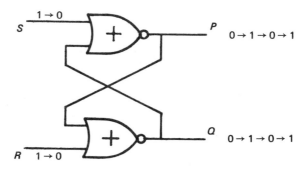

Fig. 12-6(g). Improper S-R flip-flop operation

Fig. 12-6(h) shows a timing diagram for the S-R flip-flop. Note that when S changes to 1 at time t_1, Q changes to 1 a short time (ϵ) later. (ϵ represents the response time or delay time of the flip-flop.) At time t_2, when S changes back to 0, Q does not change. At time t_3, R changes to 1, and Q changes back to 0 a short time (ϵ) later. The duration of the S (or R) input pulse must normally be at least as great as ϵ in order for a change in the state of Q to occur. If $S = 1$ for a time less than ϵ, the gate output will not change and the flip-flop will not change state.

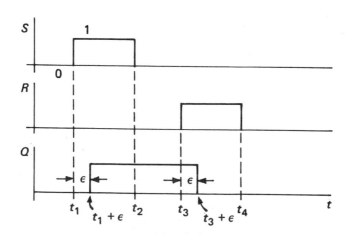

Fig. 12-6(h). Timing diagram for S-R flip-flop

The behavior of the *S-R* flip-flop is summarized by Fig. 12-6(i). The fifth row of this table means that if at some time the inputs are $S = 1$ and $R = 0$ and the output of the flip-flop is $Q = 0$, then at a time ϵ later, the flip-flop output will be $Q = 1$. Other rows are interpreted in a similar manner.

$S(t)$	$R(t)$	$Q(t)$	$Q(t + \epsilon)$
0	0	0	0
0	0	1	1
0	1	0	0
0	1	1	0
1	0	0	1
1	0	1	1
1	1	0	$-$ } inputs not allowed
1	1	1	$-$

Fig. 12-6(i)

When discussing flip-flops, we will use the term "present state" to mean the state of the Q output of the flip-flop at the time the input signals are applied (or changed), and the term "next state" to mean the state of the Q output after the flip-flop has reacted to these input signals. In the above table, $Q(t)$ represents the "present state" of the flip-flop, ϵ is the time required for a change of state to occur, and $Q(t + \epsilon)$ is the "next state" of the flip-flop. For example, if $S = 0$ and $R = 1$ at time t, the next state of the flip-flop will be $Q = 0$, regardless of its present state. Normally, we will only be concerned with the state of the flip-flop when the outputs are stable. Therefore, we will not discuss the flip-flop behavior during the interval t to $t + \epsilon$, during which the outputs may be changing.

By using a Karnaugh map for $Q(t + \epsilon)$, we can derive an equation which describes the behavior of the flip-flop. The inputs which are not allowed are treated as don't cares.

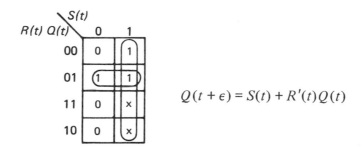

$$Q(t + \epsilon) = S(t) + R'(t)Q(t)$$

Fig. 12-6(j).   Map for $Q(t + \epsilon)$

Normally, we will write this equation without including time explicitly, using Q to represent the present state of the flip-flop and Q^+ to represent the next state:

$$Q^+ = S + R'Q \qquad (SR = 0)$$

In words, this equation tells us that the next state of the flip-flop will be 1 either if it is set to 1 with an S input, or if the present state is 1 and it is not reset. The condition $SR = 0$ implies that S and R cannot both be 1 at the same time. An equation which expresses the next state of a flip-flop in terms of its present state and inputs will be referred to as a "next-state equation" or "characteristic equation".

12.3 The Trigger Flip-Flop

The trigger or T flip-flop in Fig. 12-7(a) has a single input. Applying a pulse to this input causes it to change state. For example, if $Q = 1$ and the T input is pulsed, Q changes to 0. If T is pulsed again, Q changes back to 1. A simple T flip-flop can be constructed using an S-R flip-flop and two AND gates, shown in Fig. 12-7(b).

Fig. 12-7(a)   Fig. 12-7(b)

A timing diagram for the T flip-flop of Fig. 12-7(b) is shown in Fig. 12-7(c). If Q is 0, a pulse on T pulses S and causes the state to change to 1. If Q is 1, a pulse on T pulses R and resets the flip-flop to 0.

Fig. 12-7(c)   Fig. 12-7(d)

In order for this type of flip-flop to operate properly, there must be a finite delay (δ) between the time a pulse is applied to the S or R input and the time the flip-flop output Q changes. This delay in change of state could be accomplished by adding capacitance or extra logic circuitry within the S-R flip-flop. Fig. 12-7(d) indicates symbolically how the basic S-R flip-flop of Fig. 12-6(a) could be modified to delay the change of state. In Fig. 12-7(c), note that the T pulse must be terminated before the change of state is completed. Then no further state change can occur until another pulse is applied to T. If T is too long or the delay in the S-R flip-flop (δ) is too short, the change in Q will propagate back to the AND gate inputs in Fig. 12-7(b) while T is still 1 causing another change of state. If T remains 1, then the flip-flop will change state again and it will continue to oscillate until T becomes zero. Other types of T flip-flops change state in response to the rising or falling edge of the input pulses, in which case the pulse width is not critical.

The next state table and characteristic equation for the T flip-flop are given in Fig. 12-7(e).

$$\begin{array}{cc|c} T & Q & Q^+ \\ \hline 0 & 0 & 0 \\ 0 & 1 & 1 \\ 1 & 0 & 1 \\ 1 & 1 & 0 \end{array}$$

$$Q(t + \epsilon) = T'(t)Q(t) + T(t)Q'(t)$$

or

$$Q^+ = T'Q + TQ' = T \oplus Q$$

Fig. 12-7(e)

The above equation states that the next state of the flip-flop (Q^+) will be 1 iff the present state (Q) is 1 and no T pulse occurs or the present state is 0 and a T pulse occurs.

12.4 The *J-K* Flip-Flop

The J-K flip-flop combines the features of the S-R and T flip-flops. A 1 input applied to J or K alone acts exactly like an S or R input, respectively. That is, if $J = 1$ the flip-flop output is set to $Q = 1$; and if $K = 1$, the flip-flop output is reset to $Q = 0$. Unlike the S-R flip-flop, it is permissible to apply a 1 input simultaneously to J and K, in which case the flip-flop changes state just like a T flip-flop. For example, if $Q = 0$ and we momentarily apply a 1 input to both J and K, the flip-flop state will change to $Q = 1$. The next state table and characteristic equation for the J-K flip-flop are given in Fig. 12-8.

J	K	Q	Q⁺

$J\ K\ Q\ \ \vert\ Q^+$

0 0 0	0
0 0 1	1
0 1 0	0
0 1 1	0
1 0 0	1
1 0 1	1
1 1 0	1
1 1 1	0

Fig. 12-8(a)

$Q^+ = QK' + Q'J$

Fig. 12-8(b)

Fig. 12-8(c). Construction of a *J-K* flip-flop from an *S-R* flip-flop

Figure 12-8(c) shows one way of constructing a *J-K* flip-flop using an *S-R* flip-flop with added gates. If $Q = 0$, an input of $J = 1$ will set the flip-flop to $Q = 1$. If $Q = 1$, an input of $K = 1$ will reset the flip-flop to $Q = 0$. If the *J* and *K* inputs are pulsed simultaneously ($J = K = 1$), then the flip-flop acts just like the *T* flip-flop of Fig. 12-7(b), and a state change occurs. Again, the change of state of the *S-R* flip-flop must be delayed, as shown in Fig. 12-7(d), to assure proper operation. When *J* and *K* are pulsed at the same time, timing problems may arise if the pulses are too long or if they do not arrive at exactly the same time. To overcome such timing problems, a clocked *J-K* flip-flop of the type discussed in the next section can be used.

12.5 The Clocked *J-K* Flip-Flop

In large sequential networks, it is common practice to synchronize the operation of all flip-flops by a common clock or pulse generator. The clock pulse may be fed into each flip-flop through external gates, or internal gating may be used as is the case with most integrated circuit flip-flops. Use of the clock to synchronize the operation of several flip-flops is illustrated in Units 13 and 14. When a clock is used, all flip-flops which change state do so in response to the clock pulse rather than in response to some other input signal.

Figure 12-9(a) shows a clocked *J-K* flip-flop. This flip-flop has three inputs—*J*, *K*, and the clock input, which is often labeled *T* or *CK*. As illustrated in Fig. 12-9(b), this flip-flop changes state a short time (ε) after the falling edge of the clock pulse provided that *J* and *K* have appropriate values. If $J = 1$ during the clock pulse, *Q* will be set to 1 immediately following the clock pulse. If $K = 1$ during the clock pulse, *Q* will be set to 0 after the clock pulse. Similarly, if $J = K = 1$, *Q* will change state after the clock pulse. The change in state is initiated by the clock pulse and never by a change in *J* or *K*. Referring to Fig. 12-9(b), since $Q = 0$, $J = 1$ and $K = 0$ during the first clock pulse, *Q* changes to 1 at t_1. Since $Q = 1$, $J = 0$ and $K = 1$ during the second pulse, *Q* changes to 0 at t_2. Since $Q = 0$, $J = 1$ and

$K = 1$ during the third pulse, Q changes to 1 at t_3. The arrowhead on the flip-flop symbol identifies the clock input, and the small circle (inversion symbol) indicates that the state changes occur on a high to low transition, i.e., after the falling (rather than the rising) edge of the clock pulse.

Fig. 12-9(a). Clocked *J-K* flip-flop

Fig. 12-9(b). *J-K* flip-flop timing

The next state table and characteristic equation previously given for the unclocked *J-K* flip-flop also apply to the clocked *J-K* flip-flop, if Q is interpreted as the state of the flip-flop before the clock pulse and Q^+ as the state after the clock pulse. Thus, the presence of a clock signal is implied and does not appear explicitly in the equation.

One way of realizing the clocked *J-K* flip-flop is with two *S-R* flip-flops connected in a master-slave arrangement as shown in Fig. 12-9(c). Master-slave clocked *J-K* flip-flops are commonly constructed in integrated circuit form.

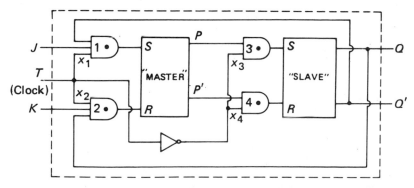

Fig. 12-9(c). Master-slave *J-K* flip-flop

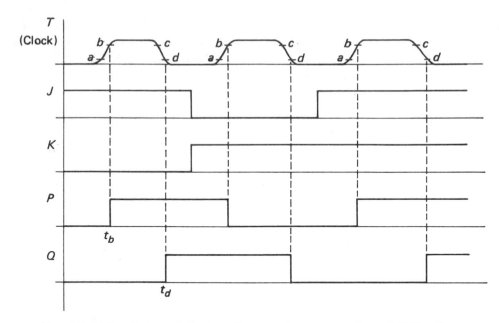

Fig. 12-9(d). Internal timing diagram for master-slave *J-K* flip-flop

Figure 12-9(d) shows a detailed timing diagram for the master-slave clocked *J-K* flip-flop. The slope of the rising and falling edges of the clock pulse has been exaggerated in order to better illustrate the internal operation. Gates 3 and 4 in Fig. 12-9(c) are designed to operate at a different time during the clock pulse than gates 1 and 2. On the rising edge of the clock pulse, gates 3 and 4 open to isolate the slave flip-flop inputs from the master at point "*a*". In other words, following point "*a*" the inputs x_3 and x_4 act like 0's so the P and P' signals cannot pass through the gates and the slave flip-flop cannot change state. Next, at point "*b*" on the rising edge of the clock pulse, gates 1 and 2 close to allow the master flip-flop to be set to the proper state. That is, the inputs x_1 and x_2 will act like 1's so that the J or K signals can pass through the gates if Q has the proper value. On the falling edge of the clock pulse, gates 1 and 2 open to isolate the inputs from the master at point *c*, and gates 3 and 4 close at point *d* so that the output of the master is transferred to the slave.

In Fig. 12-9(d), note that since $J = 1$ during the first clock pulse, P is set to 1 at time t_b and Q is set to 1 at time t_d. The state change of the master takes place on the rising edge of the clock pulse, and the state change of the slave follows on the falling edge. In order to assure that the flip-flop works properly, i.e., obeys the equation $Q^+ = JQ' + K'Q$, any changes in the J and K inputs must occur between clock pulses as illustrated in Fig. 12-9(d). The change of flip-flop state always occurs on the falling edge of the clock pulse regardless of pulse width. Therefore, as long as the clock pulse width exceeds a certain minimum value, proper operation of the flip-flop does not depend on pulse width.

Another type of clocked flip-flop is the "edge-triggered" flip-flop. Like the master-slave flip-flop, an edge-triggered flip-flop will change state in response to a change on the clock input. However, unlike the master-slave flip-flop, the other inputs may change during the clock pulse without causing improper operation. The same symbol is often used for the J-K master-slave flip-flop and the J-K edge-triggered flip-flop,* and their external behavior is the same as long as J and K do not change during the clock pulse.

12.6 The D Flip-Flop

Another flip-flop available in integrated circuit form is the clocked D (delay) flip-flop, seen in Fig. 12-10(a). The state of this flip-flop after the clock pulse (Q^+) is equal to the input (D) before the clock pulse. For example, if $D = 1$ before the clock pulse, $Q = 1$ after the clock pulse regardless of the previous value of Q. Therefore, the characteristic equation is $Q^+ = D$. Like the clocked J-K flip-flop, the arrowhead on the D flip-flop symbol designates the clock input and the small inversion circle indicates that the state changes occur on a high to low transition — i.e., after the falling edge of the clock pulse.

D	Q	Q⁺
0	0	0
0	1	0
1	0	1
1	1	1

$$Q^+ = D$$

Fig. 12-10(a). Clocked D flip-flop

If D changes at most once following each clock pulse, the output of the flip-flop is the same as the D input, except that changes in the output are delayed until after the falling edge of the clock pulse as illustrated in Fig. 12-10(b).

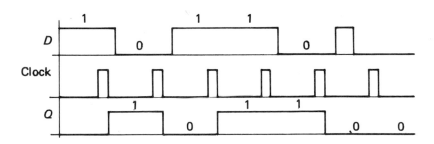

Fig. 12-10(b). Timing for clocked D flip-flop

---

*For example, the 7473 and 74LS73 have the same symbol and external connections; however, the 7473 is master-slave and the 74LS73 is edge-triggered.

12.7 Clocked Flip-Flops with Clear and Preset Inputs

Clocked integrated circuit flip-flops often have additional inputs which can be used to set the flip-flop to an initial state independent of the clock. Figure 12-9 shows a clocked *J-K* flip-flop with clear (*CLR*) and preset (*PR*) inputs. The small circles (inversion symbols) on these inputs indicate that a logic 0 (rather than a 1) is required to clear or set the flip-flop. Thus, a 0 applied to the clear input will reset the flip-flop to $Q = 0$, and a 0 applied to the preset input will set the flip-flop to $Q = 1$. These inputs override the clock and *J-K* inputs. That is, a 0 applied to the *CLR* input will reset the flip-flop regardless of the values of *J*, *K* and the clock. Under normal operating conditions, a 0 should not be simultaneously applied to *CLR* and *PR*. When the *CLR* and *PR* inputs are both held at logic 1 (or not connected), the *J*, *K* and clock inputs operate in the normal manner.

Fig. 12-11. Clocked *J-K* flip-flop with clear and preset inputs

Figure 12-12 shows two types of clocked *D* flip-flops with clear (*CLR*) inputs. The small inversion circle on the clear input indicates that a 0 (rather than a 1) will reset the flip-flop to $Q = 0$. The clear input overrides the clock and *D* inputs. When the clear input is held at 1 (or not connected), the *D* and clock inputs operate in the normal manner. In Fig. 12-12(a), the inversion symbol on the clock indicates that the flip-flop responds to a high-to-low transition – i.e., to the falling edge of the clock pulse – whereas in Fig. 12-12(b), the lack of an inversion symbol indicates that the state changes will occur on a low-to-high transition – i.e., on the rising edge of the clock. Unless otherwise specified, we will use the former type of *D* flip-flop throughout the remainder of this text.

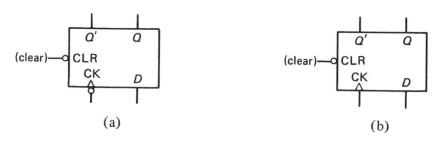

(a)   (b)

Fig. 12-12. Clocked *D* flip-flop with clear

12.8 Characteristic Equations

The characteristic equations for the flip-flops discussed in this chapter are:

$$Q^+ = S + R'Q \qquad (SR = 0) \qquad \text{(S-R flip-flop)} \qquad\qquad (12\text{-}1)$$
$$Q^+ = T \oplus Q = TQ' + T'Q \qquad \text{(T flip-flop)} \qquad\qquad (12\text{-}2)$$
$$Q^+ = JQ' + K'Q \qquad \text{(J-K flip-flop, clocked or unclocked)} \quad (12\text{-}3)$$
$$Q^+ = D \qquad \text{(clocked D flip-flop)} \qquad\qquad (12\text{-}4)$$

In each case, Q represents an initial or present state of the flip-flop, and Q^+ represents the final or next state. These equations are only valid when the appropriate restrictions on the flip-flop inputs are observed. For the S-R flip-flop, $S = R = 1$ is forbidden. If the T flip-flop is of the type shown in Fig. 12-7(b), the T pulse must be of appropriate duration. For the master-slave clocked J-K flip-flop, J and K should not change during the clock pulse.

The characteristic equations given above apply to both clocked and unclocked flip-flops, but their interpretation is different for the two cases. For example, consider the clocked T flip-flop shown in Fig. 12-13. This flip-flop will change state in response to a clock pulse if $T = 1$ but not if $T = 0$. Equation (12-2) applies to the clocked T flip-flop if we interpret Q to mean the state of the flip-flop before the clock pulse and Q^+ the state after the clock pulse. Note that the clock pulse does not explicitly appear in the equation.

Fig. 12-13.   Clocked T flip-flop

It is usually possible to convert one type of flip-flop to another by adding external gates. Figures 12-7(b) and 12-8(c) show how an S-R flip-flop can be converted to a T flip-flop or a J-K flip-flop. Next we will convert a clocked J-K flip-flop to a clocked T flip-flop. When $T = 1$, we want the flip-flop to change state, so we must have $J = K = 1$. Similarly, when $T = 0$, we want no state change, so $J = K = 0$. Therefore, we must have $J = K = T$, as shown in Fig. 12-14(a).

In many cases, the necessary flip-flop input equations can be found by determining the conditions under which the flip-flop must be set or reset (in the case of an *S-R* flip-flop), or the conditions under which the flip-flop must change state (in the case of a *T* flip-flop).

Example: Convert an *S-R* flip-flop to a clocked *D* flip-flop. Figure 12-10(a) shows the desired behavior of the flip-flop after conversion. The flip-flop must be set to 1 if $D = 1$ and a clock pulse occurs. Therefore, $S = D(CK)$ Similarly, the flip-flop must be set to 0 if $D = 0$ and a clock pulse occurs. Therefore, $R = D'(CK)$ Figure 12-14(b) shows the result of the conversion.

Fig. 12-14(a). **Conversion of a *J-K* flip-flop to a *T* flip-flop**

Fig. 12-14(b). **Conversion of an *S-R* flip-flop to a clocked *D* flip-flop**

In the above examples, an intuitive approach to conversion of one type of flip-flop to another type has been presented. In the next unit, systematic methods for deriving flip-flop input equations are described. These systematic methods can also be applied to convert one flip-flop type to another.

The most commonly used types of clocked flip-flops are the *J-K* and *D* flip-flops. Both of these types are readily available in integrated circuit form. When a *T* flip-flop is needed, a *J-K* flip-flop with *J* and *K* connected together can be used. The *S-R* flip-flop is more commonly used in asynchronous sequential network design (see Section 25.1) than in synchronous design (see Section 13.3).

PROBLEMS

12.1 Complete the timing diagram for the network shown below. Assume that both gates have a propagation delay of 5 ns.

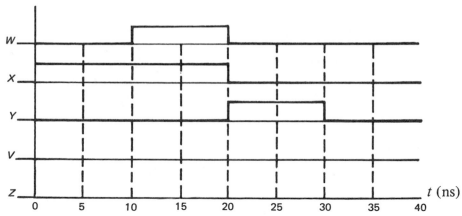

12.2 A flip-flop can be constructed from two NAND gates connected as follows:

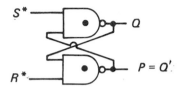

a. What restriction must be placed on $S*$ and $R*$ so that P will always equal Q' (under steady-state conditions)?

b. Construct a next state table and derive the characteristic (next state) equation for the flip-flop.

c. Complete the following timing diagram for the flip-flop.

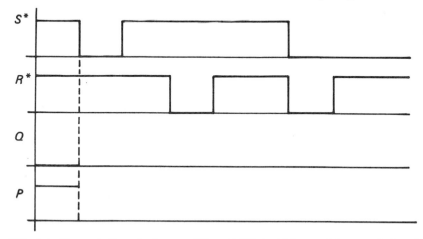

d. What is the relation between $S*$ and $R*$ in this problem and the S and R inputs of the NOR-gate flip-flop of Fig. 12-6(e)?

12.3 This problem illustrates the improper operation that can occur if both inputs to an *S-R* flip-flop are 1 and then changed back to 0. For Fig. 12-6(g) complete the timing chart given below, assuming that each gate has a propagation delay of exactly 10 ns. Note that when $t = 100$ ns, S and R are both changed to 0. Then 10 ns later, both P and Q will change to 1. Since these 1's are fed back to the gate inputs, what will happen after another 10 ns?

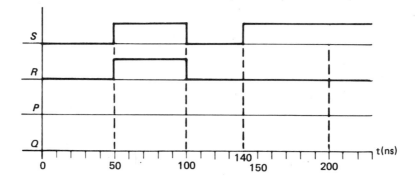

12.4 For the *T* flip-flop of Fig. 12-7(b), draw a timing diagram similar to Fig. 12-7(c), which shows what happens when *T* remains 1 for a time equal to 2.5δ.

12.5 a. Using Fig. 12-9(c), trace the signals through the master-slave *J-K* flip-flop when the following input sequence is applied starting with $J = K = P = Q = 0$: *JK* change to 11, clock pulse, *JK* change to 01, clock pulse, *JK* change to 10, clock pulse. Draw a timing diagram which includes *P, Q, J, K,* and the clock.

   b. Improper operation may occur if *J* or *K* is changed while the clock is high. Starting with $J = K = T = P = Q = 0$, the inputs are changed in the following order: $J = 1, T = 1, J = 0, K = 1, T = 0$. What is the final value of *Q*?

   c. Repeat part b when the inputs are changed in the order: $T = 1, J = 1, T = 0$. Note that the final value of *Q* is determined by the values of *J* and *K* *before* the clock pulse in part b but not in part c.

   d. What restrictions should be placed on the times at which the *J* and *K* inputs change in order to assure that the equation $Q^+ = QK' + Q'J$ holds for a master-slave *J-K* flip-flop?

12.6 Convert a clocked *D* flip-flop to a clocked *J-K* flip-flop by adding external gates.

12.7 In Section 12.5, the clock (T) input is not included explicitly in the characteristic (next state) equation for a clocked J-K flip-flop. However, we can derive a next state equation which includes T if we interpret the variables in a special way. Consider a time interval in which it is known that either a clock pulse will occur ($T = 1$) or will not occur ($T = 0$). Let Q represent the state of the flip-flop before the start of the interval, and let Q^+ represent the state of the flip-flop after the interval. Assume that J and K remain constant during the interval. Construct a truth table and derive the equation for Q^+ in terms of J, K, T and Q.

12.8 A gated latch (G-L flip-flop) behaves as follows: If $G = 0$, the flip-flop does not change state. If $G = 1$, the next state of the flip-flop is equal to the value of L.

a. Derive the characteristic (next state) equation for the flip-flop.

b. Show how an S-R flip-flop can be converted to a G-L flip-flop by adding gate(s) and inverter(s).

Hint: What values must S and R have so that the flip-flop will be set and reset at the proper time when $G = 1$? How can you prevent the flip-flop from changing state when $G = 0$?

12.9 a. Complete the following timing diagram for the flip-flop of Fig. 12-11.

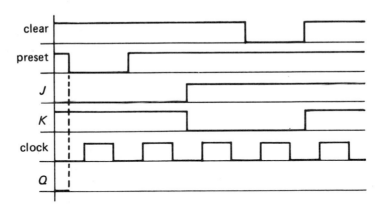

b. Complete the timing diagram for the circuit given below. Note that the CK inputs on the two flip-flops are different.

12.10 A reset-dominant flip-flop behaves like an *S-R* flip-flop, except that the input $S = R = 1$ is allowed, and the flip-flop is reset when $S = R = 1$.

    a. Derive the characteristic equation for a reset-dominant flip-flop.

    b. Show how a reset dominant flip-flop can be constructed by adding gate(s) to an *S-R* flip-flop.

12.11 Derive a characteristic equation for the flip-flop of Fig. 12-11, including the preset (*P*) and clear (*C*) inputs as well as *J* and *K*. Assume that $P = C = 0$ will never occur.

Programmed Exercise 12.12

Cover the bottom part of each page with a sheet of paper and slide it down as you check your answers.

The internal logic diagram of a clocked *D* flip-flop is shown below. This flip-flop consists of two basic *S-R* flip-flops with added gates. When the clock input (*CK*) is 1, the value of *D* is stored in the first *S-R* flip-flop (*P*). When the clock changes from 1 to 0, the value of *P* is transferred to the output flip-flop (*Q*). Thus, the operation is similar to that of the master-slave *J-K* flip-flop shown in Fig. 12-9(c).

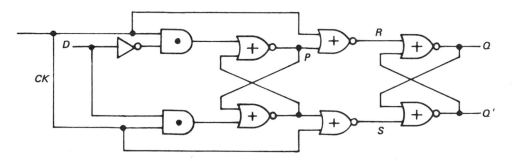

In this exercise you will be asked to analyze the operation of the clocked *D* flip-flop shown above by filling in a table showing the values of *CK, D, P, S, R* and *Q* after each change of input. It will be helpful if you mark the changes in these values on the circuit diagram as you trace the signals. Initially, assume the following signal values:

CK	D	P	S	R	Q
0	0	0	0	1	0 (stable)

Verify by tracing signals through the circuit that this is a stable condition of the circuit; i.e., no change will occur in *P, S, R* or *Q*. Now assume that *CK* is changed to 1:

	CK	D	P	S	R	Q	
1.	0	0	0	0	1	0	(stable)
2.	1	0	0	0	1	0	?
3.							

Trace the change in *CK* through the circuit to see if a change in *P, S* or *R* will occur. If a change does occur, mark row 2 of the above table "unstable" and enter the new values in row 3.

Answer:								
	2.	1	0	0	0	1	0	(unstable)
	3.	1	0	0	0	0	0	(stable)
	4.	1	1	0	0	0	0	(unstable)
	5.	1	1				?	

Verify that row 3 is stable; that is, by tracing signals show that no further change in *P, S, R* or *Q* will occur. Next *D* is changed to 1 as shown in row 4. Verify that row 4 is unstable, fill in the new values in row 5, and indicate if row 5 is stable or unstable.

Answer:		CK	D	P	S	R	Q	
	5.	1	1	1	0	0	0	(stable)
	6.	0	1	1	0	0	0	?
	7.	0	1					?
	8.	0	1					

Then *CK* is changed to 0 (row 6). If row 6 is unstable, indicate the new value of *S* in row 7. If row 7 is unstable, indicate the new value of *Q* in row 8. Then determine whether row 8 is stable or not.

Answer:		CK	D	P	S	R	Q	
	7.	0	1	1	1	0	0	(unstable)
	8.	0	1	1	1	0	1	(stable)
	9.	0	0					(stable)
	10.	1	0					
	11.	1	0					

Next *D* is changed back to 0 (row 9). Fill in the values in row 9 and verify that it is stable. *CK* is changed to 1 in row 10. If row 10 is unstable, fill in row 11 and indicate whether it is stable or not.

Answer:

9.	0	0	1	1	0	1	(stable)
10.	1	0	1	1	0	1	(unstable)
11.	1	0	0	0	0	1	(stable)
12.	0	0					
13.	0	0					
14.	0	0					

CK is changed back to 0 in row 12. Complete the rest of the table.

Answer:

12.	0	0	0	0	0	1	(unstable)
13.	0	0	0	0	1	1	(unstable)
14.	0	0	0	0	1	0	(stable)

Using the above results, plot *P* and *Q* on the timing diagram given below. Verify that your answer is consistent with the description of flip-flop operation given in the first paragraph of this exercise.

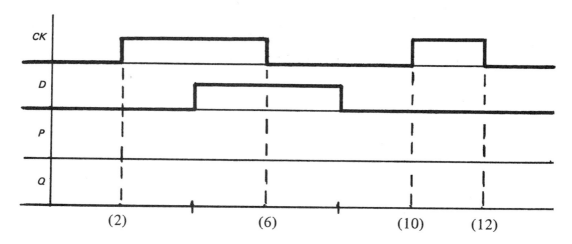

13

COUNTERS AND SIMILAR
SEQUENTIAL NETWORKS

OBJECTIVES

1. Given the present state and desired next state of a flip-flop, determine the required flip-flop inputs.

2. Given the desired counting sequence for a counter, derive the flip-flop input equations.

3. Given the desired behavior of a sequential network whose next state (i.e., the state after receiving an input clock pulse) depends only on the present state, design the network.

4. Explain the procedures used for deriving flip-flop input equations.

5. Construct a timing diagram for a counter by tracing signals through the network.

STUDY GUIDE

1. Study Section 13.1, *Design of a Binary Counter*, and Section 13.2, *Counters for Other Sequences*.

    a. For Fig. 13-2, if $ABC = 101$ and an input pulse occurs, which of the T inputs will be pulsed?

b. Complete the following timing diagram for the binary counter of Fig. 13-2.

c. Using the results of part b, draw a state graph for this binary counter (similar to Fig. 13-3).

d. Use Table 13-3 to verify that the values of T_A, T_B and T_C in Table 13-1 are correct.

e. What happens if the network of Fig. 13-5 is started in one of the "don't care" states and then an input pulse occurs? In particular, augment the state graph of Fig. 13-7 to indicate the result for starting in states 101 and 110.

f. Redraw the network of Fig. 13-5 using clocked T flip-flops. (One gate can be eliminated.)

2. Study Section 13.3, *Counter Design Using* S-R *Flip-Flops.*

    a. Referring to Table 13-4(c):

        If $Q = Q^+ = 0$, explain in words why R is a don't care.

        If $Q = Q^+ = 1$, explain in words why S is a don't care.

        If $Q = 0$ and $Q^+ = 1$, what value should S have and why?

        If $Q = 1$ and $Q^+ = 0$, what value should R have and why?

    b. For Fig. 13-8, derive the R_B and S_B maps from the B^+ map, and derive the R_C and S_C maps from the C^+ map.

    c. In Fig. 13-8, where do the gate inputs (A, B, C, etc.) come from?

    d. For Fig. 13-8(c), which flip-flop inputs will be pulsed if $ABC = 100$ and a P pulse occurs?

    e. Complete the following state graph by tracing signals in Fig. 13-8(c). Compare your answer with Fig. 13-3. What will happen if the counter is in state 001 and a P pulse occurs?

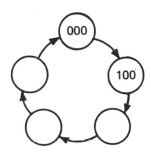

3. Study Section 13.4, *Counter Design with J-K Flip-Flops,* and Section 13.5, *Short Cut Method for Deriving J-K Flip-Flop Input Equations.*

   a. Referring to Table 13-6(c).

     If $Q = Q^+ = 0$, explain in words why K is a don't care.

     If $Q = Q^+ = 1$, explain in words why J is a don't care.

     If $Q = 0$ and $Q^+ = 1$, explain why both $JK = 10$ and $JK = 11$ will produce the required state change.

     If $Q = 1$ and $Q^+ = 0$, give two sets of values for J and K which will produce the required state change, and explain why your answer is valid.

   b. Verify that the maps of Fig. 13-9(a) can be derived from the maps of Fig. 13-9(b).

   c. Compare the number of logic gates in Figs. 13-8 and 13-9. The *J-K* realization requires fewer gates than the *S-R* realization for two reasons:

     (1) The *J-K* maps have more don't cares than the *S-R* maps.

     (2) Clocked *J-K* flip-flops are used so that it is unnecessary to provide AND gates for the input pulses.

   d. Draw in the implied feedback connections on the network of Fig. 13-9(c).

   e. By tracing signals through the network, verify that the state sequence for Fig. 13-9(c) is correct.

   f. Find a minimum expression for F_1 and for F_2. (*Hint:* No variables are required.)

BC \ A	0	1
00	×	×
01	1	×
11	×	1
10	×	×

F_1

BC \ A	0	1
00	×	×
01	0	×
11	×	×
10	×	×

F_2

g. By applying the steps of the short-cut method given on p. 280 determine J_B and K_B from the following map:

AB CD	00	01	11	10
00	1	1	1	0
01	1	0	0	1
11	0	0	1	0
10	0	1	x	1

B^+

Steps d and e of the short-cut method are easy to remember since a change from $Q = 0$ to $Q^+ = 1$ requires $J = 1$, and a change from $Q = 1$ to $Q^+ = 0$ requires $K = 1$.

4. Study Section 13.6, *Counter Design Using* D *Flip-Flops,* Section 13.7, *Design of a Code Converter,* and Section 13.8, *Shift Registers.*

   a. Verify the *J-K* flip-flop input equations, which are derived in Fig. 13-12.

   b. Sketch the network for a four-bit cyclic left shift register using clocked *J-K* flip-flops. For such a shift register, why is it possible to shift information into one flip-flop at the same time information is shifted out to the next flip-flop without causing a timing problem?

5. Study Section 13.9, *Derivation of Flip-Flop Input Equations.*

   a. Make sure that you know how to derive input equations for the different types of flip-flops. It is important that you understand the procedures for deriving the equations; merely memorizing the rules is not sufficient.

   b. Table 13-9 is provided mainly for reference. It is not intended that you memorize this table; instead you should understand the reasons for the entries in the table. If you understand the reasons why a given map entry is 0, 1 or *X*, then you should be able to derive the flip-flop input maps without reference to a table.

6. Work Problem 13.1 or Problem 13.2 as assigned. Use both the standard method and the short-cut method for part c. Work Problems 13.3 through 13.7.

7. *Lab Problem* (required). This lab exercise introduces the use of *J-K* flip-flops in lab in preparation for a sequential network design problem (Unit 17).

   a. Study the information on *J-K* flip-flops in the Laboratory Information handout and work through Study Guide Part III of this handout.

   b. Go to lab and check out your design for Problem 13.1c or 13.2c.

   c. Draw a complete state graph (of the form of Fig. 13-7) for your counter showing the state sequence observed in lab, including what happens when you start in each one of the states not in the prescribed counting sequence.

8. Bring your solution to Lab Problem 7 with you when you come to take the readiness test.

13. COUNTERS AND SIMILAR SEQUENTIAL NETWORKS

Counters are one of the simplest types of sequential networks. A counter is usually constructed from two or more flip-flops which change state in a pre-scribed sequence when input pulses are received. In this unit, you will learn pro-cedures for deriving flip-flop input equations for counters. These procedures will be applied to more general types of sequential networks in later units.

13.1 Design of a Binary Counter

The counters discussed in this chapter are all synchronous counters. This means the operation of the flip-flops is synchronized by the common input pulse (P) so that when several flip-flops must change state, the state changes occur sim-ultaneously. Ripple counters, in which the state change of one flip-flop triggers the next flip-flop in line, are not discussed in this chapter.

We will first construct a binary counter using three T flip-flops to count pulses (Fig. 13-1). We will assume that all the flip-flops change state immediately following the falling edge of the input pulse. The *state* of the counter is determined by the states of the individual flip-flops; e.g., if flip-flop A is in state 0, B in state 1, and C in state 1, the state of the counter is 011. Initially, all flip-flops will be set to the zero state. When a pulse is received, the counter will change to state 001; when a second pulse is received, the state will change to 010; etc. The sequence of flip-flop states is $ABC = 000, 001, 010, 011, 100, 101, 110, 111, 000, \ldots$

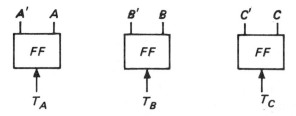

Fig. 13-1. Flip-flops for binary counter

Note that when the counter reaches state 111, the next pulse resets it to the 000 state and then the sequence repeats.

First we will design the counter by inspection of the counting sequence; then we will use a systematic procedure which can be generalized to other types of counters. The problem is to determine the flip-flop inputs—T_A, T_B and T_C. From the above counting sequence, observe that C changes state every time a pulse is received. Since pulsing T_C causes C to change state, the pulse source must be connected directly to the T_C input. Next, observe that B changes state when a pulse is received only if $C = 1$. Therefore, an AND gate is connected to T_B as shown in Fig. 13-2, so that if $C = 1$ and a pulse is received, B will change state. Similarly A changes state when a pulse is received only if B and C are both 1. An AND gate is connected to T_A so that A will change state if $B = 1$, $C = 1$, and a pulse is received.

Now we will verify that the network of Fig. 13-2 counts properly by tracing signals through the network. Initially, $ABC = 000$, so when the first pulse arrives it only gets through to T_C. The state changes to 001, so when the second pulse arrives it gets through to T_B and T_C, and the state changes to 010. This process continues until finally when state 111 is reached, the next pulse gets through to T_A, T_B, and T_C, and all flip-flops return to the zero state.

Counter Outputs

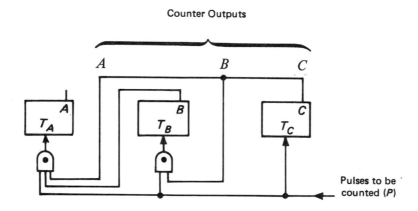

Fig. 13-2. **Synchronous binary counter**

Next we will redesign the binary counter by using a state table (Table 13-1). This table shows the present state of flip-flops A, B and C (before a pulse is received) and the corresponding next state (after the pulse is received). Although the pulse is not explicit in the table, it is understood to be the input. For example, if the flip-flops are in state $ABC = 011$ and a pulse is received, the next states will be $A^+B^+C^+ = 100$. A third column in the table is used to derive the inputs for T_A, T_B and T_C. Whenever the entries in the C and C^+ columns differ, flip-flop C must change state and T_C must be 1. Similarly, if B and B^+ differ, B must change state so T_B must be 1. For example, if $ABC = 011$, $A^+B^+C^+ = 100$ and all three flip-flops must change state, so $T_A T_B T_C = 111$.

Table 13-1. State Table for Binary Counter

present state	next state	flip-flop inputs
A B C	$A^+ B^+ C^+$	$T_A\ T_B\ T_C$
0 0 0	0 0 1	0 0 1
0 0 1	0 1 0	0 1 1
0 1 0	0 1 1	0 0 1
0 1 1	1 0 0	1 1 1
1 0 0	1 0 1	0 0 1
1 0 1	1 1 0	0 1 1
1 1 0	1 1 1	0 0 1
1 1 1	0 0 0	1 1 1

T_A, T_B and T_C are now derived from the table as functions of A, B and C. By inspection, $T_C = 1$. Karnaugh maps are plotted for T_A and T_B:

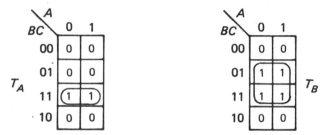

from which $T_A = BC$ and $T_B = C$. Since a pulse (P) is required to initiate each change of state, we multiply each input by P so that

$$T_A = BCP \qquad\qquad T_B = CP \qquad\qquad T_C = P$$

These equations yield the same network derived previously.

13.2 Counters for Other Sequences

In some applications, the sequence of states of a counter is not in straight binary order. Figure 13-3 shows the *state graph** for such a counter. The arrows indicate the state sequence. If this counter is started in state 000, the first pulse will take it to state 100, the next pulse to 111, etc. The count pulse is implicitly understood to be the input to the network.

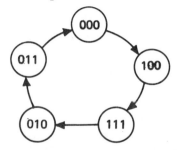

Fig. 13-3. State graph for counter

_____
*Also called a state diagram.

The corresponding state table for the counter is Table 13-2.

Table 13-2. State Table for Fig. 13-3

A	B	C	A^+	B^+	C^+
0	0	0	1	0	0
0	0	1	—	—	—
0	1	0	0	1	1
0	1	1	0	0	0
1	0	0	1	1	1
1	0	1	—	—	—
1	1	0	—	—	—
1	1	1	0	1	0

Note that the next state is unspecified for present states 001, 101 and 110.

We could derive T_A, T_B and T_C directly from this table as in the preceding example. However, it is often more convenient to plot *"next state maps"* showing A^+, B^+ and C^+ as functions of A, B and C, and then derive T_A, T_B and T_C from these maps. The next state maps in Fig. 13-4(a) are easily plotted from inspection of Table 13-2. From the first row of the table, the $ABC = 000$ squares on the A^+, B^+ and C^+ maps are filled in with 1, 0 and 0 respectively. From the second row, the $ABC = 001$ squares on all 3 maps are filled in with don't cares. From the third row, the $ABC = 010$ squares on the A^+, B^+ and C^+ maps are filled in with 0, 1 and 1 respectively. The next state maps can be quickly completed by continuing in this manner.

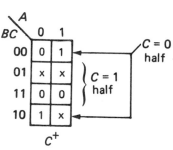

(a) Next state maps for Table 13-2

$T_A = A'B' + AB$
$\quad = (A' + B)(A + B')$

$T_B = A'C + AB' = (A' + B')(A + C)$

$T_C = A + B$

(b) Derivation of T inputs

Fig. 13-4

Next, we will derive the maps for the T inputs from the next state maps. In the following discussion, the general symbol Q represents the present state of the flip-flop (A, B, or C) under consideration and Q^+ represents the next state (A^+, B^+, or C^+) of the same flip-flop. Given the present state of a T flip-flop (Q) and the desired next state (Q^+), the T input must be pulsed ($T = 1$) whenever a change of state is required. Thus, $T = 1$ whenever $Q^+ \neq Q$ as shown in Table 13-3.

Table 13-3. Input for T Flip-Flop

Q	Q^+	T
0	0	0
0	1	1
1	0	1
1	1	0

$$T = Q^+ \oplus Q$$

In general, the next state map for flip-flop Q gives Q^+ as a function of Q and several other variables. The value written in each square of the map gives the value of Q^+, while the value of Q is determined from the row or column headings. Given the map for Q^+, we can then form the map for T_Q by simply putting a 1 in each square of the T_Q map for which Q^+ is different from Q. Thus to form the T_A map in Fig. 13-4(b) from the A^+ map in Fig. 13-4(a), we place a 1 in the $ABC = 000$ square of T_A because $A = 0$ and $A^+ = 1$ for this square. We also place a 1 in the 111 square of T_A because $A = 1$ and $A^+ = 0$ for this square.

If we don't care what the next state of a flip-flop is for some combination of variables, we don't care what the flip-flop input is for that combination of variables. Therefore, if the Q^+ map has a don't care in some square, the T_Q map will have a don't care in the corresponding square. Thus, the T_A map has don't cares for $ABC = 001$, 101 and 110 since A^+ has don't cares in the corresponding squares.

Instead of transforming the Q^+ map into the T_Q map one square at a time, we can divide the Q^+ map into two halves corresponding to $Q = 0$ and $Q = 1$, and transform each half of the map. From Table 13-3, whenever $Q = 0$, $T = Q^+$, and whenever $Q = 1$, $T = (Q^+)'$. Therefore, to transform the Q^+ map into a T map, we copy the half for which $Q = 0$ and complement the half for which $Q = 1$, leaving the don't cares unchanged.

We will apply this method to transform the A^+, B^+, and C^+ maps for our counter shown in Fig. 13-4(a) into T maps. For the first map, A corresponds to Q (and A^+ to Q^+), so to get the T_A map from the A^+ map we complement the second column (where $A = 1$) and leave the rest of the map unchanged. Similarly, to get T_B from B^+ we complement the bottom half of the B map, and to get T_C from C^+ we complement the middle two rows. This yields the maps and equations of Fig. 13-4(b) and the network shown in Fig. 13-5. The gate inputs connect directly to the corresponding flip-flop outputs as indicated by the dashed lines. To facilitate reading similar circuit diagrams, such connecting wires will be omitted in the remainder of the book.

Fig. 13-5. Counter using T flip-flops

Note that the input pulse (P) is ANDed with each of the T functions so that the flip-flops will change state only in response to an input pulse. To make sure that the pulse simultaneously reaches all of the flip-flops which must change state, the pulse has been connected to the gate closest to the flip-flop. Timing problems could result if the pulse had to pass through a different number of gates to reach each flip-flop. Clocked T flip-flops can be used to simplify the network and to eliminate such timing problems.

     The timing diagram of Fig. 13-6, derived by tracing signals through the network, verifies that the counter functions according to the state diagram of Fig. 13-3. For example, starting with $ABC = 000$, the first P pulse produces a pulse only on T_A, so the next state is 100. Note that the flip-flops always change state after the input pulse is over.

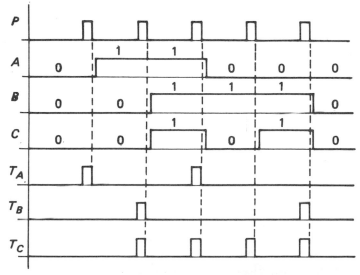

Fig. 13-6. Timing diagram for Fig. 13-5

Although the original state table for the counter (Table 13-2) is not completely specified, the next states of states 001, 101 and 110 have been specified in
the process of completing the network design. For example, if the flip-flops are
initially set to $A = 0, B = 0$ and $C = 1$ and a pulse is applied, tracing signals through
the network shows that $T_A = T_B = 1$ so that the state will change to 111. This
behavior is indicated by the dashed line in Fig. 13-7. Once state 111 is reached,
successive pulses will cause the counter to continue in the original counting
sequence as indicated on the state graph. When the power in a network is
first turned on, the initial states of the flip-flops may be unpredictable. For
this reason, all of the don't care states in a counter should be checked to make
sure that they eventually lead into the main counting sequence unless a
power-up reset is provided.

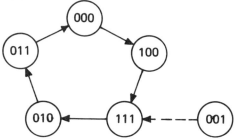

Fig. 13-7. State graph for counter

In summary, the following procedure can be used to design a counter
using T flip-flops:

a. Form a state table which gives the next flip-flop states for each combination of present flip-flop states.

b. Plot the next state maps from the table.

c. Plot a T input map for each flip-flop. When filling in the T_Q map, T_Q must
be 1 whenever $Q^+ \neq Q$. This means that the T_Q map can be formed from
the Q^+ map by complementing the $Q = 1$ half of the map and leaving the
$Q = 0$ half unchanged.

d. Find the T input equations from the maps and realize the network.

13.3 Counter Design Using *S-R* Flip-Flops

The procedures used to design a counter with *S-R* flip-flops are similar to
the procedures discussed in Sections 13.1 and 13.2. However, instead of deriving
an input equation for each T flip-flop, S and R input equations must be derived.
We will now develop methods for deriving these S and R flip-flop input equations.

Table 13-4(a) describes the behavior of the *S-R* flip-flop. Given S, R and
Q, we can determine Q^+ from this table. However, the problem we must solve is
to determine S and R given the present state Q and the desired next state Q^+. If
the present state of the flip-flop is $Q = 0$, and the desired next state is $Q^+ = 1$, a 1
must be applied to the S input to set the flip-flop to 1. If the present state is 1, and
the desired next state is 0, a 1 must be applied to the R input to reset the flip-flop
to 0. Restrictions on the flip-flop inputs require that $S = 0$ if $R = 1$, and $R = 0$ if
$S = 1$. Thus when forming Table 13-4(b), the rows corresponding to $QQ^+ = 01$

and 10 are filled in with $SR = 10$ and 01, respectively. If the present state and next state are both 0, S must be 0 to prevent setting the flip-flop to 1. However, R may be either 0 or 1 since when $Q = 0$, $R = 1$ has no effect on the flip-flop state. Similarly, if the present state and next state are both 1, R must be 0 to prevent resetting the flip-flop, but S may be either 0 or 1. The required S and R inputs are summarized in Table 13-4(b). Table 13-4(c) is the same as 13-4(b), except the alternative choices for R and S have been indicated by don't cares.

Table 13-4. S-R Flip-Flop Inputs

(a)			
S	R	Q	Q^+
0	0	0	0
0	0	1	1
0	1	0	0
0	1	1	0
1	0	0	1
1	0	1	1
1	1	0	— inputs not
1	1	1	— allowed

(b)

Q	Q^+	S	R
0	0	$\begin{cases}0 & 0\\0 & 1\end{cases}$	
0	1	1	0
1	0	0	1
1	1	$\begin{cases}0 & 0\\1 & 0\end{cases}$	

(c)

Q	Q^+	S	R
0	0	0	x
0	1	1	0
1	0	0	1
1	1	x	0

$$Q^+ = S + R'Q \quad (SR = 0)$$

Next we will redesign the counter of Fig. 13-3 using S-R flip-flops. Table 13-2 is repeated in Table 13-5 with columns added for the S and R flip-flop inputs. These columns can be filled in using Table 13-4(c). For $ABC = 000$, $A = 0$ and $A^+ = 1$, so $S_A = 1$, $R_A = 0$. For $ABC = 010$ and 011, $A = 0$ and $A^+ = 0$, so $S_A = 0$ and $R_A = x$. For $ABC = 100$, $A = 1$ and $A^+ = 1$, so $S_A = x$ and $R_A = 0$. For row 111, $A = 1$ and $A^+ = 0$, so $S_A = 0$ and $R_A = 1$. For $ABC = 001$, 101 and 110, $A^+ = x$, so $S_A = R_A = x$. Similarly, the values of S_B and R_B are derived from the values of B and B^+, and S_C and R_C are derived from C and C^+. The resulting flip-flop input functions are mapped in Fig. 13-8(a).

Table 13-5

A	B	C	A^+	B^+	C^+	S_A	R_A	S_B	R_B	S_C	R_C
0	0	0	1	0	0	1	0	0	x	0	x
0	0	1	—	—	—	x	x	x	x	x	x
0	1	0	0	1	1	0	x	x	0	1	0
0	1	1	0	0	0	0	x	0	1	0	1
1	0	0	1	1	1	x	0	1	0	1	0
1	0	1	—	—	—	x	x	x	x	x	x
1	1	0	—	—	—	x	x	x	x	x	x
1	1	1	0	1	0	0	1	x	0	0	1

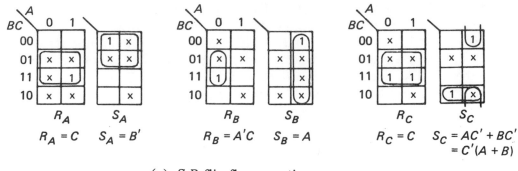

$$R_A = C \qquad S_A = B'$$
$$R_B = A'C \qquad S_B = A$$
$$R_C = C \qquad S_C = AC' + BC'$$
$$= C'(A + B)$$

(a) *S-R* flip-flop equations

(b) Next state maps

(c) Logic diagram

Fig. 13-8. Counter of Fig. 13-3 using *S-R* flip-flops

It is generally faster and easier to derive the S-R flip-flop input maps directly from the next state maps than to derive them from the state table as was done above. For each flip-flop, we will derive the S and R input maps from the next state (Q^+) map using Table 13-4(c) to determine the values for S and R. Just as we did for the T flip-flop, we will use the next state maps for A^+, B^+, and C^+ in Fig. 13-4(a) as a starting point for deriving the S-R flip-flop input equations. For convenience, these maps are repeated in Fig. 13-8(b). We will consider one half of each next state map at a time when deriving the input maps. We will start with flip-flop A ($Q = A$ and $Q^+ = A^+$) and consider the $A = 0$ column of the map. From Table 13-4(c), if $A = 0$ and $A^+ = 1$, then $S = 1$ and $R = 0$. Therefore, for every square in the $A = 0$ column where $A^+ = 1$, we plot $S_A = 1$ and $R_A = 0$ (or blank) in the corresponding squares of the input maps. Similarly, for every square in the $A = 0$ column where $A^+ = 0$, we plot $S_A = 0$ and $R_A = x$ on the input maps. For the $A = 1$ column, if $A^+ = 0$, we plot $S_A = 0$ and $R_A = 1$; if $A^+ = 1$, we plot $S_A = x$ and $R_A = 0$. Don't cares on the A^+ map remain don't cares on the S_A and R_A maps, since if we don't care what the next state is, we don't care what the input is. In a similar manner, we can derive the S_B and R_B maps from the B^+ map by working with the $B = 0$ (top) half of the map and the $B = 1$ (bottom) half of the map. As before, 1's are placed on the S or R map when the flip-flop must be set or reset. S is a don't care if $Q = 1$ and no state change is required, and $R = x$ if $Q = 0$ and no state change is required. Finally, S_C and R_C are derived from the C^+ map. Figure 13-8(c) shows the resulting network. Note that the connecting wires between the flip-flop outputs and the gate inputs have been omitted to facilitate reading the diagram. The input pulse (P) is ANDed with each flip-flop input so that a change of state only occurs when a pulse is received. This design assumes that the pulses are of the proper width so that the state of the counter will change only once for each pulse.

13.4　Counter Design Using *J-K* Flip-Flops

The procedure used to design a counter with J-K flip-flops is very similar to that used for S-R flip-flops. The J-K flip-flop is similar to the S-R flip-flop except that J and K can be 1 simultaneously, in which case the flip-flop changes state. Table 13-6(a) gives the next state (Q^+) as a function of J, K and Q. Using this table, we can derive the required input conditions for J and K when Q and Q^+ are given. Thus if a change from $Q = 0$ to $Q^+ = 1$ is required, either the flip-flop can be set to 1 by using $J = 1$ (and $K = 0$) or the state can be changed by using $J = K = 1$. In other words, J must be 1, but K is a don't care. Similarly a state change from 1 to 0 can be accomplished by resetting the flip-flop with $K = 1$ (and $J = 0$) or by changing the flip-flop state with $J = K = 1$. When no state change is required, the inputs are the same as the corresponding inputs for the S-R flip-flops. The J-K input requirements are summarized in Tables 13-6(b) and 13-6(c).

Table 13-6. J-K Flip-Flop Inputs

(a)	(b)	(c)

(a)

J	K	Q	Q^+
0	0	0	0
0	0	1	1
0	1	0	0
0	1	1	0
1	0	0	1
1	0	1	1
1	1	0	1
1	1	1	0

(b)

Q	Q^+	J	K
0	0	0	0
		0	1
0	1	1	0
		1	1
1	0	0	1
		1	1
1	1	0	0
		1	0

(c)

Q	Q^+	J	K
0	0	0	x
0	1	1	x
1	0	x	1
1	1	x	0

$$Q^+ = JQ' + K'Q$$

We will now redesign the counter of Fig. 13-3 using J-K flip-flops. Table 13-2 is repeated in Table 13-7 with columns added for the J and K flip-flop inputs. We will fill in these columns using Table 13-6(c). For $ABC = 000$, $A = 0$ and $A^+ = 1$, so $J_A = 1$ and $K_A = x$. For $ABC = 010$ and 011, $A = 0$ and $A^+ = 0$, so $J_A = 0$ and $K_A = x$. The remaining table entries are filled in similarly. The resulting J-K flip-flop input functions are plotted in Fig. 13-9(a).

Table 13-7

A	B	C	A^+	B^+	C^+	J_A	K_A	J_B	K_B	J_C	K_C
0	0	0	1	0	0	1	x	0	x	0	x
0	0	1	–	–	–	x	x	x	x	x	x
0	1	0	0	1	1	0	x	x	0	1	x
0	1	1	0	0	0	0	x	x	1	x	1
1	0	0	1	1	1	x	0	1	x	1	x
1	0	1	–	–	–	x	x	x	x	x	x
1	1	0	–	–	–	x	x	x	x	x	x
1	1	1	0	1	0	x	1	x	0	x	1

The J-K flip-flop input maps can also be derived directly from the next state maps. From Table 13-6(c), when $Q = 0$, $J = Q^+$ and $K = x$; and when $Q = 1$, $J = x$ and $K = (Q^+)'$. Thus the $Q = 0$ half of the J map is the same as Q^+ and the $Q = 1$ half is all x's. The $Q = 0$ half of the K map is all x's and the $Q = 1$ is the complement of Q^+. The next state maps of Fig. 13-4(a) are repeated in Fig. 13-9(b). We will derive the J-K maps of Fig. 13-9(a) directly from these next state maps using the method described above. The $A = 0$ half of the J_A map is the same as the corresponding half of the A^+ map, and the $A = 1$ half of the J_A map is all don't cares. The $A = 1$ half of the K_A map is the complement of the A^+ map, and the $A = 0$ half of the K_A map is all don't cares. We can derive the J_B and K_B maps from the B^+ map in a similar manner, and also derive J_C and K_C from the C^+ map.

After deriving the flip-flop input equations from the *J-K* maps, we can draw the logic diagram of Fig. 13-9(c). Since clocked *J-K* flip-flops have been used, the input pulses go directly to the clock (*CK*) inputs on the flip-flops rather than into AND gates as in Fig. 13-8(c).

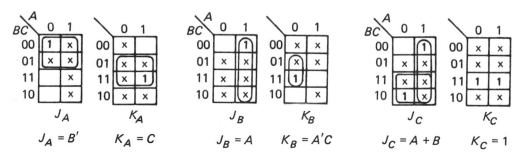

(a) *J-K* flip-flop input equations

(b) Next state maps

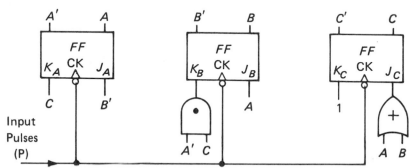

(c) Logic diagram (omitting the feedback lines)

Fig. 13-9. Counter of Fig. 13-3 using *J-K* flip-flops

13.5 Short-Cut Method for Deriving *J-K* Flip-Flop Input Equations

We will now show a method for reading the *J-K* input equations directly off the next state maps without the necessity of plotting separate *J* and *K* maps. From Fig. 13-9, note that the functions J_A and K_A do not contain the variable A. Similarly, J_B and K_B are independent of B, and J_C and K_C are independent of C. This is true in general that the minimized *J* and *K* input equations for flip-flop *Q* will not depend on *Q*. This occurs because the $Q = 1$ half of the *J* map is all don't cares. Therefore, any 1 on the $Q = 0$ half of the *J* map can be combined with a don't care on the $Q = 1$ half to eliminate the variable *Q*. A similar situation holds for *K* since the $Q = 0$ half of the *K* map is all don't cares.

From Table 13-6(c), when $Q = 0$, $J = Q^+$. Therefore, since *J* is independent of *Q*, we can read *J* directly from the $Q = 0$ half of the Q^+ map. This is illustrated in Fig. 13-10. The next state maps of Fig. 13-4(a) have been replotted with each three-variable map divided into two two-variable maps. For the A^+ map, the first column ($A = 0$) constitutes a map giving J_A as a function of B and C. Similarly, the top ($B = 0$) half of the B^+ map gives J_B as a function of A and C, and the top and bottom rows of the third map constitute a map for J_C. The *J* functions read from these maps are the same as read from the maps in Fig. 13-9(b).

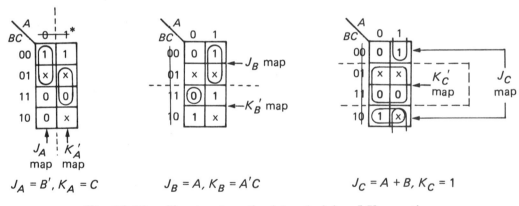

$$J_A = B', K_A = C \qquad J_B = A, K_B = A'C \qquad J_C = A + B, K_C = 1$$

Fig. 13-10. Short-cut method for deriving *J-K* equations

From Table 13-6(c), when $Q = 1$, $K = (Q^+)'$ or $K' = Q^+$. Therefore, since *K* (and hence K') is independent of *Q*, the $Q = 1$ half of the Q^+ map serves as a map for K'. We can read *K* directly from this K' map by reading the 0's instead of the 1's. For example, the $A = 1$ column of the A^+ map in Fig. 13-10 constitutes a map for K_A'. By combining the 0 on this map with a don't care, we get $K_A = C$. Similarly, we get K_B by reading the 0's on the bottom half of the B^+ map, and we get K_C from the middle two rows of the C^+ map. The *K* functions read from these maps are the same as derived in Fig. 13-9.

---

*On each map, since *J* and *K* are independent of the variable "*Q*", the values of *Q* ($Q = A, B,$ or C) have been crossed out to facilitate reading the expressions for *J* and *K*.

We can prove the general validity of the short-cut method by starting with the characteristic equation for the *J-K* flip-flop:

$$Q^+ = JQ' + K'Q \tag{13-1}$$

If we assume that Q^+ is a function of Q and n other variables, then

$$Q^+ = F(Q, X_1, X_2, \ldots, X_n) \tag{13-2}$$

Therefore, $Q^+ = JQ' + K'Q = F(Q, X_1, X_2, \ldots, X_n)$ (13-3)

Letting $Q = 0$ yields

$$Q^+\big|_{Q=0} = J = F(0, X_1, X_2, \ldots, X_n) \tag{13-4}$$

Letting $Q = 1$ yields

$$Q^+\big|_{Q=1} = K' = F(1, X_1, X_2, \ldots, X_n) \tag{13-5}$$

and

$$K = (Q^+\big|_{Q=1})' = F'(1, X_1, X_2, \ldots, X_n) \tag{13-6}$$

Given an $n + 1$ variable map for Q^+ which corresponds to (13-2), setting $Q = 0$ is equivalent to choosing the $Q = 0$ half of the map and eliminating Q. Equation (13-4) indicates that the resulting n-variable map is a map for J. Similarly, setting $Q = 1$ in (13-2) is equivalent to choosing the $Q = 1$ half of the Q^+ map and eliminating Q. The result is an n-variable map for K' as indicated by (13-5). Reading the 0's on the K' map then gives an expression for K.

In summary, the steps for determining the J and K inputs for flip-flop Q by the short-cut, method are:

a. Plot the next-state (Q^+) map.

b. Identify the $Q = 0$ and $Q = 1$ halves of the map.

c. Cross out the values of Q on the edge of the map (since J and K are independent of Q).

d. To determine J as a function of the remaining variables, loop the *1's* on the $Q = 0$ half of the map.

e. To determine K as a function of the remaining variables, loop the *0's* on the $Q = 1$ half of the map.

The short-cut method described above offers two advantages over the standard method: (1) Plotting separate maps for J and K is unnecessary. (2) The number of variables to be worked with is reduced by 1 (since the J_Q and K_Q sub-maps are independent of Q).

13.6 Counter Design Using *D* Flip-Flops

For a *D* flip-flop, $Q^+ = D$, so the *D* input map is identical to the next state map. Therefore, the equation for *D* can be read directly from the Q^+ map. For the counter of Fig. 13-3, the following equations can be read from the next state maps shown in Fig. 13-4(a):

$$D_A = A^+ = B' \qquad D_B = B^+ = A + BC' \qquad D_C = C^+ = AC' + BC' = C'(A + B)$$

This leads to the network shown in Fig. 13-11 using clocked *D* flip-flops.

Fig. 13-11. Counter of Fig. 13-3 using D flip-flops

13.7   Design of a Code Converter

The same design technique used for counters can be applied to any sequential network which has a single pulse input to initiate state changes and no other external inputs. For example, consider the design of a 8-4-2-1 BCD to excess-3 code converter using four flip-flops. Initially, one of the BCD digits 0 through 9 is stored in the flip-flops. After a pulse is applied to the network, the corresponding excess-3 coded digit should appear in the flip-flops. The state table for the converter is given by Table 13-8. Figure 13-12 gives the next state maps, the J-K input equations, and the resulting network. The short-cut method was used to derive the J-K equations. The circuitry for initially loading the BCD digit into the flip-flops has been omitted from the diagram.

Table 13-8.   State Table for Code Converter

A	B	C	D	A^+	B^+	C^+	D^+
0	0	0	0	0	0	1	1
0	0	0	1	0	1	0	0
0	0	1	0	0	1	0	1
0	0	1	1	0	1	1	0
0	1	0	0	0	1	1	1
0	1	0	1	1	0	0	0
0	1	1	0	1	0	0	1
0	1	1	1	1	0	1	0
1	0	0	0	1	0	1	1
1	0	0	1	1	1	0	0

$$J_A = BC + BD = B(C + D) \qquad K_A = 0$$
$$J_B = C + D \qquad K_B = C + D$$
$$J_C = D' \qquad K_C = D' \qquad J_D = 1 \qquad K_D = 1$$

Fig. 13-12. BCD to excess-3 code converter

13.8 Shift Registers

A shift register is a group of flip-flops in which a binary number can be stored. This number can be shifted to the left or right when a shift pulse is applied. Bits shifted out one end of the register may be lost, or if the shift register is of cyclic type, bits shifted out one end are shifted back in the other end. Figure 13-13(a) illustrates a four bit cyclic right-shift register constructed from S-R flip-flops. If the initial contents of the register is 0111, after one pulse the contents is 1011. After a second pulse, the state is 1101, then 1110, and the fourth pulse returns the register to the initial 0111 state. Note that the outputs of flip-flop A are fed into the inputs of flip-flop B through AND gates. If $A = 1$, flip-flop B is set to 1 by the shift pulse; if $A = 0$, flip-flop B is reset to 0 by the shift pulse. The other flip-flops are connected in a similar manner. The AND gates can be eliminated if clocked flip-flops are used as in Fig. 13-13(b).

To assure proper operation of the shift register of Fig. 13-13(a), the change of state of the flip-flops must be delayed until the shift pulse is completed; otherwise, several shifts could occur for one pulse. The necessary delay can be built into the flip-flop, in which case the shift pulse width must be less than the flip-flop delay. Alternately, the flip-flop can be designed to respond to the trailing edge of the pulse, in which case the pulse width is not important. In any case, the operation of the flip-flops in the shift register is synchronized by the common shift pulse so that the flip-flops change state simultaneously after the pulse is over.

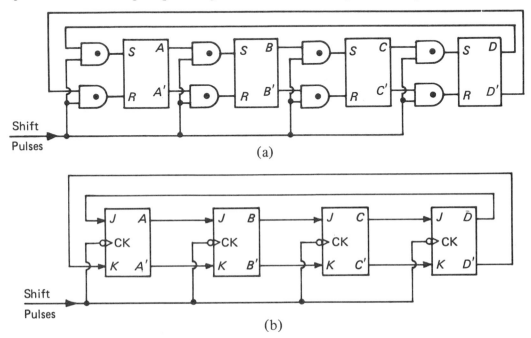

Fig. 13-13. Cyclic right-shift registers

13.9 Derivation of Flip-Flop Input Equations—Summary

The input equation for the flip-flops in a sequential network may be derived from the next state equations by using truth tables or by using Karnaugh maps. For networks with three to five variables it is convenient to first plot maps for the next state equations and then transform these maps into maps for the flip-flop inputs.

Given the present state of a flip-flop (Q) and the desired next state (Q^+), Table 13-9 gives the required inputs for various types of flip-flops. For the D flip-flop, the input is the same as the next state. For the T flip-flop the input is 1 whenever a state change is required. For the S-R flip-flop, S is 1 whenever the flip-flop must be set to 1 and R is 1 when it must be reset to 0. We don't care what S is if the flip-flop state is 1 and must remain 1; we don't care what R is if the flip-flop state is 0 and must remain 0. For a J-K flip-flop, the J and K inputs are the same as S and R respectively, except that when one input is 1 the other input is x. This difference arises because $S = R = 1$ is not allowed, but $J = K = 1$ causes a change of state.

Table 13-9. Determination of Flip-flop Input Equations from Next State Equations using Karnaugh Maps

Type of flip-flop	Input	$Q = 0$		$Q = 1$		Rules for forming input map from next state map*	
		$Q^+ = 0$	$Q^+ = 1$	$Q^+ = 0$	$Q^+ = 1$	$Q = 0$ half of map	$Q = 1$ half of map
Delay	D	0	1	0	1	no change	no change
Trigger	T	0	1	1	0	no change	complement
Set-Reset	S	0	1	0	x	no change	replace 1's with x's**
	R	x	0	1	0	replace 0's with x's**	complement
J-K	J	0	1	x	x	no change	fill in with x's
	K	x	x	1	0	fill in with x's	complement

Q^+ means the next state of Q

x is a don't care

*Always copy x's from the next state map onto the input maps first.

**Fill in the remaining squares with 0's.

Example (illustrating the use of Table 13.9):

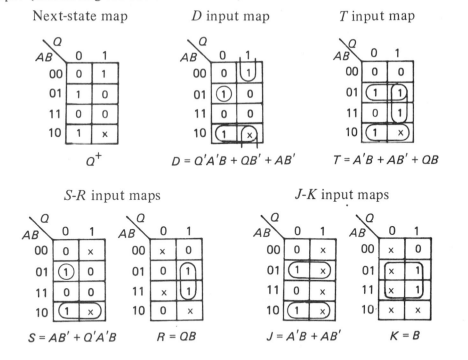

$$D = Q'A'B + QB' + AB'$$

$$T = A'B + AB' + QB$$

$$S = AB' + Q'A'B \qquad R = QB$$

$$J = A'B + AB' \qquad K = B$$

Table 13-9 summarizes the rules for transforming next state maps into flip-flop input maps. Before applying these rules, we must copy any don't cares from the next state maps onto the input maps. Then we must work with the $Q = 0$ and $Q = 1$ halves of each next state map separately. The rules given in Table 13-9 are easily derived by comparing the values of Q^+ with the corresponding input values. For example, in the $Q = 0$ column of the table, we see that J is the same as Q^+, so the $Q = 0$ half of the J map is the same as the Q^+ map. In the $Q = 1$ column, $J = x$ (independent of Q^+) so we fill in the $Q = 1$ half of the J map with x's.

For the S-R flip-flop, note that when $Q = 0$, $R = x$ if $Q^+ = 0$; and when $Q = 1$, $R = 1$ if $Q^+ = 0$. Therefore, to form the R map from the Q^+ map, replace 0's with x's on the $Q = 0$ half of the map and replace 0's with 1's on the $Q = 1$ half (and fill in 0's for the remaining entries). Similarly, to form the S map from the Q^+ map, copy the 1's on the $Q = 0$ half of the map, and replace the 1's with x's on the $Q = 1$ half.

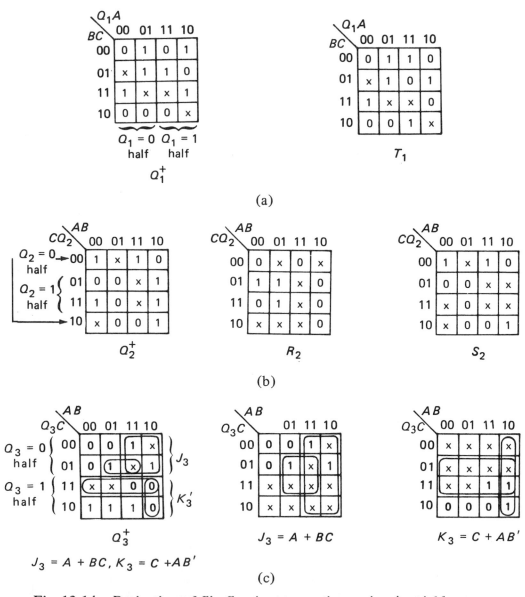

(a)

(b)

(c)

Fig. 13-14. Derivation of flip-flop input equations using 4-variable maps

Examples of deriving 4-variable input maps are given in Fig. 13-14. In each case, Q_i represents the flip-flop for which input equations are being derived and A, B and C represent other variables on which the next state depends. In Fig. 13-14(a), a 1 is placed on the T_1 map whenever Q_1 must change state. In Fig. 13-14(b), 1's are placed on the $Q_2 = 0$ half of the S_2 map whenever Q_2 must be set to 1, and 1's are placed on the $Q_2 = 1$ half of the R_2 map whenever Q_2 must be reset. Figure 13-14(c) illustrates derivation of J_3 and K_3 both by using separate J and K maps and by using the short-cut method. In the latter case, plotting separate J and K maps is not necessary because J_3 is read directly from the $Q_3 = 0$ half of the $Q_3{}^+$ map, and K_3 is read directly from the 0's of the $Q_3 = 1$ half. As will be seen in Unit 15, the methods used to derive flip-flop input equations for counters are easily extended to general sequential networks.

The procedures for deriving flip-flop input equations discussed in this unit can be extended to other types of flip-flops. If we want to derive input equations for a different type of flip-flop, the first step is to construct a table which gives the next state (Q^+) as a function of the present state (Q) and the flip-flop inputs. From this table, we can construct another table which gives the required flip-flop input combinations for each of the four possible pairs of values of Q and Q^+. Then using this table, we can plot a Karnaugh map for each input function and derive minimum expressions from the maps.

PROBLEMS

13.1 Design a counter which counts in the following sequence:

0000, 1000, 1100, 1010, 1110, 0001, 1001, 1101, 1011, 1111, 0000, . . .

    a.   Use T flip-flops, AND and OR gates

    b.   Use S-R flip-flops, AND and OR gates

    c.   Use clocked J-K flip-flops and NAND gates

    d.   Use clocked D flip-flops and NOR gates

13.2 Work Problem 13.1 using the sequence:

0000, 0010, 0100, 0110, 1000, 0001, 0011, 0101, 0111, 1101, 0000, . . .

13.3 An M-N flip-flop works as follows:

If $MN = 00$, the next state of the flip-flop is 0.
If $MN = 01$, the next state of the flip-flop is the same as the present state.
If $MN = 10$, the next state of the flip-flop is the complement of the present state.
If $MN = 11$, the next state of the flip-flop is 1.

a. Complete the following table (use don't cares when possible.):

present state Q	next state Q^+	M	N
0	0		
0	1		
1	0		
1	1		

b. Using the above table and Karnaugh maps, derive and minimize the input equations for a counter composed of 3 M-N flip-flops which counts in the following sequence:

$$ABC = 000, 001, 011, 111, 101, 100, 000, \ldots$$

13.4 A sequential network contains a register of four flip-flops. Initially a binary number N ($0000 \leqslant N \leqslant 1001$) is stored in the flip-flops. After a single input pulse is applied to the network, the register should contain $N + 0101$. In other words, the function of the sequential network is to add five to the contents of a 4-bit register. Design the network using J-K flip-flops.

13.5 A network diagram for a K-G flip-flop is given below.

a. Find an equation which gives the next state of the flip-flop (i.e., the state after the clock pulse has occurred) in terms of the present state (Q) and the inputs (K and G)

b. Complete the following table, giving all possible pairs of values for K and G in each case (don't use don't cares).

Q	Q^+	K	G
0	0		
0	1		
1	0		
1	1		

c. A logic network contains several K-G flip-flops. The desired next state of one of the K-G flip-flops is given by $Q^+ = XY + Q$, where X and Y are outputs of other flip-flops in the network. Find K and G in terms of X, Y and Q. (Several different solutions are possible for K and G. Find at least two different solutions.)

13.6 A sequential network has two registers. Each register is composed of four clocked (master-slave) J-K flip-flops. The flip-flops in the first register are labeled A, B, C, and D; the flip-flops in the second register are labeled E, F, G and H.

    a.   Show how to interconnect the flip-flops so that a single pulse (P) will interchange the contents of the two registers; that is, after the pulse the new value of A should be the value of E before the pulse and the new value of E should be the value of A before the pulse, and similarly for B and F, C and G, and D and H.

    b.   Show the required connections if S-R flip-flops and AND gates are used instead of clocked J-K flip-flops. What problem will arise if flip-flops of the type shown in Fig. 12-4(a) are used with no added delay? If S-R flip-flops with added delay as seen in Fig. 12-5(d) are used, what restriction must be placed on the pulse width to assure proper operation of the network?

13.7 By tracing signals through the network, draw a timing diagram for the counter of Fig. 13-11 showing P, A, B, C, D_A, D_B and D_C.

13.8 Design a decade counter which counts in the sequence 0000, 0001, 0010, 0011, 0100, 0101, 0110, 0111, 1000, 1001, 0000, ...

    a.   Use clocked J-K flip-flops.

    b.   Use S-R flip-flops.

    c.   Use T flip-flops.

    d.   Draw a complete state diagram for the counter of part a showing what happens when the counter is started in each of the "unused" states.

13.9 If the cyclic shift register of Fig. 13-13(b) is changed so that D is connected to the K input of flip-flop A and D' is connected to J, determine the sequence of register states. Assume that the initial state is $ABCD = 0000$, and determine the state after each shift pulse.

13.10 Redesign the network of Fig. 13-12 using

    a. unclocked T flip-flops   b.   clocked D flip-flops

13.11 Design a 3-bit counter which counts in the following sequence:
001, 011, 010, 110, 111, 101, 100, 001, . . .

    a.   Use clocked D flip-flops.   b.   Use clocked J-K flip-flops.

    c.   Use clocked T flip-flops.   d.   Use S-R flip-flops.

    e.   What will happen if the counter of part (a) is started in state 000?

13.12 Design a decade counter which counts in the 6-3-1-1 code sequence (see Table 1-1).

    a.   Use clocked D flip-flops.   b.   Use clocked T flip-flops.

    c.   Use clocked J-K flip-flops.

    d.   What will happen if the counter of part (c) is started in state 1101?

14

ANALYSIS OF CLOCKED SEQUENTIAL NETWORKS

OBJECTIVES

1. Analyze a sequential network by signal tracing.

2. Given a sequential network, write the next state equations for the flip-flops and derive the state graph or state table. Using the state graph, determine the state sequence and output sequence for a given input sequence.

3. Explain the difference between a Mealy machine and a Moore machine.

4. Given a state table, construct the corresponding state graph, and conversely.

5. Given a sequential network or a state table and an input sequence, draw a timing chart for the network. Determine the output sequence from the timing chart, neglecting any "false" outputs.

6. Draw a general model for a clocked Mealy or Moore sequential network. Explain the operation of the network in terms of these models. Explain why a clock pulse is needed to assure proper operation of the network.

STUDY GUIDE

1. Study Section 14.1, *A Sequential Parity Checker.*

   a. Explain how parity can be used for error detection.

   b. Verify that the parity checker (Fig. 14-4) will produce the output waveform given in Fig. 14-2 when the input waveform is as shown.

2. Study Section 14.2, *Analysis by Signal Tracing and Timing Charts.*

    a. What is the difference between a Mealy machine and a Moore machine?

    b. For normal operation of clocked sequential networks of the types discussed in this section, when should the inputs be changed?

    When do the flip-flops change state?

    At what times can the output change for a Moore network?

    At what times can the output change for a Mealy network?

    c. At what time (with respect to the clock) should the output of a Mealy network be read?

    d. Why can false outputs appear in a Mealy network and not in a Moore network?

    What can be done to eliminate the false outputs?

    If the output of a Mealy network is used as an input to another Mealy network synchronized by the same clock pulse, will the false outputs cause any problem? Explain.

    e. Examine the timing diagram of Fig. 14-8. Note that there are two types of false outputs. A false 0 output occurs if Z is 1 during two successive clock pulses and Z goes to 0 between the clock pulses. A false 1 output occurs if Z is 0 during two successive clock pulses and Z goes to 1 between the clock pulses. When the output is different during two successive clock pulses, the output may be temporarily incorrect immediately following the clock pulse but before the input has changed to its next value. In this case, we will not say that a false output has occurred since the sequence of outputs is still correct.

3. Study Section 14.3, *State Tables and Graphs.*

   a. In Equations (14-1) through (14-4), at what time (with respect to the clock pulse) is the right hand side evaluated?

   What does Q^+ mean?

   b. Derive the timing chart of Fig. 14-6 using Table 14-2(a).

   c. What is the difference between the state graphs for Mealy and Moore machines?

   d. For a state table, Table 14-3(b) for example, what do the terms *"present state"*, *"next* state", and *"present* output" mean with respect to the clock pulse?

   e. Why does a Moore state table have only one output column?

4. The following timing chart was derived from the network of Fig. 14-7.

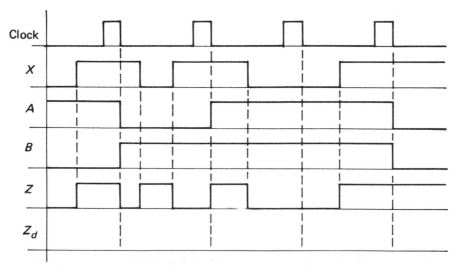

a. Noting that extra input changes which occur between clock pulses cannot affect the state of the network, what is the effective input sequence seen by the flip-flops in the network?

b. Using Table 14-3, verify the waveforms given for A, B and Z.

c. Indicate any false outputs. What is the "correct" output sequence from the network?

d. Using the effective input sequence from part a, determine the output sequence from the state graph (Fig. 14-11). This output sequence should be the same as your answer to part c. Why can't false outputs be determined from the state graph?

e. The output Z is fed into a clocked D flip-flop using the same clock (CK) as the network. Sketch the waveform for Z_d. Does Z_d have any false outputs?

f. Starting with Fig. 14-11, construct the corresponding state table. Verify that your answer is the same as Table 14-3(b). Note that the output label on a given arrow of the graph is associated with the state from which the arrow originates.

g. Assume that the flip-flops in Fig. 14-7 are changed to flip-flops which trigger on the rising edge of the clock; i.e., the inversion circles are removed from the clock inputs. Also, the clock waveform in Fig. 14-8 is replaced with

The input waveform is left unchanged. What changes, if any, would occur in the remainder of the timing diagram? Explain.

5. Consider the following state tables:

MEALY						MOORE			

<table>
<tr><td>p.s.</td><td colspan="2">n.s.</td><td colspan="2">z</td><td></td><td>p.s.</td><td colspan="2">n.s.</td><td>z</td></tr>
<tr><td></td><td>$x = 0$</td><td>1</td><td>$x = 0$</td><td>1</td><td></td><td></td><td>$x = 0$</td><td>1</td><td></td></tr>
<tr><td>S_0</td><td>S_1</td><td>S_0</td><td>0</td><td>0</td><td></td><td>S_0</td><td>S_1</td><td>S_0</td><td>0</td></tr>
<tr><td>S_1</td><td>S_0</td><td>S_2</td><td>1</td><td>0</td><td></td><td>S_1</td><td>S_3</td><td>S_2</td><td>0</td></tr>
<tr><td>S_2</td><td>S_0</td><td>S_0</td><td>1</td><td>0</td><td></td><td>S_2</td><td>S_3</td><td>S_0</td><td>0</td></tr>
<tr><td></td><td></td><td></td><td></td><td></td><td></td><td>S_3</td><td>S_3</td><td>S_0</td><td>1</td></tr>
</table>

a. Draw the corresponding state graphs.

b. Show that the same output sequence is obtained from both state graphs when the input sequence is 010 (ignore the initial output for the Moore network).

c. Using the state tables, complete the following timing diagrams for the two networks. Note that the Mealy network has a false output, but the Moore does not. Also note that the output from the Moore network is delayed with respect to the Mealy.

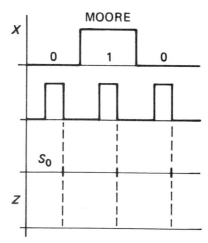

6. Study Section 14.4, *General Models for Sequential Networks.*

    a. A Mealy sequential network has the form shown below. The combinational network realizes the following equations:

$$Q_1^+ = X_1'Q_1 + X_1Q_1'Q_2' \quad Z_1 = X_1Q_1$$
$$Q_2^+ = X_1Q_2' + X_2'Q_1 \quad\quad Z_2 = X_1'Q_1 + X_2Q_2'$$

Initially, $X_1 = X_2 = 1$ and $Q_1 = Q_2 = 0$ as shown.

(1) Before the clock occurs, show the values of the four combinational network outputs on the above diagram and on the timing chart given below.

(2) Show the signal values on the network and timing chart immediately after the clock pulse.

(3) Show any further changes in signal values which will occur after the new values of Q_1 and Q_2 have pro: ·gated through the network.

(4) Next change X_1 to 0 and repeat steps (1), (2) and (3). Show values for each step on the network and on the timing chart.

(5) Next change the inputs to $X_1 = 1$ and $X_2 = 0$ and repeat steps (1), (2) and (3).

(6) Change X_2 to 1 and repeat.

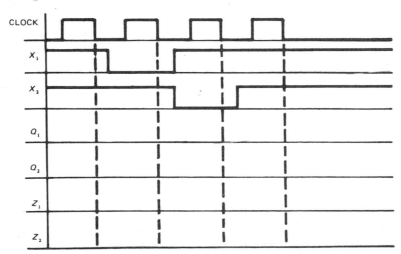

b. Draw a block diagram for a general model of a Mealy network using *J-K* flip-flops as memory elements. If the network has n output variables and k flip-flops, how many outputs will the combinational subnetwork have?

c. Why does use of a clock pulse prevent timing problems?

d. In Equations (14-5) and 14-6), what do the symbols δ and λ mean?

Equation (14-6) is for a Mealy network. What is the corresponding equation for a Moore network?

e. For Table 14-5,

$\delta(S_3, 1) = $ _____ $\lambda(S_3, 1) = $ _____

$\delta(S_1, 2) = $ _____ $\lambda(S_1, 2) = $ _____

7. Work Programmed Exercise 14.1.

8. Work Problems 14.2 through 14.5.

9. When you are satisfied that you can meet the objectives, take the readiness test.

14. ANALYSIS OF CLOCKED SEQUENTIAL NETWORKS

The sequential networks which we have considered up to this point have had no inputs other than an input pulse or clock pulse which causes the network to change state. We will now consider sequential networks which have additional inputs. In general, the sequence of outputs and the sequence of flip-flop states for such networks will depend on the input sequence which is applied to the network. Given a sequential network and an input sequence, we can analyze the network to determine the flip-flop state sequence and the output sequence by tracing the 0 and 1 signals through the network. Although signal tracing may be adequate for small networks, for larger networks it is better to construct a state graph or state table which represents the behavior of the network. Then we can determine the output and state sequences from the graph or table. Such graphs and tables are also useful for the design of sequential networks.

In this chapter we will also study the timing relationships between the inputs, clock pulse, and outputs for sequential networks by constructing timing diagrams. These timing relationships are very important when a sequential network is used as part of a larger digital system. After analyzing several specific sequential networks, we will discuss a general model for a sequential network which consists of a combinational network together with flip-flops which serve as "memory".

14.1   A Sequential Parity Checker

When binary data is transmitted or stored, an extra bit (called a parity bit) is frequently added for purposes of error detection. For example, if data is being transmitted in groups of 7 bits, an eighth bit can be added to each group of 7 bits such that the total number of ones in each block of 8 bits is odd. When the total number of one bits in the block is odd, we say that the parity is odd. (Alternately, the parity bit could be chosen such that the total number of 1's in the block is even, in which case we would have even parity.) Some examples of 8-bit words with odd parity are:

7 data bits	parity bit
0 0 0 0 0 0 0	1
0 0 0 0 0 0 1	0
0 1 1 0 1 1 0	1
1 0 1 0 1 0 1	1
0 1 1 1 0 0 0	0

If any single bit in the 8-bit word is changed from 0 to 1 or from 1 to 0, the parity is no longer odd. Thus, if any single bit error occurs in transmission of a word with odd parity, the presence of this error can be detected because the number of one bits in the word has been changed from odd to even.

As a simple example of a sequential network which has one input in addition to the clock, we will design a parity checker for serial data. (Serial implies that the data enters the network sequentially, one bit at a time.) This network has the form shown in Fig. 14-1.

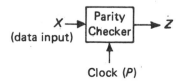

Fig. 14-1.   **Block diagram for parity checker**

When a sequence of 0's and 1's is applied to the X input, the output of the network should be $Z = 1$ if the total number of 1 inputs received is odd; i.e., the output should be 1 if the input parity is odd. Thus, if data which originally had odd parity is transmitted to the network, a final output of $Z = 0$ indicates that an error in transmission has occurred.

We will assume that the X input is synchronized with the clock and changes only between clock pulses. The value of X is determined at the time the clock is high. The clock input is necessary in order to distinguish consecutive 0's or consecutive 1's on the X input. Typical input and output waveforms are shown in Fig. 14-2.

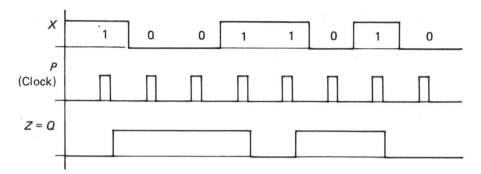

Fig. 14-2. Waveforms for parity checker

We will start the design by constructing a state graph (Fig. 14-3). The sequential network must "remember" whether the total number of 1 inputs received is even or odd; therefore, only two states are required. We will designate these states as S_0 and S_1, corresponding respectively to an even number of 1's received and an odd number of 1's received. We will start the network in state S_0 since initially zero 1's have been received and zero is an even number. As indicated in Fig. 14-3, if the network is in state S_0 (even number of 1's received) and $X = 0$ is received, the network must stay in S_0 since the number of 1's received is still even. However, if $X = 1$ is received, the network goes to state S_1 since the number of 1's received is then odd. Similarly, if the network is in state S_1 (odd number of 1's received) a 0 input causes no state change, but a 1 causes a change to S_0 since the number of 1's received is then even. The output Z should be 1 whenever the network is in state S_1 (odd number of 1's received). The output is listed below the state on the state graph.

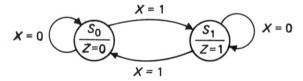

Fig. 14-3. State graph for parity checker

Table 14-1(a) gives the same information as the state graph in tabular form. For example, the table shows that if the present state is S_0, the output is $Z = 0$, and if the input is $X = 1$, the next state will be S_1.

Table 14-1. State Table for Parity Checker

(a)

present state	next state $X = 0$	$X = 1$	present output
S_0	S_0	S_1	0
S_1	S_1	S_0	1

(b)

Q	Q^+ $X = 0$	$X = 1$	T $X = 0$	$X = 1$	Z
0	0	1	0	1	0
1	1	0	0	1	1

Since only two states are required, a single flip-flop (Q) will suffice. We will let $Q = 0$ correspond to state S_0 and $Q = 1$ correspond to S_1. We can then set up a table which shows the next state of flip-flop Q as a function of the present state and X. If we use a T flip-flop, T must be 1 whenever Q and Q^+ differ.

From Table 14-1, the T input should be 1 whenever $X = 1$. Since we only want the network to change state when the clock pulse (P) is present, $T = XP$ and the following network results:

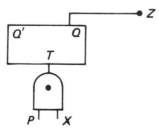

Fig. 14-4

The output waveform for this network is shown in Fig. 14-2. Note that the final value of Z is 0 since an even number of ones were received. If the number of ones received had been odd, the final value of Z would be 1. In this case, it would be necessary to reset the flip-flop to the proper initial state $(Q = 0)$ before checking the parity of another input sequence.

14.2   Analysis by Signal Tracing and Timing Charts

In this section we will analyze clocked sequential networks to find the output sequence resulting from a given input sequence by tracing 0 and 1 signals through the network. The basic procedure is as follows:

   a.   Assume an initial state of the flip-flops (all flip-flops reset to zero unless otherwise specified).

   b.   For the first input in the given sequence, determine the network output(s) and flip-flop inputs.

   c.   Apply the clock pulse to the flip-flops and determine the new set of flip-flop states.

   d.   Determine the output(s) which corresponds to the new states.

   e.   Repeat parts b, c and d for each input in the given sequence.

As we carry out the analysis, we will construct a timing chart which shows the relationship between the input signal, clock pulse, flip-flop states, and network output. We have already seen how to construct timing charts for flip-flops (Unit 12) and counters (Unit 13).

Unless otherwise specified, we will use one of the following two types of flip-flops in this unit:

   a.   Flip-flops that change state on the falling edge of the clock pulse.

   b.   Flip-flops that change state in response to a pulse of a specified width. In this case we assume that the response time of the flip-flop is greater than the clock pulse width.

In either case, the sequential network will change state shortly after the clock pulse is over, that is after the clock goes from high to low. The network inputs will normally be changed between clock pulses when the clock pulse is low. The output may change at the time the flip-flops change state or at the time the input changes depending on the type of network.

If we use flip-flops which change state on the rising edge of the clock pulse instead of the falling edge, operation of the sequential network will be similar except that the state change occurs after the clock pulse goes from low to high. In this case, the inputs will normally be changed when the clock pulse is high.

Two types of clocked sequential networks will be considered – those in which the output depends only on the present state of the flip-flops and those in which the output depends on both the present state of the flip-flops and on the value of the network inputs. If the output of a sequential network is a function of the present state only (as in Figs. 14-4 and 14-5), the network is often referred to as a *Moore machine*. The state graph for a Moore machine has the output associated with the state (as in Figs. 14-3 and 14-9). If the output is a function of both the present state and the input (as in Figs. 14-7 and 14-8), the network is referred to as a *Mealy machine*. The state graph for a Mealy machine has the output associated with the arrow going between states (as in Fig. 14-11).

As an example of a Moore network, we will analyze Fig. 14-5 using an input sequence $X = 10101$. The input is assumed to change between clock pulses and the initial state is $A = B = 0$ as shown in Fig. 14-6. Since Z is only a function of the present state (in this case, $Z = B$), the output will only change when the state changes. If $X = 1$, $J_A = K_A = J_B = 1$, and the state will change to $A = B = 1$ after the first clock pulse.* Then X is changed to 0, and no change of state or output will occur with the second clock pulse since all flip-flop inputs are 0. Then X is changed to 1, and $J_A = J_B = K_B = 1$, so the next clock pulse causes B to become 0. When the 4th clock pulse occurs, $X = 0$ and no change of state or output takes place. Then, with $X = 1$, $J_A = K_A = K_B = J_B = 1$, and the fifth clock pulse causes both flip-flops to change state, so that the final state is $A = 0$, $B = 1$. The input, state and output sequences are plotted on the timing chart of Fig. 14-6 and are also listed below:

$$X = 1\ 0\ 1\ 0\ 1$$
$$A = 0\ 1\ 1\ 1\ 1\ 0$$
$$B = 0\ 1\ 1\ 0\ 0\ 1$$
$$Z = (0)\ 1\ 1\ 0\ 0\ 1$$

If the initial 0 output is ignored, the output sequence is $Z = 11001$. Note that for the *Moore* network, the output which results from application of a given input does not appear until after the clock pulse; therefore, the output sequence is displaced in time with respect to the input sequence.

*Actually, there will be a short propagation delay between the falling edge of the clock pulse and the time the flip-flops change state. Such small delays have been omitted from Fig. 14-6 and other timing diagrams in this and subsequent units.

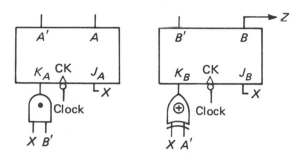

Fig. 14-5. Moore sequential network to be analyzed

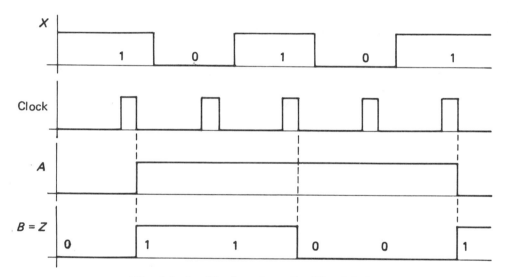

Fig. 14-6. Timing chart for Fig. 14-5

As an example of a Mealy network, we will analyze Fig. 14-7 and construct a timing chart using the input sequence $X = 10101$. The input is assumed to change between clock pulses as shown in Fig. 14-8. In this example, the output depends on both the input (X) and the flip-flop states (A and B), so Z may change either when the input changes or when the flip-flops change state. Initially, assume that the flip-flop states are $A = 0$, $B = 0$. If $X = 1$, the output is $Z = 1$ and $J_B = K_A = 1$. After the falling edge of the first clock pulse, B changes to 1 so Z changes to 0. If the input is changed to $X = 0$, Z will change back to 1. All flip-flop inputs are then 0, so no state change occurs with the second clock pulse. When X is changed to 1, Z becomes 0 and $J_A = K_A = J_B = 1$. A changes to 1 on the falling edge of the third clock pulse at which time Z changes to 1. Next, X is changed to 0 so Z becomes 0 and no state change occurs with the fourth clock pulse. Then X is changed to 1 and Z becomes 1. Since $J_A = K_A = J_B = K_B = 1$, the fifth clock pulse resets the network to the initial state. The input, state and output sequences are plotted on the timing chart of Fig. 14-8 and are also listed below:

$$X = 1 \quad 0 \quad 1 \quad 0 \quad 1$$
$$A = 0 \quad 0 \quad 0 \quad 1 \quad 1 \quad 0$$
$$B = 0 \quad 1 \quad 1 \quad 1 \quad 1 \quad 0$$
$$Z = 1(0)1 \quad 0(1)0 \quad 1 \qquad \text{(“false” outputs are indicated in parentheses)}$$

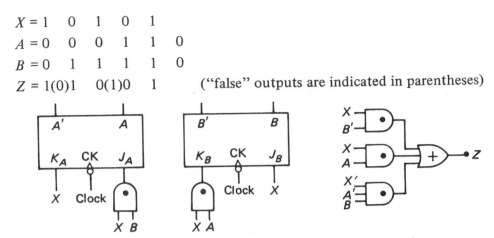

Fig. 14-7. Mealy sequential network to be analyzed

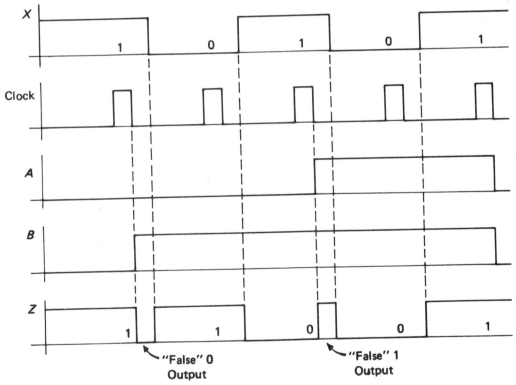

Fig. 14-8. Timing chart for network of Fig. 14-7

Careful interpretation of the output waveform (Z) of the Mealy network is necessary. For a clocked sequential network of this type, the value of the input during (and immediately preceding) the clock pulse determines the next state of the flip-flops. Extra input changes which might occur between clock pulses cannot affect the state of the flip-flops. In a similar manner, the output is only of interest during (and immediately preceding) the clock pulse, and extra output changes which might occur between clock pulses should be ignored. After the network has changed state and before the input is changed, the output may assume a "false" value as indicated on the timing chart. This "false" value arises because the network has assumed a new state but the old input associated with the previous state is still present.

Two types of "false" outputs can occur as indicated in Fig. 14-8. In one case the output Z momentarily goes to 0 when it is expected to remain 1; in the other case the output Z momentarily goes to 1 when it is expected to remain 0. In both cases, two changes of output occur when no change is expected. Ignoring the "false" outputs, by reading the output only during the clock pulse, the output sequence for the network is $Z = 11001$. The false outputs could be eliminated if the input X was only allowed to change at the same time as the falling edge of the clock pulse. If the output of the network is fed into a second sequential network which uses the same clock, the "false" outputs will not cause any problem because the inputs to the second network can only cause a change of state when a clock pulse occurs. Since the output of a Moore network can only change state when the flip-flops change state and not when the input changes, no false outputs can appear in a Moore network.

For the *Mealy* network, the output which corresponds to a given input appears immediately following application of that input. Since the correct output appears before the clock pulse, the output sequence is *not* displaced in time with respect to the input sequence as was the case for the Moore network.

14.3 State Tables and Graphs

In the previous section, we analyzed clocked sequential networks by signal tracing and construction of timing charts. Although this is satisfactory for small networks and short input sequences, construction of state tables and graphs provides a more systematic approach which is useful for analysis of larger networks and which leads to a general synthesis procedure for sequential networks.

The state table specifies the next state and output of a sequential network in terms of its present state and input. The following method can be used to construct the state table:

a. Determine the flip-flop input equations and the output equations from the network.

b. Derive the next state equation for each flip-flop from its input equations using one of the following relations:

D flip-flop	$Q^+ = D$	(14-1)
T flip-flop	$Q^+ = T \oplus Q$	(14-2)
S-R flip-flop	$Q^+ = S + R'Q$	(14-3)
J-K flip-flop	$Q^+ = JQ' + K'Q$	(14-4)

c. Plot a next-state map for each flip-flop.

    d. Combine these maps to form the state table. Such a state table, which gives the next state of the flip-flops as a function of their present state and the network inputs, is frequently referred to as a transition table.

As an example of the above procedure, we will derive the state table for the network of Fig. 14-5:

    a. The flip-flop input equations and output equation are

$$J_A = X \qquad\qquad K_A = XB' \qquad\qquad\qquad Z = B$$
$$J_B = X \qquad\qquad K_B = X \oplus A'$$

    b. The next state equations for the flip-flops are

$$A^+ = J_A A' + K_A' A = XA' + (X' + B)A$$
$$B^+ = J_B B' + K_B' B = XB' + (X \oplus A')'B = XB' + (XA' + X'A)B$$

    c. The corresponding maps are

AB＼X	0	1
00	0	1
01	0	1
11	1	1
10	1	0

A^+

AB＼X	0	1
00	0	1
01	0	1
11	1	0
10	0	1

B^+

    d. Combining these maps yields the transition table in Table 14-2(a), which gives the next state of both flip-flops (A^+B^+) as a function of the present state and input. The output function is then added to the table. In this example, the output depends only on the present state of the flip-flops and not on the input, so only a single output column is required.

    Using Table 14-2(a), we can construct the timing chart of Fig. 14-6 or any other timing chart for some given input sequence and specified initial state. Initially $AB = 00$ and $X = 1$, so $Z = 0$ and $A^+B^+ = 11$. This means that *after* the clock pulse, the flip-flop state will be $AB = 11$. Then with $AB = 11$, the output is $Z = 1$. The next input is $X = 0$, so $A^+B^+ = 11$ and the clock pulse produces no state change. Continuing in this manner, we can complete the timing chart.

Table 14-2. Moore State Tables for Fig. 14-5

(a)

AB			Z

	A^+B^+		
AB	$X = 0$	$X = 1$	Z
00	00	11	0
01	00	11	1
11	11	10	1
10	10	01	0

(b)

present state	next state $X = 0$	$X = 1$	present output (Z)
S_0	S_0	S_2	0
S_1	S_0	S_2	1
S_2	S_2	S_3	1
S_3	S_3	S_1	0

If we are not interested in the individual flip-flop states we can replace each combination of flip-flop states with a single symbol which represents the state of the network. Replacing 00 with S_0, 01 with S_1, 11 with S_2 and 10 with S_3 in Table 14-2(a) yields Table 14-2(b). The Z column is labeled "present output" because it is the output associated with the "present state". The state graph of Fig. 14-9 represents Table 14-2(b). Each node of the graph represents a state of the network, and the corresponding output is placed in the circle below the state symbol. The arrow joining two nodes is labeled with the value of X which will cause a state change between these nodes. Thus if the network is in state S_0 and $X = 1$, a clock pulse will cause a transition to state S_2.

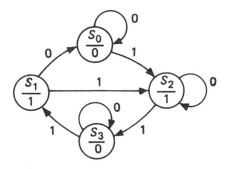

Fig. 14-9.   Moore state graph for Fig. 14-5

Next we will construct the state table and graph for the Mealy machine of Fig. 14-7. The next state and output equations are

$$A^+ = J_A A' + K_A' A = XBA' + X'A$$

$$B^+ = J_B B' + K_B' B = XB' + (AX)'B = XB' + X'B + A'B$$

$$Z = X'A'B + XB' + XA$$

The next state and output maps (Fig. 14-10) combine to form the transition table in Table 14-3(a). Given values for A, B, and X the current value of the output is determined from the Z column of this table, and the states of the flip-flops after the clock pulse are determined from the A^+B^+ columns.

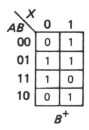

Fig. 14-10

Table 14-3. Mealy State Tables for Fig. 14-7

(a)

AB	A^+B^+ $X=0$	1	Z $X=0$	1
00	00	01	0	1
01	01	11	1	0
11	11	00	0	1
10	10	01	0	1

(b)

present state	next state $X=0$	1	present output $X=0$	1
S_0	S_0	S_1	0	1
S_1	S_1	S_2	1	0
S_2	S_2	S_0	0	1
S_3	S_3	S_1	0	1

We can construct the timing chart of Fig. 14-8 using Table 14-3(a). Initially with $A = B = 0$ and $X = 1$, the table shows that $Z = 1$ and $A^+B^+ = 01$. Therefore, after the clock pulse, the state of flip-flop B will change to 1 as indicated in Fig. 14-8. Now, from the 01 row of the table, if X is still 1, the output will be 0 until the input is changed to $X = 0$. Then the output is $Z = 1$, and the next clock pulse produces no state change. Finish stepping through the state table in this manner and verify that A, B and Z are as given in Fig. 14-8.

If we let $AB = 00$ correspond to network state S_0, 01 to S_1, 11 to S_2, and 10 to S_3, we can construct the state table in Table 14-3(b) and the state graph of Fig. 14-11. In Table 14-3(b), the "present output" column gives the output associated with the present state and present input. Thus, if the present state is S_0 and the input changes from 0 to 1, the output will immediately change from 0 to 1. However, the state will not change to the next state (S_1) until after the clock pulse. For Fig. 14-11, the labels on the arrows between states are of the form X/Z, where the symbol before the slash is the input and the symbol after the slash is the corresponding output. Thus, in state S_0 an input of 0 gives an output of 0, and an input of 1 gives an output of 1. For any given input sequence, we can easily trace out the state and output sequences on the state graph. For the input sequence $X = 10101$, verify that the corresponding output sequence is 11001. This agrees with Fig. 14-8 if the false outputs are ignored. Note that the false outputs do *not* show on the state graph since the inputs are only shown during the clock pulse interval and no provision is made for input changes between clock pulses.

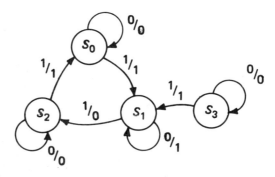

Fig. 14-11. Mealy state graph for Fig. 14-7

Table 14-4. A State Table With Multiple Inputs and Outputs

present state	next state $X_1 X_2 = 00$	01	10	11	present output $(Z_1 Z_2)$ $X_1 X_2 = 00$	01	10	11
S_0	S_3	S_2	S_1	S_0	00	10	11	01
S_1	S_0	S_1	S_2	S_3	10	10	11	11
S_2	S_3	S_0	S_1	S_1	00	10	11	01
S_3	S_2	S_2	S_1	S_0	00	00	01	01

Table 14-4 shows a state table for a Mealy sequential network with two inputs and two outputs. Figure 14-12 shows the corresponding state graph. The notation 00, 01/00 means if $X_1 = X_2 = 0$ or $X_1 = 0$ and $X_2 = 1$, then $Z_1 = 0$ and $Z_2 = 0$.

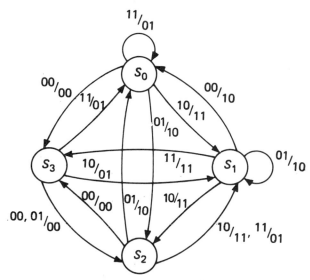

Fig. 14-12. State graph for Table 14-4

The synthesis procedure for sequential networks, discussed in detail in Units 15 through 17, is just the opposite of the procedure used for analysis. Starting with the specifications for the sequential network to be synthesized, a state graph is constructed. This diagram is then translated to a state table, and codes are assigned for each state. Flip-flop input equations are then derived, and finally the logic diagram for the network is drawn. For example, to synthesize the network in Fig. 14-7, we would start with the state graph of Fig. 14-11. Then we would derive Table 14.3(b), Table 14.3(a), the next state and output equations, and finally Fig. 14-7.

Several important points concerning the construction and interpretation of timing charts are summarized below:

   a. When constructing timing charts, note that a state change will normally occur after the falling edge of the clock pulse.

   b. The input will normally be changed in between clock pulses.

   c. For a Moore network, the output can only change when the state changes, but for a Mealy network the output can change when the input changes as well as when the state changes. A "false" output may occur between the time the state changes and the time the input is changed to its new value. (In other words, if the state has changed to its next value, but the old input is still present, the output may be temporarily incorrect.)

   d. False outputs are difficult to determine from the state graph, so use either signal tracing through the network or use the state table when constructing timing charts for Mealy networks.

   e. When using a Mealy state table for constructing timing charts, the procedure is as follows:

     (1) For the first input, read the present output and plot it.

     (2) Read the next state and plot it (following the appropriate edge of the clock pulse).

     (3) Go to the row in the table which corresponds to the next state and read the output under the old input column and plot it. (This may be a "false" output.)

     (4) Change to the next input and repeat steps (1), (2) and (3).

        (*Note:* If you are just trying to read the correct output sequence from the table, step (3) is naturally omitted.)

   f. For Mealy networks that change state on the falling edge of the clock, the best time to read the output is during the clock pulse, since the output will always be correct during that time.

14.4 General Models for Sequential Networks

A sequential network can conveniently be divided into two parts — the flip-flops which serve as memory for the network and the combinational logic which realizes the input functions for the flip-flops and the output functions. Figure 14-13 illustrates the general model for a clocked Mealy sequential network with m inputs, n outputs, and k clocked D flip-flops used as memory. Drawing the model in this form emphasizes the presence of feedback in the sequential network since the flip-flop outputs are fed back as inputs to the combinational subnetwork. The combinational subnetwork realizes the n output functions and the k next state functions, which serve as inputs to the D flip-flops:

$$Z_1 = f_1(X_1, X_2, \ldots, X_m, Q_1, Q_2, \ldots, Q_k)$$
$$Z_2 = f_2(X_1, X_2, \ldots, X_m, Q_1, Q_2, \ldots, Q_k)$$
$$\vdots$$
$$Z_n = f_n(X_1, X_2, \ldots, X_m, Q_1, Q_2, \ldots, Q_k)$$

n output functions

$$Q_1^+ = D_1 = g_1(X_1, X_2, \ldots, X_m, Q_1, Q_2, \ldots, Q_k)$$
$$Q_2^+ = D_2 = g_2(X_1, X_2, \ldots, X_m, Q_1, Q_2, \ldots, Q_k)$$

k next state
functions

$$Q_k^+ = D_k = g_k(X_1, X_2, \ldots, X_m, Q_1, Q_2, \ldots, Q_k)$$

Fig. 14-13. **General model for Mealy network using clocked D flip-flops**

When a set of inputs is applied to the network, the combinational subnetwork generates the outputs $(Z_1, Z_2, \ldots, Z_n)$ and the flip-flop inputs $(D_1, D_2, \ldots, D_k)$. Then a clock pulse is applied and the flip-flops change to the proper next state. This process is repeated for each set of inputs. Note that at a given point in time, the outputs of the flip-flops represent the present state of the network $(Q_1, Q_2, \ldots, Q_k)$. These Q_i's feed back into the combinational network, which generates the flip-flop inputs using the Q_i's and the X inputs. When D flip-flops are used, $D_i = Q_i^+$; therefore, the combinational network outputs are labeled Q_1^+, Q_2^+, etc. Although the above model uses D flip-flops, a similar model may be used for other types of clocked flip-flops, in which case the combinational network must generate the appropriate flip-flop inputs instead of the next state functions.

The clock pulse synchronizes the operation of the flip-flops and prevents timing problems. The gates in the combinational subnetwork have finite propagation delays, so when the inputs to the network are changed a finite time is required before the flip-flop inputs reach their final values. Because the gate delays are not all the same, the flip-flop input signals may contain transients and they may change at different times. Since the clock pulse is not applied until all flip-flop input signals have reached their final steady-state values, the unequal gate delays do not cause any timing problems. All flip-flops which must change state do so at the same time, usually on the falling edge of the clock pulse. When the flip-flops change state, the new flip-flop outputs are fed back into the combinational subnetwork. However, no further change in the flip-flop states can occur until the next clock pulse.

The general model for the clocked Moore network (Fig. 14-14) is similar to the clocked Mealy network. The output subnetwork is drawn separately for the Moore network because the output is only a function of the present state of the flip-flops and not a function of the network inputs. Operation of the Moore network is similar to that of the Mealy except when a set of inputs is applied to the Moore network, the resulting outputs do not appear until after the clock pulse causes the flip-flops to change state.

Fig. 14-14. General model for Moore network using clocked D flip-flops

To facilitate the study of sequential networks with multiple inputs and outputs, assignment of symbols to represent each combination of input values and each combination of output values is convenient. For example, we can replace Table 14-4 with Table 14-5 if we let $X = 0$ represent the input combination $X_1 X_2 = 00$, $X = 1$ represent $X_1 X_2 = 01$, etc., and similarly let $Z = 0$ represent the output combination $Z_1 Z_2 = 00$, $Z = 1$ represent $Z_1 Z_2 = 01$, etc. In this way we can specify the behavior of any sequential network in terms of a single input variable X and a single output variable Z.

Table 14-5. State Table with Multiple Inputs and Outputs

present state	next state $X = 0$	1	2	3	present output (Z) $X = 0$	1	2	3
S_0	S_3	S_2	S_1	S_0	0	2	3	1
S_1	S_0	S_1	S_2	S_3	2	2	3	3
S_2	S_3	S_0	S_1	S_1	0	2	3	1
S_3	S_2	S_2	S_1	S_0	0	0	1	1

Table 14-5 specifies two functions, the next-state function and the output function. The next-state function, designated δ, gives the next state of the network (i.e., the state after the clock pulse) in terms of the present state (S) and the present input (X):

$$S^+ = \delta(S, X) \tag{14-5}$$

The output function, designated λ, gives the output of the network (Z) in terms of the present state (S) and input (X):

$$Z = \lambda(S, X) \tag{14-6}$$

Values of S^+ and Z can be determined from the state table. From Table 14-5, we have

$$\delta(S_0, 1) = S_2 \qquad \delta(S_2, 3) = S_1$$

$$\lambda(S_0, 1) = 2 \qquad \lambda(S_2, 3) = 1$$

We will use the λ and δ notation introduced above when we discuss equivalent sequential networks in Unit 16.

Programmed Exercise 14.1

Cover the bottom of the page with a sheet of paper and slide it down as you check your answers.

14.1a In this exercise you will analyze the following sequential network using a state table and a timing chart.

Derive the next state and output equations.

$A^+ = $ _____

$B^+ = $ _____

$Z = $ _____

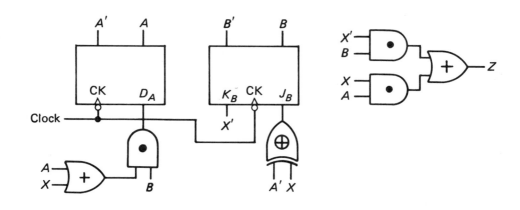

Answer: $Z = XA + X'B$, $B^+ = (A' \oplus X)B' + XB = A'B'X' + AB'X + XB$

$A^+ = B(A + X)$

14.1b Plot these equations on maps and complete the transition table:

X AB	0	1
00		
01		
11		
10		

A^+

X AB	0	1
00		
01		
11		
10		

B^+

X AB	0	1
00		
01		
11		
10		

Z

AB	A^+B^+ X = 0 1	Z 0 1
00		
01		
11		
10		

Turn to the next page and check your answer.

Answer to 14.1b:

	AB	A^+B^+ $X = 0$	1	Z 0	1
S_0	00	01	00	0	0
S_1	01	00	11	1	0
S_2	11	10	11	1	1
S_3	10	00	01	0	1

14.1c Convert your transition table to a state table using the given state numbering.

	next state $X = 0$ 1		output 0 1	
S_0				
S_1				
S_2				
S_3				

Answer to 14.1c:

	$X = 0$	1	0	1
S_0	S_1	S_0	0	0
S_1	S_0	S_2	1	0
S_2	S_3	S_2	1	1
S_3	S_0	S_1	0	1

14.1d Complete corresponding state graph.

Answer to 14.1d:

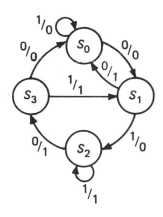

14.1e Using this graph, determine the state sequence and output sequence if the initial state is S_0 and the input sequence is $\qquad$ $X = 0, 1, 0, 1$

(1) The initial output with $X = 0$ in state S_0 is $Z =$ _____ and the next state is _____ .

(2) The output in this state when the next input ($X = 1$) is applied is $Z =$ _____ and the next state is _____ .

(3) When the third input ($X = 0$) is applied, the output is $Z =$ _____ and the next state is _____ .

(4) When the last input is applied, $Z =$ _____ and the final state is _____ .

In summary, the state sequence is $S_0,$ ___, ___, ___, ___ . The output sequence is $Z =$ _____ .

Turn to the next page and check your answer.

Answer to 14.1e: $\quad S_0, S_1, S_2, S_3, S_1 \qquad Z = 0011$

14.1f The above sequence for Z is the "correct" output sequence. Next we will determine the timing chart including any false outputs for Z. Assuming that X changes midway between clock pulses, draw the waveform for X ($X = 0, 1, 0, 1$).

Answer:

AB	A^+B^+ $X = 0$	1
00	01	00
01	00	11
11	10	11
10	00	01

14.1g Referring to the transition table, sketch the waveforms for A and B assuming that initially $A = B = 0$. The state sequence is

$$AB = 00, \underline{\quad}, \underline{\quad}, \underline{\quad}, \underline{\quad}.$$

Answer: (Note that A and B change immediately after the clock pulse.)

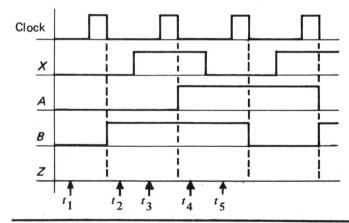

AB	Z $X = 0$	1
00	0	0
01	1	0
11	1	1
10	0	1

Check your state sequence against the answer to 14.1e, noting that $S_0 = 00$, $S_1 = 01$, $S_2 = 11$ and $S_3 = 10$.

14.1h Using the output table, sketch the waveform for Z. At time t_1, $X = A = B = 0$, so $Z = \underline{\qquad}$. At time t_2, $X = \underline{\qquad}$ and $AB = \underline{\qquad}$, so $Z = \underline{\qquad}$. At time t_3, $X = \underline{\qquad}$ and $AB = \underline{\qquad}$, so $Z = \underline{\qquad}$. Complete the waveform for Z, showing the output at t_4, t_5, etc.

Answer: (Note that Z can change immediately following the change in X or immediately following the clock pulse.)

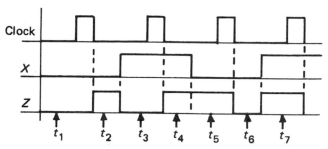

14.1i (1) Since this is a Mealy network, the correct times to read the output are during intervals t_1, _____ , _____ and _____ .

(2) The correct output sequence is therefore Z = _____ .

(3) False outputs may occur during intervals _____ , _____ and _____ .

(4) In two of these intervals, false outputs actually occur. These intervals are _____ and _____ .

Answer:

(1) t_1, t_3, t_5 and t_7

(3) t_2, t_4 and t_6

(2) Check your Z sequence against the answer to 14.1e.

(4) t_2 and t_6 (output during t_4 is not "false" because it is the same as t_5).

14.1j Finally, we will verify part of the timing chart by signal tracing on the original network (see 14.1a).

(1) Initially, $A = B = 0$ and $X = 0$ so D_A = _____ , J_B = _____ , K_B = _____ and Z = _____ .

(2) After the clock pulse A = _____ , B = _____ and Z = _____ .

(3) After X is changed to 1, D_A = _____ , J_B = _____ , K_B = _____ and Z = _____ .

(4) After the clock pulse A = _____ , B = _____ and Z = _____ .

Check your answers against the timing chart. Answer to (1) corresponds to t_1, (2) to t_2, (3) to t_3 and (4) to t_4.

PROBLEMS

14.2 Construct a state graph for the shift register shown below. (X is the input and Z is the output.)

14.3 a. For the following sequential network, find the next state equation or map for each flip-flop. Using these next state equations or maps, construct a (Moore) state table and graph for the network.

b. What is the output sequence when the input sequence is $X = 01100$?

14.4 Draw a timing chart for the following network starting with an initial state $ABC = 000$ and using an input sequence $X = 110101$. Assume that the input changes occur midway between clock pulses. Pay particular attention to the times at which the flip-flops change state and the times at which Z changes. Indicate false outputs, if any. Verify that your answer is correct by using the state table for the network.

14.5 a. For the following sequential network, write the next state equations for flip-flops A and B.

b. Using these equations, find the state table and draw the state graph.

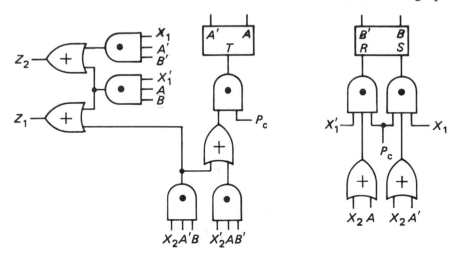

14.6 The sequential network shown in Fig. 17-3 has the transition table shown in Fig. 17-2. Draw a timing chart for the network starting with an initial state $Q_1Q_2Q_3 = 000$ and using an input sequence $X = 0101$. Assume that X changes midway between clock pulses. Specify the correct output sequence and indicate any false outputs.

14.7 A sequential network has the form shown in Fig. 14-13 with

$$D_1 = Q_1Q_3' + X' \qquad D_2 = Q_1'Q_2'Q_3$$
$$D_3 = Q_1Q_3 + X \qquad Z = X' + Q_2Q_3$$

a. Construct a state table and state graph for the network.

b. Draw a timing diagram for the network showing X, clock, Q_1, Q_2, Q_3 and Z. Use the input sequence $X = 0, 1, 0, 1, 1$ and assume that X changes midway between clock pulses. Indicate any "false" outputs on the diagram.

c. Compare the output sequence obtained from the timing diagram with that from the state graph.

d. At what time with respect to the clock should the input be changed in order to eliminate the false output(s)?

14.8 A Moore sequential network has 1 input, 1 output and 2 flip-flops. A timing chart for the network is shown below. Construct a state table and state graph for the network.

14.9 A sequential network is constructed using a ROM and two D flip-flops as shown below. The contents of the ROM is given in the table.

a. Draw a timing diagram for the network for the input sequence $X_1 X_2$ = 10, 01, 11, 10. Assume that input changes occur midway between clock pulses. Indicate any false outputs on the diagram, and specify the correct output sequence for Z_1 and Z_2.

b. Construct a transition table and state graph for the network.

Q_1	Q_2	X_1	X_2	D_1	D_2	Z_1	Z_2
0	0	0	0	0	0	1	0
0	0	0	1	0	0	1	0
0	0	1	0	0	1	1	0
0	0	1	1	0	1	1	0
0	1	0	0	1	1	0	0
0	1	0	1	1	1	1	0
0	1	1	0	1	0	0	1
0	1	1	1	1	0	1	1
1	0	0	0	1	1	0	0
1	0	0	1	0	0	0	0
1	0	1	0	1	1	0	1
1	0	1	1	0	0	0	1
1	1	0	0	1	0	0	0
1	1	0	1	0	1	0	0
1	1	1	0	1	0	0	0
1	1	1	1	0	1	0	0

15

DERIVATION OF STATE TABLES

OBJECTIVES

1. Given a problem statement for the design of a Mealy or Moore sequential network, find the corresponding state graph and table.

2. Explain the significance of each state in your graph or table in terms of the input sequences required to reach that state.

3. Check your state graph using appropriate input sequences.

STUDY GUIDE

1. Study Section 15.1, *Design of a Sequence Detector*.

    a. Verify that the state graph in Fig. 15-4 will produce the correct output sequence for Z when the input sequence for X is as given in Equation (15-1).

    b. Using Equations (15-2) and (15-3) together with $Z = XA$ construct the next state table for the network and verify that it is the same as given in Table 15-2, except that the new table will have four states because the don't cares were assigned in the process of designing the network.

    c. Complete the design of the Moore sequential network whose transition table is given by Table 15-4. Use clocked J-K flip-flops for A and B.

    d. Verify that the state graph of Fig. 15-6 gives the correct output sequence when the input sequence (15-1) is applied. (Ignore the initial output for the Moore graph.)

2. Study Section 15.2, *More Complex Design Problems*.

3. Study Section 15.3, *Guidelines for Construction of State Graphs.* Study the examples carefully and observe how some of the guidelines were applied.

4. Work through Programmed Exercises 15.1 and 15.2.

5. A very important part of deriving state tables or state graphs is knowing how to tell when your answer is right (or wrong!). One way to do this is to make up a suitable list of test sequences, apply them to the state graph, and check the resulting output sequences.

6. To gain proficiency in construction of state tables or graphs requires a fair amount of practice. Work **Problems** 15.3 through 15.7. The problems on the readiness tests will be about the same order of difficulty as these problems, so make sure that you can work them in a reasonable time.

Note: Don't look at the answers to Problems 15.3 through 15.7 in the back of the book until you have tried the problems and checked your answers using the following test sequences:

15.3 $X =$ 0 1 1 1 0 1 0 1

   $Z = (0)$ 0 0 0 0 1 1 1 1

   (Solution should have 5 self-loops*)

15.4 X = 1 1 0 0 1 0 1 X = 0 0 1 1 1 0 0 1 0 1 1

   Z_1 = 0 0 0 0 0 0 1 Z_1 = 0 0 0 0 0 0 0 0 0 0 0

   Z_2 = 0 0 0 0 0 0 0 Z_2 = 0 0 0 1 0 0 0 0 0 0 1

   (Solution should have 4 self-loops)

15.5 X_1 =   0 0 1 1 0 1 0 1 1 0 1 0 0

   X_2 =   0 1 0 1 0 0 0 1 0 1 1 1 0

   Z = (0) 0 0 0 1 1 1 1 0 0 0 1 1 1

   (Solution should have at least 4 self-loops)

15.6 a. X = 0 0 1 1 0 1 0 1 0 1 1

      Z = 1 1 0 0 0 1 1 0 0 0 1

      (Solution should have 3 self-loops)

   b. X = 1 1 1 0 0 1 0 1 0 1

      Z = 0 0 0 0 1 0 0 0 0 1

15.7 a. X_1 = 0 0 1 1 1 1 0 0 1 0 0

      X_2 = 0 1 0 1 1 0 1 0 0 1 1

      Z_1 = 0 1 1 1 0 0 0 0 1 0 0

      Z_2 = 0 0 0 0 0 1 1 1 0 1 0

   b. Should get same sequences as above after initial output of
      $Z_1 Z_2$ = 00

---

*A self-loop is an arrow which starts at one state and goes back to the same state.

7. When you are satisfied that you can meet all of the objectives, take the readiness test.

15. DERIVATION OF STATE TABLES

In Unit 14, we analyzed sequential networks using timing charts and state graphs. Now we will consider the design of sequential networks starting from a problem statement which specifies the desired relationship between the input and output sequences. The first step in the design is to construct a state table or graph which specifies the desired behavior of the network. Flip-flop input equations and output equations can then be derived from this table. Construction of the state table or graph, one of the most important and challenging parts of sequential network design, is discussed in detail in this unit.

15.1 Design of a Sequence Detector

To illustrate the design of a clocked Mealy sequential network, we will design a sequence detector. The network has the form shown in Fig. 15-1.

Fig. 15-1. Sequence detector to be designed

The network will examine a string of 0's and 1's applied to the X input and generate an output $Z = 1$ only when a prescribed input sequence occurs. It will be assumed that the input X can only change between clock pulses. Specifically, we will design the network so that any input sequence ending in 101 will produce an output $Z = 1$ coincident with the last 1. The network does not reset when a 1 output occurs. A typical input sequence and the corresponding output sequence are

$$X = 0\ 0\ 1\ 1\ 0\ 1\ 1\ 0\ 0\ 1\ 0\ 1\ 0\ 1\ 0\ 0$$
$$Z = 0\ 0\ 0\ 0\ 0\ 1\ 0\ 0\ 0\ 0\ 0\ 1\ 0\ 1\ 0\ 0 \qquad (15\text{-}1)$$
$$(\text{time: } 0\ 1\ 2\ 3\ 4\ 5\ 6\ 7\ 8\ 9\ 10\ 11\ 12\ 13\ 14\ 15)$$

Initially, we do not know how many flip-flops will be required, so we will designate the network states as S_0, S_1, etc., and later assign flip-flop states to correspond to the network states. We will construct a state graph to show the sequence of states and outputs which occur in response to different inputs. Initially, we will start the network in a reset state designated S_0. If a 0 input is received, the network can stay in S_0 since the input sequence we are looking for does not start with 0. However, if a 1 is received, we must go to a new state (S_1) to "remember" that the first input in the desired sequence has been received (Fig. 15-2).

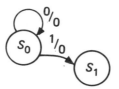

Fig. 15-2

The labels on the graph are of the form X/Z, where the symbol before the slash is the input and the symbol after the slash is the corresponding output.

When in state S_1, if we receive a 0 the network must change to a new state (S_2) to remember that the first two inputs of the desired sequence (10) have been received. If a 1 is received in state S_2, the desired input sequence (101) is complete and the output should be 1. The question arises whether the network should then go to a new state or back to S_0 or S_1. Since the network is not supposed to reset when an output occurs, we cannot go back to S_0. However, since the last 1 in a sequence can also be the first 1 in a new sequence, we can return to S_1 as indicated in Fig. 15-3.

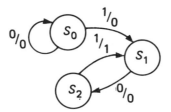

Fig. 15-3

The graph of Fig. 15-3 is still incomplete. If a 1 input occurs when in state S_1, we can stay in S_1 since the sequence is simply restarted. If a 0 input occurs in state S_2 we have received two 0's in a row and must reset the network to state S_0 since 00 is not part of the desired input sequence, and going to one of the other states could lead to an incorrect output. The final state graph is given in Fig. 15-4. Note that for a single input variable each state must have two exit lines (one for each value of the input variable) but may have any number of entry lines depending on the network specifications.

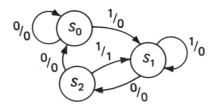

Fig. 15-4. Mealy state graph for sequence detector

State S_0 is the starting state, state S_1 indicates that a sequence ending in 1 has been received, and state S_2 indicates that a sequence ending in 10 has been received. An alternative way to start the solution would be to first define states in this manner and then construct the state graph. Converting the state graph to a state table yields Table 15-1.

Table 15-1

present state	next state		present output	
	$X = 0$	$X = 1$	$X = 0$	$X = 1$
S_0	S_0	S_1	0	0
S_1	S_2	S_1	0	0
S_2	S_0	S_1	0	1

At this point, we are ready to design a network which has the behavior described by the state table. Since one flip-flop can have only two states, two flip-flops are needed to represent the three states. Designate the two flip-flops as A and B. Let flip-flop states $A = 0$, $B = 0$ correspond to network state S_0; $A = 0$, $B = 1$ correspond to S_1; and $A = 1$, $B = 0$ correspond to network state S_2. Each network state is then represented by a unique combination of flip-flop states. Substituting the flip-flop states for S_0, S_1 and S_2 in the state table yields the transition table (Table 15-2).

Table 15-2

AB	A^+B^+		Z	
	$X = 0$	$X = 1$	$X = 0$	$X = 1$
00	00	01	0	0
01	10	01	0	0
10	00	01	0	1

From this table, we can plot the next state maps for the flip-flops and the map for the output function Z:

A^+

B^+

$Z = XA$

The flip-flop input maps are then derived from the next state maps using the same method that was used for counters (Section 13.9). If we use T flip-flops, the input maps are

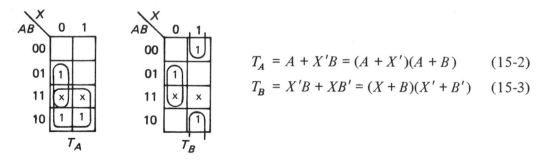

$$T_A = A + X'B = (A + X')(A + B) \qquad (15\text{-}2)$$

$$T_B = X'B + XB' = (X + B)(X' + B') \qquad (15\text{-}3)$$

Since we only want the network to change state when a clock pulse occurs, each T input is ANDed with the clock pulse. The resulting network is shown in Fig. 15-5.

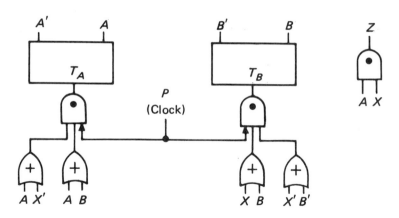

Fig. 15-5

Initially, we will reset both flip-flops to the zero state. By tracing signals in the network you can verify that an output $Z = 1$ will occur when an input sequence ending in 101 occurs.

The procedure for finding the state graph for a Moore machine is similar to that used for a Mealy machine except that the output is written with the state instead of with the transition between states. We will rework the previous example as a Moore machine to illustrate the procedure. The network should produce an output of 1 only if an input sequence ending in 101 has occurred. The design is similar to that for the Mealy machine up through the point where the input sequence 10 has occurred, except that 0 output is associated with states S_0, S_1 and S_2:

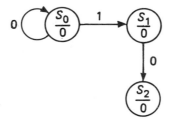

Now, when a 1 input occurs to complete the 101 sequence, the output must become 1; therefore, we cannot go back to state S_1 and must create a new state S_3 with a 1 output:

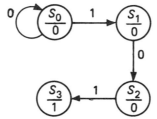

We now complete the graph as shown in Fig. 15-6. Note the sequence 100 resets the network to S_0. A sequence 1010 takes the network back to S_2 since another 1 input should cause Z to become 1 again.

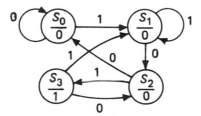

Fig. 15-6. **Moore state graph for sequence detector**

The state table corresponding to the network is given by Table 15-3. Note that there is a single column for the output since the output is determined by the present state and does not depend on X. Note that in this example the Moore machine requires one more state than the Mealy machine which detects the same input sequence.

Table 15-3

present state	next state $X = 0$	$X = 1$	present output (Z)
S_0	S_0	S_1	0
S_1	S_2	S_1	0
S_2	S_0	S_3	0
S_3	S_2	S_1	1

Since there are four states, two flip-flops are required to realize the network. Using the state assignment $AB = 00$ for S_0, $AB = 01$ for S_1, $AB = 11$ for S_2, and $AB = 10$ for S_3, the following transition table for the flip-flops results:

Table 15-4

	A^+B^+		
AB	$X = 0$	$X = 1$	Z
00	00	01	0
01	11	01	0
11	00	10	0
10	11	01	1

The output function is $Z = AB'$. Note that Z depends only on the flip-flop states and is independent of X, while for the corresponding Mealy machine, Z was a function of X. Derivation of the flip-flop input equations is straightforward and will not be given here.

15.2 More Complex Design Problems

In this section we will derive a state graph for a sequential network of somewhat greater complexity than the previous examples. The network to be designed again has the form shown in Fig. 15-1. The output Z should be 1 if the input sequence ends in either 010 *or* 1001, and Z should be 0 otherwise. Before attempting to draw the state graph, we will work out some typical input-output sequences to make sure that we have a clear understanding of the problem statement. We will determine the desired output sequence for the following input sequence:

$$X = 0\ 0\ 1\ 0\ 1\ 0\ 0\ 1\ 0\ 0\ 0\ 1\ 0\ 0\ 1\ 1\ 0$$
$$\quad\quad\quad\ \ \uparrow\ \ \ \ \uparrow\ \ \uparrow\uparrow\ \ \ \ \ \ \ \ \uparrow\ \ \ \ \uparrow$$
$$\quad\quad\quad\ \ \underline{a}\ \ \ \ \underline{b}\ \ \underline{c}\ \underline{d}\ \ \ \ \ \ \ \ \underline{e}\ \ \ \ \underline{f}$$
$$Z = 0\ 0\ 0\ 1\ 0\ 1\ 0\ 1\ 1\ 0\ 0\ 0\ 1\ 0\ 1\ 0\ 0$$

At point $\underline{a}$, the input sequence ends in 010, one of the sequences we are looking for, so the output is $Z = 1$. At point $\underline{b}$, the input again ends in 010 so $Z = 1$. Note that overlapping sequences are allowed since the problem statement does not say anything about resetting the network when a 1 output occurs. At point $\underline{c}$, the input sequence ends in 1001, so Z is again 1. Why do we have a 1 output at points $\underline{d}$, $\underline{e}$ and $\underline{f}$?

We will start construction of the state graph by working with the two sequences which lead to a 1 output. Then we will later add additional arrows and states as required to make sure that the output is correct for other cases. We start off with a reset state S_0 which corresponds to having received no inputs. Whenever an input is received which corresponds to part of one of the sequences we are looking for, the network should go to a new state to "remember" having received this input. Figure 15-7 shows a partial state graph which gives a 1 output for the sequence 010. In this graph S_1 corresponds to having received a sequence ending in 0, S_2 to a sequence ending in 01, and S_3 to a sequence ending in 010.

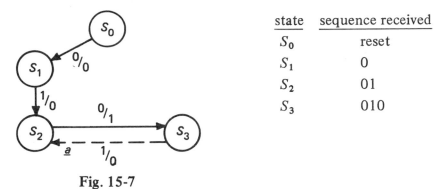

state	sequence received
S_0	reset
S_1	0
S_2	01
S_3	010

Fig. 15-7

Now, if a 1 input is received in state S_3, we again have a sequence ending in 01, which is part of the input sequence we are looking for. Therefore we can go back to state S_2 (arrow $\underline{a}$) since S_2 corresponds to having received a sequence ending in 01. Then if we get another 0 in state S_2, we go to S_3 with a 1 output. This is correct since the sequence again ends in 010.

Next we will construct the part of the graph corresponding to the sequence 1001. Again we start in the reset state S_0, and when we receive a 1 input, we go to S_4 (Fig. 15-8, arrow $\underline{b}$) to remember that we have received the first 1 in the sequence 1001. The next input in the sequence is 0, and when this 0 is received we should ask the question: Should we create a new state to correspond to a sequence ending in 10, or can we go to one of the previous states on the state graph? Since S_3 corresponds to a sequence ending in 10, we can go to S_3 (arrow $\underline{c}$). The fact that we didn't have an initial 0 this time does not matter since 10 starts off the sequence we are looking for. If we get a 0 input when in S_3, the input sequence received will end in 100 regardless of the path we took to get to S_3. Since there is no state so far corresponding to the sequence 100, we create a new state S_5 to indicate having received a sequence ending in 100.

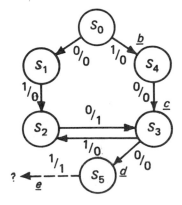

state	sequence ends in
S_0	reset
S_1	0
S_2	01
S_3	010 or 10
S_4	1
S_5	100

Fig. 15-8

If we get a 1 input when in state S_5, this completes the sequence 1001 and gives a 1 output as indicated by arrow e. Again we ask the question, can we go back to one of the previous states, or do we have to create a new state. Since the end of the sequence 1001 is 01, and S_2 corresponds to a sequence ending in 01, we can go back to S_2 (Fig. 15-9). If we get another 001, we have again completed the sequence 1001 and get another 1 output.

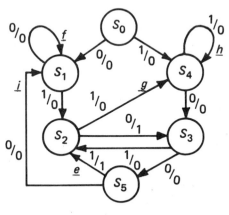

state	sequence ends in
S_0	reset
S_1	0
S_2	01
S_3	010 or 10
S_4	1
S_5	100

Fig. 15-9

We have now taken care of putting out a 1 when either the sequence 010 or 1001 is completed. Next, we will go back and complete the state graph to take care of the other input sequences which we haven't already accounted for. In state S_1, we have accounted for a 1 input but not a 0 input. If we are in S_1 and get a 0 input, to which state should we go? If a 0 input occurs in S_1, we have a sequence ending in 00. Since 00 is not part of either of the input sequences for which we are looking, we can ignore the extra 0 and stay in S_1 (arrow f). No matter how many extra 0's occur, we still have a sequence ending in 0, and we stay in S_1 until a 1 input occurs. In S_2, we have taken care of the 0 input case, but not the 1 input case. If a 1 is received, the input sequence ends in 11. Since 11 is not part of either the sequence 010 or 1001 we do not need a state which corresponds to a sequence ending in 11. We can't stay in S_2 since S_2 corresponds to a sequence ending in 01. Therefore, we go to S_4 which corresponds to having received a sequence ending in 1 (arrow g). S_3 already has arrows corresponding to 0 and 1 inputs, so we examine S_4 next. If a 1 is received in S_4, the input sequence ends in 11. We can stay in S_4 and ignore the extra 1 (arrow h) since 11 is not part of either sequence for which we are looking. In S_5, if we get a 0 input, the sequence ends in 000. Since 000 is not contained in either 010 or 1001, we can go back to S_1 since S_1 corresponds to having received a sequence ending in one (or more) 0's. This completes the state graph since every state has arrows leaving it which correspond to both 0 and 1 inputs. We should now go back and check the state graph against the original input sequences to make sure that a 1 output is always obtained for a sequence ending in 010 or 1001 and that a 1 output does not occur for any other sequence.

Next we will derive the state graph for a Moore sequential network with one input X and one output Z. The output Z is to be 1 if the total number of 1's received is odd and at least two consecutive 0's have been received. A typical input and output sequence are

$$X = 1 \quad 0 \quad 1 \quad 1 \quad 0 \quad 0 \quad 1 \quad 1$$

$$\underset{a}{\uparrow} \qquad \qquad \underset{b}{\uparrow} \qquad \underset{c}{\uparrow} \quad \underset{d}{\uparrow} \quad \underset{e}{\uparrow}$$

$$Z = 0 \quad 0 \quad 0 \quad 0 \quad 0 \quad 1 \quad 0 \quad 1$$

At points a and b in the above sequence, an odd number of 1's have been received, but two consecutive 0's have not been received, so the output remains 0. At points c and e, an odd number of 1's and two consecutive 0's have been received, so $Z = 1$. At point d, $Z = 0$ because the number of 1's is even.

We start construction of the Moore state graph (Fig. 15-10) with the reset state S_0, and we associate a 0 output with this state. First, we will consider keeping track of whether the number of 1's is even or odd. If we get a 1 input in S_0, we will go to state S_1 to indicate an odd number of 1's received. The output for S_1 is 0 since two consecutive 0's have not been received. When a second 1 is received, should we go to a new state or go back to S_0? For this problem, it is unnecessary to distinguish between an even number of 1's and no 1's received, so we can go back to S_0. A third 1 then takes us to S_1 (odd number of 1's), a fourth 1 to S_0 (even 1's), and so forth.

Fig. 15-10

If a 0 is received in S_0, this starts a sequence of two consecutive 0's, so we go to S_2 (0 output) in Fig. 15-11. Another 0 then takes us to S_3 to indicate two consecutive 0's received. The output is still 0 in S_3 since the number of 1's received is even. Now if we get a 1 input, we have received an odd number of 1's and go to S_4. (Why can't we go to S_1?) In S_4 we have received two consecutive 0's and an odd number of 1's, so the output is 1.

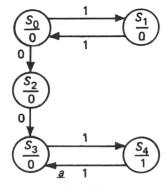

Fig. 15-11

state	sequence received
S_0	reset or even 1's
S_1	odd 1's
S_2	even 1's and 0
S_3	even 1's and 00
S_4	00 and odd 1's

If we receive a 1 in S_4, we have an even number of 1's and two consecutive 0's, so we can return to S_3 (arrow $\underline{a}$). The output in S_3 is 0, and when we get another 1 input, the number of 1's is odd, so we again go to S_4 with a 1 output. Now suppose that we are in S_1 (odd number of 1's received) and we get a 0. We cannot go to S_2 (why?) so we go to a new state S_5 (Fig. 15-12, arrow $\underline{b}$) which corresponds to an odd number of 1's followed by a 0. Another 0 results in two consecutive 0's and we can go to S_4 (arrow $\underline{c}$) which gives us a 1 output.

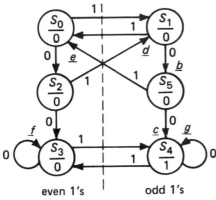

state	input sequence
S_0	reset or even 1's
S_1	odd 1's
S_2	even 1's and 0
S_3	even 1's and 00
S_4	odd 1's and 00
S_5	odd 1's and 0

Fig. 15-12

Now we must go back and complete the state graph by making sure that there are two arrows leaving each state. In S_2, a 1 input means that we have re-. ceived an odd number of 1's. Since we have not received two consecutive 0's, we must return to S_1 (arrow $\underline{d}$) and start counting 0's over again. Similarly, if we receive a 1 in S_5, we return to S_0 (why?). Now, what should happen if we receive a 0 in S_3? Referring to the original problem statement, we see that once two consecutive 0's have been received, additional 0's can be ignored. Therefore, we can stay in S_3 (arrow $\underline{f}$). Similarly, extra 0 inputs can be ignored in S_4 (arrow $\underline{g}$). This completes the Moore state diagram, and we should go back and verify that the correct output sequence is obtained for various input sequences.

15.3 Guidelines for Construction of State Graphs

Although there is no one specific procedure which can be used to derive state graphs or tables for every problem, the following guidelines should prove helpful:

a. First construct some sample input and output sequences to make sure that you understand the problem statement.

b. Determine under what conditions, if any, the network should reset to its initial state.

c. If only one or two sequences lead to a non-zero output, a good way to start is to construct a partial state graph for those sequences.

d. Another way to get started is to determine what sequences or groups of sequences must be "remembered" by the network and set up states accordingly.

e. Each time you add an arrow to the state graph, determine whether it can go to one of the previously defined states or whether a new state must be added.

f . Check your graph to make sure there is one and only one path leaving each state for each combination of values of the input variables.

g. When your graph is complete, test it by applying the input sequences formulated in part a and making sure the output sequences are correct.

Several examples of deriving state graphs or tables follow.

Example 1:   A sequential network has one input (X) and one output (Z). The network examines groups of four consecutive inputs and produces an output $Z = 1$ if the input sequence 0101 or 1001 occurs. The network resets after every four inputs. Find the Mealy state graph.

Solution: A typical sequence of inputs and outputs is

$$X = 0101 \mid 0010 \mid 1001 \mid 0100$$
$$Z = 0001 \mid 0000 \mid 0001 \mid 0000$$

The vertical bars indicate the points at which the network resets to the initial state. Note that an input sequence of either 01 or 10 followed by 01 will produce an output of $Z = 1$. Therefore, the network can go to the same state if either 01 or 10 is received. The partial state graph for the two sequences leading to a 1 output is shown in Fig. 15-13.

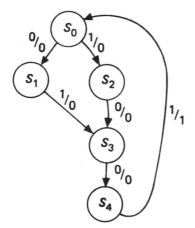

state	sequence received
S_0	reset
S_1	0
S_2	1
S_3	01 or 10
S_4	010 or 100

Fig. 15-13.   Partial state graph for Example 1

Note that the network resets to S_0 when the fourth input is received. Next we add arrows and labels to the graph to take care of sequences which do not give a 1 output as shown in Fig. 15-14.

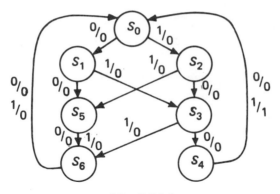

Fig. 15-14

Addition of states S_5 and S_6 was necessary so that the network would not reset to S_0 before four inputs were received. Note that once a 00 or 11 input sequence has been received (state S_5), no output of 1 is possible until the network is reset.

Example 2: Find the Mealy state graph for a sequential network which generates the output sequence 0101 $\underline{110}$ $\underline{110}$ $\underline{110}$ $\ldots$

Solution:

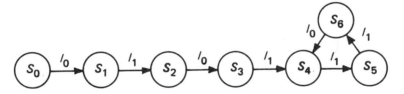

(A blank space above the slash indicates that the network has no input other than the clock.)

In general, a sequence can be divided into a non-periodic part followed by a periodic part. Therefore, the general form for a sequence generator will be a linear string of states leading into a loop as in the above example.

Example 3: A sequential network has two inputs (X_1, X_2) and one output (Z). The output remains a constant value unless one of the following input sequences occurs:

    a.   The input sequence $X_1 X_2 = 01, 11$* causes the output to become 0.

    b.   The input sequence $X_1 X_2 = 10, 11$ causes the output to become 1.

    c.   The input sequence $X_1 X_2 = 10, 01$ causes the output to change value.

Derive a Moore state graph for the network.

Solution: The only sequences of input pairs which affect the output are of length two. Therefore, the previous and present inputs will determine the output, and

---

*This notation means $X_1 = 0$, $X_2 = 1$ followed by $X_1 = 1$, $X_2 = 1$.

the network must "remember" only the previous input pair. At first it appears that three states are required, corresponding to the last input received being $X_1 X_2 = 01$, 10 and (00 or 11). Note that it is unnecessary to use a separate state for 00 and 11 since neither input starts a sequence which leads to an output change. However, for each of these states the output could be either 0 or 1, so we will initially define six states as follows:

previous input $(X_1 X_2)$	output (Z)	state designation
00 or 11	0	S_0
00 or 11	1	S_1
01	0	S_2
01	1	S_3
10	0	S_4
10	1	S_5

Using this state designation we can then set up a state table* (Table 15-5).

Table 15-5

present state	Z	$X_1 X_2 = 00$	01	11	10
S_0	0	S_0	S_2	S_0	S_4
S_1	1	S_1	S_3	S_1	S_5
S_2	0	S_0	S_2	S_0	S_4
S_3	1	S_1	S_3	S_0	S_5
S_4	0	S_0	S_3	S_1	S_4
S_5	1	S_1	S_2	S_1	S_5

The S_4 row of this table was derived as follows. If 00 is received, the input sequence has been 10, 00 so the output does not change and we go to S_0 to remember that the last input received was 00. If 01 is received, the input sequence has been 10, 01 so the output must change to 1 and we go to S_3 to remember that the last input received was 01. If 11 is received, the input sequence has been 10, 11 so the output should become 1 and we go to S_1. If 10 is received, the input sequence has been 10, 10 so the output does not change and we remain in S_4. Verify for yourself that the other rows in the table are correct. The state graph is shown in Fig. 15-15.

---

*The 6-row table given here can be reduced to 5 rows using the methods given in Unit 16.

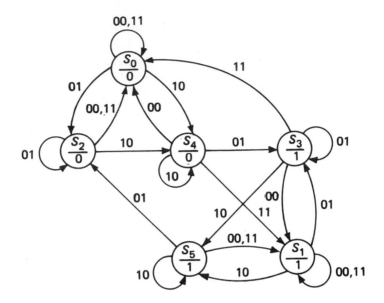

Fig. 15-15. State graph for Example 3

Programmed Exercise 15.1 (top half of this page and the next 5 pages)

Problem: A clocked Mealy sequential network with one input (X) and one output (Z) is to be designed. The output is to be 0, unless the input is 0 following a sequence of *exactly* two 0 inputs followed by a 1 input.

To make sure you understand the problem statement, specify the output sequence for each of the following input sequence:

a. $X = 0\ 0\ 1\ 0$
    $Z = $ _____

b. $X = \ldots 1\ 0\ 0\ 1\ 0$ ($\ldots$ means any input
                                    sequence)
    $Z = \ldots$ _____

c. $X = \ldots 0\ 0\ 0\ 1\ 0$
    $Z = \ldots$ _____

d. $X = 0\ 0\ 1\ 0\ 0\ 1\ 0\ 0\ 0\ 1\ 0$
    $Z = $ _____

e.   Does the network reset after a 1 output occurs? _____

Turn to the next page and check your answers.

Programmed Exercise 15.2 (bottom half of this page and the next 5 pages)

Problem: A clocked Moore sequential network should have an output of $Z = 1$ if the total number of 0's received is an even number greater than zero, provided that two consecutive 1's have never been received.

To make sure that you understand the problem statement, specify the output sequence for the following input sequence:

$X = \quad 0\ 0\ 0\ 0\ 1\ 0\ 1\ 0\ 1\ 1\ 0\ 0\ 0\ 0$
$Z = (0)$ _____

    └─this 0 is the initial output before any inputs have been received

Turn to the next page and check your answer.

Answers to 15.1:

    a. $Z = 0001$ b. $Z = \ldots 00001$

    c. $Z = \ldots 00000$ d. $Z = 00010010000$ e. NO

Note that no 1 output occurs in answer c because there are 3 input 0's in a row.

Add arrows to the following graph so that the sequence $X = 0010$ gives the correct output (don't add another state).

Turn to the next page and check your answer.

Answer to 15.2:

$$Z = (0)\ 0\ 1\ 0\ 1\ 1\ 0\ 0\ 1\ 1\ 0\ 0\ 0\ 0\ 0$$

Note that once two consecutive ones have been received, the output can never become 1 again.

To start the state graph, consider only 0 inputs and construct a Moore state graph which gives an output of 1 if the total number of 0's received is an even number greater than zero.

Now turn to the next page and check your answers.

Answer:

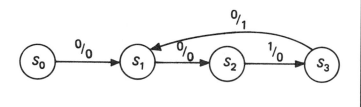

state	sequence received
S_0	(reset)
S_1	0 or
S_2	
S_3	
S_4	

Note that the arrow from S_3 returns to S_1 so that an additional input of 010 will produce another 1 output.

Add a state to the above graph which corresponds to "3 or more consecutive 0's received". Also complete the above table to indicate the sequence received which corresponds to each state.

Turn to the next page and check your answers.

Answer:

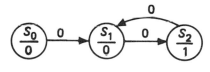

state	sequence received
S_0	(reset)
S_1	odd no. of 0's
S_2	
S_3	
S_4	

Now add states to the above graph so that starting in S_0, if two consecutive 1's are received followed by any other sequence, the output will remain 0. Also complete the above table to indicate the sequence received that corresponds to each state.

Turn to the next page and check your answers.

Answer:

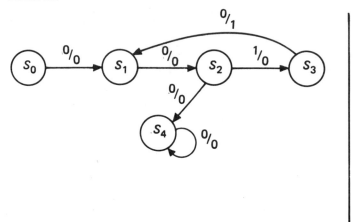

state	sequence received
S_0	(reset)
S_1	0 or 0010
S_2	00
S_3	001
S_4	3 (or more) consec. 0's

The above state graph is not complete since there is only one arrow leaving most states. Complete the graph by adding the necessary arrows. Return to one of the previously used states when possible.

Turn to the next page and check your answer.

Answer:

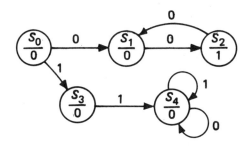

state	sequence received
S_0	(reset)
S_1	odd no. of 0's
S_2	even no. of 0's
S_3	1
S_4	11 (followed by
S_5	any sequence)
S_6	

Now complete the graph so that each state has both a 0 and 1 arrow leading away from it. Add as few extra states to the graph as possible. Also complete the above table.

Answer:

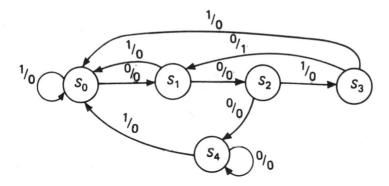

Verify that this state graph gives the proper output sequences for the input sequences listed at the start of this exercise. Write down the Mealy state table which corresponds to the above graph.

Turn to the next page and check your answer.

Answer:

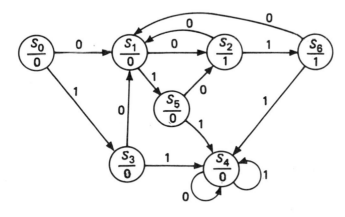

S_5 — odd no. of 0's followed by 1.

S_6 — even no. of 0's followed by 1.

Verify that this state graph gives the proper output sequence for each input sequence at the start of this exercise. Write down the Moore state table which corresponds to the above graph. (Note that a Moore table has only one output column.)

Turn to the next page and check your answer.

Answer:

present state	next state 0	1	output 0	1
S_0	S_1	S_0	0	0
S_1	S_2	S_0	0	0
S_2	S_4	S_3	0	0
S_3	S_1	S_0	1	0
S_4	S_4	S_0	0	0

Answer:

present state	next state 0	1	output
S_0	S_1	S_3	0
S_1	S_2	S_5	0
S_2	S_1	S_6	1
S_3	S_1	S_4	0
S_4	S_4	S_4	0
S_5	S_2	S_4	0
S_6	S_1	S_4	1

PROBLEMS

15.3   A sequential network has one input and one output. The output becomes one and remains one thereafter when at least two zeros *and* at least two ones have occurred as inputs, regardless of the order of occurrence. Draw a state graph (Moore type) for the network (9 states are sufficient). Your final state graph should be neatly drawn with no crossed lines.

15.4   A sequential network has one input (X) and two outputs (Z_1 and Z_2). An output $Z_1 = 1$ occurs every time the input sequence 101 is completed provided that the sequence 011 has never occurred. An output $Z_2 = 1$ occurs every time the input 011 is completed. Note that once a $Z_2 = 1$ output has occurred, $Z_1 = 1$ can never occur but *not* vice versa. Find a Mealy state graph and state table (minimum number of states is 8).

15.5   A sequential network has two inputs (X_1, X_2) and one output (Z). The output remains a constant value unless one of the following input sequences occurs:

    a.   The input sequence $X_1 X_2 = 00, 11$ causes the output to become 0.

    b.   The input sequence $X_1 X_2 = 01, 11$ causes the output to become 1.

    c.   The input sequence $X_1 X_2 = 10, 11$ causes the output to change value.

    Derive a Moore state table and state graph.

15.6   A sequential network has one input (X) and one output (Z). Draw a Mealy state graph for each of the following cases:

    a.   The output is $Z = 1$ iff the total number of 1's received is divisible by 3. (*Note:* 0, 3, 6, 9, 12, . . . are divisible by 3.)

    b.   The output is $Z = 1$ iff the total number of 1's received is divisible by 3 *and* the total number of 0's received is an even number greater than zero. (9 states are sufficient)

15.7   A sequential network has two inputs and two outputs. The inputs ($X_1 X_2$) represent a 2-bit binary number, N. If the present value of N is greater than the previous value, then Z_1 is 1. If the present value of N is less than the previous value, then Z_2 is 1. Otherwise, Z_1 and Z_2 are 0. When the first pair of inputs is received, there is no previous value of N, so we cannot determine whether the present N is greater than or less than the previous value; therefore, the "otherwise" category applies.

    a.   Find a Mealy state table or graph for the network (minimum number of states, including starting state, is 5).

    b.   Find a Moore state table for the network (minimum number of states is 11).

15.8   A Moore sequential network has one input and one output. When the input sequence 011 occurs, the output becomes 1 and remains 1 until the sequence 011 occurs again in which case the output returns to 0. The output then remains 0 until 011 occurs a third time, etc. Derive the state graph (6 states minimum).

15.9 The input to a sequential network consists of groups of 5 bits. Each group of 5 bits represents a 2-out-of-5 binary-coded decimal digit (see Table 1-1). After receiving 5 bits, the network should output a 1 and reset if the bit pattern represents a valid 2-out-of-5 BCD digit; otherwise the network should output a 0 and reset. Derive a Mealy state graph (13 states minimum).

15.10 A Mealy sequential network has two inputs and one output. If the total number of 1's received is ≥ 4 and at least 3 pairs of inputs have occurred, then the output should be 1 coincident with the last input pair in the sequence. Whenever a 1 output occurs, the network resets. Derive a state graph and state table. Specify the meaning of each pair of states. For example, S_0 means reset, S_1 means 1 pair of inputs received but no 1's received, etc.

Example:

input sequence: $\begin{array}{l}0\ 0\ 0\ 1\ 1\ 1\ 0\ 0\ 0\ 1\ 1\ 1\ 0\ 0\ 1\ 1\ 1\ 0\ 1\\ 0\ 1\ 1\ 1\ 1\ 1\ 0\ 0\ 0\ 0\ 0\ 0\ 1\ 0\ 1\ 1\ 1\ 0\ 1\end{array}$

output sequence: $0\ 0\ 0\ 1\ 0\ 0\ 1\ 0\ 0\ 0\ 0\ 0\ 1\ 0\ 0\ 1\ 0\ 0\ 1$

reset here

15.11 A Moore sequential network has one input and one output. The output should be 1 if the total number of 0's received is odd and the total number of 1's received is an even number greater than 0. Derive the state graph and table (6 states).

15.12 A sequential network has an input X and an output Z. The output is the same as the input was two clock periods previously. For example,

$$X = 0\ \ 1\ \ 0\ \ 1\ \ 1\ \ 0\ \ 1\ \ 0\ \ 1\ \ 1\ \ 0\ \ 1\ \ 0\ \ 0\ \ 0\ \ 1$$
$$Z = 0\ \ 0\ \ 0\ \ 1\ \ 0\ \ 1\ \ 1\ \ 0\ \ 1\ \ 0\ \ 1\ \ 1\ \ 0\ \ 1\ \ 0\ \ 0$$

The first two values of Z are 0. Find a Mealy state graph and table for the network.

15.13 A sequential network has an input X and two outputs, S and V. X represents a 4-bit binary number N which is input least significant bit first. S represents a 4-bit binary number equal to $N + 2$, which is output least significant bit first. At the time the fourth input occurs, $V = 1$ if $N + 2$ is too large to be represented by four bits; otherwise, $V = 0$. The network always resets after the fourth bit of X is received. Find a Mealy state graph and table for the network.

Example:

$X = 0\ \ 1\ \ 1\ \ 1$ (binary 14 with the least significant bit first)

$S = 0\ \ 0\ \ 0\ \ 0$ (since $14 + 2 = 16$, and 16 requires 5 bits)

$V = 0\ \ 0\ \ 0\ \ 1$

15.14 A sequential network has an input X and outputs Y and Z. YZ represents a 2-bit binary number equal to the number of 1's that have been received as inputs. The network resets when the total number of 1's received is 3, or when the total number of 0's received is 3. Find a Moore

16

REDUCTION OF STATE TABLES
STATE ASSIGNMENT

OBJECTIVES

1. Define equivalent states, state several ways of testing for state equivalence, and determine if two states are equivalent.

2. Define equivalent sequential networks and determine if two networks are equivalent.

3. Reduce a state table to a minimum number of rows.

4. Specify a suitable set of state assignments for a state table, eliminating those assignments which are equivalent with respect to cost of realizing the network.

5. State three guidelines which are useful in making state assignments, and apply these to making a good state assignment for a given state table.

6. Given a state table and assignment, form the transition table and derive flip-flop input equations.

STUDY GUIDE

1. Study Section 16.1, *Elimination of Redundant States.*

2. Study Section 16.2, *Equivalent States.*

   a. State in words the meaning of $\lambda_1(p, \underline{X}) = \lambda_2(q, \underline{X})$.

b. Assuming that N_1 and N_2 are identical networks with the following state graph, use Definition 16.1 to show that p is *not* equivalent to q. (Calculate $\lambda(p, \underline{X})$ and $\lambda(q, \underline{X})$ for $\underline{X} = 0$, $\underline{X} = 1$, $\underline{X} = 00$, $\underline{X} = 01$, etc.)

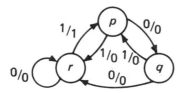

c. Suppose you were given two sequential networks (N_1 and N_2) in black boxes with only input and output terminals available. Each box has a reset button. The button on N_1 resets it to state p and the button on N_2 resets it to state q. Could you experimentally determine if $p \equiv q$ using Definition 16.1? Explain.

d. Apply Theorem 16.1 to show that in Table 16-5, $b \not\equiv c$.

e. Note the difference between the *definition* of state equivalence (Definition 16.1) and the state equivalence *theorem* (Theorem 16.1). The definition requires examination of output sequences but not next states, while the theorem requires looking at *both the output and next state* for each single input. Make sure that you know both the definition and the theorem.

Write out the definition of equivalent states:

Write out the state equivalence theorem:

When you check your answers, note that the theorem requires equal outputs and *equivalent* next states. This distinction between equal and equivalent is very important.

3. Study Section 16.3, *Determination of State Equivalence Using an Implication Table.*

    a. Fill in the implication chart given below to correspond to Table 16-5 (first pass only).

    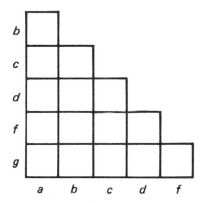

    Your answer should have 8 squares with X's, 2 squares with 1 implied pair, and 4 squares with 2 implied pairs. There should be a check in square f-g since the only non-trivial implication of f-g is f-g itself.

    b. Now go through your chart and eliminate all non-equivalent pairs (several passes may be required). What is the only equivalent state pair?

    c. Find all of the equivalent states in the following table using an implication table:

	next state		present output	
	$X = 0$	1	$X = 0$	1
a	b	c	0	1
b	d	b	0	0
c	e	a	0	1
d	d	e	0	0
e	e	e	0	0

    (You should have found 4 pairs of equivalent states. If you found only 2 pairs, reread Section 16.3).

    Reduce the table to 2 rows.

4. Study Section 16.4, *Equivalent Sequential Networks.* Define equivalent sequential networks. (Make sure you know the difference between equivalent *states* and equivalent *networks.*)

5. Study Section 16.5, *Incompletely Specified State Tables.*

   a. State two reasons why a state table might be incompletely specified.

   b. For Fig. 16-9, fill in the don't care outputs in the $X = 0$ column as 1 and 0 (instead of 0 and 1). Show that with this choice of outputs, the minimum number of states is 3.

6. Work Problems 16.1, 16.2 and 16.3 using the methods of Sections 16.3 and 16.4.

7. Section 16.6, *Determination of Equivalent States Using Next Class Tables,* is optional.

   a. You will probably find it easy to learn the procedure for finding equivalent states found in this section. However, finding the input sequences which will distinguish between two states, as in the example following Table 16-7(d), is a little trickier. In order to do this, we must find the first next class table in which we can tell the states apart and then work *back* through the tables to determine the required input sequence.

   b. Work Problems 16.4 and 16.5.

8. Study Section 16.7, *Equivalent State Assignments.*

   a. Fill in the missing assignments (numbered 8 through 18) in Table 16-9. First list the remaining assignments with 01 in the first row and then the assignments with 10 in the first row.

   b. Why is the trial-and-error method of state assignment of limited usefulness?

c. Why is it unnecessary to try all possible state assignments to be assured of finding a minimum cost network?

d. For symmetrical flip-flops, why is it always possible to assign all 0's to the starting state and still obtain a minimum network?

e. Show that each of the assignments in Table 16-9 is equivalent to one of the assignments in Table 16-10.

f. Why are the following two state assignments equivalent in cost?

A	000	011
B	001	111
C	011	101
D	101	110
E	100	010
F	010	001
G	110	000

g. Show that each of the following assignments can be generated from Table 16-10 by permuting and/or complementing columns:

10	11	01
01	01	11
00	00	00
11	10	10

h. Read Problem 16.6, and then answer the following questions regarding state assignments before you work the problem:

(1) Why should a column *not* be assigned all 0's or all 1's?

(2) Why should two columns *not* be given the same assignment?

(3) Does interchanging two columns affect the cost of realizing the network?

(4) Does interchanging two rows affect the cost?

(5) Why is an assignment which has two identical rows invalid?

(6) Consider the following 2 assignments:

	(1) (3) (5)	(3) (1) (5)
(The number at the top of each	0 0 0	0 0 0
column is the decimal equivalent	0 0 1	0 0 1
of the binary number in the	0 1 0	1 0 0
column.)	1 1 1	1 1 1

If we try the column assignment (1) (3) (5), why is it unnecessary to try (3) (1) (5)?
Why is it desirable to assign the column values in increasing numerical order?

9. Study Section 16.8, *Guidelines for State Assignment.*

   a. Why do the guidelines for making state assignments help in making an economical assignment?

   b. What should be done if all the adjacencies specified by the guidelines cannot be satisfied?

   c. The state assignment guidelines for Fig. 16-13(a) indicate that the following sets of states should be given adjacent assignments:

      (1) (S_0, S_1, S_3, S_5) (S_3, S_5) (S_4, S_6) (S_0, S_2, S_4, S_6)

      (2) (S_1, S_2) (S_2, S_3) (S_1, S_4) $(S_2, S_5)2X$ $(S_1, S_6)2X$

      Since the adjacencies from guideline 1 are generally most important, we will start by placing one of the largest groups from guideline 1 in four adjacent squares:

S_0	
S_1	
S_3	
S_5	

      Note that (S_3, S_5) is also satisfied by this grouping. Place S_2, S_4 and S_6 in the remaining squares to satisfy as many of the remaining guidelines as possible. Keeping in mind that groups labeled $2X$ should be given preference over groups which are not repeated. Compare your answer with Fig. 16-13(b).

10. Read Section 16.9, *Derivation of Flip-Flop Input Equations.*

    a. Review the short-cut method for deriving J-K flip-flop input equations (Section 13.5). The J and K input equations for flip-flop Q_i are independent of which variable?

    b. Complete the transition table for the state table of Fig. 16-15(a) using the assignment of Fig. 16-15(b).

	Q_1 Q_2 Q_3	$Q_1^+Q_2^+Q_3^+$ $X = 0$	1	0	1
A	0 0 0	000	100	0	0
B	1 1 1	011	110	0	1
C	1 0 0	100	000	0	0

c. Complete the next state and output maps, and verify that the cost of realizing the corresponding equations with an AND-OR gate network is 13 gates and 35 gate inputs.

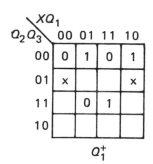

XQ_1
Q_2Q_3	00	01	11	10
00	0	1	0	1
01	x			x
11		0	1
10			

$$Q_1^+$$

XQ_1
Q_2Q_3	00	01	11	10
00	0	0	0	0
01	x			x
11		1	1
10			

$$Q_2^+$$

XQ_1
Q_2Q_3	00	01	11	10
00	0	0	0	0
01	x			x
11		1	0
10			

$$Q_3^+$$

XQ_1
Q_2Q_3	00	01	11	10
00	0	0	0	0
01	x			x
11		0	1
10			

$$Z$$

$D_1 =$ _____ $D_3 =$ _____

$D_2 =$ _____ $Z \ =$ _____

d. Using the short-cut method, find J_1 and K_1 from the Q_1^+ map.

$J_1 \ =$ _____

$K_1 =$ _____

11. Work Problems 16.7, 16.8, and 16.9.

12. When you are satisfied that you can meet all of the objectives, take the readiness test.

16. REDUCTION OF STATE TABLES STATE ASSIGNMENT

Given a description of the desired input-output behavior of a sequential network, the first step in designing the network is to derive a state table using methods similar to the ones discussed in the previous unit. Before we realize this state table using flip-flops and logic gates, reduction of the state table to a minimum number of states is desirable. In general, reducing the number of states in a table will reduce the amount of logic required, and the number of flip-flops may also be reduced. For example, if a table with 9 states is reduced to 8 states, the number of flip-flops required is reduced from 4 to 3, with a possible corresponding reduction in the amount of input logic for the flip-flops. If the table is further reduced to 6 states, 3 flip-flops are still required, but the presence of more don't cares in the flip-flop input equations will probably further reduce the required logic.

Given the reduced state table, the next step in synthesizing the network is to assign binary flip-flop states to correspond to the network states. The way in which this assignment is made will determine the amount of logic required for the network. The problem of finding a good state assignment which leads to an economical network is a difficult one, but some guidelines for achieving this are discussed in Sections 16.7−16.9.

16.1   Elimination of Redundant States

In Unit 15, we were careful to avoid introducing unnecessary states when setting up a state graph or table. We will now approach the problem of deriving the state graph somewhat differently. Initially, when first setting up the state table we will not be overly concerned with inclusion of extra states, but when the table is complete we will eliminate any redundant states. In previous units, we have used the notation $S_0, S_1, S_2, \ldots$ to represent states in a sequential network. In this unit, we will frequently use $A, B, C, \ldots$ (or $a, b, c, \ldots$) to represent these states.

We will rework Example 1 in Section 15.3. Initially, we will set up enough states to remember the first three bits of every possible input sequence. Then when the fourth bit comes in, we can determine the correct output and reset the network to the initial state. As indicated in Table 16-1, we will designate state A as the reset state. If we receive a 0, we go to state B; if we receive a 1, we go to state C. Similarly, starting in state B, a 0 takes us to state D to indicate that the sequence 00 has been received, and a 1 takes us to state E to indicate that 01 has been received. The remaining states are defined in a similar manner. When the fourth input bit is received, we return to the reset state. The output is 0 unless we are in state J or L and receive a 1, which corresponds to having received 0101 or 1001.

Next we will attempt to eliminate redundant states from the table. The input sequence information was only used in setting up the table and will now be disregarded. Looking at the table, we see that there is no way of telling states H and I apart. That is, if we start in state H the next state is A and the output is 0; similarly, if we start in state I the next state is A and the output is 0. Hence, there is no way of telling states H and I apart and we can replace I with H where it appears in the next state portion of the table. Having done this, there is no way to reach state I, so row I can be removed from the table. We say that H is *equivalent* to I ($H \equiv I$). Similarly, rows K, M, N and P have the same next state and output as H, so K, M, N and P can be replaced by H and these rows can be

Table 16-1. State Table for Sequence Detector

input sequence	present state	next state X = 0	next state X = 1	present output X = 0	present output X = 1
reset	A	B	C	0	0
0	B	D	E	0	0
1	C	F	G	0	0
00	D	H	I	0	0
01	E	J	K	0	0
10	F	L	M	0	0
11	G	N	P	0	0
000	H	A	A	0	0
001	I	A	A	0	0
010	J	A	A	0	1
011	K	A	A	0	0
100	L	A	A	0	1
101	M	A	A	0	0
110	N	A	A	0	0
111	P	A	A	0	0

deleted. Also, the next states and outputs are the same for rows J and L, so $J \equiv L$. Thus, L can be replaced with J and eliminated from the table. The result is shown in Table 16-2.

Table 16-2. State Table for Sequence Detector

present state	next state X = 0	next state X = 1	present output X = 0	present output X = 1
A	B	C	0	0
B	D	E	0	0
C	~~F~~ E	~~G~~ D	0	0
D	H	~~I~~ H	0	0
E	J	~~K~~ H	0	0
~~F~~	~~L~~ ~~J~~	~~M~~ ~~H~~	~~0~~	~~0~~
~~G~~	~~N~~ ~~H~~	~~R~~ ~~H~~	~~0~~	~~0~~
H	A	A	0	0
~~I~~	~~A~~	~~A~~	~~0~~	~~0~~
J	A	A	0	1
~~K~~	~~A~~	~~A~~	~~0~~	~~0~~
~~L~~	~~A~~	~~A~~	~~0~~	~~1~~
~~M~~	~~A~~	~~A~~	~~0~~	~~0~~
~~N~~	~~A~~	~~A~~	~~0~~	~~0~~
~~P~~	~~A~~	~~A~~	~~0~~	~~0~~

Having made these changes in the table, rows D and G are identical and so are rows E and F. Therefore, $D \equiv G$, and $E \equiv F$, so states F and G can be eliminated. Figure 16-1 shows a state diagram for the final reduced table. Note that this is identical to the state graph of Fig. 15-14 except for the designations for the states. The procedure used to find equivalent states in this example is known as *row matching*. In general, row matching is *not* sufficient to find all equivalent states, except in the special case where the network resets to the starting state after receiving a fixed number of inputs.

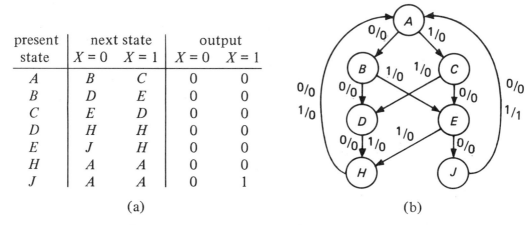

present	next state		output	
state	$X = 0$	$X = 1$	$X = 0$	$X = 1$
A	B	C	0	0
B	D	E	0	0
C	E	D	0	0
D	H	H	0	0
E	J	H	0	0
H	A	A	0	0
J	A	A	0	1

(a)   (b)

Fig. 16-1. Reduced state table and graph for sequence detector

16.2 Equivalent States

As we have seen in the previous example, state tables can be reduced by eliminating equivalent states. A state table with fewer rows often requires fewer flip-flops and logic gates to realize; therefore, determination of equivalent states is important to obtaining economical realizations of sequential networks.

Let us now consider the general problem of state equivalence. Basically, two states are equivalent if there is no way of telling them apart from observation of the network inputs and outputs. Consider two sequential networks (these may be different networks or two copies of the same network), one which is started in state p and one which is started in state q:

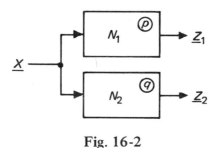

Fig. 16-2

Let $\underline{X}$ represent a sequence of inputs $X_1, X_2, ---, X_n$. Feed the same input sequence $\underline{X}$ into both networks and observe the output sequences $\underline{Z}_1$ and $\underline{Z}_2$. If these output sequences are the same, so far so good. Then reset the networks to the states p and q and try a different input sequence for $\underline{X}$ and again compare output sequences. If for every possible input sequence $\underline{X}$ these output sequences are the same, then there is no way of telling states p and q apart by observing the terminal behavior of the networks, and we say p is equivalent to q ($p \equiv q$). On the other hand, if for some input sequence $\underline{X}$ the output sequences $\underline{Z}_1$ and $\underline{Z}_2$ are different, then we can distinguish between states p and q, and they are not equivalent. Since the output sequence is a function of the initial state and the input sequence, we will write

$$\underline{Z}_1 = \lambda_1(p, \underline{X}) \qquad \underline{Z}_2 = \lambda_2(q, \underline{X})$$

We can then state formally the definition of state equivalence as follows:

> *Definition* 16.1: Let N_1 and N_2 be sequential networks (not necessarily different). Let $\underline{X}$ represent a sequence of inputs of arbitrary length. Then state p in N_1 is equivalent to state q in N_2 iff $\lambda_1(p, \underline{X}) = \lambda_2(q, \underline{X})$ for every possible input sequence $\underline{X}$.

Definition 16.1 is often difficult to apply directly in practice, since it may require testing the network with an infinite number of input sequences in order to prove that two states are equivalent. A more practical way of testing for state equivalence makes use of the following theorem:

> *Theorem* 16.1* Two states p and q of a sequential network are equivalent iff for every single input X, the outputs are the same and the next states are *equivalent*, i.e.,

$$\lambda(p, X) = \lambda(q, X) \text{ and } \delta(p, X) \equiv \delta(q, X)$$

> where $\lambda(p, X)$ is the output given the present state p and input X and $\delta(p, X)$ is the next state given the present state p and input X.

The row matching procedure previously discussed is a special case of this theorem where the next states are actually the same instead of just being equivalent.

We will use the above theorem to show that Table 14-4 has no equivalent states. By inspection of the output part of the table, the only possible pair of equivalent states is S_0 and S_2. From the table,

$$S_0 \equiv S_2 \text{ iff } S_3 \equiv S_3, S_2 \equiv S_0, S_1 \equiv S_1 \text{ and } S_0 \equiv S_1$$

But $S_0 \not\equiv S_1$ (because the outputs differ), so the last condition is not satisfied and $S_0 \not\equiv S_2$.

---

*See Appendix C.2 for proof.

16.3 Determination of State Equivalence Using an Implication Table

In this section, we will discuss a procedure for finding all of the equivalent states in a state table. If the equivalent states found by this procedure are eliminated, then the table can be reduced to a minimum number of states. We will use an implication table (sometimes referred to as a pair chart) to check each pair of states for possible equivalence. Non-equivalent pairs are systematically eliminated until only equivalent pairs remain.

Table 16-3

present state	next state $X = 0$	1	present output
a	d	c	0
b	f	h	0
c	e	d	1
d	a	e	0
e	c	a	1
f	f	b	1
g	b	h	0
h	$c.$	g	1

We will use the example of Table 16-3 to illustrate the implication table method. The first step is to construct a chart of the form shown in Fig. 16-3. This chart has a square for every possible pair of states. A square in column i and row j corresponds to state pair i-j. Thus, the squares in the first column correspond to state pairs a-b, a-c, etc. Note that squares above the diagonal are not included in the chart since if $i \equiv j$, $j \equiv i$, and only one of the state pairs i-j and j-i is needed. Also, squares corresponding to pairs a-a, b-b, etc. are omitted. To fill in the first column of the chart, we compare row a of Table 16-3 with each of the other rows. Since the output for row a is different than the output for row c, we place an X in the a-c square of the chart to indicate that $a \not\equiv c$. Similarly, we place X's in squares a-e, a-f and a-h to indicate that $a \not\equiv e$, $a \not\equiv f$, and $a \not\equiv h$ because of output differences. States a and b have the same outputs, and thus by Theorem 16.1,

$$a \equiv b \quad \text{iff} \quad d \equiv f \quad \text{and} \quad c \equiv h$$

To indicate this, we place the "implied pairs", d-f and c-h, in the a-b square. Similarly, since a and d have the same outputs, we place a-d and c-e in the a-d square to indicate that

$$a \equiv d \quad \text{iff} \quad a \equiv d \quad \text{and} \quad c \equiv e$$

The entries b-d and c-h in the a-g square indicate that

$$a \equiv g \quad \text{iff} \quad b \equiv d \quad \text{and} \quad c \equiv h$$

Next, row b of the state table is compared with each of the remaining rows of the table, and column b of the implication chart is filled in. Similarly, the remaining columns in the chart are filled in to complete Fig. 16-3. Self-implied pairs are redundant, so a-d can be eliminated from square a-d, and c-e from square c-e.

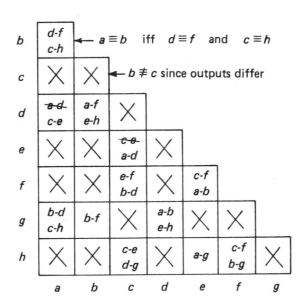

Fig. 16-3. Implication chart for Table 16-3

At this point, each square in the implication table has either been filled in with an X to indicate that the corresponding state pair is not equivalent or filled in with implied pairs. We now check each implied pair. If one of the implied pairs in square i-j is not equivalent, then by Theorem 16.1, $i \not\equiv j$. The a-b square of Fig. 16-3 contains two implied pairs (d-f and c-h). Since $d \not\equiv f$ (d-f square has an X in it), $a \not\equiv b$ and we place an X in the a-b square as shown in Fig. 16-4. Continuing to check the first column, we note that the a-d square contains the implied pair c-e. Since square c-e does not contain an X, we cannot determine at this point whether or not $a \equiv d$. Similarly, since neither square b-d nor c-h contains an X, we cannot determine immediately whether $a \equiv g$ or not. Going on to the second column, we place X's in squares b-d and b-g since we have already shown $a \not\equiv f$ and $b \not\equiv f$. In a similar manner, we check each of the remaining columns and X out squares c-f, d-g, e-f and f-h. Figure 16-4 shows the resulting chart.

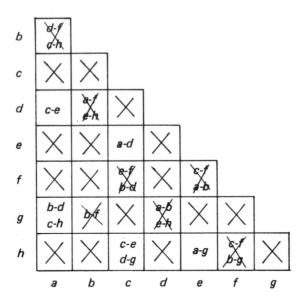

Fig. 16-4. Implication chart after first pass

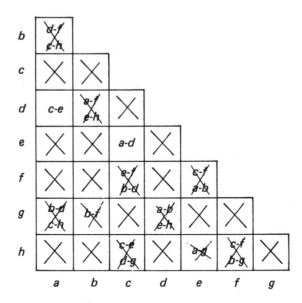

Fig. 16-5. Implication chart after second pass

In going from Fig. 16-3 to Fig. 16-4, we found several additional non-equivalent state pairs. Therefore, we must go through the chart again to see if the added *X*'s make any other pairs non-equivalent. Rechecking column *a*, we find that we can place an *X* in square *a-g* since square *b-d* has an *X*. Checking the remaining columns, we *X* out squares *c-h* and *e-h* since *d-g* and *a-g* have *X*'s.

This completes the second pass through the implication table as shown in Fig. 16-5. Since we added some X's on the second pass, a third pass is required. No new X's are added on the third pass through the table, so all squares which correspond to non-equivalent state pairs have been Xed out. The co-ordinates of the remaining squares must then correspond to equivalent state pairs. Since square a-d (in column a, row d) does not contain an X, we conclude that $a \equiv d$. Similarly, square c-e does not contain an X, so $c \equiv e$. All other squares contain X's, so there are no other equivalent state pairs. Note that we determined equivalent states from the column-row coordinates of the squares without X's, *not* by reading the implied pairs contained within the squares. If we replace d with a and e with c in Table 16-3, we can eliminate rows d and e, and the table reduces to 6 rows as shown in Table 16-4.

Table 16-4

present state	next state $X = 0$	1	output
a	a	c	0
b	f	h	0
c	c	a	1
f	f	b	1
g	b	h	0
h	c	g	1

The implication table method of determining state equivalence can be summarized as follows:

1. Construct a chart which contains a square for each pair of states.

2. Compare each pair of rows in the state table. If the outputs associated with states i and j are different, place an X in square i-j to indicate that $i \not\equiv j$. If the outputs are the same, place the implied pairs in square i-j. (If the next states of i and j are m and n for some input x, then m-n is an implied pair.) If the outputs and next states are the same (or if i-j only implies itself), place a check ($\checkmark$) in square i-j to indicate that $i \equiv j$.

3. Go through the table square-by-square. If square i-j contains the implied pair m-n, and square m-n contains an X, then $i \not\equiv j$, and an X should be placed in square i-j.

4. If any X's were added in step 3, repeat step 3 until no more X's are added.

5. For each square i-j which does not contain an X, $i \equiv j$.

If desired, row matching can be used to partially reduce the state table before constructing the implication table. Although we have illustrated this procedure for a Moore table, the same procedure applies to a Mealy table.

16.4 Equivalent Sequential Networks

Next, we will consider equivalence between sequential networks. Essentially, two sequential networks are equivalent if they are capable of doing the same "work". Equivalence between sequential networks is defined as follows:

> *Definition* 16.2: Sequential network N_1 is equivalent to sequential network N_2 if for each state p in N_1 there is a state q in N_2 such that $p \equiv q$, and conversely, for each state s in N_2 there is a state t in N_1 such that $s \equiv t$.

Thus if $N_1 \equiv N_2$, for every starting state p in N_1 we can find a corresponding starting state q such that $\lambda_1(p, \underline{X}) = \lambda_2(q, \underline{X})$ for all input sequences $\underline{X}$ (i.e., the output sequences are the same for the same input sequence). Thus, in a given application N_1 could be replaced with its equivalent network N_2.

If N_1 and N_2 have only a few states, one way to show that $N_1 \equiv N_2$ is to match up pairs of equivalent states by inspection and then show that Theorem 16.1 is satisfied for each pair of equivalent states. If N_1 and N_2 both have a minimum number of states and $N_1 \equiv N_2$, then N_1 and N_2 must have the same number of states. Otherwise, one network would have a state left over which was not equivalent to any state in the other network and Def. 16.2 would not be satisfied.

Figure 16-6 shows two reduced state tables and their corresponding state graphs. By inspection of the state graphs, it appears that if the networks are equivalent we must have A equivalent to either S_2 or S_3 since these are the only states in N_2 with self-loops. Since the outputs of A and S_2 correspond, the only possibility is $A \equiv S_2$. If we assume that $A \equiv S_2$, this implies that we must have $B \equiv S_0$, which in turn implies that we must have $D \equiv S_1$ and $C \equiv S_3$. Using the

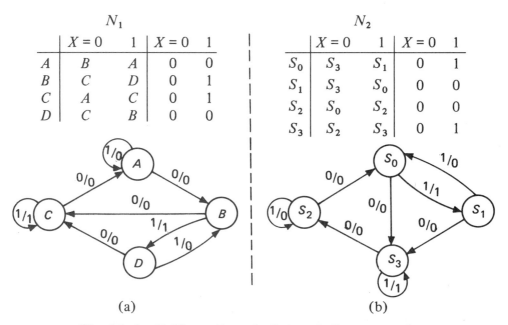

N_1	$X = 0$	1	$X = 0$	1
A	B	A	0	0
B	C	D	0	1
C	A	C	0	1
D	C	B	0	0

N_2	$X = 0$	1	$X = 0$	1
S_0	S_3	S_1	0	1
S_1	S_3	S_0	0	0
S_2	S_0	S_2	0	0
S_3	S_2	S_3	0	1

(a) (b)

Fig. 16-6. Tables and graphs for equivalent networks

state tables, we can verify that the above assumptions are correct since for every pair of assumed equivalent states the next states are equivalent and the outputs are equal when $X = 0$ and also when $X = 1$. This verifies that $N_1 \equiv N_2$.

The implication table can easily be adapted for determining equivalence of sequential networks. Since the states of one network must be checked for equivalence against states of the other network, an implication chart is constructed with rows corresponding to states of one network and columns corresponding to states of the other. For example, for the networks of Fig. 16-6 we can set up the implication table of Fig. 16-7(a). The first column of Fig. 16-7(a) is filled in by comparing row A of the state table in Fig. 16-6(a) with each of the rows in Fig. 16-6(b). Since states A and S_0 have different outputs, an X is placed in the A-S_0 square. Since states A and S_1 have the same outputs, the implied next state pairs (B-S_3 and A-S_0) are placed in the A-S_1 square, etc. The remainder of the table is filled in similarly. In the next step, Fig. 16-7(b), squares corresponding to additional non-equivalent state pairs are crossed out. Thus, square A-S_1 is crossed out because $A \not\equiv S_0$. Similarly, square B-S_3 is crossed out because $C \not\equiv S_2$, square C-S_0 because $A \not\equiv S_3$, and square D-S_2 because $B \not\equiv S_2$. Another pass through the table reveals no additional non-equivalent pairs; therefore, the remaining equivalent state pairs are

$$A \equiv S_2 \qquad B \equiv S_0 \qquad C \equiv S_3 \qquad D \equiv S_1$$

Since each state in N_1 has an equivalent state in N_2 and conversely, $N_1 \equiv N_2$.

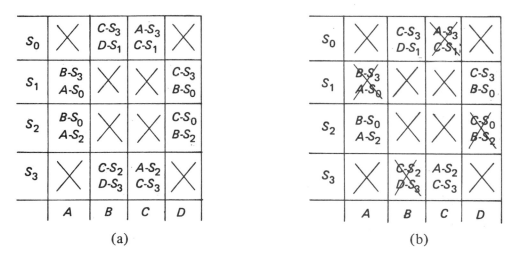

(a)   (b)

Fig. 16-7. Implication tables for determining network equivalence

16.5 Incompletely Specified State Tables

When a sequential network is used as part of a larger digital system, it frequently happens that certain sequences will never occur as inputs to the sequential network. In other cases, the output of the sequential network is only observed at certain times rather than at every clock time. Such restrictions lead to unspecified next states or outputs in the state table. When such don't cares are present, we say that the state table is incompletely specified. Just as don't cares in a truth table can be used to simplify the resulting combinational network, don't cares in a state table can be used to simplify the sequential network.

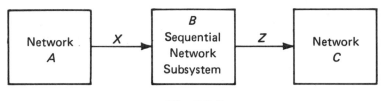

Fig. 16-8

The following example illustrates how don't cares arise in a state table. Assume that network A (Fig. 16-8) can only generate two possible output sequences, $X = 100$ and $X = 110$. Thus, the sequential network subsystem (B) has only two possible input sequences. When the third input in the sequence is received, the output of B is to be $Z = 0$ if 100 was received and $Z = 1$ if 110 was received. Assume that network C ignores the value of Z at other times so that we don't care what Z is during the first two inputs in the X sequence. The possible input-output sequences for network B are listed below, where t_0, t_1 and t_2 represent 3 successive clock times:

$$
\begin{array}{c|c}
\begin{array}{ccc} t_0 & t_1 & t_2 \end{array} & \begin{array}{ccc} t_0 & t_1 & t_2 \end{array} \\
\hline
X = \begin{array}{ccc} 1 & 0 & 0 \\ 1 & 1 & 0 \end{array} & Z = \begin{array}{ccc} - & - & 0 \\ - & - & 1 \end{array}
\end{array}
\quad (- \text{ is a don't care output})
$$

The state table of Fig. 16-9(a) will produce the required outputs. Note that the next state entry for S_0 with $X = 0$ is a don't care since 0 can never occur as the first input in the sequence. Similarly, the next state entries for S_2 and S_3 with $X = 1$ are don't cares since $X = 1$ cannot occur as the third input in the sequence. If we fill in the don't cares in the state table as indicated in Fig. 16-9(b), we can use row matching to reduce the table to two states as shown in Fig. 16-9(c).

	$X=0$	1	0	1
S_0	–	S_1	–	–
S_1	S_2	S_3	–	–
S_2	S_0	–	0	–
S_3	S_0	–	1	–

(a)

	$X=0$	1	0	1
S_0	(S_0)	S_1	(0)	–
S_1	S_0	S_3	(1)	–
S_2	S_0	(S_1)	0	–
S_3	S_0	(S_3)	1	–

(b) $S_0 \equiv S_2,\ S_1 \equiv S_3$

	$X=0$	1	0	1
S_0	S_0	S_1	0	–
S_1	S_0	S_1	1	–

(c)

Fig. 16-9. Incompletely specified state table

As illustrated in the above example, one method of reducing incompletely specified state tables is to fill in the don't cares in an appropriate manner and then reduce the table using one of the methods which apply to completely specified state tables. This procedure may be applied to small tables or to tables with only a few don't cares, but in general it does not lead to a minimum-row reduced table. Determining the best way to fill in the don't cares may require considerable trial and error, and even if the best way of filling in the don't cares is found, the resulting table cannot always be reduced to a minimum-row table. General procedures are known which will reduce an incompletely-specified state table to a minimum number of rows*, but discussion of such procedures is beyond the scope of this text.

16.6 Determination of Equivalent States Using Next Class Tables**

This section presents an alternative procedure for finding all of the equivalent states in a state table. We will use Table 16-5 to illustrate this method.

Table 16-5

	next state		present output	
	$X = 0$	1	$X = 0$	1
a	a	b	0	0
b	d	$ʾₐa$	0	1
c	$ʾₐa$	b	0	1
d	g	f	0	0
e	a	b	0	0
f	d	g	0	1
g	d	f	0	1

States a and e are equivalent by row matching, so we replace e with a and eliminate row e as indicated. Now with a single input, we can tell that certain states are *not* equivalent. For example, state a is not equivalent to states b, c, f or g because the output for state a is different from the outputs for the other states when $X = 1$. We will divide the states into classes and put those states with the same outputs in the same class:

$$S_1 = \{a, d\} \qquad S_2 = \{b, c, f, g\}$$

With a single input, we can tell states in class S_1 apart from states in S_2. To determine if the states within each class can be distinguished from each other by applying longer input sequences, we set up a "next class" table. For each state this

---

*See, for example, Hill and Peterson, *Introduction to Switching Theory and Logical Design*, 3d edition, Chapter 13.
**This section is optional.

table shows what class the next state will be in when a single input is applied. When $X = 0$ the next state of a is a, which is in class S_1. When $X = 1$, the next state of a is b, which is in class S_2. The next class table is completed in this manner as shown in Table 16-6.

Table 16-6

present class		next class $X = 0$	1
S_1	a	S_1	S_2
	d	S_2	S_2
S_2	b	S_1	S_1
	c	S_1	S_2
	f	S_1	S_2
	g	S_1	S_2

Examination of this table shows that we can now distinguish states a and d, since when $X = 0$ the next state of a is in class S_1, the next state of d is in class S_2 and we can distinguish states in S_1 from states in S_2. This in effect means that we can distinguish states a and d by an input sequence of length two. An input sequence which will distinguish the two states is 01 as illustrated by the following sequences:

```
state   → a a b      d g f
input   → 0 1        0 1
output  → 0 0        0 1      (second outputs differ)
          ↑            ↑
```

In a similar manner, Table 16-6 shows that we can distinguish state b from states c, f and g since the next class is different when $X = 1$. At this point, we have divided the states into four classes which can be distinguished from each other.

$$S_{11} = \{a\}, \quad S_{12} = \{d\}, \quad S_{21} = \{b\}, \quad S_{22} = \{c, f, g\}$$

At this point, we do not know if the states in class S_{22} are equivalent so we set up a new next class table for these states.

present class		next class $X = 0$	1
S_{22}	c	S_{11}	S_{21}
	f	S_{12}	S_{22}
	g	S_{12}	S_{22}

We can now distinguish state c from states f and g, so we subdivide class S_{22} into classes $S_{221} = \{c\}$ and $S_{222} = \{f, g\}$. An input sequence of length three is required to distinguish state c from states f and g:

```
state   → c a a b       f d g f
input   → 0 0 1         0 0 1
output  → 0 0 0         0 0 1     (third outputs differ)
           ↑               ↑
```

At this point, we do not know if f and g are equivalent so we will set up another next class table:

		next class	
		0	1
S_{222}	f	S_{12}	S_{222}
	g	S_{12}	S_{222}

Since there is no way of distinguishing states f and g, $f \equiv g$. We can then go back to the original table and eliminate g. The final result is:

	0	1	0	1
a	a	b	0	0
b	d	a	0	1
c	a	b	0	1
d	f	f	0	0
f	d	f	0	1

Summary of procedure for determining equivalent states:

1. Use row matching to reduce the table as far as possible.

2. Divide the states into classes according to the outputs.

3. Set up a next class table which shows the present class and next classes for each state.

4. If states in a given class can be distinguished from other states in the class by using the table formed in step 3, subdivide this class accordingly.

5. Using the new classes formed in step 4 along with any other classes which were not subdivided, repeat step 3 and then step 4 until the states in each class cannot be distinguished from each other. The states remaining in a given class are then equivalent.

The tables generated in the above process are also useful in generating input sequences which can be used to distinguish non-equivalent states.

As a further example of using the next class method, we will find the equivalent states in Table 16-3. There are no identical rows, so we divide the states into output classes and set up a next class table, Table 16-7(a). From the table (a), we see that b is not equivalent to a, d or g, so S_1 splits into two classes in table (b).

Table 16-7

(a)

present class		next class 0	1
class S_1	a	S_1	S_2
	b	S_2	S_2
	d	S_1	S_2
	g	S_1	S_2
class S_2	c	S_2	S_1
	e	S_2	S_1
	f	S_2	S_1
	h	S_2	S_1

(b)

present class		next class 0	1
S_{11}	a	S_{11}	S_2
	d	S_{11}	S_2
	g	S_{12}	S_2
S_{12}	b		
S_2	c	S_2	S_{11}
	e	S_2	S_{11}
	f	S_2	S_{12}
	h	S_2	S_{11}

(c)

		0	1
S_{111}	a	S_{111}	S_{21}
	d	S_{111}	S_{21}
S_{112}	g		
S_{12}	b		
S_{21}	c	S_{21}	S_{111}
	e	S_{21}	S_{111}
	h	S_{21}	S_{112}
S_{22}	f		

(d)

S_{111}	a	S_{111}	S_{211}
	d	S_{111}	S_{211}
S_{112}	g		
S_{12}	b		
S_{211}	c	S_{211}	S_{111}
	e	S_{211}	S_{111}
S_{212}	h		
S_{22}	f		

At this point, we see that g is not equivalent to a or d, and f is not equivalent to c, e or h. This leads to Table 16-7(c). Then we see that h is not equivalent to c or e.

So we form a new table (d). Now there is no way of telling a and d apart, or c and e apart, so $a \equiv d$ and $c \equiv e$. The original table reduces to Table 16-4.

Next we will demonstrate by direct application of the definition of state equivalence that $h \not\equiv c$. We do this by determining an input sequence which will distinguish between the two states. We cannot tell c and h apart in Tables 16-3, 16-7(a) or 16-7(b); however, in Table 16-7(c), a 1 input takes c and h to different next classes. From Table 16-3,

$$\delta(c, 1) = d \quad \text{and} \quad \delta(h, 1) = g$$

so our problem now becomes how to distinguish states d and g.

We see that d and g cannot be distinguished in Tables 16-3 and 16-7(a) but in Table 16-7(b), a 0 input takes d and g to different next classes. From Table 16-3,

$$\delta(d, 0) = a \quad \text{and} \quad \delta(g, 0) = b$$

so our problem now becomes how to distinguish states a and b. From Table 16-7(a), a 0 input will take a and b to different next classes. Then from Table 16-3,

$$\delta(a, 0) = d \quad \text{and} \quad \delta(b, 0) = f$$

We can tell d and f apart since they have different outputs (independent of the input). Therefore, the required input sequences and the corresponding output sequences are:

$$
\begin{array}{llll}
\text{input} & 1\ 0\ 0\ x & \quad 1\ 0\ 0\ x \\
\text{state} & c\ d\ a\ d & \quad h\ g\ b\ f \\
\text{output} & 1\ 0\ 0\ 0 & \quad 1\ 0\ 0\ 1
\end{array}
$$

The next class procedure used for finding equivalent states can also be used to determine if two networks (N_1 and N_2) are equivalent. First, combine the state tables for N_1 and N_2 into a single table using different symbols to represent the states in the two networks. Then find the classes of equivalent states using the procedure given on p. 335. If every class of equivalent states contains at least one state from both networks, then Definition 16.2 is satisfied and $N_1 \equiv N_2$. If any state in N_1 does not have an equivalent state in N_2 (or conversely), then Definition 16.2 is not satisfied and $N_1 \not\equiv N_2$.

As an example, we will show that the sequential networks represented by Tables 16-8(a) and 16-8(b) are equivalent. The two tables are first combined into a single table, the states are sorted into classes according to output, and a next class table, Table 16-8(c), is formed. When class S_0 is subdivided, the resulting next class table, Table 16-8(d), shows that $a \equiv e$, $c \equiv d$ and $b \equiv f$. The conditions of Definition 16.2 are satisfied and the two networks are equivalent.

Table 16-8. Determination of Network Equivalence

(a)

	$x=0$	1	0	1
a	b	c	0	0
b	a	b	0	1
c	c	a	0	0

(b)

	$x=0$	1	0	1
d	d	e	0	0
e	f	d	0	0
f	e	f	0	1

(c)

		$x=0$	1	0	1
S_0	a	S_1	S_0	0	0
	c	S_0	S_0	0	0
	d	S_0	S_0	0	0
	e	S_1	S_0	0	0
S_1	b	S_0	S_1	0	1
	f	S_0	S_1	0	1

(d)

		$x=0$	1
S_{00}	a	S_1	S_{01}
	e	S_1	S_{01}
S_{01}	c	S_{01}	S_{00}
	d	S_{01}	S_{00}
S_1	b	S_{00}	S_1
	f	S_{00}	S_1

16.7 Equivalent State Assignments

The cost of the logic required to realize a sequential network is strongly dependent on the way in which flip-flop states are assigned to correspond to the states in the state table. Several methods for choosing state assignments to obtain economical realizations are discussed in this unit. The trial and error method described in Section 16.7 is useful only for a small number of states. The guideline method discussed in Section 16.8 produces good solutions for some problems, but it is not entirely satisfactory in all cases. The SHR technique.[*] produces optimum solutions for J-K flip-flops with a reasonable amount of computation and is the best method to use when an optimum solution is required.

If the number of states is small, it may be feasible to try all possible state assignments, evaluate the cost of the realization for each assignment, and choose the assignment with the lowest cost. For example, with three states a, b and c and two flip-flops, Q_1 and Q_2, there are four possible assignments for state a (00, 01, 10, and 11). Choosing one of these assignments leave 3 possible assignments for state b. After state b is assigned, we have 2 possible assignments for state c. Thus, there are 24 possible state assignments, as shown in Table 16-9. In this table, the entry 01 means that flip-flops Q_1 and Q_2 are assigned values 0 and 1 respectively.

Table 16-9. State Assignments for 3-Row Tables

	1	2	3	4	5	6	7		19	20	21	22	23	24
a	00	00	00	00	00	00	01	- - -	11	11	11	11	11	11
b	01	01	10	10	11	11	00		00	00	01	01	10	10
c	10	11	01	11	01	10	10		01	10	00	10	00	01

*James R. Story, Harold J. *Harrison,* and Erwin A. *Reinhard,* "Optimum State Assignment for Synchronous Sequential Circuits," *IEEE Transactions on Computers,* Vol. C-21, Dec. 1972, pp. 1365 - 1373.

Trying all of these assignments is not really necessary. If we interchange the two columns in one of the given assignments, the cost of realization will be unchanged, because interchanging columns is equivalent to relabeling the flip-flop variables. Thus assignments 1 and 3 above have the same cost since the first column of assignment 3 is the same as the second column of assignment 1 and vice versa. Assignments 2 and 4 also have the same cost, and so do 5 and 6. Interchanging rows, however, will generally change the cost of realization. Thus, assignments 4 and 6 will have a different cost for most state tables.

If symmetrical flip-flops such as T, J-K or S-R are used, complementing one or more columns of the state assignment will have no effect on the cost of realization. Consider a J-K flip-flop imbedded in a network, Fig. 16-10(a). Leave the network unchanged and interchange the J and K leads and the Q_k and Q_k' leads, Fig. 16-10(b). If network A is started with $Q_k = p$ and network B with $Q_k = p'$, the behavior of the two networks will be identical except the value of Q_k will always be complemented in the second network because whenever J is 1 in the first network K will be 1 in the second and conversely. The state table for the second network is therefore the same as for the first except the value of Q_k is complemented for the second network. This implies that complementing one or more columns in the state assignment will not affect the cost of the realization when J-K flip-flops are used. Similar reasoning applies to T and S-R flip-flops. Thus in Table 16-9, assignments 2 and 7 have the same cost, and so do assignments 6 and 19.

(a) NETWORK A (b) NETWORK B (identical to A except leads to flip-flop Q_k are crossed)

Fig. 16-10. Equivalent networks obtained by complementing Q_k

If unsymmetrical flip-flops are used such as a D flip-flop, it is still true that permuting (i.e., rearranging the order of) columns in the state assignment will not affect the cost; however, complementing a column may require adding an inverter to the network as shown in Fig. 16-11. If different types of gates are available, the network can generally be redesigned to eliminate the inverter and use the same number of gates as the original. If network A in Fig. 16-11 is started with $Q_k = p$ and network B with $Q_k = p'$, the behavior of the two networks will be identical, except the value of Q_k will always be complemented in network B because f is the same in both networks and $D = f'$ for network B.

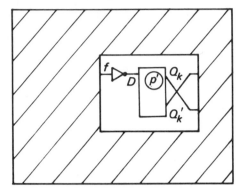

(a) NETWORK A (b) NETWORK B (identical to A except for connections to flip-flop Q_k)

Fig. 16-11. Equivalent networks obtained by complementing Q_k

The following example illustrates the effect of interchanging or complementing state assignment columns on the equations for realizing a specific state table (Fig. 16-12).

assignments			present state	next state $X = 0$ 1		output 0 1	
"a"	"b"	"c"		$X = 0$	1	0	1
00	00	11	S_1	S_1	S_3	0	0
01	10	10	S_2	S_2	S_1	0	1
10	01	01	S_3	S_2	S_3	1	0

Fig. 16-12

The J-K and D flip-flop input equations for the three assignments, derived in the usual way using Karnaugh maps, are:

assignment "a"	assignment "b"	assignment "c"
$J_1 = XQ_2'$	$J_2 = XQ_1'$	$K_1 = XQ_2$
$K_1 = X'$	$K_2 = X'$	$J_1 = X'$
$J_2 = X'Q_1$	$J_1 = X'Q_2$	$K_2 = X'Q_1'$
$K_2 = X$	$K_1 = X$	$J_2 = X$
$Z = X'Q_1 + XQ_2$	$Z = X'Q_2 + XQ_1$	$Z = X'Q_1' + XQ_2'$

$D_1 = XQ_2'$	$D_2 = XQ_1'$	$D_1 = X' + Q_2'$
$D_2 = X'(Q_1 + Q_2)$	$D_1 = X'(Q_2 + Q_1)$	$D_2 = X + Q_1Q_2$

Note that assignment *"b"* was obtained by interchanging the columns of *"a"*. The corresponding equations for assignment *"b"* are the same as for *"a"* except that subscripts 1 and 2 are interchanged. Assignment *"c"* was obtained by complementing the columns of *"a"*. The Z equation for *"c"* is the same as for *"a"* except that Q_1 and Q_2 are complemented. The K and J equations for *"c"* are the same, respectively, as the J and K equations for *"a"* with the Q's complemented. The D equations for *"c"* can be obtained by complementing those for *"a"* and then complementing the Q's. Thus, the cost of realizing Fig. 16-12 using J-K flip-flops and any kind of logic gates will be exactly the same for all three assignments. If both AND and OR (or NAND and NOR) gates are available, the cost of realizing the three sets of D equations will be the same. If only NOR gates are available, for example, then realizing D_1 and D_2 for assignment *"c"* would require two additional inverters compared with *"a"* and *"b"*.

By complementing one or more columns, any state assignment can be converted to one in which the first state is assigned all 0's. If we eliminate assignments which can be obtained by permuting or complementing columns, Table 16-9 reduces to three assignments (Table 16-10). Thus, when realizing a 3-state sequential network with symmetrical flip-flops, it is only necessary to try three different state assignments to be assured of a minimum cost realization. Similarly, only three different assignments must be tried for four states.

Table 16-10. **Non-equivalent Assignments for 3 and 4 States**

States	3-State Assignments			4-State Assignments		
	1	2	3	1	2	3
a	00	00	00	00	00	00
b	01	01	11	01	01	11
c	10	11	01	10	11	01
d	--	--	--	11	10	10

We will say that two state assignments are *equivalent* if one can be derived from the other by permuting and complementing columns. Two state assignments which are not equivalent are said to be *distinct*. Thus a four-row table has three distinct state assignments and any other assignment is equivalent to one of these three. Unfortunately, the number of distinct assignments increases very rapidly with the number of states as shown in Table 16-11. Hand solution is feasible for 2, 3 or 4 states; computer solution is feasible for 5 through 8 states; but for 9 or more states it is not practical to try all assignments even if a high-speed computer is used.

Table 16-11. Number of Distinct (Non-equivalent) State Assignments

No. of states	Minimum no. of state variables	No. of distinct assignments
2	1	1
3	2	3
4	2	3
5	3	140
6	3	420
7	3	840
8	3	840
9	4	10,810,800
.	.	.
.	.	.
.	.	.
16	4	$\approx 5.5 \times 10^{10}$

16.8 Guidelines for State Assignment

Since trying all non-equivalent state assignments is not practical in most cases, other methods of state assignment are needed. The next method to be discussed involves trying to choose an assignment which will place the 1's on the flip-flop input maps in adjacent squares so that the corresponding terms can be combined. This method does not apply to all problems, and even when applicable does not guarantee a minimum solution.

Assignments for two states are said to be adjacent if they differ in only one variable. Thus, 010, and 011 are adjacent, but 010 and 001 are not. The following *guidelines* are useful in making assignments which will place 1's together (or 0's together) on the next state maps:

1. States which have the same next state for a given input should be given adjacent assignments.

2. States which are the next states of the same state should be given adjacent assignments.

A third guideline is used for simplification of the output function:

3. States which have the same output for a given input should be given adjacent assignments.

Application of Guideline 3 will place 1's together on the output maps.

When using the state assignment guidelines, the first step is to write down all of the sets of states which should be given adjacent assignments according to the guidelines. Then, using a Karnaugh map, try to satisfy as many of these adjacencies as possible. A fair amount of trial and error may be required to fill in the map such that the maximum number of desired state adjacencies are obtained.

When filling in the map, keep in mind the following:

   a. Assign the starting state (reset state) to the "0" square on the map. Nothing is to be gained by trying to put the starting state in different squares on the map since the same number of adjacencies can be found no matter where you put the starting state. Usually, assigning "0" to the starting state simplifies initialization of the network.

   b. Adjacency conditions from Guideline 1 and adjacency conditions which are required two or more times should be satisfied first.

   c. When guidelines require that 3 or 4 states be adjacent, these states should be placed within a group of 4 adjacent squares on the assignment map.

   d. If the output table is to be considered, then Guideline 3 should also be applied. The priority given to adjacency conditions from Guideline 3 should generally be less than that given to Guidelines 1 and 2 if a single output function is being derived. If there are 2 or more output functions, a higher priority for Guideline 3 may be appropriate.

The following example should clarify application of Guidelines 1 and 2. Consider the state table given in Fig. 16-13(a). According to Guideline 1, S_0, S_2, S_4 and S_6 should be given adjacent assignments because they all have S_1 as a next state (with input 0). Similarly, S_0, S_1, S_3 and S_5 should have adjacent assignments because they have S_2 as a next state (with input 1); also S_3 and S_5 should have adjacent assignments, and so should S_4 and S_6. Application of Guideline 2 indicates that S_1 and S_2 should be given adjacent assignments since they are both next states of S_0. Similarly, S_2 and S_3 should have adjacent assignments since they are both next states of S_1. Further application of Guideline 2 indicates that S_1 and S_4, S_2 and S_5 (two times), and S_1 and S_6 (two times) should be given adjacent assignments. In summary, the sets of adjacent states specified by Guidelines 1 and 2 are

   1. (S_0, S_1, S_3, S_5) (S_3, S_5) (S_4, S_6) (S_0, S_2, S_4, S_6)

   2. (S_1, S_2) (S_2, S_3) (S_1, S_4) $(S_2, S_5)2x$ $(S_1, S_6)2x$

$x = 0$	1	0	1
S_0	S_1	S_2	0 0
S_1	S_3	S_2	0 0
S_2	S_1	S_4	0 0
S_3	S_5	S_2	0 0
S_4	S_1	S_6	0 0
S_5	S_5	S_2	1 0
S_6	S_1	S_6	0 1

(a) State table

BC \ A	0	1
00	S_0	
01	S_2	S_5
11	S_4	S_3
10	S_6	S_1

BC \ A	0	1
00	S_0	
01	S_1	S_6
11	S_3	S_4
10	S_5	S_2

(b) Assignment maps

Fig. 16-13

We will attempt to fulfill as many of these adjacency conditions as possible. A Karnaugh map will be used to make the assignments so that states with adjacent assignments will appear in adjacent squares on the map. If the guidelines require that 3 or 4 states be adjacent, these states should be placed within a group of 4 adjacent squares on the assignment map. Two possible ways of filling in the assignment maps are shown in Fig. 16-13(b). These maps were filled in by trial and error, attempting to fulfill as many of the above adjacency conditions as possible. Conditions from Guideline 1 are given preference to conditions from Guideline 2. Conditions which are required two times (such as S_2 adjacent to S_5, and S_1 adjacent to S_6) are given preference over conditions which are required only once (such as S_1 adjacent to S_2, and S_2 adjacent to S_3). The left assignment map, Fig. 16-13(b), implies the following assignments for the states of flip-flops A, B and C:

$$S_0 = 000, S_1 = 110, S_2 = 001, S_3 = 111,$$
$$S_4 = 011, S_5 = 101, S_6 = 010 \qquad (16\text{-}1)$$

A next state map for the network, Fig. 16-14(a), can be constructed using this assignment. For example, if $X = 0$ and $ABC = 000$, the next state is S_1; if $X = 1$ and $ABC = 000$, the next state is S_2. Because Guideline 1 was used in making the state assignment, S_1 appears in four adjacent squares on the next state map, S_5 appears in two adjacent squares, etc. The next state maps for the individual flip-flops, Fig. 16-14(b), can be derived in the usual manner from the next state table, or they can be derived directly from Fig. 16-14(a). Using the latter approach, wherever S_1 appears in Fig. 16-14(a), it is replaced with 110 so that 1, 1 and 0 are plotted on the corresponding squares of the A^+, B^+, and C^+ maps, respectively. The other squares on the next state maps are filled in similarly.

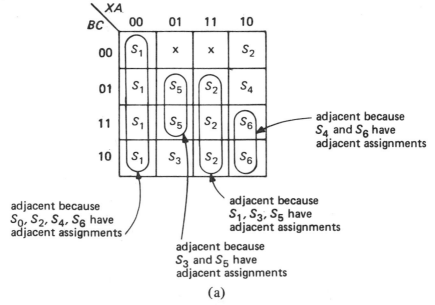

(a)

Fig. 16-14. Next state maps for Fig. 16-13

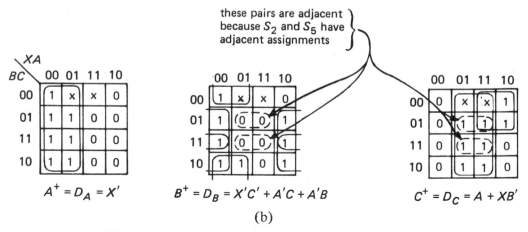

Fig. 16-14. Next state maps for Fig. 16-13 (cont.)

Once the next state maps for the flip-flops have been derived, the flip-flop input equations can be derived using the techniques developed in Unit 13. If D flip-flops are used, the maps for the D inputs are the same as the next state maps. Figure 16-14(b) gives the D input equations for the state table of Fig. 16-13(a) using the assignment of Equations (16-1). The cost of realizing these equations is 6 gates and 13 gate inputs. If a straight binary assignment ($S_0 = 000$, $S_1 = 001$, $S_2 = 010$, etc.) were used instead, the cost of realizing the flip-flop input equations would be 10 gates and 39 inputs. Although application of the guidelines gave good results in this example, this is not always the case.

	$X = 0$	1	$X = 0$	1
a	a	c	0	0
b	d	f	0	1
c	c	a	0	0
d	d	b	0	1
e	b	f	1	0
f	c	e	1	0

(a)

a = 000
b = 111
c = 100
d = 011
e = 101
f = 110

(b)

a = 100
b = 111
c = 000
d = 011
e = 101
f = 010

(c)

Fig. 16-15. State table and assignments

Next, we will apply the state assignment guidelines to Fig. 16-15(a). First, we list the sets of adjacent states specified by each Guideline:

1. (b, d) (c, f) (b, e)
2. $(a, c)2x$ (d, f) (b, d) (b, f) (c, e)
3. (a, c) (b, d) (e, f)

Next, we try to arrange the states on a map so as to satisfy as many of the above pairs as possible, but giving preference to the duplicate pairs (b, d) and (a, c) and to the remaining pairs in group 1. One such arrangement and the corresponding assignment is given in Fig. 16-15(b). All adjacencies are satisfied except (d, f) and (e, f).   Using D flip-flops with an AND-OR gate network, the cost of realizing the state table (including output) using the above assignment is 13 gates and 35 gate inputs. For this example the best known assignment for D flip-flops, given in Fig. 16-15(c), requires only 10 gates and 26 gate inputs. This assignment actually satisfies fewer of the adjacencies given by the guidelines than the first assignment. As illustrated by this example, the guidelines do not always lead to the best assignment, and more sophisticated techniques are needed to obtain a minimum solution.

The guidelines work best for D flip-flops and J-K flip-flops. They do not work as well for T and S-R flip-flops. In general, the best assignment for one type of flip-flop is not the best for another type.

16.9   Derivation of Flip-Flop Input Equations

After guidelines have been used to find a state assignment, the following procedure can be used to derive the flip-flop input equations:

1. Construct a transition table which gives the next states of the flip-flops as a function of the present states and inputs.

2. Derive next state maps from the transition table.

3. Find flip-flop input maps from the next state maps using the techniques developed in Unit 13.

The technique for deriving next state maps used in Fig. 16-14 illustrates why the adjacency guidelines lead to simplified next state functions. The usual way to derive next state maps is to first construct a transition table which gives the next states of the flip-flops in terms of the present states and inputs. Starting with the state table of Fig. 16-13(a) and using the state assignment given by Equations (16-1) we substitute 000 for S_0, 110 for S_1, 001 for S_2, etc. Table 16-12 shows the resulting transition table.

Table 16-12.   Transition Table for Fig. 16-13(a)

$$A^+B^+C^+$$

ABC	$X = 0$	1	0	1
000	110	001	0	0
110	111	001	0	0
001	110	011	0	0
111	101	001	0	0
011	110	010	0	0
101	101	001	1	0
010	110	010	0	1

This table gives the next state of flip-flops A, B and C in terms of the present states and the input X. We can fill in the next state maps, Fig. 16-14(b) directly from this table. Thus for $XABC = 0000$, we fill in $A^+ = 1$, $B^+ = 1$ and $C^+ = 0$; for $XABC = 1000$, we fill in $A^+ = 0$, $B^+ = 0$ and $C^+ = 1$; etc.

Once the next state maps have been plotted from the transition table, the D flip-flop input equations can be derived directly from the next state maps. If J-K flip-flops are used, the J and K input equations can be derived from the next state maps using the short-cut method as illustrated in Fig. 16-16. As was shown in Section 13.5, the $A = 0$ half of the A^+ map is a map for J_A and the $A = 1$ half is a map for K_A'. Therefore, we can determine J_A by looping 1's on the $A = 0$ half of the A^+ map, and we can determine K_A by looping 0's on the $A = 1$ half. We can derive J_B, K_B, J_C and K_C from the B^+ and C^+ maps in a similar manner.

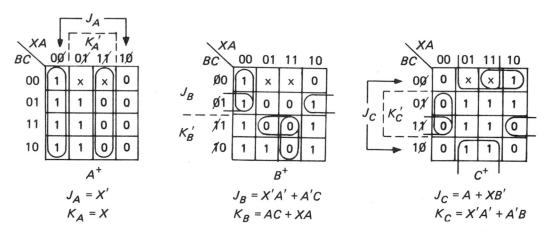

Fig. 16-16. Derivation of J-K flip-flop inputs from Table 16-13

Next, we will derive flip-flop input equations for the state table given in Fig. 16-15(a) using the state assignment of Fig. 16-15(c). By substituting the state codes in this assignment for the states in the table (100 for A, 111 for B, etc.), we obtain the transition table (Table 16-13). Then we plot the next state and output maps (Fig. 16-17) from the transition table. If D flip-flops are used, the flip-flop input equations can be read directly from these maps:

$$D_1 = Q_1^+ = X'Q_1 Q_2' + XQ_1'$$

$$D_2 = Q_2^+ = Q_3$$

$$D_3 = Q_3^+ = XQ_1'Q_2 + X'Q_3$$

and the output equation is

$$Z = XQ_2 Q_3 + X'Q_2'Q_3 + X'Q_2 Q_3'$$

Table 16-13. Transition Table for Fig. 16-15(a)

$$Q_1^+ Q_2^+ Q_3^+$$

$Q_1 Q_2 Q_3$	$X = 0$	1	$X = 0$	1
1 0 0	100	000	0	0
1 1 1	011	010	0	1
0 0 0	000	100	0	0
0 1 1	011	111	0	1
1 0 1	111	010	1	0
0 1 0	000	101	1	0

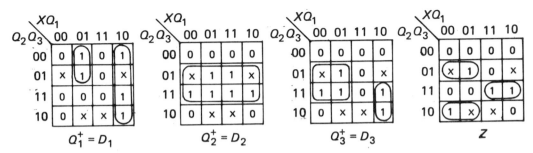

Fig. 16-17. Next state and output maps for Table 16-13

If J-K flipflops are used, the J and K equations can be read from the next state maps using the short-cut method. If T or S-R flip-flops are used, the flip-flop input maps can be derived from the next state maps using the techniques given in Section 13.9. As an example, the S-R equations for Table 16-13 are derived in Fig. 16-18. The S and R maps are derived from the corresponding Q^+ maps (Fig. 16-17) by using Table 13-4(c).

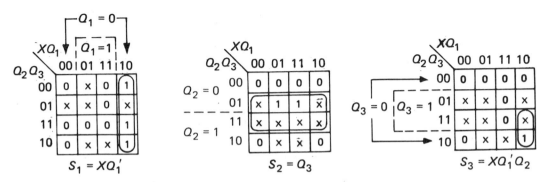

Fig. 16-18. Derivation of S-R flip-flop equations for Fig. 16-15(a)

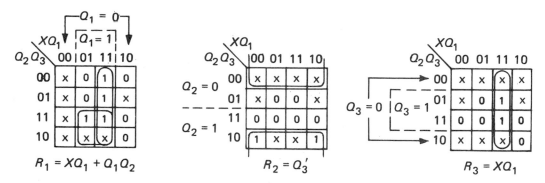

Fig. 16-18. Derivation of S-R flip-flop equations for Fig. 16-15(a) (cont.)

PROBLEMS

16.1 a. Reduce the following state table to a minimum number of states.

present state	next state $X = 0$	1	present output 0	1
a	c	f	0	0
b	d	e	—	0
c	h	g	0	0
d	b	g	0	0
e	e	b	0	1
f	f	a	0	1
g	c	g	0	1
h	c	f	0	0

b. You are given two identical sequential networks which realize the above state table. One network is initially in state "a" and the other network is initially in state "c". Specify an input sequence of length three which could be used to distinguish between the two networks, and give the corresponding output sequence from each network.

16.2 Reduce the following state table to a minimum number of states.

present state	next state $x = 0$	1	present output (z)
a	f	d	0
b	d	a	1
c	h	b	0
d	b	c	1
e	g	b	0
f	a	h	0
g	e	c	0
h	c	f	0

16.3   Digital engineer B. I. Nary has just completed the design of a sequential network which has the following state table:

	next state x = 0	1	output 0	1
S_0	S_1	S_4	0	0
S_1	S_0	S_5	0	0
S_2	S_3	S_5	0	1
S_3	S_2	S_4	0	1
S_4	S_1	S_2	0	0
S_5	S_0	S_3	0	0
S_6	S_1	S_0	0	0

His assistant, F. L. Ipflop, who has just completed this course, claims that his design can be used to replace Mr. Nary's network. Mr. Ipflop's design has the following state table:

	0	1	0	1
σ_0	σ_0	σ_1	0	0
σ_1	σ_0	σ_2	0	0
σ_2	σ_2	σ_1	0	1

a.   Is Mr. Ipflop correct? (Prove your answer.)

b.   If Mr. Nary's network is always started in state S_0, is Mr. Ipflop correct? (Prove your answer by showing equivalent states, etc.)

16.4   Work Problem 16.1 using the next class method.

16.5   a.   Work Problem 16.2 using the next class method.

b.   Demonstrate directly that state a is *not* equivalent to state e by specifying an input sequence for x (of minimum length) which will give different output sequences starting in state a and state e. Specify the input sequence, state sequence and output sequence for each case. (Use the original table.)

16.6   It is sometimes possible to save logic by using more than the minimum number of flip-flops. (This rarely results in overall savings since flip-flops are usually considerably more expensive than gates.) For both parts (a) and (b), fill in each state assignment by columns and then check for duplicate rows instead of filling in the assignments by rows and checking for permuted columns. If the columns are assigned in ascending numerical order and the first row is all 0's, then equivalent assignments will not be generated. Do not list degenerate assignments for which two columns are identical or complements of each other, or assignments where one column is all 0's or all 1's.

a.   Consider a state table with three states to be realized using three J-K flip-flops. To be sure of getting the minimum amount of logic, how many different state assignments must be tried? Enumerate these assignments.

b. For four states and three flip-flops, 29 assignments must be tried. Enumerate 10 of these, always assigning 000 to the first state.

16.7 A sequential network with one input and one output has the following state table:

present state	next state X = 0	X = 1	present output
S_1	S_5	S_4	0
S_2	S_1	S_6	1
S_3	S_7	S_8	1
S_4	S_7	S_1	0
S_5	S_2	S_3	1
S_6	S_4	S_2	0
S_7	S_6	S_8	0
S_8	S_5	S_3	1

a. For this part of the problem, do not consider the flip-flop input equations (this means that you can ignore the next state part of the table). Make a state assignment which will minimize the output equation, and derive the minimum output equation for your assignment.

b. Forget about your solution to part a; this part of the problem is entirely independent of part a. Apply Guidelines 1 and 2 to make a state assignment, assigning 000 to S_1. Derive input equations for D flip-flops using this assignment.

16.8 The following table is to be realized using J-K flip-flops.

a. Find a good state assignment using the three guidelines. (Do not reduce the table first.) Try to satisfy as many of the adjacency conditions as possible.

b. Using this assignment, derive the J-K flip-flop input equations and the output equations. Use the short-cut method.

	X = 0	1	Z X = 0	1
A	A	E	0	0
B	C	B	0	1
C	A	F	0	0
D	C	B	0	1
E	F	E	0	0
F	A	F	0	0

16.9   a. For the following state table, use the 3 guidelines to determine which
of the 3 possible non-equivalent state assignments should give the
best solution.

	$X_1 X_2 = 00$	01	11	10	$X_1 X_2 = 00$	01	11	10
							$Z_1 Z_2$	
A	A	C	B	D	00	00	00	00
B	B	B	D	D	00	00	10	10
C	C	A	C	A	01	01	01	01
D	B	B	C	A	01	01	10	10

      b. Using your answer to part a, derive T flip-flop input equations and
the output equations.

16.10 a. Reduce the following state table to a minimum number of states using
an implication chart.

      b. Repeat part a, using the next class method.

      c. Use the guideline method to determine a suitable state assignment for
the reduced table.

      d. Realize the table using D flip-flops.

      e. Realize the table using $J\text{-}K$ flip-flops.

      f. Find a minimum length input sequence which will distinguish between
states B and D in the original table.

	$X = 0$	1	Z
A	A	B	1
B	C	E	0
C	F	G	1
D	C	A	0
E	I	G	1
F	H	I	1
G	C	F	0
H	F	B	1
I	C	E	0

16.11 Make a suitable state assignment and realize the state graph of Fig. 15-9
using:

      a. D flip-flops   b. $S\text{-}R$ flip-flops

16.12 Make a suitable state assignment and realize the state graph of Fig. 15-12
using:

      a. $J\text{-}K$ flip-flops   b. T flip-flops

16.13 Reduce each of the following state tables to a minimum number of states:

a.

	XY = 00	01	11	10	Z
a	a	c	e	d	0
b	d	e	e	a	0
c	e	a	f	b	1
d	b	c	c	b	0
e	c	d	f	a	1
f	f	b	a	d	1

b.

	X = 0	1	0	1
a	b	c	1	0
b	e	d	1	0
c	g	d	1	1
d	e	b	1	0
e	f	g	1	0
f	h	b	1	1
g	h	i	0	1
h	g	i	0	1
i	a	a	0	1

16.14 Networks N and M have the state tables given below.

 a. Without first reducing the tables, determine whether networks N and M are equivalent.

 b. Reduce each table to a minimum number of states, and then show that N is equivalent to M by inspection of the reduced tables.

N

	X = 0	1	
S_0	S_3	S_1	0
S_1	S_1	S_3	1
S_2	S_2	S_0	0
S_3	S_0	S_1	0

M

	X = 0	1	
a	a	e	0
b	e	a	1
c	d	a	0
d	c	a	0
e	b	a	1

16.15 Make a suitable state assignment and realize the state table of Problem 15.4 using J-K flip-flops and NAND gates.

16.16 Reduce the state table of Problem 15.5 to a minimum number of rows. Then make a suitable state assignment and realize the state table using D flip-flops.

17

SEQUENTIAL NETWORK DESIGN

OBJECTIVES

Design, construct and test a sequential network.

STUDY GUIDE

1. Study Sections 17.1, *Summary of Design Procedure,* and 17.2, *Design Example – Code Converter.*

   a. Why are the states in the next state part of Table 17-2 listed in a different order than the states in Table 16-1?

   b. Consider the design of a sequential network to convert an 8-4-2-1 code to a 6-3-1-1 code (see Table 1-1). If the least significant bit of an 8-4-2-1 coded digit is fed into the network at t_0, can the least significant bit of the 6-3-1-1 coded digit be determined immediately? Explain. Why can't the technique described in this section be used to design the 8-4-2-1 to 6-3-1-1 code converter?

2. Work out the solution for your assigned design problem. Try two different state assignments and choose the one which requires the smallest number of logic gates.

3. Check your design carefully before going to lab. Test it "on paper" by applying a sequence of 0's and 1's and tracing signals to make sure the outputs are correct. If you wish, ask one of the proctors to look over your design.

4. Study Section 17.3, *Laboratory Testing.* Suppose that you are testing the network of Fig. 17-3, and that when you set $X = 0$ and $Q_1 Q_2 Q_3 = 011$ and pulse the clock, the network goes to state 101 instead of 100. What would you do to determine the cause of the malfunction?

5. Answer the following question *before* you test your network in lab: At which of the following times will the *output* of your network be correct?*

   a. during the clock pulse

   b. immediately following the clock pulse (before the input is changed to the next value)

   c. after the input has been changed to the next value, but before the next clock pulse occurs

6. a. Explain how it is possible to get false outputs from your network even though the network is correctly designed and working properly.

   b. If the output of your network was fed into another sequential network using the same clock, would the false outputs cause any problem? Explain.

7. Review the information on the *J-K* flip-flop in the *Laboratory Information Unit*.

8. When you get your network working properly, determine the output sequences for the given test sequences. Demonstrate operation of your network to a proctor and have him check your output sequences. After successful completion of the project, turn in your design and results of lab testing. (No readiness test is required.)

17. SEQUENTIAL NETWORK DESIGN

We have already studied the various steps in sequential network design — derivation of state tables (Unit 15), state table reduction (Unit 16), state assignment (Unit 16), and derivation of flip-flop input equations (Unit 13). This unit contains a summary of the design procedure, a comprehensive design example, and procedures for testing your network in lab.

17.1 Summary of Design Procedure

   a. Given the problem statement, determine the required relationship between the input and output sequences, and derive a state table. For many problems, it is easiest to first construct a state graph.

   b. Reduce the table to a minimum number of states. First eliminate duplicate rows by row matching, then form an implication table and follow the procedure in Section 16.3.

---

*If you are not absolutely sure that your answer is correct, review Section 14.2, paying particular attention to the timing charts for Mealy networks.

c. If the reduced table has m states ($2^{n-1} < m \leq 2^n$), n flip-flops are required. Assign a unique combination of flip-flop states to correspond to each state in the reduced table. The guidelines given in Section 16.8 may prove helpful in finding an assignment which leads to an economical network. If an optimum assignment is necessary, the SHR procedure may be used.

d. Form the transition table by substituting the assigned flip-flop states for each state in the reduced state table. The resulting transition table specifies the next states of the flip-flops and the output in terms of the present states of the flip-flops and the input.

e. Plot next state maps and input maps for each flip-flop and derive the flip-flop input equations. (Depending on the type of gates to be used, either determine the sum-of-products form from the 1's on the map or the product-of-sums form from the 0's on the map.) Derive the output functions.

f. Realize the flip-flop input equations and the output equations using the available logic gates.

g. Check your design by signal tracing, laboratory testing, or computer simulation.

17.2 Design Example—Code Converter

We will design a sequential network to convert BCD to excess-3 code. The input and output will be serial with the least significant bit first. A list of allowed input and output sequences is shown in Table 17-1.

Table 17-1 lists the desired inputs and outputs at times t_0, t_1, t_2 and t_3. After receiving four inputs, the network should reset to the initial state, ready to receive another group of four inputs. It is not clear at this point whether a sequential network can actually be realized to produce the output sequences as specified above without delaying the output. For example, if at t_0 some sequences required an output $Z = 0$ for $X = 0$ and other sequences required $Z = 1$ for $X = 0$, it would be impossible to design the network without delaying the output. For the following table we see that at t_0 if the input is 0 the output is always 1, and if the input is 1 the output is always 0; therefore, there is no conflict at t_0. At time t_1 the network will have available only the inputs received at t_1 and t_0. There will be no conflict at t_1 if the output at t_1 can be determined only from the inputs received at t_1 and t_0. If 00 has been received at t_1 and t_0, the output should be 1 at t_1 in all 3 cases where 00 occurs in the table. If 01 has been received, the output should be 0 at t_1 in all 3 cases where 01 occurs. For sequences 10 and 11 the outputs at t_1 should be 0 and 1 respectively. Therefore, there is no output conflict at t_1. In a similar manner we can check to see that there is no conflict at t_2, and at t_3 all four inputs are available so there is no problem.

We will now proceed to set up the state table (Table 17-2), using the same procedure as in Section 16.1. The arrangement of next states in the table is different from that in Table 16-1 because in this example the input sequences are

Table 17-1

X input (BCD) $t_3\ t_2\ t_1\ t_0$	Z output (excess-3) $t_3\ t_2\ t_1\ t_0$
0 0 0 0	0 0 1 1
0 0 0 1	0 1 0 0
0 0 1 0	0 1 0 1
0 0 1 1	0 1 1 0
0 1 0 0	0 1 1 1
0 1 0 1	1 0 0 0
0 1 1 0	1 0 0 1
0 1 1 1	1 0 1 0
1 0 0 0	1 0 1 1
1 0 0 1	1 1 0 0

Table 17-2.   State Table for Code Converter

time	input sequence received (least significant bit first)	present state	next state X = 0	1	present output (Z) X = 0	1
t_0	reset	A	B	C	1	0
t_1	0	B	D	F	1	0
	1	C	E	G	0	1
t_2	00	D	H	L	0	1
	01	E	I	M	1	0
	10	F	J	N	1	0
	11	G	K	P	1	0
t_3	000	H	A	A	0	1
	001	I	A	A	0	1
	010	J	A	–	0	–
	011	K	A	–	0	–
	100	L	A	–	0	–
	101	M	A	–	1	–
	110	N	A	–	1	–
	111	P	A	–	1	–

received least significant bit first, while for Table 16-1 the first input bit received is listed first in the sequence. Dashes (don't cares) appear in this table because only 10 of the 16 possible 4-bit sequences can occur as inputs to the code converter. The output part of the table is filled in using the reasoning discussed in the above paragraph. For example, if the network is in state B at t_1 and a 1 is received, this means that the sequence 10 has been received and the output should be 0.

Next we will reduce the table using row matching. When matching rows which contain dashes (don't cares), a dash will "match" with any state or with any output value. By matching rows in this manner, we have $H \equiv I \equiv J \equiv K \equiv L$ and $M \equiv N \equiv P$. After eliminating I, J, K, L, N and P, we find $E \equiv F \equiv G$ and the table reduces to 7 rows (Table 17-3).

Table 17-3. Reduced State Table for Code Converter

time	present state	next state $X = 0$	1	present output (Z) $X = 0$	1
t_0	A	B	C	1	0
t_1	B	D	E	1	0
	C	E	E	0	1
t_2	D	H	H	0	1
	E	H	M	1	0
t_3	H	A	A	0	1
	M	A	$-$	1	$-$

An alternate approach to deriving Table 17-2 is to start with a state graph. The state graph (Fig. 17-1) has the form of a tree. Each path starting at the reset state represents one of the ten possible input sequences. After the paths for the

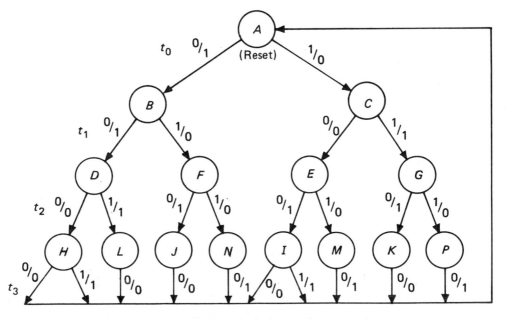

Fig. 17-1. State graph for code converter

input sequences have been constructed, the outputs can be filled in by working backwards along each path. For example, starting at t_3, the path 0 0 0 0 has outputs 0 0 1 1 and the path 1 0 0 0 has outputs 1 0 1 1. Verify that Table 17-2 corresponds to this state graph.

Three flip-flops are required to realize the reduced table since there are seven states. Each of the states must be assigned a unique combination of flip-flop states. Some assignments will lead to economical networks with only a few gates, while other assignments will require many more gates. Using the guidelines given in Section 16.8 states B and C, D and E, and H and M should be given adjacent assignments in order to simplify the next state functions. To simplify the output function, states $(A, B, E$ and $M)$ and $(C, D$ and $H)$ should be given adjacent assignments. A good assignment for this example is given on the map and table in Fig. 17-2. Flip-flops Q_1 and Q_2 have been assigned according to the four time blocks, and flip-flop Q_3 is used to distinguish between the two states in a given block. Thus flip-flops Q_1 and Q_2 form a counter which counts the number of inputs received. If two inputs have been received in a sequence, $Q_1 Q_2 = 10$ which means the network is in state D or E depending on whether Q_3 is 0 or 1. After the state assignment has been made, the transition table is filled in according to the assignment, and the next state maps are plotted as shown in Fig. 17-3. The J-K input equations are then read off the Q^+ maps as indicated.

$$
\begin{array}{c|c|c}
\multicolumn{1}{c}{Q_3} \\
Q_1 Q_2 & 0 & 1 \\
\hline
00 & A & - \\
\hline
01 & B & C \\
\hline
11 & M & H \\
\hline
10 & E & D \\
\end{array}
$$

time	present state	$Q_1 Q_2 Q_3$	$Q_1^+ Q_2^+ Q_3^+$ $X = 0$	1	Z 0	1
t_0	A	0 0 0	010	011	1	0
t_1	B	0 1 0	101	100	1	0
	C	0 1 1	100	100	0	1
t_2	D	1 0 1	111	111	0	1
	E	1 0 0	111	110	1	0
t_3	H	1 1 1	000	000	0	1
	M	1 1 0	000	---	1	-

Fig. 17-2. **Assignment map and transition table for flip-flops**

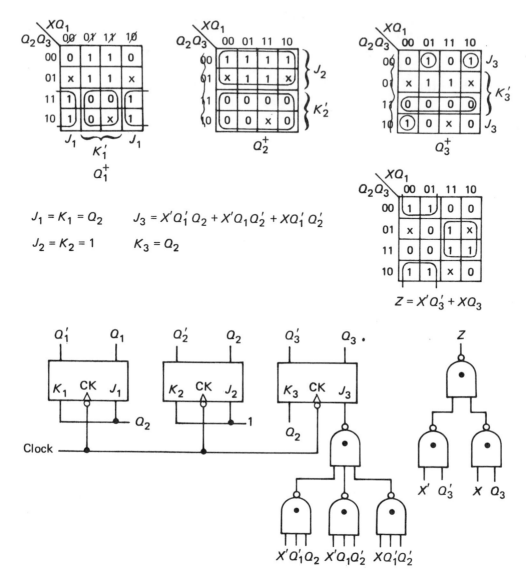

$$J_1 = K_1 = Q_2 \qquad J_3 = X'Q_1'Q_2 + X'Q_1Q_2' + XQ_1'Q_2'$$

$$J_2 = K_2 = 1 \qquad K_3 = Q_2$$

$$Z = X'Q_3' + XQ_3$$

Fig. 17-3. Completion of code converter design

17.3 Laboratory Testing

Testing of sequential networks is generally more difficult than testing combinational networks. For a sequential network with only a few states, the state table can be checked out in lab as follows:

a. Using the direct set and clear inputs, set the flip-flop states to correspond to one of the present states in the table.

b. For a Moore machine, check to see that the output is correct. For a Mealy machine, check to see that the output is correct for each input combination.

c. For each input combination, clock the network and check to see that the next state of the flip-flops is correct. (Reset the network to the proper state before each input combination is applied.)

d. Repeat parts a, b and c for each of the present states in the table.

If one of the outputs is wrong, the output network can be checked using the techniques discussed in Section 10.3. If one of the next states is wrong, this may be due to an incorrect flip-flop input or to a defective flip-flop. After determining which flip-flop goes to the wrong state, the network should be reset to the proper present state and the flip-flop inputs should be checked *before* applying another clock pulse.

Example: Assume that you have built the network of Fig. 17-3 and you are checking out the state table of Fig. 17-2. Suppose that when you set the flip-flop states to 010, set $X = 1$, and pulse the clock, the network goes to state 101 instead of 100. This indicates that flip-flop Q_3 went to the wrong state. You should then reset the flip-flops to state 010 and observe the inputs to flip-flop Q_3. Since the flip-flop is supposed to remain in state 0, J_3 should be 0. If $J_3 = 1$, this indi-. cates that either J_3 was derived wrong or that the J_3 network has a problem. Check the J_3 map and equation to make sure that $J_3 = 0$ when $X = 1$ and $Q_1 Q_2 Q_3 = 010$. If the map and equation are correct, then the J_3 network should be checked using the procedure in Section 10.3.

After you have verified that the network works according to your state table, you must then check the network to verify that it works according to the problem statement. To do this, you must apply appropriate input sequences and observe the resulting output sequence. When testing a Mealy network, you must be careful to read the outputs at the proper time to avoid reading false outputs (see Section 14.2).

So far in our discussion of sequential networks, we have assumed that the inputs are properly synchronized with the clock; i.e., all inputs change in between clock pulses. This is no problem in the laboratory if we use a manual clock, since we can easily change the inputs between clock pulses. However, if we operate our circuits at a high clock rate, then synchronization becomes a problem. We must either generate our input sequences in synchronization with the clock, or we must use a special circuit to synchronize the inputs with the clock. The former can be accomplished by loading the inputs into a shift register and then using the network clock to shift them into the network one at a time as shown in Fig. 17-4.

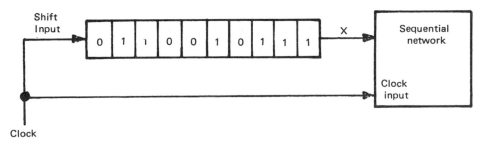

Fig. 17-4.   **Using a shift register to generate synchronized inputs**

If the input changes are not synchronized with the clock, edge-triggered D flip-flops can be used to synchronize them as shown in Fig. 17-5. In this figure, although X_1 and X_2 change at arbitrary times with respect to the clock, X_{1s} and X_{2s} always change immediately following the clock pulse; therefore, the inputs to the sequential network are properly synchronized.

Fig. 17-5(a). Synchronizer
circuit

Fig. 17-5(b). Synchronizer
inputs and outputs

DESIGN PROBLEMS

The following problems require the design of a Mealy sequential network of the form shown in Fig. 17-6. For purposes of lab testing, the input X will come from a toggle switch, and the clock pulse will be supplied manually from a push button.

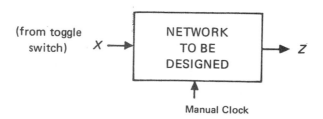

Fig. 17-6

17A. Design Specifications

Design a clocked sequential network (Fig. 17-6) which investigates an input sequence X and will produce an output of $Z = 1$ for any input sequence ending in 0010 *or* 100.

Example:

$$X = 1\ 1\ 0\ 0\ 1\ 0\ 0\ 1\ 0\ 1\ 0\ 0\ 1\ 0\ 1$$
$$Z = 0\ 0\ 0\ 1\ 0\ 1\ 1\ 0\ 1\ 0\ 0\ 1\ 0\ 1\ 0$$

Notice that the circuit does not reset to the start state when an output of $Z = 1$ occurs. However, your circuit should have a start state and should be provided with a method for manually resetting the flip-flops to the start state. A minimum solution requires 6 states. Design your network using NAND gates, NOR gates, and three *J-K* flip-flops. Any solution which is minimal for your state assignment and which uses 10 or fewer gates and inverters is acceptable; the best known solution uses 3. (Assign 000 to the start state.)

Test Procedure

First check out your state table by starting in each state and making sure that the present output and next state are correct for each input. Then, starting in the proper initial state, determine the output sequence for each of the following input sequences:

(1) 0 0 1 1 0 1 0 0 1 0 1 0 1 0 0 0 1 0 0 1 0 0 1 0

(2) 1 1 0 0 1 1 0 0 1 0 1 0 1 0 0 1 0 1 0 1 0 0 1 0

17B. Design Specifications

Design a clocked sequential network (Fig. 17-6) which investigates an input sequence X and will produce an output of $Z = 1$ for any input sequence ending in 1101 or 011.

Example:

$$X = 0\ 0\ 1\ 1\ 0\ 1\ 1\ 0\ 1\ 0\ 1\ 1\ 0\ 1\ 0$$
$$Z = 0\ 0\ 0\ 1\ 0\ 1\ 1\ 0\ 1\ 0\ 0\ 1\ 0\ 1\ 0$$

Notice that the circuit does not reset to the start state when an output of $Z = 1$ occurs. However, your circuit should have a start state and should be provided with a method for manually resetting the flip-flops to the start state. A minimum solution requires 6 states. Design your network using NAND gates, NOR gates and three *J-K* flip-flops. Any solution which is minimal for your state assignment and which uses 10 or fewer gates and inverters is acceptable; the best known solution uses 3. (Assign 000 to the start state).

Test Procedure

First check out your state table by starting in each state and making sure that the present output and next state are correct for each input. Then, starting in the proper initial state, determine the output sequence for each of the following input sequences:

    (1) 1 1 0 0 1 0 1 1 0 1 0 1 0 1 1 1 0 1 1 0 1 1 0 1

    (2) 0 0 1 1 0 0 1 1 0 1 0 1 0 1 1 0 1 0 1 0 1 1 0 1

17C. Design Specifications

Design a sequential network (Fig. 17-6) to convert excess-3 code to BCD code. The input and output should be serial with the least significant bit first. The input X represents an excess-3 coded decimal digit, and the output Z represents the corresponding BCD code. Design your network using three J-K flip-flops, NAND gates, and NOR gates. Any solution which is minimal for your state assignment and which uses 12 or fewer gates and inverters is acceptable; the best known solution uses 6. (Assign 000 to the reset state.)

Test Procedure:

First check out your state table by starting in each state and making sure that the present output and next state are correct for each input. Then, starting in the reset state, determine the output sequence for each of the ten possible input sequences and make a table.

17D. Design Specifications

Design a sequential network (Fig. 17-6) which adds six to a binary number in the range 0000 through 1001. The input and output should be serial with the least significant bit first. Find a state table with a minimum number of states. Design the network using NAND gates, NOR gates, and three J-K flip-flops. Any solution which is minimal for your state assignment and which uses 10 or fewer gates and inverters is acceptable; the best known solution uses 6. (Assign 000 to the reset state).

Test Procedure:

First check out your state table by starting in each state and making sure that the present output and next state are correct for each input. Then starting in the reset state, determine the output sequence for each of the ten possible input sequences and make a table.

17E. Design Specifications

Design a clocked sequential network (Fig. 17-6) which investigates an input sequence X and will produce an output of $Z = 1$ for any input sequence ending in 0110 *or* 101.

Example:

$$X = 0 \ 1 \ 0 \ 1 \ 1 \ 0 \ 1$$
$$Z = 0 \ 0 \ 0 \ 1 \ 0 \ 1 \ 1$$

Notice that the circuit does not reset to the start state when an output of $Z = 1$ occurs. However, your circuit should have a start state and should be provided with a method for manually resetting the flip-flops to the start state. A minimum solution requires 6 states. Design your network using NAND gates, NOR gates, and three *J-K* flip-flops. Any solution which is minimal for your state assignment and which uses 12 or fewer gates and inverters is acceptable; the best known solution uses 6. (Assign 000 to the start state.)

Test Procedure

First check out your state table by starting in each state and making sure that the present output and next state are correct for each input. Then, starting in the proper initial state, determine the output sequence for each of the following input sequences:

(1) 0 0 1 1 0 1 1 1 1 0 0 1 0 1 0 0

(2) 1 0 1 0 0 0 1 1 1 1 0 1 1 0 0 0

17 F. Design Specifications

Design a clocked sequential network which investigates an input sequence X and which will produce an output of $Z = 1$ for any input sequence ending in 0101 provided that the sequence 110 has never occurred.

Example:

$$X \ = \ 0 \ 1 \ 0 \ 1 \ 0 \ 1 \ 1 \ 0 \ 1 \ 0 \ 1$$

$$Z \ = \ 0 \ 0 \ 0 \ 1 \ 0 \ 1 \ 0 \ 0 \ 0 \ 0 \ 0$$

Notice that the circuit does not reset to the start state when an output of $Z = 1$ occurs. However, your circuit should have a start state and should be provided with a method for manually resetting the flip-flops to the start state. A minimum solution requires 6 states. Design your network using NAND gates, NOR gates, and three *J-K* flip-flops. Any solution which is minimal for your state assignment and which uses 9 or fewer gates and inverters is acceptable; the best known solution uses 7. (Assign 000 to the start state.)

Test Procedure:

First check out your state table by starting in each state and making sure that the present output and next state are correct for each input. Then, starting in the proper initial state, determine the output sequence for the following input sequences:

(1) $X = 0 \ 1 \ 0 \ 1 \ 0 \ 0 \ 0 \ 1 \ 0 \ 1 \ 1 \ 0$

(2) $X = 1 \ 0 \ 1 \ 0 \ 1 \ 0 \ 1 \ 1 \ 0 \ 1 \ 0 \ 1$

17 G.   Design Specifications

Design a clocked Mealy sequential network which investigates an input
sequence X and which will produce an output of $Z = 1$ if the total number of
1's received is even (consider zero 1's to be an even number of 1's) and the
sequence 00 has occurred at least once. *Note:* The *total* number of 1's received
includes those received before and after 00.

Example:

$$X = 1\ 0\ 1\ 0\ 1\ 0\ 0\ 1\ 1\ 0\ 1$$
$$Z = 0\ 0\ 0\ 0\ 0\ 0\ 0\ 1\ 0\ 0\ 1$$

Notice that the circuit does not reset to the start state when an output of
$Z = 1$ occurs. However, your circuit should have a start state and should be
provided with a method for manually resetting the flip-flops to the start
state. A minimum solution requires 6 states. Design your network using
NAND gates, NOR gates, and three *J-K* flip-flops. Any solution which is
minimal for your state assignment and which uses 12 or fewer gates and
inverters is acceptable; the best known solution uses 7. (Assign 000 to the
start state.)

Test Procedure:

First check out your state table by starting in each state and making
sure that the present output and next state are correct for each input. Then,
starting in the proper initial state, determine the output sequence for each of
the following input sequences:

(1) $X = 0\ 1\ 1\ 0\ 0\ 1\ 0\ 1\ 0\ 0$

(2) $X = 1\ 0\ 1\ 1\ 1\ 1\ 0\ 0\ 1\ 1\ 1\ 0$

18

ITERATIVE NETWORKS

OBJECTIVES

1. Given a problem statement, design a unilateral iterative network.

2. Explain the relationship between iterative and sequential networks.

STUDY GUIDE

1. Study Section 18.1, *Design of a Parity Checker*.

   a. If inputs 10111 are simultaneously applied to the network of Fig. 18-2(b), show the outputs of each gate on the network. If the same 5 inputs (left bit first) are applied sequentially to Fig. 18-3, give the flip-flop output (a_i) after each clock pulse. Compare these outputs with the gate outputs in the iterative network.

   b. Compare the parity checker of Fig. 18-3 with the one designed in Section 14.1.

2. Study Section 18.2, *Design of a Comparator*.

   a. Draw a state graph for the comparator of Table 18-2. Compare several pairs of binary numbers using the scheme represented by Table 18-2 and make sure you understand why this method works. Draw a network similar to Fig. 18-4 with 5 cells. Show the values of all the cell inputs and outputs if $X = 10101$ and $Y = 10011$.

b. If the state table for a typical cell of an iterative network has n states, what is the minimum number of leads required between each pair of adjacent cells?

c. Redesign the sequential comparator of Fig. 18-7 using S-R flip-flops.

3. Study Sections 18.3 and 18.4.

   a. Why is there a dead-end state in Fig. 18-8?

   b. What are some of the advantages and disadvantages of using iterative networks?

   c. How can an iterative network be converted to a sequential network?

   d. How do you determine the secondary inputs to the first cell of an iterative network (a_1 and b_1)?

4. a. Review the *Guidelines for Construction of State Graphs* in Section 15.3. These guidelines apply equally well to sequential and iterative networks.

b. Review the *Summary of Design Procedure* for sequential networks (Section 17.1). Write out a similar procedure for iterative networks.

c. Review the three *Guidelines for State Assignment* (Section 16.8). Do these guidelines also apply to iterative networks?

5. Once you understand the relationship between iterative and sequential networks, this unit *should* present no particular difficulty. The method used to construct the state graph for an iterative network is essentially the same as for a sequential network. However, many students find that going from the word statement of an iterative network problem to the state graph is a little "tricky". For this reason, it is important to work all of the problems at the end of Unit 18 carefully before you attempt the readiness test. Before you look at the answers in the back of the book for each of these problems, check your state graphs using the information given below.

18.1 The Moore state graph has two states. Each state has a self-loop for three out of the four possible input combinations. Check your solution for the following pattern of cell inputs and outputs:

$$i - 6\ 5\ 4\ 3\ 2\ 1\ 0$$
$$X_i - 0\ 1\ 0\ 1\ 0\ 1\ 0$$
$$Y_i - 0\ 0\ 0\ 1\ 1\ 1\ 0$$
$$\text{cell output } (a_{i+1}) - 1\ 1\ 0\ 0\ 0\ 1\ 1$$

18.2 Three of the four states in the Moore state graph should have self-loops. Two of the states should have a "1" output. Check your graph using the sequences given in the problem statement.

18.3 Each of the four states in the Moore state graph should have a self-loop. One of the states should have a "1" output. Check your graph using the following test sequences:

$$X = 01010111 \quad \text{gives a final output of } Z = 1$$
$$X = 00011110 \quad \text{gives a final output of } Z = 0$$

18.4 Three of the six states in the Moore state graph should have self-loops. Two of the states should have a "1" output. Check your graph using the following test sequences:

$$\text{An input } 000101000 \quad \text{gives a final output } Z = 1$$
$$\text{An input } 01010010 \quad \text{gives a final output } Z = 0$$

18.5 Five of the seven states in the Mealy state graph should have self-loops. Check your graph using the test sequence given in the problem statement and some others which you make up.

6. When you are satisfied that you can meet all of the objectives, take the readiness test.

18. ITERATIVE NETWORKS

An iterative network consists of a number of identical cells interconnected in a regular manner. The simplest form of iterative network consists of a linear array of combinational cells with signals between cells traveling in only one direction (Fig. 18-1). Each cell is a combinational network with one or more primary inputs (x_i) and possibly one or more primary outputs (z_i). In addition, each cell has one or more secondary inputs (a_i) and one or more secondary outputs (a_{i+1}). The a_i leads carry information about the "state" of the previous cell.

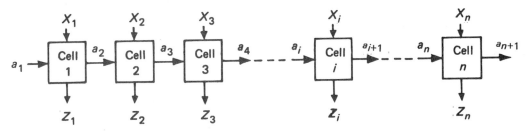

Fig. 18-1. Unilateral iterative network

The primary inputs to the cells ($x_1, x_2, \ldots, x_n$) are applied in parallel; that is, they are all applied at the same time. The a_i signals then propagate down the line of cells. Since the network is combinational, the time required for the network to reach a steady state condition is determined only by the delay times of the gates in the cells. As soon as steady state is reached, the outputs may be read. Thus the iterative network can function as a parallel-input, parallel-output device, in contrast with the sequential network in which the input and output are serial. One can think of the iterative network as receiving its inputs as a sequence in space in contrast with the sequential network which receives its inputs as a sequence in time.

18.1   Design of a Parity Checker

First we will design a parity-checking network which determines whether the number of ones in an n-bit word is even or odd. We will use a network of the form of Fig. 18-1, except that the z outputs from each cell are not needed. If the number of ones in $x_1 x_2 x_3 \ldots x_n$ is odd, we want the a_{n+1} output from the last cell to be one; otherwise, $a_{n+1} = 0$. Since all of the cells are identical, we only need to design a typical cell (cell i). We will construct a table showing the relation between the secondary input (a_i) for the typical cell and the corresponding output (a_{i+1}). The design procedure is similar to constructing a state table for a sequential network in which a_i corresponds to the present state and a_{i+1} corresponds to the next state. The a_i input must indicate whether the number of ones contained in the x-inputs to the left of cell i is even or odd, and a_{i+1} indicates whether the number of ones up to and including x_i is even or odd. Letting 0 stand for an even number of ones and 1 stand for an odd number, we obtain Table 18-1.

Table 18-1

no. of 1's	a_i	a_{i+1} $x_i = 0$	$x_i = 1$
even	0	0	1
odd	1	1	0

Note that if the number of ones to the left of cell i is even and x_i is one, the number of ones is then odd; however, if x_i is 0 the number of 1's is still even. From inspection of Table 18-1,

$$a_{i+1} = x_i' a_i + a_i' x_i = a_i \oplus x_i \qquad (18\text{-}1)$$

Thus, a typical cell can consist of a single exclusive-OR gate:

Fig. 18-2(a)

The a_1 input to the first cell must be 0 since no ones are received to the left of the first cell and 0 is an even number. The equation for the first cell can then be simplified if desired:

$$a_2 = x_1' a_1 + a_1' x_1 = x_1 \qquad (18\text{-}2)$$

Thus, cell 1 can be replaced with a wire. All of the other cells are identical to cell
i. The x inputs are fed into the network in parallel, and as soon as the signals have
had time to propagate through the network, the a_{n+1} output from the last cell
indicates whether the total number of x's which are 1 is even or odd.

Figure 18-2(b) shows the complete iterative network for $n = 5$. The output
a_6 will be 1 if an odd number of x inputs are 1.

Fig. 18-2(b).   Iterative parity checker ($n = 5$)

Table 18-1 could also be interpreted as the state table for a sequential network in which the x_i inputs are received sequentially in time. In this case, a_i
represents the present state of the network and a_{i+1} represents the next state.
The sequential network is easily constructed using a clocked D flip-flop. The next
state equation for the flip-flop is Equation (18-1), so $D = a_i \oplus x_i$ and the network is shown in Fig. 18-3.

Fig. 18-3.   Sequential parity checker

The flip-flop is initially set to the 0 state and after the x inputs have been received,
the final state of the flip-flop indicates whether the total number of ones received
is even or odd.

18.2   Design of a Comparator

Next, we will design a network which compares two n-bit binary numbers
and determines if they are equal or which one is larger if they are not equal. Direct
design as a $2n$-input combinational network is not practical for n larger than 3 or
4, so we again use the iterative approach. Designate the two binary numbers to be
compared as

$$X = x_1 x_2 \ldots x_n \quad \text{and} \quad Y = y_1 y_2 \ldots y_n$$

Figure 18-4 shows the form of the iterative network, although the number of leads between each pair of cells is not yet known. Comparison proceeds from left to right. The first cell compares x_1 and y_1 and passes on the result of the comparison to the next cell, the second cell compares x_2 and y_2, etc. Finally, x_n and y_n are compared by the last cell, and the output network produces signals to indicate if $X = Y$, $X > Y$, or $X < Y$.

Fig. 18-4. Form of iterative network for comparing binary numbers

We will now design a typical cell for the comparator. To the left of cell i, three conditions are possible: $X = Y$ so far $(x_1 x_2 \ldots x_{i-1} = y_1 y_2 \ldots y_{i-1})$, $X > Y$ so far, and $X < Y$ so far. We designate these three input conditions as states S_0, S_1, and S_2 respectively. Table 18-2 shows the output state at the right of the cell (S_{i+1}) in terms of the $x_i y_i$ inputs and the input state at the left of the cell (S_i).

Table 18-2. State Table for Comparator

		S_{i+1}			
S_i	$x_i y_i = 00$	01	11	10	$Z_1 Z_2 Z_3$
$X = Y \quad S_0$	S_0	S_2	S_0	S_1	0 1 0
$X > Y \quad S_1$	S_1	S_1	S_1	S_1	0 0 1
$X < Y \quad S_2$	S_2	S_2	S_2	S_2	1 0 0

If the numbers are equal to the left of cell i and $x_i = y_i$, the numbers are still equal including cell i, so $S_{i+1} = S_0$. However, if $S_i = S_0$ and $x_i y_i = 10$, then $x_1 x_2 \ldots x_i > y_1 y_2 \ldots y_i$ and $S_{i+1} = S_1$. If $X > Y$ to the left of cell i, then regardless of the values of x_i and y_i, $x_1 x_2 \ldots x_i > y_1 y_2 \ldots y_i$, so $S_{i+1} = S_1$. Similarly, if $X < Y$ to the left of cell i, then $X < Y$ including the inputs to cell i, and $S_{i+1} = S_2$.

The logic for a typical cell is easily derived from the state table. Since there are three states, two intercell leads are required. Using the guidelines from Section 16.8 leads to the state assignment $a_i b_i = 00$ for S_0, 01 for S_1 and 10 for S_2. Substituting this assignment into the state table yields Table 18-3. Figure 18-5 shows the Karnaugh maps, next state equations and realization of a typical cell using NAND gates. Inverters must be included in the cell since only a_i and b_i and not their complements are transmitted between cells.

Table 18-3. Transition Table for Comparator

		$a_{i+1} b_{i+1}$			
$a_i b_i$	$x_i y_i = 00$	01	11	10	$Z_1 Z_2 Z_3$
0 0	00	10	00	01	0 1 0
0 1	01	01	01	01	0 0 1
1 0	10	10 · 10	10	1 0 0

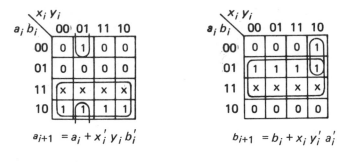

$$a_{i+1} = a_i + x'_i y_i b'_i \qquad\qquad b_{i+1} = b_i + x_i y'_i a'_i$$

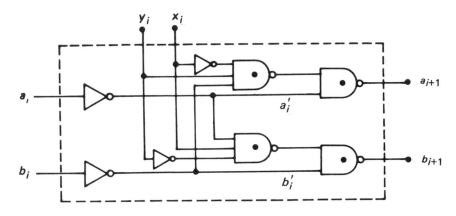

Fig. 18-5. Typical cell for comparator

The $a_1 b_1$ inputs to the left end cell must be 00 since we must assume that the numbers are equal (all zero) to the left of the most significant bit. The equations for the first cell can then be simplified if desired:

$$a_2 = a_1 + x'_1 y_1 b'_1 = x'_1 y_1$$
$$b_2 = b_1 + x_1 y'_1 a'_1 = x_1 y'_1 \qquad\qquad (18\text{-}3)$$

For the output circuit, let $Z_1 = 1$ if $X < Y$, $Z_2 = 1$ if $X = Y$, $Z_3 = 1$ if $X > Y$. Figure 18-6 shows the output maps, equations and circuit.

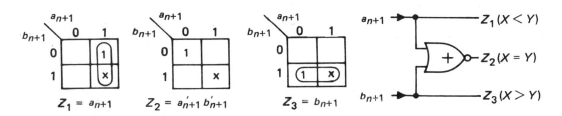

Fig. 18-6. Output network for comparator

Conversion to a sequential network is again straightforward. If x_i and y_i inputs are received serially instead of in parallel, Table 18-2 is interpreted as a state table for a sequential network, and the next state equations are the same as in Fig. 18-5. If D flip-flops are used, the typical cell of Fig. 18-5 can be used as the combinational part of the sequential network, and Fig. 18-7 shows the resulting network.

Fig. 18-7. Sequential comparator for binary numbers

After all of the inputs have been read in, the output is determined from the state of the two flip-flops as shown in Fig. 18-7.

The above two examples indicate that the design of a unilateral iterative network is very similar to the design of a sequential network. The principal difference is that for the iterative network the inputs are received in parallel as a sequence in space, while for the sequential network the inputs are received serially as a sequence in time. For the iterative network, the state table specifies the output state of a typical cell in terms of its input state and primary inputs, while for the corresponding sequential network, the same table specifies the next state (in time) in terms of the present state and inputs. If D flip-flops are used, the typical cell for the iterative network can serve as the combinational logic for the corresponding sequential network. If other flip-flop types are used, the input equations can be derived in the usual manner.

18.3   Design of a Pattern Detector

A third example illustrates the design of an iterative network to detect a given input pattern. The problem is to design an iterative network which has an output of 1 from the last cell only if the input sequence contains exactly one group of one or more consecutive ones. For example, the input sequence 000111000 will produce a 1 output from the last cell, but 001100100 will not. The network will have the same form as Fig. 18-4, except there will be only one Z output.

We will solve this problem by first constructing a state graph (Fig. 18-8). Starting in state S_0, the network will remain in S_0 as long as 0's are received. When a 1 is received, the network goes to state S_1 and remains there as long as additional 1's are received. When a 0 is received, this terminates the first group of 1's, so a change to a new state is necessary. If additional 0's are received, the network remains in S_2, but if another 1 is received, the state changes to S_3 to indicate that a second group of 1's has been started. Once this occurs, a 1 output is no longer possible since the sequence contains two groups of 1's. Therefore a 0 output is associated with S_3. S_3 is a "dead-end" state since once two groups of 1's have occurred, a 1 output is no longer possible no matter what input sequence follows. A 1 output is associated with both states S_1 and S_2, since in both cases exactly 1 consecutive group of 1's has occurred.

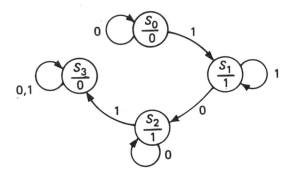

Fig. 18-8

Table 18-4(a) gives the corresponding state table for a typical cell. The states in this table have the following significance:

S_0 — starting state or all 0's received

S_1 — first 1 or group of 1's received

S_2 — first group of 1's followed by one or more 0's

S_3 — two or more groups of 1's (no 1 output possible)

The output is listed with the understanding that an output network is only required following the last cell.

Since there are four states, two intercell leads are required to carry the state information between cells. Since the next state equations for an iterative network are the same as for a corresponding sequential network, we can apply the state assignment procedures of Section 16.8. The assignment guidelines suggest the following adjacencies:

1. (S_1, S_2) (S_0, S_1) (S_2, S_3)
2. (S_0, S_1) (S_1, S_2) (S_2, S_3)
3. (S_1, S_2) (S_0, S_3)

b_i \ a_i	0	1
0	S_0	S_3
1	S_1	S_2

All the adjacencies are satisfied by the assignment

$$S_0 = 00, \quad S_1 = 01, \quad S_2 = 11, \quad S_3 = 10$$

Using this assignment, Table 18-4(b) gives the transition table for a_i and b_i from which the typical cell (Fig. 18-9) is easily synthesized. The output from the last cell is

$$Z = a'_{n+1}b_{n+1} + a_{n+1}b_{n+1} = b_{n+1}$$

Table 18-4

(a) state table for typical cell

S_{i+1}

S_i	$x_i = 0$	$x_i = 1$	Z
S_0	S_0	S_1	0
S_1	S_2	S_1	1
S_2	S_2	S_3	1
S_3	S_3	S_3	0

(b) transition table

$a_{i+1}b_{i+1}$

a_ib_i	$x_i = 0$	$x_i = 1$	Z
00	00	01	0
01	11	01	1
11	11	10	1
10	10	10	0

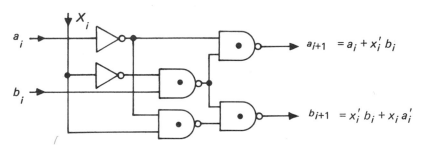

Fig. 18-9. Typical cell for Table 18-4(b)

18.4   Iterative Networks with Outputs from Each Cell

In the three examples of iterative networks given in this unit, the output was taken from the last cell only. It was convenient to assume that the output was only a function of the state of the last cell, so a Moore type state table was used. In this section, we will design an iterative network which has an output from each cell (as in Fig. 18-1). If the output of cell i depends only on the inputs of the preceding cells and not on x_i, then z_i is only a function of the secondary input state of the cell, and a Moore table should be used. On the other hand, if z_i also depends on x_i, a Mealy table is required.

The following example illustrates the design of a Mealy iterative network. The output of cell i (z_i) should be 1 iff the input to cell i (x_i) is 0 and the inputs to the cells immediately to the left of cell i consist of a group of an even number of consecutive 1's. In other words, the output of a cell is 1 if its input is a 0 which terminates a group of an even number of consecutive 1's. First, we construct a typical input-output sequence:

$$x_i = 0\ 1\ 1\ 0\ 0\ 1\ 1\ 1\ 0\ 1\ 1\ 1\ 1\ 0\ 0\ 0\ 0\ 1\ 0\ 0$$

$$z_i = 0\ 0\ 0\ 1\ 0\ 0\ 0\ 0\ 0\ 0\ 0\ 0\ 0\ 1\ 0\ 0\ 0\ 0\ 0\ 0$$

We then define 3 states: S_0 (reset), S_1 (odd number of consecutive 1's), and S_2 (even number of consecutive 1's). Figure 18-10 shows the resulting state graph. Note that the network resets whenever a 0 input is received, and that the output is 1 only when a 0 is received following an even number of 1's.

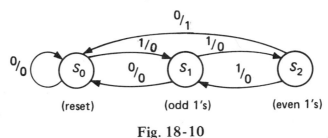

(reset)   (odd 1's)   (even 1's)

Fig. 18-10

	$a_i b_i$	$a_{i+1} b_{i+1}$		z_i	
		$x_i = 0$	1	$x_i = 0$	1
S_0	00	00	01	0	0
S_1	01	00	10	0	0
S_2	10	00	01	1	0

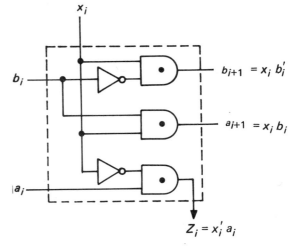

$b_{i+1} = x_i\, b_i'$

$a_{i+1} = x_i\, b_i$

$Z_i = x_i'\, a_i$

(a)   transition table   (b)   typical cell

Fig. 18-11

Figure 18-11 shows the transition table and resulting typical cell. Since the initial state is S_0, $a_1 = b_1 = 0$, and the equations for the first cell can be simplified to:

$$b_2 = x_1\ ,\quad a_2 = 0\ ,\quad z_1 = 0$$

As is shown in this unit, the procedure used to design iterative networks is very similar to that used to design sequential networks with D flip-flops. A Moore iterative network which has an output network following the last cell is analogous to a Moore sequential network in which the output is observed after the entire input sequence has been applied. A Mealy iterative network which has an output from each cell is analogous to a Mealy sequential network in which the output is observed after applying each input.

For problems where an iterative network can be used, it offers several advantages over an ordinary combinational network:

   a. It is easier to design an economical network.

   b. It is cheaper to build a large number of identical cells than to fabricate one large complex network.

   c. The iterative network is easily expanded to accommodate more inputs simply by adding more cells.

The principal disadvantage of the iterative network is that the signal must propagate through a large number of cells, so the response time will be longer than a combinational network with fewer levels.

PROBLEMS

18.1 Two binary numbers, $X = x_n \ldots x_3 x_2 x_1 x_0$ and $Y = y_n \ldots y_3 y_2 y_1 y_0$, are to be compared by an iterative network. The comparator should compare the *least* significant bits first so that the intercell signals will propagate from right to left:

Only *one* lead should be used between each pair of cells. The output from the left end cell should be $a_{n+1} = 1$ if $X \geqslant Y$ and $a_{n+1} = 0$ if $X < Y$.

Design a typical cell using NAND gates.

18.2 An iterative network has a form similar to Fig. 18-4. The output Z is to be 1 if and only if at least one of the inputs x_i is 1 and no group of 2 or more consecutive 1 inputs occurs.

For example,

$$0 0 1 0 1 0 0 0 1 0 0 \qquad \text{gives an output } Z = 1$$

but

$$0 0 1 0 1 1 0 0 0 0 0 \qquad \text{gives an output } Z = 0$$

Derive the equations and a NOR-gate network for a typical cell and for the output network.

18.3 An iterative network has a form similar to Fig. 18-4. The output Z is to be 1 if and only if the total number of x-inputs which are 1 is an odd number greater than 2.

Derive the equations and a NAND-gate network for a typical cell and the output network. Specify a_1 and b_1 and simplify the first cell.

18.4   An iterative network has an output $Z = 1$ from the last cell iff the sequence of cell inputs contains one appearance of one of the following patterns and no other 1's:

$$0\ 1\ 0$$
$$0\ 1\ 0\ 1\ 0$$
$$0\ 1\ 0\ 1\ 0\ 1\ 0$$
$$0\ 1\ 0\ 1\ 0\ 1\ 0\ 1\ 0$$
etc.

Note that the pattern may be preceded and followed by any number of 0's. Draw a state graph for the typical cell, and derive the equations for a typical cell.

18.5   Each cell of an iterative network has two inputs (x_i and y_i) and one output (z_i). The output for cell i is defined as follows:

If any three consecutive cells to the left of cell $i + 1$ have the inputs $xy = 00, 01, 10$ (in that order), the output from cell i will be 1 unless the sequence $xy = 00, 01, 10$ has occurred a second time to the left of cell $i + 1$.

Example:

i	1	2	3	4	5	6	7	8	9	10	11	12	13	14	15
$x_i y_i$	01	10	00	01	10	01	00	01	00	01	10	00	01	10	00
z_i	0	0	0	0	1	1	1	1	1	1	0	0	0	0	0

Draw a Mealy state graph (with a minimum number of states) for the typical cell. Assume that $x_i y_i = 11$ never occurs.

18.6   Each cell of an iterative network has one primary input (X_i). The output from the last cell is $Z = 1$ iff the total number of X_i inputs which are 1 is $\geqslant 4$.

a.   Find a Moore state graph with a minimum number of states.

b.   Derive the logic equations for a typical cell and for the output.

c.   Design the first three cells of the network making simplifications where possible.

18.7   Each cell of an iterative network has inputs X_i and Y_i. The network has two outputs, Z_1 and Z_2. $Z_1 = 1$ if $X_i = Y_i$ in every cell. $Z_2 = 1$ if X_i and Y_i are complements in every cell.

a.   Specify the form of the network.

b.   Find a Moore state graph with a minimum number of states.

c.   Design a typical cell using only NAND gates. Assign 00 to the initial state.

d.   Design the output network.

e.   Simplify the first cell if possible.

f.   Draw a diagram that shows how your design could be converted to a sequential network which has 1 output under the same conditions as above, except that the inputs are received serially instead of in parallel.

19

MSI INTEGRATED CIRCUITS IN SEQUENTIAL NETWORK DESIGN

OBJECTIVES

1. Analyze the operation of an integrated circuit shift register, indicate the connections required to perform various shifting functions, and draw a timing diagram.

2. Analyze the operation of an integrated circuit counter, indicate the connections required to perform various counting functions, and draw a timing diagram.

3. Design a sequential network using a counter with clear and load inputs.

4. Design a sequential network using a ROM (read-only memory) or PLA (programmable logic array) and flip-flops. Analyze such a network.

STUDY GUIDE

1. Study Section 19.1, *Integrated Circuit Shift Registers*. Note that the two inverter symbols used in Figs. 19-1(b), 19-3, and 19-7 are equivalent:

Also, $\bar{Q}$ is often used instead of Q' to indicate the complement.

a. Compare the block diagrams for the 7491 and 74178 shift registers. Which one changes state on the rising edge of the clock pulse?

The falling edge?

b. Complete the following timing diagram and table for a 7491 shift register. Assume that $A = 1$.

Clock pulse number	state of shift register during clock pulse Q_A Q_B Q_C Q_D Q_E Q_F Q_G Q_H							
1	0	0	0	0	0	0	0	0
2								
3								
4								
5								
6								
7								
8								
9								
10								
11								
12								
13								
14								
15								
16								

c. Explain the meaning of Equation (19-2) in words.

d. Write the next state equation for flip-flop Q_B of a 74178 shift register.

$$Q_B^+ = \underline{\hspace{6cm}}$$

Verify that your equation is consistent with Table 19-1.

e. Work Problems 19.1 and 19.2.

2. Study Section 19.2, *Integrated Circuit Counters.*

a. If the ripple counter of Fig. 19-5 is in state 0111, what will be the sequence of transient states after T_A changes from 1 to 0?

b. Show the required connections so that two 7493A counters will act like a single 8-bit counter.

c. Note that for the counters described in this unit, Q_A represents the least significant bit, but for the shift registers Q_A represents the most significant bit. This inconsistent notation is used to be compatible with data sheets published by manufacturers of TTL logic.

d. Note that the 7493A counter changes state on the falling edge of the clock pulse, and the 74S163 changes state on the rising edge of the pulse.

e. Explain the difference between the asynchronous clear (on the 7493A counter) and the synchronous clear (on the 74S163).

f. From Fig. 19-7, determine the conditions under which the ripple carry out will be 1.

g. After the counter of Fig. 19-10 reaches state 1101, the NAND gate output clears the counter. Why is it unnecessary to connect Q_B' to this gate?

h. Work Problems 19.3 and 19.4. Check your solution to 19.3 to make sure all state changes occur immediately following the proper clock transition. The final state of the counter should be 15.

3. Study Section 19.3, *Design of Sequential Networks Using Counters.*

a. Why is the CLEAR function derived before LOAD or *PT?*

b. Explain the don't cares which appear in the *PT* and *D* columns of Table 19-3.

c. Work Problems 19.5 and 19.6.

4. Study Section 19.4, *Register Transfers and 3-state Logic.*

   a. What are the three possible output "states" of a 3-state buffer?

   b. Referring to Fig. 19-15, how does an inversion symbol (small circle) on the enable input affect the operation of a 3-state buffer?
   How does an inversion symbol on the buffer output affect the operation?

   c. Draw a logic circuit which will realize $F = A'B' + AC$, using only 3-state buffers.

   d. Referring to Fig. 19-19, the bus is 8 bits wide; i.e., the bus consists of 8 wires. Draw the logic diagram showing the flip-flops and buffers associated with *one* of these bus wires.

   e. Work Problem 19.9.

5. Study Section 19.5, *Design of Sequential Networks Using ROMs and PLAs.*

   a. Review Section 9.6, *Read-Only Memories,* and Section 9.7, *Programmable Logic Arrays.*

   b. What size ROM would be required to realize a *state* table with 13 states, 2 input variables and 3 output variables?

   c. In going from Table 19-4(b) to Table 19-4(c), note that for $X = 0$, $Q_1 Q_2 Q_3 = 000$, $Z = 1$, and $Q_1^+ Q_2^+ Q_3^+ = D_1 D_2 D_3 = 001$; therefore, 1001 is entered in the first row of the truth table. Verify that the other truth table entries are correct.

    d. Continue the analysis of the PLA realization of the code converter which was started in the last paragraph of Section 19.5. In particular, if $Q_1 Q_2 Q_3 = 100$ and $X = 1$, what will be the PLA outputs? What will the state be after the clock?

    e. Work Problems 19.7 and 19.8.

6. Before you study Section 19.6, *Design of Sequential Networks Using PALs*, review the material on PALs in Section 9.8.

    a. Study the 16R4 PAL shown in Fig. 19-22. Verify that the X's on the diagram implement Equations (19-3).

    b. Label the pin 2 input Y. Add 1 or more X's to the diagram so that the Z output will only be enabled when $Y = 0$.

    c. Which buffer must be disabled so that pin 13 can be used as an input rather than an output?

    d. Work Problem 19.10(a).

7. Review the objectives of this unit. If you are satisfied that you can meet these objectives, take the readiness test. You will not need to memorize the type numbers of the TTL shift registers and counters discussed in this unit. How-- ever, given data which specifies the operation of these or similar integrated circuits, you should be able to use them or analyze their operation.

19. MSI INTEGRATED CIRCUITS IN SEQUENTIAL NETWORK DESIGN

    This unit introduces the use of MSI integrated circuit shift registers and counters* in sequential network design. Then the techniques used in Unit 9 for designing combinational networks with read-only memories and programmed logic arrays are extended to sequential network design. The use of such techniques simplifies the design of sequential networks and generally leads to lower overall digital system cost.

19.1 Integrated Circuit Shift Registers

    Shift registers with 4, 8 or more flip-flops are available in integrated circuit form. Figure 19-1 illustrates an 8-bit serial-in, serial-out shift register. "Serial in" means that data is shifted into the first flip-flop one bit at a time and the flip-flops cannot be loaded in parallel. "Serial out" means that data can only be read out of the last flip-flop and the outputs from the other flip-flops are not connected to terminals of the integrated circuit. Master-slave S-R flip-flops are used. These flip-flops are similar in operation to the master-slave J-K flip-flops described in Unit 12, except that the input combination $S = R = 1$ is not allowed. The inputs to the first flip-flop are $S = AB$ and $R = (AB)'$. Thus, if $AB = 1$, a 1 is shifted into the register when it is clocked, and if $AB = 0$, a 0 is shifted in. Since the clock

---

*As examples of integrated circuit shift registers and counters, several typical TTL integrated circuits are described in this unit. For further information on TTL logic, see Appendix A.3 of this text and the *TTL Data Book* published by Texas Instruments.

input goes through an inverting buffer, the flip-flops change state on the 0-1 transition (leading edge) of the input clock pulse instead of on the 1-0 transition. Figure 19-2 shows a typical timing diagram.

(a)   Block diagram

(b)   Logic diagram (courtesy of Texas Instruments)

Fig. 19-1.   7491 TTL shift register

Fig. 19-2.   Typical timing diagram for 7491 TTL shift register

Figure 19-3 shows a 4-bit parallel-in, parallel-out shift register. The shift register has two control inputs, shift enable (SH) and load enable (L). If $SH = 1$ (and $L = 1$ or $L = 0$), clocking the register causes the serial input (SI) to be shifted into the first flip-flop, while the data in flip-flops Q_A, Q_B and Q_C are shifted right. If $SH = 0$ and $L = 1$, clocking the shift register will cause the four data inputs (D_A, D_B, D_C, D_D) to be loaded in parallel into the flip-flops. If $SH = L = 0$, clocking the register causes no change of state. The input equations for the first flip-flop are

$$S_A = SH \cdot SI + SH' \cdot L \cdot D_A + SH' \cdot L' \cdot Q_A \quad \text{and} \quad R_A = S_A' \quad (19\text{-}1)$$

The next state equation is

$$Q_A{}^+ = SH \cdot SI + SH' \cdot L \cdot D_A + SH' \cdot L' \cdot Q_A \quad (19\text{-}2)$$

(a) Block diagram

(b) Logic diagram (courtesy of Texas Instruments)

Fig. 19-3. 74178 TTL shift register

Table 19-1 summarizes the operation of this shift register. All state changes occur immediately following the trailing edge (1 to 0 transition) of the clock.

Table 19-1. Operation of 74178 Shift Register

SH (shift)	L (load)	Q_A^+	Q_B^+	Q_C^+	Q_D^+	
0	0	Q_A	Q_B	Q_C	Q_D	(no change)
0	1	D_A	D_B	D_C	D_D	(parallel load)
1	x	SI	Q_A	Q_B	Q_C	(right shift)

Inputs — Next State

A typical application of this register would be conversion of parallel data to serial data. The parallel output from the last flip-flop also serves as a serial output in this case. Figure 19-4 shows a typical timing diagram. The first clock pulse loads data into the shift register in parallel. During the next four clock pulses, this data is available at the serial output. Assuming the register is initially clear ($Q_A Q_B Q_C Q_D = 0000$), that the serial input is $SI = 0$ throughout, and that the data inputs $D_A D_B D_C D_D$ are 1011 during the load time (t_0), the resulting waveforms are as shown. Shifting occurs at the end of t_1, t_2, and t_3, and the serial output can be read during these clock times. During t_4, $SH = L = 0$, so no state change occurs.

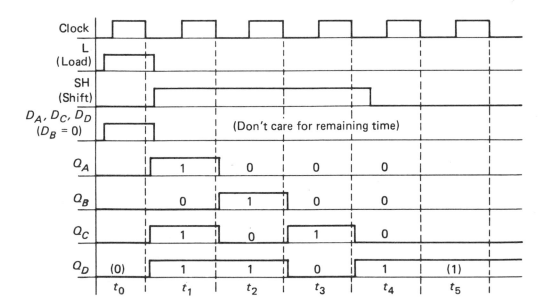

Fig. 19-4. Timing diagram for 74178 TTL shift register

19.2 Integrated Circuit Counters

Integrated circuit counters are available in two types — ripple (asynchronous) counters and synchronous counters. Operation of the latter is similar to the counters discussed in Unit 13. Analysis of a ripple counter is carried out below.

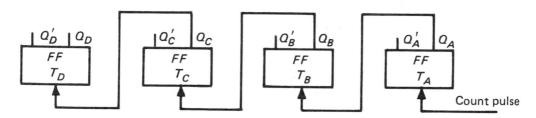

Fig. 19-5. Four-bit ripple counter

Figure 19-5 shows a 4-bit ripple counter. Each flip-flop in the counter changes state when the T input changes from 1 to 0. The count pulse goes directly to the T_A input; hence flip-flop Q_A changes state each time a count pulse is received. Since T_B is connected to Q_A, Q_B will change state each time Q_A changes from 1 to 0. Similarly, Q_C will change each time Q_B changes from 1 to 0, and Q_D changes when Q_C goes from 1 to 0. The state sequence for the counter is given below. Each time the T_A input is pulsed, the counter may go through a series of intermediate transient states (enclosed in parentheses) before reaching a final state.

$Q_D \ Q_C \ Q_B \ Q_A$

0	0	0	0	initial state
				1st count pulse changes Q_A to 1
0	0	0	1	
				2nd count pulse changes Q_A to 0
(0	0	0	0)	
				1-0 transition of T_B changes Q_B to 1
0	0	1	0	
				3rd count pulse changes Q_A to 1
0	0	1	1	
				4th count pulse changes Q_A to 0
(0	0	1	0)	
				1-0 transition of T_B changes Q_B to 0
(0	0	0	0)	
				1-0 transition of T_C changes Q_C to 1
0	1	0	0	

The counter continues to operate in this manner until state 1111 is reached.

When a count pulse is applied in state 15 ($Q_D Q_C Q_B Q_A$ = 1111), the following sequence of events occurs:

1	1	1	1	16th count pulse changes Q_A to 0
(1	1	1	0)	1-0 transition of T_B changes Q_B to 0
(1	1	0	0)	1-0 transition of T_C changes Q_C to 0
(1	0	0	0)	1-0 transition of T_D changes Q_D to 0
0	0	0	0	the counter is now reset to state 0 and the state sequence repeats.

Note that in the above analysis, a change of Q_A "ripples" through until all four flip-flops have changed state; hence the name "ripple counter".

Figure 19-6 shows a 4-bit TTL ripple counter. Since the J and K inputs of the flip-flops are all 1, the CK (clock) input acts as a T input. Since T_B is not connected to Q_A internally, an external connection is required in order to make a 4-bit counter. If both reset inputs (R_1 and R_2) are 1, the clear inputs on the flip-flops are 0, and the counter is reset to the 0000 state. The R_1 and R_2 inputs are often referred to as *asynchronous* (or direct) clear inputs because they clear the counter independently of the clock input.

(a) Block diagram

(b) Logic diagram

Fig. 19-6. 4-bit binary counter

Figure 19-7 shows a very general type of 4-bit TTL synchronous counter. In addition to performing the counting function, it has provision for clearing the flip-flops and for loading the flip-flops in parallel from the data inputs. All operations are synchronized by the clock, and all state changes take place immediately following the 0-1 transition of the clock input.

Fig. 19-7. 74S163 4-bit counter logic diagram
(courtesy of Texas Instruments)

This counter has four control inputs—CLEAR, LOAD, P and T. P and T are used to enable the counting function. Operation of the counter is as follows:

a. If CLEAR = 0, all flip-flops are set to 0 immediately following the 0-1 transition of the clock.

b. If CLEAR = 1 and LOAD = 0, the D inputs are transferred in parallel to the flip-flops immediately following the 0-1 transition of the clock.

c. If CLEAR = LOAD = 1 and $P = T = 1$, the count is enabled and the counter state will be incremented by 1 following each 0-1 transition of the clock.

Table 19-2 summarizes the operation of the counter. Note that CLEAR overrides the LOAD and count functions in the sense that when CLEAR = 0, clearing occurs regardless of the values of LOAD, P and T. Similarly LOAD overrides the count function. The CLEAR input on the 74S163 is referred to as a *synchronous* clear input because it clears the counter in synchronization with the clock, and no clearing can occur if no clock pulse is present.

Table 19-2. Operation of 74S163 Synchronous Counter

control signals		PT	next state				
CLEAR	LOAD	(ENABLE COUNT)	Q_D^+	Q_C^+	Q_B^+	Q_A^+	
0	x	x	0	0	0	0	(clear)
1	0	x	D_D	D_C	D_B	D_A	(parallel load)
1	1	0	Q_D	Q_C	Q_B	Q_A	(no change)
1	1	1	present state + 1				(increment count)

The carry output is 1 when the counter is in state 15 and $T = 1$. This carry output is useful when two or more 4-bit counters are cascaded to form longer counters. Figure 19-8 shows how two 74S163 counters can be connected to form an 8-bit counter. When the state of the first counter is 15, CARRY will be 1 so that the second counter will be enabled. When the clock pulse occurs, the first counter is incremented from state 1111 to state 0000 and the second counter is incremented by 1.

Fig. 19-8. 8-bit counter

The data inputs can be used to change the normal binary counting sequence. For example, if 5 is loaded into the counter after the counter reaches state 15, the state sequence will be

$$5, 6, 7, 8, 9, 10, 11, 12, 13, 14, 15, 5, 6, \ldots$$

The connections required to obtain this counting sequence are shown in Figure 19-9. When the counter reaches state 1111, CARRY = 1, the load is enabled, and the next clock loads 0101 into the flip-flops.

Fig. 19-9. 11-state counter

The CLEAR input can also be used to reset the counter to state 0000 when a given state is reached as shown in Figure 19-10. For this example, when the counter reaches state 1101, CLEAR = 0 and the counter is cleared by the next clock pulse. The state sequence will therefore be

$$0, 1, 2, 3, 4, 5, 6, 7, 8, 9, 10, 11, 12, 13, 0, 1, \ldots$$

More complicated counting sequences can be obtained by making the CLEAR, LOAD and data inputs all functions of the counter state.

Fig. 19-10. 14-state counter

19.3   Design of Sequential Networks Using Counters

Figure 19-11 shows the state graph for a sequential network with an input X. Note that the form of this graph is a loop of states with a few additional state transitions added. State graphs of this general form can be economically realized using a counter which has load and clear inputs. As an example, we will realize the graph using a 74S163 counter. We will apply the following procedure:

a. Use a straight binary state assignment for the states in the main loop.

b. Use the clear input when transitions to state 0 are required.

c. Activate the counting function when transitions between successive states in the main loop are required.

d. Use the load input when transitions out of the normal counting sequence (except transitions to state 0) are required.

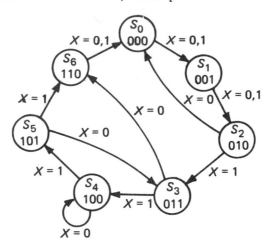

Fig. 19-11

Table 19-3. Derivation of Counter Inputs

	$C\,B\,A$	$C^+B^+A^+$	CLEAR	LOAD	$D_C\,D_B\,D_A$	PT
$X=0$	S_0 0 0 0	0 0 1	1	1	$x\ \ x\ \ x$	1
	S_1 0 0 1	0 1 0	1	1	$x\ \ x\ \ x$	1
	S_2 0 1 0	0 0 0	0	x	$x\ \ x\ \ x$	x
	S_3 0 1 1	1 1 0	1	0	1 1 0	x
	S_4 1 0 0	1 0 0	1	1	$x\ \ x\ \ x$	0
	S_5 1 0 1	0 1 1	1	0	0 1 1	x
	S_6 1 1 0	0 0 0	0	x	$x\ \ x\ \ x$	x
	1 1 1	$x\ \ x\ \ x$	x	x	$x\ \ x\ \ x$	x
$X=1$	S_0 0 0 0	0 0 1	1	1	$x\ \ x\ \ x$	1
	S_1 0 0 1	0 1 0	1	1	$x\ \ x\ \ x$	1
	S_2 0 1 0	0 1 1	1	1	$x\ \ x\ \ x$	1
	S_3 0 1 1	1 0 0	1	1	$x\ \ x\ \ x$	1
	S_4 1 0 0	1 0 1	1	1	$x\ \ x\ \ x$	1
	S_5 1 0 1	1 1 0	1	1	$x\ \ x\ \ x$	1
	S_6 1 1 0	0 0 0	0	x	$x\ \ x\ \ x$	x
	1 1 1	$x\ \ x\ \ x$	x	x	$x\ \ x\ \ x$	x

The binary state assignment is shown on the state graph, and the CBA and $C^+B^+A^+$ columns of Table 19-3 indicate the required state transitions for $X = 0$ and $X = 1$. We will now derive the counter inputs to realize these state transitions. The inputs are listed in the remaining columns of the table. Since state 111 never occurs, all inputs associated with state 111 are don't cares. Since CLEAR over-rides the other inputs, we will derive it first. We must clear the counter for state transitions S_2 to S_0 ($X = 0$) and S_6 to S_0, so CLEAR must be 0 for these transi-tions. CLEAR must be 1 to avoid clearing the counter for the other transitions. Since LOAD overrides the P and T inputs, we will derive LOAD next. State tran-sitions S_3 to S_6 and S_5 to S_3 are not in the normal counting sequence, so we will use the D inputs to load in the proper next state for these transitions. In state 011 with $X = 0$, we will set LOAD = 0 and $D_C D_B D_A = 110$ so that the next state is S_6. In state 101 with $X = 0$, we will set LOAD = 0 and $D_C D_B D_A = 011$ so that the next state is S_3. When CLEAR is 0, LOAD is a don't care since CLEAR over-rides LOAD. For the other transitions, LOAD must be 1 to prevent undesired state changes. When LOAD $\neq$ 0, the D inputs are don't cares since no loading can occur. For state transitions in the main loop, PT must be 1 to enable the counting function. In state S_4 with $X = 0$, PT must be 0 to prevent a change of state. In the remaining rows, PT is a don't care since CLEAR and LOAD override PT.

The required counter input functions can now be derived using the Kar-naugh maps in Fig. 19-12. Figure 19-13 shows the final circuit. If the same circuit is realized using $J\text{-}K$ flip-flops, 3 flip-flops and 11 gates are required.

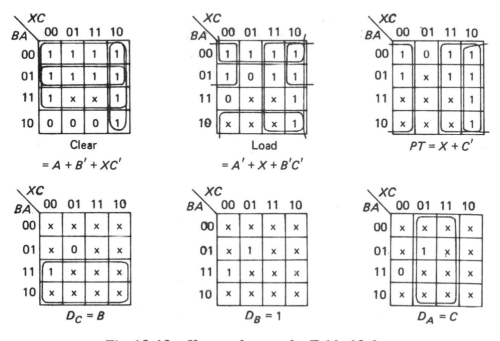

Fig. 19-12. Karnaugh maps for Table 19-3

Fig. 19-13.   Realization of Fig. 19-11

19.4   Register Transfers and 3-State Logic

In digital systems it is often necessary to transfer data back and forth between several registers. In this section we will introduce the concept of 3-state logic and show how it can be used to facilitate transfer of data among a group of registers.

Normally, a logic circuit will not operate correctly if the outputs of two or more gates or flip-flops are directly connected to each other. For example, if one gate has a 0 output (a low voltage) and another has a 1 output (a high voltage), when the gate outputs are connected together the resulting output voltage may be some intermediate value that does not clearly represent either a 0 or a 1. In some cases, damage to the gates may result if the outputs are connected together.

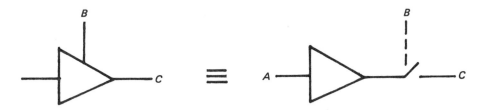

Fig. 19-14.   A 3-state buffer

Use of 3-state logic will permit the outputs of two or more gates or flip-flops to be connected together. Figure 19-14 shows a 3-state buffer and its logical equivalent. When the enable input B is 1, the output C equals A; when B is 0, the output C acts like an open circuit. In other words, when B is 0 the output C is effectively disconnected from the buffer output so that no current can flow. This is often referred to as a Hi-Z (high-impedance) state of the output, since the circuit offers a very high resistance or impedance to the flow of current.

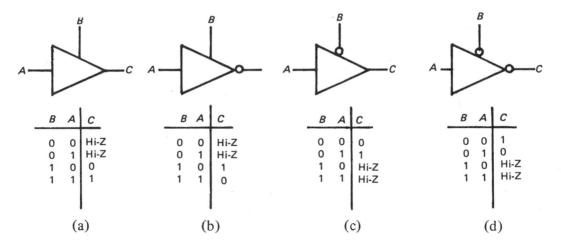

B	A	C
0	0	Hi-Z
0	1	Hi-Z
1	0	0
1	1	1

(a)

B	A	C
0	0	Hi-Z
0	1	Hi-Z
1	0	1
1	1	0

(b)

B	A	C
0	0	0
0	1	1
1	0	Hi-Z
1	1	Hi-Z

(c)

B	A	C
0	0	1
0	1	0
1	0	Hi-Z
1	1	Hi-Z

(d)

Fig. 19-15.   Four types of 3-state buffers

Figure 19-15 shows truth tables for four types of 3-state buffers. In Figs. 19-15(a) and (b) the enable input B is not inverted, so the buffer output is enabled when $B = 1$ and disabled when $B = 0$. That is, the buffer operates normally when $B = 1$, and the buffer output is effectively an open circuit when $B = 0$. In Fig. 19-15(b) the buffer output is inverted — that is, $C = A'$ when the buffer is enabled. The buffers in Figs. 19-15(c) and (d) operate the same as in (a) and (b) except that the enable input is inverted, so the buffer is enabled when $B = 0$.

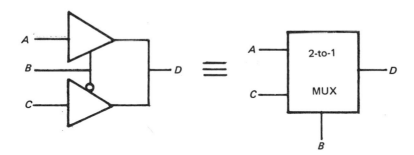

Fig. 19-16.   Data selection using 3-state buffer

In Fig. 19-16, the outputs of two 3-state buffers are tied together. When $B = 1$, the top buffer is enabled so that $D = A$; when $B = 0$, the lower buffer is enabled so that $D = C$. Therefore, $D = BA + B'C$. This is logically equivalent to using a 2-to-1 multiplexer to select the A input when $B = 1$ and the C input when $B = 0$.

Next we will consider the problem of transferring data from the outputs of two different registers into a third register. Figure 19-17 shows how this can be accomplished using 3-state buffers. If $B = 1$ and a clock is applied to register Q, the data in register A will be stored in Q; if $B = 0$, the data in register C will be stored in Q.

register A =
flip-flops A_1, A_2

register C =
flip-flops C_1, C_2

register Q =
flip-flops Q_1, Q_2

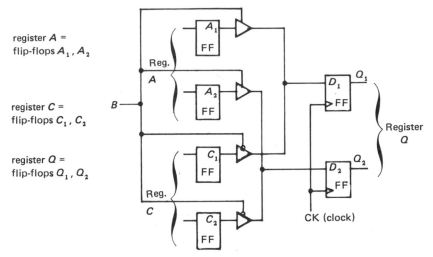

Fig. 19-17. Data transfer between registers

Figure 19-18(a) shows a 74LS374 integrated circuit register which contains 8 D flip-flops with 3-state buffers at the flip-flop outputs. These buffers are enabled when $EN = 0$. A simplified representation for this octal register is shown in Fig. 19-18(b). The notation

$$\searrow\!\!\frac{8}{}$$

is used to represent 8 wires.

(a) (b)

Fig. 19-18. Logic diagram for 74LS374, octal register
with 3-state outputs

Figure 19-19 shows how data can be transferred from one of four octal registers into a fifth register. The outputs from registers A, B, C and D are all connected in parallel to a common "bus". The D flip-flop inputs of register G are also connected to the bus. When $ENA = 0$, the 3-state outputs of register A are enabled onto the bus and loaded into register G when the next clock occurs. Similarly, the data in register B, C or D is transferred to G when ENB, ENC or END is 0, respectively. The four enable signals may be generated by a decoder. The operation can be summarized as follows:

If $EF = 00$, A is stored in G.
If $EF = 01$, B is stored in G.
If $EF = 10$, C is stored in G.
If $EF = 11$, D is stored in G.

Note that 8 bits of data are transferred in parallel by each clock pulse. As an alternative to using a bus with 3-state logic, eight 4-to-1 multiplexers could be used, but this would lead to a more complex circuit.

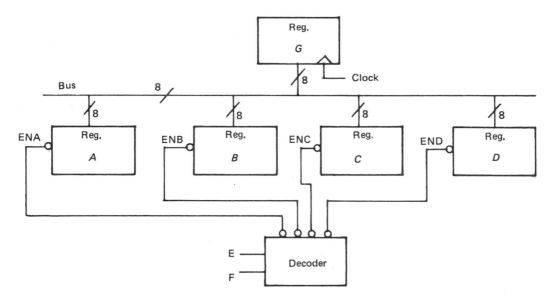

Fig. 19-19. Data transfer using a 3-state bus

19.5   Design of Sequential Networks Using ROMs and PLAs

A sequential network can easily be designed using a ROM (read-only memory) and flip-flops. Referring to the general model of a Mealy sequential network given in Fig. 14-13, the combinational part of the sequential network can be realized using a ROM. The ROM can be used to realize the output functions $(Z_1, Z_2, \ldots, Z_n)$ and the next state functions $(Q_1^+, Q_2^+, \ldots, Q_k^+)$. The state of the network can then be stored in a register of D flip-flops and fed back to the input of the ROM. Thus a Mealy sequential network with m inputs, n outputs and k state variables can be realized using k D flip-flops and a ROM with $m + k$ inputs (2^{m+k} words) and $n + k$ outputs. The Moore sequential network of Fig. 14-14 can be realized in a similar manner. The next state and output combinational subnetworks of the Moore network can both be realized with a single ROM or with separate ROMs.

Use of D flip-flops is preferable to J-K flip-flops since use of two-input flip-flops would require increasing the number of outputs from the ROM. The fact that the D flip-flop input equations would generally require more gates than the J-K equations is of no consequence since the size of the ROM depends only on the number of inputs and outputs and not on the complexity of the equations being realized. For this reason, the state assignment which is used is also of little importance, and generally a state assignment in straight binary order is as good as any.

In Section 17.2, we realized a code converter using gates and J-K flip-flops. We will now realize this converter using a ROM and D flip-flops. The state table for the converter is reproduced in Table 19-4(a). Since there are 7 states, 3 D flip-flops are required. Thus, a ROM with 4 inputs (2^4 words) and 4 outputs is required, as shown in Fig. 19-20. Using a straight binary state assignment, we can construct the transition table, seen in Table 19-4(b), which gives the next state of the flip-flops as a function of the present state and input. Since we are using D flip-flops, $D_1 = Q_1^+$, $D_2 = Q_2^+$ and $D_3 = Q_3^+$. The truth table for the ROM, shown in Table 19-4(c), is easily constructed from the transition table. This gives the ROM outputs (Z, D_1, D_2, D_3) as functions of the ROM inputs (X, Q_1, Q_2, Q_3).

Fig. 19-20. Realization of a sequential network with a ROM

Table 19-4

(a) State table

present state	next state $X = 0$	1	present output (Z) $X = 0$	1
A	B	C	1	0
B	D	E	1	0
C	E	E	0	1
D	H	H	0	1
E	H	M	1	0
H	A	A	0	1
M	A	$-$	1	$-$

(b) Transition table

	$Q_1 Q_2 Q_3$	$Q_1^+ Q_2^+ Q_3^+$ $X = 0$	$X = 1$	Z $X = 0$	$X = 1$
A	000	001	010	1	0
B	001	011	100	1	0
C	010	100	100	0	1
D	011	101	101	0	1
E	100	101	110	1	0
H	101	000	000	0	1
M	110	000	$-$	1	$-$

(c) Truth table

$X\,Q_1Q_2Q_3$	$Z\,D_1D_2D_3$
0 0 0 0	1 0 0 1
0 0 0 1	1 0 1 1
0 0 1 0	0 1 0 0
0 0 1 1	0 1 0 1
0 1 0 0	1 1 0 1
0 1 0 1	0 0 0 0
0 1 1 0	1 0 0 0
0 1 1 1	x x x x
1 0 0 0	0 0 1 0
1 0 0 1	0 1 0 0
1 0 1 0	1 1 0 0
1 0 1 1	1 1 0 1
1 1 0 0	0 1 1 0
1 1 0 1	1 0 0 0
1 1 1 0	x x x x
1 1 1 1	x x x x

Sequential networks can also be realized using PLAs (programmable logic arrays) and flip-flops in a manner similar to using ROMs and flip-flops. However, in the case of PLAs, the state assignment may be important since use of a good state assignment can reduce the required number of product terms and hence reduce the required size of the PLA.

As an example, we will consider realizing the state table of Table 19-4(a) using a PLA and 3 D flip-flops. The network configuration is the same as Fig. 19-20, except that the ROM is replaced with a PLA of appropriate size. Using a straight binary assignment leads to the truth table given in Table 19-4(c). This table could be stored in a PLA with 4 inputs, 13 product terms and 4 outputs, but this would offer no advantage over the ROM solution discussed earlier. If the state assignment of Fig. 17-2 is used, the resulting output equation and D flip-flop input equations, derived from the maps in Fig. 17-3, are:

$$D_1 = Q_1Q_2' + Q_1'Q_2$$

$$D_2 = Q_2'$$

$$D_3 = Q_2'Q_3 + X'Q_1Q_2' + XQ_1'Q_2' + X'Q_1'Q_2Q_3'$$

$$Z = X'Q_3' + XQ_3$$

(19-3)

The PLA table which corresponds to these equations is in Table 19.5.

Table 19-5

X	Q_1	Q_2	Q_3	Z	D_1	D_2	D_3
–	1	0	–	0	1	0	0
–	0	1	–	0	1	0	0
–	–	0	–	0	0	1	0
–	–	0	1	0	0	0	1
0	1	0	–	0	0	0	1
1	0	0	–	0	0	0	1
0	0	1	0	0	0	0	1
0	–	–	0	1	0	0	0
1	–	–	1	1	0	0	0

Realization of this table requires a PLA with 4 inputs, 9 product terms and 4 outputs. When the number of inputs is small, as in this example, the ROM solution is generally more economical than the PLA solution; however, when the number of input variables is large, the PLA solution becomes more attractive.

Next, we will verify the operation of the network of Fig. 19-20 using a PLA which corresponds to Table 19.5. Initially, assume that $X = 0$ and $Q_1Q_2Q_3 = 000$. This selects rows ––0– and 0––0 in the table, so $Z = 1$ and $D_1D_2D_3 = 010$. After the clock, $Q_1Q_2Q_3 = 010$. If the next input is $X = 1$, then row –01– is selected, so $Z = 0$ and $D_1D_2D_3 = 100$. After the clock, $Q_1 Q_2Q_3 = 100$. Continuing in this manner, we can verify the transition table of Fig. 17-2.

19.6   Design of Sequential Networks Using PAL

PALs provide a convenient way of realizing sequential networks. In addition to the combinational PALs listed in Table 9-2, PALs are available which contain D flip-flops with inputs driven from the programmable array logic. Figure 19-21 shows a segment of a sequential PAL. The D flip-flop is driven from an OR gate which is fed by two AND gates. The flip-flop output is fed back to the programmable AND array through a buffer. Thus, the AND gate inputs can be connected to A, A', B, B', Q or Q'. The X's on the diagram show the realization of the next-state equation

$$Q^+ = D = A'BQ' + AB'Q$$

The flip-flop output is connected to an inverting tri-state buffer, which is enabled when $EN = 1$.

Fig. 19-21. Segment of a sequential PAL

Figure 19-22 shows a 16R4 PAL, which contains a register of 4 D flip-flops. Each flip-flop output goes through a tri-state inverting buffer (output pins 14–17). One input (pin 11) is used to enable these buffers. The rising edge of a common clock (pin 1) causes the flip-flops to change state. Each D flip-flop input is driven from an OR gate, and each OR gate is fed from 8 AND gates. The AND gate inputs can come from the external PAL inputs (pins 2–9) or from the flip-flops outputs, which are fed back internally. In addition there are 4 input/output (I/O) terminals (pins 12, 13, 18 and 19) which can be used as either network outputs or as inputs to the AND gates. Thus, each AND gate can have a maximum of 16 inputs (8 external inputs, 4 inputs fed back from the flip-flop outputs, and 4 inputs from the I/O terminals). When used as an output, each I/O terminal is driven from an inverting tri-state buffer. Each of these buffers is fed from an OR gate and each OR gate is fed from 7 AND gates. An eighth AND gate is used to enable the buffer.

When the 16R4 PAL is used to realize a sequential network, the I/O terminals are normally used for the Z outputs. Thus, a single 16R4 with no additional logic could realize a sequential network with up to 8 inputs, 4 outputs and 16 states. Each next state equation could contain up to 8 terms, and each output equation could contain up to 7 terms. As an example, we will realize the code converter described by Equations (19-3). Three flip-flops are used to store Q_1, Q_2 and Q_3, and the array logic which drives these flip-flops is programmed to realize D_1, D_2 and D_3 as shown in Fig. 19-22. The X's on the diagram indicate the connections to the AND-gate inputs. The flip-flop outputs are not used externally, so the output buffers are disabled. Since the Z output comes through an inverting buffer, the array logic must realize

$$Z' = (X + Q_3)(X' + Q_3') = XQ_3' + X'Q_3$$

The Z output buffer is permanently enabled in this example, so there are no connections to the AND gate that drives it.

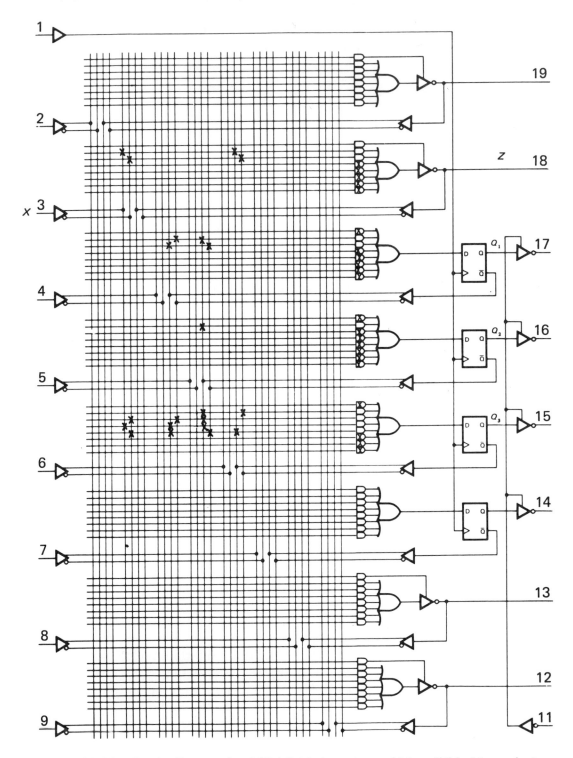

Fig. 19-22. Logic diagram for 16R4 PAL (courtesy of Monolithic Memories)

PROBLEMS

19.1 The 74178 shift register could be made to shift left by adding external connections between the Q outputs and D inputs. Indicate the appropriate connections on a block diagram of the 74178. Which input line would serve as a serial input in this case? With the connections you have made, what should SH and L be for a left shift? For a right shift?

19.2 a. Show how to connect a 74178 shift register so that a right *circular* shift is performed.

   b. Complete the following timing diagram for a 74178 shift register if it is connected as in part a. Assume that $D_A D_B D_C D_D = 1010$.

19.3 Complete the following timing diagram for a 74S163 counter. Assume that $D_D = D_B = D_A = 1, D_C = 0, T = 1$

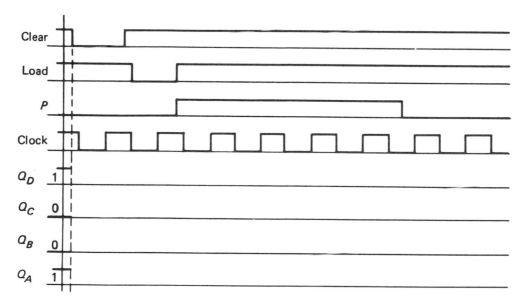

19.4 Using a 74S163 counter* and a NAND gate connected to the LOAD input, design a counter which counts in the sequence 0, 1, 2, 3, 4, 5, 13, 14, 15, 0, 1, ... Inverters may also be used if necessary. Note that 13 must be loaded into the counter when it is in state 5.

19.5 Realize the given state graph using a 74S163 counter* with added gates. Note that in state 0010, if $X = 1$, the counter must be loaded with 0101. Take advantage of the fact that the LOAD signal overrides the count.

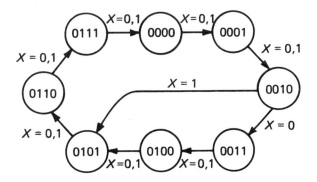

19.6 Realize the given state graph using a 74S163 counter* with added gates.

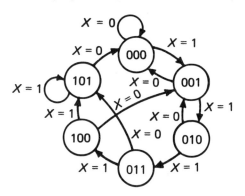

19.7 Draw a block diagram which shows how a ROM and D flip-flops could be connected to realize Table 14-4 (p. 307). Specify the truth table for the ROM using a straight binary state assignment. (Note that a *truth* table, not a *transition* table is to be specified.)

19.8 The state table of Fig. 16-13 is to be realized using a PLA and D flip-flops.

   a. Draw a block diagram.

   b. Specify the contents of the PLA in tabular form using the state assignment of Equation (16-1). (See Fig. 16-14(b) for the D equations.)

   c. If the PLA were replaced with a ROM, what size ROM would be required?

---

*Use the order $Q_D Q_C Q_B Q_A$ for the counter state variables.

19.9 A digital system contains four 74LS374 octal D flip-flop registers. The inputs *and* outputs of all four registers are connected to a common bus so that the contents of any register can be loaded into any other register. A decoder is used to selectively enable the register outputs, and each register can be clocked separately.

   a. Draw a block diagram of the system.

   b. What should be the decoder inputs and which register(s) should be clocked in order to load the contents of register B into register A? In order to load the contents of register A into both registers C and D?

19.10 a. Realize the state table of Fig. 16-13 using a 16R4 PAL. (See Fig. 16-14(b) for the next state equations.) Mark X's on a copy of the 16R4 diagram to indicate the fuse pattern.

   b. Realize the state table of Table 15-5 using a 16R4 PAL. Use a straight binary state assignment ($S_0 = 000$, $S_1 = 001$, etc.).

19.11 Work Problem 19.8 using the state table given in Problem 16.8. Derive the D equations using the state assignment given on page 652.

20

NETWORKS FOR ADDITION
AND SUBTRACTION

OBJECTIVES

1. Write negative binary numbers in sign and magnitude, 1's complement, and 2's complement forms. Add signed binary numbers using 1's complement and 2's complement arithmetic. Justify the methods used. State when an overflow occurs.

2. Design a full adder and a full subtracter.

3. Analyze, design and explain the operation of networks for parallel and serial addition or subtraction of binary numbers.

STUDY GUIDE

1. Review Section 1.3 and then study Section 20.1, *Representation of Negative Numbers.*

    a. In digital systems, why are 1's complement and 2's complement commonly used to represent negative numbers instead of sign and magnitude?

    b. State two different ways of forming the 1's complement of an *n*-bit binary number.

c. State three different ways of forming the 2's complement of an n-bit binary number.

d. If the word length is $n = 4$ bits (including sign), what decimal number does 1000_2 represent in sign and magnitude?

In 2's complement?   In 1's complement?

e. Given a negative number represented in 2's complement, how do you find its magnitude?

Given a negative number represented in 1's complement, how do you find its magnitude?

f. If the word length is 6 bits (including sign), what decimal number does 100000_2 represent in sign and magnitude?

In 2's complement?   In 1's complement?

g. What is meant by an overflow? How can you tell that an overflow has occurred when performing 1's or 2's complement addition?

Does a carry out of the last bit position indicate that an overflow has occurred?

h. Work out some examples of 1's and 2's complement addition for various combinations of positive and negative numbers.

i. What is the justification for using the end-around carry in 1's complement addition?

j. The one thing that causes the most trouble with 2's complement numbers is the special case of the negative number which consists of a 1 followed by all 0's (1000 . . . 000). If this number is n bits long, what number does it represent and why? (It is not negative zero.)

k. How would -5873 be represented in 9's complement? In 10's complement?

l. Work Problems 20.1, 20.2 and 20.3.

2. Review Section 13.8 and then work Problem 20.4.

3. Study Section 20.2, *Design of Binary Adders.*

a. Make sure that you can analyze or design any of the networks given.

b. For the network of Fig. 20-1, using 1's complement addition, indicate the sum and carry outputs for each cell if $n = 5$, $X = 15$ and $Y = -11$.

c. Note the difference between the parallel binary adder without accumulator (Fig. 20-1) and the parallel binary adder with accumulator (Fig. 20-6). In the former, the X and Y inputs could come from two different registers; the sum is available at the adder output and does not replace either X or Y. In the latter, the sum replaces the number X, and the original X is no longer available after the add pulse.

d. In Figs. 20-8 and 20-9, note that T_i is only a function of c_i and y_i even though the next state of the flip-flop (x_i^+) depends on the value of x_i. (Study the maps in Fig. 20-8 if you don't understand why.)

e. Draw a Mealy state graph for the serial adder.

4. Study Section 20.3, *Binary Subtracters.*

a. Explain how the entries in Table 20-3 were determined and carry out some subtraction examples using this table.

b. Demonstrate that the circuit of Fig. 20-10 works correctly for the following combinations

$A - B = (-3) - (-6)$ $A - B = (+3) - (+6)$

$A - B = (-6) - (-3)$ $A - B = (+6) - (+6)$

c. What modification should be made to the circuit when 1's complement is used for negative numbers?

d. For the network of Fig. 20-11, indicate the borrow and difference outputs from each cell if $n = 5$, $X = 8$ and $Y = 3$.

    c. Note that the terms "FULL ADDER" and "FULL SUBTRACTER" refer to very specific combinational logic blocks. Each of these blocks has exactly 3 inputs and 2 outputs. Make sure that you know their functions and how to design them.

5. Work Problems 20.5, 20.6 and 20.7.

6. When you are satisfied that you can meet all of the objectives, take the readiness test.

20. NETWORKS FOR ADDITION AND SUBTRACTION

    This unit applies the techniques for combinational, sequential and iterative network design to the design of binary adders and subtracters. Before proceeding with this design, the various methods used to represent negative binary numbers will be discussed.

20.1 Representation of Negative Numbers

    Several representations of negative binary numbers are possible. In most computers the first bit in a word is used as a sign bit, with 0 used for plus and 1 used for minus. The *sign and magnitude* system is similar to that which people commonly use. For an n-bit word, the first bit is the sign and the remaining $n-1$ bits represent the magnitude of the number. Thus an n-bit word can represent any one of 2^{n-1} positive integers or 2^{n-1} negative integers. Table 20-1 illustrates this for $n = 4$. Note that 1000 represents minus zero in the sign and magnitude system.

Table 20-1. Signed Binary Integers (word length $n = 4$)

$+N$	positive integers (all systems)	$-N$	Negative integers		
			sign and magnitude	2's complement N^*	1's complement $\bar{N}$
+0	0000	−0	1000	——	1111
+1	0001	−1	1001	1111	1110
+2	0010	−2	1010	1110	1101
+3	0011	−3	1011	1101	1100
+4	0100	−4	1100	1100	1011
+5	0101	−5	1101	1011	1010
+6	0110	−6	1110	1010	1001
+7	0111	−7	1111	1001	1000
		−8	——	1000	——

Design of logic networks to do arithmetic with sign and magnitude binary numbers is awkward; therefore, other representations are often used. The 2's complement and 1's complement are commonly used because arithmetic units are easy to design using these systems. For the 2's complement system, a positive number, N, is represented by a 0 followed by the magnitude as in the sign and magnitude system; however, a negative number, $-N$, is represented by its 2's complement, $N*$. If the word length is n bits, the *2's complement* of a positive integer N is defined as

$$N* = 2^n - N \tag{20-1}$$

For $n = 4$, $-N$ is represented by $16-N$ as in Table 20-1. For example, -3 is represented by $16 - 3 = 13 = 1101_2$. As is the case for sign and magnitude numbers, all negative 2's complement numbers have a 1 in the leftmost (sign bit) position.

For the 1's complement system, a negative number, $-N$, is represented by its 1's complement, $\bar{N}$. The *1's complement* of a positive integer N is defined as

$$\bar{N} = (2^n - 1) - N \tag{20-2}$$

for a word length of n bits. For $n = 4$, $-N$ is represented by $15 - N$ as in Table 20-1. Note that 1111 represents minus zero, and -8 has no representation in a 4-bit system. An alternate way to form the 1's complement is to simply complement N bit-by-bit by replacing 0's with 1's and 1's with 0's. This is equivalent to the definition, Equation (20-2), since $2^n - 1$ consists of all 1's, and subtracting a bit from 1 is the same as complementing the bit. For example, if $n = 6$ and $N = 010101$,

$$2^n - 1 = 111111$$
$$N = \underline{010101}$$
$$\bar{N} = 101010$$

From Equations (20-1) and (20-2),

$$N* = 2^n - N = (2^n - 1 - N) + 1 = \bar{N} + 1$$

so the 2's complement can be formed by complementing N bit-by-bit and then adding 1. An easier way to form the 2's complement of N is to start at the right and complement all bits to the left of the first 1. For example, if

$$N = 0101100, \quad N* = 1010100$$

From Equations (20-1) and (20-2),

$$N = 2^n - N* \quad \text{and} \quad N = (2^n - 1) - \bar{N}$$

Therefore, given a negative integer represented by its 2's complement ($N*$), we can obtain the magnitude of the integer by taking the 2's complement of $N*$. Similarly, to get the magnitude of a negative integer represented by its 1's complement ($\bar{N}$), we can take the 1's complement of $\bar{N}$.

In the 2's complement system the number of negative integers which can be represented is one more than the number of positive integers (not including 0). For example, in Table 20-1, 1000 represents -8, since a sign bit of 1 indicates a negative number, and if $N = 8$, $N* = 10000 - 1000 = 1000$. In general, in a 2's complement system with a word length of n bits, the number $100 \ldots 000$ (1 followed by $n-1$ 0's) represents a negative number with a magnitude of

$$2^n - 2^{n-1} = 2^{n-1}$$

This special case occurs only for 2's complement. However, -0 has no representation in 2's complement, but -0 is a special case for 1's complement as well as for the sign and magnitude system.

The idea of 2's and 1's complement representation of negative numbers can be extended to number systems with other bases. In general, if the base is R and the word length is n digits, the R's complement of a positive number N is defined as

$$N^* = R^n - N$$

and the $(R-1)$'s complement is defined as

$$\overline{N} = (R^n - 1) - N$$

For example, for octal numbers ($R = 8$) with $n = 4$, the 8's complement of 0345_8 is $10000_8 - 0345_8 = 7433_8$, and the 7's complement is $(10000 - 1) - 0345 = 7777 - 0345 = 7432_8$. Just as the 1's complement can be formed on a bit-by-bit basis by complementing each bit, the $(R - 1)$'s complement can be formed on a digit-by-digit basis. Thus, for octal numbers the 7's complement can be formed by subtracting each digit from 7.

Addition of 2's Complement Numbers

Addition of n-bit signed binary numbers is straightforward using the 2's complement system. Addition is carried out just as if all the numbers were positive and any carry from the sign position is ignored. This will always give the correct result except when an overflow occurs. When the word length is n bits, we say that an *overflow* has occurred if the correct representation of the sum (including sign) requires more than n bits. The different cases which can occur are illustrated below for $n = 4$.

a. Addition of 2 positive numbers, sum $< 2^{n-1}$.

+3	0011	
+4	0100	
+7	0111	(correct answer)

b. Addition of 2 positive numbers, sum $\geq 2^{n-1}$.

+5	0101	
+6	0110	
	1011	← wrong answer because of overflow (+11 requires 5 bits including sign)

c. Addition of positive and negative numbers (negative number has greatest magnitude).

+5	0101	
−6	1010	
−1	1111	(correct answer)

    d. Same as case c except positive number has greatest magnitude.

$$
\begin{array}{ll}
-5 & 1011 \\
+6 & 0110 \\
\hline
+1\ (1)\ 0001 & \leftarrow \text{correct answer when carry from sign bit is ignored} \\
& \quad\text{(this is } not \text{ an overflow)}
\end{array}
$$

    e. Addition of two negative numbers, $|\text{sum}| \leqslant 2^{n-1}$.

$$
\begin{array}{ll}
-3 & 1101 \\
-4 & 1100 \\
\hline
-7\ (1)\ 1001 & \leftarrow \text{correct answer when last carry is ignored (this is } not \\
& \quad\text{an overflow)}
\end{array}
$$

    f. Addition of two negative numbers, $|\text{sum}| > 2^{n-1}$.

$$
\begin{array}{ll}
-5 & 1011 \\
-6 & 1010 \\
\hline
(1)\ 0101 & \leftarrow \text{wrong answer because of overflow } (-11 \text{ requires 5 bits} \\
& \quad\text{including sign)}
\end{array}
$$

Note that an overflow condition (cases b and f) is easy to detect since in case b addition of two positive numbers yields a negative result and in case f addition of two negative numbers yields a positive answer (for four bits).

    Proof that throwing away the carry from the sign bit always gives the correct answer follows for cases d and e:

    Case d. $-A + B$ (where $B > A$)

$$
A* + B = (2^n - A) + B = 2^n + (B - A) > 2^n
$$

Throwing away the last carry is equivalent to subtracting 2^n, so the result is $(B - A)$, which is correct.

    Case e. $-A - B$ (where $A + B \leqslant 2^{n-1}$)

$$
A* + B* = (2^n - A) + (2^n - B) = 2^n + 2^n - (A + B)
$$

Discarding the last carry yields $2^n - (A + B) = (A + B)*$, which is the correct representation of $-(A + B)$.

Addition of 1's Complement Numbers

    Addition of 1's complement numbers is similar to 2's complement except that instead of discarding the last carry, it is added to the n-bit sum in the rightmost position. This is referred to as an "end-around" carry. Addition of positive numbers is the same as illustrated for cases a and b under 2's complement. The remaining cases are illustrated below ($n = 4$).

    c. Addition of positive and negative numbers (negative number with greatest magnitude).

$$
\begin{array}{lll}
+5 & 0101 & \\
-6 & 1001 & \\
\hline
-1 & 1110 & \text{(correct answer)}
\end{array}
$$

d. Same as case c except positive number has greatest magnitude.

$$
\begin{array}{ll}
-5 & 1010 \\
+6 & \underline{0110} \\
& (1)\,\overline{0000}
\end{array}
$$

          └────▸1   (end-around carry)

           0001   (correct answer, *no* overflow)

e. Addition of two negative numbers, $|\text{sum}| < 2^{n-1}$.

$$
\begin{array}{ll}
-3 & 1100 \\
-4 & \underline{1011} \\
& (1)\,\overline{0111}
\end{array}
$$

          └────▸1   (end-around carry)

           1000   (correct answer, *no* overflow)

f. Addition of two negative numbers, $|\text{sum}| \geqslant 2^{n-1}$.

$$
\begin{array}{ll}
-5 & 1010 \\
-6 & \underline{1001} \\
& (1)\,\overline{0011}
\end{array}
$$

          └────▸1   (end-around carry)

           0100   (wrong answer because of overflow)

Again, note that the overflow in case f is easy to detect since the addition of two negative numbers yields a positive result.

    Proof that the end-around carry method gives the correct result follows for cases d and e:

Case d. $-A + B$ (where $B > A$)

$$\bar{A} + B = (2^n - 1 - A) + B = 2^n + (B - A) - 1$$

The end-around carry is equivalent to subtracting 2^n and adding 1, so the result is $(B - A)$, which is correct.

Case e. $-A - B\ (A + B < 2^{n-1})$

$$\bar{A} + \bar{B} = (2^n - 1 - A) + (2^n - 1 - B) = 2^n + [2^n - 1 - (A + B)] - 1$$

After the end-around carry, the result is $2^n - 1 - (A + B) = (\overline{A + B})$, which is the correct representation for $-(A + B)$.

    The following examples illustrate addition of 1's and 2's complement numbers for a word length of $n = 8$:

a. Add -11 and -20 in 1's complement.

    $+11 = 00001011$ $+ 20 = 00010100$

    taking the bit-by-bit complement,

    -11 is represented by 11110100 and -20 by 11101011

$$
\begin{array}{ll}
11110100 & (-11) \\
\underline{11101011} & \underline{+(-20)} \\
(1)\,11011111 &
\end{array}
$$

         └────────▸1   (end-around carry)

          $\overline{11100000}\ = -31$

b. Add -8 and $+19$ in 2's complement

$+8 = 00001000$

complementing all bits to the left of the first 1, -8 is represented by
11111000

$$
\begin{array}{ll}
11111000 & (-8) \\
00010011 & + \ 19 \\
\hline
(1)00001011 \ = & + \ 11
\end{array}
$$

—(discard last carry)

Note that in both cases, the addition produced a carry out of the left-most bit position, but there is *no overflow* since the answer can be correctly represented with 8 bits (including sign). A general rule for detecting overflow when adding two n-bit signed binary numbers (1's or 2's complement) to get an n-bit sum is:

An overflow occurs if adding two positive numbers gives a negative answer or if adding two negative numbers gives a positive answer.

The principles used for 1's and 2's complement arithmetic can be extended to any base. If we are working with base R numbers, and negative numbers are represented in R's complement, we simply add the numbers and discard the carry from the last digit position. For example, for 4-digit octal numbers,

$$
\begin{array}{ll}
7433 & (-345) \\
+ \ 0672 & \\
\hline
10325 & \text{(which is the correct answer when the carry} \\
& \text{is discarded)}
\end{array}
$$

For $R - 1$'s complement, an end-around carry is required. If we use 7's complement to represent negative octal numbers, the above example becomes

$$
\begin{array}{ll}
7432 & (-345) \\
+ \ 0672 & \\
\hline
10324 & \\
\ \ \llcorner\!\!\rightarrow +1 & \text{(end-around carry)} \\
\hline
0325 &
\end{array}
$$

20.2   Design of Binary Adders

Parallel Adder

We will start by designing a parallel adder for two n-bit binary numbers,

$$ X = x_n x_{n-1} x_{n-2} \ldots x_3 x_2 x_1 \quad \text{and} \quad Y = y_n y_{n-1} y_{n-2} \ldots y_3 y_2 y_1 $$

We will assume an iterative network of the form shown in Fig. 20-1. The two binary numbers are fed in parallel into the cell inputs. The rightmost cell adds the least significant bits x_1 and y_1 to form a sum digit s_1 and a carry digit c_2. The next cell adds the carry c_2 to bits x_2 and y_2 to form a sum digit s_2 and a carry digit c_3. This process continues as fast as the gates in the cells can operate, and when a steady-state condition is reached the sum $s_n s_{n-1} s_{n-2} \ldots s_3 s_2 s_1$ can be read out in parallel.

End-around carry for 1's complement

Fig. 20-1. Parallel binary adder

To design the network, we must design a typical cell which adds a carry c_i to bits x_i and y_i to generate a sum digit s_i and a new carry c_{i+1}. Table 20-2 is easily filled in to specify the behavior of this typical cell. For example, for the combination $x_i = 1$, $y_i = 0$ and $c_i = 1$, binary addition yields $1 + 0 + 1 = 10$ which gives a sum digit $s_i = 0$ and a carry $c_{i+1} = 1$. The network which realizes these functions is referred to as a *full adder* and is available in integrated circuit form.

Table 20-2. Logic Functions for a Binary Adder

x_i	y_i	c_i	c_{i+1}	s_i
0	0	0	0	0
0	0	1	0	1
0	1	0	0	1
0	1	1	1	0
1	0	0	0	1
1	0	1	1	0
1	1	0	1	0
1	1	1	1	1

The functions for a typical cell are easily determined from Karnaugh maps as shown in Fig. 20-2.

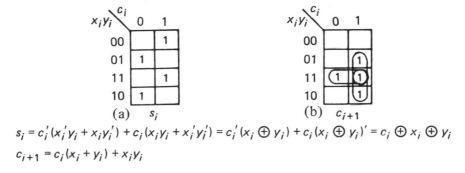

$$s_i = c_i'(x_i'y_i + x_iy_i') + c_i(x_iy_i + x_i'y_i') = c_i'(x_i \oplus y_i) + c_i(x_i \oplus y_i)' = c_i \oplus x_i \oplus y_i$$

$$c_{i+1} = c_i(x_i + y_i) + x_iy_i$$

Fig. 20-2. Maps for typical cell (full adder)

Although designed for positive binary numbers, this adder can also be used with negative numbers expressed in complement form. When 2's complement is used, the last carry (c_{n+1}) is discarded and there is no carry into the first cell. Since $c_1 = 0$, the equations for the first cell may be simplified to:

$$s_1 = x_1'y_1 + x_1y_1' \text{ and } c_2 = x_1y_1$$

When 1's complement is used, the end-around carry is accomplished by connecting c_{n+1} to the c_1 input as shown by the dashed line in Fig. 20-1. Even though the network has the form of a closed loop, carries cannot propagate continuously around the loop and a steady-state condition will always be reached. In order to start a carry propagating, we must have a cell with $x_i = 1$ and $y_i = 1$, which generates a carry $c_{i+1} = 1$ (regardless of the value of c_i). Even if this carry propagates around the loop causing c_i to change value, c_{i+1} remains 1 and steady state is reached.

Serial Adder

Next we will design a serial adder in which the binary numbers X and Y are fed in serially, one pair of bits at a time. First x_1 and y_1 are fed in; a sum digit s_1 is generated and the carry c_2 is stored. At the next clock time, x_2 and y_2 are fed in and added to c_2 to give the next sum digit s_2 and the new carry c_3, which is stored. This process continues until all bits have been added. Table 20-2 still applies, so we can use the same full adder circuit to generate the sum and carry bits. Adding a delay unit to store the carry gives the serial adder shown in Fig. 20-3(a). It is assumed that the inputs are synchronized with the delay so that the new x and y inputs are present at the same time the previous carry is available at the delay output. In practice, a clocked D flip-flop could be used to achieve this synchronization as seen in Fig. 20-3(b).

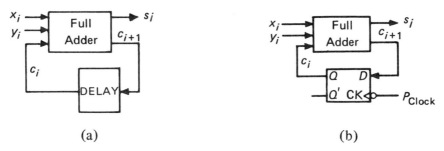

(a)   (b)

Fig. 20-3.   Serial adder

We will now modify the serial adder of Fig. 20-3 to use an S-R flip-flop to store the carry instead of the delay. In this case, the c_i column in Table 20-2 can be interpreted as the present state of the carry flip-flop, and the c_{i+1} column as the next state. The next state map and the derived S-R input maps for the carry flip-flop are shown in Fig. 20-4. The resulting serial adder circuit is shown in Fig. 20-5.

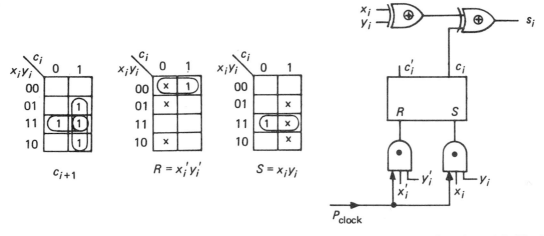

x_iy_i \ c_i	0	1
00		
01		1
11	1	1
10		1

c_{i+1}

x_iy_i \ c_i	0	1
00	x	1
01	x	
11		
10	x	

$R = x_i'y_i'$

x_iy_i \ c_i	0	1
00		
01		x
11	1	x
10		x

$S = x_iy_i$

Fig. 20-4

Fig. 20-5. **Serial adder with flip-flop for carry storage**

Parallel Adder with Accumulator

In computer circuits, it is frequently desirable to store one number in a register of flip-flops (called an accumulator) and add a second number to it leaving the result stored in the accumulator. One way to build a parallel adder with an accumulator is to add a flip-flop register to the adder of Fig. 20-1, resulting in the network of Fig. 20-6. First the number X is entered into the accumulator (by additional gating not shown). The number Y is applied to the full adder inputs, and after the carry has propagated through the adders, the sum appears at the adder outputs. An add pulse (P_{add}) is used to transfer the adder outputs into the accumulator flip-flops. If $s_i = 1$, $J_i = 1$ and $K_i = 0$, so the next state of flip-flop x_i will be 1. If $s_i = 0$, $J_i = 0$ and $K_i = 1$, so the next state of flip-flop x_i will be 0. Thus, $x_i^+ = s_i$, and when the add pulse occurs, the number X in the accumulator is replaced with the sum of X and Y.

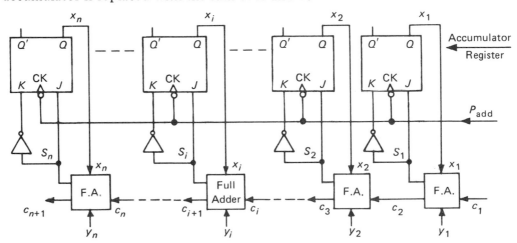

Fig. 20-6. **Parallel adder with accumulator**

An alternate design is possible by using the accumulator flip-flops to do part of the logic. We will assume an iterative sequential network of the form shown in Fig. 20-7. Here T flip-flops are used, so our problem is to derive T_i for a typical cell. The adder works as follows: First X is entered into the flip-flops. The flip-flop outputs and Y are fed into the typical cells of the adder, and the carry signal is allowed to propagate between cells. Then, after the add line is pulsed, the sum of X and Y appears in the accumulator flip-flops. Table 20-2 still applies, except s_i is now the next state of the accumulator flip-flop, i.e., $s_i = x_i^+$. Thus, the next state map for x_i in Fig. 20-8(a) is the same as Fig. 20-2(a). The corresponding input map for T_i seen in Fig. 20-8(b) is derived from x_i^+ in the usual way. The carry function (c_{i+1}) is the same as for the ordinary parallel adder shown in Fig. 20-2(b), but note that we now generate T_i instead of the more complex function, s_i. Fig. 20-9 shows the resulting typical cell.

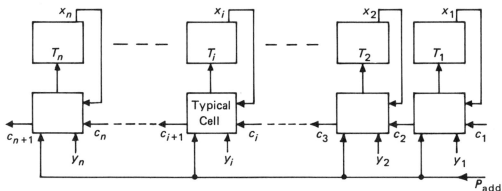

Fig. 20-7. Simplified parallel adder with accumulator

$$x_i^+ = s_i$$

(a)

$$T_i = y_i c_i' + y_i' c_i = c_i \oplus y_i$$

(b)

Fig. 20-8

Fig. 20-9. Typical cell for adder of Fig. 20-7

20.3 Binary Subtracters

Subtraction of binary numbers is more easily accomplished by adding the complement of the number to be subtracted. To compute $A - B$, the complement of B is added to A. Either 1's or 2's complement is used depending on the type of adder employed.

The circuit of Fig. 20-10 may be used to form $A - B$ using the 2's complement representation for negative numbers. The 2's complement of B can be formed by first finding the 1's complement and then adding 1. The 1's complement is formed by inverting each bit of B, and the addition of 1 is effectively accomplished by putting a 1 into the carry input of the first full adder.

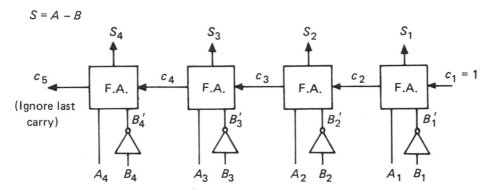

Fig. 20-10. Binary subtracter using full adders

Example: $A = 0110$ $(+6)$
$B = 0011$ $(+3)$

The adder output is

$$
\begin{array}{rl}
0110 & (+6) \\
+1100 & (\text{1's complement of 3}) \\
+\quad 1 & (\text{first carry input}) \\
\hline
(1)\ 0011 & = 3 = 6 - 3
\end{array}
$$

Alternatively, direct subtraction can be accomplished by employing a full subtracter in a manner analogous to a full adder. A block diagram for a parallel subtracter which subtracts Y from X is shown in Fig. 20-11. The first two bits

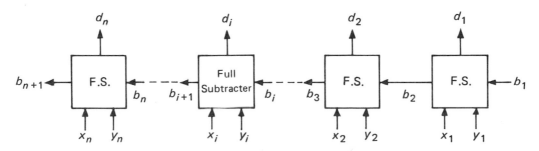

Fig. 20-11. Parallel subtracter

are subtracted in the rightmost cell and a borrow signal ($b_2 = 1$) is generated if it is necessary to borrow from the next column. In cell i, bits b_i and y_i are subtracted from x_i to form the difference d_i, and a borrow signal ($b_{i+1} = 1$) is generated if it is necessary to borrow from the next column.

Table 20-3 gives the truth table for a binary full subtracter. Consider the following case, where $x_i = 0$, $y_i = 1$ and $b_i = 1$:

	column i before borrow	column i after borrow
x_i	0	10
$-b_i$	−1	−1
$-y_i$	−1	−1
d_i		0 ($b_{i+1} = 1$)

Note that in column i, we cannot immediately subtract y_i and b_i from x_i. Hence, we must borrow from column $i + 1$. Borrowing 1 from column $i + 1$ is equivalent to setting b_{i+1} to 1 and adding 10 (2_{10}) to x_i. We then have $d_i = 10 - 1 - 1 = 0$. Verify that Table 20-3 is correct for the other input combinations and use it to work out several examples of binary subtraction.

Table 20-3. Truth Table for Binary Full Subtracter

$x_i y_i b_i$	$b_{i+1} d_i$
0 0 0	0 0
0 0 1	1 1
0 1 0	1 1
0 1 1	1 0
1 0 0	0 1
1 0 1	0 0
1 1 0	0 0
1 1 1	1 1

PROBLEMS

20.1 By analogy with 1's complement, define the 9's complement of an n-digit decimal number and state a rule for 9's complement addition. Note that a sign digit of 9 indicates a negative number. Add -2489 and $+5367$ using 5-digit numbers. Use 9's complement to represent the negative number.

20.2 Add the following numbers in binary using 2's complement to represent negative numbers. Use a word length of 5 bits (including sign) and indicate if an overflow occurs.

   a. $(-9) + (-11)$ b. $(-9) + (-7)$ c. $(-9) + 11$

   d. $11 + 7$ e. $(-10) + (-5)$

   Repeat using 1's complement to represent negative numbers.

20.3 A computer has a word length of 8 bits (including sign). If 2's complement is used to represent negative numbers, what range of integers can be stored in the computer? If 1's complement is used? (Express your answers in decimal.)

20.4 Given four flip-flops and four input signals (x_1, x_2, x_3, and x_4), show the required connections so that when a transfer pulse occurs, the values of the inputs will be transferred to the flip-flops. In other words the next state of flip-flop Q_i should be $Q_i^+ = x_i$ regardless of the present state of flip-flop. Solve this problem for clocked J-K flip-flops, S-R flip-flops, and T flip-flops. In each case, add as few gates and inverters as possible.

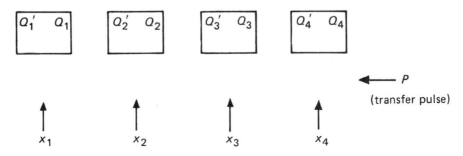

20.5 This problem concerns the design of a parallel adder for adding three positive binary numbers. These numbers are designated $x_n \ldots x_3 x_2 x_1$, $y_n \ldots y_3 y_2 y_1$ and $z_n \ldots z_3 z_2 z_1$. A typical cell for the adder is of the form:

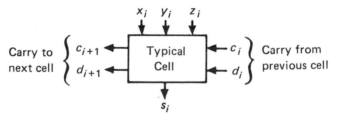

Note that there are two carry signals propagating between ceils. Two carry signals are required because when three binary digits are added to the carry coming into the cell, the carry to the next cell may be either 0, 1, or 2 (coded as 00, 01 and 10 respectively).

a. Derive a truth table which specifies the operation of a typical cell. (Your table should contain some don't cares.)

b. Derive an equation for s_i in minimum form. (Equations for c_{i+1} and d_{i+1} are not required.)

20.6 Design a parallel subtracter with accumulator using T flip-flops and without using full adders or full subtracters. Your design should be similar to Fig. 20-7, except that the borrow will propagate between cells instead of the carry.

20.7 a. Assume that the parallel binary adder of Fig. 20-1 is used to add signed binary numbers (1's or 2's complement). Design an overflow indicator network which has an output of 1 when an overflow occurs.

b. Assume that the parallel binary subtracter of Fig. 20-11 is used to subtract signed binary numbers (2's complement). Design an overflow indicator network.

20.8 Redesign the parallel adder with accumulator of Fig. 20-6 so that S-R flip-flops (with added gates) are used instead of J-K flip-flops.

20.9 Subtract each of the following pairs of 5-bit binary numbers by adding the complement of the subtrahend to the minuend. Indicate when an overflow occurs. Assume that negative numbers are represented in 1's complement.

$$\begin{array}{ccccc} 01001 & 10101 & 10110 & 00101 & 11100 \\ -11010 & -10000 & -01101 & -01010 & -10101 \end{array}$$

Repeat using 2's complement.

20.10 Design a 4-bit binary adder-subtracter with accumulator for signed binary numbers. Use 4 D flip-flops and 4 full adders together with any necessary gates. Use 1's complement to represent negative numbers. The network should have one control input, S. If $S = 1$, the input is subtracted from the accumulator; if $S = 0$, it is added to the accumulator.

a. Draw the complete logic diagram including provision for overflow detection.

b. If the accumulator contains 1110, the input is 0010 and $S = 1$, indicate on the diagram the logic values of all of the full adder inputs and outputs at a time just before the answer is clocked into the accumulator.

20.11 The excess-3 code (Table 1-1) is said to be self-complementing because the code for the 9's complement of each decimal digit can be formed by taking the bit-by-bit complement of the corresponding code. For example, the 9's complement of 6 is 3, and the bit-by-bit complement of the code for 6 (1001) is 0110, which is the code for 3. Construct a 2-4-2-1 code that is self-complementing.

21

NETWORKS FOR ARITHMETIC OPERATIONS

OBJECTIVES

1. Analyze and explain the operation of various networks for adding, subtracting, multiplying, and dividing binary numbers and for similar operations.

2. Draw a block diagram and design the control network for various networks for adding, subtracting, multiplying, and dividing binary numbers and for similar operations.

STUDY GUIDE

1. Study Section 21.1, *Serial Adder with Accumulator.*

   a. Study Fig. 21-2 carefully to make sure you understand the operation of this type of adder. Work out a table similar to Table 21-1 starting with $X = 6$ and $Y = 3$:

	X	Y	c_i	s_i	c_i^+
t_0	0110	0011			
t_1					
t_2					
t_3					
t_4					

   b. What changes would be made in the above table if the D input to the addend register (Fig. 21-1) was connected to a logic 0 instead of to y_1?

c. Work Problems 21.1 and 21.2.

2. Study Section 21.2, *Design of a Parallel Multiplier.*

a. For the binary multiplier of Fig. 21-6, if the initial contents of the accumulator is 000001101 and the multiplicand is 1111, show the sequence of add and shift pulses and the contents of the accumulator at each time step.

b. For the state diagram of Fig. 21-7, what is the maximum number of clock pulses required to carry out the multiplication? The minimum number?

c. For Fig. 21-6, how many bits would be required for the product register if the multiplier was 6 bits and the multiplicand was 8 bits?

d. Work Problems 21.3 and 21.4.

e. The control circuit of the binary multiplier of Fig. 21-6 is replaced with the multiplier control shown in Fig. 21-8(a). The counter is two bits wide and $K = 1$ when the counter is in state 11. Complete the following table, which shows the operation of the control circuit when 1101 is multiplied by 1011. (The sequence of product register states will be the same as shown at the top of page 461.)

state	counter	N	M	K	P_a	P_s
S_0	00	0	1	0	0	0
S_0	00	1	1	0	1	0
S_1	00	0	1	0	0	1

f. Work Programmed Exercise 21.10.

3. Study Section 21.3, *Design of a Binary Divider.*

   a. Using the state diagram of Fig. 21-10 to determine when to shift or subtract, work through the division example given at the start of this section.

   b. What changes would have to be made in Fig. 21-11 if the subtraction was done using full adders rather than full subtracters?

   c. For the block diagram of Fig. 21-9, under what conditions will an overflow occur and why?

   d. Work Programmed Exercise 21.11.

   e. Derive the control circuit equations, Equations (21-1).

   Hint: Construct the Karnaugh map for *Sh* by setting *Sh* = 1, *Su* = *V* = 0 in Table 21-2.

   f. In Fig. 21-11, why is b_4 set equal to 0? Why is one of the inputs to the leftmost full subtracter set to 0?

   g. Work Problems 21.5, 21.6 and 21.7.

4. Optional lab exercises:

   a. Redesign the serial adder of Fig. 20-5 to use a clocked *J-K* flip-flop, build it in lab and test it.

   b. Connect two 4-bit shift registers to the inputs of the adder that you built in part a to form a serial adder with accumulator (as in Fig. 21-1). Supply the shift pulse manually so that a control circuit is unnecessary. Test your adder using binary numbers in the range 000 to 111.

   c. Build the control circuit of Fig. 21-5, connect it to the network which you built in part b, and test it.

5. When you are satisfied that you can meet all of the objectives, take the readiness test.

21. NETWORKS FOR ARITHMETIC OPERATIONS

This unit introduces the concept of using a control network to control a sequence of operations in a digital network. A control network is a sequential network which puts out a sequence of control signals. These signals cause operations like addition or shifting to take place at appropriate times.

The following notation will be used for shift registers in this unit:

Arrows entering and leaving the ends of the register indicate a serial input and output. Arrows entering and leaving the sides of the register indicate parallel inputs and outputs. A long arrow through the register indicates the shift pulse input and the direction of the shift.

21.1 Serial Adder with Accumulator

Figure 21-1 shows a block diagram of a serial adder with an accumulator. Two shift registers are used to hold the numbers to be added, X and Y. The long arrow drawn through the shift register in Fig. 21-1 is the shift pulse input. When this input is pulsed, the contents of the register is shifted right one position and the bit at the D input is entered into x_4 (or y_4). The X-register serves as the accumulator, and after four shift pulses, the number X is replaced with the sum of X and Y. The addend register is connected as a cyclic shift register (similar to the type shown in Fig. 13-13) so that after four shift pulses it is back in its original state and the number Y is not lost. The serial adder in the diagram is identical to the one in Fig. 20-3(b). At each clock time, one pair of bits is added. The shift pulse (P_{shift}) stores the sum bit in the accumulator, stores the carry bit in the carry flip-flop, and causes the addend register to cycle right.

Fig. 21-1. Block diagram for serial adder with accumulator

Figure 21-2 illustrates the operation of the serial adder. In this figure, t_0 is the time before the first shift pulse, t_1 is the time after the first shift pulse, t_2 is the time after the second shift pulse, etc. Initially, at time t_0, the accumulator contains X and the addend register contains Y. Since the full adder is a combinational network, x_1, y_1 and c_1 are added immediately to form the sum s_1 and carry c_2. When the first shift pulse occurs, s_1 is shifted into the accumulator and the remaining accumulator digits are shifted right one position. The same shift pulse stores c_2 in the carry flip-flop and cycles the addend register right one position. The next pair of bits, x_2 and y_2, are now at the full adder input, and the adder generates the sum and carry, s_2 and c_3 as seen in Figure 21-2(b). The second shift pulse shifts s_2 into the accumulator, stores c_3 in the carry flip-flop, and cycles the addend register right. Bits x_3 and y_3 are now at the adder input as seen in Figure 21-2(c), and the process continues until all bit pairs have been added, shown in Figure 21-2(e).

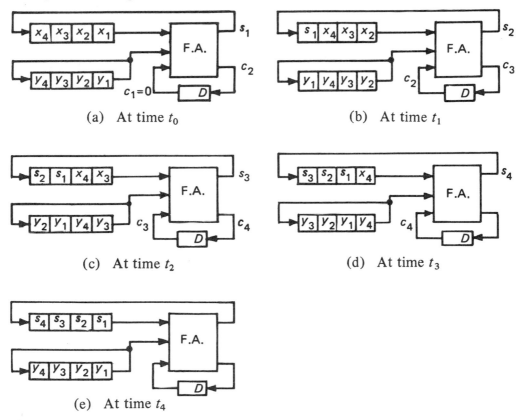

(a) At time t_0

(b) At time t_1

(c) At time t_2

(d) At time t_3

(e) At time t_4

Fig. 21-2. Operation of serial adder

Table 21-1 shows a numerical example of the serial adder operation. Initially, the accumulator contains 0101 and the addend register contains 0111. At t_0, the full adder computes $1 + 1 + 0 = 10$, so $s_i = 0$ and $c_i^+ = 1$. After the first shift pulse (time t_1) the first sum bit has been entered into the accumulator, the carry has been stored in the carry flip-flop, and the addend has been cycled right. After four pulses (time t_4) the sum of X and Y is in the accumulator and the addend register is back to its original state.

Table 21-1. Operation of Serial Adder

	X	Y	c_i	s_i	c_i^+
t_0	0101	0111	0	0	1
t_1	0010	1011	1	0	1
t_2	0001	1101	1	1	1
t_3	1000	1110	1	1	0
t_4	1100	0111	0	(1)	(0)

The control circuit for the adder must now be designed so that after receiving a start signal, the control circuit will put out four shift pulses and then stop. Figure 21-3 shows the state graph and table for the control circuit. The network remains in S_0 until a start signal is received, at which time the network outputs a shift pulse and goes to S_1. Then at successive clock times 3 more shift pulses are outputted. It will be assumed that the start signal is terminated before the network returns to state S_0 so that no further output occurs until another start signal is received. Dashes appear on the graph because once S_1 is reached the network operation continues regardless of the value of N.

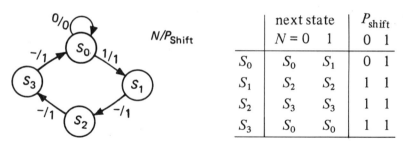

	next state		P_{shift}	
	$N = 0$	1	0	1
S_0	S_0	S_1	0	1
S_1	S_2	S_2	1	1
S_2	S_3	S_3	1	1
S_3	S_0	S_0	1	1

Fig. 21-3.   State graph for serial adder control

When the state graph for a sequential network forms a single loop of states, as in Fig. 21-3, the network has the form of a counter. For this reason, a state assignment which consists of a sequence of consecutive binary numbers usually leads to an economical network. Starting with the state table of Fig. 21-3 and using a straight binary state assignment, the control network equations are derived in Fig. 21-4 using the short-cut method for J and K.

		A^+B^+	
	AB	0	1
S_0	00	00	01
S_1	01	10	10
S_2	10	11	11
S_3	11	00	00

AB\\N	0	1
00	0	0
01	1	1
11	0	0
10	1	1

A^+

$J_A = B$
$K_A = B$

AB\\N	0	1
00	0	1
01	0	0
11	0	0
10	1	1

B^+

$J_B = N + A$
$K_B = 1$

AB\\N	0	1
00	0	1
01	1	1
11	1	1
10	1	1

P_{shift}

$P_{\text{shift}} = N + A + B$

Fig. 21-4.   Derivation of control network equations

Figure 21-5 shows the resulting network. The clock pulse is ANDed with $(N + A + B)$ since P_{shift} is connected to the clock inputs of the shift registers.

Fig. 21-5. Control circuit for serial adder

21.2   Design of a Parallel Multiplier

Next we will design a parallel multiplier for positive binary numbers. As illustrated in the example on p. 12, binary multiplication requires only shifting and adding. The same example is reworked below using a slight variation in the procedure. Instead of forming all of the partial products first and then adding, each partial product is added in as soon as it is formed. This eliminates the need for adding more than two binary numbers at a time.

$$
\begin{array}{rl}
\text{Multiplicand} \longrightarrow & 1101 \quad (13) \\
\text{Multiplier} \longrightarrow & 1011 \quad (11) \\
\hline
& 1101 \\
& 1101 \\
\hline
& 100111 \\
& 0000 \\
\hline
& 100111 \\
& 1101 \\
\hline
\text{Product} \longrightarrow 1& 0001111 \quad (143)
\end{array}
$$

Multiplication of two four-bit numbers requires a 4-bit multiplicand register, a 4-bit multiplier register, and an 8-bit register for the product. The product register serves as an accumulator to accumulate the sum of the partial products. Instead of shifting the multiplicand left each time before it is added in as was done in the above example, it is more convenient to shift the product register to the right each time. Figure 21-6 shows a block diagram for such a parallel multiplier. As indicated by the arrows on the diagram, 4 bits from the accumulator and 4 bits from the multiplicand register are connected to the adder inputs; the 4 sum bits and the carry output from the adder are connected back to the accumulator. (The actual connections are similar to the parallel adder with accumulator shown in Fig. 20-6.) When an add pulse (P_a) occurs, the adder outputs are transferred to the accumulator, thus causing the multiplicand to be added to the accumulator. An extra bit at the left end of the product register temporarily stores any carry which is generated when the multiplicand is added to the accumulator.

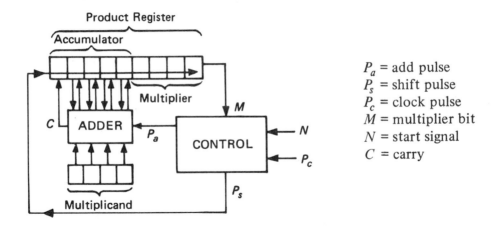

Fig. 21-6. Block diagram for parallel binary multiplier

Since the lower four bits of the product register are initially unused, we will store the multiplier in this location instead of in a separate register. As each multiplier bit is used, it is shifted out the right end of the register to make room for additional product bits. A pulse P_s causes the contents of the product register (including the multiplier) to be shifted right one place. The control circuit puts out the proper sequence of add and shift pulses after a start signal ($N = 1$) has been received. If the current multiplier bit (M) is one, the multiplicand is added to the accumulator followed by a right shift; if the multiplier bit is zero, the addition is skipped and only the right shift occurs. The multiplication example (13×11) is reworked below showing the location of the bits in the registers at each clock time.

initial contents of product register $0\ 0\ 0\ 0\ |1\ 0\ 1\ 1 \longleftarrow M$ (11)
(add multiplicand since $M = 1$) $1\ 1\ 0\ 1|$ (13)
after addition $0\ 1\ 1\ 0\ 1\ 1\ 0\ 1\ 1$
after shift $0\ 0\ 1\ 1\ 0\ 1\ 1\ 0\ 1 \longleftarrow M$
(add multiplicand since $M = 1$) $1\ 1\ 0\ 1$
after addition $1\ 0\ 0\ 1\ 1\ 1\ 1\ 0\ 1$
after shift $0\ 1\ 0\ 0\ 1\ 1\ 1\ 1\ 0 \longleftarrow M$
(skip addition since $M = 0$)
after shift $0\ 0\ 1\ 0\ 0\ 1\ 1\ 1\ 1 \longleftarrow M$
(add multiplicand since $M = 1$) $1\ 1\ 0\ 1$
after addition $1\ 0\ 0\ 0\ 1\ 1\ 1\ 1\ 1$
after shift (final answer) $0\ 1\ 0\ 0\ 0\ 1\ 1\ 1\ 1$ (143)
dividing line between product and multiplier

The control circuit must be designed to output the proper sequence of add and shift pulses. Figure 21-7 shows a state graph for the control circuit. The notation used on this graph is slightly different than that used previously. MN/P_a means if $MN = 1$, then the output P_a is 1 (and the other outputs are 0). M'/P_s means if $M' = 1$ ($M = 0$), then the output P_s is 1 (and the other outputs are 0). In general, we will use the following notation on state diagrams for control networks: X_iX_j/Z_pZ_q means if inputs X_i and X_j are 1 (we don't care what the other input values are), the outputs Z_p and Z_q are 1 (and the other outputs are 0). That is, for a network with four inputs (X_1, X_2, X_3 and X_4) and four outputs (Z_1, Z_2, Z_3 and Z_4), X_1X_4'/Z_2Z_3 is equivalent to 1 - - 0/0110. This type of notation is very useful for large control networks where there are many inputs and outputs.

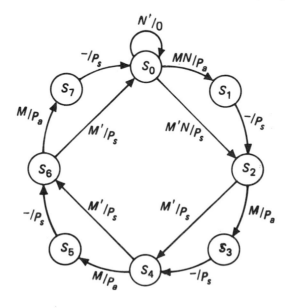

Fig. 21-7.   State graph for multiplier control

In Fig. 21-7, S_0 is the reset state, and the network stays in S_0 until a start signal ($N = 1$) is received. Then, if $M = 1$, an add pulse is generated, and if $M = 0$, a shift pulse is generated. Similarly, in states S_2, S_4 and S_6, M is tested to determine whether to generate an add or shift pulse. A shift pulse is always generated at the next clock time following an add pulse (states S_1, S_3, S_5 and S_7). After four shift pulses have been generated, the control network returns to the initial state and terminates the multiplication process.

As the state graph indicates, the control performs two functions— generating add or shift signals as needed and counting the number of shifts. If the number of bits is large, it is convenient to divide the control network into a counter and an add-shift control as shown in Fig. 21-8(a). First, we will derive a state graph for the add-shift control which tests M and N and outputs the proper sequence of add and shift pulses (Fig. 21-8(b)). Then we will add a completion signal (K) from the counter which stops the multiplier after the proper number of shifts have been completed. Starting in S_0 in Fig. 21-8(b), when a start signal ($N = 1$) is received, if $M = 1$, an add pulse is generated and the network goes to

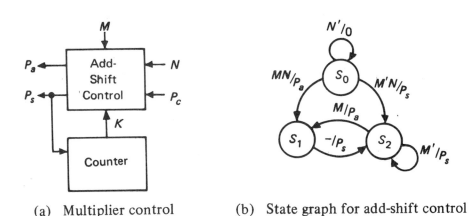

(a) Multiplier control   (b) State graph for add-shift control

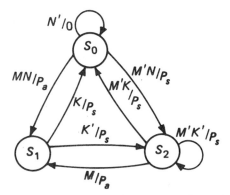

(c) Final state graph for add-shift control

Fig. 21-8

state S_1, and if $M = 0$, a shift pulse is generated and the network goes to S_2. In S_1, a shift pulse is generated since a shift always follows an add. In S_2, the next multiplier bit (M) is tested to determine whether to add or shift. The graph of Fig. 21-8(b) will generate the proper sequence of add and shift pulses, but it has no provision for stopping the multiplier.

In order to determine when the multiplication is completed, the counter is incremented each time a shift pulse is generated. If the multiplier has n bits, n shift pulses are required, and we will design the counter so that a completion signal (K) is generated after n-1 shifts have occurred. Then when K is 1, the network should output one more shift pulse and stop. In Fig. 21-8(c), the control operation is the same as Fig. 21-8(b) as long as $K = 0$. In state S_1, if $K = 1$, we output one more shift pulse and return to S_0. In state S_2, if $K = 1$, we test M as usual. If $M = 0$, we output the final shift pulse and stop; however, if $M = 1$, we add before shifting. The last shift pulse will reset the counter to 0 when the add-shift control returns to the stop state. For example, if $n = 8$, a 3-bit counter is used. After 7 shift pulses, the counter is in state 111 and $K = 1$. The last shift pulse increments the counter so that it returns to state 000.

21.3   Design of a Binary Divider

We will consider the design of a parallel divider for positive binary numbers. As an example, we will design a network to divide a 6-bit dividend by a 3-bit divisor to obtain a 3-bit quotient. The following example illustrates the division process:

$$
\begin{array}{r}
101 \leftarrow \text{quotient} \\
\text{divisor} \rightarrow 110\overline{)100010} \quad (34 \div 6 = 5 \text{ with a remainder of } 4) \\
\underline{110} \qquad \text{dividend} \\
101 \\
\underline{000} \\
1010 \\
\underline{110} \\
100 \leftarrow \text{remainder}
\end{array}
$$

Just as binary multiplication can be carried out as a series of add and shift operations, division can be carried out by a series of subtract and shift operations. To construct the divider, we will use a 7-bit dividend register and a 3-bit divisor register as shown in Fig. 21-9. During the division process, instead of shifting the divisor right before each subtraction, we will shift the dividend to the left. Note that an extra bit is required on the left end of the dividend register so that a bit is not lost when the dividend is shifted left. Instead of using a separate register to store the quotient, we will enter the quotient bit-by-bit into the right end of the dividend register as the dividend is shifted left.

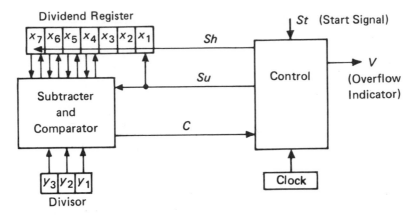

Fig. 21-9. Block diagram for parallel binary divider

The above division example ($34 \div 6$) is reworked below showing the location of the bits in the registers at each clock time. Initially, the dividend and divisor are entered as follows:

0	1	0	0	0	1	0

1	1	0

Subtraction cannot be carried out without a negative result, so we will shift before we subtract. Instead of shifting the divisor one place to the right, we will shift the dividend one place to the left:

```
1 0 0 0 1 0 0 ◄─────── dividing line between dividend and quotient
  1 1 0      ◄─────── Note that after the shift, the rightmost
                      position in the dividend register is "empty."*
```

Subtraction is now carried out and the first quotient digit of 1 is stored in the unused position of the dividend register:

```
0 0 1 0 1 0 1 ◄─────── first quotient digit
```

Next we shift the dividend one place to the left:

```
0 1 0 1 0 1 0
  1 1 0
```

Since subtraction would yield a negative result, we shift the dividend to the left again, and the second quotient bit remains zero:

```
1 0 1 0 1 0 0
  1 1 0
```

A final subtraction is carried out and the third quotient bit is set to 1:

```
0 1 0 0 1 0 1
remainder quotient
```

The final result agrees with that obtained in the first example.

---

*In effect, the quotient bit is initially set to 0 and if subtraction occurs, it is changed to 1.

If as a result of a division operation, the quotient would contain more bits than are available for storing the quotient, we say that an *overflow* has occurred. For the divider of Fig. 21-9, an overflow would occur if the quotient is greater than 7, since only 3 bits are provided to store the quotient. It is not actually necessary to carry out the division to determine if an overflow condition exists, since an initial comparison of the dividend and divisor will tell if the quotient will be too large. For example, if we attempt to divide 34 by 4, the initial contents of the registers would be:

    0 1 0 0 0 1 0
      1 0 0

Since subtraction can be carried out with a non-negative result, we should subtract the divisor from the dividend and enter a quotient bit of 1 in the rightmost place in the dividend register. However, we cannot do this because the right most place contains the least significant bit of the dividend, and entering a quotient bit here would destroy that dividend bit. Therefore, the quotient would be too large to store in the 3 bits we have allocated for it, and we have detected an overflow condition. In general, for Fig. 21-9, if initially $x_7 x_6 x_5 x_4 \geqslant y_3 y_2 y_1$ (i.e., if the left four bits of the dividend register exceed or equal the divisor), the quotient will be greater than 7 and an overflow occurs.

The operation of the divider can be explained in terms of the block diagram of Fig. 21-9. A shift signal (Sh) will shift the dividend one place to the left. A subtract signal (Su) will subtract the divisor from the four leftmost bits in the dividend register and set the quotient bit (the rightmost bit in the dividend register) to 1. If the divisor is greater than the four leftmost dividend bits, the comparator output is $C = 0$; otherwise, $C = 1$. The control circuit generates the required sequence of shift and subtract pulses. Whenever $C = 0$, subtraction cannot occur without a negative result, so a shift signal is generated. Whenever $C = 1$, a subtract signal is generated and the quotient bit is set to one.

Figure 21-10 shows the state diagram for the control circuit. Initially, the 6-bit dividend and 3-bit divisor are entered into the appropriate registers. The circuit remains in the stop state (S_0) until a start signal (St) is applied to the control circuit. If the initial value of C is 1, the quotient would require four or more bits. Since space is only provided for a three-bit quotient, this condition constitutes an overflow, so the divider is stopped and the overflow indicator is set by the V output. Normally, the initial value of C is 0, so a shift will occur first and the control circuit will go to state S_1. Then, if $C = 1$ subtraction occurs. After the subtraction is completed, C will always be 0, so the next clock pulse will produce a shift. This process continues until three shifts have occurred and the control is in state S_3. Then a final subtraction occurs if necessary, and the control returns to the stop state. For this example, we will assume that when the start signal (St) occurs, it will be 1 for one clock time, and then it will remain 0 until the control network is back in state S_0. Therefore, St will always be 0 in states S_1, S_2 and S_3.

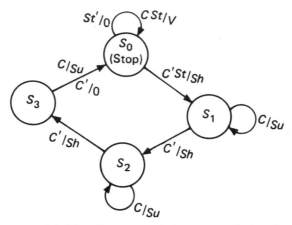

Fig. 21-10. State graph for control circuit

Table 21-2 gives the state table for the control circuit. Since we assumed that $St = 0$ in states S_1, S_2 and S_3, the next states and outputs are don't cares for these states when $St = 1$. The entries in the output table indicate which outputs are 1. For example, the entry Sh means $Sh = 1$ and the other outputs are 0. Using the state assignment shown in Table 21-2 for J-K flip-flops A and B, the following equations can be derived for the control circuit:

$$J_A = BC', \qquad K_A = B', \qquad J_B = St\,C', \qquad K_B = AC'$$
$$Sh = (St + B)C', \qquad Su = C(B + A), \qquad V = C \cdot St \qquad (21\text{-}1)$$

Table 21-2. State Table for Fig. 21-10

AB		St C 00	01	11	10	00	01	11	10
00	S_0	S_0	S_0	S_0	S_1	0	0	V	Sh
01	S_1	S_2	S_1	–	–	Sh	Su	–	–
11	S_2	S_3	S_2	–	–	Sh	Su	–	–
10	S_3	S_0	S_0	–	–	0	Su	–	–

Figure 21-11 shows a logic diagram for the subtracter/comparator, dividend register and control network. The subtracter is constructed using four full subtracters. When the numbers are entered into the divisor and dividend registers, the borrow signal will propagate through the full subtracters before the subtracter output is transferred to the dividend register. If the last borrow signal (b_8) is 1, this means that the result would be negative if subtraction were carried out. Hence, if b_8 is 1, the divisor is greater than $x_7 x_6 x_5 x_4$, and $C = 0$. Therefore, $C = b_8'$ and a separate comparator circuit is unnecessary. Gating is added to the flip-flops in the dividend register so that if $Sh = 1$ a left shift will take place when the clock pulse occurs, and if $Su = 1$ the subtracter output will be transferred to the dividend register when the clock pulse occurs. For example,

$$D_4 = Su \cdot d_4 + Sh \cdot x_3 = x_4^+$$

If $Su = 1$ and $Sh = 0$, $x_4^+ = d_4$ and the subtracter output is transferred to the register of flip-flops. If $Su = 0$ and $Sh = 1$, $x_4^+ = x_3$ and a left shift occurs. Since $D_1 = Su$, the quotient bit (x_1) is cleared when shifting occurs ($Su = 0$) and the quotient bit is set to 1 during subtraction ($Su = 1$). Note that the clock pulse is gated so that flip-flops x_7, x_6, x_5, x_4 and x_1 are clocked when Su or Sh is 1, while flip-flops x_3 and x_2 are clocked only when Sh is 1.

Fig. 21-11. Logic diagram for binary divider

PROBLEMS

21.1   Design a serial subtracter with accumulator for 4-bit binary numbers. Assume that negative numbers are represented by 2's complement. (Use a network of the form of Fig. 21-1, except that the serial adder is replaced with a serial subtracter.) Use clocked J-K flip-flops and any kind of gates.

21.2   A network which adds one to the contents of a shift register has the following form:

The control circuit puts out a pulse p_i to set the ONE ADDER to the proper initial state, followed by the required number of shift pulses (p_s). Design the box labeled "ONE ADDER" using NOR gates and a clocked J-K flip-flop with set and clear inputs.

Example: Contents of shift register before: 000010111
             Contents of shift register after p_i and 9 shift pulses: 000011000

21.3   Design a parallel binary multiplier which multiplies two 3-bit binary numbers to form a 6-bit product. This multiplier is to be a combinational network consisting of an array of full adders and AND gates (no flip-flops). Demonstrate that your network works by showing all of the signals which are present when 111 is multiplied by 111.

(*Hint:*   The AND gates can be used to multiply by 0 or 1 and the full adders can be used to add 2 bits plus a carry. Six full adders are required.)

21.4   The binary multiplier of Fig. 21-6 is to be redesigned so that whenever addition occurs the multiplier bit (M) will be set to 0. Thus, if M is 1 at a given clock time and addition takes place, M will be 0 at the next clock time. Thus, we can always add when $M = 1$ and always shift when $M = 0$. This means that the control circuit will not have to change state when $M = 1$, and the number of states can be reduced from 8 to 5. Draw the resulting state graph for the multiplier control.

21.5 In order to allow for a larger number of bits, the control circuit of the binary divider is to be redesigned so that it uses a separate counter and a subtract-shift control which is analogous to Fig. 21-8(a). Draw the state graph for the subtract-shift control.

21.6 This problem concerns the design of a parallel divider to divide two positive binary numbers (8 bits ÷ 4 bits). The design should be similar to the one shown in Fig. 21-11, except that in order to speed up operation of the divider, a shift and subtract operation should take place simultaneously during a single clock pulse. In order to accomplish this, the wires from the dividend register to the full subtracter inputs must be shifted one position with respect to the wires from the full subtracter outputs to the dividend register. In this way the division can be completed in four clock times.

   a.   Draw a block diagram for the divider using

      (1)   8 clocked D flip-flops
      (2)   5 full subtracters to perform the necessary subtraction
      (3)   a 4-bit register which holds the divisor
      (4)   a block labeled "control circuit" which puts out the required four pulses when a start signal is applied
      (5)   any other necessary gates and inverters

      Show in detail how the full subtracter inputs and outputs are connected and how the D flip-flops are connected. The difference output from the leftmost subtracter is not used. Note that it will be necessary to gate the subtracter outputs so that when the last borrow bit is $B = 1, 0$ will be subtracted from the dividend register during the shift and subtract operation, and when the borrow bit is 0, the divisor will be subtracted from the leftmost 5 bits of the dividend register during the shift and subtract operation.

   b.   If the dividend register initially contains 10010000 and the divisor register contains 1101, show the contents of the dividend register after each clock pulse.

   c.   Draw the state graph for the control circuit assuming that once the start signal (N) is set to 1 it will remain 1 for one or more clock times past the completion of the division operation. Then the start signal will be changed to 0 some time between the completion of the division and the start of the next division cycle.

   (Note: Design of an overflow detector for this type of divider is fairly difficult and is not required for this problem.)

21.7 A serial logic unit has two 8-bit shift registers, X and Y, as shown below. Inputs K_1 and K_2 determine the operation to be performed on X and Y. When $N = 1$, X and Y are shifted into the logic network one bit at a time and replaced with new values. If $K_1 K_2 = 00$, X is complemented and Y is unchanged. If $K_1 K_2 = 01$, X and Y are interchanged. If $K_1 K_2 = 10$, Y is set to 0 and each bit of X is replaced with the exclusive-OR of the corresponding bits of X and Y; that is, the new value of x_i is $x_i \oplus y_i$. If $K_1 K_2$ = 11, X is unchanged and Y is set to all 1's.

a. Derive logic equations for x_{in} and y_{in}.

b. Derive a state graph for the control network. Assume that once N is set to 1 it will remain 1 until all 8 bits have been processed. Then N will be changed back to 0 some time before the start of the next computation cycle.

c. Realize the logic network using two 4-to-1 multiplexers and a minimum number of added gates.

d. Realize the control network using a 74S163 counter.

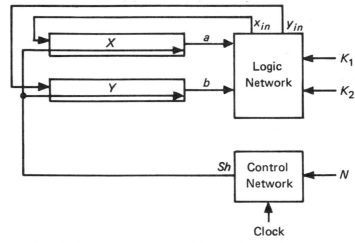

21.8 a. Draw a block diagram for a parallel multiplier that can multiply two binary numbers, where the multiplier is 3 bits and the multiplicand is 4 bits. Use an 8-bit shift register along with other necessary blocks.

b. Draw a state graph for the multiplier control.

c. Illustrate the operation of the multiplier when 11 is multiplied by 5. Specify the sequence of add and shift pulses generated by the control network and specify the contents of the 8-bit register at each clock time.

d. Draw the logic diagram for the multiplier using two 74178 shift registers, four full adders, two J-K flip-flops and any necessary gates.

21.9 A serial Boolean logic unit has two 16-bit shift registers, A and B. A control signal (C) is used to select the Boolean operation to be performed. If $C = 0$, the contents of A are serially replaced by the bit-by-bit Boolean AND of A and B. If $C = 1$, the contents of A are serially replaced by the bit-by-bit exclusive-OR of A and B. After the numbers have been placed in A and B, and C is set to 0 or 1, a start signal (N) sets the circuit in operation. A counter is used to count the number of shifts. When the counter reaches state 15, it outputs a signal $K = 1$, which causes the control network to stop after one more shift. Assume that N remains 1 and C does not change until the operation is completed. The control then remains in the stop state until N is changed back to 0.

a. Draw a block diagram of the system, which includes the shift registers, the counter, the control circuit, and a logic network that generates the serial input (SI) to the A register.

b. Draw a state graph for the control network (3 states).

c. Design the control network using a PLA and D flip-flops.

d. Design a logic network that generates SI.

Programmed Exercise 21.10

This exercise concerns the design of a network which forms the 2's complement of a 16-bit binary number. The network consists of three main components—a 16-bit shift register which initially holds the number to be complemented, a control network, and a counter which counts the number of shifts. The control network processes the number in the shift register one bit at a time and stores the 2's complement back in the shift register. Draw a block diagram of the network. Show the necessary inputs and outputs for the control network including a start signal (N) which is used to initiate the 2's complement operation.

Turn to the next page and check your answer.

Programmed Exercise 21.11

This exercise concerns the design of a binary divider to divide an 8-bit number by a 4-bit number to find a 4-bit quotient. The right 4 bits of the dividend register should be used to store the quotient. Draw a block diagram for the divider.

Turn to the next page and check your answer.

Answer to 21.10:

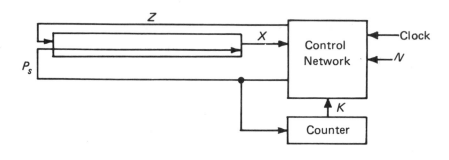

State a rule for forming the 2's complement which is appropriate for use with the above block diagram.

Turn to the next page and check your answer.

Answer to 21.11:

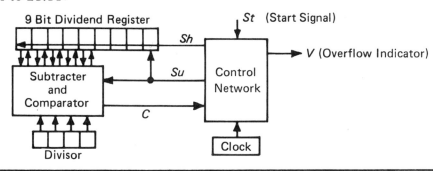

If the contents of the dividend register is initially 10000111 and the divisor is 1101, show the contents of the dividend register after each of the first three clock pulses. Also, indicate whether a shift or subtract should occur next.

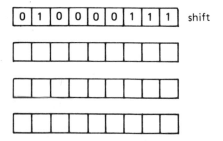

Turn to the next page and check your answer.

Answer: Starting with the least significant bit, complement all of the bits to the left of the first 1.

Draw a state graph for the control network (3 states) which implements the above rule. The 2's complement operation should be initiated when $N = 1$. (Assume that N will be 1 for only one clock time.) When drawing your graph, do *not* include any provision for stopping the network. (In the next step you will be asked to add the signal K to your state graph so that the network will stop after 16 shifts.) Explain the meaning of each state in your graph.

Turn to the next page and check your answer.

Answer:

```
0 1 0 0 0 0 1 1 1   shift
1 0 0 0 0 1 1 1 0   subtract
0 0 0 1 1 1 1 1 1   shift
0 0 1 1 1 1 1 1 0   shift
```

Now show the remaining steps in the computation, and check your answer by conversion to decimal.

Turn to the next page and check your answer.

Answer:

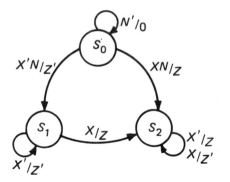

S_0 reset

S_1 no 1 received, don't complement X

S_2 a 1 has been received, complement X

The counter will generate a completion signal (K) when it reaches state 15. Modify your state graph so that when $K = 1$, the network will complete the 2's complement operation and return to the initial state. Also add the P_S output in the appropriate places.

Turn to the next page and check your answer.

Answer:

$$\begin{array}{cccccccccc}
0 & 1 & 1 & 1 & 1 & 1 & 1 & 0 & 0 & \text{subtract} \\
0 & 0 & 0 & 1 & 0 & 1 & 1 & 0 & 1 & \text{shift} \\
0 & 0 & 1 & 0 & 1 & 1 & 0 & 1 & 0 & \text{(finished)}
\end{array}$$

remainder   quotient

If the dividend register initially contained 001101011 and the divisor is 0101, can division take place? Explain.

Turn to the next page and check your answer.

NETWORKS FOR ARITHMETIC OPERATIONS / **475**

Answer: Check the input labels on all arrows leaving each state of your graph. Make sure that two of the labels on arrows leaving a given state cannot have the value 1 at the same time. Make any necessary corrections to your graph and then turn to the next page to check your final answer.

Answer: No. Since $0110 > 0101$, subtraction should occur first, but there is no place to store the quotient bit. In other words, the quotient would be greater than 4 bits so that an overflow would occur.

Draw a state graph for the divider which will produce the necessary sequence of Su and Sh signals. Assume that the comparator output is $C = 1$ if the upper 5 bits of the dividend register is greater than the divisor. Include a stop state in your graph which is different than the reset state. Assume that the start signal (N) will remain 1 until the division is completed. The network should go to the stop state when division is complete or when an overflow is detected. The network should then reset when $N = 0$.

Turn to the next page to check your answer.

Answer:

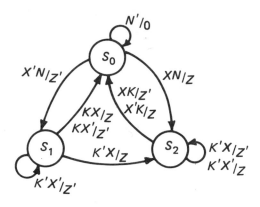

NOTE: P_S should be added to the graph everywhere z or z' appears.

Answer:

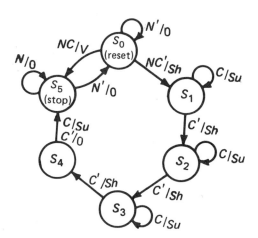

22

STATE MACHINE DESIGN
WITH SM CHARTS

OBJECTIVES

1. Explain the different parts of an SM chart.

2. Given the input sequence to a state machine, determine the output sequence from its SM chart, and construct a timing diagram.

3. Convert a state graph to an SM chart.

4. Construct an SM chart for the control network for a multiplier, divider, or other simple digital system.

5. Determine the next state and output equations for a state machine by tracing

6. Realize an SM chart using a PLA or ROM and flip-flops.

STUDY GUIDE

1. Study Section 22.1, *State Machine Charts*.

    a. For the example of Fig. 22-2, if $X_1 = 0$ and $X_2 = 1$ when the machine is in state S_1, specify the values of all of the outputs and the exit path number.

    b. For Figs. 22-6(a) and (b), trace the link paths and determine the outputs when $X_1 = X_3 = 1$.

    c. Verify that the SM chart and state graph of Fig. 22-7 are equivalent.

    d. Construct a timing chart for Fig. 22-7(b) when the input sequence is $X = 0, 1, 1, 0$.

    e. Work Problems 22.1, 22.2 and 22.6.

2. Study Section 22.2, *Derivation of SM Charts.*

    a. Using the SM chart of Fig. 22-9 to determine when to subtract and when to shift for the binary divider of Fig. 21-9, show the contents of the dividend register at each time step when 28 is divided by 5.

    b. Compare the SM chart of Fig. 22-10 with the state graph of Fig. 21-8 and verify that in each state they will generate the same outputs when the inputs are the same.

    c. Compare the flowchart for the dice game (Fig. 22-12) with the SM chart. Note that the "ROLL DICE" box on the flow chart requires two states to implement on the SM chart. In the first state, the machine waits for the roll button to be pressed; in the second state, it generates a roll signal which lasts until the roll button is released. In state S_1, four variables are tested; if they are all 0, SP is generated so that the sum will be stored in the point register at the same time the transition from S_1 to S_4 occurs.

    d. Work Problems 22.7, 22.8 and 22.9.

3. Study Section 22.3, *Realization of SM Charts.*

    a. For Fig. 22-7(b) find simplified equations for A^+ and B^+.

    b. Verify Tables 22-1 and 22-2. For Table 22-2, why is $SP = 1$ only in row 7, and $WIN = 1$ in both rows 8 and 9?

    c. Expand row 17 of Table 22-2 to give the corresponding rows of the ROM table.

    d. Work Problems 22.11a, 22.12, 22.13a and 22.14.

22. STATE MACHINE DESIGN WITH SM CHARTS

    Another name for a sequential network is an algorithmic state machine or simply a state machine. These names are often used when the sequential network is used to control a digital system that carries out a step-by-step procedure or algorithm. The state graphs in Figs. 21-3, 21-7, 21-8 and 21-10 define state machines for controlling adders, multipliers and dividers. As an alternative to using state graphs, a special type of flowchart, called a state machine flowchart or SM chart, may be used to describe the behavior of a state machine. This unit describes the properties of SM charts and how they are used in the design of state machines.

22.1   STATE MACHINE CHARTS

Just as flowcharts are useful in software design, flowcharts are useful in the hardware design of digital systems. In this section we introduce a special type of flowchart called a sequential machine flowchart, or SM chart for short. SM charts are also called ASM (algorithmic state machine) charts. We will see that the SM chart offers several advantages. It is often easier to understand the operation of a digital system by inspection of the SM chart instead of the equivalent state graph. A given SM chart can be converted into several equivalent forms, and each form leads directly to a hardware realization.

An SM chart differs from an ordinary flowchart in that certain specific rules must be followed in constructing the SM chart. When these rules are followed, the SM chart is equivalent to a state graph, and it leads directly to a hardware realization. Figure 22-1 shows the three principal components of an SM chart. The state of the system is represented by a *state box*. The state box may contain an *output list*, and a *state code* may be placed outside the box at the top. The *state name* is placed in a circle to the left of the state box. A *decision box* is represented by a diamond-shaped symbol with true and false branches.. The *condition* placed in the box is a Boolean expression that is evaluated to determine which branch to take. The *conditional output box*, which has curved ends, contains a *conditional output list*. The conditional outputs depend on both the state of the system and the inputs.

An SM chart is constructed from *SM blocks*. Each SM block (Fig. 22-2) contains exactly one state box together with the decision boxes and conditional output boxes associated with that state. An SM block has exactly one *entrance path* and one or more *exit paths*. Each SM block describes the machine operation during the time that the machine is in one state. When a digital system enters the state associated with a given SM block, the outputs on the output list in the state box become true. The conditions in the decision boxes are evaluated to determine which path (or paths) are followed through the SM block. When a conditional output box is encountered along such a path, the corresponding conditional outputs become true. A path through an SM block from entrance to exit is referred to as a *link path*.

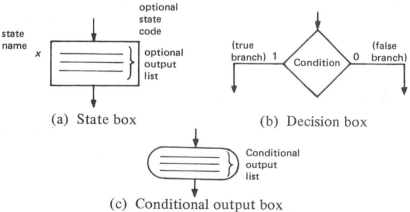

(a) State box   (b) Decision box

(c) Conditional output box

Fig. 22-1.   Components of an SM chart

Fig. 22-2. **Example of an SM block**

For the example of Fig. 22-2, when state S_1 is entered, outputs Z_1 and Z_2 become 1. If inputs X_1 and X_2 are both equal to 0, Z_3 and Z_4 are also 1, and at the end of the state time the machine goes to the next state via exit path 1. On the other hand, if $X_1 = 1$ and $X_3 = 0$, the output Z_5 is 1 and exit to the next state will occur via exit path 3.

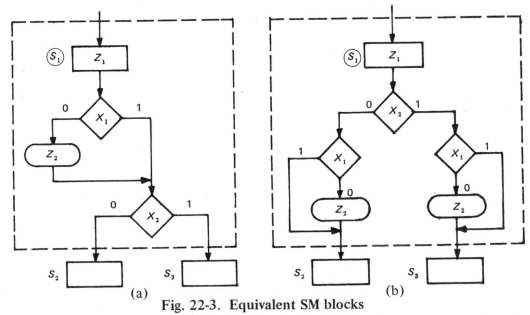

Fig. 22-3. **Equivalent SM blocks**

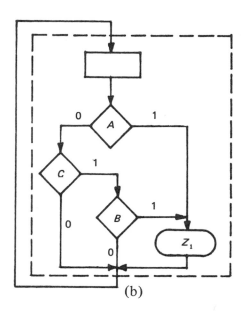

(a)

(b)

Fig. 22-4. Equivalent SM charts for a combinational network

A given SM block can generally be drawn in several different forms. Figure 22-3 shows two equivalent SM blocks. In both (a) and (b), the output $Z_2 = 1$ if $X_1 = 0$; the next state is S_2 if $X_2 = 1$ and S_3 if $X_2 = 0$.

The SM chart of Fig. 22-4(a) represents a combinational network since there is only one state and no state change occurs. The output is $Z_1 = 1$ if $A + BC = 1$; else $Z_1 = 0$. Figure 22-4(b) shows an equivalent SM chart in which the input variables are tested individually. The output is $Z_1 = 1$ if $A = 1$ or if $A = 0$, $B = 1$ and $C = 1$. Hence,

$$Z_1 = A + A'BC = A + BC$$

which is the same output function realized by the SM chart of Fig. 22-4(a).

Certain rules must be followed when constructing an SM block. First, for every valid combination of input variables, there must be exactly one exit path defined. This is necessary since each allowable input combination must

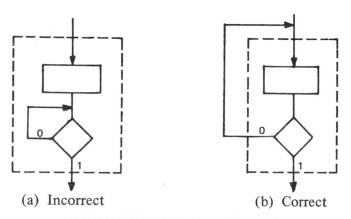

(a) Incorrect

(b) Correct

Fig. 22-5. SM block with feedback

lead to a single next state. Second, no internal feedback within an SM block is allowed. Figure 22-5 shows an incorrect and correct way of drawing an SM block with feedback.

As shown in Fig. 22-6(a), an SM block can have several parallel paths which lead to the same exit path, and more than one of these paths can be "active" at the same time. For example, if $X_1 = X_2 = 1$ and $X_3 = 0$, the link paths marked with dashed lines are active, and the outputs Z_1, Z_2 and Z_3 will be 1. Although Fig. 22-6(a) would not be a valid flowchart for a program for a serial computer, it presents no problems for a state machine implementation. The state machine can have a multiple-output network that generates Z_1, Z_2 and Z_3 at the same time. Figure 22-6(b) shows a serial SM block, which is equivalent to Fig. 22-6(a). In the serial block only one active link path between entrance and exit is possible. For any combination of input values the outputs will be the same as in the equivalent parallel form. The link path for $X_1 = X_2 = 1$ and $X_3 = 0$ is shown with a dashed line, and the outputs encountered on this path are Z_1, Z_2 and Z_3. Regardless of whether the SM block is drawn in serial or parallel form, all of the tests take place within one clock time.

A state graph for a sequential machine is easy to convert to an equivalent SM chart. The state graph of Fig. 22-7(a) has both "Moore" and "Mealy" outputs. The equivalent SM chart has three blocks — one for each state. The

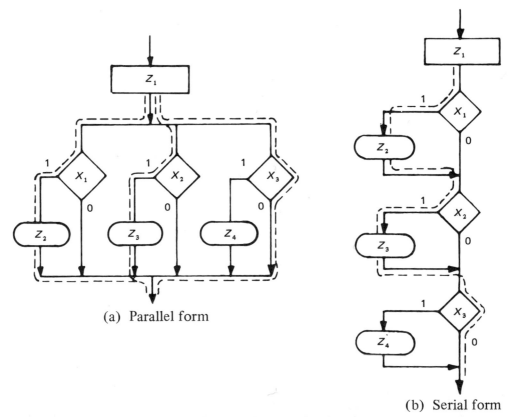

(a) Parallel form

(b) Serial form

Fig. 22-6. Equivalent SM blocks

"Moore" outputs (Z_a, Z_b, Z_c) are placed in the state boxes since they do not depend on the input. The "Mealy" outputs (Z_1, Z_2) appear in conditional output boxes since they depend on both the state and input. In this example, each SM block has only one decision box since only one input variable must be tested. For both the state graph and SM chart, Z_c is always 1 in state S_2. If $X = 0$, $Z_1 = 1$ and the next state is S_0. If $X = 1$, $Z_2 = 1$ and the next state is S_2.

(a) State graph

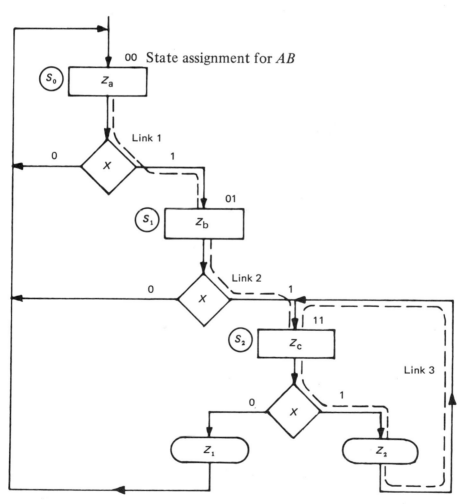

(b) Equivalent SM chart

Fig. 22-7. Conversion of a state graph to an SM chart

Fig. 22-8. Timing chart for Fig. 22-7

Figure 22-8 shows a timing chart for the SM chart of Fig. 22-7 with an input sequence $X = 1, 1, 1, 0, 0, 0$. In this example, all state changes occur immediately after the rising edge of the clock. Since the Moore outputs (Z_a, Z_b, Z_c) depend on the state, they can only change immediately following a state change. The Mealy outputs (Z_1, Z_2) can change immediately after a state change or an input change. In any case, all outputs will have their correct value during the active edge of the clock.

22.2 DERIVATION OF SM CHARTS

The method used to derive an SM chart for a sequential control network is similar to that used to derive the state graph. First, we should draw a block diagram of the system we are controlling. Next we should define the required input and output signals to the control network. Then we can construct an SM chart that tests the input signals and generates the proper sequence of output signals.

In this section, we will give several examples of SM charts. The first example is an SM chart for control of the parallel binary divider shown in Fig. 21-9. As described in Section 21.3, binary division requires a series of subtract and shift operations. Derivation of an SM chart to generate the proper sequence of subtract and shift signals is very similar to derivation of the state graph of Fig. 21-10. For the SM chart of Fig. 22-9, S_0 is the starting state. In S_0, the start signal (St) is tested, and if $St = 1$, the compare signal (C) is tested. If $C = 1$, the quotient would be larger than 3 bits, so an overflow signal ($V = 1$) is generated and no state change occurs. If $C = 0$, Sh becomes 1, so at

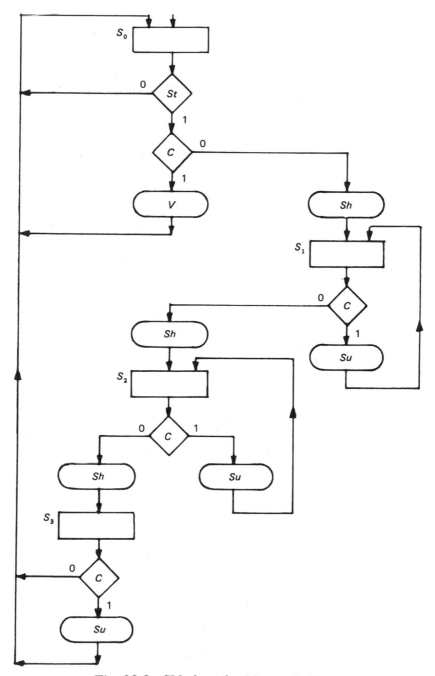

Fig. 22-9. SM chart for binary divider

the next clock the dividend is shifted left and the state changes to S_1. C is tested in state S_1. If $C = 1$, subtraction is possible, so Su becomes 1 and no state change occurs. If $C = 0$, $Sh = 1$ and the dividend is shifted as the state changes to S_2. The action in state S_2 is identical to that in state S_1. In state S_3 the next state is always S_0, and $C = 1$ causes subtraction to occur.

Next we will derive the SM chart for the multiplier control of Fig. 21-8(a). This control generates the required sequence of add and shift pulses for a binary multiplier of the type shown in Fig. 21-6. The counter counts the number of shifts and outputs $K = 1$ just before the last shift occurs. The SM chart for the multiplier control (Fig. 22-10) corresponds closely to the state graph of Fig. 21-8(c). In state S_0, when the start signal N is 1, the multiplier bit M is tested to determine whether to add or shift. If $M = 1$, an add signal is generated and the next state is S_1. In S_1 a shift signal is generated since a shift must always follow an add. If $K = 1$, the network returns to S_0 at the time of the last shift; otherwise, the next state is S_2. In S_2, M is tested to determine whether to add or shift. The add is always followed by a shift (state S_1), and after a shift, S_2 is re-entered unless $K = 1$.

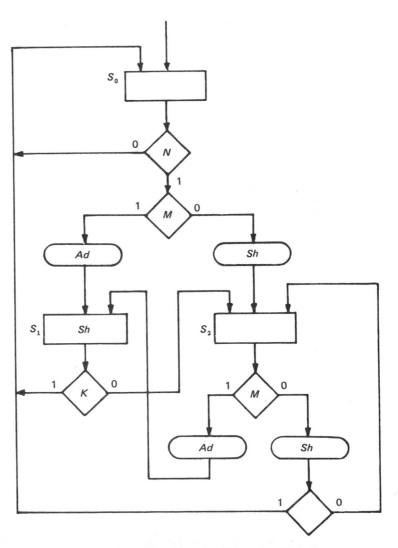

Fig. 22-10. SM chart for binary multiplier

Fig. 22-11. **Block diagram for dice game**

As a third example of SM chart construction, we will design an electronic dice game. Figure 22-11 shows the block diagram for the dice game. Two counters are used to simulate the roll of the dice. Each counter counts in the sequence 1, 2, 3, 4, 5, 6, 1, 2, ... Thus, after the "roll" of the dice, the sum of the values in the two counters will be in the range 2 through 12. The rules of the game are as follows:

1. After the first roll of the dice, the player wins if the sum is 7 or 11. He loses if the sum is 2, 3 or 12. Otherwise, the sum which he obtained on the first roll is referred to as his "point" and he must roll the dice again.
2. On the second or subsequent roll of the dice, he wins if the sum equals his point, and he loses if the sum is 7. Otherwise, he must roll again until he finally wins or loses.

The inputs to the dice game come from two push buttons*, RB (roll button) and RESET. RESET is used to initiate a new game. When the roll button is pushed, the dice counters count at a high speed, so the values cannot be read on the display. When the roll button is released, the values in the two counters are displayed and the game can proceed. If the WIN light or LOSE light is not on, the player must push the roll button again.

Figure 22-12 shows a flowchart for the dice game. After rolling the dice, the sum is tested. If it is 7 or 11, the player wins; if it is 2, 3 or 12, he loses. Otherwise the sum is saved in the point register and the player rolls again. If the new sum equals the point, he wins; if it is 7, he loses. Otherwise, he rolls again. After winning or losing, he must push reset to begin a new game.

---

*We will assume at this point that the push buttons are properly debounced and that changes in RB are properly synchronized with the clock. Methods for debouncing and synchronization are discussed in later units.

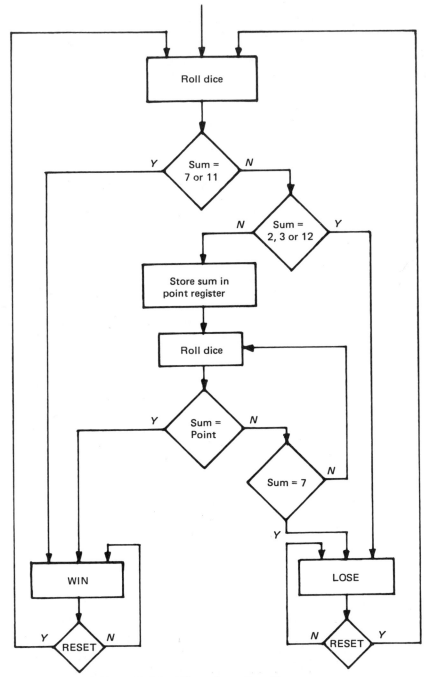

Fig. 22-12. Flowchart for dice game

The components for the dice game shown in the block diagram (Fig. 22-11) include an adder which adds the two counter outputs, a register to store the "point", test logic to determine conditions for win or lose, and a control network. Input signals to the control network are defined as follows:

$D_7 = 1$ if the sum of the dice is 7
$D_{11} = 1$ if the sum of the dice is 11
$D_{2312} = 1$ if the sum of the dice is 2, 3 or 12
EQ = 1 if the sum of the dice equals the number stored in the point
       register
RB = 1 when the roll button is pressed
RESET = 1 when the reset button is pressed
Outputs from the control network are defined as follows:
ROLL = 1 enables the dice counters
SP = 1 causes the sum to be stored in the point register
WIN = 1 turns on the win light
LOSE = 1 turns on the lose light

We can now convert the flowchart for the dice game to an SM chart for the control network using the control signals defined above. Figure 22-13 shows the resulting SM chart. The control network waits in state S_0 until the roll button is pressed (RB = 1). Then it goes to state S_1, and the roll counters are enabled as long as RB = 1. As soon as the roll button is released (RB = 0), D_7 and D_{11} are tested. If the sum is 7 or 11, it goes to state S_2 and turns on the WIN light; otherwise, D_{2312} is tested. If the sum is 2, 3 or 12, it goes to state S_3 and turns on the LOSE light; otherwise, the signal SP becomes 1 and the sum is stored in the point register. It then enters S_4 and waits for the player to "roll the dice" again. In S_5, after the roll button is released, if EQ = 1, the sum equals the point and state S_2 is entered to indicate a win. If $D_7 = 1$, the sum is 7 and S_3 is entered to indicate a lose. Otherwise, control returns to S_4 so that the player can roll again. When in S_2 or S_3, the game is reset to S_0 when the RESET button is pressed.

22.3 REALIZATION OF SM CHARTS

Methods used to realize SM charts are similar to the methods used to realize state graphs. As with any sequential network, the realization will consist of a combinational subnetwork together with flip-flops for storing the state of the network (see Fig. 14-13). The first step is to make a state assignment which relates the flip-flop states to the network states. Then the next state and output equations can be derived and realized using logic gates, a ROM or a PLA.

As an example, consider the SM chart of Fig. 22-7(b). We have made the state assignment $AB = 00$ for S_0, $AB = 01$ for S_1 and $AB = 11$ for S_2. After a state assignment has been made, output and next state equations can be read directly from the SM chart. Since the Moore output Z_a is 1 only in state 00, $Z_a = A'B'$. Similarly, $Z_b = A'B$ and $Z_c = AB$. The conditional output $Z_1 = ABX'$ since the only link path through Z_1 starts with $AB = 11$ and takes the $X = 0$ branch. Similarly, $Z_2 = ABX$. There are three link paths (labeled link 1, link 2 and link 3), which terminate in a state that has B = 1. Link 1 starts with a present state $AB = 00$, takes the $X = 1$ branch and terminates on a state in which

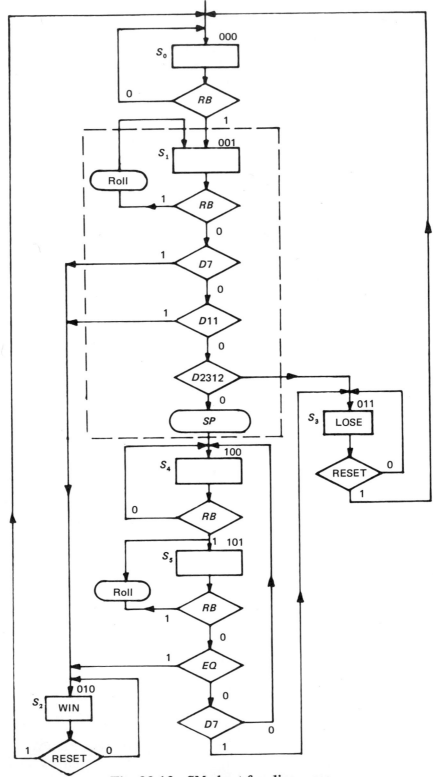

Fig. 22-13. SM chart for dice game

$B = 1$. Therefore, the next state of B (B^+) equals 1 when $A'B'X = 1$. Link 2 starts in state 01, takes the $X = 1$ branch, and ends in state 11, so B^+ has a term $A'BX$. Similarly, B^+ has a term ABX from link 3. The next state equation for B thus has 3 terms corresponding to the 3 link paths:

$$B^+ = \underbrace{A'B'X}_{\text{link 1}} + \underbrace{A'BX}_{\text{link 2}} + \underbrace{ABX}_{\text{link 3}}$$

Similarly, two link paths terminate in a state with $A = 1$, so

$$A^+ = A'BX + ABX$$

The above output and next state equations can be simplified with a Karnaugh map using the unused state assignment ($AB = 10$) as a don't care condition.

As illustrated above, the next state equation for a flip-flop Q can be derived from the SM chart as follows:

1. Identify all of the states in which $Q = 1$.
2. For each of these states, find all of the link paths that lead *into* the state
3. For each of these link paths, find a term that is 1 when the link path is followed. That is, for a link path from S_i to S_j, the term will be 1 if the machine is in state S_i and the conditions for exiting to S_j are satisfied.
4. The expression for Q^+ (the next state of Q) is formed by ORing together the terms found in step 3.

Next, consider the SM chart for the divider control (Fig. 22-9). We can realize this SM chart using gates and flip-flops in the same way we realized the state graph (Fig. 21-10), which leads to the network of Fig. 21-11. As an alternative, we will realize the SM chart with a PLA or ROM and two D flip-flops, using a network of the form shown in Fig. 19-14. As indicated in Table 22-1, the PLA has 4 inputs and 5 outputs. Each row in the table corresponds to one of the link paths in the SM chart. Since S_0 has 3 exit paths, the table has 3 rows for present state S_0. The first row corresponds to the $St = 0$ exit path, so the next state and outputs are 0. In the next row, $St = 1$ and $C = 0$, so the next state is 01 and the other PLA outputs are 100. Since St is not tested in states S_1, S_2 and S_3, St is a don't care in the corresponding rows. The outputs for each row can be filled in by tracing the corresponding link paths on the SM chart. For the last row, the link path from S_3 to S_0 passes through the conditional output Su when $C = 1$, so $Su = 1$ in this row.

If a ROM is used instead of a PLA, each row in the PLA table which has a dash must be replaced with two rows. For example, the first row is replaced with

$$0\,0\,0\,0 \qquad 0\,0\,0\,0\,0$$
$$0\,0\,0\,1 \qquad 0\,0\,0\,0\,0$$

since a dash in the C column of the PLA table indicates that the outputs are the same for $C = 0$ and $C = 1$. The final ROM table will have $2^4 = 16$ rows since there are 4 input variables.

Finally, we will realize the SM chart for the dice game using a PLA and three D flip-flops as shown in Fig. 22-14. The PLA has 9 inputs and 7 outputs,

Table 22-1. PLA Table for Divider Control

present state	PLA inputs $Q_1 Q_2$ St C	PLA outputs Q_1^+ Q_2^+ Sh Su V
S_0	0 0 0 - 0 0 1 0 0 0 1 1	0 0 0 0 0 0 1 1 0 0 0 0 0 0 1
S_1	0 1 - 0 0 1 - 1	1 0 1 0 0 0 1 0 1 0
S_2	1 0 - 0 1 0 - 1	1 1 1 0 0 1 0 0 1 0
S_3	1 1 - 0 1 1 - 1	0 0 0 0 0 0 0 0 1 0

which are listed at the top of Table 22-2. In state $ABC = 000$, the next state is $A^+B^+C^+ = 000$ or 001 depending on the value of RB. Since state 001 has five exit paths, the PLA table has five corresponding rows. When RB is 1, ROLL is 1 and there is no state change. When RB = 0 and D_7 or D_{11} is 1, the next state is 010. When RB = 0 and $D_{2312} = 1$, the next state is 011. For the link path from state 001 to 100, RB, D_7, D_{11} and D_{2312} are all 0, and SP is a conditional

Fig. 22-14. PLA realization of dice game controller

Table 22-2. PLA Table for Dice Game

	ABC	RB	RESET	D_7	D_{11}	D_{2312}	EQ	A^+	B^+	C^+	WIN	LOSE	Roll	SP
1	000	0	-	-	-	-	-	0	0	0	0	0	0	0
2	000	1	-	-	-	-	-	0	0	1	0	0	0	0
3	001	1	-	-	-	-	-	0	0	1	0	0	1	0
4	001	0	-	1	-	-	-	0	1	0	0	0	0	0
5	001	0	-	0	1	-	-	0	1	0	0	0	0	0
6	001	0	-	0	0	1	-	0	1	1	0	0	0	0
7	001	0	-	0	0	0	-	1	0	0	0	0	0	1
8	010	-	0	-	-	-	-	0	1	0	1	0	0	0
9	010	-	1	-	-	-	-	0	0	0	1	0	0	0
10	011	-	0	-	-	-	-	0	1	1	0	1	0	0
11	011	-	1	-	-	-	-	0	0	0	0	1	0	0
12	100	0	-	-	-	-	-	1	0	0	0	0	0	0
13	100	1	-	-	-	-	-	1	0	1	0	0	0	0
14	101	1	-	-	-	-	-	1	0	1	0	0	1	0
15	101	0	-	-	-	-	1	0	1	0	0	0	0	0
16	101	0	-	0	-	-	0	1	0	0	0	0	0	0
17	101	0	-	1	-	-	0	0	1	1	0	0	0	0

output. This path corresponds to row 7 of the PLA table, which has SP = 1 and $A^+B^+C^+$ = 100. In state 010, the WIN signal is always on, and the next state is 010 or 000 depending on the value of RESET. Similarly, LOSE is always on in state 011. In state 101, $A^+B^+C^+$ = 010 if EQ = 1; otherwise, $A^+B^+C^+$ = 011 or 100 depending on the value of D_7.

If a ROM is used instead of a PLA, the PLA table must be expanded to 2^9 = 512 rows. To expand the table, the dashes in each row must be replaced with all possible combinations of 0's and 1's. For example, row 5 would be replaced with the following 8 rows:

001	0	**0**	0	1	**0**	**0**	0	1	0	0	0	0	0
001	0	**0**	0	1	**0**	**1**	0	1	0	0	0	0	0
001	0	**0**	0	1	**1**	**0**	0	1	0	0	0	0	0
001	0	**0**	0	1	**1**	**1**	0	1	0	0	0	0	0
001	0	**1**	0	1	**0**	**0**	0	1	0	0	0	0	0
001	0	**1**	0	1	**0**	**1**	0	1	0	0	0	0	0
001	0	**1**	0	1	**1**	**0**	0	1	0	0	0	0	0
001	0	**1**	0	1	**1**	**1**	0	1	0	0	0	0	0

The added entrees have been printed in boldface.

The above example illustrates one way of realizing an SM chart using a PLA or ROM. Alternative procedures are available which make it possible to reduce the size of the PLA or ROM by adding some components to the network. These methods are generally based on transformation of the SM chart to different forms and encoding the inputs or outputs of the network.

PROBLEMS

22.1   Construct an SM block that has 3 input variables (D, E, F), 4 output variables (P, Q, R, S), and 2 exit paths. For this block, output P is always 1, and Q is 1 if $D = 1$. If D and F are 1 or if D and E are 0, $R = 1$ and exit path 1 is taken. If $(D = 0$ and $E = 1)$ or $(D = 1$ and $F = 0)$, $S = 1$ and exit path 2 is taken.

22.2   Convert the state graphs of Fig. 14-9 and 14-11 to SM charts.

22.3   Convert the state graphs of Figs. 15-4 and 15-6 to SM charts. Use conditional outputs for Fig. 15-4.

22.4   Convert the state graph of Fig. 14-12 to an SM chart. Test only one variable in each decision box. Try to minimize the number of decision boxes.

22.5   Convert the state graph shown in Fig. 21-7 to an SM chart.

22.6   Complete the following timing diagram for the SM chart of Fig. 22-10. Assume $N = 1$.

22.7   Solve Problem 21.4 using an SM chart instead of a state graph.

22.8   Work through Programmed Exercise 21.8 using an SM chart instead of a state graph.

22.9   Solve Problem 21.5 using an SM chart instead of a state graph.

22.10   Solve Problem 21.6(c) using an SM chart instead of a state graph.

22.11a. For the SM chart of Fig. 22-9, make the following state assignment for flip-flops A and B: S_0, $AB = 00$; S_1, $AB = 01$; S_2, $AB = 11$; S_3, $AB = 10$. Derive the next state and output equations by tracing link paths on the SM chart. Simplify the equations and then draw the network using D flip-flops and NAND gates.

   b. Repeat for the SM chart of Fig. 22-10 using the state assignment: S_0, $AB = 00$; S_1, $AB = 01$; S_2, $AB = 10$.

22.12a. Write the next state and output equations for the dice game by tracing link paths on the SM chart (Fig. 22-13).
   b. Design the block labeled "test logic" on Fig. 22-11.

22.13a. Realize the SM chart of Fig. 22-7(b) using a PLA and two D flip-flops. Draw the block diagram and give the PLA table.
   b. Repeat for Fig. 22-10. Use the same state assignment as in Problem 22.11b.

22.14   For the SM chart given below
   a. Draw a timing chart that shows the clock, the state (S_0, S_1 or S_2), the inputs X_1 and X_2, and the outputs. Assume that $X_3 = 0$ and the input sequence for $X_1 X_2$ is 01, 00, 10, 11, 01, 10.
   b. Make the same state assignment as in Problem 22.11b. Derive the next state and output equations by tracing link paths. Simplify these equations using the don't care state ($AB = 11$) and draw the corresponding network.
   c. Realize the chart using a PLA and D flip-flops. Give the PLA table.
   d. If a ROM is used instead of a PLA, what size ROM is required? Give the first 5 rows of the ROM table.

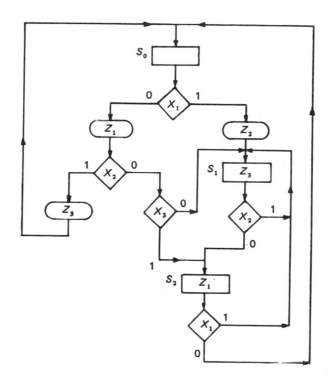

23

ANALYSIS OF ASYNCHRONOUS ·SEQUENTIAL NETWORKS

OBJECTIVES

1. Explain the differences between asynchronous and synchronous networks. Define fundamental mode operation.

2. Explain the difference between total state and internal state and between unstable and stable total states.

3. Given an asynchronous sequential network of gates or of gates and S-R flip-flops:

   a. Derive the flow table.

   b. Derive the output sequence given the input sequence.

   c. Sketch timing diagrams.

4. Given a flow table, locate critical races, non-critical races, and cycles.

STUDY GUIDE

1. Study Section 23.1, *Introduction*.

   a. What are the principal differences between synchronous and asynchronous networks?

   b. Classify each of the following counters as synchronous or asynchronous and explain your answer.

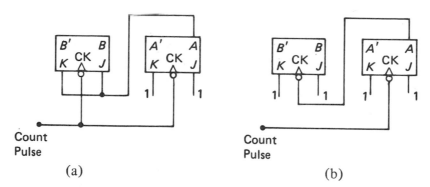

Fig. 23-1. Counters

2. Study Section 23.2, *Analysis of an Asynchronous Network with* S-R *Flip-flops.*

   a. Verify the analysis of Table 23-1 by tracing signals through the network.

   b. Show how Table 23-1 can be derived (except for the flip-flop inputs) using the transition table of Fig. 23-3 and output table of Fig. 23-5.

   c. If the input to a sequential network is changed only when it is in a stable total state, to what mode of operation does this correspond?

   d. Given a network diagram and a specified total state, how can you tell if the specified total state is stable or unstable without constructing a flow table?

3. Study Section 23.3, *Analysis of an Asynchronous Gate Network.*

   a. Verify that the tables in Fig. 23-7 are correct.

   b. When writing the output sequence for an asynchronous network, use the following convention:

   For each input in the input sequence, specify the resulting output when the network reaches a stable state. If transient outputs occur when the network passes through unstable total states, specify these outputs in parentheses. The output sequence may be condensed by omitting any transient output which is the same as one of the adjacent outputs in the sequence.

   For the flow table and associated output table given below, verify that for the input sequence

   $$x_1 x_2 = 00, \qquad 01, \qquad 11, \qquad 10, \qquad 00$$

   the output sequence is

   $$z = 0, \quad (1)\ (0)\ 1, \quad (0) \quad 1, \quad \cancel{(1)}\ \cancel{(0)}\ 0, \quad (1) \quad 0$$

   Note that the transient outputs nave been enclosed in parentheses. The sequence may be condensed by crossing out two of the transient outputs as indicated.

X_1X_2

	00	01	11	10
a	ⓐ	b	b	ⓐ
b	a	c	ⓑ	ⓑ
c	ⓒ	ⓒ	d	b
d	a	ⓓ	ⓓ	c

X_1X_2

	00	01	11	10
a	0	1	1	0
b	1	0	1	0
c.	0	1	0	0
d	0	1	1	1

Z

c. For Fig. 23-7, starting in stable total state $X_1 X_2 Q_1 Q_2 = 1100$, determine the complete output sequence (including transient outputs) for the input sequence 11, 10, 00, 01. Then write the sequence in condensed form.

d. If we start at some point in a network and can trace through a series of gates (in the direction of signal flow) and get back to the same point, we say that the network contains a *closed loop*. For the network of Fig. 23-9, find three closed loops that pass through point c.

e. For Fig. 23-9 indicate two possible choices for sets of 3 state variables other than a, c and d.

f. Can "ripple" occur in a synchronous network? Explain.

4. Study Section 23.4, *Race Conditions and Cycles*.

a. Verify that the table given in Fig. 23-11 is correct for the given network.

b. Trace signals through the network of Fig. 23-11 for $X = 1$ and verify that a cycle occurs.

c. Find any race conditions which exist in the table of Fig. 23-7(b) and tell whether they are critical or non-critical.

d. Sketch the resulting timing diagrams for X, Q_1 and Q_2 for the given transition table if the input is changed from 1 to 0 while the network is in internal state 11 and

(1) Q_1 changes before Q_2.

(2) Q_2 changes before Q_1.

(3) Q_1 and Q_2 change state simultaneously.

Q_1Q_2 \ X	0	1
00	⓪⓪	
01	00	
11	00	⑪
10	11	

5. Work Problems 23.1, 23.2, 23.3 and 23.4. When drawing timing diagrams for asynchronous networks, exaggerate the time between successive variable changes and use dotted lines if necessary (as in Fig. 23-6) so that the order in which variable changes occur is clearly indicated.

6. When you are satisfied that you can meet the objectives of this unit, take the readiness test.

23. ANALYSIS OF ASYNCHRONOUS SEQUENTIAL NETWORKS

23.1 Introduction

The sequential networks we have been studying so far fall in the category of *clocked synchronous networks.* In such networks, a change of state occurs only in response to a clock pulse. When this change of state requires several of the flip-flops to change state, they do so simultaneously because they are synchronized by the common clock pulse. Input changes are assumed to occur in between clock pulses, and the output may be read during (or immediately preceding) the clock pulse. Thus the input and output must be in synchronization with the clock pulse. When interpreting the state table for clocked synchronous networks, it is understood that when the input changes, the network does not immediately change state, but rather the network enters the next state *only* upon receiving a subsequent clock pulse.

Although clocked synchronous sequential networks are very useful, there are many applications where they are not suitable. Three situations in which synchronous networks may be unsuitable are:

a. The network has inputs which may change at any time and which cannot be synchronized with a clock.

b. The network is large enough and the response of the logic elements fast enough so that the time taken for the signals to travel down the wires is significant; in this case it may be very difficult to assure that the clock pulse arrives at all flip-flops simultaneously as is necessary to assure proper synchronous operation.

c. We want the network to operate as fast as possible and do not want to have to wait for a clock pulse after the input changes.

In these cases, it may be necessary to use asynchronous sequential networks. As the name implies, the operation of the network is not synchronized by a common clock or other means. When an input change occurs, the state of the network can change almost immediately without waiting for a clock pulse. If several flip-flops must change state, there is no guarantee that they will change at the same time. In fact, we may deliberately design the asynchronous network so that a single input change may produce a sequence of state changes.

The design of asynchronous networks is more difficult than synchronous because of the timing problems involved. In a properly designed synchronous network, timing problems are eliminated because we wait long enough after the external input changes for all flip-flop inputs to reach a steady value before applying the clock pulse. However, for an asynchronous network, special design techniques will be required to eliminate timing problems resulting from unequal delays through various paths in the network. To simplify the analysis and design, we will assume that our asynchronous networks operate in the *fundamental mode.* Fundamental mode operation assumes that the input signals will only be changed when the circuit is in a stable condition, that is, only when no internal signals are changing.

In a fundamental mode network, all of the input signals are considered to be levels. In another type of asynchronous network, called *pulse mode,* the inputs are pulses rather than levels. Operation of pulse-mode networks is similar to that of clocked synchronous networks, except that state changes are triggered by the input pulses rather than by the clock. The following restrictions are usually placed on the input pulses to pulse-mode networks:

a.   All input pulses must be of proper duration to trigger a flip-flop.

b.   Separation between two successive input pulses (on the same or different input lines) must be sufficient so that the network has time to respond to one pulse before the next one occurs.

When the above restrictions are met, analysis and design of pulse mode networks is straightforward.*

23.2   Analysis of an Asynchronous Network with S-R Flip-Flops

In order to gain some insight into the performance of asynchronous sequential networks, we will first analyze the network of Fig. 23-2 by tracing signals using the input sequence $X_1 X_2 = 00, 10, 11, 01, 11, 10, 00$.

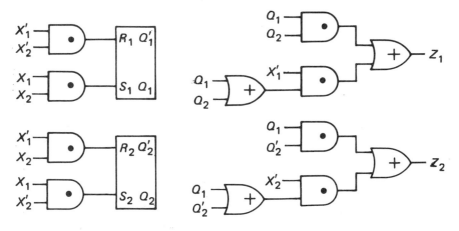

Fig. 23-2.   Asynchronous delay network

In this analysis we will assume that the propagation delay in the flip-flops is much greater than the propagation delays in the gates. The timing problems which can result from gate delays will be considered in a later unit. The first column of Table 23-1 lists the present values of the input variables and flip-flop outputs at successive times during the analysis of the network starting with the initial input of $X_1 X_2 = 00$ and the assumed starting state of $Q_1 Q_2 = 00$. Each combination of

---

*For a discussion of the design of pulse-mode networks, see Hill and Peterson, *Introduction to Switching Theory and Logical Design, Second Edition,* Chapter 11.

values for the circuit inputs and memory outputs (flip-flop outputs in this case) will be called a *total state* of the network. To avoid confusion with the total state, we will often refer to the state of the flip-flops as the *internal state*. For each total state encountered in the analysis of Fig. 23-2, the outputs and flip-flop inputs are calculated using the equations

$$R_1 = X_1'X_2' \qquad S_1 = X_1X_2 \qquad R_2 = X_1'X_2 \qquad S_2 = X_1X_2'$$

$$Z_1 = Q_1Q_2 + X_1'(Q_1 + Q_2) \qquad Z_2 = Q_1Q_2' + X_2'(Q_1 + Q_2')$$

and the next internal states are determined from the flip-flop inputs. Thus for total state $X_1X_2Q_1Q_2 = 0000$, the next internal state is $Q_1^+Q_2^+ = 00$. If for a given total state, the next internal state is the same as the present internal state, no change of state will occur and we say that the network is in a *stable total state*. Thus total state $X_1X_2Q_1Q_2 = 0000$ is stable. When we change the input to 10, the network enters total state 1000 which is *unstable* since $Q_1^+Q_2^+ \neq Q_1Q_2$. Subsequently, Q_1Q_2 will change to 01, and the network enters total state 1001, which is stable. The input is then changed to 11 and the network enters total state 1101 which is unstable because $Q_1^+Q_2^+ \neq Q_1Q_2$ and the network will change to stable total state 1111 without any further input change. The analysis is continued in this manner as illustrated in Table 23-1. The stable total states have been underlined. Since we are assuming fundamental mode operation, the input is only

Table 23-1. Analysis of Fig. 23-2

present total state $X_1X_2Q_1Q_2$	flip-flop inputs $R_1S_1R_2S_2$	outputs Z_1Z_2	next internal state $Q_1^+Q_2^+$
0 0 0 0	1 0 0 0	0 1	0 0
1 0 0 0	0 0 0 1	0 1	0 1
1 0 0 1	0 0 0 1	0 0	0 1
1 1 0 1	0 1 0 0	0 0	1 1
1 1 1 1	0 1 0 0	1 0	1 1
0 1 1 1	0 0 1 0	1 0	1 0
0 1 1 0	0 0 1 0	1 1	1 0
1 1 1 0	0 1 0 0	0 1	1 0
1 0 1 0	0 0 0 1	0 1	1 1
1 0 1 1	0 0 0 1	1 1	1 1
0 0 1 1	1 0 0 0	1 1	0 1
0 0 0 1	1 0 0 0	1 0	0 1

changed when the total state is stable, never when it is unstable. The input and output sequences (from Table 23-1) are

$$X_1 X_2 = 00, 10, 11, 01, 11, 10, 00$$

$$Z_1 Z_2 = 01, 00, 10, 11, 01, 11, 10$$

Except for the initial output, the output for any stable total state is equal to the previous input; thus this network is referred to as an asynchronous delay.

Although the method of analysis illustrated in Table 23-1 is sufficient for analysis of small networks, it is more systematic to analyze the network using a state table. First a *transition* table is constructed which shows the next states of the flip-flops as a function of the present state and inputs. This table can be formed in the same manner as for synchronous networks by mapping the next state equations for the network. For Fig. 23-2, the next state equations are

$$Q_1^+ = S_1 + R_1' Q_1 = X_1 X_2 + (X_1 + X_2) Q_1$$

$$Q_2^+ = S_2 + R_2' Q_2 = X_1 X_2' + (X_1 + X_2') Q_2$$

These equations have been mapped in Fig. 23-3. Each column of this table corresponds to a specific combination of values of the input variables, or to an *input state*. Each row corresponds to a specific assignment of values to the memory variables, or to a present internal state. Each square in the table corresponds to a total state, and the entry in that square is the next internal state for that total state. For example, the square labeled "a" in Fig. 23-3 corresponds to a *present* total state $X_1 X_2 Q_1 Q_2 = 1100$, and the corresponding next internal state is $Q_1^+ Q_2^+ = 10$. Whenever the next internal state is the same as the present internal state (i.e., $Q_1^+ Q_2^+ = Q_1 Q_2$) the corresponding total state is stable; if $Q_1^+ Q_2^+ \neq Q_1 Q_2$, the corresponding total state is unstable. Stable total states are designated on the map by circling the corresponding next internal state entry. For example, in Fig. 23-3 total stable state $X_1 X_2 Q_1 Q_2 = 1001$ has next internal state 01 circled since $Q_1^+ Q_2^+ = Q_1 Q_2 = 01$.

A change of input state corresponds to a change between columns of the transition table without any row change. If the new total state is unstable, a row change (internal state change) takes place to the row with the corresponding next

$Q_1 Q_2$ \ $X_1 X_2$	00	01	11	10
00	(00)	(00)	10 *a*	01
01	(01)	00	11	(01)
11	01	10	(11)	(11)
10	00	(10)	(10)	11

$$Q_1^+ Q_2^+$$

Fig. 23-3. Transition table for Fig. 23-2

internal state. For example, starting in total state 0000 if the input is changed to 10 we change to the 10 column and then to the 01 row as indicated by the arrows on Fig. 23-3.

The transition table may be converted to a state table in which each internal state or each stable total state is labeled with an arbitrary designation as in Fig. 23-4. The state table of Fig. 23-4(a) is used exactly like the state table for a clocked synchronous network except that for the synchronous case the internal state change does not occur when the input changes but rather when the clock pulse occurs, while for the asynchronous case the internal state change occurs immediately following the input change as fast as the network response will permit. The state table for an asynchronous network is often called a *flow table* to emphasize this difference. In the flow table of Fig. 23-4(b), the rows are not numbered, but if an input change takes the network to an uncircled total state entry, the state changes to the corresponding circled (stable) total state entry. Figure 23-4(b) can be derived from Fig. 23-4(a) by giving each stable *total* state a distinct number and then filling in each unstable entry with the corresponding next total state.

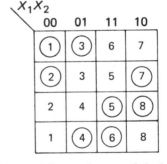

(a)   internal states labeled   (b)   stable total states labeled

Fig. 23-4.   Flow tables for Fig. 23-2

The flow table, along with the output table, can be used to find the output sequence of the network for any given input sequence. The output table is derived in the usual manner by mapping the output equations. For example, for Fig. 23-2, we will find the output sequence, starting in total state 0000, given the input sequence

$$X_1 X_2 = 00, 10, 11, 01, 11, 10, 00$$

Using one of the flow tables from Fig. 23-4 along with the output table as shown in Fig. 23-5, we get

$$Z_1 Z_2 = 01, 00, 10, 11, 01, 11, 10$$

This sequence, illustrated by the arrows drawn on the flow table in Fig. 23-5, is the same as obtained by the analysis of Table 23-1.

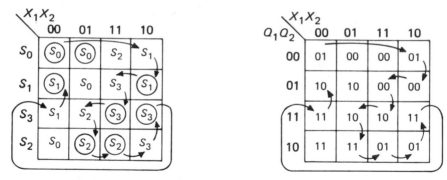

Fig. 23-5.   Flow table and output table for Fig. 23-2

The above input and output sequences are also illustrated on the timing diagram of Fig. 23-6 where ϵ is the response time for the output to change after the input changes. The value of ϵ may be different for each path through the network or for each state change associated with a given present state and input.

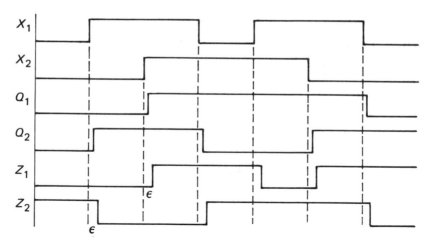

Fig. 23-6.   Timing diagram for Fig. 23-2

23.3 Analysis of an Asynchronous Gate Network

Construction of asynchronous networks using only gates and without using flip-flops or other explicit memory elements is often possible. Consider, for example, the network of Fig. 23-7 with the "delays" enclosed in dashed boxes not present. Note that there are two feedback paths from the OR gate outputs back to the AND gate inputs. We will associate the state variables Q_1 and Q_2 with these feedback paths. Each gate in the network has some delay associated with it, that is, the output will occur at some non-zero time after the corresponding gate input changes. For purposes of analysis, it is convenient to lump all of the delay associated with each feedback path into a single box labeled "delay". We then

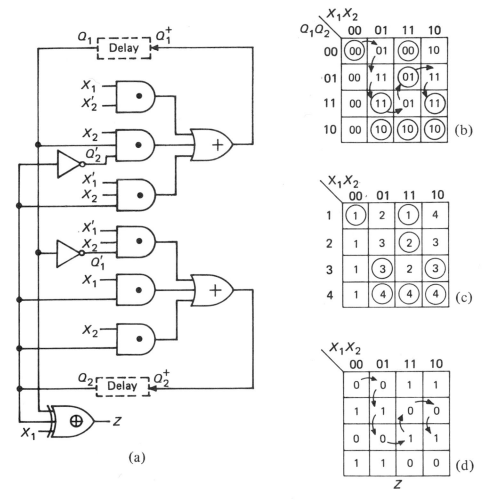

Fig. 23-7. Asynchronous network constructed from gates

associate a state variable with each delay output. If at a given instant of time the input to a delay is 0 (or 1), the output will be 0 (or 1) after the delay time elapses. Hence the delay input represents the next state of the delay output and the delay with the Q_1 output has its input labeled Q_1^+.

Once we have identified the state variables, construction of the flow table is straightforward. The network is described by the equations

$$Q_1^+ = X_1 X_2' + X_1' X_2 Q_2 + X_2 Q_1 Q_2'$$

$$Q_2^+ = X_1' X_2 Q_1' + X_1 Q_2 + X_2 Q_2$$

$$Z = X_1 \oplus Q_1 \oplus Q_2$$

These equations are plotted in Figs. 23-7(b) and (d), and the flow table of Fig. 23-7(c) is constructed by replacing each combination of state variables with a state symbol. Circled entries represent stable total states. For any given input sequence, the state and output sequences can be determined from Figs. 23-7(b) or (c), and (d). Starting in total state $X_1 X_2 Q_1 Q_2 = 0000$ if the input is changed to 01, the internal state will change to 01 and then to 11. Note that a single input change produces two internal state changes before a stable total state is reached.* If the input is next changed to 11, the network goes to unstable total state 1111 and then to stable state 1101. An input change to 10 will then take the network to unstable total state 1001 followed by stable total state 1011. The output sequence, as indicated on the map of Fig. 23-7(d), is 0 (0) (1) 0 (1) 0 (0) 1, where the outputs in parentheses correspond to unstable total states. Since two successive outputs which are the same cannot be distinguished by an asynchronous network, the output sequence can be condensed to the form 0 (1) 0 (1) 0 1. This sequence has two transient 1 outputs which occur when the network is switching between stable states. Such transient outputs can be eliminated by proper design of the output network as described in Section 25.4.

The best choice of state variables for analysis of an asynchronous network is not always obvious. State variables should be chosen so that if we cut the branch associated with each state variable, all of the closed loops (feedback loops) in the network will be opened. If explicit delays and flip-flops are present, we must associate a state variable with each delay and flip-flop output. If cutting the branches associated with these outputs does not open all closed loops, then additional state variable branches must be chosen. Generally, we wish to choose a minimum set of branches which, when cut, will open all of the remaining closed loops. When such state variable branches have been chosen, a dummy delay element may be placed in each branch (as in Fig. 23-7) in order to define Q^+ and Q. There are often several ways of choosing state variable branches, and a judicious choice will simplify the analysis. As indicated in Fig. 23-8, if a gate output fans out to connect to several gate inputs, the state variable branch should normally be chosen directly at the gate output rather than in one of the fanning branches.

Fig. 23-8. Selection of state variable branch

Figure 23-9 shows an asynchronous network to be analyzed. If we make cuts at points e and f, it would still be necessary to make two additional cuts (at a and c, for example) in order to open all closed loops. This would then require four state variables. More careful inspection of the circuit shows that making cuts at points a, c and d will open all closed loops and only three state vari-

---

*When a single input change produces two or more successive internal state changes, this is sometimes referred to as "ripple" because the effect of the input change ripples through the network to produce a sequence of state changes.

ables are required. For purposes of analysis, delay elements may be inserted at points a, c and d in order to define the state variables (Q_1, Q_2 and Q_3). The next states and outputs can then be written as functions of X, Q_1, Q_2 and Q_3.

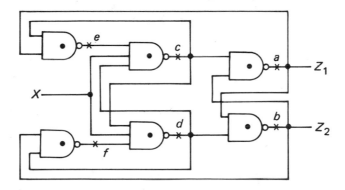

Fig. 23-9. Asynchronous network to be analyzed

Figure 23-10 shows a general model for an asynchronous sequential network. The delays may either represent the lumped effect of the gate delays in the combinational network, or they may represent explicit delays added to the network. This model is similar to the general model for a synchronous network (Section 14.4) except that no method is provided for synchronizing the operation of the delays. Thus a single input change may propagate through the different feedback paths at different times. This may cause timing problems that result in improper operation of the network. Such timing problems are discussed in Section 23.4 and in Unit 26. These timing problems are avoided in a synchronous network by synchronizing the operation of the delays with a clock.

Fig. 23-10. General model for an asynchronous sequential network

23.4 Race Conditions and Cycles

Consider the network of Fig. 23-11(a) with its corresponding transition table. Note that there is only one stable total state, $XQ_1Q_2 = 000$. If we start in this stable state, then let X change from 0 to 1, we get the condition of Fig. 23-11(c). Immediately after X changes, the present state is 00 and the next state is 10. As soon as the circuit switches to state 10, the next state is 11. From state 11, the network switches to 01 and then back to state 00, all with no further changes in the input. In fact, the circuit will cycle through the unstable states until X is made 0 again. This type of behavior is therefore called a *cycle*.

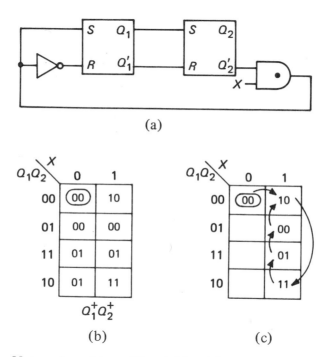

(a)

(b)   (c)

Fig. 23-11. Network and transition table with non-critical race and cycle

If X is changed back to 0 when the circuit is in internal state 10, several state change sequences are possible as indicated in Fig. 23-12. When the present internal state is $Q_1Q_2 = 10$ and $X = 0$, the next state should be $Q_1^+Q_2^+ = 01$. That is, Q_1 should change from 1 to 0 at the same time Q_2 changes from 0 to 1. Since different flip-flops may have different propagation delays, it is possible for Q_2 to change to 1 before Q_1 can change to 0, in which case the circuit is momentarily in the $Q_1Q_2 = 11$ row of the flow table. Then the next state is 01, so the circuit goes to the $Q_1Q_2 = 01$ row, and from there to stable state 00. If the two flip-flops had changed simultaneously, the circuit would have gone directly from state 10 to 01, and then on to 00. If in state 10, Q_1 changes to 0 before Q_2 changes, the network will go directly to state 00.

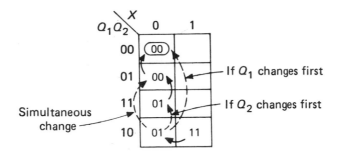

Fig. 23-12. Non-critical race

Whenever two or more flip-flops must change state in response to a single change in input, the result is a *race condition* between the flip-flops. If the resulting stable state is the same no matter in what order the flip-flops change, as in the above example, it is called a *non-critical* race. If it is possible to end up in two or more different stable states depending on the order in which the flip-flops change state, then it is a *critical* race.

The flow table of Fig. 23-13 illustrates a critical race. Starting in total state $XQ_1Q_2 = 000$, if X is changed to 1 both Q_1 and Q_2 are required to change from 0 to 1. However, if Q_2 changes to 1 before Q_1 due to unequal propagation delays, the network will get "stuck" in stable total state 101 and no further state change will occur. On the other hand, if Q_1 changes first the internal state becomes 10 and the network will get stuck in total state 110. Hence the race is critical because the network will go to the proper next state only if both Q_1 and Q_2 change simultaneously.

Several distinct differences between asynchronous and clocked circuits are evident in the networks analyzed in this unit. First, for asynchronous circuits, state changes occur as soon as the input change propagates through the network so that each possible input change must be taken into account when designing asynchronous networks. In a clocked circuit, many input changes may occur between clock pulses, but only the final input value before the clock pulse influ-

Fig. 23-13. Flow table with critical race

ences the next state. Also, in asynchronous networks several state changes may occur in response to a single input change. An input sequence like 00, 00, 01, 01, 11 is recognized as a sequence of 5 inputs by a synchronous network; however, since an asynchronous network only responds to input changes, it would treat the above sequence as if it were 00, 01, 11.

PROBLEMS

23.1 Initially, $Q_1 = Q_2 = 0$. Construct a flow table for the following network, and use this flow table to determine the shortest input sequence for $X_1 X_2$ which will give an output of $Z = 1$. (A simultaneous change of input variables is not allowed.)

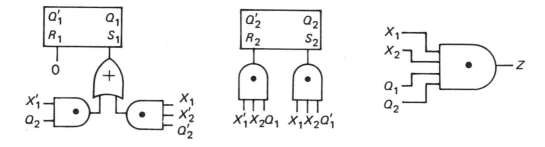

23.2 Construct a flow table for the following network and describe what happens when X is changed from 0 to 1. If the network is started with $Q_1 = Q_2 = 0$, how can an output of $Z = 1$ be obtained? Draw a timing diagram showing X, Q_1, Q_2, and Z indicating the time at which X must change in order to get an output $Z = 1$.

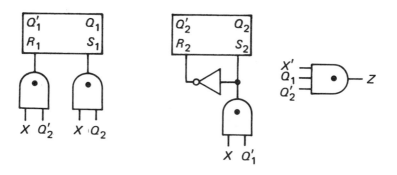

23.3   Analyze the following network using a flow table. What is the output
sequence for the following input sequence: $X_1 X_2 = 00, 10, 11, 01, 11, 10,$
$00, 01, 00$?

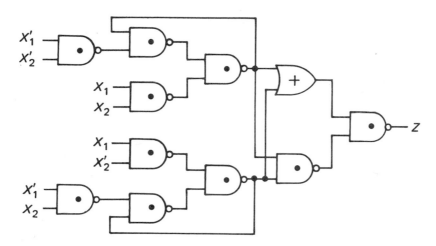

23.4   a.   Analyze the following asynchronous network using a flow table.
Starting in the stable total state for which $X = Z = 0$, determine the
state and output sequences when the input sequence is $X = 0, 1, 0, 1, \ldots$

b.   Find any critical races which are present in the table.

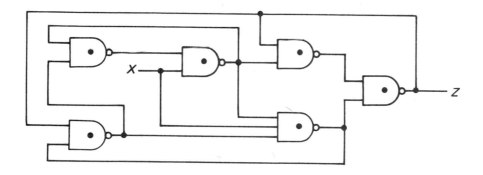

24

DERIVATION AND REDUCTION OF PRIMITIVE FLOW TABLES

OBJECTIVES

Carry out the following steps in the synthesis of a fundamental mode asynchronous sequential network:

1. Derive a *primitive* flow table from the problem statement.
2. Reduce the flow table to a minimum number of rows.

STUDY GUIDE

1. Study Section 24.1, *Derivation of Primitive Flow Tables*.

    a. Define a *primitive* flow table.

    b. For a primitive table, why must every allowable input change result in a state change?

    c. For the table of Fig. 24-1(c), why are there two different stable total states with the same output in column 01?

d. Why is there exactly one dash in each row of the table?

e. Study *Example* 2. Take a sheet of paper and construct the table of Fig. 24-3 row by row making sure you understand the reason for each entry.

f. Study *Example* 3. Verify that the output sequences obtained from Fig. 24-6 are correct for the various input waveforms indicated in Fig. 24-4.

2. Study Section 24.2, *Reduction of Primitive Flow Tables*.

a. What is the difference in the definition of equivalent internal states and equivalent stable total states?

b. Why is it possible to ignore the outputs when constructing the merger diagram for a reduced primitive flow table?

c. Consider the following merger diagram. Find two different ways of merging to obtain a minimum-row table (3 rows).

d. Work Programmed Exercise 24.1.

3. Work Problems 24.2 through 24.6.

4. When you are satisfied that you can meet the objectives of this unit, take the readiness test.

24. DERIVATION AND REDUCTION OF PRIMITIVE FLOW TABLES

The basic design procedure for asynchronous networks is similar to that for synchronous networks. First a state (or flow) table is constructed from the problem statement, then the table is reduced to a minimum number of rows, a state assignment is made, and the table is realized using appropriate logic elements. However, the details of each step are somewhat different for asynchronous networks.

24.1 Derivation of Primitive Flow Tables

The starting point for asynchronous synthesis is usually a *primitive* flow table. The primitive flow table is defined as a flow table which has exactly one stable total state per row. The primitive table can usually be reduced to a table with fewer rows. However, in order to be sure of obtaining a final reduced table with a minimum number of rows, for most problems it is necessary to start with the primitive table rather than trying to construct the reduced table directly.

The following examples illustrate construction of the primitive flow table from the problem statement. To avoid the timing problems which can result when two input variables change simultaneously, we will assume that only one input variable changes at a time and the input changes are spaced so that the network will always reach a stable total state between changes (fundamental mode operation). When constructing a *primitive* flow table, every change in input must result in a state change since only one stable state per row is allowed.

Example 1: An asynchronous network has two inputs and one output. The input sequence $X_1 X_2 = 00, 01, 11$ causes the output to become 1. The next input change then causes the output to return to 0. No other input sequence will produce a 1 output.

The first row of the flow table in Fig. 24-1(a) is constructed as follows. Stable total state (1) represents a reset state in which the input is 00. If the input changes to 01, we change to stable total state (2) to indicate the sequence 00, 01 has been received, and similarly if the input changes to 10, we change to (3) . Note that each time the input changes we go through *one* unstable total state on the way to the corresponding stable total state. The dash in the third column indicates that the double input change, 00 to 11, is not allowed.

		00	01	11	10	Z
(reset)	1	(1)	2	–	3	0
(00, 01)	2		(2)			0
(00, 10)	3				(3)	0

Fig. 24-1(a)

We then fill in rows 2 and 3 of the table in Fig. 24-1(b). Starting in (2) , an input change 01 to 00 causes a return to the reset state ((1)) since 00 starts the desired sequence over again. From (2) , an input change 01 to 11 completes the desired input sequence, so we go to (4) with an output $Z = 1$. Starting in (3) , an input change 10 to 00 resets the network to (1) . From (3) , an input change 10 to 11 does *not* complete the desired sequence so we cannot go to (4) which has a 1 output. Therefore, we introduce a new state in the 11 column ((5)) which has a zero output. The dashes in rows 2 and 3 are present because double input changes 01 to 10 and 10 to 01 are not allowed.

		00	01	11	10	Z
(reset)	1	①	2	–	3	0
(00, 01)	2	1	②	4	–	0
(00, 10)	3	1	–	5	③	0
(00, 01, 11)	4			④		1
(00, 10, 11)	5			⑤		0

Fig. 24-1(b)

Next we fill in rows 4 and 5, and then add row 6 to complete the primitive table in Fig. 24-1(c). Starting in ④ an input change 11 to 01 must change the output to 0, but we cannot go to ② because we should not get another 1 output until the circuit resets. Therefore, in the 01 column we introduce a new state (⑥) with 0 output. From ④ , a 11 to 10 change must change the output to 0; in this case we can go to ③ since ③ cannot lead to a 1 output without resetting first. Starting in ⑤ , we cannot get a 1 output without resetting so a change to input 01 or 10 can take us to state 6 or 3 respectively. Starting in ⑥ , a change to input 00 resets the circuit and a change to 11 takes us back to state ⑤ .

		X_1X_2				
		00	01	11	10	Z
(reset)	1	①	2	–	3	0
(00, 01)	2	1	②	4	–	0
*	3	1	–	5	③	0
(00, 01, 11)	4	–	6	④	3	1
*	5	–	6	⑤	3	0
*	6	1	⑥	5	–	0

*These states cannot lead to a 1 output without first resetting.

Fig. 24-1(c). Primitive flow table

Figure 24-2 shows the state diagram for the primitive flow table of Fig. 24-1(c). Note that on the state diagram for a primitive table all arrows leading into a given state must have the same input.

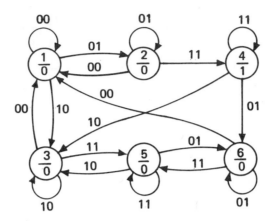

Fig. 24-2.   State diagram for primitive flow table

Example 2:   This example illustrates the design of a clocked *T* flip-flop shown in Fig. 24-3(a). Although this flip-flop is used as a component in synchronous networks, the internal design of the flip-flop is an asynchronous problem. The flip-flop has two inputs, *T* and *P*. The flip-flop will change state if *T* = 1 when the clock (*P*) changes from 1 to 0. Under all other input conditions, *Q* should remain constant. We will assume that *T* and *P* do not change simultaneously.

		TP				Q
		00	01	11	10	
(*TP* = 00)	1	①	2	–	3	0
(*TP* = 01)	2	1	②	4	–	0
(*TP* = 10)	3	1	–	4	③	0
(*TP* = 11)	4	–	2	④	5	0
(*TP* = 10)	5	6	–	7	⑤	1
(*TP* = 00)	6	⑥	8	–	5	1
(*TP* = 11)	7	–	8	⑦	3	1
(*TP* = 01)	8	6	⑧	7	–	1

(a) Clocked *T* flip-flop   (b) Primitive flow table

Fig. 24-3

Figure 24-3(b) shows the primitive flow table. Because the table is primitive, the state must change each time the input changes. In this example, there is one stable total state for each combination of values of *T*, *P* and *Q*. The values of *T* and *P* associated with each stable total state have been listed beside the corresponding rows for reference. Note that the output (*Q*) only changes when the input changes from *TP* = 11 to 10.

Example 3: A clock signal (C) is to be gated on and off by another signal (S). The gating network must be such that only complete clock pulses appear at the output (Z) even though S may change in the middle of a clock pulse. Figure 24-4 shows the timing diagram for the network to be designed. Even though a clock is present, this is an asynchronous problem because the input S is allowed to change at any time with respect to the clock. We will assume that S will always be on or off for at least two complete clock pulses.

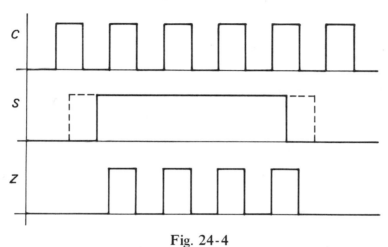

Fig. 24-4

The flow table can be derived as follows. Starting in state ① if C goes to 1 and back to 0, we go to state ② and back to ① with no change in output. From state ① , if S goes to 1, we go to state ③ and wait for C to go to 1.

	CS 00	01	11	10	Z
1	①	3		2	0
2	1			②	0
3		③	4		0
4		3	④		1

Fig. 24-5

Then when C goes to 1, we go to state ④ with a 1 output. As C goes to 0 we go back to ③ with a 0 output. We then cycle back and forth between ③ and ④ as C turns on and off. This action continues until S goes to 0. If S goes to 0 in state ③ , we can immediately reset to state ① . However, if S goes to 0 in state ④ we must wait until the termination of the input clock pulse before Z goes to 0; therefore, we go to ⑤ to maintain the 1 output. From ⑤, the next input change must be C going to 0, in which case we reset to ①. To complete the flow table (Fig. 24-6), we must consider the case where S turns on in the middle of a clock pulse. From ② we go to ⑥ and wait for C to go to 0 (we can't go to ④ because we don't want Z to become 1 until the next clock pulse). From ⑥, we then go to ③, so the Z can be cycled on and off as C goes on and off. If we assume that double changes of input cannot occur, the remaining table entries are don't cares. Note that in ⑤, the input change 10 to 11 cannot occur since S is assumed to be off for at least two clock pulses.

	CS				
	00	01	11	10	Z
1	①	3	–	2	0
2	1	–	6	②	0
3	1	③	4	–	0
4	–	3	④	5	1
5	1	–	–	⑤	1
6	–	3	⑥	–	0

Fig. 24-6

24.2 Reduction of Primitive Flow Tables

After formulation of the primitive flow table, the next step in the synthesis of an asynchronous sequential network is reduction of the flow table to a minimum number of rows. This reduction will usually reduce the number of state variables required to realize the table. In general, this will make it easier to complete the design of the network and will reduce the amount of logic required.

Two methods of reducing the primitive flow table are possible. The first method requires two steps — first a minimum-row *primitive* flow table is found, and then this table is further reduced by merging rows. The second method carries out the complete reduction in one step by applying the general reduction method for incompletely specified state tables.* The first method is generally less work to carry out and will be discussed here.

A minimum-row *primitive* flow table can be found by eliminating redundant stable total states. To do this, we must find equivalent stable total states. Two stable total states are equivalent iff they have the same inputs and the associated internal states are equivalent. Thus two stable total states are equivalent if (a) their inputs are the same, (b) their outputs are the same, and (c) their next states are equivalent for each possible next input. The following example illustrates determination of equivalent stable total states.

We will reduce the table of Fig. 24-7 to obtain a minimum-row primitive flow table. From the first column (input 00) states ②, ⑥ and ⑧ have the

---

* See Hill and Peterson, *Introduction to Switching Theory and Logical Design,* 2nd ed., Chapters 12 and 13.

same outputs. From the second column ⑤ and ⑫ have the same outputs, from the third column ③ and ⑩ do, and from the last column ④ and ⑪ do. Therefore the sets of potentially equivalent states are

$$(2, 6, 8) \quad (5, 12) \quad (3, 10) \quad (4, 11)$$

	$X_1 X_2$				$Z_1 Z_2$
	00	01	11	10	
1	①	7	—	4	1 1
2	②	5	—	4	0 1
3	—	7	③	11	1 0
4	2	—	3	④	0 0
5	6	⑤	9	—	1 1
6	⑥	7	—	11	0 1
7	1	⑦	14	—	1 0
8	⑧	12	—	4	0 1
9	—	7	⑨	13	0 1
10	—	.7	⑩	4	1 0
11	8	—	10	⑪	0 0
12	6	⑫	9	—	1 1
13	8	—	14	⑬	1 1
14	—	12	⑭	11	0 0

Fig. 24-7. Primitive table to be reduced

Next we examine the next states of the states in each group. With input 01, the next states of ② and ⑥ are 5 and 7. Since $5 \neq 7$, ② $\neq$ ⑥. Similarly, the next states of ⑥ and ⑧ are 7 and 12. Since $7 \neq 12$, ⑥ $\neq$ ⑧. However, for ② and ⑧, with input 01 the next states are 5 and 12, and with input 10 both next states are 4. For ⑤ and ⑫, both next states are 6 for input 00, and both are 9 for input 11. For ③ and ⑩, both next states are 7 for input 01, and the next states are 4 and 11 for input 10. Finally for ④ and ⑪ the next states are 2 and 8, and 3 and 10, for inputs 00 and 11, respectively. Since we have found no additional non-equivalent states, the remaining sets of equivalent states are

$$(2, 8) \quad (5, 12) \quad (3, 10) \quad (4, 11)$$

After eliminating redundant states 8, 10, 11 and 12, the reduced primitive flow table is given by Fig. 24-8.

	00	01	11	10	
1	①	7	–	4	11
2	②	5	–	4	01
3	–	7	③	4	10
4	2	–	3	④	00
5	6	⑤	9	–	11
6	⑥	7	–	4	01
7	1	⑦	14	–	10
9	–	7	⑨	13	01
13	2	–	14	⑬	11
14	–	5	⑭	4	00

Fig. 24-8. **Reduced primitive table for Fig. 24-7**

Next, we will return to the primitive flow tables derived for Examples 1 and 2 of this unit to determine if these tables can be reduced. For the primitive table of Fig. 24-1(c) the only stable total states with the same inputs and outputs are ② and ⑥. The next states of ② and ⑥ for input 11 are 4 and 5. Since 4 ≢ 5, ② ≢ ⑥, and there are no equivalent stable total states. Therefore, this primitive table already has a minimum number of rows.

For the primitive table of Fig. 24-3, since states ① and ⑥ have different outputs, as do states ② and ⑧, ④ and ⑦, and ③ and ⑤, there are no equivalent stable total states.

Each of the minimum-row primitive tables discussed above can be further reduced by merging rows. So far, all of the primitive tables we have worked with have been in Moore form (output a function of the present state only). We can proceed to merge rows in the Moore table, or first convert the Moore table to a Mealy table. The latter procedure is generally preferable since it sometimes leads to a reduced table with fewer rows.

For the table of Fig. 24-1(c), the corresponding Mealy form is given in Fig. 24-9. The Mealy table is formed from the Moore table by associating the output for each row with the corresponding stable total state in that row.* Thus for row 2, stable state ② is in the 01 column, so the corresponding output of 0 is placed in the 01 column of the Mealy output table. After all of the outputs associated with stable states have been filled in, the remaining outputs are temporarily left unspecified (as indicated by the dashes in the output table). When the network is in a stable state, the outputs from the Mealy and Moore tables will be identical. After the Mealy table has been reduced and a state assignment has been made, the outputs associated with unstable states will be filled in to avoid transients in the output.

---

*This type of Moore-Mealy conversion applies only to asynchronous tables. A different conversion procedure is used for synchronous tables because of timing differences.

X_1X_2	00	01	11	10	00	01	11	10
1	①	2	–	3	0	–	–	–
2	1	②	4	–	–	0	–	–
3	1	–	5	③	–	–	–	0
4	–	6	④	3	–	–	1	–
5	–	6	⑤	3	–	–	0	–
6	1	⑥	5	–	–	0	–	–

Fig. 24-9. Primitive Mealy flow table for Fig. 24-1(c)

After all redundant stable total states have been removed from the primitive table, we will call the resulting table a *reduced primitive flow table*. Two rows of a *reduced* primitive Mealy flow table are compatible and can be merged into a single row iff there are no state conflicts in any column. Thus for Fig. 24-9 rows 1 and 2 can be merged because column 00 contains ① and 1, column 01 contains 2 and ②, 11 contains – and 4, and 10 contains 3 and –. Merging rows 1 and 2 yields

	00	01	11	10	00	01	11	10
1, 2	①	②	4	3	0	0	–	–

Note that a stable total state and the corresponding unstable state were merged to form a stable total state. Thus, in the (1, 2) row, an input change of 00 to 01 takes us directly from ① to ②, while in the original table the change between stable states ① and ② goes through an intermediate unstable total state 2. Rows 2 and 3 of Fig. 24-9 cannot be merged because of the state conflict in column 11. (We already know that ④ ≢ ⑤ because all redundant stable total states have been removed from the table.)

To facilitate selection of rows to be merged, we will draw a *merger diagram* (Fig. 24-10). In this diagram, we draw a line between any pair of states which are compatible and can be merged. To form this merger diagram, we first compare row 1 of the reduced primitive table with rows 2 through 6 and find that row 1 is compatible with row 2 and with row 3. Row 2 is then compared with rows 3 through 6, and no further compatible rows are found. Comparing row 3 with rows 4, 5 and 6 shows that 3 and 5 are compatible as are 3 and 6. Row 4 is compatible with neither 5 nor 6, and finally rows 5 and 6 are compatible. The merger diagram indicates that the following row mergers are possible: (1, 2), (1, 3), and (3, 5, 6). Note that 1, 2 and 3 cannot be merged together since 2 and 3 are not compatible. We can form a 3-row table (Fig. 24-11) by merging rows (1, 2) and (3, 5, 6). To complete the reduced table, the don't cares in the output part of the table must be filled in using the procedure described in Section 25.4.

Fig. 24-10. Merger diagram for Fig. 24-9

		00	01	11	10	00	01	11	10
a	(1, 2)	①	②	4	3	0	0	—	—
b	(3, 5, 6)	1	⑥	⑤	③	—	0	0	0
c	4	—	6	④	3	—	—	1	—

Fig. 24-11. Reduced table for Fig. 24-9

For a given input sequence, the sequence of stable total states and the output sequence will be the same for the reduced primitive table (Fig. 24-9) and the final reduced flow table (Fig. 24-11). The only difference is that in the primitive table every change between stable states goes through an intermediate unstable state, but in the final table some transitions between some stable total states are direct.

When two rows of the reduced primitive Mealy flow table are merged, there will never be any conflicts between outputs. The reason for this is that the outputs are only associated with the *stable* total states. Since we never merge two rows with different *stable* total states in the same column, there are never any output conflicts. Consequently, we can completely ignore the output part of the reduced primitive flow table when merging rows, and then fill in the Mealy output table after the rows have been merged.

Returning to the reduced primitive table of Fig. 24-8, and comparing each row with all of the following rows, we see that row 1 can merge with 3 and 7, row 2 with 4 and 14, and row 3 with 4 and 6. From the corresponding merger diagram (Fig. 24-12) we can merge rows (1, 7), (2, 4) and (3, 6) to form a 7-row table (Fig. 24-13). Then we form the Mealy output table by entering the output associated with each stable total state. Thus state ① has output 11, ② has output 01, etc.

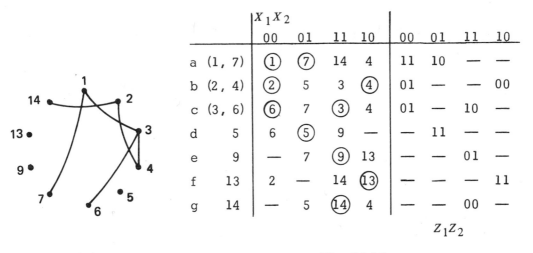

	X_1X_2				Z_1Z_2			
	00	01	11	10	00	01	11	10
a (1, 7)	①	⑦	14	4	11	10	—	—
b (2, 4)	②	5	3	④	01	—	—	00
c (3, 6)	⑥	7	③	4	01	—	10	—
d 5	6	⑤	9	—	—	11	—	—
e 9	—	7	⑨	13	—	—	01	—
f 13	2	—	14	⑬	—	—	—	11
g 14	—	5	⑭	4	—	—	00	—

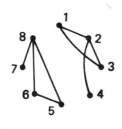

Fig. 24-12   Fig. 24-13

The minimum-row flow table is generally not unique. Figure 24-14 gives the merger diagram for Fig. 24-3. Either of the following mergers will give a 4-row table:

$$(1, 2, 3) \quad (4) \quad (5, 6, 8) \quad (7) \quad \text{or} \quad (1, 3) \quad (2, 4) \quad (5, 6) \quad (7, 8)$$

Using the first merger, the table can be reduced to Fig. 24-15.

	TP							
	00	01	11	10	00	01	11	10
a	①	②	4	③	0	0	—	0
b	—	2	④	5	—	—	0	—
c	⑥	⑧	7	⑤	1	1	—	1
d	—	8	⑦	3	—	—	1	—

Fig. 24-14   Fig. 24-15

In summary, a primitive flow table can be reduced to a minimum-row Mealy table using the following procedure:

a. Find a reduced *primitive* flow table by eliminating redundant stable total states:

   (1) Write down the sets of stable total states which have the same input and output. The states in each set are potentially equivalent.

   (2) Let S_i and S_j be a pair of potentially equivalent states found in (1). Determine the next states when the input is changed to column X_k.

These next states are $\delta(S_i, X_k)$ and $\delta(S_j, X_k)$. If $\delta(S_i, X_k)$ and $\delta(S_j, X_k)$ are not in the same one of the sets found in (1), then $\delta(S_i, X_k) \neq \delta(S_j, X_k)$ and consequently $S_i \neq S_j$. In this manner check each set of states found in (1) for each possible input change and eliminate the non-equivalent states. Repeat this process until all non-equivalent states have been found and only sets of equivalent states remain.

(3) Using the sets of equivalent states found in (2), construct a reduced primitive table using only one state from each set.

b. Construct a minimum-row Mealy flow table from the reduced primitive table found in step a(3):

(1) Compare each row of the reduced primitive table with all of the succeeding rows and construct a merger diagram. If there are no state conflicts between a pair of rows, these rows are compatible and a line is drawn between the corresponding row numbers on the merger diagram.

(2) Select a minimum set of merged rows from the merger diagram and merge the corresponding rows of the reduced primitive table to form a minimum-row table.

(3) Construct a Mealy output table for the minimum row table by associating the appropriate output with each stable total state.

The procedure outlined above will always reduce a primitive table to a minimum number of rows provided that the only don't cares in the original table arise from forbidden input changes (for example, if only single input variable changes are allowed). If the original table contains don't cares which arise from other conditions, use of the more general procedure for reduction of incompletely specified state tables may be necessary.

In this unit, we have only specified the outputs associated with the stable total states in the minimum-row Mealy flow table. After making a state assignment using the methods discussed in Unit 25, we will fill in the unspecified entries so as to avoid unwanted transients in the network output. In some cases, the flow table must be modified in order to make a proper state assignment. For this reason, it is usually desirable to wait to complete the output table until the state assignment has been made.

Programmed Exercise 24.1

Cover the bottom of the page with a sheet of paper and slide it down as you check your answers.

This example illustrates the process of reducing a primitive flow table to a minimum number of rows using the procedure described on page 474.

    a. For the given state table, list the sets of potentially equivalent stable total states. (Total states in each set must have the same inputs and outputs.)

	$X_1 X_2$ 00	01	11	10	Z
1	①	2	3	4	0
2	8	②	7	9	1
3	1	2	③	9	0
4	1	6	7	④	1
5	⑤	6	7	4	0
6	5	⑥	3	4	1
7	8	2	⑦	9	0
8	⑧	2	3	4	0
9	5	10	3	⑨	1
10	1	⑩	7	9	0
11	5	10	⑪	4	0

Answer to a: (1, 5, 8) (2, 6) (3, 7, 11) (4, 9)

    b. For convenience in checking the next states, we will rewrite the state table with the potentially equivalent states grouped together. (This step is not necessary, but for large tables it may be helpful.)

	00	01	11	10
1	①	2	3	4
5	⑤	6	7	4
8	⑧	2	3	4
2	8	②	7	9
6	5	⑥	3	4
3	1	2	③	9
7	8	2	⑦	9
11	5	10	⑪	4
4	1	6	7	④
9	5	10	3	⑨

Are the next states of (1, 5, 8) potentially equivalent for the 01 column?

_____

for the 11 column? _____

for the 10 column? _____

Are the next states of (2, 6) potentially equivalent for all columns? _____

Are the next states of (3, 7, 11) potentially equivalent for all columns? _____

At this point, can you conclude that any of the pairs (3, 7), (3, 11), (7, 11) are not equivalent? _____

What can you say about the equivalence of 4 and 9? _____
Why? _____

List the sets of states which are still potentially equivalent:

Programmed Exercise 24.1 (continued)

Answers to b: yes;   yes;   yes;   yes;   no; $2 \not\equiv 10$; $3 \not\equiv 11; 7 \not\equiv 11; 4 \not\equiv 9$
because $6 \not\equiv 10$; $(1, 5, 8)$ $(2, 6)$ $(3, 7)$

---

c. Since we found some non-equivalent states in part b, we must recheck the potentially equivalent states listed above.

At this point, are the next states of $(1, 5, 8)$ potentially equivalent for all columns? _____

What can you say about the equivalence of states 2 and 6? _____
Why? _____

At this point, are 3 and 7 still potentially equivalent? _____

List the sets of states which are still potentially equivalent:

Answers to c: yes; $2 \not\equiv 6$ because $4 \not\equiv 9$;   yes; $(1, 5, 8)$ $(3, 7)$

---

d. Since we found some non-equivalent states in part c, we are not done yet.

Are any of the pairs $(1, 5)$, $(1, 8)$, $(5, 8)$, $(3, 7)$ not equivalent? _____
Why? _____

At this point we have eliminated all pairs of non-equivalent stable total states. Which pairs of equivalent stable total states remain?

_____

Answers to d: $1 \not\equiv 5$ and $5 \not\equiv 8$ because $2 \not\equiv 6$; $1 \equiv 8$ and $3 \equiv 7$

---

e. Write out the minimum row primitive flow table by eliminating states 7 and 8 from the original table.

	$X_1 X_2$				Z
	00	01	11	10	
1					
2					
3					
4					
5					
6					
9					
10					
11					

Programmed Exercise 24.1 (continued)

Answer to e:

	$X_1 X_2$				Z
	00	01	11	10	
1	①	2	3	4	0
2	1	②	3	9	1
3	1	2	③	9	0
4	1	6	3	④	1
5	⑤	6	3	4	0
6	5	⑥	3	4	1
9	5	10	3	⑨	1
10	1	⑩	3	9	0
11	5	10	⑪	4	0

f. Although the above table is a minimum-row *primitive* flow table, we can convert it to a non-primitive Mealy flow table by merging rows. Using a merger diagram, indicate which rows in the above table can be merged.

Merge appropriate rows in the above table and give the merged rows below (including the corresponding rows of the Mealy output table).

Answer to f:

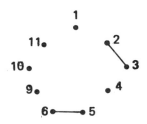

Note that rows 2 and 3 can be merged in spite of the fact that row 2 has a 1 output and row 3 has a 0 output. The merged rows are:

| 1 | ② | ③ | 9 | – | 1 | 0 | – |
| ⑤ | ⑥ | 3 | 4 | 0 | 1 | – | – |

PROBLEMS

24.2 An asynchronous sequential switching network has two inputs and two outputs. All possible input sequences and the required output sequences are tabulated as follows:

Input sequence: 00, 10, 11, 01, 00
Output sequence: 00, 00, 10, 00, 00

Input sequence: 00, 01, 11, 10, 00
Output sequence: 00, 00, 01, 00, 00

Input sequence: 00, 10, 00, 01, 00
Output sequence: 00, 00, 00, 00, 00

Input sequence: 00, 01, 00, 10, 00
Output sequence: 00, 00, 00, 00, 00

Find a minimum-row flow table.

24.3 A common feature of computer consoles is a step control, which enables the operator to step the computer through a program one cycle at a time. This requires a circuit where a push-button can be used to parcel out the clock pulses, one clock pulse each time the push-button is pressed. The timing diagram is shown below. The timing of the push-button signal is random, except that the duration and interval is long compared to clock duration and interval. Find a minimum-row flow table.

24.4 A sequential network has two inputs $(X_1 X_2)$ and one output (Z). If the input sequence 00, 01, 11 occurs, Z becomes 1 and remains 1 until the input sequence 11, 01, 00 occurs. In this case Z becomes 0 and remains 0 until the first sequence occurs again. (Note that the last input in one sequence may be the first input in the other sequence.) Find a minimum-row flow table.

24.5 For the following primitive flow table, find the equivalent stable total states and reduce the table accordingly. Complete the reduction by row merger and then derive a corresponding output table. Is the minimum-row flow table unique?

$X_1 X_2$

00	01	11	10	$Z_1 Z_2$
①	11	4	10	01
5	②	–	3	11
5	2	13	③	11
12	–	④	15	00
⑤	–	8	–	10
14	⑥	–	10	11
⑦	6	8	3	01
7	–	⑧	3	00
⑨	11	13	10	01
12	6	13	⑩	11
5	⑪	–	3	11
⑫	2	4	15	01
1	–	⑬	10	00
⑭	–	8	–	10
1	6	4	⑮	11

24.6 One type of clocked D flip-flop works as follows:

On the trailing edge of the clock pulse (1 to 0 transition) the output Q assumes the same state which the input D had on the leading edge of the clock pulse (0 to 1 transition). The output does not change at any other time. D may change at any time with respect to the clock. When D changes simultaneously with the leading edge of the clock, the value D had immediately before the change should determine the output after the clock pulse. Find a minimum-row flow table.

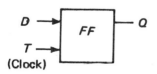

25

STATE ASSIGNMENT AND
REALIZATION OF FLOW TABLES

OBJECTIVES

1. Given any flow table, find a state assignment which avoids critical races and construct the expanded flow table.

2. Find a shared row assignment for a given flow table. Know and be able to use standard assignments for 4, 5 and 8 row tables.

3. Fill in the output table to avoid transient outputs.

4. Realize a given flow table using gates and S-R flip-flops or gates only.

STUDY GUIDE

1. Study Section 25.1, *Introductory Example*.

    a. What is the most important consideration in making state assignments for asynchronous networks?

    b. Given a transition table for an asynchronous network, how can you determine if any races are present?

    Verify that Fig. 25-3 is free of races.

    c. Review Section 13.3 on derivation of S-R flip-flop input equations, if necessary.

2. Study Section 25.2, *State Assignments for 3- and 4-Row Tables.*

    a. Verify that Figs. 25-8 and 25-10 are free of critical races.

    b. Is the following assignment valid for Fig. 25-6? Justify your answer.

a	
b	
	c
	d

    c. What are the relative advantages of the assignments of Figs. 25-7 and 25-9?

3. Study Section 25.3, *Shared-Row Assignments.*

    a. Is Fig. 25-13(c) a valid assignment for Fig. 25-12(a)?

    b. Why isn't the following assignment valid for Fig. 25-12(a)?

a	
b	
d	f
c	e

    c. A student has derived the following assignment map for a 6-row table:

1	3
5	2
6	
α	4

In column 10 of the flow table, the following transitions are required:

$$5 \rightarrow 2 \quad \text{and} \quad 3, 4 \rightarrow 1$$

In the student's solution, the transition from state 3 to 1 is direct, and the transition from 4 to 1 is directed through α in order to avoid a critical race. Using the same map, what is a better way of handling the 4 to 1 transition without going through α?

    d. The following transitions are required in a 5-row flow table:

        column 00: $d \rightarrow a$ $b, e \rightarrow c$ column 01: $c \rightarrow a$ $e \rightarrow d$

        column 11: $b, c \rightarrow d$ $a \rightarrow e$ column 10: $a, d, e \rightarrow b$

Complete the following assignment map so as to avoid critical races. Indicate the transitions for each column by arrows on a copy of the assignment map. Arrange your assignment so that no transitions pass through the shaded square on the map.

e. What are two possible disadvantages of using the universal assignment of Fig. 25-16?

f. Given the following flow table and assignment map, modify the flow table as required so that all required transitions between rows are race-free. Do *not* add any rows to the table; however, you may fill in the don't cares if necessary.

	00	01	11	10
a	ⓐ	c	—	d
b	c	ⓑ	ⓑ	ⓑ
c	ⓒ	ⓒ	e	d
d	—	b	ⓓ	ⓓ
e	a	ⓔ	ⓔ	—

4. Study Section 25.4, *Completion of the Output Table.*

a. The output portion of the following table is to be filled in to avoid transient outputs. Assume that *all* input changes are possible.

Q_1Q_2		00	01	11	10	00	01	11	10
0 0	1	①	2	2	①	0	$(0)_{-a}$	$-b$	0
0 1	2	1	②	②	3	$(0)_{-c}$	0	1	$-d$
1 1	3	2	4	③	③	$-e$	$-f$	1	1
1 0	4	④	④	3	1	0	1	$(1)_{-g}$	$-h$

(1) Why was output *a* assigned 0?

(2) What should output *f* be?

(3) Why was *c* assigned 0?

(4) Why can b and e remain $-$'s?

(5) What should d be?

(6) What should h be?

b. Fill in the output table associated with the following transition table so as to avoid output transients. (Give all possible ways of filling in the first output column.)

	00	01	11	10	00	01	11	10
00	00	01	–	10	0		–	
01	00	01	01	11	1		1	
11	01	–	01	11	–			0
10	11	10	11	10	1			1

c. Work Programmed Exercise 25.1.

5. Work Problems 25.2–25.6.

6. Study Section 25.5, *The One-Hot Assignment.* *

a. A one-hot assignment is made for Fig. 25-12(a) with $Q_1 = 1$ for row a, $Q_2 = 1$ for row b, etc. The next state equation for row d is

$$Q_4^+ = \underbrace{Q_4 Q_2' Q_5'}_{\text{holding term}} + \underbrace{X_1' X_2 (Q_3 + Q_6) + X_1 X_2' (Q_1 + Q_3)}_{\text{transition terms}}$$

Explain each of the terms in the equation, noting that there are two transitions leaving row d, and 4 transitions entering row d.

b. Suppose that Fig. 25-22 is to be realized using *S-R* flip-flops using the given one-hot assignment. By inspection of Equations (25-1), write the corresponding *S-R* equations. *Hint:* Each next state equation is of the following form:

$$Q_i^+ = Q_i R' + S$$

c. Work Problem 25.7.

7. When you are satisfied that you can meet the objectives, take the readiness test.

---

*This section is optional.

25. STATE ASSIGNMENT AND REALIZATION OF FLOW TABLES

Once a reduced flow table has been derived for an asynchronous sequential network, the next step in the design is making a state assignment. In choosing a state assignment for *synchronous* networks, the primary objective was simplification of the logic. However, for *asynchronous* networks the primary objective in choosing a state assignment is prevention of critical races, and simplification of the logic becomes a secondary consideration. After a state assignment has been made which is free of critical races, the asynchronous network can be realized using gates and *S-R* flip-flops or using gates only.

25.1 Introductory Example

We now will complete the design for Example 1 of Unit 24. Figure 25-1 gives the reduced flow table of Fig. 24-11 with the next states labeled in terms of the internal states a, b and c. The outputs for the unstable total states will be filled in after the state assignment has been made. Note that in the 00 column a transition is required from row b to row a, in the 01 column a transition is required from row c to row b, in the 11 column from row a to row c, and in column 10 from a to b and from c to b. The state transition diagram, Fig. 25-2(a), indicates the required transitions. A line drawn between a pair of states indicates a required transition between that pair of states.

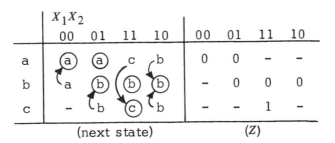

(next state)   (Z)

Fig. 25-1

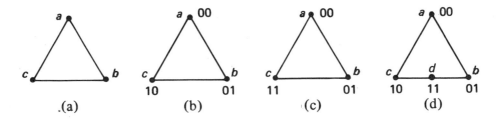

Fig. 25-2

Two state variables are required to realize the 3-row flow table. To avoid critical races we must find a state assignment such that only one state variable changes during each state transition. Two attempts to find such an assignment are indicated in Fig. 25-2(b) and (c). In the first case there is a critical race going from state c to state b (10 to 01), and in the second case a critical race going from a to c (00 to 11). In fact, it is impossible to find a race-free assignment in this way. If a single variable changes going from a to b, a single variable changes from b to c, and a single variable changes going from c to a, then there are three single variable changes in all. However, to get back where we started each variable must change an even number of times. Therefore, we cannot make a race-free assignment for the given 3-row table and we must expand the table to four rows.

If we add an extra row to the table and direct the transition from row c to row b through row d, then we can make the race-free assignment shown in Fig. 25-2(d). Using this assignment, we can construct the transition table of Fig. 25-3. In column 01, starting in row c, the state variables change from 10 to 11 to 01, thus avoiding a critical race. In column 10, we could also have directed the transition from row c to row b through row d; however, since a transition is already required from row a to row b, we can direct the transition from c to a to b (10 to 00 to 01) as shown in the transition table.

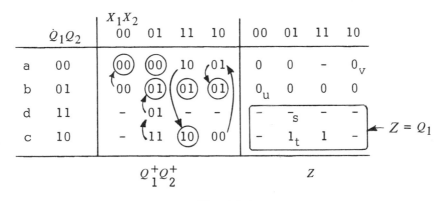

Fig. 25-3

The outputs corresponding to the unstable total states must then be filled in to avoid momentary false outputs during the transitions between stable total states. One way of filling in the output table to do this is indicated in Fig. 25-3. Detailed procedures for completing the output table are discussed in Section 25-4.

Having found a race-free state assignment, we now proceed to realize the network. First we will realize it using gates and delays as shown in Fig. 25-4(a). The next state maps for state variables Q_1 and Q_2 are plotted from the transition table of Fig. 25-3, and the output function is $Z = Q_1$. The next state functions, Q_1^+ and Q_2^+ lead directly to the network of Fig. 25-4(a). In most cases, the internal delay in the gates is sufficient to assure proper operation of the network and the delays indicated in the network diagram can be eliminated.

$$Q_1^+ = X_1 X_2 Q_2' + X_2 Q_1 Q_2'$$

$$Q_2^+ = X_1 X_2' Q_1' + X_1' Q_1 + X_2 Q_2$$

Fig. 25-4(a). Gate realization of Fig. 25-3

Figure 25-4(b) shows an alternate realization using *S-R* flip-flops. The flip-flop input functions are derived by converting the next state maps to *S* and *R* maps using the same rules as for synchronous networks. Each *S-R* flip-flop can be constructed from two cross-coupled NOR gates as discussed in Unit 12.

As an alternative to using *S-R* flip-flops constructed from cross-coupled NOR gates, flip-flops constructed from cross-coupled NAND gates may be used. Analysis of the NAND-gate flip-flop* in Fig. 25-5(a) shows that a 0 applied to the *U* input will set *Q* to 1, and a 0 applied to the *V* input will reset the flip-flop to *Q* = 0. Normally, *U* = *V* = 0 is not allowed since this would produce 1 outputs from both NAND gates. Figure 25-5(b) shows the inputs required to change the flip-flop state. Comparison with a similar table for the *S-R* flip-flop, Table 13-4(c), shows that *U* = *S'* and *V* = *R'*. Therefore the design procedure using NAND gate flip-flops is the same as for *S-R* flip-flops except that the *S* and *R* functions must be complemented. Figure 25-5(c) shows the realization of Fig. 25-3 using NAND-gate flip-flops. The flip-flop inputs are the complements of the *S* and *R* inputs in Fig. 25-4(b).

*See Problem 12.2.

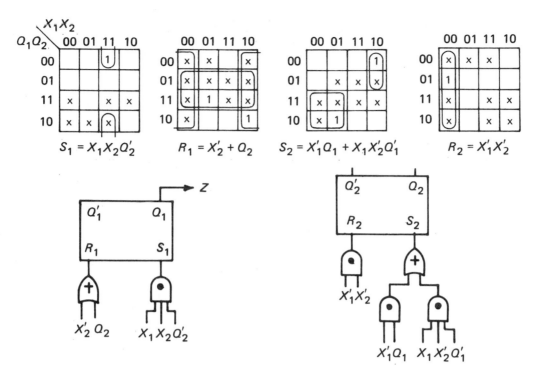

Fig. 25-4(b). *S-R* flip-flop realization of Fig. 25-3

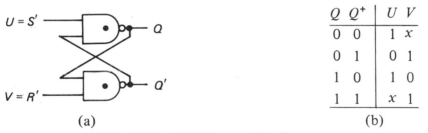

Q	Q^+	U	V
0	0	1	x
0	1	0	1
1	0	1	0
1	1	x	1

(a)   (b)

Fig. 25-5. NAND-gate flip-flop

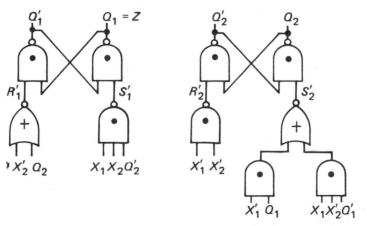

Fig. 25-5(c). NAND flip-flop realization of Fig. 25-3

25.2   State Assignments for 3- and 4-Row Tables

A race-free assignment for any 3-row flow table can be found using two state variables. If, as in the previous example, transitions between all 3 pairs of rows are required, a fourth row is added to the table. Then races can be eliminated by directing the transition between one pair of rows through the added row.

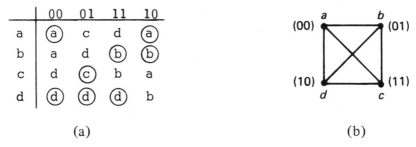

(a)   (b)

Fig. 25-6.   General 4-row table and state transition diagram

Although a race-free assignment for some 4-row tables requires only two state variables, many 4-row tables require three state variables. In the most general case for a 4-row table, transitions are required between all pairs of rows as illustrated in Fig. 25-6. The transitions for each column are as follows:

$$\text{column 00} \qquad b \to a, \ c \to d$$
$$\text{column 01} \qquad a \to c, \ b \to d$$
$$\text{column 11} \qquad a \to d, \ c \to b$$
$$\text{column 10} \qquad c \to a, \ d \to b$$

As can be seen from the state transition diagram, any assignment using two state variables will have critical races. Therefore, at least three state variables are needed. Figure 25-7 shows a universal state assignment map which will work for any 4-row table. Since states in adjacent squares differ in only one variable, direct transitions can be made from a to b, b to c, and b to d. On the other hand the transition from a to d is directed through state e so that only one state variable changes at a time. Similarly, the transition from c to d is directed through g, and c to a goes through f. Using the assignment given by the map, the four row table (Fig. 25-6) can be expanded to a 7-row table which is free of races (Fig. 25-8). Note that in every row of this table, the present state and next state differ in at most one state variable.

Figure 25-9 shows another universal assignment for four-row tables. In making this assignment, each state in the original table is replaced by a pair of equivalent states. For example, a is replaced with a_1 and a_2, where $a \equiv a_1 \equiv a_2$. Note that a_1 is adjacent to b_2, c_1 and d_1; b_1 is adjacent to a_2, c_1 and d_1; and each state is adjacent to three states of different types. Thus it is always possible to change from a state of a given type to one of the other types by changing a single state variable.

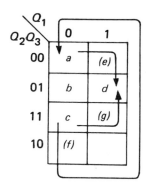

Fig. 25-7. Universal state assignment for 4-row tables

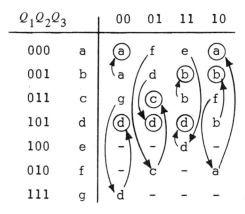

$Q_1Q_2Q_3$		00	01	11	10
000	a	(a)	f	e	(a)
001	b	a	d	(b)	(b)
011	c	g	(c)	b	f
101	d	(d)	(d)	(d)	b
100	e	–	–	d	–
010	f	–	c	–	a
111	g	d	–	–	–

Fig. 25-8. Expanded 4-row table

Figure 25-10 shows the table of Fig. 25-6 in expanded form using the state assignment of Fig. 25-9. The expanded table is formed as follows. First, each row in the original table is replaced with two rows, and the stable total states in each row are filled in. For example, row a is replaced by rows a_1 and a_2, and the stable total states (a_1) and (a_2) are entered in columns 00 and 10. After all stable total states have been entered, the unstable states are filled in by reference to the assignment map. When choosing the next state entry for a given present state, a state which is adjacent to the present state is selected from the map. In the original table, the next states of b are a and d for inputs 00 and 01 respectively. In the expanded table, the next states for row b_1 are a_2 and d_1 because a_2 and d_1 are adjacent to b_1 on the map; similarly, the next states for b_2 are a_1 and d_2.

For the table of Fig. 25-10, if we start in any stable total state and change the input, only one state variable will change in going to the next stable total state. This is in contrast to Fig. 25-8 where transitions between some stable total states

$Q_1Q_2Q_3$		00	01	11	10
000	a_1	(a_1)	c_1	d_1	(a_1)
111	a_2	(a_2)	c_2	d_2	(a_2)
011	b_1	a_2	d_1	(b_1)	(b_1)
100	b_2	a_1	d_2	(b_2)	(b_2)
010	c_1	d_2	(c_1)	b_1	a_1
101	c_2	d_1	(c_2)	b_2	a_2
001	d_1	(d_1)	(d_1)	(d_1)	b_1
110	d_2	(d_2)	(d_2)	(d_2)	b_2

Fig. 25-9. Universal assignment for 4-row tables

Fig. 25-10. Expanded 4-row table

require two successive state variable changes. Thus, a network based on Fig. 25-9 will generally be faster than one based on Fig. 25-7; however, more logic is required for the former because there are fewer don't cares in the table. Also, when each of the original stable states is represented by two or more states in the final network, observation of network behavior is more difficult. This may lead to increased system development time and maintenance costs.

When unspecified next state entries (don't cares) are present in the state table, they can often be used in the process of making a race-free state assignment. Consider Fig. 25-11(a), for example. The transitions needed for each column are

$$\text{column 00} \quad d \to a \qquad \text{column 01} \quad a \to b, \ c \to d$$
$$\text{column 11} \quad b \to c \qquad \text{column 10} \quad a \to c, \ b \to d$$

Since all possible transitions between pairs of rows are needed, it first appears that adding rows to the table will be necessary in order to achieve a race-free assignment. However, this is not the case because of the don't cares in the table. If we make a 4-row assignment, the transitions in columns 01 and 10 must be satisfied directly since there are no don't cares in these columns. Therefore, we will make a state assignment based on the following transition diagram:

With this assignment, all of the transitions in columns 01 and 10 can be made without races. For column 00, the transition d to a cannot be made directly since this would lead to a critical race; however, since there is a dash in row c, we can make a transition from d to c to a. Similarly, in column 11 the direct transition b to c would lead to a critical race, but by using the $-$ in row a, we can make a transition from b to a to c. Figure 25-11(b) shows the resulting flow table with the necessary modifications made to columns 00 and 11 so that all critical races are eliminated.

(a) Flow table with don't cares

(b) Flow table with don't cares filled in to eliminate races

Fig. 25-11

25.3   Shared-Row Assignments

This section discusses a general approach to making state assignments in which extra rows are added to the flow table to resolve critical races. An extra row of the flow table may be used in different columns as an intermediate state between different pairs of rows, hence the term shared row.

	00	01	11	10
a	①	2	5	4
b	⑦	②	3	⑩
c	1	8	③	4
d	7	⑧	5	④
e	1	⑨	⑤	6
f	⑪	8	3	⑥

(a)

Required transitions:

column 00: $e, c \to a$ $d \to b$

column 01: $a \to b$ $c, f \to d$

column 11: $b, f \to c$ $a, d \to e$

column 10: $a, c \to d$ $e \to f$

(b)

Fig. 25-12

Consider the 6-row table of Fig. 25-12(a). At least three state variables are required and more may be needed to obtain a race-free assignment. The first step in making a state assignment is to list the required transitions in Fig. 25-12(b). The notation $e, c \to a$ means that states e and c must go to state a. There is some flexibility in the way these transitions are carried out. Several possibilities are:

e directly to a and c directly to a

e to c to a

c to e to a

any of the above, but going through an intermediate state (or states) during one (or more) of the transitions

Thus, to avoid critical races, the only requirement is that e, c and a be placed in a series of adjacent squares on the assignment map, or that they be placed in a series of adjacent squares with intermediate blank squares. Generally, use of intermediate blank squares should be avoided when possible. If blank squares are not filled in, this will leave more don't cares in the transition table and hence lead to a more economical realization.

The transitions listed in Fig. 25-12(b) imply that the states in each of the following adjacency sets must be placed in a series of adjacent squares:

column 00: $(a, c, e)(b, d)$

column 01: $(a, b)(c, d, f)$

column 11: $(b, c, f)(a, d, e)$

column 10: $(a, c, d)(e, f)$

We proceed to do this by trial and error, starting with a 3-variable map. State "a" can always be placed in the 000 square with no loss of generality. Then b is placed adjacent to a to satisfy the adjacency set (a, b), and d adjacent to b to satisfy the set (b, d):

OR

To satisfy the adjacency set (a, d, e), e is placed adjacent to a and d:

OR

Then f is placed adjacent to e:

OR

Now we try placing c in different squares so as to satisfy the remaining adjacency sets $[(a, c, e), (c, d, f), (b, c, f), (a, c, d)]$ as shown in Fig. 25-13.

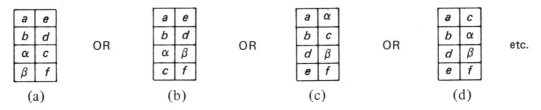

OR   OR   OR   etc.

(a)   (b)   (c)   (d)

Fig. 25-13

For the map of Fig. 25-13(a), the set (c, d, f) is satisfied directly, set (a, c, e) is satisfied by including α and β in the chain of adjacent squares; i.e., e, a, β, α and c form a string of adjacent squares. Similarly, (b, c, f) is satisfied by including α; and (a, c, d) is satisfied by including α and β. For the map of Fig. 25-13(b), the set (a, c, e) is satisfied directly. Set (c, d, f) is satisfied by including β; (b, c, f) by including α; and (a, c, d) by including α and β. Expanding Fig. 25-12(a) using the assignment of Fig. 25-13(b) yields Fig. 25-14.

		00	01	11	10
000	a	a	b	e	c
001	b	b	b	α	b
010	c	a	f	c	α
101	d	b	d	e	d
100	e	a	e	e	f
110	f	f	β	c	f
011	α	–	–	c	β
111	β	–	d	–	d

Fig. 25-14. Expanded table of Fig. 25-12(a) using assignment of Fig. 25-13(b)

In column 01 of Fig. 25-14, the transition from c to d is directed through f and $β$ since $c, f, β$ and d form a string of adjacent map squares. Similarly, in column 11 the transition from b to c goes through row $α$ since $b, α$ and c form a string of adjacent squares. In column 10, the transition from a to d goes by way of $c, α$ and $β$. In the expanded table, only one state variable changes in each transition between rows; hence there are no races (critical or otherwise). Row $α$ is "shared" between columns 11 and 10 and has a different next state in each of these columns.

When making shared-row assignment, it is often possible to take advantage of don't cares which are present in the flow table. Instead of adding rows to the table, it may be possible to eliminate critical races by directing some of the state transitions through the don't care states as was done in Fig. 25-11.

Most 5-row tables, including all tables with 14 or fewer columns, can be realized using three state variables with an assignment of the form shown in Fig. 25-15. This is not a universal assignment in the sense of Figs. 25-7 and 25-9 because the assignment will only work if the proper correspondence is established between $α, β, γ, δ$ and $ε$ and the five rows of the table. In other words the states of the table must be arranged on the assignment map in the pattern indicated in Fig. 25-15, and the order of the states on the map must be such that all transitions can be made without races.

α	
β	
γ	δ
	ε

Fig. 25-15. Assignment form for most 5-row tables

Fig. 25-16. Universal assignment for 8-row tables

Figure 25-16 shows a universal assignment for 8-row tables. For each column of the table the state transitions must be directed through the unused squares on the map in such a way as to avoid races. For example if the required transitions in a column are *a* to *c*, *b* to *h*, *d* to *f*, and *e* to *g*, the transitions would be directed as shown in Fig. 25-16. The 8-row universal assignment will also work for 6- or 7-row tables. However, many 6-, 7- and 8-row tables can be realized using only 3 state variables, and such an assignment should be attempted before using the universal assignment which requires 4 state variables.

The assignments discussed in this section have the disadvantage that several successive single state variable changes may be required when going from one stable total state to another. The fact that several *successive* changes are needed slows down the operation of the network. Faster operation can be achieved by allowing several state variables to change simultaneously, and making the state assignment such that all races are *non-critical.* In this way it is possible to make all transitions between stable total states without going through any intermediate rows. Such assignments are referred to as STT (single transition time) assignments. In general, STT assignments will require more state variables than shared row assignments. Methods for obtaining STT assignments are discussed by Unger* and others and will not be discussed here.

25.4 Completion of the Output Table

After a state assignment has been made which avoids critical races, the next step in designing an asynchronous sequential network is to complete the output table. At this point, the output has been specified for all of the stable total states. The unspecified entries in the Mealy output table must now be filled in so that momentary false outputs do not occur when the network is switching between stable total states. In synchronous networks, a momentary false output will cause no problem if it occurs between clock pulses. However, a momentary false output from an asynchronous network can cause problems if the output is used as an input to another asynchronous network.

A procedure for specifying the outputs for the unstable total states so as to avoid momentary false outputs is described below. Consider the partial flow table of Fig. 25-17 and the four possible output configurations given. In case (a), states ① and ② both have 0 output, so the "−" must be replaced with 0 so that a constant 0 output will be maintained during the transition from ① to ②. Similarly, in case (d), the "−" must be assigned a value 1 to prevent a momentary 0 output during the transition from ① to ②. In cases (b) and (c), the "−" may remain as a don't care since the output changes from 0 to 1 (or 1 to 0) anyway. Thus in case (b) if "−" is assigned a value 0, the output will only change once from 0 to 1 during the transition from state ① to ②; similarly, if "−" is assigned a value 1, the output only changes once during the state transition.

---

*S. H. Unger, *Asynchronous Sequential Switching Circuits*, Wiley, 1969, pp. 75-96.

Fig. 25-17

If a given input column can be reached starting in two (or more) different stable total states, then both (all) of the transitions must be considered in filling in the output table. Consider Fig. 25-18 for example. Starting in ①, the output changes from 1 to 0 so the "−" could be left as a don't care; however starting in ②, the output must remain a constant 0, so the "−" must be replaced with a 0.

Fig. 25-18

Figure 25-19 shows a partial flow table in which the transition between stable total states ⓐ and ⓒ goes through two intermediate unstable total states and the output changes from 0 to 1. Both of the don't cares in output table (a) cannot be assigned arbitrary values, because this could lead to the output sequence 0 (1) (0) 1, and this sequence contains unwanted transients. If one of the don't cares is assigned a value as in (b) and (c), then the other don't care can be assigned an arbitrary value (0 or 1) without introducing transients. Thus, when filling in the output table we can specify either (b) or (c), but we cannot leave both don't cares in the table as in (a).

a	ⓐ	b
b		c
c		ⓒ

(a)   (b)   (c)

Fig. 25-19

In the output table of Fig. 25-3, the entry labeled u must be 0 as indicated to maintain a constant 0 output when switching between total states $X_1 X_2 Q_1 Q_2 = 0101$ and 0000. Similarly, entry v must be 0 to avoid an output transient when switching between 0000 and 1001. The entries labeled s and t could also be 0 and "−", respectively. However, s and t cannot both be don't cares because this would allow the possibility of a 1010 output sequence during the transition from row c to d to b. The best choice for s and t is "−" and 1 since this simplifies the output function as shown in Fig. 25-3.

When the output table has two or more output variables, each of the outputs must be considered individually when replacing dashes with 0's or 1's. Figure 25-20 illustrates a case where the output changes from $Z_1 Z_2 = 01$ to 11. The intermediate output is filled in as −1 since Z_1 is changing and Z_2 is not.

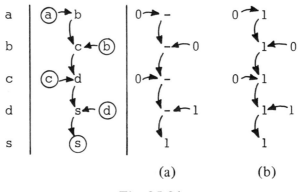

Fig. 25-20

Filling in the output table to eliminate all transients is always possible. If all unstable total states which lead to a stable total state ⓢ are assigned the same output as the output for state ⓢ, then when the input is changed the output will immediately assume its final value and no transient outputs will appear. Consider Fig. 25-21 for example. If the "−'s" in output table (a) are all changed to 1's as in (b), then the output will immediately assume its final value of 1 when the input is changed regardless whether the initial stable total state is ⓐ, ⓑ, ⓒ or ⓓ. This method of filling in the output has the advantage that the response to an input change is fast. It has the disadvantage that the don't cares are eliminated, and this may lead to an uneconomical output network.

(a)   (b)

Fig. 25-21

After the output table has been completed, the procedure used for realizing the network is similar to that used for synchronous networks. The transition table is formed by substituting the assigned values of the state variables for each state in the flow table. The next state maps are then plotted from the transition table. If the network is to be realized without using flip-flops, the next state functions are read from the maps and realized using the available logic gates. If S-R flip-flops are to be used, the S-R flip-flop input maps are derived from the next state maps in the usual manner. The S and R input functions are then read from the maps and realized using the available logic gates. If the state assignment used is free of critical races and if the output table is filled in correctly, a network realized by the above procedure should, in theory, work correctly. However, timing problems, which cause the network to malfunction, may arise due to gate delays. The detection and correction of such timing problems is the subject of the next unit.

25.5 The One-Hot Assignment

This section describes another method for finding a race-free state assignment. The one-hot assignment uses one state variable for each row of the flow table. The assignment is made such that when the network is in a stable state exactly one of the state variables is 1. In row i of the table, state variable Q_i is 1 and all other state variables are 0. When a transition between row i and row j is required, first state variable Q_j is set to 1 (so that both Q_i and Q_j are 1), and then Q_i is set to 0. Thus each transition between two rows in the flow table goes through one intermediate row and thus requires two state transition times.

The following example illustrates application of the one-hot assignment to Fig. 25-22. Starting in row a, when $x_1x_2 = 01$, a transition to row b is required; therefore, row e (with Q_1 and Q_2 both equal to 1) is added to the table and the transition from a to b is directed through row e. Starting in row a, when $x_1x_2 = 11$, a transition to row c is required; therefore row f (with Q_1 and Q_3 both equal to 1) is added to the table, and the transition from a to c is directed through row f. In a similar manner, rows g, h, i and j are added to the table so that every transition in the original table is directed through one of the added rows.

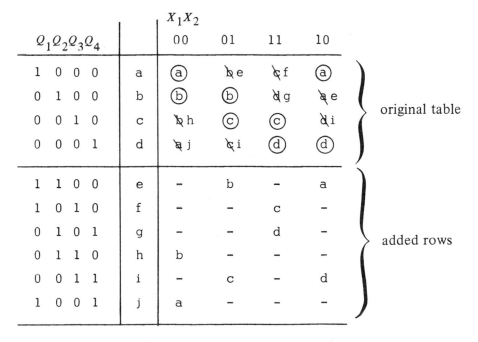

Fig. 25-22. One-hot assignment

The next state equations can be derived from Fig. 25-22 in the usual manner; however, they can also be derived by inspection of the original table *without* actually writing down the rows added to the table. Considering the original table in Fig. 25-22 and starting in a stable state in row $a(Q_1 = 1)$, if the input is changed to 01, first Q_2 must be set to 1 and then Q_1 must be set to 0. Therefore, the next state equation for Q_2 must contain a term $x_1'x_2Q_1$ in order to set Q_2 to 1. The next state equation for Q_1 should contain a term Q_1Q_2' which will keep Q_1 equal to 1 until Q_2 becomes 1. So far we have

$$Q_1^+ = Q_1Q_2' \ldots$$
$$Q_2^+ = x_1'x_2Q_1 + \ldots$$

Since a transition from row a to row c is required when the input is changed to 11, the next state equation for Q_3 contains a term $x_1x_2Q_1$ in order to set Q_3 to 1. To set Q_1 back to 0 when Q_3 becomes 1, we multiply the Q_1Q_2' term by Q_3' which gives

$$Q_1^+ = Q_1Q_2'Q_3' + \ldots$$
$$Q_2^+ = x_1'x_2Q_1 + \ldots$$
$$Q_3^+ = x_1x_2Q_1 + \ldots$$

Transitions from row b to rows d and a are required for inputs 11 and 10, respectively. Therefore we introduce a term $x_1x_2Q_2$ in the Q_4^+ equation and add $x_1x_2'Q_2$ to the Q_1^+ equation. To keep Q_2 equal to 1 until Q_4 or Q_1 becomes 1, we add $Q_2Q_1'Q_4'$ to the Q_2^+ equation. At this point we have

$$Q_1^+ = Q_1Q_2'Q_3' + x_1x_2'Q_2 + \ldots$$
$$Q_2^+ = Q_2Q_1'Q_4' + x_1'x_2Q_1 + \ldots$$
$$Q_3^+ = x_1x_2Q_1 + \ldots$$
$$Q_4^+ = x_1x_2Q_2 + \ldots$$

After adding in terms which correspond to the transitions from rows c and d, the final equations are

$$Q_1^+ = Q_1Q_2'Q_3' + x_1x_2'Q_2 + x_1'x_2'Q_4$$
$$Q_2^+ = Q_2Q_1'Q_4' + x_1'x_2Q_1 + x_1'x_2'Q_3$$
$$Q_3^+ = Q_3Q_2'Q_4' + x_1x_2Q_1 + x_1'x_2Q_4$$
$$Q_4^+ = Q_4Q_1'Q_3' + x_1x_2Q_2 + x_1x_2'Q_3 \tag{25-1}$$

$$\underbrace{}_{\substack{\text{holding} \\ \text{term}}} \quad \underbrace{}_{\substack{\text{transition} \\ \text{terms}}}$$

Each of these equations has a "holding term" which holds the given state variable in the 1 state until another state variable becomes 1. In addition, each equation contains one or more "transition terms" which cause the state variable to become 1 when the network is in an appropriate state and the appropriate input is applied.

In general, if transitions are required from row i to rows j, k, ... , the holding term for the Q_i^+ equation is of the form

$$Q_i Q_j' Q_k' \cdots$$

If a transition is required from row i to row j when input X is 1, then the Q_j^+ equation will contain a term of the form $Q_i X$.

As can be seen from the discussion, the logic equations for the one-hot assignment are relatively simple and easy to derive. Transitions from one row of the original table to another row are always carried out in two steps changing one state variable at a time, so the solution is free of races. The main disadvantage of the one-hot solution is the large number of state variables required.

Programmed Exercise 25.1

We will make a state assignment and complete the output table for the example of Fig. 24-13. This figure is reproduced below with the next state part of the table converted to internal state notation.

	00	01	11	10	00	01	11	10
a	ⓐ	ⓐ	g	b	11	10	--	--
b	ⓑ	d	c	ⓑ	01	--	--	00
c	ⓒ	a	ⓒ	b	01	--	10	--
d	c	ⓓ	e	–	--	11	--	--
e	–	a	ⓔ	f	--	--	01	--
f	b	–	g	ⓕ	--	--	--	11
g	–	d	ⓖ	b	--	--	00	--

$$Z_1 Z_2$$

List the state transitions which are required for each column:

        00   01   11   10

List the corresponding sets of adjacent states required for each column:

Programmed Exercise 25.1 (continued)

(Cover the bottom of the page with a sheet of paper and slide it down as you check your answers.)

Answers:

00: $d \to c$	01: $g, b \to d$	11: $a, f \to g$	10: $a, c, g \to b$
$f \to b$	$c, e \to a$	$b \to c; d \to e$	$e \to f$
$(c, d)(b, f)$	$(b, d, g)(a, c, e)$	$(a, f, g)(b, c)(d, e)$	$(a, b, c, g)(e, f)$

We will attempt to satisfy the required *pairs* of adjacent states first. Try to arrange the states $b, c, d,$ e and f on a map so that as many of the pairs (c, d) $(b, f) (b, c) (d, e)$ and (e, f) as possible are in adjacent squares.

Answer: Four of the five pairs can be made adjacent. Many different solutions are possible. We will work with the one shown at the right.

Add a to the map so that (a, c, e) forms a string of adjacent squares. Also add g so that (a, b, c, g) forms a string of adjacent squares. After these additions, which sets of adjacent squares are not directly satisfied?

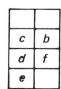

Answer: The map shown at the right directly satisfies all adjacency sets except:

$$(b, d, g) (a, f, g) (e, f)$$

Which of these sets can be satisfied by adding an extra row to the table?

Programmed Exercise 25.1 (continued)

Answer: (a, f, g) (e, f) can be satisfied by using row α.

a	g
c	b
d	f
e	α

At first it appears that (b, d, g) cannot be satisfied by this assignment and we will have to start over again. However, note that (b, d, g) is required for the 01 column and row f has a $-$ in the 01 column. Therefore, the transition can be made from row g to row b to row d by way of row f. Using the above assignment complete the expanded flow table below so that no races are present.

	00	01	11	10
a	ⓐ	ⓐ		
b	ⓑ			ⓑ
c	ⓒ		ⓒ	
d		ⓓ		
e			ⓔ	
f				ⓕ
g			ⓖ	
α				

Answer:

	00	01	11	10	0 0	0 1	1 1	1 0
a	ⓐ	ⓐ	g	c	1 1	1 0		
b	ⓑ	f	c	ⓑ	0 1			0 0
c	ⓒ	a	ⓒ	b	0 1		1 0	
d	c	ⓓ	e	–		1 1		– –
e	–	a	ⓔ	α	– –		0 1	
f	b	d	α	ⓕ				1 1
g	–	b	ⓖ	b	– –		0 0	
α	–	–	g	f	– –	– –		

Programmed Exercise 25.1 (continued)

Next we will fill in the blanks in the above output table so that no momentary false outputs will occur. We will use don't cares whenever possible. Double input changes were prohibited for the original primitive table from which this table was derived; therefore, we will only consider single changes of input when filling in the output table. The last column of the output table will be filled in as follows:

Row *c*: Possible transitions are indicated below. Why must "? ?" be replaced with 00?

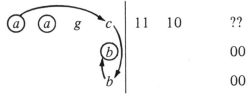

Row *a*: Why should " ? ? " be replaced with −−?

Row *e*: Why must *t* and *v* be replaced with 1's?
Why should *s* and *u* be replaced with " − " and 1 or 0 and " − ", respectively?

$$- \quad a \quad \textcircled{e} \quad \alpha \quad \Big| \quad -- \qquad 01 \quad s\,t$$
$$\textcircled{f} \qquad \qquad 11$$
$$\,f \qquad \qquad uv$$

Answer: Check for yourself to verify that when the outputs are filled in as indicated, no momentary false outputs will occur.

When a single input change produces only a single change of internal state variable, filling in the corresponding output entries is straightforward. Identify several such cases in the above flow table and fill in the corresponding output entries.

Programmed Exercise 25.1 (continued)

Answer: (new entries in the table are underlined)

	00	01	11	10	00	01	11	10
a	ⓐ	ⓐ	g	c	11	10	$\underline{-0}$	--
b	ⓑ	f	c	ⓑ	01		$\underline{-0}$	00
c	ⓒ	a	ⓒ	b	01	$\underline{10}$	10	00
d	c	ⓓ	e	–	$\underline{-1}$	11	-1	--
e	–	a	ⓔ	α	--	$\underline{--}$	01	-1
f	b	d	α	ⓕ	$\underline{-1}$			11
g	–	b	ⓖ	b	--		00	$\underline{00}$
α	–	–	g	f	--	--		11

Now fill in the remaining entries in the 11 column.

Answers: Two of the possibilities are

$$\begin{array}{cc} -\,- & 1\ 1 \\ & \text{and} \\ 0\ 0 & -\,- \end{array}$$

If you feel that you need more practice, fill in the remaining entries in the 01 column.

Answer: Two of the possibilities are

$$\begin{array}{ccc} 0\ 1 & & -\ 1 \\ -\ 1 & \text{and} & 1\ 1 \\ 0\ - & & 0\ - \end{array}$$

PROBLEMS

25.2 Make a proper assignment of internal state variables for each of the following flow tables. In each case, 3 internal state variables are sufficient. Specify the final state tables in terms of internal states.

X_1X_2

	00	01	11	10
a	①	4	⑦	10
b	1	⑤	⑧	11
c	2	⑥	8	⑩
d	②	④	9	⑪
e	3	6	⑨	10
f	③	5	7	⑫

X_1X_2

	00	01	11	10
a	①	4	⑦	11
b	②	6	⑧	10
c	③	6	7	⑩
d	2	④	9	10
e	1	⑤	9	10
f	3	⑥	7	11
g	2	6	⑨	11
h	1	5	7	⑪

25.3 Using the following assignment for Fig. 25-6, find the expanded flow table. Note that although a direct transition from a_1 to c_1 or c_2 is not possible, a transition from a_1 to a_2 to c_1 is possible since a_1 and a_2 are equivalent states.

a_1	b_1
a_2	b_2
c_1	c_2
d_1	d_2

25.4 Realize Fig. 24-15 using:

a. two S-R flip-flops and gates,

b. gates only.

25.5 Make a proper state assignment for the following table using the assignment form of Fig. 25-15, and give the expanded table.

X_1X_2

	00	01	11	10
a	①	7	②	10
b	5	③	9	④
c	⑤	⑥	8	10
d	1	⑦	⑧	4
e	1	3	⑨	⑩

25.6 Make a state assignment for Problem 24.6 such that the output is equal to one of the state variables.

25.7 Make a "one-hot" assignment for the table of Problem 25.5 and derive the next state equations.

26

HAZARDS

OBJECTIVES

1. Define static 0- and 1-hazards and dynamic hazards and give examples of networks containing such hazards. Explain why hazards in the combinational part of a sequential network can cause the network to go to the wrong state.

2. Given a combinational network, find all of the static 0- and 1-hazards. For each hazard, specify the order in which the gates must switch in order for the hazard to actually produce a false output.

3. Given a switching function, find a two-level network to realize it which is free of static and dynamic hazards (for single input variable changes). Be able to transform this network to a higher level network which is also hazard free.

4. Find all of the essential hazards in an asynchronous network by using a flow table. For any given essential hazard, specify the order in which the network elements must switch in order for the network to go to the wrong state. Eliminate essential hazards by adding delays in appropriate places in the network.

5. Find a hazard-free realization of a flow table using S-R flip-flops or cross-coupled NAND gates.

STUDY GUIDE

1. Study Section 26.1, *Hazards in Combinational Networks*.

   a. Review the discussion of gate delays in Section 12.1. Even though all of the gates in a network are of the same type, each individual gate may have a different propagation delay. For example, for one type of TTL NAND gate the manufacturer specifies a minimum propagation delay of 5 nano-seconds (*ns*) and a maximum delay of 30 *ns*. Sketch the gate outputs for the following network when the *x* input changes from 1 to 0, assuming the following gate delays:

gate 1 - 5 *ns*,   gate 2 - 20 *ns*,   gate 3 - 10 *ns*.

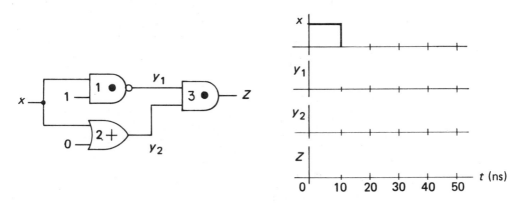

b. Consider the network of Fig. 26-1 for the case where $x_1 = y = 1$ and x_2 changes from 0 to 1. For this case, in what order must the gate outputs change in order for the hazard to show up at the network output?

c. Define static 0-hazard, static 1-hazard, and dynamic hazard.

2. Study Section 26.2, *Detection of Static Zero and One Hazards.*

a. When computing the transient output function, F^t, why must each variable and its complement be treated like separate variables?

b. Using a Karnaugh map, explain why $F = a'b + ac$ has a 1-hazard for the input change $abc = 011$ to 111, but not for 011 to 010. Then explain it without using the map.

c. Explain why $F = (a' + b')(b + c)$ has a 0-hazard for the input change $abc = 100$ to 110, but not for 100 to 000.

3. Study Section 26.3, *Dynamic Hazards.*

For $a = b = 1$, note that Z^t reduces to $Z^t = c' + cc' = (c + c')c'$.

If c changes from 0 to 1, in what order must the c's in these expressions change in order for the dynamic hazard to show up?

4. Study Section 26.4, *Design of Hazard-Free Combinational Networks.*

a. State two conditions which are sufficient to assure that a sum-of-products expression for F^t represents a hazard-free two-level AND-OR network.

b. State two conditions which are sufficient to assure that a product-of-sums expression for F^t represents a hazard-free two-level OR-AND network.

c. Why does transforming a network of AND and OR gates to NAND or NOR gates introduce no hazards?

5. Study Section 26.5, *Essential Hazards.*

a. How can essential hazards be determined from the flow table?

b. For Fig. 26-12, find two more essential hazards in addition to those mentioned in the text.

c. How can essential hazards be eliminated from a network?

d. If the network of Fig. 26-10 is started in stable total state $\textcircled{c}$ and the input is changed from 0 to 1, specify the sequence of events which must occur in order for the network to go to an incorrect stable total state. At what *one* point in the network should a delay be added to eliminate this essential hazard?

6. Study Section 26.6, *Hazard-Free Realizations Using* S-R *Flip-Flops.*

   a. Why is it permissible to have 1-hazards, but not 0-hazards, in the input networks for an *S-R* flip-flop?

   b. How can a network be designed which is free of 0-hazards?

   c. Why is it permissible to have 0-hazards, but not 1-hazards, in the input networks for a NAND-gate flip-flop?

   d. The following network is part of the realization of a flow table which contains essential hazards. Assume that initially $x_1 = 1$, $x_2 = 0$, $y_1 = 0$ and $y_2 = 1$. If x_2 changing to 1 causes y_2 to go to 0, what sequence of events would cause y_1 to go to the wrong state?

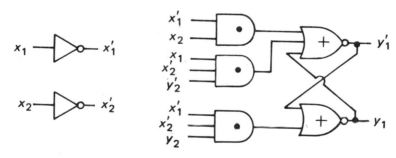

   e. Assuming that the network delays are concentrated mainly in the gate outputs, how should the above gate structure be changed to eliminate any essential hazards?

   f. The following gate is one of the input gates to a NAND flip-flop as in Fig. 26-16(b). Assuming that the network delays are concentrated mainly in the gate outputs, how should the gate be changed to eliminate any essential hazards?

7. Work Problems 26.1 through 26.4.

8. When you are satisfied that you can meet the objectives, take the readiness test.

26. HAZARDS

Even though an asynchronous sequential network is designed with a race-free state assignment using the procedures described in Unit 25, the network still may malfunction due to timing problems. Such timing problems, which arise due to gate and wiring delays, are referred to as hazards. This unit describes how to detect and eliminate these hazards so that the asynchronous network will function properly.

26.1 Hazards in Combinational Networks

When the input to a combinational network changes, unwanted switching transients may appear at the network output. These transients occur because different paths through the network from input to output may have different propagation delays. For example, consider the network of Fig. 26-1.

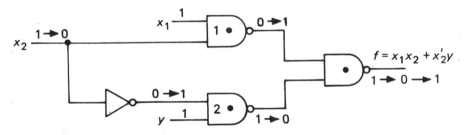

Fig. 26-1.   Network with 1-hazard

Consider the case where $x_1 = y = 1$ and x_2 changes from 1 to 0. The network output should remain a constant 1; however, the network output may momentarily go to 0 if the gate outputs switch in the following sequence: gate 1 output goes to 1, then f goes to 0, then the inverter output goes to 1, then gate 2 output goes to 0, and finally f goes back to 1.

If, in response to an input change and for some combination of propagation delays, a network output may momentarily go to 0 when it should remain a constant 1, we say that the network has a *static 1-hazard*. Similarly, if the output may momentarily go to 1 when it should remain a constant 0, we say that the network has a *static 0-hazard*. If, when the output is supposed to change from 0 to 1 (or 1 to 0), the output may change three or more times, we say that the network has a *dynamic hazard*. Fig. 26-2 illustrates possible outputs from a network with hazards. In each case the steady-state output of the network is correct, but a switching transient appears at the network output when the input is changed.

In the example of Fig. 26-1, note that although in the steady state x_2 and x_2' are complements, under transient conditions they are not. Thus in the analysis of a network for hazards, we must treat a variable and its complement as if they were two independent variables. The hazard in Fig. 26-1 can be eliminated by adding a redundant gate as shown in Fig. 26-3. During the time when x_2 is switching and $x_2 = x_2' = 0$, the term $x_1 y$ remains 1; hence f remains 1, and no false 0 appears at the network output. In Sections 26.2 and 26.4 we will study a general method for eliminating hazards from combinational networks.

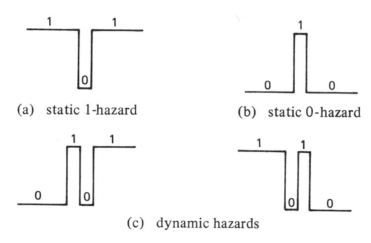

(a) static 1-hazard   (b) static 0-hazard

(c) dynamic hazards

Fig. 26-2. Types of hazards

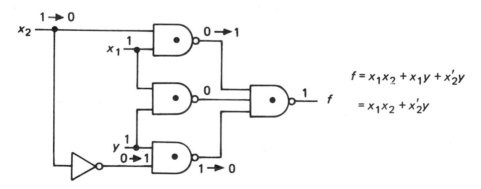

$$f = x_1 x_2 + x_1 y + x_2' y$$

$$= x_1 x_2 + x_2' y$$

Fig. 26-3. Network of Fig. 26-1 with hazard removed

Hazards in the combinational part of a sequential network can cause the sequential network to malfunction. Hazards in the output network can cause momentary false outputs, which may be a serious problem if the output serves as the input to another asynchronous network. As illustrated by the following example (Fig. 26-4) hazards in the next state part of the network may cause the network to go to the wrong stable total state. If the network is in stable total state ④ ($x_1 = x_2 = y = 1$) and the x_2 input is changed to 0, the next stable total state should be ⑤. However, if because of the 1-hazard in the network, y momentarily goes to 0, and this feeds back before the x_2' signal goes to 1, the output of gate 2 will remain 1 and the network will end up in state ②. This malfunction can be eliminated by adding an extra gate as in Fig. 26-3.

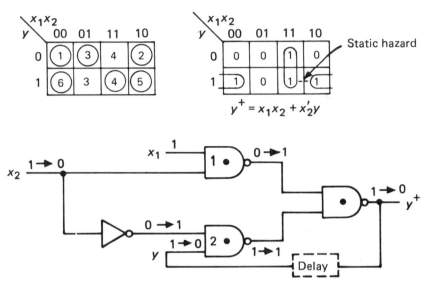

Fig. 26-4. Sequential network with hazard

26.2 Detection of Static Zero and One Hazards

This section presents a systematic approach for detecting the presence of static hazards in a combinational network. We will only consider hazards which occur when a single input variable changes. Analysis begins by determining the *transient output function, F^t*, which represents the behavior of the network under transient conditions. The transient output function for a network is determined in the same way as the ordinary (steady-state) output function except a variable x_i and its complement x_i' are treated as independent variables. This must be done since during transient conditions x_i and x_i' may both momentarily assume the same values. This means that the following theorems of Boolean algebra *cannot* be used when manipulating F^t:

$$XX' = 0, \; X + X' = 1, X + X'Y = X + Y, XY + X'Z + YZ = XY + X'Z, \text{ etc.}$$

The associative, distributive, and DeMorgan's laws as well as $XX = X$, $X + XY = X$, etc., *can* be used.

The following example illustrates how F^t is used to detect hazards. For Fig. 26-5(a), the transient output function is

$$F^t = abc + (a + d)(a' + c') = abc + aa' + ac' + a'd + c'd \qquad (26\text{-}1)$$

To check for static 1-hazards, the 1-terms of F^t are plotted on a Karnaugh map as in Fig. 26-5(b). (If F is in sum-of-products form, each product term is called a 1-term of F.) The term aa' can momentarily go to 1 when a is changing; however, this cannot cause a 1-hazard since the momentary 1 cannot cause F to go to 0. Similarly, any term which contains the product of a variable and its complement cannot cause a 1-hazard. Thus, such terms can be ignored when checking for 1-hazards (they can't be plotted on the map anyway).

If two 1's in adjacent squares on the map of F^t are covered by the same 1-term, changing the input to the network between the corresponding two input states cannot cause a hazard.

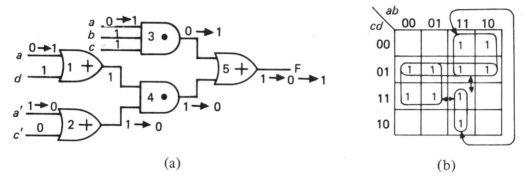

(a)   (b)

Fig. 26-5. Detection of static 1-hazards

For example, in Fig. 26-5(b), changing the input from $abcd = 1100$ to 1000 cannot cause a hazard because the corresponding 1's on the map are both covered by the term ac'. This means that when b is changing, the ac' term remains a constant 1; hence F^t remains a constant 1, and there is no 1-hazard. However, if two 1's in adjacent squares on the map are not covered by a single 1-term, a hazard is present. For example, an input change from 0111 to 1111 causes a hazard because the corresponding 1's are not covered by a single 1-term. For this input change, the term $a'd$ must change from 1 to 0 while the term abc changes from 0 to 1. Since all of the other 1-terms are 0 during this transition, F^t can go to 0 if the $a'd$ term goes to 0 before the abc term goes to 1; therefore, a 1-hazard is present. This hazard will actually show up at the network output, as indicated in Fig. 26-5(a), if the gate outputs change in the order: 2, 4, 5, 3, 5. The other two input changes which cause 1-hazards are indicated by arrows on the map.

The term aa' which is present in F^t indicates a possible 0-hazard since this term can momentarily go to 1 when it is supposed to remain 0. This 0-hazard is actually present only if the other terms of F^t are 0 while a is changing. If we set $d = 0$, $c' = 0$ ($c = 1$) and $b = 0$, F^t reduces to aa'. Therefore if $b = 0$, $c = 1$, $d = 0$, and a changes, F^t can momentarily go to 1, which indicates the presence of a 0-hazard. Although 0-hazards can be detected by careful inspection of the sum-of-products form of F^t, a more systematic approach uses the product-of-sums form. Factoring F^t by using the second distributive law, $X + YZ = (X + Y)(X + Z)$, gives

$$F^t = (abc + a + d)(abc + a' + c')$$

$$= (a + d)(a + a' + c')(b + a' + c')(c + a' + c')$$

Terms like $a + a' + c'$ and $c + a' + c'$ either remain a constant 1 or momentarily go to 0 and cannot cause a 0-hazard. The remaining 0-terms* of F^t are plotted on the map of Fig. 26-6(b). Note that the 0's on this map are in the same location as the implied 0's on the map of Fig. 26-5(b); however, we cannot determine how the 0's are grouped from Fig. 26-5(b).

An alternate procedure for mapping the 0-terms of F^t uses the fact that the 1-terms of $(F^t)'$ are the 0-terms of F^t. From Equation (26-1),

$$(F^t)' = (a' + b' + c')(a'd' + ac)$$

$$= a'd' + a'ac + \cancel{a'b'd'} + ab'c + \cancel{a'c'd'} + acc'$$

Note that two terms were eliminated using $X + XY = X$. When the terms $a'd'$ and $ab'c$ are plotted on the map using 0's instead of 1's, we obtain the same plot of 0-terms of F^t as in Fig. 26-6(b).

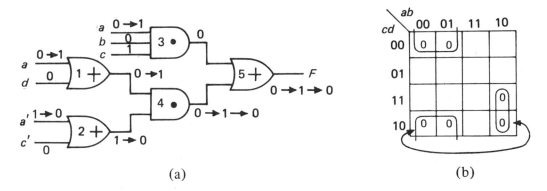

(a)　　　　　　　　　　　　　　(b)

Fig. 26-6. Detection of static 0-hazards

To detect 0-hazards, we examine pairs of adjacent 0's on the map of Fig. 26-6(b). Two adjacent 0's covered by the same 0-term cannot lead to a 0-hazard. For example, when $abcd$ is changed from 0000 to 0100, no 0-hazard is present because the term $a + d$ remains a constant 0 during this transition and F^t cannot change. If two adjacent 0's are not covered by the same 0-term, a 0-hazard is present. For example, if $abcd$ changes from 0010 to 1010, $a + d$ must change 0 to 1 while $a' + b + c'$ changes 1 to 0; therefore, both terms can momentarily be equal to 1, which indicates a 0-hazard. This 0-hazard will show up at the network output as indicated in Fig. 26-6(a) if the gates switch in the order: 1, 4, 5, 2, 4, 5.

In summary, the following procedure can be used to find all of the static 1- and 0-hazards in a network due to single input variable changes:

---

*If F is in product-of-sums form, each sum term is called a 0-term of F.

a. Determine the transient output function of the network F^t, and reduce F^t to sum-of-products form treating each variable and its complement as separate variables.

b. Examine each pair of adjacent input states for which F^t is 1. If there is no 1-term which includes both input states of the pair, a 1-hazard is present. (This is conveniently accomplished by plotting the 1-terms of F^t on a Karnaugh map and checking each pair of adjacent 1's on the map.)

c. If the sum of products for F^t *does not* contain the product of a variable and its complement, no 0-hazards are present. If the sum of products for F^t *does* contain the product of a variable and its complement, a 0-hazard *may* be present. To detect all 0-hazards,

 (1) Obtain the product-of-sums for F^t by factoring or other means (still treating x_i and x_i' as separate variables).

 (2) Examine each pair of adjacent input states for which F^t is 0. If there is no 0-term which includes both input states of the pair, a 0-hazard is present. (This is conveniently done by plotting the 0-terms of F^t on a Karnaugh map and checking each pair of adjacent 0's on the map.)

Static 1- and 0-hazards can be eliminated by adding additional gates to the network to produce the missing 1-terms and 0-terms. A procedure for designing hazard-free networks is given in Section 26.4.

26.3 Dynamic Hazards

Dynamic hazards due to a change in an input variable x_i can only occur if there are three or more paths between the x_i (and/or x_i') input and the network output. This is necessary since a dynamic hazard involves a triple change in output, so the effect of the input change must reach the output at three different times. A network may have a dynamic hazard even if it is free of static hazards as illustrated by the example of Fig. 26-7. For this network, the transient output function is

$$Z^t = (ac' + bc)(a' + c') = a'ac' + \underline{a'bc} + \underline{ac'} + bcc'$$

$$= (ac' + b)(ac' + c)(a' + c') = (a + b)(b + c')(a + c)(c + c')(a' + c')$$

Plotting the 1-terms and 0-terms of Z^t on the map of Fig. 26-7(b) reveals that there are no 1-hazards or 0-hazards. Inspection of the network shows that the only input variable which could cause a dynamic hazard when it changes is c (since c is the only variable with 3 paths to the output). If we choose $a = b = 1$, the effect of a change in c can propagate to the output along all three paths. If the gate outputs change in the order shown in Fig. 26-7(c), the $G3$ output undergoes a 1-0-1 change before the $G4$ output changes 1 to 0, and the dynamic hazard shows up at the output.

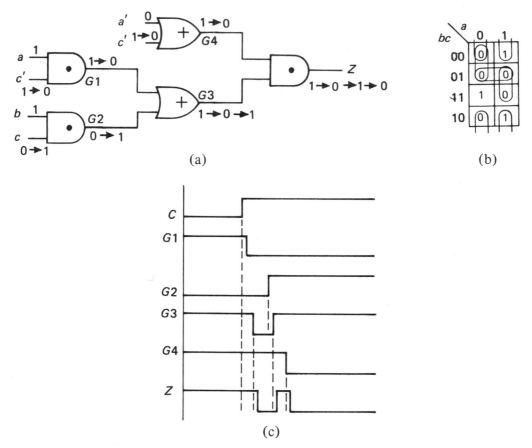

Fig. 26-7. Network with a dynamic hazard

The procedure used to detect static hazards can be extended to allow the detection of all dynamic hazards; however, this is beyond the scope of this text.*

26.4 Design of Hazard-Free Combinational Networks

In this section, we will discuss a procedure for designing networks which are free of static 0- and 1-hazards as well as dynamic hazards. The procedure is based on the following theorems:

Theorem 26.1 If the 1-terms of F^t satisfy the following conditions, the network will not contain static or dynamic hazards:

    a. For each pair of adjacent input states that produce a 1 output, there is at least one 1-term that includes both input states of the pair.

    b. There are no 1-terms that contain exactly one pair of complementary literals.

---

*See McCluskey, E. J., *Introduction to the Theory of Switching Circuits* for a description of the procedure used to find dynamic hazards.

Theorem 26.2 If the 0-terms of F^t satisfy the following conditions, the network will not contain static or dynamic hazards:

   a. For each pair of adjacent input states that produce a 0 output, there is at least one 0-term that includes both input states of the pair.

   b. There are no 0-terms that contain exactly one pair of complementary literals.

Condition a of Theorem 26.1 assures that the network does not contain 1-hazards, and condition b eliminates the possibility of 0-hazards and dynamic hazards. Alternatively, condition a of Theorem 26.2 assures that the network does not contain 0-hazards, and condition b eliminates the possibility of 1-hazards and dynamic hazards. Thus we can use either Theorem 26.1 or 26.2 to design a hazard free network.

Based on Theorem 26.1, a design procedure for hazard-free networks is:

   a. Find a sum-of-products expression (F^t) for the output in which every pair of adjacent 1's is covered by a 1-term. (The sum of all prime implicants will always satisfy this condition.)

   b. Manipulate F^t to the desired form (by factoring*, DeMorgan's laws, etc.) treating each x_i and x_i' as independent variables so as to prevent introduction of hazards.

An alternative procedure, based on Theorem 26.2 is

   a. Find a product-of-sums expression (F^t) for the output in which every pair of adjacent 0's is covered by a 0-term.

   b. Manipulate F^t to the desired form without introducing hazards.

The following example illustrates the design of a network which is free of static and dynamic hazards. We will realize

$$f(a, b, c, d) = \Sigma m(1, 5, 7, 14, 15)$$

first using NAND gates and then using NOR gates. When f is read from the map (Fig. 26-8), a redundant term is included so that all pairs of adjacent 1's are covered and f is free from 1-hazards. Since no terms containing products of literals like xx' are included, f is automatically free of 0-hazards and dynamic hazards. Since simple factoring and application of DeMorgan's laws do not introduce any hazards, f can be realized using NAND gates as shown.

To realize f using NOR gates, we start by reading the 0's from the map (Fig. 26-9). Redundant terms are included so that all adjacent 0's are covered, so f is free of 0-hazards. Since no terms containing sums like $x + x'$ are included, f is automatically free of 1-hazards and dynamic hazards. Since factoring and applying DeMorgan's laws do not introduce any hazards, f can be realized using NOR gates as shown.

---

*Simple factoring using the ordinary distributive law does not introduce hazards; however, factoring using $XY + X'Z = (X + Z)(X' + Y)$ can introduce hazards.

$f = a'c'd + a'bd + bcd + abc$
$= a'd(b + c') + bc(a + d)$
$= \{[a'd(b + c')]' \cdot [bc(a + d)]'\}'$
$= \{[a'd(b'c)']' \cdot [bc(a'd')']'\}'$

Fig. 26-8

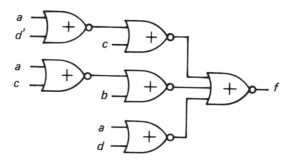

$f' = c'd' + ab' + ac' + b'c + a'd'$
$f = [c'd' + ab' + ac' + b'c + a'd']'$
$= [c'(a + d') + b'(a + c) + a'd']'$
$= \{[c + (a + d')']' + [b + (a + c)']'$
$+ [a + d]'\}'$

Fig. 26-9

26.5   Essential Hazards

Even though an asynchronous sequential network is free of critical races and the combinational part of the network is free of static and dynamic hazards, timing problems due to propagation delays may still cause the network to malfunction and go to the wrong state. Consider, for example, the network of Fig. 26-10. Clearly, there are no hazards in the combinational part of the network, and inspection of the flow table shows that there are no critical races. If we start in state (a) and change X to 1, the network should go to state (d). However, consider the following possible sequence of events:

a. X changes 0 to 1

b. gate 2 output changes 0 to 1

c. flip-flop y_1 output changes 0 to 1

d. gate 4 output changes 0 to 1

e. flip-flop y_2 output changes 0 to 1

f. inverter output X' changes 1 to 0

g. gate 1 output changes 0 to 1, gate 2 output changes back to 0, gate 4 output changes back to 0

h. flip-flop output y_1 changes back to 0

Note that the final state of the network is ⓑ instead of ⓓ. This came about because the delay in the inverter was longer than the other delays in the network, so that in effect part of the network saw the value $X = 1$ while the other part of the network saw the value $X = 0$. The net result was that the network acted as if the input X had changed three times instead of once so that the network went through the sequence of states $y_1 y_2 = 00, 10, 11, 01$.

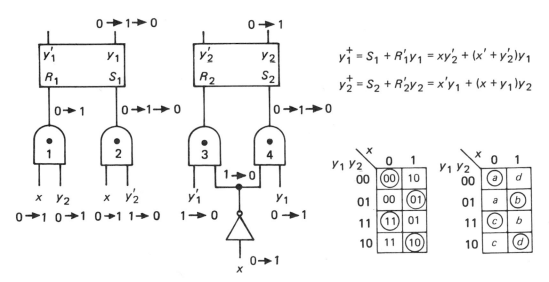

$$y_1^+ = S_1 + R_1' y_1 = xy_2' + (x' + y_2')y_1$$

$$y_2^+ = S_2 + R_2' y_2 = x'y_1 + (x + y_1)y_2$$

Fig. 26-10. Network with essential hazards

The malfunction illustrated in the previous example is referred to as an *essential hazard*. Essential hazards can be located by inspection of the flow table. We will define an essential hazard as follows:

A flow table has an *essential hazard* starting in stable total state ⓢ for input variable x_i iff the stable total state reached after one change in x_i is different from the stable total state reached after three changes in x_i.

If an essential hazard exists in the flow table for stable total state ⓢ and input x_i, then when the network is realized there will be some combination of propagation delays which will cause the network to go to the wrong state when x_i is changed starting in (s). This occurs because the change in x_i reaches different parts of the network at different times. Fig. 26-11 illustrates portions of several flow tables. Essential hazards exist for state (a) in cases (d) and (e).

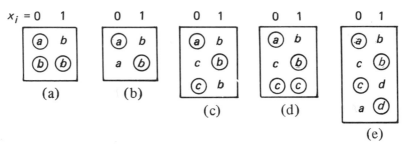

Fig. 26-11

In order to test a flow table for essential hazards, it is necessary to test each stable total state for each possible input change using the definition given above. For example, the flow table of Fig. 26-12 has essential hazards starting in (1) and changing x_1, starting in (5) and changing x_1, and starting in (4) and changing x_2.

$x_1 x_2$

$y_1 y_2$	00	01	11	10
00	①	2	–	5
01	3	②	6	⑤
11	③	2	⑥	7
10	1	④	6	⑦

Fig. 26-12. Flow table with essential hazards

Essential hazards can be eliminated by adding delays to the network. For the example of Fig. 26-10, if we add a sufficiently large delay to the output of flip-flop y_1, then the change in X will propagate to all of the gates before the change in y_1 does and the essential hazard is eliminated. For Fig. 26-12, to eliminate the essential hazard starting in (1), it is necessary to delay the change in y_2 until the change in x_1 has had a chance to propagate through the network.

In summary, in order to design an asynchronous network which is free of timing problems, we must:

   a. Make a state assignment which is free of critical races.

   b. Design the combinational part of the network so that it is free of hazards (this may require adding redundant gates).

   c. Add delays in the feedback paths for the state variables as required to eliminate essential hazards.

26.6 Hazard-Free Realizations Using S-R Flip-Flops

Use of *S-R* flip-flops·simplifies the design of hazard-free asynchronous networks. A momentary 1 applied to the *S* or *R* input can set or reset the flip-flop; however, a momentary 0 applied to *S* or *R* will have no effect on the flip-flop state. Therefore, the networks realizing *S* and *R* must be free of 0-hazards (since a 0-hazard can produce a momentary false 1), but the *S* and *R* networks may contain 1-hazards. A minimum two-level sum-of-products expression may contain 1-hazards, but it is inherently free of 0-hazards. For this reason, the minimum sum of products can be used as a starting point for realizing the *S* or *R* flip-flop input equations. In the process of realizing *S* and *R*, simple factoring or other transformations which do not introduce 0-hazards can, of course, be applied to the minimum sum-of-products expressions.

Figure 26-13(a) shows a typical network structure with the *S-R* flip-flop constructed from cross-coupled NOR gates. If multiple-input NOR gates are available, the OR gates can be eliminated as shown in Fig. 26-13(b). The two structures are equivalent since in both cases

$$Q = (P + R_1 + R_2 + \ldots)' \text{ and } P = (Q + S_1 + S_2 + \ldots)'$$

Even if an asynchronous network is realized using *S-R* flip-flops, and the *S* and *R* networks are free of 0-hazards, essential hazards may still be present. Such essential hazards may be eliminated as discussed in Section 26.5 by adding delays in the feedback paths for the state variables. An alternative method for eliminating essential hazards[*] involves changing the gate structure of the network.

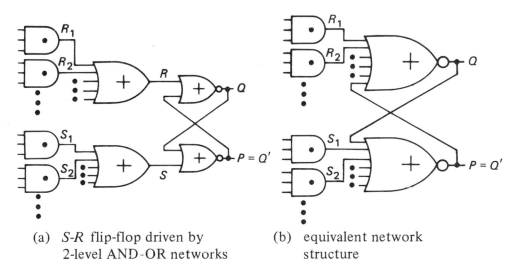

(a) *S-R* flip-flop driven by
      2-level AND-OR networks

(b) equivalent network
      structure

Fig. 26-13. Gate structures for *S-R* flip-flop realization of flow table

[*]Armstrong, Friedman, and Menon, "Realization of Asynchronous Sequential Circuits Without Inserted Delay Elements," *IEEE Transactions on Computers,* Vol. C-17, pp. 129-134, February 1968.

This alternative method can be applied only if the wiring delays in the network are small compared with the gate delays and if we can assume that all of the gate delays are concentrated at the gate outputs.

As illustrated in Section 26.5, the following sequence of events is required for an essential hazard to cause a network to malfunction:

a. An input variable changes.

b. A state variable changes in response to the input variable change.

c. The effect of the state variable change propagates through the network and initiates another state variable change before

d. the original input variable change has propagated through the entire network.

Thus, in an asynchronous network with S-R flip-flops, we can eliminate the essential hazards by arranging the gate structure so that the effect of any input change will propagate to all flip-flop inputs before any state variable changes can propagate back to the flip-flop inputs. For example, we can eliminate the essential hazard in Fig. 26-10 by replacing the R_2 and S_2 networks with Fig. 26-14. Assuming that wiring delays are negligible and that the gate delay is concentrated at the gate output, any change in x will propagate to R_2 and S_2 before flip-flop y_1 can change state and this change in y_1 can propagate to R_2 and S_2. This eliminates the essential hazard.

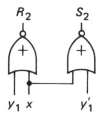

Fig. 26-14

Next, we will consider a more general case in which the network is of the form of Fig. 26-13(b). Each AND gate can have inputs of the form shown in Fig. 26-15(a), where the x's are external inputs to the network and the y's are fed back from flip-flop outputs. If there are essential hazards in the flow table, then the network could malfunction due to the inverter delays. If we replace the AND gate with the NOR-AND network of Fig. 26-15(b), the inverters on the x variables are eliminated. In the revised circuit, a change in any x will propagate to the S_i (or R_i) terminal before a flip-flop can change state and the corresponding y signal can propagate to S_i or R_i. Therefore, if we replace all of the AND gates in Fig. 26-13 with NOR-AND combinations as indicated in Fig. 26-15, all of the essential hazards will be eliminated. (We are still assuming that the network delays are largely concentrated at the gate outputs. Given a sufficiently long propagation delay in one of the x wires, an essential hazard could still cause a malfunction.)

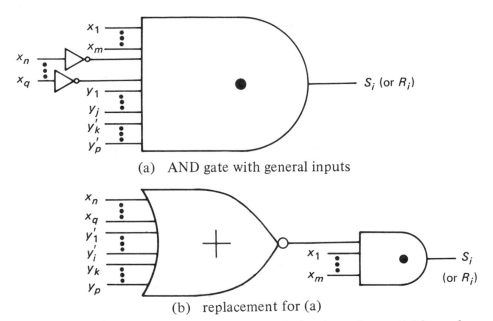

(a)   AND gate with general inputs

(b)   replacement for (a)

Fig. 26-15.   A gate transformation for elimination of essential hazards

Figure 26-16 shows two of the possible gate configurations when NAND flip-flops are used to realize a state variable in an asynchronous network. If minimum sum-of-products expressions are derived for S and R, then the complements of these expressions will be minimum product-of-sums expressions for S' and R'. If S and R are free of 0-hazards, S' and R' will be free of 1-hazards. This is exactly what is needed for the NAND flip-flops since a 0 applied to S' or R' can change the flip-flop state but a 1 cannot. If multiple-input NAND gates are available, Fig. 26-16(a) can be transformed to Fig. 26-16(b) by eliminating the AND gates and replacing the OR gates by NAND gates with complemented inputs. Note that for both networks

$$Q = (P \cdot U_1 \cdot U_2 \ldots)' \quad \text{and} \quad P = (Q \cdot V_1 \cdot V_2 \ldots)'$$

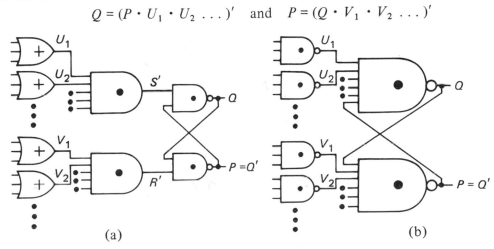

(a)

(b)

Fig. 26-16.   Gate structure for NAND flip-flop realization of flow table

If a network constructed using the configuration of Fig. 26-16(b) contains essential hazards, they can be eliminated by replacing each NAND gate (except the flip-flop) with a NOR-NAND configuration or equivalent, using a transformation similar to Fig. 26-15.

The example of Fig. 26-17 illustrates realization of a flow table using the gate structure of Fig. 26-16(b). First, the transition table is formed from the flow table using the given race-free state assignment. The flip-flop input equations, derived from the transition table in the usual manner, are:

$$S_1' = (X_1' X_2' Y_2)'(X_1 X_2 Y_2')' \qquad R_1' = (X_1' X_2' Y_2')'(X_1 X_2 X_2)'$$
$$S_2' = (X_1' X_2 Y_1')'(X_1 X_2' Y_1)' \qquad R_2' = (X_1' X_2 Y_1)'(X_1 X_2' Y_1')'$$

Figure 26-17(c) shows the resulting network. Assuming that the gate delays are largely concentrated at the gate outputs, the essential hazards can be eliminated by making the transformation shown in Fig. 26-17(d).

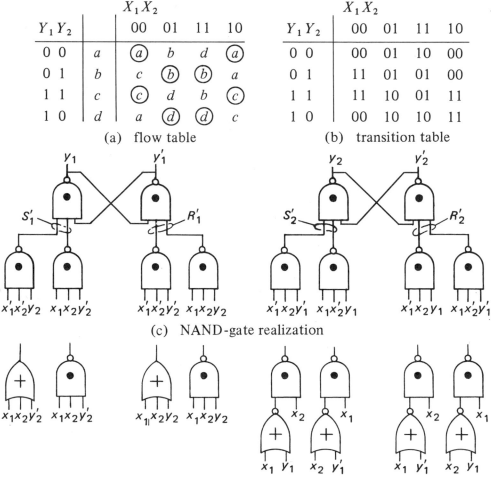

Fig. 26-17

PROBLEMS

26.1 Find all of the static hazards in the following network. For each hazard, specify the values of the variables which are constant and the variable which is changing. Indicate how all of these hazards could be eliminated by adding gates to the existing network. (This means that you can add gates or gate inputs to the network as it stands, but you cannot change any of the connections in the given network.)

26.2 a. Find all of the static hazards in the following network. For each hazard, specify the values of the input variables and which variable is changing when the hazard occurs. Also specify the order in which the gate outputs must change.

b. There is a dynamic hazard which occurs when the output of the network changes from 0 to 1. Specify the values of the input variables before and after. In which order must the gate outputs switch in order for this hazard to occur?

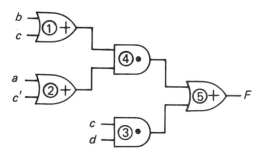

26.3 Find a hazard-free realization of the following function using only 3-input NOR gates.

$$f(a, b, c, d) = \Sigma m(0, 2, 6, 7, 8, 10, 13)$$

26.4 Find all of the essential hazards in the flow table of Fig. 24-15. Make any necessary changes so that your solution to Problem 25.4 is free of all hazards.

27

ASYNCHRONOUS SEQUENTIAL NETWORK DESIGN

OBJECTIVES

1. Use the short-cut method to derive *S-R* flip-flop input equations for an asynchronous network.

2. Design, construct and test an asynchronous sequential network.

STUDY GUIDE

1. Study Section 27.1, *Summary of Design Procedure.*

2. Study Section 27.2, *Short-Cut Method for Deriving* S-R *Flip-Flop Input Equations.*

   a. Under what conditions can the short-cut method be applied for deriving *S-R* input equations?

   b. If you are interested in a proof of the method, read Appendix C.3.

   c. Given the next state map for flip-flop Q_i, how do you read S_i from the map when using the short-cut method? How do you read R_i?

3. Read Section 27.3, *Design Example.*

   a. Verify that the flow table of Fig. 27-5 meets the problem specifications.

b.   Verify that the designs of Figs. 27-12 and 27-13 are correct and free of hazards.

4.   Read pages 586-587, *DESIGN PROBLEMS.*   When a toggle switch is used as an input to an asynchronous network, why is a switch filter necessary?

5.   Work out the solution for your assigned design problem. Check to see that your solution meets all of the design specifications.

6.   Carry out the lab testing as specified for your problem. If you have difficulty getting your circuit to work, try starting in each stable total state and verify that the output is correct and that the circuit goes to the proper next state when the input is changed.

7.   When you get your network working properly, demonstrate its operation to a proctor. After successful completion of the project, turn in your design and results of lab testing. (No readiness test is required.)

27.   ASYNCHRONOUS SEQUENTIAL NETWORK DESIGN

We have already studied the various steps in the design of asynchronous sequential networks—derivation and reduction of flow tables (Unit 24), state assignment to avoid critical races (Unit 25), and derivation of hazard-free realizations (Unit 26). This unit contains a summary of the design procedure and a comprehensive design example.

27.1   Summary of Design Procedure

a.   Given the problem statement, determine the required relationship between the input and output. Derive a primitive flow table which has one stable total state per row, and specify the output associated with each stable total state.

b.   Reduce the primitive flow table to a minimum number of rows. This may conveniently be done in two steps. First, determine equivalent stable total states and find a minimum-row *primitive* flow table. Then merge rows in this table to find the final reduced table. A merger diagram may be helpful in selecting rows to be merged.

c.   Find a state assignment which eliminates all critical races between state variables. In this process it may be necessary to expand the flow table by adding rows.

d.   Form the transition table by substituting the assigned values of the state variables for each state in the expanded flow table. If a Mealy output table is used, fill in unspecified entries as required to avoid transients in the output. Plot the next state maps and output maps from the transition table.

e. If flip-flops are not used, find a hazard-free realization for each next state function using available logic gates.

f. If *S-R* flip-flops are used, plot the flip-flop input maps and find a realization which is free of 0-hazards for each *S* and *R*. (If NAND-gate flip-flops are used, the flip-flop inputs are the complements of *S* and *R* and must be free of 1-hazards.)

g. Find a hazard-free realization of the output functions.

h. If essential hazards are present in the flow table, add delays in the feed-back paths or modify the gate structure as required to eliminate the essential hazards.

i. Check your design by laboratory testing or computer simulation.

27.2 Short-Cut Method for Deriving S-R Flip-Flop Input Equations

Most asynchronous networks are designed so that no cycles are present in the flow table. When the state assignment procedures discussed in Unit 25 are used, the resulting transition table will generally be free of all races (both critical and non-critical). This section introduces a fast method for deriving *S-R* flip-flop input equations which can be applied to any cycle-free asynchronous flow table provided that a race-free state assignment is used. This method is based on the following theorem:

If a cycle-free asynchronous flow table is realized with *S-R* flip-flops using a race-free state assignment, then for each flip-flop Q_i, there exist *S* and *R* equations which are independent of Q_i.

Note, for example, that in Fig. 25-4(b), the *S-R* equations for flip-flop Q_1 depend on Q_2, but not on Q_1. Similarly, the *S-R* equations for flip-flop Q_2 depend on Q_1, but not on Q_2. (A general proof of the above theorem is given in Appendix C.3.)

From Table 27-1, observe that when $Q_i = 0$, $S_i = Q_i^+$; similarly, when $Q_i = 1$, $R_i = (Q_i^+)'$.

Table 27-1

Q_i	Q_i^+	S_i	R_i
0	0	0	x
0	1	1	0
1	0	0	1
1	1	x	0

Thus, since S_i is independent of Q_i, we can read S_i directly from the $Q_i = 0$ half of the Q_i^+ map. Similarly, we can read R_i directly from the 0's of the $Q_i = 1$ half of the Q_i^+ map. Note that this is exactly the same procedure as for the short-cut method for deriving J-K flip-flop input equations (Section 13.5) except that J is replaced with S and K with R. The S-R equations will be exactly the same as the J-K equations, and the short-cut method for deriving J-K equations can be applied. In general, the short-cut method for deriving S-R equations does *not* apply to *synchronous* networks because state assignments for synchronous networks permit two or more state variables to change simultaneously.

The next state maps from Fig. 25-4(a) are reproduced in Fig. 27-1 to illustrate the short-cut method. Note that the resulting S-R equations are the same as those derived from the S-R maps in Fig. 25-4(b).

$$S_1 = X_1 X_2 Q_2' \qquad R_1 = X_2' + Q_2$$

$$S_2 = X_1' Q_1 + X_1 X_2' Q_1' \qquad R_2 = X_1' X_2'$$

Fig. 27-1.   Derivation of S-R equations by short-cut method

27.3   Design Example

Figure 27-2 shows a system of pipes with flowmeters to measure the fluid flowing through pipes A and B. The flowmeter in pipe A puts out a series of pulses with a pulse rate proportional to the flow in pipe A, and similarly the pulse rate from the other flowmeter is proportional to the rate of flow in pipe B. A "digital pulse subtracter" is to be designed to determine the rate of flow in pipe C. Thus the output pulse rate from the subtracter should be equal to the difference of the pulse rates from flowmeters A and B.

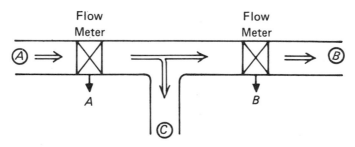

Fig. 27-2.   System of pipes with flowmeters

Figure 27-3(b) shows a typical timing diagram for the pulse subtracter. Input lines A and B each receive a series of pulses of varying frequency and pulse width. Under normal operation, the pulse frequency on line A is greater than that on line B and the number of pulses on the output line is the difference of the number of pulses received on lines A and B. Should the pulse frequency on line B

Fig. 27-3. **Digital pulse subtracter**

exceed that of A, the extra B pulses are ignored and no pulses are output on line Z. The output pulses should have the same width as the A pulses.

We will design the network so that when an A pulse occurs, an output pulse will occur. However, if a B pulse starts before (or during) an A pulse, we cancel the effect of the next A pulse so that it does not produce an output pulse. The output will never be turned on or off in the middle of an A pulse. In constructing the primitive flow table, we will assume that only one input variable changes at a time. (In actual practice, A and B might occasionally change simultaneously, but this will occur so infrequently that the error produced by ignoring simultaneous changes will be negligible compared with the error in the flowmeters.)

Sketching the various waveforms which can occur (Fig. 27-4) is helpful in constructing the primitive flow table. The circled numbers under each waveform indicate the corresponding stable total states which are reached in the primitive flow table (Fig. 27-5).

a. If no B pulse occurs, $Z = A$:

b. If a B pulse is started before an A pulse, the A pulse is cancelled:

c. If several A pulses occur during a B pulse, only the first one is cancelled:

 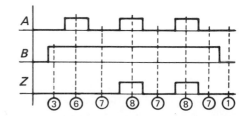

d. If a B pulse starts in the middle of an A pulse, the next A pulse is cancelled:

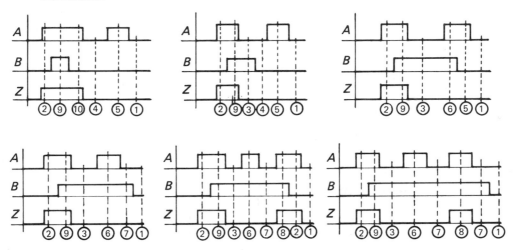

e. If the B pulse frequency is higher than A, the extra B pulses are ignored:

Fig. 27-4. Timing diagrams for pulse subtracter

Figure 27-5 shows the resulting primitive flow table together with the significance of each stable total state.

		AB 00	01	11	10	Z
reset	1	①	3	–	2	0
A on, Z on	2	1	–	9	②	1
B on, cancel next A	3	4	③	6	–	0
cancel next A	4	④	3	–	5	0
A on (cancelled)	5	1	–	6	⑤	0
A on (cancelled), B on	6	–	7	⑥	5	0
B on (don't cancel next A)	7	1	⑦	8	–	0
A on, B on, Z on (don't cancel next A)	8	–	7	⑧	2	1
A on, B on, Z on, cancel next A	9	–	3	⑨	10	1
A on, Z on, cancel next A	10	4	–	9	⑩	1

Fig. 27-5. **Primitive flow table for pulse subtracter**

For the primitive table of Fig. 27-5, the sets of stable total states which have the same inputs and outputs are

$$(1, 4) \quad (3, 7) \quad (8, 9) \quad \text{and} \quad (2, 10)$$

However, $1 \not\equiv 4$ because the next states in column 10 (2 and 5) are not equivalent. Similarly, $3 \not\equiv 7$ because $6 \not\equiv 8$, $8 \not\equiv 9$ because $3 \not\equiv 7$, and $2 \not\equiv 10$ because $1 \not\equiv 4$. Therefore, this primitive table has a minimum number of rows. The merger diagram of Fig. 27-6 shows the table can be reduced to five rows (Fig. 27-7).

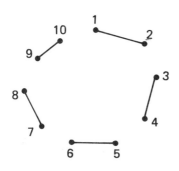

Fig. 27-6. **Merger diagram for Fig. 27-5**

	AB 00	01	11	10
a	①	3	9	②
b	④	③	6	5
c	1	7	⑥	⑤
d	1	⑦	⑧	2
e	4	3	⑨	⑩

Fig. 27-7. **Reduced table**

The following transitions between rows are required in Fig. 27-7:

$$e \to b \quad c, d \to a; \quad a, e \to b \quad c \to d; \quad b \to c \quad a \to e; \quad b \to c \quad d \to a$$

To avoid critical races, we must construct a state assignment which has the following adjacency sets:

$$(b, e) \quad (a, c, d); \quad (a, b, e) \quad (c, d); \quad (b, c) \quad (a, e); \quad (b, c) \quad (a, d)$$

The map of Fig. 27-8 satisfies all of these adjacencies directly except (b, c), and (b, c) is satisfied by adding row f. Figure 27-9 gives the expanded flow table based on this assignment.

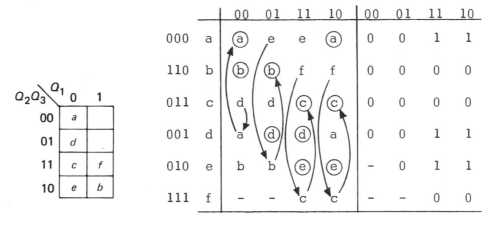

Q_2Q_3 \ Q_1	0	1
00	a	
01	d	
11	c	f
10	e	b

Fig. 27-8. State assignment for Fig. 27-7

		00	01	11	10	00	01	11	10
000	a	ⓐ	e	e	ⓐ	0	0	1	1
110	b	ⓑ	ⓑ	f	f	0	0	0	0
011	c	d	d	ⓒ	ⓒ	0	0	0	0
001	d	a	ⓓ	ⓓ	a	0	0	1	1
010	e	b	b	ⓔ	ⓔ	–	0	1	1
111	f	–	–	c	c	–	–	0	0

Fig. 27-9. Expanded flow table

$Q_1Q_2Q_3$	AB 00	01	11	10	00	01	11	10
0 0 0	000	010	010	000	0	0	1	1
0 0 1	000	001	001	000	0	0	1	1
0 1 0	110	110	010	010	–	0	1	1
0 1 1	001	001	011	011	0	0	0	0
1 1 0	110	110	111	111	0	0	0	0
1 1 1	–	–	011	011	–	–	0	0

$$Q_1^+ Q_2^+ Q_3^+ \qquad\qquad Z$$

Fig. 27-10. Transition table

Figure 27-10 shows the transition table. The *S-R* flip-flop equations are derived from the transition table using Karnaugh maps as shown in Fig. 27-11. The output equation, also derived from a Karnaugh map, is

$$Z = AQ_1'Q_3' + AQ_2'$$

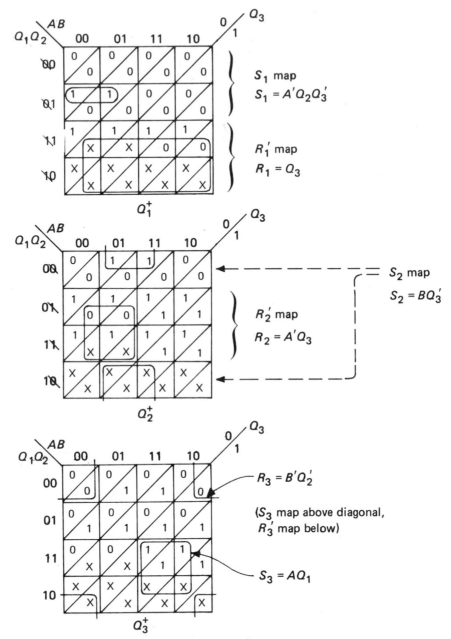

Fig. 27-11. Derivation of *S-R* equations by short-cut method

Figure 27-12 shows the resulting network. The *S-R* input functions are hazard-free since each requires only one gate, and the *Z* function is also free of hazards. However, inspection of Fig. 27-9 shows that there are essential hazards starting in the following total states:

$$b - 01, d - 01, d - 11, e - 11, e - 10$$

Therefore, it may be necessary to add delays to the flip-flop outputs in order to assure proper operation of the network.

Fig. 27-12. Realization of pulse subtracter using S-R flip-flops

Figure 27-13 shows an alternate realization using NAND flip-flops. The flip-flop inputs are the complements of those in Fig. 27-12. The gate structure has been chosen so as to eliminate the essential hazards, assuming that the network delays are largely concentrated at the gate outputs. Note that A and B require no inverters, and that they appear as inputs to the same gates as the Q's which feed back from the flip-flop outputs.

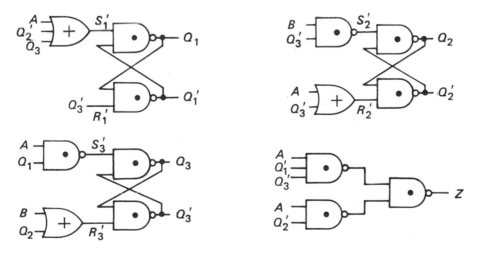

Fig. 27-13. Realization of pulse subtracter with NAND flip-flops

DESIGN PROBLEMS

The following problems each require the design and testing of a fundamental mode asynchronous sequential network. For purposes of lab testing, the
inputs will normally come from toggle switches. When a mechanical switch is
operated, the switch contact will vibrate or bounce several times before coming to
rest. This means that when a switch is closed, its output will contain a series of
noise pulses instead of simply changing from 0 to 1. The spurious 1 or 0 output
pulses can cause an asynchronous network to malfunction. For this reason, it is
important that the toggle switch outputs be filtered to eliminate the effects of
contact bounce. If the switches available in lab are not filtered, a simple filter can
be built using a NAND-gate flip-flop (Fig. 27-14). A single-pole double-throw
switch is connected to the flip-flop inputs. When the switch is moved to the upper
position, a 0 is applied to the S' input and X becomes 1. Even if the switch
bounces and makes intermittent contact in the upper position, the flip-flop cannot change state and its output will remain 1 until the switch is moved to the
lower position. When the switch is moved to the lower position, a 0 is applied to
R' and X becomes 0. Again, the flip-flop state will be unaffected by contact
bounce. Thus, the X and X' outputs from the flip-flop will not contain spurious
noise pulses and can be used as inputs to an asynchronous network.

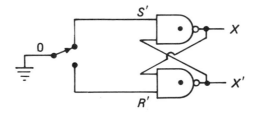

Fig. 27-14.   Contact bounce filter

When a network contains hazards, these hazards may or may not cause the
network to malfunction depending on the distribution of gate and wiring delays
in the network. For this reason, it may be necessary to insert added delay into the
network in order to actually observe the presence of hazards. Also, it may be
necessary to insert delay in the feedback paths of some networks to eliminate
essential hazards. Normally, 2, 4 or 6 inverters in series will provide sufficient delay for these purposes. If necessary, a resistor-capacitor network can be placed
between two of the inverters to increase the delay, or a special delay module
may be used.

If your asynchronous network does not function properly when you build
it in laboratory, determining the cause of the malfunction will generally be more
difficult than for a clocked synchronous network. If you find that your network

goes to the wrong state in response to some input change, the following procedure is suggested for tracking down the error:

a. Open all feedback loops and connect the state variables to switches as indicated in Fig. 27-15.

b. Set the switches to correspond to a given present state. Read the corresponding next state from the Q^+ outputs. If the next state is not correct, track down the error in the combinational network in the usual way.

c. If the network always generates the correct next state with the feedback loops open, but it goes to the wrong state when the switches are removed and the feedback loops are closed, this indicates that a race or hazard is present.

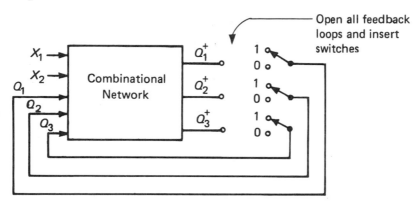

Fig. 27-15. Troubleshooting an asynchronous network

27 A. Design Specifications

Figure 27-16(a) illustrates a small room with a display set up. The room will hold only two people at a time. Visitors can enter or exit only through the turnstiles as shown. Each turnstile puts out a 1 signal whenever someone is in it. Whenever there are two people in the room, the entrance turnstile is locked to prevent additional entries and is not unlocked until one of the two people in the room starts to leave. It is unlocked at all other times. The room light is to be on whenever someone is entering, in, or leaving the room.

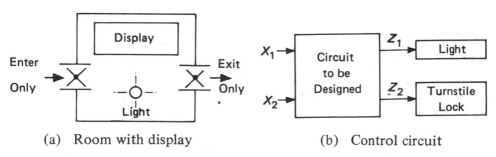

(a) Room with display   (b) Control circuit

Fig. 27-16

Design an asynchronous circuit for Fig. 27-16(b) to furnish the signals indicated.

$X_1 = 1$ if the entrance turnstile is in use, and $X_2 = 1$ if the exit turnstile is in use.

$Z_1 = 1$ should turn on the light, and $Z_2 = 1$ should lock the entrance turnstile.

Assume both inputs will not change simultaneously, although both inputs may be 1 simultaneously.

(1) Derive a minimum-row flow table (6 rows).

(2) Design the network using NAND gates and inverters only (no flip-flops or gates connected as flip-flops). Make sure your realization is free of combinational logic hazards.

(3) Find all of the essential hazards. For one of the essential hazards indicate the order in which the gate outputs must change in order for the hazard to cause the network to go to the wrong state. Indicate where a delay element should be added to the network in order to eliminate this hazard.

(4) Determine a suitable input sequence to test the network.

Lab Testing

(5) Construct and test the network designed in part (2) using the sequence determined in part (4).

(6) If no essential hazards show up, add delay to the appropriate gate output so that the essential hazard analyzed in part (3) will show up. Then add delay in the appropriate place(s) to eliminate the essential hazard(s) which were observed, and demonstrate that the network functions properly.

27 B.   Design Specifications

An "inhibited-toggle" flip-flop (Fig. 27-17) has a trigger input, T, and inhibit inputs, I_0 and I_1. The flip-flop output (Q) will change state if $I_0 = 1$ when T changes from 0 to 1, or if $I_1 = 1$ when T changes from 1 to 0. The flip-flop will not change state under any other conditions. You may assume that I_0 and I_1 will always be constant when T is changing.

Fig. 27-17

(1) Find a minimum-row flow table for the flip-flop (4 rows). (List the input variables in the order TI_0I_1.)

(2)   Design the flip-flop using NAND gates and inverters only (no flip-flops or gates connected as flip-flops). First design the network without eliminating hazards. Using your flow table and maps, indicate how one of the static hazards can cause the network to go to the wrong state. For this hazard, indicate the order in which the gates must change for the hazard to actually show up.

(3)   Add the necessary gates to the network designed in part (2) to eliminate the combinational logic hazards.

Lab Testing

(4)   Construct and test the network designed in part (3). If any essential hazards show up, add delays to eliminate them.

(5)   Remove the gates which were added to eliminate the combinational hazards so that you can test the design of part (2). Demonstrate that the static hazard which you analyzed in part (2) will actually cause the network to malfunction. You will probably have to add some delay to one of the gate outputs in order to make the hazard show up.

(6)   Reconnect the gates which were removed leaving any added delay in place and demonstrate that the network again functions properly.

27 C. Design Specifications

A push-button combination lock (Fig. 27-18) for a door operates as follows:

When locked, the following input sequence will unlock the door:
$X_1 X_2 = 00, 01, 11, 10, 00$

After the door is unlocked, (1) each time X_1 is depressed, the electric door opener will operate, and (2) depressing and releasing X_2 will relock the door.

Any sequence other than those given above will ring the alarm. For example, if the door is locked, the sequence 00, 01, 00 will ring the alarm; if the door is unlocked, the sequence 10, 11 will ring the alarm. Once the alarm starts ringing, it will keep ringing until the power is shut off.

You may assume that simultaneous input changes do not occur.

Fig. 27-18

(1) Derive a minimum-row flow table (7 rows).

(2) Design the network using NAND gates and inverters only (no flip-flops or gates connected as flip-flops). Make sure your realization is free of combinational logic hazards.

(3) Find all of the essential hazards. For one of the essential hazards indicate the order in which the gate outputs must change in order for the hazard to cause the network to go to the wrong state. Indicate where a delay element should be added to the network in order to eliminate each of the essential hazards.

Lab Testing

(4) Construct and test the network designed in (2).

(5) If no essential hazards show up, add delay to the appropriate gate output so that the essential hazard analyzed in (3) will show up. Then add delay in the appropriate place(s) to eliminate the essential hazard(s) which were observed, and demonstrate that the network functions properly.

27 D. Design Specifications

This problem concerns the design of an asynchronous sequential switching network (Fig. 27-19) to detect the direction of rotation of a shaft. A cam mounted on the shaft actuates two switches as shown. The single output of the circuit is to be 1 when the shaft is rotating clockwise and 0 when the shaft is rotating counterclockwise. If the direction of rotation changes, the output should change as soon as possible.

(1) Synthesize the network using only NAND and NOR gates (no flip-flops or gates connected as flip-flops). Design two different output networks, one which is minimum and one which is free of hazards.

(2) Synthesize the network using two NAND-gate flip-flops and NAND and NOR gates. The output network should be the same as in (1).

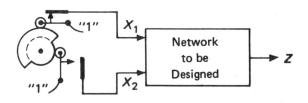

$x_1 x_2 = 10$ for the cam position shown

Fig. 27-19

Lab Testing

(3) Test the design of part (1) using the minimum output network.

(4) Test the design of part (2) using each of the output networks. Check the output for transients by connecting Z to the T (clock) input of a J-K flip-flop. If the hazard doesn't show up when using the minimum output network, add some delay in the appropriate place so that the hazard will become apparent. Then make sure that your output is transient-free when the hazard-free output network is used.

27 E.   Design Specifications

Same as Problem 27A except:

(2) Design the network using NAND gates connected as flip-flops. Use the gate configuration of Fig. 26-16(b).

In parts (3) and (6), do not use delays to eliminate the essential hazards. Instead, change the gate structure to eliminate the essential hazards using the technique described in Section 26.6.

27 F.   Design Specifications

Same as Problem 27C except:

(2) Design the network using NAND gates connected as flip-flops. Use the gate configuration of Fig. 26-16(b).

In parts (3) and (5), do not use delays to eliminate the essential hazards. Instead, change the gate structure to eliminate the essential hazards using the technique described in Section 26.6.

28

REVIEW OF SYNCHRONOUS SEQUENTIAL NETWORKS

OBJECTIVES

This unit reviews synchronous sequential networks and iterative networks. The objectives of this unit are essentially the same as Units 12 through 19 and include the following:

1. Given a sequential network, analyze it to find a state table and graph, timing diagram, and output sequence.

2. Given a problem statement, design an economical sequential or iterative network to realize it.

STUDY GUIDE

1. Study Unit 28, and review the steps in designing a sequential network:

   a. Given a problem statement, construct the state graph and table.

   b. Determine equivalent states and reduce the table to a minimum number of rows.

   c. Choose a suitable state assignment for the flip-flop states.

   d. Find the next state maps, input maps and input equations for the flip-flops, output maps and equations.

   e. Realize the network.

2. Review the objectives of Units 12 through 19. If you cannot meet some of these objectives, review the pertinent material in the units. Also, review the following:

   a. Construction of timing charts for Mealy and Moore networks (Section 14.2).

b. Derivation of flip-flop input equations for different types of flip-flops (see Problems 13.3 and 13.5, for example).

c. The design procedure and design example in Unit 17.

3. Work the Review Problems.

4. When you are satisfied that you can meet the objectives of Units 12 through 19, take the readiness test.

28. REVIEW OF SYNCHRONOUS SEQUENTIAL NETWORKS

28.1 Flip-Flops

Flip-flops are commonly used as memory elements in sequential networks. An S-R flip-flop can be constructed from cross-coupled NOR gates:

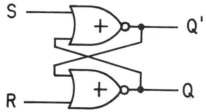

Since $S = 1$ sets the flip-flop to $Q = 1$ and $R = 1$ resets the flip-flop to $Q = 0$, the next state of such a flip-flop is given by

$$Q^+ = S + R'Q \qquad (SR = 0) \tag{28-1}$$

where Q is the present state and Q^+ is the state after the flip-flop has had time to react to the present inputs.

T and J-K flip-flops can be constructed by adding gates and delay to the basic S-R flip-flop. The T flip-flop changes state every time the T input is pulsed, and thus has the next state equation

$$Q^+ = T \oplus Q \tag{28-2}$$

The unclocked J-K flip-flop acts like the S-R flip-flop ($J = 1$ sets the flip-flop to $Q = 1$ and $K = 1$ resets it) except that it changes state if J and K are pulsed simultaneously.

To avoid timing problems, clocked flip-flops are commonly used when constructing synchronous sequential networks. For clocked flip-flops, a change of state can be initiated only by a pulse on the clock input. The next state equations for clocked D and J-K flip-flops are

$$Q^+ = D \tag{28-3}$$

$$Q^+ = JQ' + K'Q \tag{28-4}$$

where Q^+ is the state of the flip-flop after the clock pulse and J, K and D represent the input values before (and during) the clock pulse. A master-slave J-K flip-flop is internally constructed from two S-R flip-flops with added gating. The "master" flip-flop is set to the proper state (as determined by the inputs) on the leading edge of the clock and the "slave" assumes this state value on the trailing edge of the clock.

28.2   Analysis of Sequential Networks

Sequential networks are commonly analyzed using state tables, state graphs, and timing charts. Two ways of deriving a state table from a network are:

a.   Assume a present state for the flip-flops and an input value. Trace signals through the network to determine the output and flip-flop inputs. Determine the next state of each flip-flop from the values of its inputs. Repeat for each present state and input combination.

b.   Write down the equations for the network outputs and the equation for each flip-flop input in terms of the flip-flop outputs and network inputs. Substitute these flip-flop input equations into the appropriate flip-flop next state equations, such as Equations (28-1), (28-2), (28-3), or (28-4). Using the resulting equations, tabulate the next state and output values for each combination of present state and network inputs.

For a Moore network, the output is only a function of the present state, and when drawing the state graph an output is associated with each state. For a Mealy network, the output is a function of both the present state and the input, so the output is associated with the transition between states on the state graph. The response of the network to a given input sequence can easily be determined from inspection of the state graph.

A timing chart which shows at which times the outputs and flip-flops change state can be constructed by tracing signals through the network or by using the state table. For a Moore network, the output changes can only occur at the same time as state changes (neglecting any gate delays). For a Mealy network, the output can change both when the state changes and when the input changes. This can give rise to false outputs during the time interval between when the state changes and when the input changes.

28.3   Derivation of State Graphs and Tables

The hardest part of designing a sequential network is often deriving the state graph from the problem statement. The first step is to write down enough input and output sequences to make sure that you understand the problem statement. When you construct the state graph (see guidelines in Section 15.3) ask yourself such questions as, "under what conditions (if any) should the network reset to the initial state?", "when can the network return to a previously used state and when must a new state be added?", etc. Be especially careful when using self-loops. If you are trying to keep track of whether the total number of 0's (or 1's) is even or odd, you cannot introduce a self-loop. However, if any number of successive 0's (or 1's) can occur in a sequence without affecting the output, a self-loop is appropriate. When your graph is complete, check it for two things:

a. Does it give the proper output when one of the specified input sequences occurs?

b. Does it give an output of 1 (or 0) for some input sequence for which the output should remain 0 (or 1)?

28.4   State Table Reduction

Before realizing a state table, it is usually desirable to reduce the table to a minimum number of rows by eliminating equivalent states. The basic *definition* of equivalent states is that states s_i and s_j are equivalent iff for every input sequence $\underline{X}$, the output sequences obtained by starting in s_i and s_j are the same, i.e.

$$s_i \equiv s_j \quad \text{iff} \quad \lambda(s_i, \underline{X}) = \lambda(s_j, \underline{X}) \quad \text{for every input sequence } \underline{X}$$

The state equivalence *theorem* tells us that two states are equivalent iff for every single input x, the next states are equivalent and the outputs are the same, i.e.

$$s_i \equiv s_j \quad \text{iff} \quad \delta(s_i, x) \equiv \delta(s_j, x) \quad \text{and } \lambda(s_i, x) = \lambda(s_j, x) \text{ for all } x.$$

Some states in the table can often be eliminated by direct application of this theorem. After any initial reduction in this way, further state equivalences can be found by constructing an implication chart which contains a square for each pair of states. Then, if states i and j have different outputs, place an X in square i-j to indicate that $i \not\equiv j$; otherwise, place the implied next state pairs in the square (see p. 329 for details). Place a check in square i-j to indicate $i \equiv j$ if both the outputs and next states of states i and j are the same. Then cycle through the chart and place an X in each square that contains an implied pair m-n for which square m-n contains an X. Repeat this process until all non-equivalent state pairs have been eliminated. Then if square i-j does not contain an X, $i \equiv j$. Finally, reduce the original state table by eliminating rows which correspond to equivalent states.

An alternative way to find equivalent states (Section 16.6) is to first divide the states into classes according to their associated outputs. A next class table is then formed, and if states within a given class can be distinguished, the class is subdivided. This procedure is repeated until no further states can be distinguished. Then any states remaining in the same class are equivalent. The next class tables, together with the original state table, can be used to determine the shortest input sequence which is required to distinguish two states. This is done starting with the first next class table in which the states can be distinguished and working backwards table by table until different outputs are obtained.

Two sequential machines are equivalent if every state in the first machine has an equivalent state in the second and every state in the second machine has an equivalent state in the first. The implication chart method can be adapted to determination of equivalent machines by listing the states of one machine along the side of the chart and the states of the other machine along the bottom. Then the procedure described above is used to determine equivalent states.

28.5   State Assignment

Given the reduced state table, the next step in the sequential network design is to assign flip-flop states to correspond to the network states. If the network has m states, where

$$2^{n-1} < m \leqslant 2^n$$

a minimum of n flip-flops are required. If two state assignments differ only in that one assignment can be formed from the other by permuting columns (*not* rows), the cost of realizing the state table will be the same for both assignments. For symmetrical flip-flops (T, J-K, S-R) complementing one or more columns of the state assignment does not effect the cost either. Thus, for this case, one can always assign all 0's to the first state without loss of generality. For a state table with 3 or 4 states, only 3 non-equivalent assignments must be tried in order to be sure of getting the minimum solution. However, for more states, it is usually not feasible to try all possible non-equivalent assignments. In this case, the following guidelines help to place 1's or 0's in adjacent squares on the next state (or output) maps and hence help to simplify the required logic:

1. States which have the same next state for a given input should be given adjacent assignments.

2. States which are the next states of the same state should be given adjacent assignments.

3. States which have the same output for a given input should be given adjacent assignments.

These guidelines work best with D and J-K flip-flops. They usually lead to good, but not necessarily minimum solutions.

28.6   Derivation of Flip-Flop Input Equations

To derive the flip-flop input equations, the state table is first converted to a transition table by substituting the assigned flip-flop states for each state in the table. The resulting table gives the next state of each flip-flop as a function of the present flip-flop states and the network inputs. Next state maps are then plotted for each flip-flop. For flip-flop Q, the Q^+ map is converted to flip-flop input maps as follows:

$Q\,Q^+$	D	T	S	R	J	K
0 0	0	0	0	X	0	X
0 1	1	1	1	0	1	X
1 0	0	1	0	1	X	1
1 1	1	0	X	0	X	0

The conversion can be carried out rapidly by first working with the $Q = 0$ half of the map and then with the $Q = 1$ half. The resulting flip-flop input equations are then simplified and realized using the available types of logic gates.

J and K equations can also be read directly off the Q^+ map. The $Q = 0$ half of the map serves as a map for J, and the $Q = 1$ half serves as a map for K'.

28.7 Iterative Networks

The design procedures for unilateral iterative networks are essentially the same as for sequential networks. For iterative networks, the inputs are received as a sequence in space rather than as a sequence in time, and the state information is passed by leads connected between adjacent cells rather than being stored in flip-flops. Derivation of the state table and graph and state assignment are exactly the same as for sequential networks. The next state maps are used to determine the equations which describe a typical cell. Initial state information is fed into the first cell, and this sometimes permits the logic in the first cell to be simplified. Depending on the application, each cell may have its own output network, or a single output network may be used with the last cell.

28.8 Design Using Shift Registers, Counters, ROMs and PLAs

Use of MSI integrated circuits such as counters and shift registers rather than individual gates and flip-flops can greatly simplify the design of digital systems. Integrated circuit shift registers are available with 4, 8 or more bits. These shift registers range in complexity from simple serial-in, serial-out unidirectional shift registers to parallel-in, parallel-out bidirectional shift registers.

An integrated circuit counter which has parallel load inputs is useful in designing networks which require special counting sequences. For example, the 74S163 4-bit synchronous counter operates as follows:

If CLEAR = 0, set the counter to 0000.

If CLEAR = 1 and LOAD = 0, load the counter from the parallel inputs.

If CLEAR = LOAD = 1 and PT = 1, enable the counter.

By making these control inputs functions of the counter state or of external inputs, state graphs which have several states in a loop can economically be realized using a 74S163 counter with added gates.

A sequential network can be realized using a ROM or PLA together with D flip-flops (see Fig. 19-20, for example). The ROM (or PLA) is used to generate the flip-flop input equations and output equations. A sequential network with m inputs, n outputs and k state variables requires a ROM with $2^{(m+k)}$ words and $n + k$ outputs. The size of the ROM is independent of the state assignment used, but the number of product terms in the PLA may depend on the state assignment.

REVIEW PROBLEMS

28.1 A logic designer who had not taken this course designed a sequential network with an input W using 3 T flip-flops. The input equations for these
flip-flops are:

$$T_A = W'A'B + W'BC' + A'BC' + AB'C + WB'C + WAC$$

$$T_B = W'A'C + W'A'B + A'BC + AB'C' + WB'C' + WAC'$$

$$T_C = W'AC + W'B'C' + WBC + WA'C'$$

and the output equation is $Z = W'A'BC'$.

Find an equivalent sequential network which uses fewer states. Try to
minimize the amount of logic required.

28.2 Design a sequential circuit having one input and one output which will
produce a 1 output for every second "zero" it receives, and for every second "one" it receives. *Example:*

X (input) $= 0\ 1\ 1\ 0\ 1\ 1\ 1\ 0\ 0\ 0\ 0\ 1\ 0\ 1\ 1\ 0\ 0\ 1\ 0\ 1\ 1\ 0\ 1\ 0$

Z (output) $= 0\ 0\ 1\ 1\ 0\ 1\ 0\ 0\ 1\ 0\ 1\ 1\ 0\ 0\ 1\ 1\ 0\ 0\ 1\ 1\ 0\ 0\ 1\ 1$

a. Design a Mealy sequential network using J-K flip-flops, showing a
reduced state graph, and equations for the output and J-K inputs. It
should be a reasonably economical design.

b. Design a Moore sequential network using T flip-flops to do the same
task, showing a state graph and input equations for a reasonably economical design.

28.3 a. Reduce the following state table to a minimum number of states:

	next state		output	
	$X = 0$	1	0	1
a	e	g	0	1
b	d	f	0	1
c	e	c	1	0
d	b	f	0	1
e	g	f	0	1
f	b	d	1	0
g	e	c	1	0

b. Using the basic definition of state equivalence, show that state a is *not*
equivalent to state b.

28.4 Given the following timing chart for a sequential network, construct as much of the state table as possible.

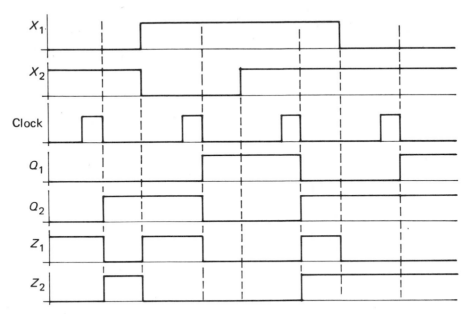

28.5 An iterative network has an output of 1 from the last cell iff the input pattern 1011 or 1101 has occurred as inputs to any 4 adjacent cells in the network.

    a. Find a Moore state graph or table with a minimum number of states.

    b. Make a suitable state assignment and derive one of the equations for a typical cell.

    c. Derive the output equation.

28.6 Realize the following state table using a minimum number of AND and OR gates together with:

    a. a clocked $J\text{-}K$ flip-flop (use the short-cut method)

    b. a clocked D flip-flop

    c. a T flip-flop

    d. an $S\text{-}R$ flip-flop

    e. For part d, what would happen if $x_1 = 0$, $x_2 = 1$, $x_3 = 1$ and the clock pulse is too long?

$x_1 x_2 x_3$	000	001	010	011	100	101	110	111	Z
A	A	A	B	B	B	B	A	A	0
B	A	B	B	A	A	B	B	A	1

28.7 a. Draw a state graph for the sequential network given below. The table gives the contents of the PLA. (All PLA outputs are 0 for input combinations not listed in the table).

b. Draw a timing diagram showing the clock, X, Q_1, Q_2 and Z for the input sequence $X = 10011$. Assume that initially $Q_1 = Q_2 = 0$.

X	Q_1	Q_2	D_1	D_2	Z
0	1	–	1	0	0
1	0	1	1	0	0
0	–	1	0	1	1
1	0	0	0	1	1
1	1	0	0	0	1

c. Identify any false outputs in the timing diagram. What is the correct output sequence for Z?

28.8 Design a sequential network to multiply an 8-4-2-1 binary-coded decimal digit by 3 to give a 5-bit binary number. For example, if the input is 0111 the output should be 10101. The input and output to the network should be serial with the least significant bit first. Assume that the input will be 0 at the fifth clock time and reset the network after the fifth output bit.

a. Derive a state table with a minimum number of states.

b. Design the network using J-K flip-flops and NAND and NOR gates.

c. Design the network using a PLA and D flip-flops. Give the PLA table.

d. Design the network using a PAL. Give the PAL type and fuse pattern.

Appendix A

DISCRETE AND INTEGRATED CIRCUIT LOGIC GATES

OBJECTIVES

1. Given the circuit diagram for a network of diode AND and OR gates, determine the function realized for positive and negative logic.

2. Explain the operation of a simple transistor logic circuit, assuming that the transistors act like ideal switches.

3. Be familiar with the operation of TTL logic gates.

4. Explain the operation of a MOS logic circuit, assuming that the MOSFETs act like ideal switches.

STUDY GUIDE

1. Study Section A.1, *Diode AND and OR Gates.*

   a. Review Section 3.5, *Positive and Negative Logic.*

   b. For Fig. A-2, if $e_1 = 2$, $e_2 = 5$, $e_3 = 1$, $E = +8$ volts, which diodes will be conducting and what will e_o be?

   c. For Fig. A-3, if $e_1 = 2$, $e_2 = 5$, $e_3 = 1$, $E = -2$ volts, which diodes will be conducting and what will e_o be?

d. The bias voltage for a diode gate should always be chosen so that it forces current through the diodes and one of the diodes will always be conducting (or on the verge of conduction with zero voltage across the diode and zero current through the diode). When choosing values for the bias voltage (E), note the following:

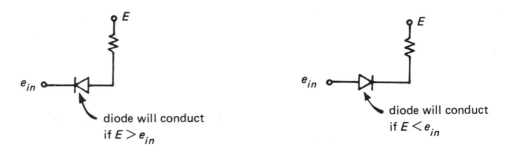

diode will conduct if $E > e_{in}$

diode will conduct if $E < e_{in}$

For the following gates, what range must E be so that one of the diodes always conducts if the input voltages can be -3 or $+3$?

e. Work Problems A.1 and A.2.

f. Diodes can be connected in a regular pattern to form a memory array for a read-only memory (ROM) or a programmed logic array (PLA). If the switching elements in the memory array of Fig. 9-22 are diodes (connected to point in the same direction as the arrows on the switching elements), verify that these diodes form a set of OR gates which realize the functions given in Equations (9-9). If the switching elements in Fig. 9-26 are replaced with diodes, verify that resulting diode array is equivalent to the AND and OR gate array shown in Fig. 9-27.

2. Study Section A.2, *Transistor Logic Circuits.*

   a. Complete the following table for the network of Fig. A-6(a) and verify that the network realizes the NOR function for positive logic.

A	B	C	F
0	0	0	
0	0	+V	
0	+V	0	
0	+V	+V	
+V	0	0	
+V	0	+V	
+V	+V	0	
+V	+V	+V	

   b. Complete the following table for the network of Fig. A-7(a) and verify that the network realizes the NAND function for positive logic.

A	B	C	F
0	0	0	
0	0	+V	
0	+V	0	
0	+V	+V	
+V	0	0	
+V	0	+V	
+V	+V	0	
+V	+V	+V	

   c. For the networks of Figs. A-6(a) and A-7(a), if all transistors are replaced by PNP and the supply voltage is changed to $-V$, what functions would be realized if $-V$ is a logic 1 and 0 volts is a logic 0?

   d. For the networks of Figs. A-6(a) and A-7(a), if no changes are made in the network but 0 volts is a logic 1 and $+V$ is a logic 0, what functions would be realized? (*Hint:* negative logic theorem).

   e. Work Problem A.3.

3. Study Section A.3, *TTL Integrated Circuit Logic.*

   a. Referring to Table A-3, if standard TTL integrated circuit packages are used what type and how many IC's would you use to implement Fig. 8-16(b)?

   b. Referring to Table A-4, what TTL family would you select to obtain the lowest power consumption if speed of operation was not important? _____

      What TTL family would you select if fast operation was the most important consideration? _____

   c. Referring to Fig. A-10, an input of 0.3 volts will act like a logic _____, an input of 4.2 volts will act like a logic _____, and an input of 1.5 volts _____. If the input is a logic 0, the output voltage will be in the range _____ and if the input is a logic 1, the output voltage will be in the range _____.

4. Study Section A.4, *MOS and CMOS Logic.*

   a. For the following MOS logic network, draw a switch analog and determine the function realized by the network.

   b. Work Problems A.4 and A.5.

A.1 Diode AND and OR Gates

AND and OR gates can be realized with a variety of circuits. This section describes how such gates can be constructed using diodes. The logic function realized by a given diode circuit configuration depends on whether we interpret the input and output voltage levels according to positive or negative logic.*

Figure A-1(a) shows the symbol used for a diode. The arrow in the diode symbol indicates the normal direction of current flow. The diode characteristic in Fig. A-1(b) shows the diode current (i) as a function of the voltage drop across the diode ($v = v_a - v_b$). When the diode is conducting in the forward direction (i positive), the voltage drop across the diode is very small; when a negative voltage is applied across the diode, the current flowing in the reverse direction is very small. Thus, the diode can act as a two-state switching device. In the conducting state, $v \approx 0$; in the non-conducting state $i \approx 0$. For purposes of analysis, we will assume that the forward voltage drop and reverse current are both negligible so that the diode has an ideal characteristic as shown in Fig. A-1(c). Thus we will treat the diode as a switch which closes if $v_a > v_b$ and opens if $v_a < v_b$.

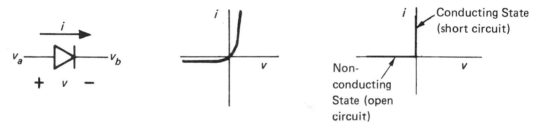

(a) Diode symbol   (b) Diode characteristic   (c) Ideal diode characteristic

Fig. A-1

Consider the diode gate circuit shown in Fig. A-2. The sources e_1, e_2, and e_3 represent external signals applied to the gate. The voltage source labeled "E" is sometimes referred to as the *bias* voltage. E is chosen so that

$$e_1 \leqslant E, \quad e_2 \leqslant E, \quad e_3 \leqslant E$$

With this restriction at least one of the diodes will be conducting or at its breakpoint ($i = 0, v = 0$). It is easy to verify that the output voltage e_o will be the *minimum* of the three input voltages e_1, e_2, and e_3. For example if $e_1 < e_2$ and $e_1 < e_3$, then diode D_1 will conduct. Since the forward drop across D_1 is negligible, the output voltage will be $e_o = e_1$. Since e_o is then less than e_2 and e_3, diodes D_2 and D_3 will have a negative voltage applied and will not conduct.

When this gate is used to perform logic functions, the input voltages are restricted to a pair of values. For example, if we choose voltages 0 and $+V$ as input

---

*See Section 3.5 for a definition of positive and negative logic.

signals, we can complete a table of voltages (Table A-1) using the relation

$$e_o = \text{minimum } (e_1, e_2, e_3)$$

Table A-1

e_1	e_2	e_3	e_o
0	0	0	0
0	0	+V	0
0	+V	0	0
0	+V	+V	0
+V	0	0	0
+V	0	+V	0
+V	+V	0	0
+V	+V	+V	+V

Fig. A-2. Diode gate with external inputs

Table A-1 is identical to Table 3-1. If we translate this table according to positive logic (0 volts is a logic 0 and +V volts is a logic 1), we see that e_o is 1 if e_1, e_2 and e_3 are all 1, so the gate of Fig. A-2 performs the AND function for positive logic. If we translate the table according to negative logic (0 volts is a logic 1 and +V volts is a logic 0), we see that e_o is 1 if e_1 or e_2 or e_3 is 1, so the gate performs the OR function for negative logic.

Consider the diode gate circuit shown in Fig. A-3. The voltage E is chosen so that $E \leqslant e_1$, $E \leqslant e_2$, $E \leqslant e_3$. With this restriction at least one of the diodes will be conducting or at its breakpoint, and the output voltage e_o will be the *maximum* of the three input voltages e_1, e_2 and e_3. To verify this, consider the case where $e_1 > e_2$ and $e_1 > e_3$. Then diode D_1 will conduct, so the output voltage will be $e_o = e_1$. Since e_o is then greater than e_2 and e_3, diodes D_2 and D_3 will have a negative voltage applied and will not conduct. If we choose voltages 0 and +V as input signals, we can complete Table A-2 using the relation

$$e_o = \text{maximum } (e_1, e_2, e_3)$$

Table A-2

e_1	e_2	e_3	e_o
0	0	0	0
0	0	+V	+V
0	+V	0	+V
0	+V	+V	+V
+V	0	0	+V
+V	0	+V	+V
+V	+V	0	+V
+V	+V	+V	+V

Fig. A-3. Diode gate with external inputs

Table A-2 is identical to Table 3-2(a). If we translate this table according to positive logic, we see that e_o is 1 if e_1 or e_2 or e_3 is 1, so the gate performs the OR function for positive logic. If we translate the table according to negative logic, we see that e_o is 1 if e_1, e_2 and e_3 are all 1, so the gate of Fig. A-3 performs the AND function for negative logic. Unless otherwise specified, we will use positive logic so that Fig. A-2 is an AND gate and Fig. A-3 is an OR gate.

Practical circuit design considerations limit the number of diode gates which can be cascaded in series to two or three. The number of diode gate inputs which a given diode gate output can drive is also sharply limited. If these limits are exceeded, the voltage levels at the gate outputs may change appreciably from their nominal values so that it is no longer possible to reliably distinguish between a logic 0 and a logic 1. For this reason, diode gates are often used in conjunction with transistor amplifiers so that proper voltage levels can be maintained.

A.2 Transistor Logic Circuits

Transistor logic circuits offer several advantages over diode gate circuits. Transistor gates can realize inversion, they are capable of driving more gate inputs, and they generally operate faster than diode gates.

We will first analyze an inverter which uses an NPN transistor shown in Fig. A-4(a). The current which flows from the collector (C) to the emitter (E) in the transistor is controlled by the input voltage (e_i) applied to the base (B) circuit. In this discussion we will treat transistors like ideal switches. We will assume that when a transistor is cut off, the leakage current flowing from collector to emitter is so small that we can treat the transistor like an open circuit. When the input is 0 volts, the transistor is cut off, no current flows in the collector resistor (R_c), and the output voltage (e_o) is equal to the supply voltage ($+V$). When a transistor is saturated, we will assume that the voltage drop from collector to emitter is so small that we can treat the transistor like a short circuit. The base resistor (R_b) is chosen so that when the input (e_i) is $+V$, the base current will be large enough to cause saturation and the output voltage will be approximately 0. Thus, the operation of the transistor is analogous to a switch in Fig. A-4(b) which is open when e_i is 0 and closed when e_i is $+V$. Figure A-4(c) summarizes the relation between the input and output voltages for the networks of Fig. A-4(a) and A-4(b).

e_i	e_o
0	$+V$
$+V$	≈ 0

(a) NPN inverter   (b) Switch analog   (c) Table for (a) and (b)

Fig. A-4. Transistor inverters

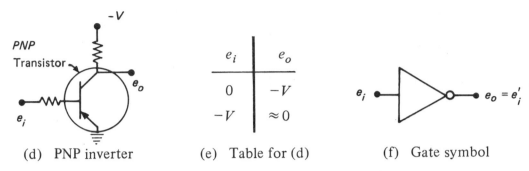

(d) PNP inverter   (e) Table for (d)   (f) Gate symbol

Fig. A-4. Transistor inverters (cont.)

The transistor inverter of Fig. A-4(a) can also be analyzed by drawing a load line on the transistor characteristics as shown in Fig. A-5. The current flowing into the base is

$$i_B \approx e_i / R_b$$

When e_i is 0, i_B is 0, and the transistor operates at the cutoff point on the load line with $e_0 = +V$. When e_i is $+V$, $i_B \approx V/R_b$, and the transistor operates at the saturation point on the load line with $e_o \approx 0$.

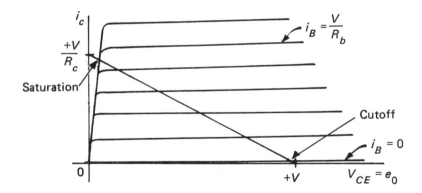

Fig. A-5. Load-line analysis of Fig. A-4

The operation of the PNP inverter in Fig. A-4(d) is similar to the NPN case except that the signs of all the voltages are reversed. The inverter symbol seen in Fig. A-4(f) can represent either type of inverter.

For convenience, we will use positive logic ($+V$ for a logic 1, 0 volts for a logic 0) for NPN transistors and negative logic ($-V$ for a logic 1, 0 volts for a logic 0) for PNP transistors. Then in either case a logic 1 used as a base input will turn on (i.e., saturate) the transistor, and a logic 0 will turn off the transistor. With this convention, an NPN transistor logic circuit and the corresponding circuit with PNP transistors (and the signs of all voltages reversed) will perform the same logic function. The remainder of this discussion will consider only NPN transistors and positive logic, but all of the results apply equally well to PNP transistors and negative logic.

For the parallel-transistor circuit of Fig. A-6(a), if input A or input B or input C is a logic 1, the corresponding transistor is "on" (saturated) and the output (F) is 0. Hence $F' = A + B + C$, and $F = (A + B + C)' = A'B'C'$. This network performs the OR function followed by inversion and is called an OR-NOT gate, or more commonly, a NOR gate. Symbolically it is represented by an OR gate with an inversion symbol (circle) at the output as in Fig. A-6(b). Fig. A-6(c) shows the switch network analog. If A or B or C is 1, the corresponding switch is closed, there is a path to ground ($\frac{1}{\overline{=}}$) and F is 0. If A, B and C are all 0, all the switches are open and F is $+V$ (logic 1).

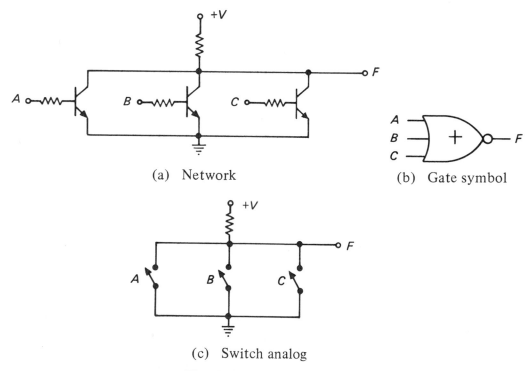

(a) Network

(b) Gate symbol

(c) Switch analog

Fig. A-6. NPN NOR gate

For the series-transistor network of Fig. A-7(a), if input A and input B and input C are all "1", then all the transistors are on, and the output is 0. Therefore, $F' = ABC$ and $F = (ABC)' = A' + B' + C'$. This network performs the AND function followed by inversion. It is called an AND-NOT gate, or more commonly, a NAND gate. Symbolically, it is represented by an AND gate with an inversion symbol at the output as in Fig. A-7(c).

(a) Network   (b) Switch network analog   (c) Gate symbol

Fig. A-7. NPN NAND gate

A.3 TTL Integrated Circuit Logic

Logic gates are commonly built in integrated circuit form rather than using discrete components. All of the diodes, transistors and resistors which form a gate are fabricated on a tiny (typically less than .1 inch square) "chip" of silicon. Several integrated circuit gates are usually sealed in a small plastic package (typically .3 by .8 inches). In addition to small size, integrated circuit gates have the advantages of low power consumption and greater reliability as compared with gates built from discrete components. Medium- and large-scale integration techniques permit fabrication of a complete functional unit (like a shift register, counter, memory or microprocessor) on a single semiconductor chip.

Several types of integrated circuit gates are available including RTL (resistor-transistor logic), DTL (diode-transistor logic), TTL (transistor-transistor logic), ECL (emitter-coupled logic), MOS (metal-oxide-semiconductor) logic, and CMOS (complementary MOS). RTL NOR gates use a circuit which is equivalent to that shown in Fig. A-6(a). DTL NAND gates combine a diode AND gate with a transistor inverter as shown in Fig. A-8. TTL logic is one of the most commonly used forms of integrated circuit logic and will be discussed in more detail in this section. MOS and CMOS logic is described in Section A.4.

Fig. A-8. Simplified DTL NAND gate

Figure A-9 shows a TTL NAND gate. The input transistor (Q_1), which has multiple emitters, effectively takes the place of the AND gate in Figure A-8. If one or more of the inputs (A, B, C) is low, transistor Q_1 is turned on, and the input to Q_2 is low. Transistor Q_2 is off, so the input to Q_4 is high and the input to Q_3 is low. Therefore, Q_4 is on, Q_3 is off, and the gate output voltage is high. On the other hand, if all of the inputs to Q_1 are high, Q_4 is off, Q_3 is on, and the gate output is low. Since the output is a logic 0 iff $ABC = 1$, the output function is $F = (ABC)'$, and the gate performs the NAND function for positive logic.

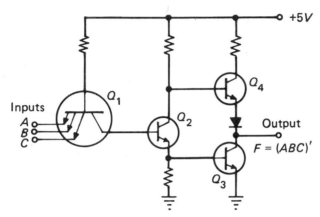

Fig. A-9. TTL NAND gate

Table A-3 lists some commonly available TTL gates. A typical TTL integrated circuit package contains six inverters, four 2-input gates, three 3-input gates or two 4-input gates. The reader should refer to a TTL data book for detailed specifications on these and other types of TTL integrated circuits.

Table A-3. Common TTL Gates

Type number	Type of gate	No. of inputs per gate	No. of gates per IC package
7404	INVERTER	1	6
7400	NAND	2	4
7410	NAND	3	3
7420	NAND	4	2
7430	NAND	8	1
7402	NOR	2	4
7427	NOR	3	3
7408	AND	2	4
7411	AND	3	3
7421	AND	4	2
7432	OR	2	4
7486	EXCLUSIVE-OR	2	4

In addition to standard TTL, several other families of TTL integrated circuits are available. These families differ in amount of propagation delay and power dissipation as indicated in Table A-4. All of the example type numbers represent a TTL integrated circuit with four 2-input NAND gates. The letters S, LS, AS or ALS are added to the type number to indicate the family.

Table A-4. TTL Integrated Circuit Families

TTL family	example type number	typical power dissipation (milliwatts)	propagation delay (nanoseconds) typical	maximum
standard	7400	40	7	22
Schottky	74S00	75	3	5
low-power Schottky	74LS00	8	9	15
advanced Schottky	74AS00	54	3	4.5
advanced low-power Schottky	74ALS00	7.5	7	11

The output of a TTL logic gate typically can drive 10 gate inputs of the same family. Figure A-10 shows the transfer characteristic (output voltage vs input voltage) of a TTL inverter with a 5.0 volt supply voltage and 10 gate inputs connected to its output. Manufacturer's specifications guarantee that any input voltage in the range 0 to 0.8 volts will act like a logic 0 and any input voltage in the range 2 volts to 5 volts will act like a logic 1. The output voltage is typically 3.6 volts for a logic 1 and 0.2 volts for a logic 0. The specifications guarantee that under all normal operating conditions a logic 1 output voltage will always be greater than 2.4 volts and a logic 0 output less than 0.4 volts.

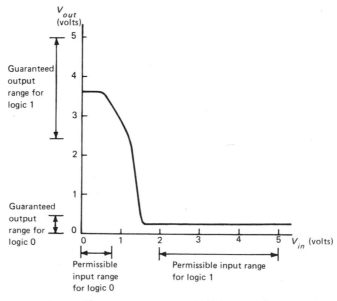

Fig. A-10. Typical TTL inverter transfer characteristic

A.4 MOS and CMOS Logic

MOS logic is based on the use of MOSFETs (metal-oxide-semiconductor field-effect transistors) as switching elements. Figure A-11 shows symbols used to represent MOSFETS. The substrate (or body) is a thin slice of silicon. The gate is a thin metallic layer deposited on the substrate and insulated from it by a thin layer of silicon dioxide. A voltage applied to the gate is used to control the flow of current between the drain and source.

In normal operation of an N-channel MOSFET shown in Fig. A-11(a), a positive voltage (V_{DS}) is applied between the drain and source. If the gate voltage (V_{GS}) is 0, there is no channel between the drain and source and no current flows. When V_{GS} is positive and exceeds a certain threshold, an N-type channel is formed between the drain and source, which allows current to flow from D to S. Operation of a P-channel MOSFET is similar, except V_{DS} and V_{GS} are negative. When V_{GS} assumes a negative value less than the threshold, a P-type channel is formed between drain and source, which allows current to flow from S to D.

The symbol in Fig. A-11(c) may be used to represent either a P- or N-channel MOSFET. When this symbol is used, it is generally understood that the substrate is connected to the most positive circuit voltage for P-channel MOSFETs (or the most negative for N-channel). We will use positive logic for N-channel MOS circuits and negative logic for P-channel MOS circuits. Using this convention, a logic 1 applied to the gate will switch the MOSFET to the "ON" state (low resistance between drain and source) and a logic 0 will switch it to the "OFF" state (high resistance between drain and source).

(a) N-channel MOSFET   (b) P-channel MOSFET   (c) General MOSFET symbol

Fig. A-11. MOSFET symbols

Figure A-12(a) shows a MOS inverter. When a logic 0 is applied to the gate, the MOSFET is in a high-resistance or OFF state, and the output voltage is approximately V_{DD}. When a logic 1 is applied to the gate, the MOSFET switches to a low-resistance or ON state, and the output voltage is approximately 0. Thus, operation of the MOSFET is analogous to the operation of a switch in Fig. A-12(b) which is open when V_{in} is a logic 0 and closed when V_{in} is a logic 1. In Fig. A-12(d), a second MOSFET serves as a load resistor. The geometry of this MOSFET and the gate voltage V_{GG} are chosen so that its resistance is high compared with the ON resistance of the lower MOSFET, so that the switching operation of Fig. A-12(d) is essentially the same as Fig. A-12(a).

(a)   (b)   (c)   (d)

Fig. A-12. MOS inverter

As shown in Fig. A-13, MOSFETs can be connected in parallel or series to form NOR or NAND gates. Operation is similar to that of the bipolar transistor NOR and NAND gates shown in Figs. A-6 and A-7. In Fig. A-13(a), a logic 1 applied to A or B turns on the corresponding MOSFET and F becomes 0. Thus $F' = A + B$ and $F = (A + B)'$. In Fig. A-13(c), a logic 1 applied to the A and B inputs turns on both MOSFETs and F becomes 0. In this case $F' = AB$ and $F = (AB)'$. More complex functions can be realized by using series-parallel combinations of MOSFETs. For example, the network of Fig. A-13(e) performs the exclusive-OR function. The output of this network has a conducting path to ground and $F = 0$ if A and B are both 1 of if A' and B' are both 1. Thus, $F' = AB + A'B'$ and $F = A'B + AB' = A \oplus B$.

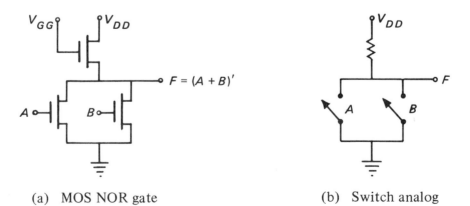

(a)   MOS NOR gate   (b)   Switch analog

Fig. A-13. MOS gates

(c) MOS NAND gate   (d) Switch analog

(e) MOS exclusive-OR gate

Fig. A-13. MOS gates (cont.)

CMOS (complementary MOS) logic performs logic functions using a combination of p-channel and n-channel MOSFETs. Compared with TTL, CMOS has the advantage of much lower power dissipation. Figure A-14 shows a CMOS inverter. When 0 volts (logic 0) is applied to the gate inputs, the p-channel MOSFET (Q_1) is ON and the n-channel MOSFET (Q_2) is OFF, so the output is $+V$ (logic 1). When $+V$ (logic 1) is applied to the gate inputs, Q_1 is OFF and Q_2 is ON, so the output is 0 volts (logic 0).

Figure A-15 shows a CMOS NAND gate. If A or B is 0 volts, then Q_1 or Q_2 is ON and the output is $+V$. If A and B are both $+V$, then Q_3 and Q_4 are both ON and the output is 0 volts. This gate therefore performs the NAND function for positive logic as indicated in Fig. A-15(b).

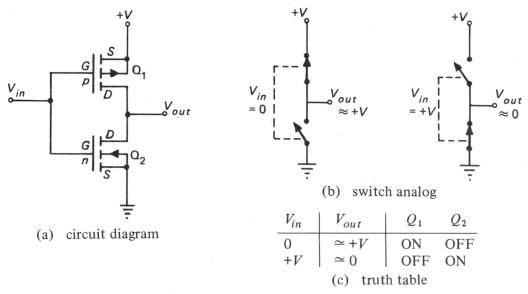

(a) circuit diagram

(b) switch analog

V_{in}	V_{out}	Q_1	Q_2
0	$\simeq +V$	ON	OFF
$+V$	$\simeq 0$	OFF	ON

(c) truth table

Fig. A-14. CMOS inverter

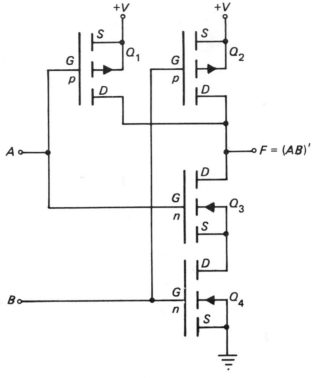

(a)   circuit diagram

A	B	F	Q_1	Q_2	Q_3	Q_4
0	0	$+V$	ON	ON	OFF	OFF
0	$+V$	$+V$	ON	OFF	OFF	ON
$+V$	0	$+V$	OFF	ON	ON	OFF
$+V$	$+V$	0	OFF	OFF	ON	ON

(b)   truth table

Fig. A-15.   CMOS NAND gate

PROBLEMS

A.1 a. If 0 volts corresponds to a logic 0, and −3 volts to a logic 1, what logic
function does the following circuit realize?

b. If 0 volts corresponds to a logic 1, and −3 volts corresponds to a logic 0,
what logic function does the following circuit realize?

A.2 a. Assuming that −5 volts is a logic 0, and +5 volts is a logic 1, what function is realized by the following diode gate network?

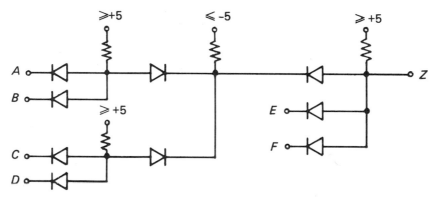

b. What changes would have to be made in the network to realize the same
function if +5 volts is a logic 0 and −5 volts is a logic 1?

A.3 Determine the function F realized by the following diode-transistor network:
$$(+V = \text{logic } 1, 0 \text{ volts} = \text{logic } 0)$$

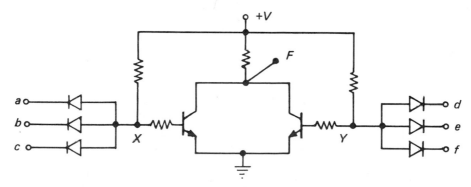

What would F be if $+V = $ logic 0 and 0 volts = logic 1?

A.4 For the following CMOS network, make a table similar to Fig. A-15(b).
What type of CMOS gate is this?

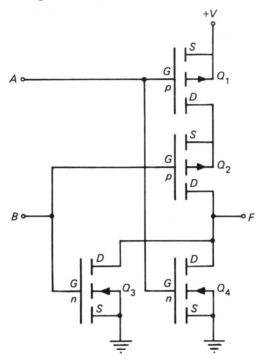

A.5 MOSFETs can be connected in a regular pattern to form the memory array
for a read-only memory (see Fig. 9-21) or a programmed logic array (see
Fig. 9-25). For the 4 word $\times$ 4 bit read-only memory shown below, determine the four output functions realized by the MOS array.

Appendix B

OTHER LOGIC SYMBOLS

B.1   Alternative Symbols for Gates and Flip-Flops

Engineers who design complex digital systems often find it convenient to use more than one representation for a given type of gate. Figure B-1 shows some alternative representations for AND, OR, NAND and NOR gates, where each small circle represents a complement operation. These equivalent gate symbols are based on the identities

$$AB = (A' + B')', \quad A + B = (A'B')', \quad (AB)' = A' + B', \quad (A + B)' = A'B'$$

The Institute of Electrical and Electronics Engineers has published a new standard* for logic symbols. This standard presents a general notation for logic diagrams that is consistent with international standards. It provides for representation of devices ranging from simple gates to complex integrated circuits. Although traditional symbols for AND and OR gates are permitted, the standard emphasizes the use of rectangular symbols throughout. Figure B-2 shows some gate symbols that are consistent with the new standard. The ≥ 1 symbol used in the OR gate implies that the output is 1 if one or more of the inputs are 1.

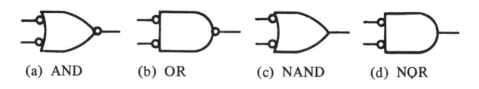

(a) AND   (b) OR   (c) NAND   (d) NOR

Fig. B-1. Alternative gate symbols

IEEE Standard Graphic Symbols for Logic Functions (ANSI/IEEE Std 91-1984), Institute of Electrical and Electronics Engineers, 1984.

Fig. B-2. Rectangular gate symbols

The standard provides for two types of inversion symbols as illustrated in Fig. B-3. When positive logic is used throughout a digital system, the circle and half-arrow inversion symbols have essentially the same meaning; however, there is a subtle difference between the two. A circle at an input means a logic 0 at the input produces an internal logic 1 as shown in Fig. B-3(a); a half-arrow at an input means that a low level (L) at the input produces an internal logic 1 as shown in Fig. B-3(b). Similarly, an output circle indicates an internal logic 0 produces an external 1. A half-arrow at the output indicates that an internal logic 1 produces an external low level (L). Figure B-4 shows four possible inverter symbols using these symbols. The half-arrow inversion symbol is intended for use when circuit functions are described in terms of H and L levels rather than in terms of logic 0's and 1's.

Fig. B-3. Standard inversion symbols

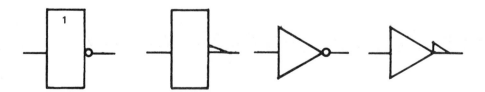

Fig. B-4. Four symbols for an inverter.

The following example will further clarify the difference between the two types of inversion symbols. Figure B-5(a) represents a physical device described externally in terms of H and L levels. As is evident from the truth table, it performs an OR function for positive logic and an AND function for negative logic. Figure B-5(b) represents a logical device described externally in terms of logic 0's and 1's. It performs the same OR function regardless of whether all external signals are defined in terms of positive or negative logic, but its physical realization would be different in the two cases. The two symbols are equivalent when positive logic is used, but the symbols have different meanings for negative logic.

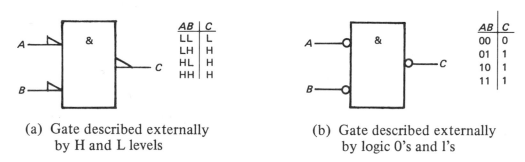

(a) Gate described externally by H and L levels		(b) Gate described externally by logic 0's and 1's

Fig. B-5

An edge-triggered J-K flip-flop with preset and clear, such as shown in Fig. 12-11, can be represented by Fig. B-6(a). The preset and clear inputs are labeled S and R internally. The inversion half-arrow indicates that these inputs are activated when the corresponding preset and clear signals are low (logic 0 for positive logic). The general symbol for a control input is C, so the clock input is labeled C1 to indicate control input 1. The internal arrow indicates that this is a dynamic (edge-triggered) input, and the inversion half-arrow indicates that it responds to a H to L transition (falling edge) of the clock signal. The 1 in front of J and K in the labels 1J and 1K indicates that these inputs are activated by control input C1.

Figure B-6(b) shows a dual edge-triggered D flip-flop with preset and clear. As in the J-K flip-flop example, S and R designate the active-low preset and clear inputs. C1 and C2 designate the two clock inputs that respond to an L-to-H transition (rising edge) of the clock; 1D and 2D are D inputs that are activated by C1 and C2, respectively.

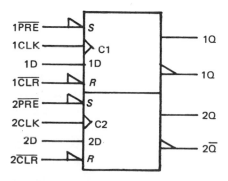

(a) J-K flip-flop with preset and clear.

(b) Dual D flip-flop with preset and clear.

Fig. B-6

B.2 Representation of MSI Functions

This section gives examples of how several MSI functions can be represented by the new IEEE standard notation. Figure B-7 shows the standard symbol for the 7442 4-line to 10-line decoder of Fig. 9-17. The notation BCD/DEC identifies this as a decoder which accepts a BCD (binary-coded decimal) input and outputs the corresponding decimal digit. The output inversion symbols indicate that the decimal outputs are active-low, that is the output for the selected decimal digit is L (logic 0 for positive logic).

Figure B-8 represents a 74151 8-to-1 multiplexer similar to the one shown in Figs. 9-10 and 9-11, except that it has an additional enable input ($\overline{\text{EN}}$) and an inverted output as well as a non-inverted output. The outputs are activated only when $\overline{\text{EN}}$ is L. The three control inputs to the multiplexer are identified by

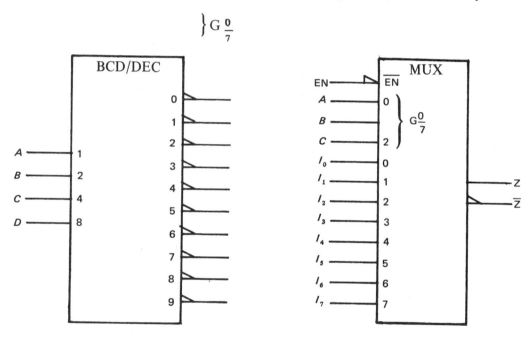

Fig. B-7. 4-to-10 line
decoder

Fig. B-8. 8-to-1
multiplexer

A common control block may be used when a circuit has one or more inputs which are common to more than one element in the circuit. The common control block has a distinctive shape as shown in Fig. B-9. This figure represents a quadruple tri-state buffer with a common enable. The first triangle in the symbol indicates that the outputs are buffered, that is, they have a higher than normal driving capability. The second triangle indicates that the outputs are tri-state. These outputs are enabled when EN is high.

**Fig. B-9. Quad tristate buffer
with common control input**

Fig. B-10. 74178 shift register

The symbol for the 74178 4-bit parallel-in, parallel-out shift register (Fig. 19-3) is shown in Fig. B-10. The notation SRG4 identifies this as a 4-bit shift register. C3 identifies the clock input that is activated by an H-to-L transition (falling edge) of CLK. The notation $\overline{1}$, 2, 3D indicates that the corresponding D flip-flop input is active when M1 = 0, M2 = 1, and the active edge of C3 occurs; /1→ means that shifting occurs in response to the clock when M1 = 1.

The 74S163 4-bit synchronous binary counter of Figs. 19-7 and 19-8 is represented by Fig. B-11. CTRDIV16 indicates a divide by 16 counter. C5 is the clock input which is activated by an *L*-to-*H* transition (rising edge) of CLK. C5 is followed by /2, 3, 4+, which means that the clock increments the counter when M2 = G3 = G4 = 1. The notation 5CT = 0 by the clear input indicates that the counter is set to 0 when the clock (C5) is active and $\overline{CLR}$ is L. The ripple carry output (RCO) is H when G3 is 1 and the count is 15, as indicated by 3CT = 15. The condition for parallel loading the D flip-flops is indicated by 1, 5D, which means that the D input is active when M1 = 1 ($\overline{LOAD}$ is L) and the clock (C5) is active.

Figure B-12 gives the symbol for the octal D flip-flop register of Fig. 19-18. The small triangle near the flip-flop output indicates that the outputs are tri-state. The EN and C1 inputs to the control block are common to all of the flip-flops. When $\overline{OC}$ is L (EN = 1) all outputs are enabled, and an L-to-H transition on CLK (0 to 1 transition on C1) clocks all of the D inputs into the flip-flops.

Fig. B-11. 74S163 counter

Fig. B-12. 74374 octal D flip-flop

Appendix C

PROOFS OF THEOREMS

C.1 Essential Prime Implicants

Section 6.4 presents a method for finding all of the essential prime implicants which is based on finding adjacent 1's on a Karnaugh map. The validity of the method is based on the following theorem:

> If a given minterm m_j of F and all of its adjacent minterms are covered by a single term p_j, then p_j is an essential prime implicant of F.

Proof:

   a. Assume p_j is *not* a *prime* implicant. Then it can be combined with another term p_k to eliminate some variable x_i and form another term which does not contain x_i. Therefore, $x_i = 0$ in p_j and $x_i = 1$ in p_k, or vice versa. Then p_k covers a minterm m_k which differs from m_j only in the variable x_i. This means that m_k is adjacent to m_j, but m_k is not covered by p_j. This contradicts the original assumption that all minterms adjacent to m_j are covered by p_j; therefore, p_j is a prime implicant.

   b. Assume p_j is *not essential*. Then there is another prime implicant p_h which covers m_j. Since p_h is not contained in p_j, p_h must contain at least one minterm m_h which is adjacent to m_j and not covered by p_j. This is a contradiction, so p_j must be essential.

C.2 State Equivalence Theorem

The methods for determining state equivalence presented in Unit 16 are based on Theorem 16.1:

> Two states p and q of a sequential network are equivalent if and only if for every single input x, the outputs are the same and the next states are equivalent.

Proof: We must prove both (a), the "if" part of the theorem, and (b), the "only if" part.

a. Assume that $\lambda(p, x) = \lambda(q, x)$ and $\delta(p, x) \equiv \delta(q, x)$ for every input x. Then from Definition 16.1, for every input sequence $\underline{X}$,

$$\lambda[\delta(p, x), \underline{X}] = \lambda[\delta(q, x), \underline{X}]$$

For the input sequence $\underline{Y} = x$ followed by $\underline{X}$, we have

$$\lambda(p, \underline{Y}) = \lambda(p, x) \text{ followed by } \lambda[\delta(p, x), \underline{X}]$$
$$\lambda(q, \underline{Y}) = \lambda(q, x) \text{ followed by } \lambda[\delta(q, x), \underline{X}]$$

Hence $\lambda(p, \underline{Y}) = \lambda(q, \underline{Y})$ for every input sequence $\underline{Y}$, and $p \equiv q$ by Definition 16.1.

b. Assume that $p \equiv q$. Then by Definition 16.1, $\lambda(p, \underline{Y}) = \lambda(q, \underline{Y})$ for every input sequence $\underline{Y}$. Let $\underline{Y} = x$ followed by $\underline{X}$. Then

$$\lambda(p, x) = \lambda(q, x) \text{ and } \lambda[\delta(p, x), \underline{X}] = \lambda[\delta(q, x), \underline{X}]$$

for every sequence $\underline{X}$. Hence from Definition 16.1, $\delta(p, x) \equiv \delta(q, x)$.

C.3 Justification of Short-Cut Method for Deriving *S-R* Input Equations

The short-cut method for deriving *S-R* input equations is based on the following theorem:

If a cycle-free asynchronous flow table is realized with *S-R* flip-flops using a race-free state assignment, then for each flip-flop Q_i, there exist S and R equations which are independent of Q_i.

Proof: Consider two present states S_j and S_k whose state assignment differs only in the state variable Q_i. Let the state assignments be $0t$ and $1t$, respectively, where 0 and 1 are the values of Q_i, and t represents the values of the other state variables. Since the assignment is race-free, only one state variable can change at a time. For a given input column, the possible next states for S_j are $0u$ and $1t$, and for S_k are $1v$ and $0t$, where u and v differ in at most one state variable from t. There are four cases to be considered:

	present state		next state	S_i	R_i	
case 1	S_j	$0t$	$0u$	0	x	choose $x = 0$, then S_i and R_i
	S_k	$1t$	$1v$	x	0	do not depend on Q_i
case 2	S_j	$0t$	$0u$	0	x	choose $x = 1$, then S_i and R_i
	S_k	$1t$	$0t$	0	1	do not depend on Q_i
case 3	S_j	$0t$	$1t$	1	0	choose $x = 1$, then S_i and R_i
	S_k	$1t$	$1v$	x	0	do not depend on Q_i
case 4	S_j	$0t$	$1t$	1	0	S_i and R_i depend on Q_i,
	S_k	$1t$	$0t$	0	1	but there is a cycle

$$\uparrow \qquad \uparrow$$
$$Q_i \qquad Q_i^+$$

The above analysis applies to every pair of present states S_j and S_k whose assignments differ only in Q_i and to every input column. Thus, the don't cares can always be chosen so that S_i and R_i are independent of Q_i unless a cycle or race is present.

REFERENCES

The following list of basic textbooks in switching theory and logic design is provided for those students who wish to do additional reading concerning the topics covered in this text and their application to digital system design.

References 1, 2, 3, 11, 16, 21 and 22 are particularly applicable to Units 1, 20 and 21 (number systems and arithmetic operations).

References 2, 5, 8, 9, 10, 12, 15, 17, 18, 19, 20, 21, 22 and 24 are particularly applicable to Units 2 through 11 (Boolean algebra and combinational networks).

References 2, 4, 7, 8, 9, 10, 12, 15, 17, 18, 22 and 24 are particularly applicable to Units 12 through 19 and 28 (synchronous sequential networks).

References 6, 7, 18, 23 and 28 are particularly applicable to Unit 22 (SM charts).

References 8, 12, 15, 19, 20, 22 and 27 are particularly applicable to Units 23 through 27 (asynchronous sequential networks).

References 2, 13 and 25 discuss the circuit aspects of digital devices and are particularly applicable to Appendix A.

References 1, 2, 3, 5, 6, 9, 11, 16, 23 and 28 extend the material in the text and apply it to digital systems and computer design.

1. Abd-alla, A. M., and Meltzer, A. C. *Principles of Digital Computer Design.* Englewood Cliffs, N.J.: Prentice-Hall, 1976.

2. Barna, Arpad, and Porat, Dan I. *Integrated Circuits in Digital Electronics.* New York: John Wiley, 1973.

3. Bartee, Thomas C. *Digital Computer Fundamentals.* New York: McGraw-Hill, 6th ed. 1985.

4. Birkner, John M., and Coli, Vincent. *PAL Handbook.* Santa Clara, Calif.: Monolithic Memories, 3d ed. 1983.

5. Blakeslee, Thomas R. *Digital Design with Standard MSI and LSI.* New York: John Wiley, 2d ed. 1979.

6. Clare, Christopher R. *Designing Logic Systems Using State Machines.* New York: McGraw-Hill, 1973.

7. Comer, David J. *Digital Logic and State Machine Design.* New York: Holt, Rinehart and Winston, 1984.

8. Dietmeyer, D. L. *Logic Design of Digital Systems.* Boston: Allyn and Bacon, 2d ed. 1978.

9. Fletcher, William. *An Engineering Approach to Digital Design.* Englewood Cliffs, N.J.: Prentice-Hall, 1980.

10. Friedman, Arthur D. *Logical Design of Digital Systems.* Woodland Hills, Calif.: Computer Science Press, 1975.

11. Gschwind, Hans W., and McCluskey, E. J. *Design of Digital Computers.* New York: Springer-Verlag, 2d ed. 1975.

12. Hill, F. J., and Peterson, G. R. *Introduction to Switching Theory and Logical Design.* New York: John Wiley, 3d ed. 1981.

13. Holt, Charles A. *Electronic Circuits, Digital and Analog.* New York: John Wiley, 1978.

14. Institute of Electrical and Electronics Engineers. *IEEE Standard Graphic Symbols for Logic Functions* (ANSI/IEEE Std 91-1984). New York: IEEE, 1984

15. Kohavi, Z. *Switching and Finite Automata Theory.* New York: McGraw-Hill, 2d ed. 1978.

16. Kostopoulos, George K. *Digital Engineering.* New York: John Wiley, 1975.

17. Lee, Samuel C. *Digital Circuits and Logic Design.* Englewood Cliffs, N.J.: Prentice-Hall, 1976.

18. Mano, Morris M. *Digital Design.* Englewood Cliffs, N.J.: Prentice-Hall, 1984.

19. Marcus, Mitchell P. *Switching Circuits for Engineers.* Englewood Cliffs, N.J.: Prentice-Hall, 3d ed. 1975.

20. McCluskey, E. J. *Introduction to the Theory of Switching Circuits.* New York: McGraw-Hill, 1965.

21. Mowle, Frederic J. *A Systematic Approach to Digital Logic Design.* Reading, Mass.: Addison-Wesley, 1976.

22. Nagle, H. Troy; Carroll, B. D.; and Irwin, J. David. *An Introduction to Computer Logic.* Englewood Cliffs, N.J.: Prentice-Hall, 1975.

23. Peatman, John B. *Digital Hardware Design.* New York: McGraw-Hill, 1980.

24. Rhyne, V. Thomas *Fundamentals of Digital Systems Design.* Englewood Cliffs, N.J.: Prentice-Hall, 1973.

25. Taub, Herbert, and Schilling, Donald. *Digital Integrated Electronics.* New York: McGraw-Hill, 1977.

26. Texas Instruments Staff. *The TTL Data Book.* Dallas: Texas Instruments, 2d ed. 1981. Also Vol. 1, 1984.

27. Unger, Stephen H. *Asynchronous Sequential Switching Circuits.* New York: Wiley-Interscience, 1969.

28. Winkler, David, and Prosser, Franklin. *The Art of Digital Design.* Englewood Cliffs, N.J.: Prentice-Hall, 1980.

ANSWERS TO SELECTED STUDY GUIDE QUESTIONS AND PROBLEMS

This section contains answers to some of the more difficult study guide questions and answers to all of the problems which are referenced in the study guides. Answers to the remaining problems are not included here, but they are available in the instructor's manual.

Unit 1   Study Guide Answers

2 e.   Two of the rows are:

1110	16	14	E
1111	17	15	F

3 b. $1100_2 - 101_2 = [1 \times 2^3 + 1 \times 2^2 + 0 \times 2^1 + 0 \times 2^0]$

$\qquad\qquad -[\qquad\qquad 1 \times 2^2 + 0 \times 2^1 + 1 \times 2^0]$ ——— note borrow from column 1

$= [1 \times 2^3 + 1 \times 2^2 + (0 - 1) \times 2^1 + (10 + 0) \times 2^0]$

$\quad -[\qquad\qquad 1 \times 2^2 + \qquad 0 \times 2^1 + \qquad 1 \times 2^0]$ ——— note borrow from column 2

$= [1 \times 2^3 + (1 - 1) \times 2^2 + (10 - 1) \times 2^1 + 10 \times 2^0]$

$\quad -[\qquad\qquad 1 \times 2^2 + \qquad 0 \times 2^1 + 1 \times 2^0]$ ——— note borrow from column 3

$= [(1 - 1) \times 2^3 + (10 - 0) \times 2^2 + 1 \times 2^1 + 10 \times 2^0]$

$\quad -[\qquad\qquad\qquad 1 \times 2^2 + 0 \times 2^1 + 1 \times 2^0]$

$= [\qquad 0 \times 2^3 + \qquad 1 \times 2^2 + 1 \times 2^1 + 1 \times 2^0] = 111_2$

5 a.

BCD:	0001	1000	0111
excess-3:	0100	1011	1010
6-3-1-1:	0001	1011	1001
2-out-of-5:	00101	10100	10010

Unit 1   Answers to Problems

1.1 a. 1365.2_8, 1011110101.010_2

  b. 173.127_8, 1111011.001010111_2

1.2 a. 273.4_8, 187.5_{10} b. 155.3_8, 109.375_{10}

1.3

	Add	Subtract	Multiply
a.	11010	100	10100101
b.	10000011	1111	1000010001010

1.4　　341.12$_5$ (96.2857$_{10}$)

1.5 a.
$$2 \quad B \quad D \;.\; 1 \quad E_{16}$$
$$\downarrow \;\; \downarrow \;\; \downarrow \;\; \downarrow \;\; \downarrow$$
$$02 \;\; 23 \;\; 31 \;.\; 01 \;\; 32_4$$

b.

Hex.	Base 4
0	00
1	01
2	02
3	03
4	10
5	11
6	12
7	13
8	20
9	21
A	22
B	23
C	30
D	31
E	32
F	33

c.　2748.8125$_{10}$

1.6

	5	3	2	1
0	0	0	0	0
1	0	0	0	1
2	0	0	1	0
3	0	0	1	1
4	0	1	0	1
5	0	1	1	0
6	0	1	1	1
7	1	0	1	0
8	1	0	1	1
9	1	1	0	1

1101 0011 1010 0001

$\underbrace{}$　$\underbrace{}$　$\underbrace{}$　$\underbrace{}$

9　　3　　7　　1

1.9 a.
$$11 \quad 11$$
$$11011011$$
$$- \;\; 1101101$$
$$\overline{1101110}$$

b.
$$11 \quad 111$$
$$10001100$$
$$- \;\; 1100101$$
$$\overline{0100111}$$

Unit 2　Study Guide Answers

2 d.　1; 0; 1; 1

e.　1, 1; 0, 0; 0; 1

3 a.　4 variables, 10 literals

d.　$F = (A'B)'$

e.　$F = (A + B')C$

f.　network should have 2 OR gates, 3 AND gates, and 3 inverters

4 b.　$A, 0, 0, A; \;\; A, 1, A, 1$

6 c.　$Z = ABC$

7 a.   sum of products
neither
product of sums (here A and B' are each considered to be separate terms
in the product)
neither

  b.   fewer terms are generated

  c. $D[A + B'(C + E)] = D(A + B')(A + C + E)$

8 a. $AE + B'C' + C'D$

  b. $C'DE + AB'CD'E$

Unit 2   Answers to Problems

2.1 a. $XY + XY' = X(Y + Y') = X \cdot 1 = X$

  d. $(A + B)(A + C) = AA + AB + AC + BC = A + AB + AC + BC$
$$= A + AC + BC = A + BC$$

2.2 a.

                            b.

2.3 a.   1 (Theorem 5)   b. $AB + CD'E$ (Th. 8D)

  c. $A + B'C$ (Th. 10)   d. $AB' + (C + D)'$ (Th. 11D)

  e. $(AB + C'D')EF$ (Th. 11)

2.4 a. $BC'D + AE$ b. $C + A'B'$

2.5 a. $(D + F')(E + F')(D + G')(E + G')$

  c. $(C + E')(D + E')(C + F)(D + F)(A' + B + E')(A' + B + F)$

  d. $E(A + D')(B + C' + D')$

  f. $(H + I + K')(H + J' + K')(H + I + L)(H + J' + L)$

2.6 a.   b.

2.7 a. $X = B'$ b. $Y = A + B$

Unit 3   Study Guide Answers

2 a. $a' + b + c$ b. $ab'c'd$

  c. $a(b' + c')$ d. $(a + b)(c' + d')$

  e. $a' + b(c + d')$

8 b. $(b' + d)(b + a)(b + c)$ $(a + d)(b + d)(a' + b' + c)$

c. $w'y' + x'y'z' + xy + wyz$

11 e. $x \oplus y$

12 a. $+ \ - \ $ no

b. $Z^D = (AB' + C' + D)(A' + B + D') + E'F$

c. dual of X' is X'

Unit 3 Answers to Problems

3.3 a. $[(w' + x') + (y + z')(y' + z)][(w + x) + yz' + y'z]$

b. $[(a' + b')c + (d + e') \cdot 0][g' + h \cdot 1][w']$

c. $(a' + b)[d' + (e + f)(g + h')] + a[b' + c' + d' + e(f + g')]$

3.4 a. $[(w + x) + (y' + z)(y + z')][(w' + x') + y'z + yz']$

b. $[(a + b)c' + (d' + e) \cdot 0][g + h' \cdot 1][w]$

c. $(a + b')[d + (e' + f')(g' + h)] + a'[b + c + d + e'(f' + g)]$

3.6 a. $ABC' + ABD' + A'B'C + A'CD$

b. $B'C + AB'D + BC' + A'BD'$ <u>or</u> $B'C + AC'D + BC' + A'CD'$

3.7 a. $(A + B' + D')(A + C' + D')(A' + B + D)(A' + C' + D)$

b. $(A + B' + C)(A + B + D)(A' + C + D')(A' + C' + D)$

3.9 a. $F = A$ b. $G = XYZ'$

3.12 $F = ABC' + ABD' + AB'CD + A'CD'$

3.13 a. No   b. $[(x \equiv y) \equiv z] = [x \equiv (y \equiv z)]$

3.16 a. $e_o = (e_1 \equiv e_2)$ b. $e_o = e_1 \oplus e_2$

3.17 a. $e_o = e_1 e_2 e_3$ b. $e_o = e_1 + e_2 + e_3$

Unit 4 Study Guide Answers

1 b. $A'B'C + BC'D' + AB'D' + BCD$ c. add BCD; eliminate $A'BD$, ABC

Unit 4 Answers to Problems

4.4 a. $ABC' + AB'D + A'BD'$ b. $W'Y' + WX'Y + WXZ$

c. $(A + B + C)(A' + C + D)(B' + C' + D')$

4.6 a. y b. $xz + y'z$

c. 1   d. $bc + b'c' + a'bd' + a'b'd$
                                  (other solutions possible)

e. $x'y' + yz + w'z'$

f. $A'BD + B'EF + CDE'G$ g. $abd + b'd' + c'd$

4.7 $(A + B')(A' + C)(B + C')$ <u>or</u> $(A' + B)(A + C')(B' + C)$

4.8 $(A + D)(A + E)(C + D' + B' + E) = AC + AD' + AB' + DE$

4.10 $BD' + A'D + AB' + AC'$

4.13 a. Valid.   b. Not valid.

    c. Valid.

Unit 5   Study Guide Answers

2 d. $ab'c'd$ e. $a + b + c' + d'$

  g. $(a + b' + c)(a' + b + c')(a' + b' + c)(a' + b' + c')$

3 c. $\Sigma m(0, 1, 3, 4)$ $\Pi M(2, 5, 6, 7)$

  h. (1) neither   (4) neither

     (2) maxterm   (5) minterm

     (3) maxterm   (6) minterm

4 b. m_{19} c. $A'BCD'E$

  e. M_{19} f. $(A + B' + C' + D + E')$

5 a. 65536

  d. $(a_0 m_0 + a_1 m_1 + a_2 m_2 + a_3 m_3)(b_0 m_0 + b_1 m_1 + b_2 m_2 + b_3 m_3) = \ldots$

    $= a_0 b_0 m_0 + a_1 b_1 m_1 + a_2 b_2 m_2 + a_3 b_3 m_3$

  f. $\Pi M(2, 5, 6)$ $\Sigma m(2, 5, 6)$ $\Pi M(0, 1, 3, 4, 7)$

6 b. $\Sigma m(0, 5) + \Sigma d(1, 3, 4)$

Unit 5   Answers to Problems

5.1 answers should be of the form:

    a. $F = ABC'$ b. $F = XY + X'Y'$

    c. $G = AB'(CD + EF)$

5.2 a. $Z = (A'B'C'D'E' + ABCDE)'$ b. $Y = A'B'CD'E$

5.3 a. $a = \Sigma m(3, 5, 6, 7) = w'xy + wx'y + wxy' + wxy$

    $b = \Sigma m(1, 2, 4, 7) = w'x'y + w'xy' + wx'y' + wxy$

  b. $a = \Pi M(0, 1, 2, 4) = (w + x + y)(w + x + y')(w + x' + y)(w' + x + y)$

    $b = \Pi M(0, 3, 5, 6) = (w + x + y)(w + x' + y')(w' + x + y')(w' + x' + y)$

5.4 a. $F = \Sigma m(7, 10, 11, 13, 14, 15)$

      $= A'BCD + AB'CD' + AB'CD + ABC'D + ABCD' + ABCD$

  b. $F = \Pi M(0, 1, 2, 3, 4, 5, 6, 8, 9, 12) = (A + B + C + D)(A + B + C + D') \ldots$

5.5 a. $\Sigma m(0, 1, 2, 3, 6)$ b. $\Pi M(4, 5, 7)$

  c. $\Sigma m(4, 5, 7)$ d. $\Pi M(0, 1, 2, 3, 6)$

5.6 a. $\Sigma m(1, 2, 3, 6, 9, 11, 12)$ b. $\Pi M(0, 4, 5, 7, 8, 10, 13, 14, 15)$

   c. $\Sigma m(0, 4, 5, 7, 8, 10, 13, 14, 15)$ d. $\Pi M(1, 2, 3, 6, 9, 11, 12)$

5.7 a. $\Sigma m(0, 1, 2, 3, 4, 8, 9, 12) = A'B'C'D' + A'B'C'D + \ldots$

   b. $\Pi M(5, 6, 7, 10, 11, 13, 14, 15) = (A + B' + C + D')(A + B' + C' + D) \ldots$

5.8 General rule: product of all maxterms in F_1 or F_2.

5.9 a. 16

   b. $F(x, y) = 0$; $x'y'$; $x'y$; x'; xy'; y'; $x'y + xy'$; $x' + y'$; xy;
                $x'y' + xy$; y; $x' + y$; x; $x + y'$; $x + y$; 1

5.12

ABC	DEF
000	0xx
001	xxx
010	x11
011	0xx
100	110
101	xxx
110	0xx
111	101

Unit 6   Study Guide Answers

2 d.   e.   0, 3, 6

   j. $G = bc + a'c' + ab'$ or $b'c' + ac + a'b$

3 d. 6, 10, 12, 15;   0, 12, 9, 10

   g. $f_1 = a'b + bc' + a'cd + ac'd$ $f_2 = b'c + cd + a'bd + ab'd'$

4 a. $a'b'd'$, $b'c'd'$, $ac'd'$, $ac'd$, $a'b'cd$, etc.

   b. $AB'C'$ and $AC'D$ are prime implicants

5 c. no   f. yes

   i. $A'D'$ because of m_4, $B'D'$ because of m_{10}

6 b. $A'D'$ is not essential because all of its minterms are covered by other prime
      implicants. BC' is essential because of m_{13}. $B'CD$ is essential because of m_{11}.
      minimum sum $= B'CD + BC' + BD' + A'B'$

   d. $A'C' + ACD + (AB$ or $BC')$

8 a. 8, 16, 25, 26, 28

   c. $P_1 + P_2 + P_3 + P_4 + BCDE + AC'E$

   f. $AC'E' + A'DE + ACE + B'CE + (AB'C$ or ADE' or $ACD)$

Unit 6   Answers to Problems

6.3   b. $Z = \Sigma m(3, 7, 11, 13, 15) = CD + ABD$

   c. $Z = \Pi M(0, 1, 2, 4, 5, 6, 8, 9, 10, 12, 14) = D(A + C)(B + C)$

   e.

6.4   a. $f_1 = a'c + ac'$ b. $f_2 = e'f + de' + df$

   c. $f_3 = r + t'$ d. $f_4 = z' + xy' + x'y$

6.5   b. $F = B' + A'D + ACD'$

   c. $F = (A + B' + D)(A' + B' + D')[(B' + C + D)$ or $(A' + B' + C)]$

6.6   a. $f = b'c' + a'd' + abd + (bcd$ or $a'bc)$ [1 other min. solution]

   b. $f = bc + bd + a'cd + b'c'd' + ad'$

   c. $f = ac'd' + a'c'd + abc + (a'b'c$ OR $b'c'd')$ [5 other min. solutions]

6.7   b. $Z = C_1 C_2 + C_2 X_2 + C_1 X_1$

6.8   a. $f_1 = a'b + ab'c' + b'd$ b. $f_2 = (a + c)(b' + c' + d')(a' + c' + d)$

6.9 $F = \underline{bc'd'} + \underline{b'c} + \underline{cd} + ad + (ab$ OR $ac)$ [1 other min. solution]
        $m_4 \quad\quad m_2 \quad m_7$

6.10 a. $c'd'e'$ (m_{16}, m_{24}) b. $a'b'de, a'd'e', cd'e, a'ce', a'b'c,$
       $a'ce'$ (m_{14}) $ace, b'ce, c'd'e', a'cd'$

       ace (m_{31})

       $a'b'de$ (m_3)

6.11 $F = \underline{BCDE'} + \underline{A'B'CD} + \underline{AB'C'D} + \underline{B'C'E'} + \underline{A'BC'} + BCD'E + A'E'$

6.12 $F = \underline{AC'D'E'} + \underline{A'B'C'E'} + \underline{BDE} + \underline{A'BC} + AB'C'E + A'B'D'$

6.13 a. $F = \Pi M(6, 7, 9, 10, 13, 14, 15)$
        $= (A + B' + C' + D)(A + B' + C' + D')(A' + B + C + D')$
        $(A' + B + C' + D)(A' + B' + C + D')(A' + B' + C' + D)$
        $(A' + B' + C' + D')$

   b. $F' = AC'D + ACD' + BC$

   c. $F = (A' + C + D')(A' + C' + D)(B' + C')$

   d. $F^D = A'CD' + A'C'D + B'C'$

6.14 Minterms 0, 1, 2, 3, 4, 5, 7, 8, 10, 11.

Unit 7   Study Guide Answers

2 f.   (2, 6)

3 a. m_0 - $a'b'c'$ $\qquad\qquad$ (m_0, m_1) - $a'b'$ $\quad\Big\rbrace$

$\qquad$ m_1 - $a'b'c$ $\qquad\qquad\quad$ (m_1, m_5) - $b'c$ $\quad\Big\rbrace$ $\quad$ prime

$\qquad$ m_5 - $ab'c$ $\qquad\qquad\quad$ (m_5, m_7) - ac $\quad\Big\rbrace$

$\qquad$ m_7 - abc

$\quad$ d. $A'B'C'$ and ABC are not prime implicants.

4 b. $a'c'd'$, bc', $ab'c$

Unit 7   Answers to Problems

7.2 a. $a'c'd$ $\quad$ (1, 5) $\qquad\qquad\qquad$ b. $a'b'c'$ $\quad$ (0, 1)

$\qquad$ $b'c'd$ $\quad$ (1, 9) $\qquad\qquad\qquad\qquad$ $b'c'd'$ $\quad$ (0, 8)

$\qquad$ $a'b\,d$ $\quad$ (5, 7) $\qquad\qquad\qquad\qquad$ $a\,b'd'$ $\quad$ (8, 10)

$\qquad$ $a\,b'd$ $\quad$ (9, 11) $\qquad\qquad\qquad\quad$ $a\,c\,d'$ $\quad$ (10, 14)

$\qquad$ $a\,b\,d'$ $\quad$ (12, 14) $\qquad\qquad\qquad$ $a'd$ $\qquad$ (1, 3, 5, 7)

$\qquad$ $b\,c\,d$ $\quad$ (7, 15) $\qquad\qquad\qquad\qquad$ $b\,c$ $\qquad$ (6, 7, 14, 15)

$\qquad$ $a\,c\,d$ $\quad$ (11, 15)

$\qquad$ $a\,b\,c$ $\quad$ (14, 15)

7.3 a. $f = a'c'd + ab'd + abd' + bcd$ <u>or</u> $f = b'c'd + a'bd + abd' + acd$

$\quad$ b. $f = a'd + bc +$ $\left\{\begin{array}{c} a'b'c' + ab'd' \\ \text{or} \\ b'c'd' + acd' \\ \text{or} \\ b'c'd' + ab'd' \end{array}\right\}$

7.4 a. $f = b'cd' + bc' + a'd + (a'b$ OR $a'c)$ $\qquad\qquad$ [1 other solution]

$\quad$ b. $f = bc'd' + b'c + cd + ab + (ad$ OR $b'd)$ $\qquad\qquad$ [1 other solution]

7.9 a. $F = A'B + A'C'\,D' + AB'D + A'C'E + BCDE$

$\quad$ b. $Z = A'B' + ABD + EB'C' + EA'C + FAB + GBD$
$\qquad$ [several other solutions]

Unit 8   Study Guide Answers

1 b.   6 gates, 13 inputs; 5 gates, 11 inputs

2 a.   0; 1; 1, 1; 0, 0; 1, 1, 1; 0, 0, 0; 0, 0; 1, 1

$\quad$ c. $F = de + abd + bcd + acd + abe + bce + ace$

6 b. $(a \equiv b') \equiv (c \equiv d)$ <u>or</u> $(a' \equiv b) \equiv (c \equiv d)$

Unit 8   Answers to Problems

8.1 a.   **b.**

8.2 a.   **b.**

                                        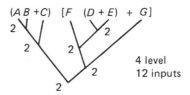

$(A + B')$ $(CD' + E + AC'D)$

3 level
12 inputs

$(AB + C)$ $[F (D + E) + G]$

4 level
12 inputs

8.3 NOR for $+$ logic, NAND for $-$ logic

8.4 a. yes   **b.** no   **c.** yes   **d.** yes

8.5

8.6   NAND - NAND   OR - NAND   NOR - OR

NOR - NOR   AND - NOR   NAND - AND

8.7 $f = (a + c' + e)(a' + c + d)(c + d + e')(b + c' + e)(b + d' + e')$

   2 level, 6 gates, 20 inputs

   $f = (ab + c' + e)(a'e' + c + d)(b + d' + e')$ 3 level, 6 gates, 16 inputs

8.8 $f = (a + b)(a' + d' + b'c')$

8.9 $F = A'[B' + (D' + E)(C' + D)]*$ or $A'B' + A'(C'D' + DE)$

8.10 $F = B'(A'D' + C'D')$

8.11 a. $wxy + xyz'$ b. $AD' + A'B'C + ABC$

Unit 9 Study Guide Answers

2 a. (1) no   (2) yes   (3) no

  c. 5 gates, 10 inputs; using common gate: 4 gates, 9 inputs

  d. $F_1 = \underline{a'cd} + \underline{acd} + ab'c'$

     $F_2 = \underline{a'cd} + \underline{bcd} + a'bc' + acd'$

     $F_3 = \underline{bcd} + \underline{acd} + a'c'd$

4 a. $Z = a'I_0 + aI_1$

  b. $Z = A'C'I_0 + A'CI_1 + AC'I_2 + ACI_3$

    $I_0 = B'$ $I_1 = B'$ $I_2 = 0$ $I_3 = 1$

  c. $I_0 = 1$ $I_1 = A'$ $I_2 = 0$ $I_3 = 1$ $I_4 = A$ $I_5 = 0$ $I_6 = 1$ $I_7 = A'$

  d. $I_0 = B'$ $I_1 = B + D$ $I_2 = D'$ $I_3 = B \oplus D$

  e. $I_0 = A'$ $I_1 = 0$ $I_2 = A$ $I_8 = 1$

5 a. inputs BCD; $A = 0$

6 a. 32 words $\times$ 4 bits; 1024 $\times$ 8

  b. 16 words $\times$ 5 bits; 16 $\times$ 10

7 a. 4 inputs
    7 terms (m_3, m_7, m_{11}, m_{12}, m_{13}, m_{14}, m_{15})
    3 outputs

c.

$ABCD$	$F_1 F_2 F_3$
1 1 - -	1 0 1
1 - 1 1	1 1 0
1 1 0 -	0 1 0
0 - 1 1	0 1 1

Unit 9 Answers to Problems

9.1 $f_1 = \underline{a'c'd'} + \underline{ab'c} + a'c$ 6 gates,   compared to original f_1 and f_2
     $f_2 = \underline{a'c'd'} + \underline{ab'c} + ac'$ 16 inputs   which require 8 gates, 18 inputs

---

*This solution requires a NAND gate connected as an inverter at the network output.

9.2 $f_1 = A'BC' + \underline{BC'D'} + AB'C$

$f_2 = B'C'D' + B'CD + \underline{A'C'D'} + \left.\begin{cases} A'B'D \\ A'B'C' \end{cases}\right\}$ 11 gates

$f_3 = \underline{A'C'D'} + \underline{BC'D'} + ACD'$ 34 inputs

9.3 $f_1 = b'd' + \underline{ac'd}$

$f_2 = a'd + \underline{ac'd}$ $\left.\right\}$ 8 gates

$f_3 = b'c + \underline{ac'd} + ab'$ 18 inputs

9.4 $xs\text{-}3 = abcd$ $W = ab + acd = a(b + cd)$ $\left.\right\}$ 9 gates,

$BCD = WXYZ$ $X = b'(\underline{c' + d'}) + bcd$

$Y = (\underline{c' + d'})(c + d)$ 19 inputs

$Z = d'$

9.5 $f_1 = (a + b + c)(b' + d)$ $f_2 = (\underline{a + b + c})(\underline{b' + c + d})(a' + c)$

$f_3 = (\underline{b' + c + d})(a + c)(b + c')$

9.6 a. Replace all gates in the AND-OR network which corresponds to Equation 9-2(b) with NAND gates. Invert the c input to the f_2 output gate.

b. Replace all gates in answer to 9.5 with NOR.

9.7 a.

b.

9.8 a. Mux inputs: $I_0 = I_1 = I_7 = 1$, $I_2 = B'$, $I_3 = B$, $I_4 = I_5 = I_6 = 0$

b. $I_0 = 1$, $I_2 = 0$, $I_3 = D$, $I_1 = B'D' + BD = B' \oplus D$ (control inputs A, C)

9.9 Answer similar to Fig. 9-18 with four 5-input NAND-gates:

$W = (m'_5 m'_6 m'_7 m'_8 m'_9)'$, $X = (m'_1 m'_2 m'_3 m'_4 m'_9)'$,

$Y = (m'_0 m'_3 m'_4 m'_7 m'_8)'$, $Z = (m'_0 m'_2 m'_4 m'_6 m'_8)'$

9.10 $X = A'BD + C'D + AB' + AB'C'D'$ ROM table:

$Y = A'BD + BCD + AB'$

$Z = A'BD + BCD + ABC + AB'C'D'$

$A\,B\,C\,D$	$X\,Y\,Z$
0 0 0 0	0 0 0
0 0 0 1	1 0 0
0 0 1 0	0 0 0
0 0 1 1	0 0 0
0 1 0 0	0 0 0
0 1 0 1	1 1 1
$\vdots$	$\vdots$
1 1 1 1	0 1 1

9.11 a.

$x_3x_2x_1x_0y_3y_2y_1y_0$	$s_3\,s_2\ s_1\,s_0\,c$
0 0 0 0 0 0 0 0	0 0 0 0 0
0 0 0 0 0 0 0 1	0 0 0 1 0
. . . .	. . . . .
0 1 0 1 0 0 1 1	1 0 0 0 0
0 1 0 1 0 1 0 0	1 0 0 1 0
. . . .	. . . . .
1 0 0 1 1 0 0 0	0 1 1 1 1
1 0 0 1 1 0 0 1	1 0 0 0 1
1 0 0 1 1 0 1 0	x x x x x
1 0 0 1 1 0 1 1	x x x x x
. . . .	. . . . .

b. 8 inputs, 100 words, 5 outputs

Unit 11 Answers to Problems

11.1 $1BD.1C7$, $\underline{0001}$, $\underline{1011}$, $\underline{1101}$, $\underline{0001}$, $\underline{1100}$, $\underline{0111}$,

11.2 $abd' + b'ce = (b + c)(b + e)\,(b' + a)(b' + d')$

11.3 a. $F = \Pi M(0, 1, 2, 4, 8) = (A + B + C + D)(A + B + C + D')\ldots$ etc.

b. $F = (A + C + BD)(B + D + AC)$ 5 gates, 12 inputs

11.4 a. $F_1 = (a + b + c + d)(a + c' + d')(a' + d')$

$F_2 = (a + b + c + d)(a + c' + d')(c + d')$

b.

	$abcd$	$F_1\,F_2$
(cd')	- - 1 0	1 1
(bd')	- 1 - 0	1 1
(ad')	1 - - 0	1 1
(ac)	1 - 1 -	0 1
$(a'c'd)$	0 - 0 1	1 0

11.5 a. $A'BC'E(m_{11})$, $A'B'CD(m_6)$, $AB'C'E'(m_{18})$

  b. $F = A'BC'E + A'B'CD + AB'C'E' + ACD'E' + A'BCD' + AC'D'E$
      $+ AB'CE$

  c. $A'BC'E$, $A'B'CD$, $AB'C'E'$, $ACD'E'$, $A'BCD'$, $AC'D'E$, $AB'CE$, $AB'D'$,
      $BCD'E'$, $BC'D'E$, $A'BD'E$, $B'CDE$

  e. $I_0 = I_1 = I_2 = a$, $I_3 = 0$, $I_4 = I_5 = a$, $I_6 = a'$, $I_7 = 1$, $I_8 = 0$, $I_9 = 1$, $I_{10} = 0$,
      $I_{11} = a'$, $I_{12} = 1$, $I_{13} = a'$, $I_{14} = I_{15} = 0$

11.6 b.

b
c
a'

11.7 $F = b'c' + a'bd + ac$ 11.8 $b'cd' + ab' + ac'd$

Unit 12 Study Guide Answers

1 a. $Z = 1$ between $t = 50$ and $t = 110$

2 b. $P = Q = 0$ c. $S = R = 1$ is not allowed

3 c. flip-flop would change state more than once per T pulse

4 b. $Q^+ = QK' + Q'J$

  c. Pulse width must be long enough to cause FF to change state, but shorter
      than the FF delay time, ϵ.

5 b. Clocked $-Q^+$ represents the state after a clock pulse.
      Unclocked $-Q^+$ is the state of the FF at time ϵ (response time) after input
      pulses on J, K.

6 b. Q becomes 1 on the trailing edge of the first clock pulse and returns to 0 on
      the trailing edge of the third clock pulse.

7 clear $= 1$, preset $= 0$; clear $= 0$

8 b. $S = Q'T$, $R = QT$

Unit 12 Answers to Problems

12.1 V changes to 1 at 15 ns and back to 0 at 25 ns
      Z changes to 1 at 20 ns and back to 0 at 35 ns

12.2 a. R^* and S^* cannot be zero simultaneously.

  b. $Q^+ = (S^*)' + R^*Q$ c.

  d. $S^* = S'$, $R^* = R'$

12.5 a.

    b. $Q = 1$ c. $Q = 1$ d. inputs must change between clock pulses

12.6 $D = Q^+ = Q'J + QK'$

12.7 $Q^+ = T'Q + K'Q + JTQ'$

12.8   a. $Q^+ = G'Q + GL$ b. $R = GL'$ $S = GL$

12.9   a.

    b.

Unit 13   Study Guide Answers

1   a. T_C and T_B

    e.   101 goes to 110 which goes to 011; 001 goes to 111

2   c.   from the flip-flop outputs

    e.   In state 001, $R_A = S_A = 1$, so A^+ is undefined. $B^+ = 0$ and $C^+ = 0$.

3   e. $F_1 = 1$, $F_2 = 0$

    f. $J_B = A'C' + C'D + ACD'$, $K_B = A'D + C'D$

4   Q and Q' from leftmost flip-flop connect to J and K of rightmost flip-flop, etc. Flip-flops do not change state until after the pulse is over.

Unit 13 Answers to Problems

13.1 a.

b.

c.

d.

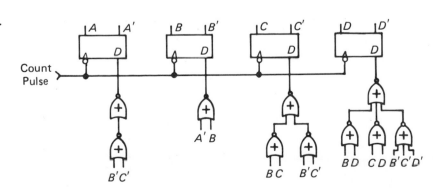

13.2 a. $T_A = A + BC$ $T_B = AB + B'C + CD'$ $T_C = A'$ $T_D = A$

b. $R_A = C'$ or A $R_B = A + BCD'$ $R_C = C$ $R_D = AD$ or AB
    $S_A = BC$ $S_B = B'C$ $S_C = A'C'$ $S_D = AB'$ or AD'

c. $J_A = BC$ $J_B = C$ $J_C = A'$ $J_D = A$
    $K_A = 1$ $K_B = A + CD'$ $K_C = 1$ $K_D = A$

d. $D_A = BC$ $D_B = B'C + CD + A'BC'$ $D_C = A'C'$ $D_D = A'D + AD'$
    or $A'D + AB'$

13.3 a.

Q	Q^+	M	N
0	0	0	x
0	1	1	x
1	0	x	0
1	1	x	1

b. $M_A = B, N_A = C;$
    $M_B = A'C, N_B = A';$
    $M_C = A', N_C = A' + B$

13.4

13.5 a. $Q^+ = KG + QK'$

b.

Q	Q^+	K	G
		0	0
0	0	0	1
		1	0
0	1	1	1
1	0	1	0
		0	0
1	1	0	1
		1	1

c. $K = XYQ', G = 1$ or $K = 1, G = Q + XY$

13.6 a.

b.

If the *S-R* flip flops have no delay, *A* may switch before *E* does (or vice versa) and cause loss of information; or one flip-flop may switch twice in the same pulse—as if the new state of *E* gets back to *A* before *P* turns off. If delay is added then *P* must be shorter than the delay time; then the new state of *E* cannot affect *A*, etc.

13.7 *P*, *A*, *B* and *C* should be the same as in Fig. 13-6.

Unit 14 Study Guide Answers

2 a. Mealy: output a function of both input and state
   Moore: output a function of state only

   b. change inputs between clock pulses
   state changes immediately following the clock pulse
   Moore: output changes only when the flip-flops change state
   Mealy: output can change when input changes or when state changes

   c. during the clock pulse or immediately preceding it

   d. Mealy: false outputs can appear when the state has changed to its next value but the input has not yct changed
   Moore: no false outputs because output is not a function of input

   Changing the inputs at the same time the state change occurs will eliminate false outputs.

3 a. before the clock pulse
   Q^+ means the state of flip-flop Q after the clock (i.e., the next state of flip-flop Q)

   c. Mealy: output associated with transitions between states
   Moore: output associated with state

    d. present: before the clock pulse
next: after the clock pulse

    e. output depends only on the state and not on the input

4 a. 1 1 0 1   c. 1 0 0 1

    e. No false outputs, but Z_d is delayed by one clock time.

6 a. Without the clock, flip-flops would change state at different times with respect to each other because of unequal propagation delays through the network. Also, without a clock, as soon as one state change was completed another change could occur without waiting for the next input.

    b. for a Moore network, $Z = \lambda(s)$

Unit 14 Answers to Problems

14.2

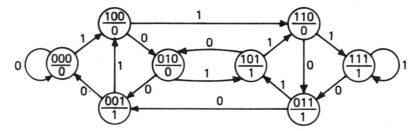

14.3 a. $A^+ = A(B' + X) + A'(BX' + B'X)$
         $B^+ = AB'X + B(A' + X')$

    b. $Z = (0)\ 00101$

Present State	Next State (A^+B^+)		Z
AB	$x = 0$	$x = 1$	
00	00	10	0
01	11	01	0
11	01	10	1
10	10	11	0

14.4

Clock

X

A

B

C

Z

False outputs

14.5 a. $A^+ = AB + AB'X_2 + A'BX_2$ <u>or</u> $A^+ = AB + AX_2 + A'BX_2$
 $B^+ = X_1A' + X_1X_2 + BX_1 + A'BX_2'$

b.

		$X_1X_2 =$				$X_1X_2 =$			
AB		00	01	11	10	00	01	11	10
00	S_0	S_0	S_0	S_1	S_1	00	00	01	01
01	S_1	S_1	S_3	S_2	S_1	00	10	10	00
11	S_2	S_3	S_3	S_2	S_2	11	11	00	00
10	S_3	S_0	S_3	S_2	S_0	00	00	00	00

$$Z_1Z_2$$

Unit 15 Study Guide Answers

1 b. $A^+ = T_A \oplus A = X'A'B$ $B^+ = T_B \oplus B = X$
   c. $J_A = BX'$ $K_A = X \oplus B$ $J_B = A + X$ $K_B = A$ $Z = AB'$

Unit 15 Answers to Problems

15.3

15.4

	$x = 0$	1	$x = 0$	1
S_0	S_4	S_1	00	00
S_1	S_2	S_1	00	00
S_2	S_4	S_3	00	10
S_3	S_2	S_5	00	01
S_4	S_4	S_3	00	00
S_5	S_6	S_5	00	00
S_6	S_6	S_7	00	00
S_7	S_6	S_5	00	01

$$Z_1Z_2$$

15.5

previous input	output	present state	next state $X_1 X_2 =$ 00	01	10	11	
00	0	S_0	S_0	S_1	S_2	S_3	
01	0	S_1	S_0	S_1	S_2	S_7	
10	0	S_2	S_0	S_1	S_2	S_7	
11	0	S_3	S_0	S_1	S_2	S_3	
00	1	S_4	S_4	S_5	S_6	S_3	
01	1	S_5	S_4	S_5	S_6	S_7	
10	1	S_6	S_4	S_5	S_6	S_3	
11	1	S_7	S_4	S_5	S_6	S_7	

Note: a 4 state solution is also possible

15.6 a.   b.

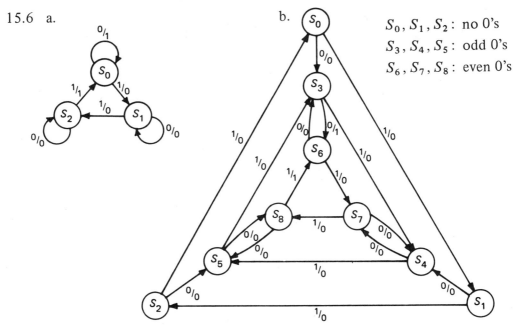

S_0, S_1, S_2 : no 0's
S_3, S_4, S_5 : odd 0's
S_6, S_7, S_8 : even 0's

15.7 a.   b.

	$X_1 X_2 =$ 00	01	10	11	00	01	10	11
S_0	S_1	S_2	S_3	S_4	00	00	00	00
S_1	S_1	S_2	S_3	S_4	00	10	10	10
S_2	S_1	S_2	S_3	S_4	01	00	10	10
S_3	S_1	S_2	S_3	S_4	01	01	00	10
S_4	S_1	S_2	S_3	S_4	01	01	01	00

$Z_1 Z_2$

	$X_1 X_2 =$ 00	01	10	11	$Z_1 Z_2$
S_0	S_1	S_4	S_7	S_{10}	00
S_1	S_1	S_3	S_6	S_9	00
S_2	S_1	S_3	S_6	S_9	01
S_3	S_2	S_4	S_6	S_9	10
S_4	S_2	S_4	S_6	S_9	00
S_5	S_2	S_4	S_6	S_9	01
S_6	S_2	S_5	S_7	S_9	10
S_7	S_2	S_5	S_7	S_9	00
S_8	S_2	S_5	S_7	S_9	01
S_9	S_2	S_5	S_8	S_{10}	10
S_{10}	S_2	S_5	S_8	S_{10}	00

Unit 16   Study Guide Answers

2 b. $\lambda(p, 01) = 00$ and $\lambda(q, 01) = 01$; therefore, $p \not\equiv q$

  c.   No. You would have to try an infinite number of test sequences to be sure the networks were equivalent.

  d. $b \equiv c$ iff $a \equiv d$ and $a \equiv b$, but $a \not\equiv b$ because the outputs are different.

3 a.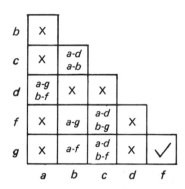

  b. $f - g$

  c. $a \equiv c, \quad b \equiv d, \quad b \equiv e, \quad d \equiv e$

	0	I	0	1
a	b	a	0	1
b	b	b	0	0

8 c.   Interchanging columns or complementing columns does not affect network cost for symmetric flip-flops.

  f.   Numbering columns from left to right, column 3 is same as column 4, column 2 is column 5 complemented, column 1 is column 6 complemented.

10 c. $D_1 = XQ_1' + XQ_3 + Q_2Q_3' + X'Q_1Q_2'$ or $D_1 = XQ_1' + XQ_2 + Q_2'Q_3 + X'Q_1Q_3'$
   $D_2 = Q_3, \ D_3 = X'Q_3 + XQ_2Q_3' + (Q_1'Q_3 \ \text{OR} \ Q_1'Q_2)$
   $Z = XQ_2Q_3 + X'Q_2'Q_3 + X'Q_2Q_3'$

  d. $J_1 = X, \ K_1 = X'Q_2Q_3 + XQ_2'Q_3'$

Unit 16   Answers to Problems

16.1 a.   Reduced Table:

	0	1	0	1
a	c	e	0	0
c	a	g	0	0
e	e	a	0	1
g	c	g	0	1

  b.

state	a	f	f	a		c	g	c	g
input	1	0	1			1	0	1	
output	0	0	1			0	0	0	

OR

state	a	f	a	f		c	g	g	g
input	1	1	1			1	1	1	
output	0	1	0			0	1	1	

16.2   Reduced Table:

	next state $x = 0$ $\quad 1$		output
a	f	b	0
b	b	a	1
e	g	b	0
f	a	f	0
g	e	a	0

16.3 a. No, because there is no state equivalent to S_6.

    b. Yes.

16.4 Answer same as 16.1.

16.5 a. Answer same as 16.2.   b.

a	f	h	f		e	g	c	b
$x = 0$	1	1	–		0	1	1	–
$z = 0$	0	0	0		0	0	0	1

16.6 a. Only <u>one</u> assignment - 000   001

                                011 OR 010 etc.

                                101   100

    b.

000	000	000	000	000	000	000	000	000	000	
001	001	001	001	001	001	001	001	001	001	etc.
010	010	010	010	011	011	011	011	110	110	
100	101	110	111	100	101	110	111	010	011	

16.7 a.

$Z = A$

    b.

$D_A = A^+ = A'B' + XA' + X'AC'$

$D_B = B^+ = $ etc.

$D_C = C^+ = $ etc.

16.8 a. The following assignment satisfies all of the adjacency conditions except (E, F):

    b. $J_1 = XQ_2', \quad K_1 = Q_2 Q_3' + X'Q_3', \quad J_2 = X'Q_1 + Q_3, \quad K_2 = X'Q_3'$

       $J_3 = 0, \qquad K_3 = X', \qquad Z = XQ_3$

16.9 a. $A = 00, \quad B = 01, \quad C = 10, \quad D = 11$

    b. $T_1 = X_1' X_2 Q_2' + X_1' Q_1 Q_2 + X_1 Q_1' Q_2 + X_1 X_2'$

       $T_2 = X_1 Q_1' Q_2' + X_1 Q_1 Q_2, \quad Z_1 = X_1 Q_2, \quad Z_2 = X_1' Q_1 + Q_1 Q_2'$

Unit 17   Study Guide Answers

1   because the input sequences are listed in reverse order

4   Reset the state to 010, and check the value of J_3. If $J_3 = 1$ and Q_3 does not change state when the clock is pulsed, the flip-flop may be defective. If $J_3 = 0$, then check the network which realizes J_3.

5   a. yes   b. not necessarily (see below)   c. yes

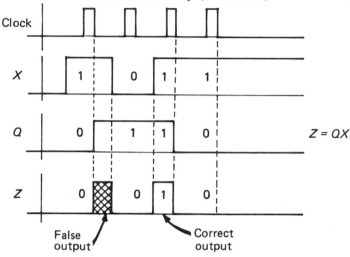

6   a. After the state changes (after the clock pulse), and before the input changes, the input and hence the output may temporarily have the wrong value.

   b. No. The output is correct during the clock pulse.

Unit 18   Study Guide Answers

2   b. m leads, where $2^{m-1} < n \leqslant 2^m$

   c. $R_a = 0$ $S_a = x'yb'$ $R_b = 0$ $S_b = xy'a'$

3. a. Once two groups of 1's have occurred, a 1 output is no longer possible no matter what input sequence follows.

4   c. yes

Unit 18   Answers to Problems

18.1

	Input State	a_i	Output State $x_i y_i =$ 00	01	11	10	a_{i+1} $x_i y_i =$ 00	01	11	10
$X \geqslant Y$	S_0	1	S_0	S_1	S_0	S_0	1	0	1	1
$X < Y$	S_1	0	S_1	S_1	S_1	S_0	0	0	0	1

$$a_{i+1} = x_i y_i' + y_i' a_i + x_i a_i$$

$$Z = a_{n+1}$$

18.2

$x_i = 0$	1	Z
S_0	S_0	S_1	0
S_1	S_2	S_3	1
S_2	S_2	S_1	1
S_3	S_3	S_3	0

b_i \ a_i	0	1
0	S_0	S_2
1	S_3	S_1

$$a_{i+1} = x_i' a_i + x_i b_i'$$
$$= (x_i + a_i)(x_i' + b_i')$$
$$b_{i+1} = x_i + a_i' b_i$$
$$Z = a_{n+1}$$

18.3

$x_i = 0$	1	Z
S_0	S_0	S_1	0
S_1	S_1	S_2	0
S_2	S_2	S_3	0
S_3	S_3	S_2	1

b_i \ a_i	0	1
0	S_0	S_1
1	S_2	S_3

$$a_{i+1} = x_i a_i' + x_i' a_i$$
$$b_{i+1} = b_i + x_i a_i$$
$$a_0 = 0 \qquad b_0 = 0$$
$$a_1 = x_0 \qquad b_1 = 0$$

18.4

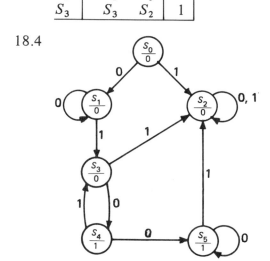

BC \ A	0	1
00	S_0	S_1
01	S_5	S_4
11	S_2	
10	S_3	

$$a_{i+1} = x_i' c_i'$$
$$b_{i+1} = b_i c_i + x_i$$
$$c_{i+1} = b_i + x_i a_i' + x_i' c_i$$

18.5

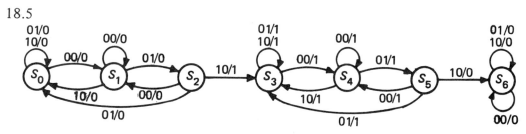

Unit 19   Study Guide Answers

1 b.

clock pulse	Q_A	Q_B	Q_C	Q_D	Q_E	Q_F	Q_G	Q_H
3	1	0	0	0	0	0	0	0
7	1	0	0	0	1	0	0	0
10	0	0	1	1	0	0	0	1
14	0	0	0	0	0	0	1	1

Q_H is 1 during clock pulses 10, 14 and 15

2 a. 0111, <u>0110</u>, <u>0100</u>, <u>0000</u>, 1000

   b. connect Q_D of right counter to A input of left counter

4 b. 64 words × 7 bits

Unit 19   Answers to Problems

19.1   Connections: serial input to D_D, Q_D to D_C, Q_C to D_B, Q_B to D_A
serial output from Q_A ; for left shift $SH = 0$, $L = 1$;
for right shift, $SH = 1$, $L = X$

19.2   a.   connect Q_D to SI (serial input).

   b. Q_D starts at 0 and changes value immediately following the trailing
   edge of clock pulses 2, 3, 4, 5 and 6

19.3 Q_D, Q_C, Q_B, and Q_A can only change value on the 0-1 transition of the
clock. Successive values of Q_D, Q_C, Q_B, Q_A are 1001, 0000, 1011, 1100,
1101, 1110, 1111, 1111, 1111 .

19.4 $D_D = D_C = D_A = 1, D_B = 0$;   LOAD $= (Q_D' Q_C Q_B' Q_A)'$

19.5   CLEAR $= (Q_C Q_B Q_A)'$ LOAD $= (X Q_C' Q_B Q_A')'$ $PT = 1$

19.6   CLEAR $= (X'B'A)'$ LOAD $= X + B'C'$ $PT = CA' + XC'$
$D_C = A$, $D_B = 0$, $D_A = 1$ or $PT = XA' + XC'$

19.7   The block diagram is similar to Fig. 19-14, except it has X_1 and X_2
inputs, Z_1 and Z_2 outputs, and 2 flip-flops.

X_1	X_2	Q_1	Q_2	D_1	D_2	Z_1	Z_2
0	0	0	0	1	1	0	0
0	0	0	1	0	0	1	0
0	0	1	0	1	1	0	0
0	0	1	1	1	0	0	0
0	1	0	0	1	0	1	0
0	1	0	1	0	1	1	0
0	1	1	0	0	0	1	0
0	1	1	1	1	0	0	0
1	0	0	0	0	1	1	1

etc.

19.8   a.   Similar to Fig. 19-14, except change ROM to PLA

   b.

X	A	B	C	Z	D_A	D_B	D_C
0	–	–	–	0	1	0	0
0	–	–	0	0	0	1	0
–	0	–	1	0	0	1	0
–	0	1	–	0	0	1	0
–	1	–	–	0	0	0	1
1	–	0	–	0	0	0	1
0	1	0	–	1	0	0	0
1	0	1	0	1	0	0	0

(0101 may be used
in place of 010–)

   c.   16 words X 4 bits

Unit 20 Study Guide Answers

1 f. sign & mag: -0,   2's comp: -32,   1's comp: -31

  g. Overflow occurs when adding n-bit numbers and the result requires $n + 1$ bits for proper representation. You can tell that an overflow has occurred when the sum of two positive numbers is negative or the sum of two negative numbers is positive.
  A carry out of the last bit position does <u>not</u> indicate overflow has occurred.

3 e.

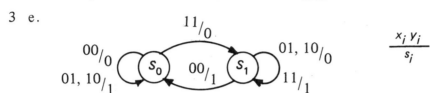

$$\dfrac{x_i \, y_i}{s_i}$$

4 d. $d_5 = 0$, $d_4 = 0$, $d_3 = 1$, $d_2 = 0$, $d_1 = 1$
  $b_6 = 0$, $b_5 = 0$, $b_4 = 1$, $b_3 = 1$, $b_2 = 1$

Unit 20 Answers to Problems

20.1 9's comp. of N $= (10^n - 1) - N$
  9's comp. of 02489 $= 99999 - 02489$
                  $= 97510$

  Check: $+ 05367$
  5367 $\overline{(1)\,02877}$
  -2489 $\quad\quad\longrightarrow 1$ Use end-around carry
  2878   02878

20.2 2's complement:

  a. 10111 (-9)   b. 10111 (-9)
    $\underline{10101}$ (-11) $\underline{11001}$ (-7)
    (1)01100   overflow   (1)10000 (-16)

  c. 10111 (-9)   d. 01011 ($+11$)
    $\underline{01011}$ ($+11$) $\underline{00111}$ ($+7$)
    (1)00010 ($+2$)   10010 overflow

  e. 10110 (-10)   1's complement:
    $\underline{11011}$ (-5)   a. 01011 overflow   b. 01111 overflow
    (1)10001 (-15)   c. 00010 ($+2$)   d. 10010 overflow
                      e. 10000 (-15)

20.3 2's complement: -128 to $+127$
   1's complement: -127 to $+127$

20.4 Each J-K flip-flop requires 1 inverter for the K input.
   Each S-R flip-flop requires 1 inverter and 2 AND gates.
   Each T flip-flop requires 1 EXCLUSIVE-OR gate and 1 AND gate.

20.5 a.

$x_i y_i z_i c_i d_i$	$c_{i+1} d_{i+1} s_i$
0 0 0 0 0 0	0 0 0
1 0 0 0 0 1	0 0 1
2 0 0 0 1 0	0 1 0
3 0 0 0 1 1	x x x
.	.
.	.
.	.
28 1 1 1 0 0	0 1 1
29 1 1 1 0 1	1 0 0
30 1 1 1 1 0	1 0 1
31 1 1 1 1 1	x x x

b. $S_i = x_i y_i' z_i' d_i' + x_i' y_i' z_i d_i' + x_i y_i z_i d_i'$
$+ x_i' y_i z_i' d_i' + x_i' y_i' z_i' d_i + x_i y_i' z_i' d_i$
$+ x_i' y_i z_i d_i + x_i y_i z_i' d_i$
$= x_i \oplus y_i \oplus z_i \oplus d_i$

20.6 Same as Fig. 20-7 except replace c_i with b_i and replace P_{add} with P_{sub}.
Equations for typical cell are $T_i = b_i \oplus y_i$, $b_{i+1} = x_i' y_i + x_i' b_i + y_i b_i$.

20.7 a. OVERFLOW $= x_n y_n s_n' + x_n' y_n' s_n$
b. OVERFLOW $= x_n y_n' d_n' + x_n' y_n d_n$

Unit 21 Study Guide Answers

1 a. t_1 1011 1001 0 0 1
t_3 0010 0110 1 1 0

2 a.

```
         0 0 0 0 0 1 1 0 1
add      1 1 1 1
         0 1 1 1 1 1 1 0 1
shift  0 0 1 1 1 1 1 1 0
shift  0 0 0 1 1 1 1 1 1
add      1 1 1 1
         1 0 0 1 0 1 1 1 1
shift  0 1 0 0 1 0 1 1 1
add      1 1 1 1
         1 1 0 0 0 0 1 1 1
shift  0 1 1 0 0 0 0 1 1
```

b. 8, 4   c. 15

3 b. Change Y to 2's complement by inverting each bit and adding 1 (by setting the carry input to the first full adder to 1). Also change C so that it is equal to the carry out of the last full adder.

c. Since only 3 bits are available to store the quotient, an overflow will occur if the quotient would be greater than 7 (111). An overflow is easily detected since if initially $x_7 x_6 x_5 x_4 \geq y_3 y_2 y_1$, subtraction is possible but there is no place to store the resulting quotient bit.

Unit 21 Answers to Problems

21.1

The control circuit is the same as for a serial adder. The logic equations for the control circuit are:

$$J_A = K_A = B$$
$$J_B = N + A, K_B = 1 \text{ or}$$
$$J_B = K_B = N + A + B$$
$$P_s = (N + A + B) \text{ Clock}$$

21.2 The ONE ADDER is similar to a serial adder, except that there is only one input. This means that the carry will be added to X. Thus if the carry flip-flop is initially set to 1, 1 will be added to the input. The p_i pulse can be used to set the carry flip-flop to 1. The p_s pulses then can be used as clock pulses for the adder. Assuming that p_i is used to set the adder network to an initial state of S_1, the state graph is

Q	Q^+ $X = 0$	1	Z 0	1
S_0 0	0	0	0	1
S_1 1	0	1	1	0

$$Z = XQ' + X'Q$$
$$= (X' + Q')(X + Q)$$

21.3

21.4

21.5

21.6 a.

b. $X = 1\ 0\ 0\ 1\ 0\ 0\ 0\ 0$ (initial)
   $0\ 1\ 0\ 1\ 0\ 0\ 0\ 1$ (after 1 pulse)
   $1\ 0\ 1\ 0\ 0\ 0\ 1\ 0$ (after 2)
   $0\ 1\ 1\ 1\ 0\ 1\ 0\ 1$ (after 3)
   $0\ 0\ 0\ 1\ 1\ 0\ 1\ 1$ (after 4)

   rem.   quotient

c.

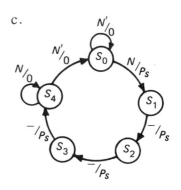

21.7 a. $X_{in} = K_1'K_2'a' + K_1'K_2b + K_1K_2'\,(a \oplus b) + K_1K_2a$

   $Y_{in} = K_1'K_2'b + K_1'K_2a + K_1K_2'\cdot 0 + K_1K_2\cdot 1$

b. state graph requires 9 states (wait in last state for $N = 0$)

d. $Sh = NQ'_D$ $PT = NQ'_D$ CLEAR $= N$ LOAD $= 1$

Unit 22   Study Guide Answers

1 b. Z_1, Z_2, Z_4 (for both charts)

d.

2 a.

0 0 1 1 1 0 0	$C = 0$, *Sh*
0 1 1 1 0 0 0	$C = 1$, *Su*
0 0 1 0 0 0 1	$C = 0$, *Sh*
0 1 0 0 0 1 0	$C = 0$, *Sh*
1 0 0 0 1 0 0	$C = 1$, *Su*
0 0 1 1 1 0 1	(result)

3 a. $A^+ = BX$

$$B^+ = A'X + BX$$

Unit 22   Answers to Problems

22.1

(1)   (2)

22.2b

22.6

22.7

22.9

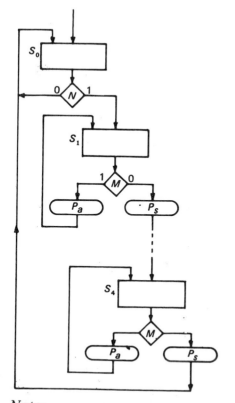

Note:
SM blocks for S_2 & S_3 are
the same as S_1.

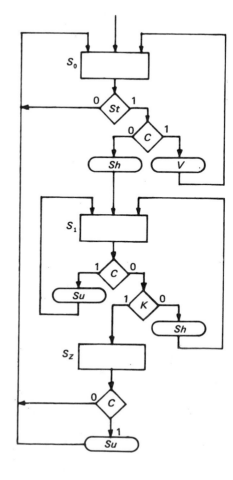

22.11 a. $A^+ = AB + BC'$ $B^+ = A'B'C' St + BC$

$V = A'B'C \cdot St$ $Su = AC + BC$ $Sh = A'C'St + BC'$

22.12 a. $A^+ = A'B'C \cdot RB'D7'D11'D2312' + AB'C' + AB' \cdot RB + AB'EQ'D7'$

$B^+ = A'B'C \cdot D7 + A'B'C \cdot D11 + A'B \cdot \text{RESET}' + AB'C \cdot RB'EQ'D7'$

$C^+ = A'B'RB + A'BC \cdot \text{RESET}' + B'C'RB + AB'C \cdot RB'EQ'D7$

(These equations could be further simplified using don't cares.)

22.13 a.

$A^+ = BX$ $Z_a = A'B'$ $Z_1 = ABX'$

$B^+ = A'X + BX$ $Z_b = A'B$ $Z_2 = ABX$

                $Z_c = AB$

X	A	B	A^+	B^+	Z_a	Z_b	Z_c	Z_1	Z_2
1	-	1	1	1	0	0	0	0	0
1	0	-	0	1	0	0	0	0	0
-	0	0	0	0	1	0	0	0	0
-	0	1	0	0	0	1	0	0	0
-	1	1	0	0	0	0	1	0	0
0	1	1	0	0	0	0	0	1	0
1	1	1	0	0	0	0	0	0	1

22.14 b.

$A^+ = A'X_1'X_2'X_3 + BX_2'$ $Z_1 = A + B'X_1'$

$B^+ = A'B'X_1 + BX_2$ $Z_2 = A'B'X_1$

                      $Z_3 = B + A'X_1'X_2$

c.

A	B	X_1	X_2	X_3	A^+	B^+	Z_1	Z_2	Z_3
0	-	0	0	1	1	0	0	0	0
-	1	-	0	-	1	0	0	0	0
0	0	1	-	-	0	1	0	1	0
-	1	-	1	-	0	1	0	0	0
1	-	-	-	-	0	0	1	0	0
-	0	0	-	-	0	0	1	0	0
-	1	-	-	-	0	0	0	0	1
0	-	0	1	-	0	0	0	0	1

d.

A	B	X_1	X_2	X_3	A^+	B^+	Z_1	Z_2	Z_3
0	0	0	0	0	0	0	1	0	0
0	0	0	0	1	1	0	1	0	0
0	0	0	1	0	0	0	1	0	1
0	0	0	1	1	1	0	1	0	1
0	0	1	0	0	0	1	0	1	0

Unit 23 Study Guide Answers

1 b. counter (a) is synchronous; (b) is asynchronous since flip-flop B changes state in response to a change in A rather than in response to the clock

2 d. stable if flip-flop excitation is such that no flip-flop will change state

3 e. *b, c, d* *a, c, f* *b, d, e* etc.

   f. no; each clock pulse can produce only a single state change

4 c. non-critical race occurs starting from $X_1 X_2 Q_1 Q_2 = 0011$

Unit 23 Answers to Problems

23.1

$X_1 X_2$

$X_1 X_2$	00	01	11	10
0	⓪	⓪	1	2
1	3	3	①	①
3	③	2	③	③
2	②	②	②	②

$X_1 X_2 = 00, 01, 11, 10, 00, 10, \underline{11}$

$Z = 1$

23.2

X

X	0	1
0	⓪	1
1	0	3
3	2	2
2	②	0

When X changes from 0 to 1, the network enters a cycle. One method to get $Z = 1$:

23.3 Output sequence: 1, 0, 1, 0, 0, 1, 0, 1, 1

23.4 a. State sequence will depend on how state variables are chosen (3 are sufficient). Flow table has 4 stable states.

$$X = 0, \ 1, \ 0, \ 1, \ \ldots$$
$$Z = 0, \ 1, \ 1, \ 0, \ \ldots$$

   b. The network contains critical races (starting in some of the unstable states).

Unit 24 Study Guide Answers

1 a. a flow table which has exactly one stable total state per row

   d. because double input changes are prohibited

2 a. equivalent stable total states must also have the same inputs

   b. because the outputs are only associated with stable total states and two rows with stable total states in the same column are never merged

   c. (4, 5, 6, 7) (1, 2, 8) (3)   or   (4, 5, 6, 7) (1, 2, 3) (8)

Unit 24 Answers to Problems

24.2 *

	00	01	11	10	00	01	11	10	**
A	(A)	B	(A)	(A)	00		10	00
B	A	(B)	(B)	A		00	01	

24.3 *

	PC 00	01	11	10	00	01	11	10	**
A	(A)	(A)	(A)	B	0	0	0	
B	–	–	C	(B)	–	–		0
C	–	–	(C)	D	–	–	1	
D	A	A	(D)	(D)			0	0

Z

24.4

$X_1 X_2$	00	01	11	10	Z
1	(1)	(1)	2	3	0
2	1	(2)	(2)	4	1
3	1	(3)	(3)	(3)	0
4	(4)	(4)	2	(4)	1

24.5 * Equivalent states: $(5, 14)\ (2, 11)\ (1, 9, 12)\ (4, 13)\ (10, 15)$

	$X_1 X_2$ 00	01	11	10	00	01	11	10	**
a 1, 4	(1)	2	(4)	10	01		00	
b 2, 3	5	(2)	4	(3)		11		11
c 5, 6	(5)	(6)	8	10	10	11		
d 7, 8	(7)	6	(8)	3	01		00	
e 10	1	6	4	(10)				11

$Z_1 Z_2$

---

*The minimum row table for these problems is not unique.

**The blank entries in the output table can be filled in using the technique described in Section 25.4.

24.6

	D Clock				Q
	00	01	11	10	
1	①	①	①	3	0
2	6	②	②	4	0
3	1	2	2	③	0
4	6	④	④	④	1
5	1	⑤	⑤	3	1
6	⑥	5	5	4	1

Unit 25   Study Guide Answers

2 b. yes (by adding 4 rows to the table and directing transitions through them, all transitions can be made without races)

   c. Fig. 25-7 may require less logic; Fig. 25-9 may be faster.

3 a. yes

   b. there is no way to direct the transitions in column 11 to avoid critical races

   c. direct 4 to 1 through 3

   f. direct the transitions as follows:
       column $00 - b$ to d to c, column $11 - c$ to a to e, column $10 - a$ to e to d

4 a. (2) 1, (5) 1, (6) 0

   b.

00	01	11	10
0	–	–	–
0	1	1	–
0	–	1	0
–	1	1	1

6 b. $R_1 = Q_2 + Q_3$, $S_1 = X_1 X_2' Q_2 + X_1' X_2' Q_4$, etc.

Unit 25 Answers to Problems

25.2 a.

a	c
x	y
b	d
f	e

$X_1 X_2$

	00	01	11	10
a	Ⓐ	x	Ⓐ	c
b	x	Ⓑ	Ⓑ	d
c	y	Ⓒ	y	Ⓒ
d	Ⓓ	Ⓓ	e	Ⓓ
e	f	c	Ⓔ	c
f	Ⓕ	b	a	Ⓕ
x	a	y	b	–
y	d	d	x	–

b.

a	d
h	e
f	g
c	b

25.3

	00	01	11	10
a_1	Ⓐ₁	a_2	d_1	Ⓐ₁
a_2	Ⓐ₂	c_1	a_1	Ⓐ₂
b_1	a_1	d_2	Ⓑ₁	Ⓑ₁
b_2	a_2	b_1	Ⓑ₂	Ⓑ₂
c_1	d_1	Ⓒ₁	c_2	a_2
c_2	d_2	Ⓒ₂	b_2	c_1
d_1	Ⓓ₁	Ⓓ₁	Ⓓ₁	d_2
d_2	Ⓓ₂	Ⓓ₂	Ⓓ₂	b_1

25.4 Using the assignment shown yields the following equations:

$$Y_1^+ = P'Y_2 + PY_1 \qquad\qquad Y_2^+ = T'Y_1 + TPY_1' + P'Y_2$$
$$R_1 = P'Y_2' \qquad\qquad\qquad R_2 = T'Y_1' + TPY_1$$
$$S_1 = P'Y_2 \qquad\qquad\qquad S_2 = TPY_1' + T'Y_1$$
$$Q = Y_1$$

Y_2 \ Y_1	0	1
0	a	d
1	b	c

25.5

a	d	e	γ
α	β	b	c

25.6

C \ AB			
0	1	3	2
1	5	6	4

$Q = C$

25.7 Using the assignment $a = 10000$, $b = 01000$, etc. yields the following next state equations:

$$Q_1^+ = Q_1 Q_4' Q_5' + X_1' X_2' Q_4 + X_1' X_2' Q_5$$
$$Q_2^+ = Q_2 Q_3' Q_5' + X_1 X_2' Q_4 + X_1' X_2 Q_5$$
$$Q_3^+ = Q_3 Q_4' Q_5' + X_1' X_2' Q_2$$
$$Q_4^+ = Q_4 Q_1' Q_2' + X_1' X_2 Q_1 + X_1 X_2 Q_3$$
$$Q_5^+ = Q_5 Q_1' Q_2' + X_1 X_2' Q_1 + X_1 X_2 Q_2 + X_1 X_2' Q_3$$

Unit 26 Study Guide Answers

1 a. $Z = 1$ between $t = 25$ and 40 ns.

   b. First the inverter output, then gate 2, followed by f, followed by gate 1, and finally f again.

3 $Z^+ = (c_1 + c_2') c_3'$ $c_2'(1 \rightarrow 0), c_1(0 \rightarrow 1), c_3'(1 \rightarrow 0)$ to get 1-0-1-0

5 b. Start in ③ or ⑦ and change X_1

   d. 1. X changes 0 to 1
       2. gate 1 output changes 0 to 1
       3. flip-flop y_1 output changes 1 to 0
       4. gate 4 output changes 1 to 0, gate 3 output changes 0 to 1
       5. flip-flop y_2 output changes 1 to 0
       6. inverter output X' changes 1 to 0
       7. gate 1 output changes back to 0, gate 2 output changes to 1
       8. flip-flop y_1 output changes back to 1

   Final state is 10 instead of 01. This essential hazard can be eliminated by delaying the change in y_1' until X' has reached its final value.

6 d. x_2 changes to 1, y_2' changes to 1, $x_1 x_2' y_2'$ AND gate output changes to 1, y_1' changes to 0 and y_1 changes to 1, and x_2' changes to 0 (too late!)

   e. Replace lower 2 AND gates with

   and

Unit 26 Answers to Problems

26.1 1-hazard: $a = 0, b = 1, d = 1, c$ changing. To eliminate, add $a'bd$ term to the OR gate at the output.

   0-hazard: $a = 0, b = 0, c = 1, d$ changing. To eliminate, add $(a + b + c')$ to AND gate which realizes $c(b + d')(a + d)$.

26.2 a. 1-hazard: $a = 0, b = 1, d = 1, c$ changing. Gate outputs $-$ 2, 4, 5, 3, 5 (for c 0 $\rightarrow$ 1) or 3, 5, 2, 4, 5 (for c 1 $\rightarrow$ 0)

   0-hazard: $a = 0, b = 0, d = 0, c$ changing. Gate outputs $-$ 1, 4, 5, 2, 4, 5 (c 0 $\rightarrow$ 1) or 2, 4, 5, 1, 4, 5 (c 1 $\rightarrow$ 0)

   b. $abcd = 0001 \rightarrow 0011$. Gate outputs $-$ 1, 4, 5, 2, 4, 5, 3, 5.

26.3 $f = [d' + b(a + c)(a' + c')](a' + b' + c'd)(b' + c + ad)$ -9 gates, 22 inputs

or

$f' = (b + d)(a' + b' + c + d')(a + c' + b'd)$ – 6 gates, 15 inputs

26.4 essential hazards starting in states ③, ④, ⑤ and ⑦ and changing variable P.

25.4(a) – add delays to flip-flop outputs } to eliminate

25.4(b) – add delays to Y_1 and Y_2 } essential hazards

To eliminate 1-hazards, add $Y_1 Y_2$ to Y_1^+ and $TY_1' Y_2$ to Y_2^+.

Unit 28 Answers to Problems

28.1 Reduced State Table:

	$w = 0$	1	0	1
0	0	0	0	0
2	4	7	1	0
4	7	6	0	0
6	2	4	0	0
7	6	2	0	0

Z

BC \ A	0	1
00	0	2
01		7
11		4
10		6

$T_A = 0$

$T_B = W'A$

$T_C = WA + AB'$

$Z = W'AB'C'$

28.2 a.

	$x = 0$	1	$x = 0$	1
S_0	S_2	S_1	0	0
S_1	S_3	S_0	0	1
S_2	S_0	S_3	1	0
S_3	S_1	S_2	1	1

B \ A	0	1
0	0	3
1	1	2

$J_A = X'$ $K_A = X'$

$J_B = 1$ $K_B = 1$

$Z = X'A + AB' + XA'B$

28.2 b.

	$x = 0$	1	Z
S_0	S_2	S_5	0
S_1	S_2	S_5	1
S_2	S_1	S_6	0
S_3	S_1	S_6	1
S_4	S_6	S_1	1
S_5	S_6	S_1	0
S_6	S_4	S_3	0

BC \ A	0	1
00	S_0	S_5
01	S_1	S_4
11	S_6	S_3
10	X	S_2

$T_A = 1$

$T_B = X'$

$T_C = AC' + A'B'C$

$Z = B'C + AC$

28.3 a. Reduced Table:

	0	1	0	1
a	e	c	0	1
b	b	f	0	1
c	e	c	1	0
e	c	f	0	1
f	b	b	1	0

b. Minimum length input sequences which will distinguish between states a and b are 000, 001, 110, 111.

28.4

		$Q_1^+ Q_2^+$				$Z_1 Z_2$			
$Q_1 Q_2$	$X_1 X_2 = 00$	01	11	10	00	01	11	10
0 0	?	01	?	?	?	10	?	?
0 1	?	11	?	10	?	01	11	10
1 1	?	?	?	?	?	01	?	?
1 0	?	?	01	?	?	?	00	00

? indicates cannot be determined from timing chart

28.5 a.

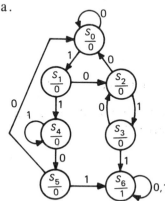

b.

BC \ A	0	1
00	0	6
01	2	5
11	4	X
10	1	3

$A_{i+1} = X_i A_i + A_i B_i' C_i'$
$\quad + X_i B_i' C_i$
$\quad + X_i' B_i C_i$

$B_{i+1} = X_i A_i'$

$C_{i+1} = X_i' B_i + A_i' B_i$

c. $Z = A_{n+1} B_{n+1}' C_{n+1}'$

28.6 a. $J = x_1' x_2 + x_1 x_2' \quad K = x_2' x_3' + x_2 x_3 \quad Z = Q$

b. $D = x_1' x_2 Q' + x_1 x_2' Q' + x_2' x_3 Q + x_2 x_3' Q$

c. $T = (x_1' x_2 Q' + x_1 x_2' Q' + x_2' x_3' Q + x_2 x_3 Q)\text{CLOCK}$

d. $S = (x_1' x_2 Q' + x_1 x_2' Q')\text{CLOCK} \qquad R = (x_2' x_3' Q + x_2 x_3 Q)\text{CLOCK}$

e. flip-flop would oscillate

28.7 a.

b.

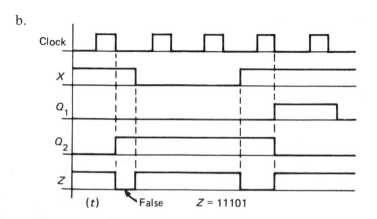

(t)   False $Z = 11101$

Appendix A   Study Guide Answers

1 b. $D3$, 1 volt   c. $D2$, 5 volts   e. $E < -3$, $E > +3$

2 c. $F = (A + B + C)'$, $F = (ABC)'$ d. $F = (ABC)'$, $F = (A + B + C)'$

3 a.   one 7400 and one 7410

   b.   advanced low-power; advanced Schottky

   c.   0, 1, is not permissible, 2.4 to 5, 0 to 0.4

4 a. $F = (AB + C)'$

Appendix A   Answers to Problems

A.1 a. $F = (AB + C)D$ b. $F = (A + B) C + D$

A.2 a. $Z = (AB + CD)EF$ b.   Reverse the diodes and voltage polarities.

A.3 $F = (a' + b' + c')(d' + e' + f')$

A.4

A	B	F	Q_1	Q_2	Q_3	Q_4	
0	0	$+V$	ON	ON	OFF	OFF	
0	$+V$	0	ON	OFF	ON	OFF	NOR gate
$+V$	0	0	OFF	ON	OFF	ON	
$+V$	$+V$	0	OFF	OFF	ON	ON	

A.5 $F_0 = (A'B' + AB)' = A'B + AB'$, $F_1 = A'B'$, $F_2 = A + B'$, $F_3 = B$

INDEX